뉴텝스
실전
모의고사

실전6회분

뉴텝스 실전 모의고사 실전 6회분

지은이 김무룡 · TEPS콘텐츠개발팀
펴낸이 임상진
펴낸곳 (주)넥서스

초판 1쇄 발행 2019년 1월 20일
초판 20쇄 발행 2024년 2월 15일

출판신고 1992년 4월 3일 제311-2002-2호
10880 경기도 파주시 지목로 5
Tel (02) 330-5500 Fax (02) 330-5555

ISBN 979-11-89432-84-3 13740

이 도서의 국립중앙도서관 출판예정도서목록(CIP)은
서지정보유통지원시스템 홈페이지(http://seoji.nl.go.kr)와
국가자료공동목록시스템(http://www.nl.go.kr/kolisnet)에서 이용하실 수
있습니다.
(CIP제어번호 : CIP2018041933)

www.nexusbook.com

How to
TEPS

기출의 재구성, 실제 시험 그대로 **6회분** 수록

뉴텝스
실전

김무룡·TEPS콘텐츠개발팀 지음

모의고사

실전 **6회분**

넥서스ENGLISH

TEPS 점수 환산표 [TEPS → NEW TEPS]

TEPS	NEW TEPS	TEPS	NEW TEPS	TEPS	NEW TEPS	TEPS	NEW TEPS
981~990	590~600	771~780	433~437	561~570	303~308	351~360	185~189
971~980	579~589	761~770	426~432	551~560	298~303	341~350	181~184
961~970	570~578	751~760	419~426	541~550	292~297	331~340	177~180
951~960	564~569	741~750	414~419	531~540	286~291	321~330	173~177
941~950	556~563	731~740	406~413	521~530	281~285	311~320	169~173
931~940	547~555	721~730	399~405	511~520	275~280	301~310	163~168
921~930	538~546	711~720	392~399	501~510	268~274	291~300	154~163
911~920	532~538	701~710	387~392	491~500	263~268	281~290	151~154
901~910	526~532	691~700	381~386	481~490	258~262	271~280	146~150
891~900	515~525	681~690	374~380	471~480	252~257	261~270	140~146
881~890	509~515	671~680	369~374	461~470	247~252	251~260	135~139
871~880	502~509	661~670	361~368	451~460	241~247	241~250	130~134
861~870	495~501	651~660	355~361	441~450	236~241	231~240	128~130
851~860	488~495	641~650	350~355	431~440	229~235	221~230	123~127
841~850	483~488	631~640	343~350	421~430	223~229	211~220	119~123
831~840	473~481	621~630	338~342	411~420	217~223	201~210	111~118
821~830	467~472	611~620	332~337	401~410	212~216	191~200	105~110
811~820	458~465	601~610	327~331	391~400	206~211	181~190	102~105
801~810	453~458	591~600	321~327	381~390	201~206	171~180	100~102
791~800	445~452	581~590	315~320	371~380	196~200		
781~790	438~444	571~580	309~315	361~370	190~195		

※ 출처: 한국영어평가학회

보다 세분화된 환산표는
www.teps.or.kr에서
내려받을 수 있습니다.

뉴텝스 최신 기출 경향

청해 영역의 두드러진 최신 경향으로는 대화와 담화의 소재가 보다 풍부해졌다는 점을 들 수 있다. 해외 취업 제의에 대한 입장과 같은 이전 텝스의 소재뿐만 아니라, 디자이너의 세련된 감각을 보증할(vouch) 수 있다는 내용의 소재도 활용된다. 또한 민족식물학(ethnobotany)과 같은 매우 생소한 내용이나, 러시아의 라스푸틴과 같은 역사적 인물에 대한 내용도 출제되고 있다. 또한 지문에서 단순히 영향을 미쳤다고 말하는 것인지와 감소하거나 증가했다고 말하는 것인지를 구별해야 하는 매우 까다로운 유형도 등장했다.

어휘와 문법 영역은 청해와 독해 영역에 비해 변화가 심한 편은 아니다. 그렇지만 어휘 영역에서는 sit on the fence(사태를 관망하다)처럼 이전 텝스에서 중요하게 다뤄졌던 숙어뿐만 아니라, put ~ on a pedestal(~을 완벽한 인물처럼 받들다)과 같은 생소한 숙어가 출제되기 때문에, 보다 풍부한 어휘를 익혀야 한다. 문법 영역에서는 이전 텝스와 달리, 가정법의 출제 비중이 조정되었고, 불가산 명사뿐만 아니라 가산명사의 특성도 측정하는 경향이 나타났다. 문법이 실제 대화나 담화에서 어떻게 활용되는지에 주목하도록 유도하는 경향이 강한 것으로 분석된다.

독해 영역은 새로운 소재의 활용뿐만 아니라, 보다 심층적인 이해를 요구하는 문항의 등장이 뚜렷한 최신 경향이다. 신진대사와 골관절염의 관계와 같이 다소 생소할 수 있는 소재가 제시되고 있기 때문에 과학과 의학, 그리고 예술 분야의 다양한 소재를 미리 접해야 한다. 또한 이메일이나 메신저 대화 내용의 경우에는 내포된 의미를 알아야만 정확히 풀어낼 수 있는 추론 문항들이 등장했다. 이 문항 유형은 전달하려는 의도가 명시적으로 분명하게 제시되지 않기 때문에 전체 내용의 흐름 속에서 어떤 의미를 말하고자 하는지를 포착해 내야 한다.

종합적으로 볼 때, 뉴텝스는 청해와 독해에서 단순히 지문의 뜻을 이해하는 능력뿐만 아니라, 화자와 저자의 의도(intention)를 파악하는 능력까지도 요구한다. 이와 같은 의도 파악 능력은 지문에서 나타나는 상황이나 맥락이 어떤 것인지를 이해하려고 노력해야만 충분히 길러질 수 있다. 따라서 영어 대화나 담화를 접하면서, 항상 이것이 어떤 맥락에서 하는 말일까를 생각해 보는 습관을 들여야 한다. 또한 오랜 기간 동안 텝스 분야에서 탁월한 교재를 출간해 온 넥서스의 다양한 뉴텝스 교재를 통해 착실하게 연습을 한다면, 반드시 목표로 하는 성과를 거두게 될 것이라고 확신한다. 모든 독자들이 목표로 하는 바를 이루기를 바란다.

뉴텝스 만점 저자 김무룡

Contents

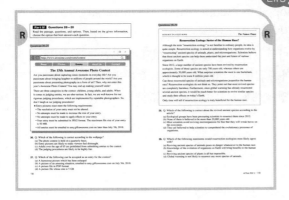

최신 경향을 가장 잘 반영한 6회분 모의고사

NEW TEPS 최신 기출 문제를 영역별로 완벽하게 파악하여 기출과 가장 유사하게 구성했습니다. 실제 시험과 가장 가까운 6회분 문제를 꼼꼼하게 풀면서 실전 감각을 제대로 갖출 수 있습니다.

스크립트 · 정답 · 해설이 한 권에

별도로 해설집을 살 필요가 없습니다. 청해 스크립트와 함께 모든 영역의 정답 및 해설까지 한 권에 종합적으로 담겨 있습니다.

MP3 · 단어장
VOCA TEST
정답 자동 채점

3가지 버전
MP3

모바일 단어장
& VOCA TEST

받아쓰기
정답자동채점

어휘 리스트
& 테스트

부가 제공 자료

언제 어디서든 편하게 학습할 수 있도록 QR 코드를 통해 모바일 단어장 및 VOCA TEST를 제공하며, 추가로 어휘 리스트 & 테스트를 넥서스 홈페이지(www.nexusbook.com) 에서 다운로드할 수 있습니다.

TEPS란?

TEPS는 Test of English Proficiency developed by Seoul National University의 약자로 서울대학교 언어교육원에서 개발하고, TEPS관리위원회에서 주관하는 국가공인 영어 시험입니다. 1999년 1월 처음 시행 이후 2018년 5월 12일부터 새롭게 바뀐 NEW TEPS가 시행되고 있습니다. TEPS는 정부기관 및 기업의 직원 채용이나 인사고과, 해외 파견 근무자 선발과 더불어 국내 유수의 대학과 특목고 입학 및 졸업 자격 요건, 국가고시 및 자격 시험의 영어 대체 시험으로 활용되고 있습니다.

1 / NEW TEPS는 종합적 지문 이해력 평가를 위한 시험으로, 실제 영어 사용 환경을 고려하여 평가 효율성을 높이고 시험 응시 피로도는 낮춰 수험자의 내재화된 영어 능력을 평가합니다.

2 / 편법이 없는 시험을 위해 청해(Listening)에서는 시험지에 선택지가 제시되어 있지 않아 눈으로 읽을 수 없고 오직 듣기 능력에만 의존해야 합니다. 청해나 독해(Reading)에서는 한 문제로 다음 문제의 답을 유추할 수 있는 가능성을 배제하기 위해 1지문 1문항을 고수해 왔지만 NEW TEPS부터 1지문 2문항 유형이 새롭게 추가되었습니다.

3 / 실생활에서 접할 수 있는 다양한 주제와 상황을 다룹니다. 일상생활과 비즈니스를 비롯해 문학, 과학, 역사 등 학술적인 소재도 출제됩니다.

4 / 청해, 어휘, 문법, 독해의 4영역으로 나뉘며, 총 135문항에 600점 만점입니다. 영역별 점수 산출이 가능하며, 점수 외에 5에서 1+까지 10등급으로 나뉩니다.

NEWTEPS 시험 구성

영역	문제 유형	문항수	제한 시간	점수 범위
청해 Listening Comprehension	**Part I** : 한 문장을 듣고 이어질 대화로 가장 적절한 답 고르기 (문장 1회 청취 후 선택지 1회 청취)	10	40분	0~240점
	Part II : 짧은 대화를 듣고 이어질 대화로 가장 적절한 답 고르기 (대화 1회 청취 후 선택지 1회 청취)	10		
	Part III : 긴 대화를 듣고 질문에 가장 적절한 답 고르기 (대화 및 질문 **1회 청취** 후 선택지 1회 청취)	10		
	Part IV : 담화를 듣고 질문에 가장 적절한 답 고르기 (1지문 1문항) (담화 및 질문 2회 청취 후 선택지 1회 청취)	6		
	Part V : 담화를 듣고 질문에 가장 적절한 답 고르기 (1지문 2문항) (담화 및 질문 2회 청취 후 선택지 1회 청취)	신유형 4		
어휘 Vocabulary	**Part I** : 대화문의 빈칸에 가장 적절한 어휘 고르기	10	변경 통합 25분	0~60점
	Part II : 단문의 빈칸에 가장 적절한 어휘 고르기	20		
문법 Grammar	**Part I** : 대화문의 빈칸에 가장 적절한 답 고르기	10		0~60점
	Part II : 단문의 빈칸에 가장 적절한 답 고르기	15		
	Part III : 대화 및 문단에서 문법상 틀리거나 어색한 부분 고르기	5		
독해 Reading Comprehension	**Part I** : 지문을 읽고 빈칸에 가장 적절한 답 고르기	10	40분	0~240점
	Part II : 지문을 읽고 문맥상 어색한 내용 고르기	2		
	Part III : 지문을 읽고 질문에 가장 적절한 답 고르기 (1지문 1문항)	13		
	Part IV : 지문을 읽고 질문에 가장 적절한 답 고르기 (1지문 2문항)	신유형 10		
총계	**14개 Parts**	135문항	105분	0~600점

청해 (Listening Comprehension) _40문항

정확한 청해 능력을 측정하기 위하여 문제와 보기 문항을 문제지에 인쇄하지 않고 들려줌으로써 자연스러운 의사소통의 인지 과정을 최대한 반영하였습니다. 다양한 의사소통 기능(Communicative Functions)의 대화와 다양한 상황(공고, 방송, 일상생활, 업무 상황, 대학 교양 수준의 강의 등)을 이해하는 데 필요한 전반적인 청해력을 측정하기 위해 대화문(dialogue)과 담화문(monologue)의 소재를 균형 있게 다루었습니다.

어휘 (Vocabulary) _30문항

문맥 없이 단순한 동의어 및 반의어를 선택하는 시험 유형을 배제하고 의미 있는 문맥을 근거로 가장 적절한 어휘를 선택하는 유형을 문어체와 구어체로 나누어 측정합니다.

문법 (Grammar) _30문항

밑줄 친 부분 중 오류를 식별하는 유형 등의 단편적이며 기계적인 문법 지식 학습을 조장할 우려가 있는 분리식 시험 유형을 배제하고, 의미 있는 문맥을 근거로 오류를 식별하는 유형을 통하여 진정한 의사소통 능력의 바탕이 되는 살아 있는 문법, 어법 능력을 문어체와 구어체를 통하여 측정합니다.

독해 (Reading Comprehension) _35문항

교양 있는 수준의 글(신문, 잡지, 대학 교양과목 개론 등)과 실용적인 글(서신, 광고, 홍보, 지시문, 설명문, 양식 등)을 이해하는 데 요구되는 총체적인 독해력을 측정하기 위해서 실용문 및 비전문적 학술문과 같은 독해 지문의 소재를 균형 있게 다루었습니다.

청해 Listening Comprehension

★ PART I (10문항)

두 사람의 질의응답 문제를 다루며, 한 번만 들려줍니다. 내용 자체는 단순하고 기본적인 수준의 생활 영어 표현으로 구성되어 있지만, 교과서적인 지식보다는 재빠른 상황 판단 능력이 필요합니다. **Part I**에서는 속도 적응 능력뿐만 아니라 순발력 있는 상황 판단 능력이 요구됩니다.

Choose the most appropriate response to the statement.

W I heard that it's going to be very hot tomorrow.
M _____

(a) It was the hottest day of the year.
(b) Be sure to dress warmly.
(c) Let's not sweat the details.
(d) It's going to be a real scorcher.

W 내일은 엄청 더운 날씨가 될 거래.
M _____

(a) 일 년 중 가장 더운 날이었어.
(b) 옷을 따뜻하게 입도록 해.
(c) 사소한 일에 신경 쓰지 말자.
(d) 엄청나게 더운 날이 될 거야.

정답 (d)

★ PART II (10문항)

짧은 대화 문제로, 두 사람이 **A-B-A** 순으로 보통의 속도로 대화하는 형식입니다. 소요 시간은 약 **12초** 전후로 짧습니다. Part I과 마찬가지로 한 번만 들려줍니다.

Choose the most appropriate response to complete the conversation.

M Would you like to join me to see a musical?
W Sorry no. I hate musicals.
M How could anyone possibly hate a musical?
W _____

(a) Different strokes for different folks.
(b) It's impossible to hate musicals.
(c) I agree with you.
(d) I'm not really musical.

M 나랑 같이 뮤지컬 보러 갈래?
W 미안하지만 안 갈래. 나 뮤지컬을 싫어하거든.
M 뮤지컬 싫어하는 사람도 있어?
W _____

(a) 사람마다 제각각이지 뭐.
(b) 뮤지컬을 싫어하는 것은 불가능해.
(c) 네 말에 동의해.
(d) 나는 그다지 음악에 재능이 없어.

정답 (a)

앞의 두 파트에 비해 다소 긴 대화를 들려줍니다. NEW TEPS에서는 대화와 질문 모두 한 번만 들려 줍니다. 대화의 주제나 주로 일어나고 있는 일, 화자가 갖고 있는 문제점, 세부 내용, 추론할 수 있는 것 등에 대해 묻습니다.

Choose the option that best answers the question.

W   I just went to the dentist, and he said I need surgery.
M   That sounds painful!
W   Yeah, but that's not even the worst part. He said it will cost $5,000!
M   Wow! That sounds too expensive. I think you should get a second opinion.
W   Really? Do you know a good place?
M   Sure. Let me recommend my guy I use. He's great.

Q: Which is correct according to the conversation?
(a) The man doesn't like his dentist.
(b) The woman believes that $5,000 sounds like a fair price.
(c) The man thinks that the dental surgery is too costly for her.
(d) The woman agrees that the dental treatment will be painless.

W   치과에 갔는데, 의사가 나보고 수술을 해야 한대.
M   아프겠다!
W   응. 하지만 더 심한 건 수술 비용이 5천 달러라는 거야!
M   왜! 너무 비싸다. 다른 의사의 진단을 받아 보는 게 좋겠어.
W   그래? 어디 좋은 곳이라도 알고 있니?
M   물론이지. 내가 가는 곳을 추천해 줄게. 잘하시는 분이야.

Q   대화에 의하면 다음 중 옳은 것은?
(a) 남자는 담당 치과 의사를 좋아하지 않는다.
(b) 여자는 5천 달러가 적당한 가격이라고 생각한다.
(c) 남자는 치과 수술이 여자에게 너무 비싸다고 생각한다.
(d) 여자는 치과 시술이 아프지 않을 것이라는 점에 동의한다.

정답 (c)

이전 파트와 달리, 한 사람의 담화를 다룹니다. 방송이나 뉴스, 강의, 회의를 시작하면서 발제하는 것 등의 상황이 나옵니다.

Part IV, Part V는 담화와 질문을 두 번씩 들려줍니다. 담화의 주제와 세부 내용, 추론할 수 있는 것 등에 대해 묻습니다.

Choose the option that best answers the question.

Tests confirmed that a 19-year-old woman recently died of the bird flu virus. This was the third such death in Indonesia. Cases such as this one have sparked panic in several Asian nations. Numerous countries have sought to discover a vaccine for this terrible illness. Officials from the Indonesian Ministry of Health examined the woman's house and neighborhood, but could not find the source of the virus. According to the ministry, the woman had fever for four days before arriving at the hospital.

Q: Which is correct according to the news report?
(a) There is an easy cure for the disease.
(b) Most nations are unconcerned with the virus.
(c) The woman caught the bird flu from an unknown source.
(d) The woman was sick for four days and then recovered.

최근 19세 여성이 조류 독감으로 사망한 것이 검사로 확인되었고, 인도네시아에서 이번이 세 번째이다. 이와 같은 사건들이 일부 아시아 국가들에게 극심한 공포를 불러 일으켰고, 많은 나라들이 이 끔찍한 병의 백신을 찾기 위해 힘쓰고 있다. 인도네시아 보건부의 직원들은 그녀의 집과 이웃을 조사했지만, 바이러스의 근원을 찾을 수 없었다. 보건부에 의하면, 그녀는 병원에 도착하기 전 나흘 동안 열이 있었다.

Q 뉴스 보도에 의하면 다음 중 옳은 것은?
(a) 이 병에는 간단한 치료법이 있다.
(b) 대부분의 나라들은 바이러스에 대해 관심이 없다.
(c) 여자는 알려지지 않은 원인에 의해 조류 독감에 걸렸다.
(d) 여자는 나흘 동안 앓고 나서 회복되었다.

정답 (c)

★ PART V (2지문 4문항)

이번 NEW TEPS에 새롭게 추가된 유형으로 1지문 2문항 유형입니다. 2개의 지문이 나오므로 총 4문항을 풀어야 합니다. 주제와 세부 내용, 추론 문제가 섞여서 출제되며, 담화와 질문을 두 번씩 들려줍니다.

Choose the option that best answers each question.

Most of you have probably heard of the Tour de France, the most famous cycling race in the world. But you may not be familiar with its complex structure and award system. The annual race covers about 3,500 kilometers across 21 days of racing. It has a total of 198 riders split into 22 teams of 9. At the end of the tour, four riders are presented special jerseys.

The most prestigious of these is the yellow jerseys. This is given to the rider with the lowest overall time. The white jersey is awarded on the same criterion, but it's exclusive to participants under the age of 26. The green jersey and the polka-dot jersey are earned based on points awarded at every stage of the race. So what's the difference between these two jerseys? Well, the competitor with the most total points gets the green jersey, while the rider with the most points in just the mountain sections of the race receives the polka-dot one.

Q1: What is the talk mainly about?
(a) How the colors of the Tour de France jerseys were chosen.
(b) How the various Tour de France jerseys are won.
(c) Which Tour de France jerseys are the most coveted.
(d) Why riders in the Tour de France wear different colored jerseys.

Q2: Which jersey is given to the rider with the most points overall?
(a) The yellow jersey   (c) The green jersey
(b) The white jersey   (d)   The polka-dot jersey

여러분은 아마도 세계에서 가장 유명한 사이클링 대회인 투르 드 프랑스에 대해 들어보셨을 것입니다. 하지만 여러분은 그 대회의 복잡한 구조와 수상 체계에 대해서는 잘 모를 것입니다. 매년 열리는 이 대회는 21일 동안 약 3,500킬로미터를 주행하게 되어있습니다. 이 대회에서 총 198명의 참가자가 각각 9명으로 구성된 22팀으로 나뉩니다. 대회 마지막에는 4명의 선수에게 특별한 저지를 수여합니다.

가장 영예로운 것은 노란색 저지입니다. 이것은 가장 단시간에 도착한 참가자에게 수여됩니다. 흰색 저지는 같은 기준에 의하여 수여되는데, 26세 미만의 참가자에게만 수여됩니다. 녹색 저지와 물방울무늬 저지는 대회의 매 단계의 점수에 기반하여 주어집니다. 그럼 이 두 저지의 차이점은 무엇일까요? 자, 가장 높은 총점을 딴 참가자는 녹색 저지를 받고, 산악 구간에서 가장 많은 점수를 딴 참가자는 물방울무늬 저지를 받습니다.

Q1 담화문의 주제는 무엇인가?

(a) 투르 드 프랑스 저지의 색깔은 어떻게 정해지는가
(b) 다양한 투르 드 프랑스 저지가 어떻게 수여되는가
(c) 어떤 투르 드 프랑스 저지가 가장 선망의 대상이 되는가
(d) 투르 드 프랑스의 선수들이 다양한 색의 저지를 입는 이유는 무엇인가   정답 (b)

Q2 가장 많은 총점을 획득한 선수에게 어떤 저지가 주어지는가?

(a) 노란색 저지   (c) 녹색 저지
(b) 흰색 저지   (d) 물방울무늬 저지   정답 (c)

어휘 Vocabulary

★ PART I (10문항)

구어체로 되어 있는 A와 B의 대화 중 빈칸에 가장 적절한 단어를 고르는 문제입니다. 단어의 단편적인 의미보다는 문맥에서 쓰인 의미가 더 중요합니다. 한 개의 단어로 된 선택지뿐만 아니라 두세 단어 이상의 구를 이루는 선택지도 있습니다.

Choose the option that best completes the dialogue.

A Congratulations on your _____ of the training course.

B Thank you. It was hard, but I managed to pull through.

(a) improvement
(b) resignation
(c) evacuation
(d) completion

A 훈련 과정을 완수한 거 축하해.
B 고마워. 어려웠지만 가까스로 끝낼 수 있었어.

(a) 개선
(b) 사임
(c) 철수
(d) 완료

정답 (d)

★ PART II (20문항)

하나 또는 두 개의 문장 속의 빈칸에 가장 적당한 단어를 고르는 문제입니다. 어휘력을 늘릴 때 한 개씩 단편적으로 암기하는 것보다는 하나의 표현으로, 즉 의미 단위로 알아 놓는 것이 제한된 시간 내에 어휘 시험을 정확히 푸는 데 많은 도움이 됩니다. 후반부로 갈수록 수준 높은 어휘가 출제되며, 단어 사이의 미묘한 의미의 차이를 묻는 문제도 출제됩니다.

Choose the option that best completes the sentence.

Brian was far ahead in the game and was certain to win, but his opponent refused to _____.

(a) yield
(b) agree
(c) waive
(d) forfeit

브라이언이 게임에 앞서 가고 있어서 승리가 확실했지만 그의 상대는 굴복하려 하지 않았다.

(a) 굴복하다
(b) 동의하다
(c) 포기하다
(d) 몰수당하다

정답 (a)

문법 Grammar

★ PART I (10문항)

A와 B 두 사람의 짧은 대화를 통해 구어체 관용 표현, 품사, 시제, 인칭, 어순 등 문법 전반에 대한 이해를 묻습니다. 대화 중에 빈칸이 있고, 그곳에 들어갈 적절한 표현을 고르는 형식입니다.

Choose the option that best completes the dialogue.

A   I can't attend the meeting, either.
B   Then we have no choice _____ the meeting.

(a) but canceling
(b) than to cancel
(c) than cancel
(d) but to cancel

A   저도 회의에 참석할 수 없어요.
B   그러면 회의를 취소하는 수밖에요.
(a) 그러나 취소하는
(b) 취소하는 것보다
(c) 취소하는 것보다
(d) 취소하는 수밖에

정답 (d)

★ PART II (15문항)

Part I에서 구어체의 대화를 나눴다면, Part II에서는 문어체의 문장이 나옵니다. 서술문 속의 빈칸을 채우는 문제로 수 일치, 태, 어순, 분사 등 문법 자체에 대한 이해도는 물론 구문에 대한 이해력이 중요합니다.

Choose the option that best completes the sentence.

_____ being pretty confident about it, Irene decided to check her facts.

(a) Nevertheless
(b) Because of
(c) Despite
(d) Instead of

그 일에 대해 매우 자신감이 있었음에도 불구하고 아이린은 사실을 확인하기로 했다.
(a) 그럼에도 불구하고
(b) 때문에
(c) 그럼에도 불구하고
(d) 대신에

정답 (c)

---

① A-B-A-B의 대화문에서 어법상 틀리거나 문맥상 어색한 부분이 있는 문장을 고르는 문제입니다. 이 영역 역시 문법 뿐만 아니라 정확한 구문 파악과 대화 내용을 이해하는 능력이 중요합니다.

Identify the option that contains a grammatical error.

(a) A: What are you doing this weekend?

(b) B: Going fishing as usual.

(c) A: Again? What's the fun in going fishing? Actually, I don't understand why people go fishing.

(d) B: For me, I like being alone, thinking deeply to me, being surrounded by nature.

(a) A 이번 주말에 뭐해?

(b) B 평소처럼 낚시 가.

(c) A 또 가? 낚시가 뭐 재미있니? 솔직히 난 사람들이 왜 낚시를 하러 가는지 모르겠어.

(d) B 내 경우엔 자연에 둘러 싸여서 혼자 깊이 생각해 볼 수 있다는 게 좋아.

정답 (d) me → myself

---

② 한 문단을 주고 그 가운데 문법적으로 틀리거나 어색한 문장을 고르는 문제입니다. 문법적으로 틀린 부분을 신속하게 골라야 하므로 독해 문제처럼 속독 능력도 중요합니다.

Identify the option that contains a grammatical error.

(a) The creators of a new video game hope to change the disturbing trend of using violence to enthrall young gamers. (b) Video game designers and experts on human development teamed up and designed a new computer game with the gameplay that helps young players overcome everyday school life situations. (c) The elements in the game resemble regular objects: pencils, erasers, and the like. (d) The players of the game "win" by choose peaceful solutions instead of violent ones.

(a) 새 비디오 게임 개발자들은 어린 게이머들의 흥미 유발을 위해 폭력적인 내용을 사용하는 불건전한 판도를 바꿔 놓을 수 있기를 바란다. (b) 비디오 게임 개발자들과 인간 발달 전문가들이 공동으로 개발한 새로운 컴퓨터 게임은 어린이들이 매일 학교에서 부딪히는 상황에 잘 대처할 수 있도록 도와준다. (c) 실제로 게임에는 연필과 지우개 같은 평범한 사물들이 나온다. (d) 폭력적인 해결책보다 비폭력적인 해결책을 선택하면 게임에서 이긴다.

정답 (d) by choose → by choosing

★ PART I (10문항)

지문 속 빈칸에 알맞은 것을 고르는 유형입니다. 글 전체의 흐름을 파악하여 문맥상 빈칸에 들어갈 내용을 찾아야 하는데, 주로 지문의 주제와 관련이 있습니다. 마지막 두 문제, 9번과 10번은 빈칸에 알맞은 연결어를 고르는 문제입니다. 문맥의 흐름을 논리적으로 파악할 수 있어야 합니다.

Read the passage and choose the option that best completes the passage.

Tech industry giants like Facebook, Google, Twitter, and Amazon have threatened to shut down their sites. They're protesting legislation that may regulate Internet content. The Stop Online Piracy Act, or SOPA, according to advocates, will make it easier for regulators to police intellectual property violations on the web, but the bill has drawn criticism from online activists who say SOPA will outlaw many common internet-based activities, like downloading copyrighted content. A boycott, or blackout, by the influential web companies acts to

_____.

(a) threaten lawmakers by halting all Internet access
(b) illustrate real-world effects of the proposed rule
(c) withdraw web activities the policy would prohibit
(d) laugh at the debate about what's allowed online

페이스북, 구글, 트위터, 아마존과 같은 거대 기술업체들이 그들의 사이트를 닫겠다고 위협했다. 그들은 인터넷 콘텐츠를 규제할지도 모르는 법령의 제정에 반대한다. 지지자들은 온라인 저작권 침해 금지 법안으로 인해 단속 기관들이 더 쉽게 웹상에서 지적 재산 침해 감시를 할 수 있다고 말한다. 그러나 온라인 활동가들은 저작권이 있는 콘텐츠를 다운로드하는 것과 같은 일반적인 인터넷 기반 활동들이 불법화될 것이라고 이 법안을 비판하고 있다. 영향력 있는 웹 기반 회사들에 의한 거부 운동 또는 보도 통제는 발의된 법안이 현실에 미치는 영향을 보여 주기 위한 것이다.

(a) 인터넷 접속을 금지시켜서 입법자들을 위협하기 위한
(b) 발의된 법안이 현실에 미치는 영향을 보여 주기 위한
(c) 그 정책이 금지하게 될 웹 활동들을 중단하기 위한
(d) 온라인에서 무엇이 허용될지에 대한 논쟁을 비웃기 위한

정답 (b)

글의 흐름상 어색한 문장을 고르는 문제로, 전체 흐름을 파악하여 지문의 주제나 소재와 관계없는 내용을 고릅니다.

Read the passage and identify the option that does NOT belong.

For the next four months, major cities will experiment with new community awareness initiatives to decrease smoking in public places. (a) Anti-tobacco advertisements in recent years have relied on scare tactics to show how smokers hurt their own bodies. (b) But the new effort depicts the effects of second-hand smoke on children who breathe in adults' cigarette fumes. (c) Without these advertisements, few children would understand the effects of adults' hard-to-break habits. (d) Cities hope these messages will inspire people to think about others and cut back on their tobacco use.

향후 4개월 동안 주요 도시들은 공공장소에서의 흡연을 줄이기 위해 지역 사회의 의식을 촉구하는 새로운 계획을 시도할 것이다. (a) 최근에 금연 광고는 흡연자가 자신의 몸을 얼마나 해치고 있는지를 보여 주기 위해 겁을 주는 방식에 의존했다. (b) 그러나 이 새로운 시도는 어른들의 담배 연기를 마시는 아이들에게 미치는 간접흡연의 영향을 묘사한다. (c) 이러한 광고가 없다면, 아이들은 어른들의 끊기 힘든 습관이 미칠 영향을 모를 것이다. (d) 도시들은 이러한 메시지가 사람들에게 타인에 대해서 생각해 보고 담배 사용을 줄이는 마음이 생기게 할 것을 기대하고 있다.

정답 (c)

글의 내용 이해를 측정하는 문제로, 글의 주제나 대의 혹은 전반적 논조를 파악하는 문제, 세부 내용을 파악하는 문제, 추론하는 문제가 있습니다.

Read the passage, question, and options. Then, based on the given information, choose the option that best answers the question.

In theory, solar and wind energy farms could provide an alternative energy source and reduce our dependence on oil. But in reality, these methods face practical challenges no one has been able to solve. In Denmark, for example, a country with some of the world's largest wind farms, it turns out that winds blow most when people need electricity least. Because of this reduced demand, companies end up selling their power to other countries for little profit. In some cases, they pay customers to take the leftover energy.

Q: Which of the following is correct according to the passage?

(a) Energy companies can lose money on the power they produce.

(b) Research has expanded to balance supply and demand gaps.

(c) Solar and wind power are not viewed as possible options.

(d) Reliance on oil has led to political tensions in many countries.

이론상으로 태양과 풍력 에너지 발전 단지는 대체 에너지 자원을 제공하고 원유에 대한 의존을 낮출 수 있다. 그러나 사실상 이러한 방법들은 아무도 해결할 수 없었던 현실적인 문제에 부딪친다. 예를 들어 세계에서 가장 큰 풍력 에너지 발전 단지를 가진 덴마크에서 사람들이 전기를 가장 덜 필요로 할 때 가장 강한 바람이 분다는 것이 판명되었다. 이러한 낮은 수요 때문에 회사는 결국 그들의 전력을 적은 이윤으로 다른 나라에 팔게 되었다. 어떤 경우에는 남은 에너지를 가져가라고 고객에게 돈을 지불하기도 한다.

Q 이 글에 의하면 다음 중 옳은 것은?

(a) 에너지 회사는 그들이 생산한 전력으로 손해를 볼 수도 있다.

(b) 수요와 공급 격차를 조정하기 위해 연구가 확장되었다.

(c) 태양과 풍력 에너지는 가능한 대안으로 간주되지 않는다.

(d) 원유에 대한 의존은 많은 나라들 사이에 정치적 긴장감을 가져왔다.

정답 (a)

이번 NEW TEPS에 새롭게 추가된 유형으로 1지문 2문항 유형입니다. 5개의 지문이 나오므로 총 10문항을 풀어야 합니다.
주제와 세부 내용, 추론 문제가 섞여서 출제됩니다.

Read the passage, questions, and options. Then, based on the given information, choose the option that best answers each question.

You seem exasperated that the governor's proposed budget would triple the funding allocated to state parks. What's the problem? Such allocation hardly represents "profligate spending," as you put it. Don't forget that a third of all job positions at state parks were cut during the last recession. This left the parks badly understaffed, with a dearth of park rangers to serve the 33 million people who visit them annually. It also contributed to deterioration in the parks' natural beauty due to a decrease in maintenance work.

These parks account for less than 1% of our state's recreational land, yet they attract more visitors than our top two largest national parks and national forests combined. They also perform a vital economic function, bringing wealth to nearby rural communities by attracting people to the area. The least we can do is to provide the minimum funding to help keep them in good condition.

Q1:   What is the writer mainly trying to do?
(a) Justify the proposed spending on state parks
(b) Draw attention to the popularity of state parks
(c) Contest the annual number of state park visitors
(d) Refute the governor's stance on the parks budget

Q2:   Which statement would the writer most likely agree with?
(a) Low wages are behind the understaffing of the state parks.
(b) State parks require more promotion than national parks.
(c) The deterioration of state parks is due mainly to overuse.
(d) The state parks' popularity is disproportionate to their size.

여러분은 주립 공원에 할당된 예산을 세배로 증가시키려는 주지사의 제안을 듣고 분노할지도 모른다. 무엇이 문제일까? 그와 같은 할당은 여러분들이 말하듯이 '낭비적인 지출'이라고 말하기 힘들다. 지난 경제 침체기 동안 주립 공원 일자리의 1/3이 삭감되었다는 사실을 잊지 말기 바란다. 이 때문에 공원은 부족한 관리인들이 매년 공원을 방문하는 3천3백만 명의 사람들을 처리해야 하는 인력 부족에 시달리고 있다. 또 그 때문에 관리 작업 부족으로 공원의 자연 경관이 망가지게 되었다.

이 공원들은 주의 여가지의 1%도 차지하지 않지만, 규모가 가장 큰 2개의 국립공원과 국립 숲을 합친 것보다 많은 방문객을 끌어들인다. 그들은 사람들을 그 지역으로 끌어들여 부를 주변의 공동체에게 가져다줌으로써 중요한 경제적 기능을 한다. 우리가 할 수 있는 최소한의 일은 공원이 잘 관리될 수 있도록 최소한의 자금을 조달하는 것이다.

Q1 작가가 주로 하고 있는 것은?

(a) 주립 공원 예산안을 정당화하기

(b) 주립 공원 인기에 대한 주의를 환기시키기

(c) 매년 주립 공원을 방문하는 사람 수에 대한 의문 제기하기

(d) 공원 예산에 대한 주지사의 입장에 대해 반박하기

정답 (a)

Q2 저자가 동의할 것 같은 내용은?

(a) 인력난에 시달리는 주립 공원의 배경에는 낮은 임금이 있다.

(b) 주립 공원은 국립공원보다 더 많은 지원이 필요하다.

(c) 주립 공원은 지나친 사용 때문에 망가지고 있다.

(d) 주립 공원의 인기는 그 규모와는 어울리지 않는다.

정답 (b)

※ 독해 Part 4 뉴텝스 샘플 문제는 서울대텝스관리위원회에서 제공한 문제입니다. (www.teps.or.kr)

NEWTEPS 성적표

TEPS
SCORE REPORT

YOUR SCORES

Total Score	**418**	Level	**2+**	Percentile Rank	**81.33**

L	V	G	R
149	**35**	**38**	**196**
Average 110	Average 32	Average 32	Average 110
Percentile Rank **74**	Percentile Rank **56**	Percentile Rank **55**	Percentile Rank **90**

YOUR ENGLISH PROFICIENCY

Advanced level of English proficiency. A score at this level typically indicates an advanced level of English proficiency for a non-native speaker. A test taker at this level is able to perform general tasks after short-term training.

Section	Subskill	Proficiency
Listening	- Understanding the connection of ideas across turns in spoken texts - Understanding the main ideas of spoken texts - Understanding specific information in spoken texts - Making inferences based on given information in spoken texts	Intermediate Advanced Advanced Intermediate
Vocabulary	- Understanding vocabulary used in spoken contexts - Understanding vocabulary used in written contexts	Intermediate Basic
Grammar	- Understanding grammar used in spoken contexts - Understanding grammar used in written contexts	Intermediate Intermediate
Reading	- Understanding the main ideas of written texts - Understanding specific information in written texts - Making inferences based on given information in written texts - Understanding the connection of ideas across sentences in written texts	Advanced Advanced Advanced Intermediate

NAME
HONG GIL DONG

DATE OF BIRTH
JUL. 12, 1990

GENDER
MALE

REGISTRATION NO.
0123456

TEST DATE
MAY 12, 2018

VALID UNTIL
MAY 12, 2020

Barcode

NO : RAAAA0000BBBB

THE TEPS COUNCIL

※ 자료 출처: www.teps.or.kr

23

NEW TEPS Q&A

1 / 시험 접수는 어떻게 해야 하나요?

정기 시험은 회차별로 지정된 접수 기간 중 인터넷(www.teps.or.kr) 또는 접수처를 방문하여 접수하실 수 있습니다. 정시 접수의 응시료는 42,000원입니다. 접수기간을 놓친 수험생의 응시편의를 위해 마련된 추가 접수도 있는데, 추가 접수 응시료는 45,000원입니다.

2 / 텝스관리위원회에서 인정하는 신분증은 무엇인가요?

아래 제시된 신분증 중 한 가지를 유효한 신분증으로 인정합니다.

일반인, 대학생	주민등록증, 운전면허증, 기간 만료전의 여권, 공무원증, 장애인 복지카드, 주민등록(재)발급 확인서 *대학(원)생 학생증은 사용할 수 없습니다.
중 · 고등학생	학생증(학생증 지참 시 유의 사항 참조), 기간 만료 전의 여권, 청소년증(발급 신청 확인서), 주민등록증(발급 신청 확인서), TEPS신분확인증명서
초등학생	기간 만료 전의 여권, 청소년증(발급신청확인서), TEPS신분확인증명서
군인	주민등록증(발급신청확인서), 운전면허증, 기간만료 전의 여권, 현역간부 신분증, 군무원증, TEPS신분확인증명서
외국인	외국인등록증, 기간 만료 전의 여권, 국내거소신고증(출입국 관리사무소 발행)

*시험 당일 신분증 미지참자 및 규정에 맞지 않는 신분증 소지자는 시험에 응시할 수 없습니다.

3 / TEPS 시험 볼 때 꼭 가져가야 하는 것은 무엇인가요?

신분증, 컴퓨터용 사인펜, 수정테이프(컴퓨터용 연필, 수정액은 사용 불가), 수험표입니다.

4 / TEPS 고사장에 도착해야 하는 시간은 언제인가요?

오전 9시 30분까지 입실을 완료해야 합니다. (토요일 시험의 경우 오후 2:30까지 입실 완료)

5 / 시험장의 시험 진행 일정은 어떻게 되나요?

	시험 진행 시간	내용	비고
시험 준비 단계 (입실 완료 후 30분)	10분	답안지 오리엔테이션	1차 신분확인
	5분	휴식	
	10분	신분확인 휴대폰 수거 (기타 통신전자기기 포함)	2차 신분확인
	5분	최종 방송 테스트 문제지 배부	
본 시험 (총 105분)	40분	청해	쉬는 시간 없이 시험 진행 각 영역별 제한시간 엄수
	25분	어휘/문법	
	40분	독해	

*시험 진행 시험 당일 고사장 사정에 따라 변동될 수 있습니다.
*영역별 제한 시간 내에 해당 영역의 문제 풀이 및 답안 마킹을 모두 완료해야 합니다.

6 / 시험 점수는 얼마 후에 알게 되나요?

TEPS 정기시험 성적 결과는 시험일 이후 2주차 화요일 17시에 TEPS 홈페이지를 통해 발표되며 우편 통보는 성적 발표일로부터 7~10일 가량 소요됩니다. 성적 확인을 위해서는 성적 확인용 비밀번호를 반드시 입력해야 합니다. 성적 확인 비밀번호는 가장 최근에 응시한 TEPS 정기 시험 답안지에 기재한 비밀번호 4자리입니다. 성적 발표일은 변경될 수 있으니 홈페이지 공지사항을 참고하시기 바랍니다. TEPS 성적은 2년간 유효합니다.

※자료 출처 : www.teps.or.kr

NEWTEPS 등급표

등급	점수	영역	능력검정기준(Description)
1+	526~600	전반	**외국인으로서 최상급 수준의 의사소통 능력** 교양 있는 원어민에 버금가는 정도로 의사소통이 가능하고 전문분야 업무에 대처할 수 있음 (Native Level of English Proficiency)
1	453~525	전반	**외국인으로서 최상급 수준에 근접한 의사소통능력** 단기간 집중 교육을 받으면 대부분의 의사소통이 가능하고 전문분야 업무에 별 무리 없이 대처할 수 있음 (Near-Native Level of Communicative Competence)
2+	387~452	전반	**외국인으로서 상급 수준의 의사소통능력** 단기간 집중 교육을 받으면 일반 분야업무를 큰 어려움 없이 수행할 수 있음 (Advanced Level of Communicative Competence)
2	327~386	전반	**외국인으로서 중상급 수준의 의사소통능력** 중장기간 집중 교육을 받으면 일반분야 업무를 큰 어려움 없이 수행할 수 있음 (High Intermediate Level of Communicative Competence)
3+	268~326	전반	**외국인으로서 중급 수준의 의사소통능력** 중장기간 집중 교육을 받으면 한정된 분야의 업무를 큰 어려움 없이 수행할 수 있음 (Mid Intermediate Level of Communicative Competence)
3	212~267	전반	**외국인으로서 중하급 수준의 의사소통능력** 중장기간 집중 교육을 받으면 한정된 분야의 업무를 다소 미흡하지만 큰 지장 없이 수행할 수 있음 (Low Intermediate Level of Communicative Competence)
4+	163~211	전반	**외국인으로서 하급수준의 의사소통능력** 장기간의 집중 교육을 받으면 한정된 분야의 업무를 대체로 어렵게 수행할 수 있음 (Novice Level of Communicative Competence)
4	111~162		
5+	55~110	전반	**외국인으로서 최하급 수준의 의사소통능력** 단편적인 지식만을 갖추고 있어 의사소통이 거의 불가능함 (Near-Zero Level of Communicative Competence)
5	0~54		

Listening
Comprehension

DIRECTIONS

1. In the Listening Comprehension section, all content will be
    presented orally rather than in written form.

2. This section contains five parts. For each part, you will receive
    separate instructions. Listen to the instructions carefully, and
    choose the best answer from the options for each item.

MP3 바로 듣기
받아쓰기 테스트
모바일 단어장

Part I　**Questions 1—10**

You will now hear ten individual spoken questions or statements, each followed by four spoken responses. Choose the most appropriate response for each item.

Part II　**Questions 11—20**

You will now hear ten short conversation fragments, each followed by four spoken responses. Choose the most appropriate response to complete each conversation.

You will now hear ten complete conversations. For each conversation, you will be asked to answer a question. Before each conversation, you will hear a short description of the situation. After listening to the description and conversation once, you will hear a question and four options. Based on the given information, choose the option that best answers the question.

L

Part IV **Questions 31—36**

You will now hear six short talks. After each talk, you will be asked to answer a question. Each talk and its corresponding question will be read twice. Then you will hear four options which will be read only once. Based on the given information, choose the option that best answers the question.

Part V **Questions 37—40**

You will now hear two longer talks. After each talk, you will be asked to answer two questions. Each talk and its corresponding questions will be read twice. However, the four options for each question will be read only once. Based on the given information, choose the option that best answers each question.

Vocabulary & Grammar

DIRECTIONS

These two sections test your vocabulary and grammar knowledge. You will have 25 minutes to complete a total of 60 questions: 30 from the Vocabulary section and 30 from the Grammar section. Be sure to follow the directions given by the proctor.

Part I **Questions 1—10**

Choose the option that best completes each dialogue.

1. A: Don't you want any pizza?
   B: No thanks. All that grease will make me _____.
   (a) come to
   (b) settle down
   (c) move on
   (d) break out

2. A: I can't look at any more pictures of the earthquake.
   B: I know. The _____ is tragic.
   (a) condolence
   (b) devastation
   (c) ambience
   (d) repression

3. A: Rebecca's haughtiness is getting on my nerves.
   B: Mine too. She can be quite _____.
   (a) modest
   (b) aloof
   (c) noble
   (d) resolute

4. A: This is the loveliest hotel lobby I've ever been in.
   B: Yes, every design decision exhibits _____ taste.
   (a) implacable
   (b) insouciant
   (c) impeccable
   (d) indecorous

5. A: How's the report coming?
   B: It'll take me hours to _____ all this data.
   (a) round out
   (b) sort through
   (c) watch over
   (d) glide about

6. A: The court appears set to strike down the tax law today.
   B: I assume you're in support of its _____.
   (a) nullification
   (b) depredation
   (c) lucidity
   (d) caprice

7. A: I take it Raquel is still moping about losing the game.
   B: Yes, she's looking particularly _____ today.
   (a) grave
   (b) dry
   (c) sedate
   (d) glum

8. A: Did you confront Jared to get him to do the work?
   B: Yes, but all that happened was more _____.
   (a) prevarication
   (b) exorbitance
   (c) attenuation
   (d) improvidence

9. A: Do you accept criticism of your work?
   B: Only if it's constructive. I won't stand for outright _____.
   (a) indigence
   (b) denigration
   (c) soliloquy
   (d) emollients

10. A: I want you to know I meant you no harm.
    B: Don't worry. I _____ no ill will against you.
    (a) regard
    (b) harbor
    (c) board
    (d) remit

Choose the option that best completes each sentence.

11. As long as sales continue to
    _____, the company will resist
    employees' calls for pay raises.

    (a) shirk
    (b) tick
    (c) rend
    (d) lag

12. Several natural aquifers in central Texas
    were dangerously _____ during
    the four-year drought.

    (a) repulsed
    (b) eradicated
    (c) asserted
    (d) depleted

13. Dreams of striking it rich _____
    many people into purchasing lottery
    tickets.

    (a) defect
    (b) exonerate
    (c) beguile
    (d) impugn

14. Writers of nonfiction may engage in
    embellishment, but they do not have
    _____ to fabricate events.

    (a) diversion
    (b) probate
    (c) tribute
    (d) license

15. Patients suffering from _____
    pain are urged to consult their doctors
    before taking painkillers.

    (a) timeless
    (b) chronic
    (c) immortal
    (d) abiding

16. After reviewing the case, the judge ruled
    that the officers' _____ of the
    man's property was unconstitutional.

    (a) seizure
    (b) deficiency
    (c) barrage
    (d) liability

17. Heavy rains and the _____
    landslides left over 20 people dead on
    the small Philippine island.

    (a) ensuing
    (b) vociferous
    (c) limpid
    (d) bludgeoned

18. The United States risks being
    _____ a hypocrite if it does not
    apply its trade policies equally to all
    countries.

    (a) assigned
    (b) redoubled
    (c) branded
    (d) daubed

19. Contact emergency services immediately
    if you _____ the solution, or if it
    comes into contact with your eye.

    (a) ingest
    (b) sterilize
    (c) cultivate
    (d) dispatch

20. Critics applauded the actor's
    _____ of Chilean dictator
    Augusto Pinochet in the Broadway play.

    (a) heresy
    (b) proponent
    (c) portrayal
    (d) depletion

21. Despite the mainstream culture becoming more _____ by the day, many in the country continue to maintain their religious faith.

(a) secular
(b) didactic
(c) meager
(d) opaque

22. Investors worry that yesterday's unstable stock prices _____ further turmoil in the weeks ahead.

(a) portend
(b) allay
(c) cajole
(d) weave

23. Federal _____ to corn growers give them an unfair market advantage over other unsupported farmers.

(a) accolades
(b) precincts
(c) subsidies
(d) snubs

24. *Web Design Intermediate* is a textbook for those who have previously _____ in web design but are serious about advancing their skills.

(a) dabbled
(b) ogled
(c) traversed
(d) ousted

25. Prior to the advent of modern paving techniques, roads in the Midwest would become _____ after even a small amount of rain.

(a) destitute
(b) impassable
(c) barren
(d) oblivious

26. Warren Buffet has pledged to donate the majority of his wealth to charity and encourages other moguls to follow _____.

(a) suit
(b) cash
(c) copy
(d) step

27. The metropolis of Kuala Lumpur is situated at the _____ of the Gombak and Klang Rivers.

(a) confluence
(b) mishmash
(c) rejoinder
(d) assemblage

28. While Ms. Lee's earlier works exhibited some fresh and unconventional prose, her latest offering is disappointingly _____.

(a) arcane
(b) rampant
(c) choleric
(d) prosaic

29. The flower species typically displays a _____ petal, with alternating bands of mauve and cyan.

(a) variegated
(b) temperate
(c) nonplussed
(d) laconic

30. On the heels of the plagiarism scandal came the news that Professor Martinez had _____ his resignation from the university.

(a) tendered
(b) substantiated
(c) underwritten
(d) divested

You have finished the Vocabulary questions. Please continue on to the Grammar questions.

Part I   Questions 1—10

Choose the option that best completes each dialogue.

1. A: Congratulations on taking first prize at the science fair!
    B: Well, I couldn't have done it if it _____ for you.
    (a) weren't to be
    (b) didn't have
    (c) hadn't been
    (d) as wasn't

2. A: Should I visit Paris or Shanghai on my vacation?
    B: You'll have a great time no matter _____ you choose.
    (a) that
    (b) which
    (c) whose
    (d) whatever

3. A: I'm going to make you a fabulous dinner this evening.
    B: Please don't _____ just for me.
    (a) put yourself out
    (b) put out yourself
    (c) put you out
    (d) you put out

4. A: I haven't seen Kim all day, have you?
    B: She's still in her office _____ that report.
    (a) finishing
    (b) to finishing
    (c) to be finished
    (d) going to finish

5. A: Is your mom still in hospital? It's been a while.
    B: Yes. _____ hospitalized for a year next month.
    (a) She was
    (b) She has been
    (c) She had been
    (d) She'll have been

6. A: It seems like everyone's talking about the new war movie.
    B: Yes, there's _____ around it that I doubt it can live up to expectations.
    (a) so hype
    (b) such hype
    (c) hype a lot
    (d) much of the hype

7. A: Diana is becoming the new CEO, right?
    B: The board _____ yet, but I believe so.
    (a) announced isn't official
    (b) hasn't officially announced it
    (c) officially hasn't it announced
    (d) isn't having officially announced

8. A: Isn't there a party in one of the firm's offices today?
    B: Yes, although I forget _____ it's being held.
    (a) whose
    (b) which
    (c) in whose
    (d) to whom

9. A: What will you do if it turns out Peter took your notebook?
    B: I'll demand that he _____ it at once, of course.
    (a) return
    (b) returns
    (c) had returned
    (d) is returning

10. A: I really wish we hadn't lost that client's account.
    B: We can't spend time worrying about _____.
    (a) could be what to have
    (b) what could have been
    (c) having what could be
    (d) being what could have

G

11. The criminal was caught _____ around the premises of the bank after hours.

    (a) prowls
    (b) prowler
    (c) to prowl
    (d) prowling

12. The collection of antique dolls _____ by a trust from the American Historical Society.

    (a) can maintain
    (b) is maintained
    (c) has maintained
    (d) has been maintaining

13. According to the financial commission, none of the electronic trades made _____ the power blackouts were recorded.

    (a) while
    (b) from
    (c) once
    (d) during

14. It was customary for Genghis Khan's armies to show _____ mercy to their enemies during battle.

    (a) the
    (b) none
    (c) any
    (d) no

15. All vertebrates alive today are believed _____ from a common ancestor millions of years ago.

    (a) to be descending
    (b) being descended
    (c) having to descend
    (d) to have descended

16. Mr. Damon would be shift supervisor by now _____ been involved in the embezzlement scandal.

    (a) not having him
    (b) had he not
    (c) he hadn't
    (d) hadn't he

17. When the disgraced politician addressed the media, he spoke _____ nothing untoward had occurred.

    (a) regardless of
    (b) rather than
    (c) whether
    (d) as if

18. Investors agreed that Wilmer Holding's revenue increase last quarter was _____.

    (a) a surprised event that most turned
    (b) a most surprising turn of events
    (c) more surprising turned event
    (d) more of a surprise event turn

19. Abu Dhabi's government provided the funding, _____ the building project might still be awaiting completion.

    (a) so that
    (b) of whose
    (c) towards what
    (d) without which

20. _____ from the marathon, the runner was rushed to an area hospital.

    (a) Exhausted
    (b) Exhausting
    (c) He was exhausted
    (d) Had been exhausted

21. A judge, after hearing arguments from several consumer groups, found that the excise tax had been raised by an amount greater _____.

    (a) than reasonable
    (b) than was reasonable
    (c) it reasonably could be
    (d) of any that reasonable was

22. All entities, citizens and corporations alike, _____ as a result of the oil spill, are entitled to remuneration.

    (a) disadvantaging
    (b) disadvantaged
    (c) were disadvantaged
    (d) having disadvantaged

23. Not even a message of reassurance from the Pope _____ could stem the rising tide of accusations.

    (a) of his
    (b) himself
    (c) he gave
    (d) had given him

24. As far as we know, the committee responsible for awarding the grant money has yet _____.

    (a) to decide whose proposal to accept
    (b) whose proposal decided to accept
    (c) to decide to accept whose proposal
    (d) decided to accept whose proposal

25. While visible on close inspection, the brushstrokes in the painting are _____ for the average viewer to note.

    (a) finer
    (b) so fine
    (c) too fine
    (d) the finest

G

Part III **Questions 26—30**

Read each dialogue or passage carefully and identify the option that contains a grammatical error.

26. (a) A: Have you ever had an MRI scan before?
    (b) B: Yes, when I tore a ligament in my knee last year.
    (c) A: Did you find the experience frightening at all?
    (d) B: Not really, but I hear that some people do find.

27. (a) A: Have you already eaten, Monique?
    (b) B: Yes, lunch will provide for free at the conference today.
    (c) A: So you don't want any of this lasagna that I made?
    (d) B: I'd love to try some later if there's any left.

28. (a) In May of 2013, Earth's atmospheric concentration of carbon dioxide was measured at 400 parts per million (ppm). (b) This was the first time such a level had been reached and marks an alarming increase from the baseline 280 ppm measured in pre-industrial times. (c) In fact, some scientists believe this is the highest concentration in the last two thousand years. (d) Atmospheric carbon dioxide is considered the main driver of climate change, to trap the sun's heat in the atmosphere and at Earth's surface.

29. (a) In the 1400s, the Chinese Admiral Zheng He commanded a series of maritime expeditions of tremendous scope. (b) While the initial impetus for these seven "treasure voyages" is unknown, there is no doubt about their outcome. (c) China's fleet was able to bring a number of neighboring kingdoms under its military and political control. (d) After that, Ming Dynasty rulers benefited from the riches extracted from these lesser powers for decades coming.

30. (a) The hackberry belongs to a genus of deciduous tree native to many regions of the Northern Hemisphere, including southern and central North America. (b) It was once categorized as a member of the elm family, though current classifications include it in the broader hemp group. (c) Hackberries are considered a nuisance by some, for the tree is so successful at reproducing than it can spread with similar tenacity to weeds. (d) However, its drought tolerance makes it popular in dry regions, and its wood is useful in cabinetry.

You have reached the end of the Vocabulary & Grammar sections. Do NOT move on to the Reading Comprehension section until instructed to do so. You are NOT allowed to turn to any other section of the test.

Reading
Comprehension

R

Read the passage and choose the option that best completes the passage.

1. Timothy Leary was both celebrated and reviled by the general public. A lecturing psychologist and researcher at Harvard University, Leary began experimenting with psychedelic drugs in 1960 and adopted anti-establishment views. This resulted in his expulsion from Harvard faculty in 1963, and his publicized calls on students everywhere to drop out of society. While many Americans regarded Leary as a symbol of cultural degeneration, others disagreed. They considered his

   _____.

   (a) views on society and culture to be unorthodox
   (b) social rebellion necessary to bring about change
   (c) behavior a serious threat to the health of society
   (d) outbursts a sign of an undiagnosed mental illness

2. Novelist Andrew Combe captured our imaginations with his 1995 bestseller *City of the Fountain*. Three years later, his sequel *Mountains and Valleys*, while not matching the high bar set by his first novel, nonetheless continued to excite readers. Since then, however, it's been one flop after another as Combe has attempted to write in genres other than science fiction. His latest effort, *Along the Winding Brook*, is an over-sentimentalized love story set in the countryside of Victorian England. In the opinion of this reviewer, Combe _____.

   (a) ought to have not returned to science fiction
   (b) can basically turn his hand to any kind of genre
   (c) would have been better off sticking to nonfiction
   (d) should not have deviated from a winning formula

3. The Scots are often viewed as one people within the larger entity of the United Kingdom. This is ironic given _____. Nine hundred years ago, the area now known as Scotland was inhabited by a number of distinct tribes. One of the primary groupings was that of the Picts, whom the Romans fought unsuccessfully during their campaigns of conquering the British Isles. Other tribal ethnicities included those of the Gaels, Britons, and Angles, all of whom eventually coalesced to form today's Scottish identity.

(a) it is largely the result of ancient Roman conquest
(b) that the Scots long ago fought against the Romans
(c) the nation should be more unified than it is
(d) a regional history of anything but unity

4. Electric fish are uniquely equipped with electric fields emanating from their bodies for either hunting or defending against predators. Electric eels, for example, emit shocks of up to 600 volts to incapacitate or kill prey. The cells in their organs have the ability to generate a small electrical potential and, when discharged in unison with hundreds of thousands of other similar cells, contributes to a strong electric pulse. On the other hand, weakly electric fish rely on low voltage fields _____. When a predator enters its electric field, the fish perceives the disturbance and is able to avoid capture.

(a) to protect themselves from the cold
(b) for sensing rather than hunting
(c) for intra-species communication
(d) to insulate their internal organs

5. Economics revolves around the study of consumer choice and behavior. Yet more and more it seems the field of economics is hobbled by analysis only of statistical modeling far removed from actual events. This predicament arises from a trend in economics wherein pure theory is revered and anything that deviates from the abstract ideal (applied economic theory, for example) is not deemed worthy of serious consideration. So economists are becoming increasingly reliant on mathematical formulae for their theories about human decision-making. Their calculations as a result _____.

(a) rather accurately follow consumer trends
(b) have no basis in real-world markets
(c) must be carried out by computers
(d) are viewed as eminently relevant

6.

> Best Food for Dogs with Allergies
>
> You create meals that are free of allergens, _____.
> We introduce Alison's Canine Allergy-Conscious Cuisine, formulated specifically
> for your pet and guaranteed to promote the health of your animal companions.
> Alison's is unique in that we create custom-tailored food based on your dog's allergy
> profile. All you have to do is register online at www.alisonscacc.com, submit your
> veterinarian-conducted allergy test results, and we'll do the rest. You'll receive 7-day
> meal shipments once a week, straight from our kitchen to your doggie dish!

(a) yet dogs are not known to suffer from allergies
(b) while other allergies are caused by house pets
(c) and your best friend deserves nothing less
(d) but be careful not to feed scraps to pets

7. When slacklining was first conceived, _____. The
practice consisted of a half-inch-wide strip of fabric tied between two points low to the
ground across which a person walked. Some ridiculed it as nothing more than amateur
tightrope walking. Soon enough, though, the more athletic practitioners began performing
stunts such as handstands and backflips on the line. The next innovation was that of the
"highline," a slackline strung hundreds of feet above the ground, as between two cliff
faces. Onlookers gaped as daredevils walked the slackline, often without a safety rope.

(a) no one understood its design
(b) it was a rather tame activity
(c) it proved too dangerous to be popular
(d) athletes introduced daredevil elements

8. What an atomic bomb explosion looks like is common knowledge, but not so
_____. First of all, the type of energy in question is
gamma radiation, released in a matter of microseconds following detonation. The
explosion's gamma rays penetrate living cells and dislodge electrons from molecules of
water that surround our DNA. These water molecules, now unstable free radicals, co-opt
electrons from DNA molecules, damaging them and introducing the risk of cancer and
other maladies.

(a) the distances that radiation is able to spread
(b) how people in proximity are actually vaporized
(c) why different kinds of radiation enter the atmosphere
(d) the mechanism by which radiation harms living tissue

9. It was the intention of management to replace Miriam Duke quickly following her abdication as Chief Investment Officer. _____, though now a month following her departure, we have yet to determine a suitable successor. At this point, our preference would be to hire an outside consultant to cull a selection of exemplary candidates with a range of skills and professional backgrounds. Of course, the expense of employing consultant services is not inconsequential, and so there is a delay while the proposal is being reviewed by the board.

(a) Wherefore
(b) Therefore
(c) However
(d) Likewise

10. The limited liability company (LLC) falls somewhere between sole proprietorship and a corporation. Similar to a corporation, an LLC provides its owner(s) with limited liability. That is, the personal wealth and property of the owner(s) is protected in the event that a suit is brought against the company. _____, an LLC also resembles a sole proprietorship when it comes to taxation. The revenue earned by the company is considered personal income for the owner(s) and is thus taxed at personal income levels.

(a) On the other hand
(b) In short
(c) Subsequently
(d) For all that

R

Read the passage and identify the option that does NOT belong.

11. Open from dawn to dusk, Manukau Canoes and Kayaks located on Adler Road is dedicated to providing you maximum enjoyment on the water. (a) Come in this week, when all of our boat rental prices will be discounted 20% to celebrate the arrival of summer. (b) We stock a range of craft, from traditional kayaks and canoes to stand-up paddleboards and bicycle boats. (c) Also be sure to retrofit all your marine equipment to comply with new safety ordinances effective this year. (d) All of our boats are safety-certified and come with a lifetime guarantee for your uninterrupted water sport leisure.

12. In the fall of 1781, the slave ship Zong was crossing the Atlantic, carrying 442 slaves from Africa to the Caribbean. (a) As a result of navigation errors, the ship expended its store of drinking water prior to making landfall. (b) The crew thereby made the decision to murder 142 of the slaves by drowning them in the ocean. (c) Though none of the crew was ever tried for this crime, the incident sparked abolitionist movements in Europe and the US. (d) The American abolitionist John Brown led an unsuccessful raid on the federal armory at Harpers Ferry almost 80 years later.

Read the passage, question, and options. Then, based on the given information, choose the option that best answers each question.

R

13.

Dear Mr. Lynn,

Thank you for your interest in the Blake Museum of Fine Arts and its ongoing roster of events and special exhibits. In answer to your question, we are not currently accepting monetary contributions from the general public, as the majority of our funding comes in the form of an endowment from the National Arts Institute. You certainly may support us by becoming a member of the museum. Annual memberships start at $65 and can be acquired through our website, www.blake-art. org.

Sincerely,
Laura Berg
Director of Outreach

Q: What is the main purpose of the email?
(a) To respond to an inquiry about donations
(b) To solicit a national grant for the museum
(c) To promote the museum's schedule of events
(d) To encourage a patron to renew membership

14. After months of anticipatory buzz, the video game manufacturer PRF Entertainment was finally set to unveil its next-generation GEX-2 console. In speeding their product to market, the company hoped to grab customers ahead of Reginald's upcoming Kazam 3.0 release slated for later this year. Industry insiders in attendance at PRF's launch event broadcast a live play-by-play of their reactions as they waited for their first look at the new console—which never came. "Announcing a new console without actually showing it?" sneered a reporter from Gamer Insider magazine. "That's lame."

Q: What is the passage mainly about?
(a) A company not revealing its new product
(b) A rivalry between two top game console companies
(c) Poor initial sales of a hyped game console
(d) Media frenzy at a gaming industry event

15. Hydropower is a method of electricity generation that channels the energy contained in moving water into a usable form. The conventional generation method capitalizes on the potential energy contained within a dammed reservoir. As the water flows through an aperture in the dam, it turns the blades of a massive turbine, which rotates the central shaft it is attached to. At the other end of the shaft, a component called the rotor spins in unison with the turbine and the shaft. As the rotor moves, the magnets inside it cycle past a stationary coil of copper wire. This moves electrons in the wire, causing electricity to flow.

Q: What is mainly being described in the passage?

(a) The various methods of generating hydropower
(b) The technology involved in hydropower operation
(c) The benefits of hydropower over other energy sources
(d) The sustainability of hydropower electricity generation

16. Two distinct cultures and ethnicities collide in the region around the Langtang Valley in central Nepal. To the south lies the Kathmandu Valley, an area of lower elevations and the site of the country's capital and largest city, Kathmandu. It is home mainly to Nepalis for whom Hinduism is the primary religion. The Langtang Valley, though proximate in distance, hosts a strikingly different population, made up of ethnic Tibetans and the related Tamang group, both of whom are adherents of the Buddhist faith.

Q: What is the best title for the passage?

(a) Nepal's Approach to Cultural Diversity
(b) Distinct Cultures in One Country
(c) A Paradox of Religion and Ethnicity
(d) The Religious Conflict in Kathmandu

17.

Economy News

This week, the British pound dropped to its lowest value against the dollar in over two years, with one pound trading at 1.5073 dollars. In recent months, the value of British currency compared to the dollar has diminished by about 7 percent. And given that financial analysts say the outlook for Britain's economy is dismal, the pound is not expected to make gains against the dollar anytime soon. At the same time, the euro has skyrocketed, gaining 7.5 percent against the pound this year alone.

R

Q: Which of the following is correct according to the passage?
(a) One British pound still trades for less than one dollar.
(b) The dollar lost value against the pound by 7 percent.
(c) The pound was worth 1.5073 euros at its lowest value.
(d) The euro and dollar gained on the pound this year.

18. For most it is a recreational pastime that can be enjoyed from time to time, but for about 2 percent of the population, gambling represents a pathological impulse that causes lasting harm. While it is officially recognized as a psychiatric condition called gambling addiction, the disorder is often an invisible one, disguised by other afflictions that may accompany it, like depression or insomnia. Effective treatments for gambling addiction exist, and in certain respects treating pathological gambling is like rehabilitating substance abusers. But of course, gambling habits are not physical addictions and cannot be medically assessed in the way drug abuse can.

Q: Which of the following is correct according to the passage?
(a) Gambling is not identified as a psychiatric disorder.
(b) Two percent of gamblers practice pathological gambling.
(c) Treatments for gambling resemble those for other addictions.
(d) Gambling impulses are measured by objective medical tests.

19. Earlier this week, it was announced that auto manufacturer TL Motors will be teaming up with Fair Skies Energy to offer car buyers a special benefit: discount solar panels. Starting next month, when consumers purchase a new electric vehicle from TL Motors, they will be eligible for $200 off a solar panel system from Fair Skies Energy. A spokesperson for TL Motors said the discount program is designed to attract consumers who are interested in reducing their carbon emissions. Fair Skies Energy is confident that their solar products will appeal to TL Motors' environmentally conscious customer base.

Q: What benefit will customers receive when they buy an electric vehicle?

(a) A $200 rebate from a government energy initiative
(b) A free solar panel system for home-energy use
(c) A discount on a product from Fair Skies Energy
(d) An extended warranty voucher from TL Motors

20. While certain factions of the Jewish diaspora always advocated for a return to the Land of Israel, this was not typically a majority viewpoint until around the mid-1800s. It was during this time that anti-Semitic sentiment was growing stronger in Europe, prompting an increasing number of Jews to view a Jewish homeland as a necessity. This movement, known as Zionism, won a major victory with Great Britain's Balfour Declaration in 1917, which backed the creation of a Jewish state in Palestine. Just over 30 years later, the Zionist vision became reality.

Q: Which of the following is correct according to the passage?

(a) The yearning for a homeland was long a part of Jewish history.
(b) Jews experienced less anti-Semitism after the mid-1800s.
(c) Discrimination drove the advocacy of a Zionist state.
(d) The Balfour Declaration marked Israel's founding.

21. The three years since our launch have been incredibly fast-moving for our team of designers and web developers here at Curb. Since our founding, we have pushed ourselves to explore the boundaries of digital creative expression and to arrive at technological innovations. The priority of user experience is a hallmark of our work and a principle we will never compromise on. Indeed, clients regularly report that our diligence in researching and serving the needs of their customer base has yielded fresh and invaluable insights they could never have achieved alone.

Q: Which of the following is correct about Curb?

(a) It is becoming successful after a slow start.
(b) It outsources its technological development.
(c) It focuses on technology over client relations.
(d) It conducts customer research to assist its clients.

22. One of the most interesting characteristics of the jumping spider is its excellent vision, made possible by four pairs of eyes. One of two pairs positioned on the face of the spider, the anterior median eyes are the largest of all the pairs and equip the jumping spider with three-dimensional vision. This enables the jumping spider to locate prey with exceptional precision, and as a consequence, its leaping attacks are quite deadly. The spider's vision is much more sensitive than human eyesight, which is limited to a tiny segment of the electromagnetic spectrum. Jumping spiders can perceive ultraviolet light, a range of the light spectrum invisible to humans.

Q: Which of the following is correct about the jumping spider?

(a) Half of its eight eyes are located on its face.
(b) Its 3D vision is primarily used to escape attack.
(c) Ultraviolet vision is used to detect all of its prey.
(d) Its visual acuity is similar to that of humans.

23. In 1938, radio listeners heard something astonishing on the news—the planet was being conquered by alien life forms. Of course, no such invasion was taking place the night of October 30, 1938. It was only a dramatized version of H. G. Wells' 1898 classic science fiction novel *The War of the Worlds*, produced by a theater company as a Halloween special. Because the performance emulated the style of reporting that listeners were accustomed to hearing in news reports, many panicked. Heightened anxiety about real-life Nazi German military aggression played into the believability of invasion.

Q: What can be inferred from the passage?
(a) The original novel did not allude to a German invasion.
(b) The performance featured a veteran news reporter.
(c) Radio was a new medium for the distribution of news.
(d) The US government financed the radio production.

24. The winter of 1609-1610 is known by historians as the "starving time" for the British settlement of Jamestown, Virginia. It is an appellation that arguably downplays the true scope of the disaster that swept Jamestown that season, when 80 percent of the residents perishing. Conditions were so dire that corpses were removed from their graves to be eaten. In 2012, forensic anthropologists recovered physical evidence of cannibalism in skull fragments gouged by the chopping and cutting utensils, ostensibly wielded by colonists cannibalizing their deceased peers.

Q: What can be inferred about the settlement of Jamestown?
(a) It never recovered from the devastating die-off.
(b) Some of its residents murdered one another for food.
(c) Its population was ill equipped for the conditions there.
(d) Historians consider it an anomaly among British colonies.

25.

Movie Review

With *The Etiquette of Iron*, director Dana Morrison returns to the saga of her luckless lovers, Curin and Mallory, and a relationship stymied by the forces of fate. It was 15 years ago that Morrison directed her first movie *Nights in Genoa* about a love buoyed by sweet idealism only the young can afford to possess. Her life experience since then has earned her deeper insights as a movie director. In her new film, Morrison's lens focuses on different details, the meaningful glances of her protagonists, the realities of making a living. The brazen passion that characterized that directorial debut has been replaced with a subtler portrayal of romance, which, while quieter and more understated, is all the more meaningful for its realism.

Q: What can be inferred from the review?

(a) *Nights in Genoa* received mixed reviews from critics.
(b) *The Etiquette of Iron* is a retelling of Morrison's earlier film.
(c) Morrison's new film was informed by her own personal maturation.
(d) Morrison's sequel to *Nights in Genoa* covers a period of 15 years.

Part IV   Questions 26—35

Read the passage, questions, and options. Then, based on the given information, choose the option that best answers each question.

R

Questions 26-27

Does Your Blood Type Determine Your Personality?

A large number of people in Japan and South Korea firmly believe that their blood types "dictate" their personality traits. Does this belief have scientific merit? Or is it just a myth?

Interestingly, even Aristotle, one of the greatest biologists in history, believed that your blood type played a major role in allowing your ancestors to pass down their personality traits to you. Nevertheless, the majority of scientists agree that there is little evidence that your blood type affects your personality in any significant ways.

According to Mari Yamaguchi, this "theory" was used by the Nazis in an effort to justify discriminating against non-Germans, including Jews. Blood types A and O are extremely common among Germans, while blood type B is quite common among Jews and other ethnic groups. The Nazis claimed that such differences were proof that Germans were superior to other peoples. However, even the Nazis eventually abandoned this theory because it was too unscientific.

It was Masahiko Nomi who revived and popularized this unscientific theory in the 1970s. Since then, this myth has been negatively influencing Japan and South Korea in many ways, which will be covered in our next issue of *Life & Science*.

---

26. Q: Which of the following is correct according to the article?

(a) Japan and South Korea share common myths about the ethnic traits of Jews.
(b) Aristotle's theory of personality traits was based on empirical evidence.
(c) Yamaguchi has been trained in the medical field for a long time.
(d) The lack of scientific merit compelled the Nazis to renounce the theory.

27. Q: What can be inferred from the article?

(a) It has been scientifically proven that personality traits are dictated by blood types.
(b) The concept of heredity was first proposed by Aristotle.
(c) The Nazis believed that Germans were allowed to discriminate against inferior peoples.
(d) Nomi strongly supported the extreme ideologies of the Nazis.

Local Business Groups Demand Consistency

On Wednesday, local business groups and associations, including the Richville Chamber of Commerce, demanded that the city government be consistent in pursuing important policies affecting the city. In particular, they expressed concern that the government's policy on foreign direct investment (FDI) has been vacillating for too long.

According to the chamber of commerce, the city of Richville had traditionally been open to FDI. However, in 2016, the government suddenly changed course and implemented many anti-FDI policies. The city government has been inconsistent with regard to FDI since then. As a result, large numbers of multinational corporations feel reluctant to directly invest in the city. At the same time, too many citizens now believe that FDI is detrimental to the local economy.

The chamber of commerce points out that in this globalized world, FDI is a major factor in bringing economic prosperity to the city. Of course, the local business associations ask that the city government be aware of that fact. For now, however, they wish the government's policies were at least consistent with regard to FDI. Such consistency would help all interested parties make informed investment decisions.

28. Q: What do the business groups and associations mainly want the city government to do?

(a) To make more profitable investment decisions
(b) To send clear messages to all parties concerned
(c) To become far more competitive in the globalized world
(d) To make efforts to help them expand into foreign markets

29. Q: What can be inferred from the passage?

(a) Only a few citizens of Richville are vehemently opposed to FDI.
(b) The chamber of commerce might want multinational corporations to invest directly in Richville.
(c) The city government is likely to decide to attract more FDI to the city for political gain.
(d) The role of FDI in bringing economic growth is vastly overrated.

R

Notice to Residents

For many people, Blue Hill Village conjures up images of comfortable living. However, not many people know that we provide ample chances for residents to interact socially with each other. The reason why we value social interaction so much is that it is the real key to happiness. We want all our residents to be genuinely happy.

The following programs are designed to promote social interaction among the residents.

- Movie watching groups: At present, there are six movie watching groups, and you can choose to join any of them.

- Meditation groups: For now, eight different meditation groups are open to residents.

- Religious activity groups: Fifteen religious activity groups welcome anyone interested in pursuing spirituality.

- Exercise groups: Nine exercise groups are open to anyone interested in getting fit.

If you want to pursue your spirituality, contact Melanie Johnson at melanie_j@ bluehillvillage.com. For other pursuits, email Julia Black at julia_b@bluehillvillage. com.

30. Q: Who is most likely to email Johnson?
(a) Amanda, who has been studying the health effects of meditation
(b) John, who has been interested in Christianity since childhood
(c) Cynthia, whose favorite genre of movie is horror
(d) Richard, who is developing anaemia

31. Q: What can be inferred from the notice?
(a) Blue Hill Village is a well-respected nursing home with dedicated doctors.
(b) The number of exercise groups has been increasing sharply these days.
(c) Religious activity groups have had tense relationships with movie watching groups.
(d) Non-residents may not be eligible to join meditation groups.

Our Heritage

Today, Greenbaum Pharmaceutical is one of the most respected pharmaceutical companies in the world. Each year, billions of consumers purchase our medical products because they trust us completely. We have never taken that trust for granted.

When Jennifer Greenbaum founded Greenbaum Pharmaceutical with her sisters, Laura and Rebecca, in 1899, it was just a small company dedicated to improving the health conditions of patients. Now, we are one of the largest pharmaceutical companies in the world. Our miraculous growth would have been impossible without the trust of our valued customers.

That is one of our greatest heritages, in which we have taken pride. Without any reservation, we can assure our customers that they can always rely upon us. We will never betray their trust.

32. Q: Which of the following is correct according to the webpage?

(a) The core values of the company include generosity and perseverance.
(b) Jennifer was far older than Rebecca when she founded the company.
(c) The company is one of the oldest pharmaceutical companies in the world.
(d) The company started as a family-owned company.

33. Q: What can be inferred from the webpage?

(a) The company has billions of lines of pharmaceutical products.
(b) The company is likely to have many regular customers.
(c) Rebecca is highly likely to be the current CEO of the company.
(d) The company was originally based in Germany.

◄ Susan ☰

> Hi, Susan. I just can't wait to see you in July. At the same time, I must tell you that I'm suspicious of this guy called James. Why would he be willing to pick you up at the airport? He hasn't even met you yet.
>
> Of course, online relationships may grow into something beautiful. However, we need to keep in mind that it takes time to build a real relationship with someone else. How about waiting a little longer to see if you can really trust James? I just want you to be safe.

me

> Hi, Jack. It's always a great pleasure for me to talk with you. Your kind words make me smile, which I greatly appreciate. Of course, I look forward to seeing you in July. We created so many happy memories in Toronto, and I hope we have another such chance in Tokyo.
>
> Thank you for caring about my safety. Well, I don't think James is a bad guy. But as the saying goes, "Better safe than sorry." I've decided to use public transportation. Again, thank you for your sound advice.

34. Q: Why did Jack send the message?

(a) To warn Susan that James will kidnap her
(b) To recommend a safe course of action for Susan
(c) To remind Susan that he will pick her up at the airport
(d) To advise Susan not to meet people online

35. Q: What can be inferred from the chat messages?

(a) Susan is extremely popular online.
(b) Susan has been corresponding with James for a long time.
(c) Susan and Jack are likely to meet in Tokyo in July.
(d) Susan firmly believes that James has heinous motives.

You have reached the end of the Reading Comprehension section. Please remain seated until you are dismissed by the proctor. You are NOT allowed to turn to any other section of the test.

Listening
Comprehension

DIRECTIONS

1. In the Listening Comprehension section, all content will be presented orally rather than in written form.

2. This section contains five parts. For each part, you will receive separate instructions. Listen to the instructions carefully, and choose the best answer from the options for each item.

Part I **Questions 1—10**

You will now hear ten individual spoken questions or statements, each followed by four spoken responses. Choose the most appropriate response for each item.

Part II **Questions 11—20**

You will now hear ten short conversation fragments, each followed by four spoken responses. Choose the most appropriate response to complete each conversation.

You will now hear ten complete conversations. For each conversation, you will be asked to answer a question. Before each conversation, you will hear a short description of the situation. After listening to the description and conversation once, you will hear a question and four options. Based on the given information, choose the option that best answers the question.

L

Part IV **Questions 31—36**

You will now hear six short talks. After each talk, you will be asked to answer a question. Each talk and its corresponding question will be read twice. Then you will hear four options which will be read only once. Based on the given information, choose the option that best answers the question.

Part V Questions 37—40

You will now hear two longer talks. After each talk, you will be asked to answer two questions. Each talk and its corresponding questions will be read twice. However, the four options for each question will be read only once. Based on the given information, choose the option that best answers each question.

L

Vocabulary & Grammar

DIRECTIONS

These two sections test your vocabulary and grammar knowledge. You will have 25 minutes to complete a total of 60 questions: 30 from the Vocabulary section and 30 from the Grammar section. Be sure to follow the directions given by the proctor.

Part I **Questions 1—10**

Choose the option that best completes each dialogue.

1. A: What do you think of your brother's new girlfriend?
   B: Honestly, she doesn't _____ up to my expectations.
   (a) measure
   (b) commit
   (c) impress
   (d) feature

2. A: The news said Northeast Airlines is being sued for malfeasance.
   B: That kind of _____ can ruin a company.
   (a) alternative
   (b) exposure
   (c) regimen
   (d) collision

3. A: Mr. Edwards says I have to come in early again.
   B: You don't have to _____ his demands, you know.
   (a) come across
   (b) switch up
   (c) cover for
   (d) submit to

4. A: Look, the café has a free table over there.
   B: But it hasn't been _____ yet.
   (a) bused
   (b) raked
   (c) cast
   (d) lubed

5. A: Doctor, these pills are doing nothing for my backache.
   B: Let's try doubling the _____.
   (a) dosage
   (b) malady
   (c) symptom
   (d) placebo

6. A: I thought you liked the song "All the Way Around."
   B: Are you kidding? I _____ the song.
   (a) taunt
   (b) uphold
   (c) loathe
   (d) embroil

7. A: Is it time to go already?
   B: Yes, so whatever you're doing, please _____.
   (a) win it over
   (b) wrap it up
   (c) stick it out
   (d) keep it down

8. A: Will Samantha come mountain biking with us this weekend?
   B: I think she's still _____ from her ankle injury.
   (a) recuperating
   (b) badgering
   (c) accruing
   (d) endorsing

9. A: How did the workers and management come to an agreement?
   B: They enlisted a third party to conduct _____.
   (a) debility
   (b) arbitration
   (c) concision
   (d) polemic

10. A: Tim tells me he's only making eight dollars an hour.
    B: I just can't _____ why he would work for so little pay.
    (a) enthrall
    (b) digress
    (c) resign
    (d) fathom

11. Some linguists maintain that Chinese is made up of different _____ while others claim these are in fact distinct languages.
    (a) associates
    (b) dialects
    (c) synonyms
    (d) homophones

12. Nazi Germany's move to _____ Poland is what drew the nations of Europe into World War II.
    (a) ascertain
    (b) apprehend
    (c) adjourn
    (d) annex

13. Corn-based ethanol has long been _____ as an environmentally friendly alternative to petroleum, though doubts about this claim are now being raised.
    (a) borne
    (b) surged
    (c) lofted
    (d) touted

14. The details of the crime were so _____ that they were typically not included in news reports covering it.
    (a) deferential
    (b) assiduous
    (c) cloistered
    (d) heinous

15. Nineteenth-century general stores often allowed customers to make purchases on _____ because cash was much scarcer then.
    (a) demand
    (b) term
    (c) credit
    (d) leave

16. By pooling their vast financial resources, the members of the _____ were able to prop up the ailing company.
    (a) divestment
    (b) matrimony
    (c) consortium
    (d) accumulation

17. While the mayor insisted his support for the orphanage project was genuine, his detractors suggested he had _____ motives.
    (a) exterior
    (b) anterior
    (c) ulterior
    (d) posterior

18. The furniture craftsmanship of the Amish in the Midwest is known for its _____ attention to detail.
    (a) engendering
    (b) groundbreaking
    (c) vituperative
    (d) painstaking

19. The summer season, when most television networks turn to reruns, can be a time of _____ for the average TV viewer.
    (a) quarries
    (b) doldrums
    (c) tyrannies
    (d) catalysts

20. As long as the government continues to _____ big business with subsidies and tax breaks, there will continue to be protests.
    (a) coddle
    (b) saddle
    (c) meddle
    (d) riddle

21. For paramedics presented with a gunshot victim, the first order of business is to _____ the bleeding.

    (a) deign
    (b) loll
    (c) tamp
    (d) stanch

22. Following a _____ of faith in which he faced overwhelming doubts about his calling, the priest left the Church.

    (a) plight
    (b) disaster
    (c) trauma
    (d) crisis

23. After _____ funds from the corporate ledger into her personal account for years, the chairwoman was finally convicted of embezzlement.

    (a) siphoning
    (b) slathering
    (c) subverting
    (d) scuttling

24. The researcher, combing the _____ of the nation's history, discovered something unexpected about one of its earliest and most revered leaders.

    (a) dirges
    (b) annals
    (c) mallets
    (d) sinews

25. The _____ lifestyle and traditions of many Native American tribes precluded the Europeans' insistence that they settle and practice agriculture.

    (a) clandestine
    (b) arable
    (c) felicitous
    (d) peripatetic

26. To cut down on air pollution, an ordinance was passed to prohibit _____ delivery trucks from being left in parking lots.

    (a) idling
    (b) drafting
    (c) flocking
    (d) sapping

27. Thomas Edison led a relatively _____ early life, dropping out of primary school after just three months and taking on a variety of odd jobs.

    (a) feckless
    (b) puissant
    (c) meretricious
    (d) canonical

28. When the Secretary of Finance testified before the Senators, she faced a(n) _____ of questions concerning her handling of the downturn.

    (a) gambit
    (b) fusillade
    (c) platitude
    (d) umbrage

29. The public relations manager _____ the visiting potential investors with tales of his firm's record-setting profit margins and unprecedented market domination.

    (a) effaced
    (b) besmirched
    (c) regaled
    (d) abated

30. The characteristic depiction of herbivorous dinosaurs as _____ behemoths is belied by the fact that their joints seem designed for quick movement.

    (a) arresting
    (b) embossed
    (c) plodding
    (d) abraded

You have finished the Vocabulary questions. Please continue on to the Grammar questions.

Part I **Questions 1—10**

Choose the option that best completes each dialogue.

G

1. A: How do you keep in such good shape?

   B: I _____ football in the park.

   (a) had played
   (b) will play
   (c) played
   (d) play

2. A: So, you'll help me by writing this essay?

   B: That's not exactly _____ I meant by "help."

   (a) what
   (b) which
   (c) in that
   (d) of whatever

3. A: Do you think Mindy really stole the computer files?

   B: She _____ it even if she'd wanted to.

   (a) shouldn't do
   (b) wouldn't be doing
   (c) must not have done
   (d) couldn't have done

4. A: What did you think of the lemon-lime soda?

   B: I'd love _____ if you have one.

   (a) others
   (b) another
   (c) one other
   (d) the others

5. A: Did the man really leave the scene of the crime?

   B: Yes. Never have I seen _____ disregard for public safety.

   (a) much
   (b) such
   (c) too
   (d) so

6. A: Any word on the job you applied for?

   B: Not yet, but I _____ by this time next week.

   (a) will be notifying
   (b) had to be notified
   (c) have been notified
   (d) will have been notified

7. A: I'm very sorry that I broke your model airplane.

   B: There isn't _____ that can be done about it now.

   (a) a lot
   (b) any
   (c) many
   (d) a few

8. A: The book report is supposed to be turned in on Friday.

   B: Sadly, I have yet to _____ for it.

   (a) select which book to read
   (b) read which book selection is
   (c) read the book which selected
   (d) have selected which book read

9. A: That new scarf looks very becoming on you.

   B: _____ to tell me that, thank you.

   (a) Very kind how you are
   (b) You're how very kind
   (c) How very kind of you
   (d) Are you very kind how

10. A: Traveling abroad seems terrifying in a lot of ways.

    B: People often fear _____ they know nothing about.

    (a) if only
    (b) once again
    (c) that which
    (d) whether or not

Part II Questions 11–25

Choose the option that best completes each sentence.

11. The environmental advisor could not in good conscience condone _____ forward with the mining operation.

    (a) having moved
    (b) moving
    (c) to move
    (d) moves

12. Among the victims of the tsunami were several Americans who _____ there at the time.

    (a) happened to be vacationing
    (b) were happening to vacation
    (c) vacationed to and happened
    (d) had happened on vacation

13. _____ the recent spate of school shootings, Hamerline Elementary is hiring an additional security guard.

    (a) Gave
    (b) Given
    (c) To give
    (d) Having given

14. There are around 850 ficus species, _____ fig trees, which grow around the world.

    (a) to refer more common as
    (b) as to refer more commonly
    (c) more commonly referred to as
    (d) commonly referred to more as

15. Both the criminal and _____ aided him are subject to the full measure of federal law.

    (a) they of whom
    (b) those who
    (c) them
    (d) theirs

16. Prior to his death from cancer, Hugo Chavez nominated Nicolas Maduro _____ him as party leader.

    (a) succeeds
    (b) to succeed
    (c) succeeding
    (d) for succeeding

17. _____ the support of a majority of conservative organizations, the embattled congressman felt he had no choice but to resign.

    (a) Having lost
    (b) Lost
    (c) To lose
    (d) He lost

18. Charles Hughes _____ the 29th US President had a few thousand more Californians voted for him over Wilson.

    (a) could have been very mighty
    (b) might have been very well
    (c) might very well have been
    (d) was mighty well to be

19. Nun and Kun are the Himalayan mountains _____ heights the 9-mile-long Shafat Glacier flows.

    (a) by that
    (b) to what
    (c) of which
    (d) from whose

20. A+ Dogs' training courses offer a range of discipline techniques _____ your pet's individual needs.

    (a) guarantee the suiting of
    (b) to guarantee suiting
    (c) guaranteed to suit
    (d) guaranteed suit

21. Within the last few decades, Greece has demanded _____ of hundreds of artifacts taken from its borders by Western European explorers.

(a) returning
(b) a return
(c) the return
(d) some return

22. _____ face the threat of censorship in North America, the novelist chose to publish his work in Europe.

(a) Not
(b) If only to
(c) Rather than
(d) Far greater than

23. The tech giant will be forced to shut down its factories in Dubai if its competitor _____ the lawsuit.

(a) wins
(b) will win
(c) had won
(d) would win

24. The automobile engine, once quite cacophonous, let out _____ a splutter after being properly tuned.

(a) so much but not
(b) not so much as
(c) as much as not
(d) not much at all

25. Earthen levees, _____ as they are to collapse during severe floods, are widely used to protect surrounding areas from inundation.

(a) prone
(b) are prone
(c) to be prone
(d) having been prone

Read each dialogue or passage carefully and identify the option that contains a grammatical error.

26. (a) A: Looks like this restaurant doesn't accept credit cards.
(b) B: But I have no cash which to pay with.
(c) A: That's okay. I'll cover this and you can pay me back.
(d) B: Oh, thanks. Our next lunch will be on me.

27. (a) A: Remember when you used to work the reception desk?
(b) B: I'd still be there, too, if you wouldn't support my promotion.
(c) A: Well, I thought you'd really fit in the sales department.
(d) B: Yes, it's suiting me fine and I'm enjoying the work.

28. (a) We all cope differently with the pressure brought on by public speaking, which is experienced to some degree by even most accomplished orators. (b) Some spend their pre-speech minutes performing meditation, focusing on their breathing to clear their minds. (c) Others may require human interaction and conversation to take their attention off their nervousness. (d) Still others swear by the technique of visualization, intently picturing exactly what they will say and how they will say it.

29. (a) Never has the world come closer to nuclear annihilation than during the Cuban Missile Crisis of 1962. (b) So close to stepping the brink seemed to affect the superpowers on either side of the confrontation, the United States and the USSR. (c) Indeed, just a few months later, the countries established the Moscow-Washington "hotline." (d) This was a direct line of communication that would, in theory, facilitate negotiation and conflict resolution during future crises.

30. (a) Prior to the arrival of Europeans, the state of Missouri was heavily forested and home to a healthy population of black bears. (b) But by the 1920s, a combination of unregulated hunting and habitat destruction have decimated the Missouri black bear population. (c) In the '50s and '60s, a reintroduction campaign was initiated, transporting bears from other regions to the Ozark forests of southern Missouri. (d) Now, biologists estimate that hundreds of bears again call the state home.

You have reached the end of the Vocabulary & Grammar sections. Do NOT move on to the Reading Comprehension section until instructed to do so. You are NOT allowed to turn to any other section of the test.

Reading
Comprehension

Part I **Questions 1—10**

Read the passage and choose the option that best completes the passage.

1. While many regions of the country continue to struggle economically, once-forsaken pockets of the United States are booming. These include the plains of North Dakota, in the area around Minot and Williston, and the flats of South Texas. The unifying characteristic of these two regions is the existence of large formations of oil and natural gas deep beneath the ground. The recent commercialization of hydraulic fracturing has enabled the accessing of hitherto untapped deposits. Thus, both locations have seen _____.

   (a) upturns in their grassroots industries
   (b) lower fuel tax rates than other regions
   (c) stagnation in economic diversification
   (d) immense infusions of capital and labor

2.

Terronetti Duffel Pack

Who says you can't _____? Introducing the Terronetti Duffel Pack, an innovative luggage solution for the modern traveler. With an 80-liter main compartment and two sturdy top-side handles, this is the ultimate duffel bag at an affordable price. But wait—simply undo the Velcro straps at either end of the handles, extend them fully, and your duffel bag is now a comfortable backpack! Whether you want the handling convenience of a duffel or the hands-free option of a backpack, the Terronetti Duffel Pack is the bag for you.

   (a) have all in one on a budget
   (b) trust the strength of Velcro
   (c) go backpacking as an adult
   (d) convert a duffel to a suitcase

3. Czar Peter I, also known as Peter the Great, ruled Russia from 1682 to 1725. At the behest of his advisors, many of whom hailed from Western European countries such as France, Peter the Great implemented various cultural changes. These included the mandatory shaving of beards and adoption of French fashions among the noblemen. In addition, he reorganized his military to mimic those of the Western powers and initiated a great navy-building enterprise. Many in the country strongly resented these top-down changes. However, the result was that Russia _____.

(a) underwent a number of significant changes despite Peter's hesitancy
(b) abandoned medieval traditions to become as modern Europeans
(c) developed its own fashions to compete with those of the West
(d) became the undisputed overlord of France's former colonies

4.

Weather Forecast

Heavy rain has been falling steadily throughout the Henderson area since early this afternoon, with some neighborhoods having received over an inch. Forecasts predict the rainstorm to continue overnight, accompanied by a drop in temperatures that will likely lead to freezing. The resultant icy road conditions are categorized as extremely hazardous, and all residents are encouraged to stay indoors tonight unless absolutely necessary. In light of these conditions, which will continue into the morning and possibly longer, _____.

(a) your usual outdoor activities should be sustained
(b) snow falls are expected to continue unabated
(c) school is suspended tomorrow for all students
(d) a ban on driving has been lifted by the mayor

5. Regardless of our level of interest in the arts, we all need an outlet to express our inner creativity. That's the founding principle of Meet-Create, an online community that aids individuals in discovering new creative pursuits and people with whom to share them. Community members form groups based on common activity interests, such as painting, knitting, woodworking, and much more. Within each group, lessons are made available, projects are described and shared, and positive support is provided. In some cases, real-life meet-ups have been organized within the metropolitan area. Join Meet-Create today and _____.

(a) jump-start your creativity with the help of like-minded people
(b) meet accomplished artists who live in communities near you
(c) receive your first shipment of art supplies at reduced cost
(d) meet individuals who also want to focus on painting skills

6. When you look at a calendar in the Western world, chances are it is a Gregorian calendar. Established in 1582, its aim was to keep important religious events, in particular Easter, more consistently tied to the same solar day each year. _____ the earlier and more primitive calendrical system, the Julian calendar initiated by Julius Caesar, had resulted in a gradual "drift" of calendar days compared to true solar days. The new Gregorian calendar refined those calculations by trimming those excessive leap years when the year was divisible by 100, thus ensuring that the calendar more accurately reflected the length of a solar year.

(a) The use of solstice and equinox for calibration by
(b) A similar misconception about a day's length in
(c) A simplified employment of leap years by
(d) The influence on its design received from

7. While most comets visible from Earth are at a great distance and appear and reappear at prescribed times according to their orbit of the sun, Lexell's Comet _____. First sighted on June 14, 1770, by the astronomer Charles Messier, it was found to have a trajectory that brought it shockingly close to our planet. At its nearest point, it was 1.4 million miles from Earth, just six times the distance of the moon. Yet this was also the last time anyone ever observed Lexell's Comet. Due to reasons unknown, its orbit was altered after 1770 and it is now considered lost.

(a) has a trajectory that is regularly inconsistent
(b) disproves the theories of comet composition
(c) nearly collided with Earth at one point
(d) is anomalous on both of those counts

8. The plant pathogen Phytophthora infestans is best known for precipitating the Irish Potato Famine of the 1840s, but this devastating fungus is still causing trouble today. In fact, it is estimated that P. infestans costs the world over $6 billion each year in lost crops and ongoing eradication efforts. Most troubling is the fact that the modern manifestation of the species is even more virulent than its infamous predecessor. This transformation is likely the result of human attempts to breed strains of potatoes that resist infection. All of this raises worries that _____.

(a) another mass potato failure is in the realm of possibility
(b) the damaging fungus will cause more genetic mutations
(c) other unknown plant pathogens may be poised to strike
(d) the potato will one day cease to be a dietary staple

9. The seed of castor oil plant, the castor bean, has been harvested for centuries and processed for its unique oil. Castor oil has been put to use for everything from medicinal healing, to industrial lubrication, to food preservation. _____, the toxic level of the compound ricin found in the raw beans presents a serious health hazard. Ingesting four to eight seeds is considered a lethal dose. So the plant is unique in possessing a duality of potential helpfulness and potential harmfulness to humans.

(a) Simultaneously
(b) Consequently
(c) Wherefore
(d) Inevitably

10. Babies may take as long as a year to develop any capacity for speech, making it difficult for parents to comprehend what their baby is thinking and feeling. _____, babies themselves may be able to precisely identify the emotional state of other babies. This is according to new developmental psychology research that found that by five months of age, babies can identify and mimic an emotion being expressed by another infant. At six months, they obtain the ability to do so for familiar adults, meaning that babies may understand their parents better than parents do their babies.

(a) In other words
(b) What's more
(c) In contrast
(d) In sum

Part II **Questions 11—12**

Read the passage and identify the option that does NOT belong.

11. We tend to imagine that any heretofore undiscovered animal species must be endemic to the deepest rainforests or remotest deserts. (a) It is assumed that surely any creature cohabiting a region with humans would have been observed and catalogued centuries ago. (b) For instance, as of today, over 10,000 recognized species of birds around the world have been catalogued. (c) The addition to the science books of the Cambodian Tailorbird in 2013 refutes this notion. (d) First noted in 2009 and ascertained as a distinct species four years later, the bird had been living all along in plain sight in Phnom Penh, the capital and largest city of Cambodia.

12. Drivers on the Trans-Canada Highway passing through Banff National Park should expect some unusual sights. (a) Banff is actually the oldest member of Canada's national park system, and one of the most visited parks in the world. (b) Within the park limits, two arched overpasses are covered in vegetation and are not intended for human traffic. (c) These are wildlife overpasses, specially designed and monitored to allow the safe passage of animals over the four lanes of speeding highway traffic. (d) Less noticeable but equally effective are 22 underpasses that let wildlife cross beneath the Trans-Canada Highway.

Part III **Questions 13—25**

Read the passage, question, and options. Then, based on the given information, choose the option that best answers each question.

R

13. When psychologists conduct studies on groups of individuals, they assume the behaviors they observe are representative of the behaviors exhibited by those individuals in their everyday lives. But the Hawthorne Effect calls this assumption into question. The effect was observed in an experiment conducted at the Hawthorne Works electrical plant to determine whether increasing the level of lighting in the workspace leads to increased productivity. While researchers found that some workers became more productive, it was not because of better lighting. They determined that the workers had altered their normal behavior because they knew they were participating in an experiment.

    Q: What is the passage mainly about?
    (a) A strategy for engendering productivity in employees
    (b) Effects on people who do research on social behavior
    (c) The need for psychological studies into work practices
    (d) Skewed results from behavior change during experiments

14. Production of coffee beans can be one of the most exploitative industries on the planet, but it also has the potential to be one of the most economically empowering. That's our guiding belief at Bright Roasters, where we source all of our beans from sustainably and ethically run coffee plantations. Our partner farmers in Central America and Southeast Asia are dedicated to following stringent environmental standards and treating and paying their workers fairly. That's why, when you order a latte made from Bright Roasters beans at a local café, you can rest assured that your money supports fair workplace practices.

    Q: What is mainly being advertised?
    (a) A human rights organization against exploitation
    (b) An ethically responsible retailer of coffee beans
    (c) A local café that serves Bright Roasters coffee
    (d) An ecofriendly coffee plantation company

15.

> Dear Editor,
>
> In your newspaper's edition of Tuesday, July 5, there appeared an opinion piece entitled "In Defense of Authoritarianism – The Economic Argument for Chile's Pinochet." This op-ed purported to show that the people of Chile were in fact better off today as a result of the authoritarian economic reforms instituted under the dictator Augusto Pinochet. As a woman of Chilean descent, I was outraged by the author's callous and irreverent treatment of the issue. To reduce decades of human rights abuses to a platitudinous economic analysis is unconscionable, and so I have suspended my subscription to your publication.
>
> Janet Alvarez

Q: What is Ms. Alvarez mainly doing in the letter?

(a) Expressing disapproval of an opinion piece in the media
(b) Correcting erroneous reporting by a paper's journalist
(c) Inquiring into the reason for her canceled subscription
(d) Asserting an alternative view on Chile's economic success

16. The Mississippi River is perhaps the most celebrated body of water in North America, the subject and setting of countless songs, stories, and other cultural touchstones. Yet, in several key respects, it is actually outshined by one of its main tributaries. The Missouri River, which rises in Montana and joins the Mississippi at their confluence in St. Louis, is actually longer than its more famous counterpart. In addition, the Missouri River wins out in the area of its drainage basin compared to the Mississippi.

Q: What is the main idea of the passage?

(a) The Missouri River contributes the most water to the Mississippi.
(b) The Mississippi has shaped how Americans think about rivers.
(c) The Missouri rivals the Mississippi in geographic vastness.
(d) The Mississippi's tributaries outnumber those of the Missouri.

17. Age-related macular degeneration, or AMD, is a relatively common condition that leads to blindness in elderly adults. Sadly, the progressive blurriness that affects their vision as the condition worsens is untreatable through only contact lenses. But researchers have recently succeeded in fabricating a new type of contact lens, one that can provide telescopic functionality and correct the effects of retinal damage in AMD patients. Despite containing dual mirrored surfaces, the lens is only a millimeter thick and should prove both comfortable and convenient for everyday use.

Q: Which of the following is correct according to the report?

(a) Blindness can afflict AMD sufferers from young to old.
(b) Special glasses that help AMD patients are still used.
(c) A special contact lens can improve vision in AMD patients.
(d) Contact lenses for correcting AMD are still rather bulky.

18. The Lord Chamberlain's Men, famous as the Elizabethan drama company which William Shakespeare long worked for, constructed the original Globe Theatre in 1599. For 14 years, it served as the premier staging venue for performances of some of Shakespeare's plays. Tragically, in June of 1613, the Globe was destroyed by fire. According to contemporary accounts, the firing of a cannon for dramatic effect during the staging of Shakespeare's *Henry VIII* ignited the wood and thatch components of the structure. A second iteration of the theater was raised the following year and served for nearly three decades before being shuttered in 1642.

Q: Which of the following is correct according to the passage?

(a) The original Globe Theatre staged all of Shakespeare's plays.
(b) Shakespeare's colleagues blamed him for the Globe's fire.
(c) Shakespeare commissioned the Globe Theatre to be built.
(d) The second Globe Theatre lasted longer than the first.

19. In the United States, the business of lawmaking is conducted through a form of representative democracy. Citizens elect members of Congress to represent them, and those members are then charged with proposing and passing laws based on the desires of their constituents. This is counter to direct democracy, wherein individual citizens suggest and vote on laws themselves. The Founders of the United States saw direct democracy with doubt, wary of majorities who may tyrannically impose their will on the minority opinion. Still, direct democracy is practiced in some US states via the referendum, in which citizens may vote to annul or uphold a law.

Q: Which of the following is correct according to the passage?

(a) The job of the US Congress is to do the bidding of business lobbyists.
(b) Direct democracy was seen as superior to representative democracy.
(c) The US's founders believed minorities should have their way.
(d) Some states allow direct democracy in deciding on certain laws.

20.

≡ **ENTERTAINMENT TODAY**   🔍

Music > Jazz

Hot Fusion's New Album

The Jazz trio Hot Fusion demonstrates a triumphant return to their bebop roots in their newest release, *Some Like It Hot*. The album will come as a huge relief to many fans who were perturbed by the band's decade-long experiment with acid jazz and other nontraditional genres. The last three offerings from Hot Fusion, though critically acclaimed, fell flat in the sales department, which reportedly provided the impetus for the group to get back to basics. Said trumpet player Max Maloney, "While we're revisiting bebop, I think we're approaching it in a new way."

Q: Which of the following is correct about Hot Fusion's newest album according to the article?

(a) It marks a return after a decade of inactivity.
(b) It was conceived as part of an acid jazz phase.
(c) It probably is unconcerned with sales figures.
(d) It is a departure from the band's previous album.

21. Amid the complexities of today's real estate market, the average consumer likely has more questions than answers. Is now the best time to buy or sell a home? What are the benefits of homeownership versus renting? Who can I turn to for help? As industry leaders, we are all too familiar with these questions, which is why we've decided to launch *The Business of Home*, a quarterly publication dedicated to lifting the veil on the workings of the property market. Subscribe now and you'll receive a full year for the discounted rate of $20.

Q: Which of the following is correct about *The Business of Home* according to the advertisement?
(a) It is focused primarily on buying and selling homes.
(b) It is written by and for the average homeowners.
(c) It provides industry advice to those in the field.
(d) It is offered through subscription at $5 per issue.

22.

Dear Valued User,

Mapview has always upheld the principle of transparency in our dealings with the public, particularly our users. We feel this is a major reason why Mapview is the #1 social media free mapping site, allowing people to personalize their maps of any place on the globe. Recent technological developments have prompted us to update our terms of service (TOS) to accommodate industry-wide changes to privacy policies. You can see a list of modifications and read our new TOS in full by clicking the Read More link below. As always, we value your opinion and welcome your input.

Sincerely,
The Mapview Team

Q: Which of the following is correct about the company according to the email?
(a) They will now start charging for personal maps.
(b) They are modifying terms based on user feedback.
(c) They are conforming to new user privacy standards.
(d) They will show the TOS for review upon request.

23. Newspaper printing changed forever upon Ottmar Mergenthaler's invention of the linotype machine in 1884. Previously, printers had employed the centuries-old technique of letter-by-letter typesetting, in which pre-cast metal letters and punctuation marks were assembled individually to form a line of text. The linotype machine made it possible to construct entire lines all at once, by inputting the text into a keyboard and then custom-casting a single metal piece, or slug, with that text. This revolutionized the way newspapers could be printed, increasing both the length and frequency of newspaper publication around the world.

Q: What can be inferred about the linotype machine from the passage?

(a) It gave rise to the invention of the typewriter.
(b) It is still used for some kinds of newspaper printing.
(c) It helped lead to the newspaper as we know it today.
(d) It produced less artistic type than traditional typesetting.

24. The Black Paintings, a series of works by the Spanish master Francisco Goya, are unique in the medium in which they were created. Goya, later in life, painted them directly onto the interior plaster walls of his Madrid home. Numbering 14 in total and bearing no titles, the works portray dark, haunting scenes of death, violence, and loneliness. From the fact that Goya never spoke or wrote of them to anyone, we can assume that he never intended the Black Paintings to be exhibited. Forty-six years after his death, they were transferred from plaster to canvas and moved to a Madrid museum.

Q: What can be inferred about the Black Paintings according to the passage?

(a) They were shown to the public before Goya's death.
(b) They are named for the themes they address.
(c) They were among Goya's most lucrative works.
(d) They are the earliest example of plaster painting.

25. For decades, we have understood DNA, the building blocks of life, to be passed down through family lines more or less uninfluenced by environmental factors. But new findings imply that such factors can shape our genes in ways that reverberate through generations. Individuals that experience severe stress during their youth, such as a prolonged period of malnutrition, have been shown to produce offspring more susceptible to stress themselves. Also some data, though too limited to prove correlation, shows that this vulnerability could be present two generations on in the original subject's grandchildren.

Q: What can be inferred from the passage?

(a) Healthy DNA has a natural defense against environmental stress.
(b) Those who experience extreme stress cannot produce children.
(c) Proof of multi-generational transmittance is still pending.
(d) Damage to genes early in life is more harmful than in later life.

R

Part IV **Questions 26—35**

Read the passage, questions, and options. Then, based on the given information, choose the option that best answers each question.

Questions 26-27

Microloans for Small Business Owners

■ **Purpose**

Since its establishment in 1992, the New Life Foundation (NLF) has been working hard to improve the lives of small business owners. We firmly believe that they are literally the backbone of our society. If they were in constant financial woes, the stability of our society would be severely undermined. That is why we have been operating the NLF microloans programs. These award-winning programs will help small business owners survive and thrive so that they can help keep our society stable and prosperous.

■ **Eligibility Requirements**

In order to apply for our NLF microloans programs, you must meet the following requirements:
· You must have an acceptable credit history.
· You must not be delinquent on any loans.
· You must have at least 2 years of experience in running a small business.
· You must complete our Innovative Management courses.
· You must be willing to work with a mentor for at least 6 months.

26. Q: Which of the following is correct about the NLF microloans programs according to the webpage?

(a) The NLF has been operating them for more than 30 years.
(b) It has not been approved of by the general public.
(c) The NLF believes that they can help to buttress social stability.
(d) They were originally proposed by several small business owners.

27. Q: Which of the following can be one of the eligibility requirements for the NLF microloans programs?

(a) A slightly dubious credit history.
(b) Up to 2 years of experience in managing a small business.
(c) A willingness to learn from a fellow business owner for six years.
(d) An ability to remain solvent.

POLITICS > LOCAL   *Pasadena Today*

The Identity Crisis of Pasadena

Since his election as mayor in 2017, Richard Miller has been a controversial political figure. In fact, some of his critics even argue that Mayor Miller is the worst enemy of the city of Pasadena. According to them, since his election, Pasadena has been constantly faced with an identity crisis.

Sarah Foster, one of the prominent detractors of Mayor Miller, says that the city used to be the beacon of American ideals such as liberty and justice. Thanks to the mayor's regressive policies, including the ban on street demonstrations, Pasadena seems to be governed by dictatorship. To make matters worse, tensions between different ethnic groups are at all-time high.

According to Foster, Mayor Miller will continue to attack those ideals that used to define Pasadena. In order to resolve this identity crisis, all the citizens must transcend their party affiliations and do everything in their power to re-establish the city as the driving force for American ideals.

28. Q: Which of the following is correct about Mayor Miller according to the article?
(a) He has been striving to embody American ideals by implementing democratic reforms.
(b) His policies may be aggravating ethnic tensions in Pasadena.
(c) He has been experiencing an identity crisis since 2016.
(d) His policies are aimed at upholding the values of liberty and justice.

29. Q: Which of the following statements would Foster most likely agree with?
(a) The procedure for impeaching Mayor Miller should be initiated immediately.
(b) The city government's progressive policies have sparked a backlash against the mayor.
(c) People's power is necessary for defending liberty and justice in Pasadena.
(d) It is time Pasadena relinquished its status as the guardian of American ideals.

R

St. John's Wort: A Placebo or the Real Thing?

In many parts of the world, St. John's wort has been believed to have medicinal properties. In the United States, a large number of people think of the herbal medicine as an effective means of treating depression. However, many organizations, including the National Institute of Mental Health, warn the public that the effectiveness of St. John's wort has not been scientifically proven.

Interestingly enough, some studies have shown that St. John's wort is as effective as antidepressants in curing mild depression. Nevertheless, in treating moderately severe depression, neither St. John's wort nor antidepressants are effective to a significant extent. Further, the National Institute of Mental Health discourages the public from combining both medicines.

Then, is St. John's wort a placebo or the real thing? Well, it may be both. There is another thing you should consider: the side effects of St. John's wort. We will cover this important topic in our next issue of the *Your Health* magazine.

30. Q: What is the main topic of the article?

(a) The effectiveness of St. John's wort in curing mild depression
(b) How to combine St. John's wort and antidepressants
(c) The reason why St. John's wort is more effective than a placebo
(d) The efficacy of St. John's wort in treating a mental illness

31. Q: Which of the following is correct according to the article?

(a) St. John's wort has been used as a medicine for hundreds of years.
(b) Ordinary Americans' perception of St. John's wort may be erroneous.
(c) Antidepressants are far more effective than St. John's wort in curing severe depression.
(d) When used therapeutically, St. John's wort has no known side effects.

How to Resolve Noise Complaints

Advised by Lowland City Council

These days, a lot of citizens make complaints about a noise nuisance. In many cases, however, it is not easy to determine whether or not your noise constitutes a nuisance. There are so many factors to take into account in making that determination.

Therefore, it is always a good idea for you to consult with your neighbors before you make some "noise." Discuss any matters with them. Surprisingly, most citizens are much more understanding than you think they are. They will inevitably make some noise, after all.

In some cases, however, your neighbors make noise complaints. The Lowland City Council usually deals with them by issuing a warning notice or imposing penalties. When the Council determines that your noise constitutes a noise offense, it will be addressed by the Department of the Environment. The Department has the authority to recommend prosecution.

For more detailed information, visit us at http://www.lowlandcitycouncil.gov/.

32. Q: What is the Council most likely to do when it decides that your noise is a noise offense?

(a) It will seek to circumvent the regulations of the Department of the Environment.
(b) It will refer the matter to the relevant department.
(c) It will directly contact prosecuting attorneys.
(d) It will issue a stern warning notice to your neighbors.

33. Q: What can be inferred from the passage?

(a) Noise pollution takes a heavy toll on public health.
(b) Not all noises are regarded as a nuisance by the Council.
(c) Residents of Lowland are always courteous to each other.
(d) The Department of the Environment does not have the authority to impose penalties.

R

From:	Dr. Julia Smith <jsmith@bremser.edu>
To:	Cynthia Spencer <c_spencer@cmail.com>
Date:	Sat, May 5 at 9:33 AM
Subject: You Are Insightful	

Dear Ms. Spencer,

This is Dr. Julia Smith, and I would like to thank you for submitting your insightful article to our *Journal of Biological Research*. As you already know, this journal is jointly published by Bremser University and the British Association of Biologists. We accept submissions from both professors of biology and graduate students majoring in biology.

In your paper, you criticize Charles Darwin's theory of evolution on the basis of the concept of species. In addition, you point out that the history of the Earth is too short for Darwinian evolution to occur.

I must assume that you are familiar with the mainstream theory of evolution. Nevertheless, that theory is still a theory. Although I respect the wisdom of the mainstream theory, I also encourage graduate students to freely explore and challenge the existing theories. Only then can we find the truth.

Again, thank you for your insightful paper. You will be notified within the next 20 days regarding your submission.

Best regards,

Dr. Julia Smith

34. Q: What is the main purpose of the email?
    (a) To appreciate Spencer's attempt to attack a mainstream theory in biology
    (b) To notify the recipient that her paper will be published in the journal
    (c) To advise the recipient to distinguish between laws and theories
    (d) To encourage Spencer to join the British Association of Biologists

35. Q: What can be inferred about Spencer from the email?
    (a) She is a professor of biology at Bremser University.
    (b) Her understanding of evolutionary theory is inadequate.
    (c) She is majoring in both chemistry and geology.
    (d) She is highly likely to be a graduate student.

You have reached the end of the Reading Comprehension section. Please remain seated until you are dismissed by the proctor. You are NOT allowed to turn to any other section of the test.

TEPS

Listening
Comprehension

MP3 바로 듣기
받아쓰기 테스트
모바일 단어장

L

Part I **Questions 1—10**

You will now hear ten individual spoken questions or statements, each followed by four spoken responses. Choose the most appropriate response for each item.

Part II **Questions 11—20**

You will now hear ten short conversation fragments, each followed by four spoken responses. Choose the most appropriate response to complete each conversation.

You will now hear ten complete conversations. For each conversation, you will be asked to answer a question. Before each conversation, you will hear a short description of the situation. After listening to the description and conversation once, you will hear a question and four options. Based on the given information, choose the option that best answers the question.

Part IV Questions 31—36

You will now hear six short talks. After each talk, you will be asked to answer a question. Each talk and its corresponding question will be read twice. Then you will hear four options which will be read only once. Based on the given information, choose the option that best answers the question.

Part V Questions 37—40

You will now hear two longer talks. After each talk, you will be asked to answer two questions. Each talk and its corresponding questions will be read twice. However, the four options for each question will be read only once. Based on the given information, choose the option that best answers each question.

Vocabulary & Grammar

DIRECTIONS

These two sections test your vocabulary and grammar knowledge. You will have 25 minutes to complete a total of 60 questions: 30 from the Vocabulary section and 30 from the Grammar section. Be sure to follow the directions given by the proctor.

Part I **Questions 1—10**

Choose the option that best completes each dialogue.

1. A: I freeze whenever I meet a guy I like.
B: You need to stop being so
_____ and speak up.

(a) reticent
(b) audacious
(c) clamorous
(d) impertinent

2. A: I can't believe Peter got promoted before me!
B: Well, his skills far _____ yours.

(a) amend
(b) surpass
(c) validate
(d) endorse

3. A: Do you need a ride for the marathon tomorrow?
B: We're _____ at City Hall Square at 7 am sharp, so I'd very much appreciate a ride.

(a) dispersing
(b) convoluting
(c) congregating
(d) disseminating

4. A: I hope you enjoyed the concert tonight.
B: Oh, I was really impressed by your _____ performance.

(a) culpable
(b) expedient
(c) delinquent
(d) impeccable

5. A: I'm not going to put up with any sort of humiliation this time!
B: _____. A hot temper won't get you anywhere.

(a) Act up
(b) Chip in
(c) Tag along
(d) Simmer down

6. A: Look at the sports car I bought!
B: You shouldn't have _____ your money on that.

(a) scattered
(b) devoured
(c) depleted
(d) squandered

7. A: Can I trust you on this matter?
B: Sure, I promise I'll never _____ your secrets to anyone.

(a) divulge
(b) protest
(c) construe
(d) manifest

8. A: How did you end up being an actress?
B: Well, Tom _____ me into doing a part in the play he was directing.

(a) cajoled
(b) reproached
(c) commended
(d) reprimanded

9. A: Look at this leftover dish in the fridge! It's got mold on it.
B: I know. It's also giving off a _____ odor.

(a) foul
(b) rough
(c) bland
(d) cruel

10. A: How would you describe your father?
B: Well, he's a very _____ type who won't take no for an answer.

(a) colossal
(b) obedient
(c) tenacious
(d) meticulous

Choose the option that best completes each sentence.

11. The agency _____ an inspection of the health-supplement factory.

    (a) escorted
    (b) delivered
    (c) regulated
    (d) conducted

12. This Wi-Fi repeater will _____ network dead spots by extending your existing router's signal to greater distances.

    (a) eliminate
    (b) disband
    (c) hinder
    (d) omit

13. After receiving a(n) _____ critique, the novelist almost gave up his career as a writer.

    (a) sympathetic
    (b) banishing
    (c) amiable
    (d) harsh

14. Any fibrous material can get tangled and _____ the garbage disposal unit.

    (a) jam
    (b) dump
    (c) loosen
    (d) merge

15. As a safety measure, tourists are _____ to travel in big groups and not to visit dangerous areas.

    (a) urged
    (b) enticed
    (c) dissected
    (d) promoted

16. _____ your windows with bubble wrap can cut the heat loss by about half.

    (a) Investing
    (b) Inserting
    (c) Inscribing
    (d) Insulating

17. People sometimes poke fun at others without realizing they are overdoing the _____ and may even be causing deep humiliation.

    (a) parody
    (b) mimicry
    (c) mockery
    (d) pretense

18. This detergent is effective at getting _____ out, cutting through grease, and lifting grime even in cold water.

    (a) blemishes
    (b) smirches
    (c) stigmas
    (d) stains

19. The trial will resume after it _____ for one day.

    (a) retreats
    (b) adjourns
    (c) withdraws
    (d) progresses

20. Researchers found that a fetus could be damaged by a mother consuming _____ fish.

    (a) tarnished
    (b) distorted
    (c) loathsome
    (d) contaminated

21. The child's behavior was very
_____, but the worse thing was
that his parents allowed it.

   (a) brisk
   (b) decrepit
   (c) pungent
   (d) obnoxious

22. Freelancing can be _____ if you
are in the right place at the right time,
earning more money than working at a
company.

   (a) lousy
   (b) crappy
   (c) lucrative
   (d) partial

23. The _____ economy is forcing
some people in their 60s to continue
working to rebuild their retirement nest-
eggs.

   (a) sturdy
   (b) astute
   (c) ardent
   (d) sluggish

24. The Arts Center has been the region's
premier fine arts _____ for
decades.

   (a) zone
   (b) niche
   (c) venue
   (d) abode

25. A fierce _____ is expected to
drop about 2-3 feet of snow and any
outdoor activity is discouraged.

   (a) tornado
   (b) blizzard
   (c) drizzle
   (d) frost

26. The employment rate _____ in
the wake of market crash and subsequent
recession.

   (a) recuperated
   (b) skyrocketed
   (c) plummeted
   (d) intervened

27. The term "home" may have a bad
_____ for someone who
experienced pain and trauma growing up.

   (a) rendition
   (b) elucidation
   (c) denotation
   (d) connotation

28. Abdominal fat can _____ several
future health problems such as heart
disease, high blood pressure and even
Alzheimer's.

   (a) integrate
   (b) compound
   (c) foreshadow
   (d) accommodate

29. All _____ raised from the auction
will support the church's restoration
project.

   (a) perks
   (b) stakes
   (c) capitals
   (d) proceeds

30. The 1960s in the US was a tumultuous
period characterized by political and
social _____.

   (a) apathies
   (b) upheavals
   (c) tranquilities
   (d) stagnations

You have finished the Vocabulary questions. Please continue on to the Grammar questions.

Part I **Questions 1—10**

Choose the option that best completes each dialogue.

G

1. A: I'm sick and tired of living in this small apartment.
    B: Don't worry. _____ enough money to move to a bigger one by next year.
    (a) We'll be saved
    (b) We saved
    (c) We had saved
    (d) We'll have saved

2. A: What size does your mother wear?
    B: She is _____ and wears size 55.
    (a) as me slim
    (b) slim as me
    (c) as slim as me
    (d) as me as slim

3. A: My life is so mundane after retirement.
    B: You should _____ to do.
    (a) find something to be exciting
    (b) be excited to find something
    (c) something find to excite
    (d) find something exciting

4. A: Why don't you have a piece of cake?
    B: Sorry, but I made _____ any sweets.
    (a) a rule to not eat
    (b) not to eat a rule
    (c) it a rule not to eat
    (d) it not to eat a rule

5. A: Is the managerial position listed on the company's job openings page?
    B: Not at the moment but it _____.
    (a) will
    (b) will be
    (c) will to be
    (d) will do it

6. A: What did you tell Pamela to do about her skin problem?
    B: I recommended that she _____ a doctor.
    (a) will see
    (b) sees
    (c) saw
    (d) see

7. A: Did you agree to appear on TV?
    B: No, I _____.
    (a) decided not do it
    (b) didn't decide to
    (c) decided not to
    (d) not decided

8. A: We shouldn't be kept in the dark about new policies.
    B: No, it's imperative that we _____ of them.
    (a) have been informed
    (b) are being informed
    (c) be informed
    (d) inform

9. A: Did Jim get promoted?
    B: _____ to the company, he actually got demoted.
    (a) A big loss causing
    (b) A big loss was caused
    (c) Having caused a big loss
    (d) Has been causing a big loss

10. A: So you had many problems after your father's business collapsed?
    B: Yes, _____ such financial difficulties before.
    (a) never my family had experienced
    (b) had my family never experienced
    (c) never had my family experienced
    (d) my family had experienced never

Part II **Questions 11—25**

Choose the option that best completes each sentence.

G

11. _____ a severe flood last summer, the city is planning to build a big dam this year.

(a) Experiencing
(b) To experience
(c) It experienced
(d) Having experienced

12. There were references to historical events _____ the movie.

(a) of
(b) for
(c) through
(d) throughout

13. One tends to develop certain chronic conditions that affect quality of life _____ one grows older.

(a) as
(b) since
(c) whereas
(d) although

14. The singer's romantic baritone voice helped to keep the audience _____.

(a) amusing
(b) amused
(c) amuses
(d) amuse

15. The speaker added that _____ of black women in teaching and nursing careers.

(a) a heavy concentration there continues to be
(b) there continues to be a heavy concentration
(c) a continuation of heavy concentration there is
(d) there is continuing a heavy concentration

16. Those who got into top schools said that they spent a certain amount of time each day _____ the materials they had learned.

(a) review
(b) in review
(c) reviewing
(d) to be reviewing

17. If you are sick of replacing your blenders often, you can rely on this product _____.

(a) service lasting you many years
(b) of many years of service to last
(c) to last you many years of service
(d) will last you many years of service

18. To succeed in an online degree program, one must be strict about setting aside _____ to complete the course work.

(a) certain time
(b) certain times
(c) the certain time
(d) the certain times

19. The auction was cancelled because no bids reached the reserve price, the level _____ was as usual undisclosed.

(a) that
(b) what
(c) which
(d) of which

20. _____ will actually make you fatter than reducing your fat intake.

(a) Carbohydrates eating too much
(b) Too much carbohydrates eating
(c) Too much eating carbohydrates
(d) Eating carbohydrates too much

21. Experts said that unfortunately almost _____ could have prevented the storm damage that happened last Friday.

(a) something
(b) everything
(c) anything
(d) nothing

22. The social worker was exhausted by the time she got home because she _____ calls at work all day long.

(a) has been answering
(b) had been answering
(c) have been answering
(d) has answered

23. _____ by his wife about his educational background, Jeff began to remain aloof from her.

(a) To be mocked
(b) Mocked
(c) He was mocked
(d) To being mocked

24. Outraged minority groups _____ even if they are promised future improvements.

(a) will not appease
(b) will appease not
(c) will be not appeased
(d) will not be appeased

25. A change in the number of available microhabitats should result in a corresponding change in _____.

(a) numbers of fish population
(b) fish population number
(c) the size of fish population
(d) fish population sizes

Part III **Questions 26—30**

Read each dialogue or passage carefully and identify the option that contains a grammatical error.

G

26. (a) A: Are you going to the school reunion?

(b) B: What school reunion? I haven't heard anything about it.

(c) A: That's strange. I was notified of it about a month ago.

(d) B: Well, they should have forgotten to inform me.

27. (a) A: Oh, no. I have to make the soup base again.

(b) B: What's wrong with the one you're making?

(c) A: I just realized I had been boiled it with too much chili.

(d) B: Oh, then I guess you need to make the soup afresh.

28. (a) The number of people either with a job or looking for one was tumbled by about 498,000 in March. (b) That shifted the labor force rate to go down to 63.3% of the working-age population. (c) Of this reduction in the working force in March, 120,000 were aged 55 and older. (d) Also, the number of people 65 and older regarded as active in the labor force increased by 27,000, adding to the rise of 72,000 in February.

29. (a) Human psychology plays a big part in the relationship between price and demand. (b) Consumers generally have the unquestioned view that the cheapest products are of poor quality. (c) For example, rather than buying the least expensive wine, a customer will think he or she is getting better quality by buying a little more expensive something. (d) Basing every purchase decision on price, however, consumers can be easily duped by unscrupulous sellers with overpriced products.

30. (a) A study was done on the degree to which the types of values held in a family environment affect their overall sense of well-being. (b) Mothers and their adolescents were surveyed on how highly they regarded three intrinsic values and three extrinsic values. (c) Results showed that mothers typically placed greater emphasis on intrinsic over extrinsic values than did adolescents. (d) Interestingly, the happiness index of both adolescents and mothers were associated with the extent to which they prioritized intrinsic values over extrinsic ones.

You have reached the end of the Vocabulary & Grammar sections. Do NOT move on to the Reading Comprehension section until instructed to do so. You are NOT allowed to turn to any other section of the test.

Reading
Comprehension

DIRECTIONS

This section tests your ability to comprehend reading passages. You will have 40 minutes to complete 35 questions. Be sure to follow the directions given by the proctor.

Part I **Questions 1—10**

Read the passage. Then choose the option that best completes the passage.

R

1.

Dear Mr. Walker,

I really enjoyed speaking with you about the job at the Williams Agency. It seems to be exactly what I have been looking for. The structured approach to account management which you illustrated confirmed my desire to work with you. If I do get the job, I will do my very best to be an essential member of the team by bringing in excellent writing skills, enthusiasm for the work, as well as by being cooperative with other members of the department.

I look forward to _____.

Sincerely,
Terence Jones

(a) visiting your company for a business meeting
(b) speaking with you about the vacancy soon
(c) introducing you to the other members
(d) hearing from you about this position

2. _____ has been found to be an important component to losing weight. People who lost 15 kg for over five years did so thanks to the type of breakfast they had. They mostly ate protein-rich foods like eggs or nuts rather than sugar-heavy cereals and pastries, which can spike and then dip your blood sugar levels. Fruits also help because their fiber content slows the absorption of their sugars. Having such wholesome foods early in the day raises metabolism and burns calories.

(a) Avoiding sugary snacks
(b) Waking up early every day
(c) Eating a healthy breakfast
(d) Favoring protein over carbohydrates

3.

> ## Movie Review
>
> Based on the best-selling novel, this film is a magical adventure story centering on a boy living in Indonesia. It has some awesome special effects, providing extraordinary visual experience in 3-D, which makes it definitely worth a trip to the cinema. My only complaint is that the film lacks substance. It is largely just effects driven. So while the film is an amazing adventure, it fizzles on an emotional level. Still, it's
> _____.

(a) not advisable for young children to watch
(b) a touching story for the whole family
(c) a rollercoaster ride of emotions
(d) good enough to recommend

4. As a specialized context for learning, _____.
First, it is a poor substitute for the real world. Intercultural communication and experiential culture learning is only simulated at a desk and on paper. Second, the curriculum is generally designed to encourage mostly just deductive reasoning and rule-ordered pedagogy. Last, the institutional context provides little "natural input" and is traditionally dedicated to language learning, not language acquisition.

(a) real world applications should be taught by teachers
(b) a school offers a relatively safe place to practice
(c) the language teacher must encourage peer learning
(d) the language classroom has some demerits

5. The new John Dexter novel explores the idea of whether people make their own choices or whether their destinies are determined ahead of time. Essentially it is about the freedom of one's will versus pre-destination. These two contrasting philosophies are examined in relation to war and in terms of the decisions men and women make when caught up in it. There is a constant tension between what they can and cannot control. So this novel will appeal most to people interested in the
_____.

(a) wartime fiction and historical novelizations
(b) importance of making right choices in wartime
(c) philosophical implications of every action we take
(d) opposing notions of free will versus fatalism

6. Chris Cox's new historical production on at the Reece Theater enlivens history by
_____. As an everyman, Samuel's concern for survival
makes him selfish and duplicitous. Yet he's not as culpable as the pampered politician
Richard whose craving for position tolerates little virtue. His corrupt political dealings
come to a head with the idealism of Morgan. But whereas Morgan maintains his values
throughout, the cowardly Nathan caves into threats. While the time frame of the play is
the Gilded Age of the early 20th century, the ethical conflicts and issues brought up are
timeless and resonant with us today.

(a) showing that anybody is capable of the most heinous behavior
(b) detailing the corruption that was rife during the Gilded Age
(c) creating a moral drama with realistic character portrayals
(d) staging a political thriller with allusions to contemporary events

7. Europe is facing a grave problem of _____. The
population of some nations is stagnant or already dwindling, which will reduce the future
workforce and hinder continued economic growth. Workers everywhere are getting older
and heading for retirement without enough workers to replace them. Furthermore, with
the increasing number of retirees, there is a greater burden to providing healthcare and
pensions. European nations on average have a worker-to-pensioner ratio of 4 to 1. By
2050, the ratio will have dropped to just 2 to 1.

(a) needing immigration to supplement a falling fertility rate
(b) high unemployment combined with delayed retirement
(c) supporting more pensioners with fewer workers
(d) automation replacing workers in the labor market

8. Not all people learn a foreign language in the same way. A person's personality,
motivation, and learning style can lead to different results. An introvert tends to be
reluctant to speak up in a communicative language learning environment. An extrovert,
on the other hand, will make most use of the ample opportunity to practice. A holistic
learner does not heed details while an analytical learner pays a lot of attention to details.
Some people are inspired by certain activities while others may not be. It stands to
reason that in order to provide the most conducive learning environment and provide
effective learning strategies, teachers _____.

(a) can benefit by analyzing their own style of teaching
(b) will ideally cater to these individual differences
(c) should avoid accommodating lazy language learners
(d) need carefully prepared lesson plans for each class

9. The only reliable way to lose weight is to eat less and exercise more. However, many reject this tried-and-true method in favor of fad or crash diets that do not work because they are too extreme, too demanding, or too restrictive to follow for any length of time. _____ these diets may seem to succeed at first, it is all too often only temporary. Often a succession of different diets are attempted, which turns into a pattern of losing and regaining weight, each new attempt more difficult than the one before. Such weight fluctuations can also increase the risk of illnesses.

(a) Hence
(b) Since
(c) In case
(d) Even though

10. A recession is a period when the economy as a whole contracts over several business quarters. This period is often marked by macroeconomic indicators showing less spending on investment, greater unemployment, and lowered individual incomes and business profits. _____, it is also the best time for governments to implement expansionary spending programs and fine-tune their monetary policies. So while an economic recession is tough on companies and workers, there are some compensatory measures to take in the form of government assistance and the call to decrease taxes.

(a) Besides
(b) Likewise
(c) However
(d) Moreover

Part II **Questions 11—12**

Read the passage and identify the option that does NOT belong.

11. With its oak forests and skins as raw material for making leather footwear, Northamptonshire's tradition of handcrafted shoes dates back centuries. (a) After the Second World War, the region continued to be a center for the modern shoe industry in Britain. (b) Then came cheaper overseas products and many local factories converted into private residences. (c) The heritage of craftsmanship is currently riding the tide of global luxury trends while domestic demand remains subdued. (d) Its reputation was bolstered by having both the legendary Robin Hood and character James Bond as patrons.

12. Statistics on arranged marriages show them to be more resilient than love marriages. (a) While marriages based on love are resulting in divorce nearly half the time in the US, only 4% of arranged marriage couples get separated. (b) The reason for that may be due to the way arranged marriages are constructed in the first place. (c) It is certainly a part of harmonious relations, for example, to maintain the important practice of compromise. (d) Since the parents do the matching in an arranged marriage, partners are presumably pre-selected for compatibility in values, education, and finances.

Part III **Questions 13—25**

Read the passage, question, and options. Then, based on the given information, choose the option that best answers each question.

R

13. Some people maintain that it is all right to cry at work, especially in creative fields where emotions can run high among sensitive types. However, not everyone agrees with the opinion that the occasional meltdown is acceptable. When someone begins sobbing at work, it can bring the entire office to a stop. It's tough not to notice. What's more, crying at work is viewed by some to be a sign of weakness, especially if men do it. Researchers have found that around 9% of men have cried at work in contrast to 41% of women.

Q: What is the passage mainly about?
(a) Explaining the emotional necessity of crying for women
(b) Differing opinions on crying in the workplace
(c) The effect of individuals crying in a work environment
(d) The emotional overreacting of people in creative fields

14.

Dear Director Smith,

I must say that I was greatly flattered by your offer to have me back in my old post after all these years. I have nothing but fond memories of working with you guys at Caldwell during my stay there. And so while I did take some time to consider it, and after discussing the matter with my wife, I have decided that I just cannot accept the offer at this time. So much time has passed, and health considerations further prevent me from performing at my best level. Please take this as appreciation for your kindness, and I truly hope that you find someone great who can handle the task.

Yours sincerely and best regards,
Kris Zanth

Q: What is the writer's main idea in the letter?
(a) He is still too ill to return to his position.
(b) He decided not to return to a previous job.
(c) He feels honored to be asked to return.
(d) He is hoping for a promotion in the company.

15. Using sunscreen protects against the damaging effects of UV radiation, a known cancer-causing agent. The research showed that applying sunscreen does not cause vitamin D deficiency and protects against skin carcinoma and premature aging due to sun exposure. Nevertheless, some concern exists on the harmfulness of the chemical oxybenzone used in sunscreens. High levels of it have been linked to low-weight births in some studies. Nanoparticles of zinc oxide and titanium dioxide are also seen as being easily absorbed into the skin and possibly causing free radical formation.

Q: What is the main topic of the passage?

(a) Proving the harmlessness of sunscreen formulations
(b) The cancer causing dangers of UV radiation exposure
(c) The effect of sunscreens in combating skin cancers
(d) Research findings on the safety of sunscreens

16. Studies on the texting behavior of teenagers report that the average teenager sends about 35 texts even after lying down to bed. Teens feel obliged to answer every tag, update, mention, and text. This urge to connect with others via text messaging can become all-consuming, transcending norms of personal boundaries in time and space. As an uncontrollable addiction, it can negatively impact their mental and physical health. Late-night texting appears to contribute toward sleep deprivation and its associated health concerns such as increased risk of infection, weight gain, anxiety, and depression.

Q: What is the passage mainly about?

(a) Why teenage texting interrupts valuable study time
(b) Keeping texting habits from becoming an addiction
(c) How much time teens spend on late-night texting
(d) Late-night texting among teens and its effects

17. Early diagnosis of Alzheimer's disease is now possible using Magnetic Resonance Imaging (MRI) which can track Glutathione (GSH), a brain component associated with the disease. In a test on 85 subjects, overall mean GSH content was found to be higher in healthy young females than in males. Treatment that helps deter the progression of Alzheimer's has also become possible since the efficacy of any medication can be checked by monitoring GSH level. This new technique could help prevent this debilitating disease from reaching the widespread brain impairment stage.

Q: Which of the following is correct according to the passage?
(a) The GSH tracking technique helps recovery from Alzheimer's.
(b) More GSH content has been detected in healthy males.
(c) The effectiveness of treatment can be gauged by GSH tracking.
(d) An Alzheimer's patient can only be partly monitored for GSH.

18. The recently uncovered skeleton ascertained to be the remains of King Richard III (1452-1485) show signs of idiopathic adolescent-onset scoliosis. In the 1400s, the disease was thought to have been caused by an imbalance in the body's humors. Treatments at the time included ointments, massages, and possibly traction or a back brace made of wood or metal. If he suffered from the condition, it would have restricted his lung capacity. It is speculated that he may have been treated for the disease, but no sign of such treatments have been found on the bones.

Q: Which of the following is correct about Richard III according to the passage?
(a) His disease is thought to have started at an early age.
(b) His options for treatment were limited to ointments.
(c) He probably suffered from restricted breathing.
(d) He wore a back brace for his condition.

19. Never pour large quantities of cooking fats or grease down the kitchen sink because it causes your pipes to clog. The addition of boiling water or mincing the fatty scraps with a garbage disposal unit does not mitigate the effect. In fact, using garbage disposal units at all should probably be done at a minimum. Not only will that reduce the potential for clogged sewer lines, but it will also cut down on maintenance and repair costs. Some municipality districts have even banned garbage disposals in new residences and restaurants. They even require by law their removal when ownership changes or major remodeling is done.

Q: Which of the following is correct according to the passage?
(a) Hot water is effective in breaking up fatty food waste.
(b) Garbage disposals are practical for getting rid of leftovers.
(c) Some districts encourage home garbage disposal installations.
(d) Removing old garbage disposal units is sometimes mandated.

20.

Volcano Safety Tips

There are many things you can do to protect yourselves from dangers of volcanic eruptions. If a volcano erupts in your area, evacuate only as directed by authorities to stay clear of lava, mud flows, and flying rocks and debris. Avoid river areas and low-lying regions. Change into long-sleeved shirts and long pants and use goggles or eyeglasses, not contacts. Wear an emergency mask or hold a damp cloth over your face. If staying indoors, close windows and doors and block chimneys. Be aware that ash may put excess weight on your roof and will need to be swept away. Also, air-borne ash can damage engines and metal parts, so it is best to avoid driving.

Q: Which of the following is advised in case of a volcanic eruption?
(a) Seek out river areas for water and safety.
(b) Ensure your face is adequately protected.
(c) Avoid climbing your roof to clear away ash.
(d) It is all right to drive after an eruption is over.

21. A new vaccine has been developed for children with autism to help fight intestinal bacteria, which may also help to regulate some of the symptoms of autism. It is carb-based and fights the intestinal bacteria which contributes to gastrointestinal (GI) disorders and somehow shows up more often in children with autism. More than 90 percent of children with autism suffer from chronic GI issues, and of those 90 percent, 75 percent suffer from diarrhea. Unfortunately, clinical and human trials of the vaccine could take more than 10 years.

Q: Which of the following is correct according to the study?

(a) All the symptoms of autism can be cured by the new vaccine.
(b) It is unclear why intestinal bacteria is more frequent in autistic kids.
(c) About 75 percent of children with autism suffer from diarrhea.
(d) It took 10 years for the vaccine to pass clinical and human trials.

22. About 1% of people in the US are known to possess the characteristics of narcissistic personality disorder. They have an exaggerated view of their own abilities, and they are arrogant, conceited, and crave constant praise and attention. Also, they are very sensitive to any form of reproach since it is usually regarded as a personal attack. Unfortunately, these people rarely seek out treatment since they are often unwilling to acknowledge their illness. If they do begin therapy, it is at the urging of family members or to treat out-of-control symptoms of the disorder.

Q: Which of the following is correct about narcissists according to the passage?

(a) They often have heightened skill capabilities.
(b) They like to have others validate their actions.
(c) They are unwilling to retract criticism of others.
(d) They often have families that need treatment.

23. It has been a year since I quit my job. It was a bit early to retire, and so people keep asking me when I would start looking for another job. They seem to worry about how I will pay for my retirement years. Well, I have worked at a company for 20 years, and I am hesitant to go back to the hustle and bustle of the corporate world. I would rather search for what I really want to do for the rest of my life. In that sense, I plan to explore my interests and options and to discuss them with friends and family and only then decide on a path to take.

Q: What can be inferred about the writer from the passage?

(a) He lacks confidence in his own abilities.
(b) He will probably go on a long vacation somewhere.
(c) He is unlikely to ever work for a company again.
(d) He has been dreaming of pursuing hobbies his whole life.

24. There are signs of trouble everywhere. The shop vacancy rate has increased from 5% to 15% and housing sales have plummeted by 50%. Yet these are mere statistics for most people, who carry on with their lives much as before. The current downturn is generally assessed not so much by the fall in output from previous peaks but rather by the lack of growth. From another perspective, we find that since the early 1990s, personal disposable incomes have risen by about 70%. This absence of economic growth still leaves many people at a higher standard of living than 20 years ago.

Q: What can be inferred from the passage?

(a) The economic slump is making people frugal with their money.
(b) The extent of economic decline has been improperly gauged.
(c) The nation as a whole is poorer though the rich get richer.
(d) The downturn has hardly impacted the standard of living.

25. Acculturation happens when cultures adopt the beliefs and practices of other cultures. In modernizing its nation, Japan acculturated to the West and transitioned from feudal agrarianism to industrial capitalism. The diet of its people, in particular, was Westernized to the extent that higher instances of cardiovascular disease among Japanese men is now a real public health issue. Acculturation to Western ways has also been linked with more instances of mental disease and drug abuse, with differences seen by gender.

Q: What can be inferred about acculturation from the passage?

(a) It most affects the liberal segments of the population.
(b) It has profound repercussions on individual lifestyles.
(c) It is an overall benefit to a culture despite the problems.
(d) It affects all ages and both genders in similar ways.

Part IV **Questions 26—35**

Read the passage, questions, and options. Then, based on the given information, choose the option that best answers each question.

R

Questions 26-27

| News | Photos | **Events** | About Us | Contact |

The 15th Annual Awesome Photo Contest

Are you passionate about capturing comic moments in everyday life? Are you passionate about bringing laughter to millions of people around the world? Are you passionate about presenting photography as a form of art? Then, why not enter this year's Awesome Photo Contest? You may end up making yourself smile!

There are three categories in the contest: children, young adults, and adults. When it comes to judging entries, we are uber-serious. In fact, we are well-known for our rigorous judging procedures, which are implemented by reputable photographers. So, don't laugh at our judging procedures!

■ Entry pictures must meet the following requirements:
- The resolution of your entry must not be altered.
- No attempts must be made to increase the size of your entry.
- No attempts must be made to apply effects to your entry.
- Your entry must be submitted in JPEG format. The maximum file size of your entry is 50 MB.
- All entries must be emailed to amy.g@awesome.com no later than July 7th.

26. Q: Which of the following is correct according to the webpage?

(a) The photo contest is held on a quarterly basis.
(b) Entry pictures are likely to make viewers feel distraught.
(c) Adults over the age of 65 are prohibited from submitting entries to the contest.
(d) The judging procedures are likely to be highly fair.

27. Q: Which of the following can be accepted as an entry for the contest?

(a) A humorous picture which has been enlarged
(b) A picture of an amusing situation, emailed to amy.g@awesome.com on July 5th.
(c) A picture file in PDF format
(d) A picture file whose size is 5 GB

118

ECOLOGY > LATEST NEWS *The Nature Times*

R

Resurrection Ecology: Savior of the Human Race?

Although the term "resurrection ecology" is not familiar to ordinary people, its idea is quite simple. Resurrection ecology is aimed at understanding how organisms evolve by "resurrecting" ancient species of animals, plants, and microorganisms. Scientists believe that those ancient species can help them understand the past and future of various organisms on Earth.

Since 2012, a large number of ancient species have been revived by resurrection ecologists. Some of those species are only 700 years old, whereas others are approximately 30,000 years old. What surprises scientists the most is one bacterium, which is thought to be some 8 million years old.

Can those resurrected species of animals and microorganisms jeopardize the human race? Resurrection ecologists do not think so. They point out that most revived species are completely harmless. Furthermore, since global warming has already resurrected several ancient species, it would be much better for scientists to revive similar species and study their effects on today's Earth.

Only time will tell if resurrection ecology is truly beneficial for the human race.

28. Q: Which of the following is correct about the revived ancient species according to the article?

(a) Ecological groups have been pressuring scientists to resurrect them since 2012.
(b) None of them is believed to be more than 30,000 years old.
(c) Most scientists avoid reviving microorganisms for fear that they will wreak havoc on the ecosystem.
(d) They are believed to help scientists to comprehend the evolutionary processes of organisms.

29. Q: Which of the following statements would resurrection ecologists most likely agree with?

(a) Reviving ancient species of animals poses no danger whatsoever to the human race.
(b) Knowledge of the evolution of organisms on Earth will bring benefits to the human race.
(c) Reviving ancient species of plants is all but impossible.
(d) Global warming is not likely to resurrect any more species of animals.

R

Igor Stravinsky: A Revolutionary in Music

When commissioned by Serge Diaghilev to compose three ballets for the Ballets Russes, Igor Stravinsky was an almost "inexperienced" composer. Nevertheless, the three ballets that Stravinsky wrote for Diaghilev were revolutionary in many ways. In particular, *The Rite of Spring*, the last of those ballets, is still highly regarded by many music historians.

Many critics observe that the music of *The Rite of Spring* is composed of distinctive sounds, such as "shrieks" and "snarls." On the other hand, some detractors of Stravinsky, such as Julius Harrison, maintain that those sounds are simply "hideous."

However, even such critics agree that Stravinsky was successful in taking bitonality to the next level. Although the other two ballets that he wrote for the Ballets Russes experimented with bitonality, *The Rite of Spring* refined that technique to the highest degree, which contributed significantly to Stravinsky's reputation as an avant-garde musician.

30. Q: What is the main point of the passage?

(a) *The Rite of Spring* provoked considerable controversy among music critics.
(b) *The Rite of Spring* helped Stravinsky establish a reputation as a radical musician.
(c) Stravinsky's musical career was defined by his constant efforts to refine bitonality.
(d) Not all music historians have been impressed by Stravinsky's experimental ballets.

31. Q: What can be inferred about Stravinsky from the passage?

(a) He recognized Diaghilev's potential as a revolutionary ballet dancer.
(b) He was in his early twenties when commissioned by Diaghilev to compose ballets for the Ballets Russes.
(c) His approach to bitonality might have been considerably different from those of other composers.
(d) He maintained a strained relationship with Harrison throughout his entire career.

From:	Cynthia Taylor <cynthia_t@leadership.com>
To:	Jack Harper <jack_h@jmail.com>
Date:	Fri, June 8 at 2:33 PM
Subject:	The 13th International Leadership Conference

We are pleased to invite you to attend the 13th International Leadership Conference, which is slated to be held from 13th through 15th July. This year's conference will be hosted at the Metro Toronto Convention Centre, in Toronto, Ontario.

By attending the conference, you will definitely gain insights into the true nature of leadership. According to Kate Porter, one of the keynote speakers, leadership is not about leading people. Instead, it is more about serving other people so that they can realize their full potential. Interestingly, other speakers will present different views on leadership.

As always, there will be Q&A sessions and interactive discussions. You can register for the conference by visiting the following link: http://www.international-leadership-conference.com.

Should you have any questions and suggestions, just feel free to email me at cynthia_t@leadership.com.

Yours sincerely,

Cynthia Taylor
Coordinator, International Leadership Conference

32. Q: What is the main purpose of the email?
   (a) To request the recipient to be present at an international event
   (b) To invite the recipient to make suggestions as to how to improve the international leadership conference
   (c) To ask the recipient to preside over the Q&A sessions
   (d) To suggest that the recipient register for the international conference by emailing Ms. Taylor.

33. Q: What can be inferred about Ms. Porter from the email?
   (a) In her speech, she is likely to attack the weaknesses of servant leadership.
   (b) She may believe that servant leadership is the true form of leadership.
   (c) She is scheduled to deliver her keynote address on July 15th.
   (d) She will answer questions asked by Mr. Harper after her presentation.

Subjectivity Defines Individuality

According to Søren Kierkegaard, "the single individual" has long been overlooked in traditional philosophy, for it values objectivity and universality. Kierkegaard observes that such concepts do not help to reveal the true meaning of the single individual.

He points out that when religious faith conflicts with universal ethics, an individual can have a chance to become "individually" meaningful. He takes the example of Abraham, who is divinely ordered to sacrifice his son.

If Abraham follows universal ethics and refuses to follow the divine order, his existence becomes "universally" meaningful, in that his intentions are dictated by universally applicable ethics. If Abraham follows the divine order, however, his existence becomes "individually" meaningful. This is mainly because his intentions are uniquely governed by his individual faith.

For this reason, Kierkegaard believes that subjectivity, not objectivity, can help to define the single individual. For the Danish philosopher, subjectivity defines individuality.

34. Q: What is the main point of the passage?
   (a) Kierkegaard believes that there is no meaningful relation between subjectivity and individuality.
   (b) Kierkegaard argues that the meaning of the single individual can be revealed by subjectivity.
   (c) Kierkegaard maintains that traditional philosophy has long hindered the manifestation of individuality.
   (d) Kierkegaard understands that religious faith is inevitably incompatible with universal ethics.

35. Q: Why does Kierkegaard take the example of Abraham?
   (a) To assert that religious faith constantly defies universally applicable ethics
   (b) To illustrate how religious faith helps to define individuality
   (c) To claim that divine orders must be abided by at all costs
   (d) To explain that Abraham's faith leads to his blindness to the truth

Listening
Comprehension

DIRECTIONS

1. In the Listening Comprehension section, all content will be presented orally rather than in written form.

2. This section contains five parts. For each part, you will receive separate instructions. Listen to the instructions carefully, and choose the best answer from the options for each item.

MP3 바로 듣기
받아쓰기 테스트
모바일 단어장

○ 정답 P 82

Part I Questions 1—10

You will now hear ten individual spoken questions or statements, each followed by four spoken responses. Choose the most appropriate response for each item.

Part II Questions 11—20

You will now hear ten short conversation fragments, each followed by four spoken responses. Choose the most appropriate response to complete each conversation.

L

Part IV **Questions 31—36**

You will now hear six short talks. After each talk, you will be asked to answer a question. Each talk and its corresponding question will be read twice. Then you will hear four options which will be read only once. Based on the given information, choose the option that best answers the question.

Part V   Questions 37—40

You will now hear two longer talks. After each talk, you will be asked to answer two questions. Each talk and its corresponding questions will be read twice. However, the four options for each question will be read only once. Based on the given information, choose the option that best answers each question.

Vocabulary & Grammar

DIRECTIONS

These two sections test your vocabulary and grammar knowledge. You will have 25 minutes to complete a total of 60 questions: 30 from the Vocabulary section and 30 from the Grammar section. Be sure to follow the directions given by the proctor.

Part I   Questions 1—10
Choose the option that best completes each dialogue.

1. A: I found out from Judy where you were last night.
B: I wish you'd stop _____ in my affairs.
(a) serving
(b) wading
(c) intruding
(d) conforming

2. A: Hello, 911? My friend just fell off a ladder and seriously injured his head!
B: Please stay calm and I'll _____ an ambulance.
(a) forward
(b) send
(c) label
(d) ship

3. A: Why do you like walking in the park?
B: I find it _____ me after a long workday.
(a) heeds
(b) accords
(c) obfuscates
(d) revitalizes

4. A: I appreciate your honest feedback about my writing.
B: It would be _____ of me not to tell you what I really think.
(a) pragmatic
(b) gallant
(c) devoid
(d) remiss

5. A: Do you have any suggestions for improving my work?
B: No, I would _____ as you have.
(a) think through
(b) carry on
(c) spin out
(d) tune in

6. A: Are there any side effects of your new medication?
B: It tends to make me a little _____ in the mornings.
(a) courteous
(b) insolent
(c) lethargic
(d) suspect

7. A: The driver of that van nearly rear-ended us!
B: It was a(n) _____ error, I'm sure.
(a) expedited
(b) inadvertent
(c) conspicuous
(d) magnanimous

8. A: Cheryl certainly likes to win at sports.
B: That _____ her attitude to life in general.
(a) partakes
(b) diverts
(c) subordinates
(d) exemplifies

9. A: What happened to your face?
B: I got into a little _____ after the basketball game last night.
(a) dribble
(b) scuffle
(c) mettle
(d) bobble

10. A: I miss the days when you could smoke in bars.
B: Well, don't expect the government to _____ the ban.
(a) make way for
(b) do away with
(c) miss out on
(d) fall back on

Choose the option that best completes each sentence.

11. Live theater was a popular _____
among the general public in Elizabethan
England.

   (a) mission
   (b) pastime
   (c) relief
   (d) station

12. Wealth alone is not enough to
_____ a meaningful sense of
living.

   (a) coax
   (b) ensure
   (c) fulfill
   (d) submit

13. According to the team physician, the
fullback will require a full three months
to _____ from his injury.

   (a) recover
   (b) deepen
   (c) wander
   (d) shelter

14. Hotel staff will be sure to _____
to all of your needs for the duration of
your stay.

   (a) count
   (b) attend
   (c) remark
   (d) conduct

15. _____ of the new human
resources service will have to wait until
the staff completes the training.

   (a) Implementation
   (b) Accommodation
   (c) Embarkation
   (d) Divination

16. The man didn't convince his indignant
friend with the claim that his remark was
an attempt at being _____.

   (a) ironic
   (b) abusive
   (c) succinct
   (d) trivial

17. Many Native American cultures
_____ certain supernatural
attributes to natural objects such as rocks
and trees.

   (a) ascribed
   (b) described
   (c) subscribed
   (d) inscribed

18. After years of campaigning for the right
to vote, American women were granted
_____ in 1920.

   (a) surveillance
   (b) suffrage
   (c) clemency
   (d) constitution

19. The principal caught one of the students
_____ just outside of the
teachers' lounge.

   (a) eavesdropping
   (b) undervaluing
   (c) instigating
   (d) collating

20. Not surprisingly, the chairman of
the board was _____ to his
authority being undermined by the board
members.

   (a) inimical
   (b) apocryphal
   (c) mercurial
   (d) diabolical

21. Should electricity be knocked out by a storm, the _____ power system will automatically engage.

    (a) burrowed
    (b) auxiliary
    (c) streamlined
    (d) entrepreneurial

22. Newton showed that a beam of sunlight can be _____ by a prism and then reconstituted by a second prism.

    (a) impaired
    (b) extended
    (c) demolished
    (d) refracted

23. Karen was beset by _____ looking on the toy she had played with as a child.

    (a) austerity
    (b) limbo
    (c) disparity
    (d) nostalgia

24. A handful of participants are _____ each year during Spain's *Running of the Bulls*, while others suffer less severe injuries.

    (a) gored
    (b) embalmed
    (c) pecked
    (d) garbled

25. Tools like tasers and pepper spray allow police to _____ suspects without causing any long-term physical harm.

    (a) pursue
    (b) maim
    (c) incapacitate
    (d) demote

26. The court ruled that the corporation should pay the family $38,500 in _____ for the contaminated property.

    (a) munificence
    (b) restitution
    (c) stipend
    (d) bastion

27. After cornering the Senator, protesters proceeded to _____ her for opposing the tax reform bill.

    (a) harangue
    (b) subject
    (c) waive
    (d) subpoena

28. Company sales were seen to _____ in the fourth quarter, despite the optimistic estimates that were forecasted.

    (a) goad
    (b) belittle
    (c) egress
    (d) slacken

29. After undergoing a purported religious experience, the criminal gave up his _____ ways and dedicated himself to serving others.

    (a) heinous
    (b) rancorous
    (c) dexterous
    (d) solicitous

30. The manager, never one to _____ words, told the laggard employee exactly what he thought of him.

    (a) mince
    (b) castrate
    (c) pique
    (d) grit

You have finished the Vocabulary questions. Please continue on to the Grammar questions.

Part I **Questions 1—10**

Choose the option that best completes each dialogue.

1. A: Were you late getting out of your sales meeting?

   B: Yes, I never expected _____.

   (a) it takes so long
   (b) so it takes long
   (c) to take it so long
   (d) it to take so long

2. A: Unfortunately, we don't have a booking under your name.

   B: But my reservation _____ nearly two months ago.

   (a) made
   (b) had made
   (c) was made
   (d) to be made

3. A: Do you think Bert will be free to join our soccer team?

   B: _____, or we find someone else.

   (a) Either able is he
   (b) Neither is he able
   (c) Either he's able to
   (d) Neither of them is able to

4. A: You must be really busy at work these days.

   B: Yes, I _____ to have such a demanding schedule.

   (a) was forgetting like it was
   (b) forgot what it was like
   (c) was like forgetting that
   (d) like what I forgot

5. A: I don't think you're ever going to get that promotion.

   B: That fact has _____ than it is now.

   (a) to me never be clearer
   (b) to be clearer never to me
   (c) never been clearer to me
   (d) been clearer that I've never

6. A: I can't believe you missed the conference call.

   B: Well, I wouldn't have if you _____ me.

   (a) could remind
   (b) had reminded
   (c) reminded
   (d) remind

7. A: Have you made a selection?

   B: Yes, I'd like to purchase _____ purses.

   (a) three brown leather all
   (b) all three leather brown
   (c) three leather brown all
   (d) all three brown leather

8. A: So, the air conditioner is a little too high for you?

   B: Yes, I'm just not _____ low temperatures.

   (a) to be accustomed
   (b) too accustomed for
   (c) accustomed to such
   (d) such as accustomed

9. A: Does visiting here bring back some memories?

   B: Oh, it's just _____.

   (a) as remembering I was
   (b) I remember as was it
   (c) as I remember it to be
   (d) I remembered to be it

10. A: I dare you to eat one of these hot chilies.

    B: I _____ if you have one first.

    (a) do
    (b) do it
    (c) dare
    (d) will

Part II **Questions 11—25**

Choose the option that best completes each sentence.

11. _____ to gain traction in the polls, the politician withdrew from the primary race.

   (a) Failed
   (b) Having failed
   (c) He failed
   (d) To have failed

12. Europe is the region most of the students would visit if they _____ the opportunity to travel abroad.

   (a) will be given
   (b) were given
   (c) had given
   (d) gave

13. The news that the dog had been found came as _____ to its owner, who had been worried sick.

   (a) the relief
   (b) a relief
   (c) reliefs
   (d) relieving

14. The study's findings, if _____, will have far-reaching consequences in the field of astrobiology.

   (a) confirmed
   (b) confirming
   (c) they confirm
   (d) to be confirmed

15. _____ regret, the company was forced to lay off workers following the worst quarter in its history.

   (a) Though with not
   (b) Not though with no
   (c) Not though without
   (d) Though not without

16. The man with the strange accent _____ the reporter received the tip turned out to be a foreign spy.

   (a) of which
   (b) to whom
   (c) for which
   (d) from whom

17. _____ to court to answer for his crimes, the suspect fled the country and has not been seen since.

   (a) Summoning
   (b) Was summoned
   (c) To have summoned
   (d) Having been summoned

18. It was less than a year after Mr. Chang's departure _____ was dismissed by the fickle board.

   (a) yet another CEO before
   (b) before another CEO yet
   (c) yet before another CEO
   (d) before yet another CEO

19. The cell sample _____ the enzyme immediately withered following the procedure.

   (a) which did the scientist extract from
   (b) from which did the scientist extract
   (c) the scientist extracted from which
   (d) from which the scientist extracted

20. Some child specialists recommend that young children _____ out of preschool until their fourth birthday.

   (a) might be keeping
   (b) could have kept
   (c) should be kept
   (d) ought to keep

21. During the first half of the season, the Baltimore Orioles were winning games at _____.

    (a) a high pace record
    (b) high pace of record
    (c) a near record pace
    (d) near record high

22. Should your pencil break while taking the test, please notify a proctor and you will be given _____.

    (a) others
    (b) another
    (c) any other
    (d) the others

23. The Lockheed C-130 Hercules is a massive four-engine aircraft _____ cargo and troops to where they're needed.

    (a) transporter used to
    (b) used as a transporter
    (c) used to transport often
    (d) often used to transport

24. A $20 surcharge will be levied for any changes _____ within 48 hours of the scheduled flight.

    (a) have to be requested
    (b) having requested
    (c) can be requested
    (d) requested

25. Immigration issues may be complex, but _____ that we tackle them head on.

    (a) why is it that important
    (b) it's so important is why
    (c) it is why that's important so
    (d) that is why it's so important

Read each dialogue or passage carefully and identify the option that contains a grammatical error.

26. (a) A: Why did you drink so much beer last night?
    (b) B: Well, I have been having a really tough day, OK?
    (c) A: I know, but you promised me you wouldn't drink anymore.
    (d) B: I'll do better from now on, I promise.

27. (a) A: I'm so sorry I couldn't make it last night.
    (b) B: That's OK, I ended up having a fun time anyway.
    (c) A: Hasn't it been snowing so hard, I could've gotten there.
    (d) B: Really, don't worry. I went to the club and danced all night!

28. (a) A comparative study of ancient Martian meteorites found on Earth and rocks on Mars has yielded an astounding discovery. (b) Based on the findings, scientists believe an oxygen-rich atmosphere existed on Mars some 4 billion years ago. (c) That is a full 1.5 billion years prior to the same conditions developed on Earth. (d) The implications are that complex life may have evolved and perished on Mars even while it was still in its nascent stages on our own planet.

29. (a) Squirrels can be a real pest for homeowners by ruining the garden, destroying insulation, and even starting fires by chewing on electrical lines. (b) To put your mind at ease, try our high-tech ultrasonic pest repellent, the Squirrel Be Gone 5000. (c) Contained within this small metal box is a radio transmitter that emits a frequency that high you can't hear it. (d) But squirrels sure can and to them it is very loud, causing them to stay well away from your house!

30. (a) It was with high hopes that the famed metal band White Anchor launched its so-called Revival Tour last fall. (b) Unfortunately for them, it seems the band's once legion of fans failed to get the memo. (c) Attendance for the concerts played in eight of the Northeast's biggest arenas was absolutely pitiful. (d) A warning let this be to other former greats who think they can magically resurrect the past.

You have reached the end of the Vocabulary & Grammar sections. Do NOT move on to the Reading Comprehension section until instructed to do so. You are NOT allowed to turn to any other section of the test.

Reading
Comprehension

Part I Questions 1—10

Read the passage. Then choose the option that best completes the passage.

1. In the interest of transparency, this following outlines _____.
Upon registering for a Spoonful account, you authorize the acquisition and retention of personal information including your IP address, mobile network, location, and operating system. Spoonful may place a small data file on your hard disk in order to audit aggregate traffic and usage trends to help us enhance our services. By using our services, you consent to the collection of personal data described herein.

(a) the tracking and marketing of your data
(b) the conditions of using our service
(c) your consent to our privacy policy
(d) how to monitor our usage of your data

2. At the beginning of the twentieth century, Britain's HMS *Dreadnought* represented a major technological advance in naval engineering. Its presence intimidated other countries into scrapping their older ships and building new ones to maintain a naval presence on the world stage. This was especially true of South American countries: Brazil started work on not one, but three Dreadnought-like warships. Not to be outdone, Argentina and Chile commissioned two "dreadnoughts" of their own. They were forced to take action and _____.

(a) keep pace with Britain as naval powers
(b) show military expenditure was not in their interest
(c) prevent the Dreadnought from becoming a threat
(d) enter a regional clash for maritime supremacy

3.

Movie Review

This summer's much-hyped blockbuster *Rancor of Truth* debuted in August. Dealing with a future dystopia divided into haves and have-nots, the film had the potential to reflect thoughtfully on our own times. Yet producer Katia Nerkoff only delves into the issue superficially, instead loading up the film with the obligatory gun play and dazzling pursuits on foot and vehicle. In the end, audiences are left with a film that is _____.

(a) full of stunts yet also carries a social message
(b) critical of the way violence shapes our society
(c) reflective of the world's growing wealth gap
(d) action packed but bereft of deeper meaning

4.

Dear Mr. White,

We have received your request for account termination, submitted via email on October 12. Unfortunately, as stipulated in the contract agreed upon at the outset, your account term is 24 months and any termination prior to the conclusion of the term will incur a penalty of $130. We are unable to process termination until we receive payment of this penalty in full. Please remit payment by check or money order to the address printed on the reverse. Alternatively, maintain your account in good standing until February 2, the end of your 24-month term. After that time,

_____.

Doug Wallace
Account Support

(a) you will be eligible for a renewal
(b) your penalty would have been fully paid
(c) you may close the account at no cost
(d) your payment will be refunded in full

5. In the late nineteenth century, Swedish hot air balloonist Salomon Andrée became enamored of the idea of _____. In particular, the as yet unexplored polar regions held an irresistible allure. The King of Sweden financed Andrée's North Pole expedition, which, after three years of planning, departed in July of 1897. However, the crew was lost and a rescue mission was futile since, lacking an understanding of the wind patterns in the upper atmosphere, no one knew where to focus their recovery efforts.

(a) reaching isolated destinations by balloon
(b) exploring the world by a balloon in 80 days
(c) becoming the first to trek to the North Pole
(d) measuring how balloons react to wind patterns

6. As every Canaveral fan knows, cold and drizzly autumn nights can make an evening at Falmouth Stadium a chilly affair. Safeguard yourself against this with the official Canaveral Loggerheads All-Weather Blanket. Manufactured from two-ply fleece and featuring a water-repellant external cover, the blanket combines the waterproofing of nylon fabric with the softness and comfort of traditional fleece. It blocks 95% of wind yet remains breathable, and insulates without being bulky. As tough as the Loggerheads themselves, it _____.

    (a) can bear whatever Mother Nature throws at it
    (b) is ideal for cleaning your sports equipment in all weather
    (c) will be a welcome companion in all seasons of the year
    (d) proudly bears the logos of all your favorite sports teams

7. Ice sheets such as those covering much of Greenland are actually resting on continental bedrock, where the structure of the terrain may be much more complex than the uniform flatness of the ice suggests. For example, beneath Greenland's ice lies a massive canyon that is longer than and nearly as deep as the Grand Canyon in Arizona. Researchers believe that, prior to the icing of the island some millions of years ago, the canyon contained a major river system. This recent finding suggests that _____.

    (a) we do not know Earth's surface as well as we think
    (b) it is clear that global warming is affecting Greenland
    (c) ice sheets tend to form where fresh water is flowing
    (d) the Grand Canyon was once covered by a large ice sheet

8. Ancient pictographs by the Pueblo peoples attest to the desert bighorn's _____. Populations of this native sheep declined drastically in the mid-nineteenth century, when the westward expansion of civilization drove the animals to near extinction. Now, desert bighorns range across only about a third of their original territory and populations remain unstable and vulnerable. This is despite conservation efforts such as a recolonization campaign by ecologists in 1991. They sought to capture and relocate isolated bighorns in the hope of rebuilding a viable population in protected habitats across Utah and the Dakotas.

    (a) resilience in the face of environmental pressures
    (b) former abundance in the American Southwest
    (c) scarcity and value to Native American peoples
    (d) rapid biological evolution over only a few millennia

9. In the minds of many, the idea of a vacation conjures up tropical sandy shorelines lapped by crystal clear waters. _____, more and more summer merrymakers are rejecting the stultifying pace of a beach vacation in favor of a more stimulating urban getaway. Urban vacations make more fiscal sense for individuals with restrictive schedules and finite budgets. More accessible than beach destinations, visiting cities can actually reduce travel time and cost less for the flight.

(a) Furthermore
(b) That said
(c) Otherwise
(d) Once again

10. Discussions of anthropogenic or human-caused climate change tend to focus on the climate-altering impact of carbon dioxide. While it is the predominant form of greenhouse gas emitted by humans, it is by no means the only one, or even the most pernicious. Methane, a greenhouse gas byproduct of the agricultural industry, is 25 times heavier per molecule than carbon dioxide. _____, nitrous oxide is an ozone-depleting gas emitted by manufacturing and agriculture that traps heat more than 300 times more per molecule than CO_2.

(a) Still
(b) Regardless
(c) Consequently
(d) Similarly

Part II **Questions 11–12**

Read the passage and identify the option that does NOT belong.

11. Known in West African cultures since ancient times, the kola nut has cultural and religious significance in Nigeria. (a) Among the Igbo people, an ethnic group in Nigeria, the kola nut has a particular symbolic relevance in social interactions. (b) Additionally, yams are grown by the Igbo and are accorded great importance in their culture. (c) The kola nuts are passed around while delivering proverbs, invocations to ancestors, and intercessions for the people of the community. (d) After this, they are divided into pieces and distributed according to the status of the individual.

12. Solar System objects known as Trojans are asteroids that inhabit the same orbit as a planet. (a) Astronomy classifies the largest of such objects as Trojan moons and, in theory, there could even be Trojan planets. (b) They trail or lead a planet along its orbital path at stable positions called Lagrangian points. (c) These asteroids, with widths up to hundreds of kilometers, are basically held in place by gravity. (d) They are not locked in place forever, however, as subtle shifts in regional gravity can knock them out of sync with their planet.

Part III **Questions 13—25**

Read the passage, question, and options. Then, based on the given information, choose the option that best answers each question.

R

13. Spurred on by evidence showing that meditation enhances productivity, a workplace trend toward offering meditation classes to employees promises to boost company returns. Yet, practitioners of meditation cannot deny the uncomfortable gulf between the personal growth-oriented objectives of meditation and the profit-motivated calculations of the companies promoting it. Meditation teachers thus find themselves driven into a discomfiting compromise. Their training in spiritual traditions that teach selflessness and detachment from material possession stand in stark contrast to capitalism's central tenet: profit above all else.

   Q: What is the best title for the passage?
   (a) Meditation Instructors Are Not Worth Their Pay
   (b) Corporate Meditation and Its Paradoxical Goals
   (c) Capitalists Make Money off Spiritual Meditation
   (d) Doubts about the Efficacy of Workplace Meditation

14.
   Dear Conference Participant,

   Congratulations and thank you for registering to attend the 6th annual International Travel Bloggers Conference, held this year in Berlin, Germany. Your username and password, with which you can enjoy access to the conference's dedicated online platform, can be found at the bottom of this email. You can connect with your fellow travel bloggers as well as schedule in-person meetings with the dozens of destination marketing organizations (DMOs) that will have representatives in attendance. Get started today as appointments fill up fast during this industry conference you won't want to miss!

   Jack Forsythe
   Travel Bloggers Conference

   Q: What is the email mainly about?
   (a) Selecting a unique username and password
   (b) Applying for jobs with travel-industry firms
   (c) Voting on the location of a travel conference
   (d) Travel networking via an online forum

15.

> ## Notice
>
> According to the most recent National Weather Service report, last updated at 6:15 am, conditions on Mt. Norse are forecast to be pristine, with unlimited visibility and a light west wind between 3 and 7 miles per hour. The King Pine and Mountain Shuttle chairlifts, therefore, will commence operation as scheduled, but be forewarned that at this altitude weather conditions can fluctuate precipitously. In the event of heavy fog or strong wind gusts, chairlift operation will cease. By purchasing a lift ticket, you assume responsibility for your safety on the mountain and accept liability for hazards incidental to a high-altitude ski facility.

Q: What is the main idea of the announcement?

(a) Skiers are often liable to suffer altitude sickness.
(b) Tourists must realize the lift could stop at any time.
(c) Conditions are rough but the weather is improving.
(d) Lifts are open but care must be taken for safety.

16. Proteins like gliadin and glutenin that are present in flour combine to form a complex called gluten, the substance that confers elasticity and chewiness in bread. During the mechanical action of kneading, gluten molecules align into sheets and spread throughout the dough, forming a network of scaffolding that holds the mass together. Not only that, carbon dioxide released by the chemical reactions of yeast becomes trapped within the porous gluten scaffold, forming pockets that raise the dough into its customary porous form.

Q: What is the main topic of the passage?

(a) Gluten's role in many of the attributes of bread
(b) Various glutens yielded from different types of flour
(c) Chemical reactions resulted from the gluten in bread
(d) The importance of yeast in making various breads

17. One of the most venerated figures in Cuban ballet, Alicia Alonso began establishing her reputation in the 1930s. However, problems with her vision obligated Alonso to suspend her career and undergo a series of surgeries, necessitating long-term bed rest. Unable to pursue the art she loved during this time, Alonso engaged in mental rehearsals, visualizing herself as the archetypal lead in *Giselle*, a dream role for a ballerina. Then, while recuperating in 1943, Alonso was invited to fill in for another ballerina and danced the role of Giselle, earning acclaim for her unparalleled interpretation of the role.

Q: Which of the following is correct about Alicia Alonso according to the passage?
(a) She appeared in a production of *Giselle* in the 1930s.
(b) She suffered from poor eyesight for most of her life.
(c) Her recuperation often involved dance rehearsals.
(d) Her 1943 return to the stage was well received.

18. Ringforts were stone or earthwork fortifications constructed throughout Ireland during the Iron Age. As many as 50,000 are believed to exist and others may have been destroyed over the centuries. Various explanations as to the purpose of these ancient outposts have been proposed, though none are definitive. Some appear to have been no more than enclosures for livestock, while other, larger ringforts may have fulfilled an economic role as an industrial or trading hub. Still other theories postulate a defensive purpose, as they could have been used as protective embankments during a raid.

Q: Which of the following is correct according to the passage?
(a) Ireland used to be home to 50,000 ringforts in the Bronze Age.
(b) Irish ringfort remains are only located in the north of Ireland.
(c) It is proven that ringforts were used to confine livestock.
(d) Experts are unsure what specific function ringforts served.

19. Mans' relationship with the practice of entomophagy, or eating insects and arachnids, is a complex one. Bugs were consumed as a source of sustenance in many ancient cultures, and in fact millions of people around the world continue to eat them. But especially within the societies of developed nations, entomophagy has come to represent a taboo, as bugs are primarily seen as "gross." That may soon change, however, with a number of experts calling for the adoption of entomophagy as an environmentally sound alternative to the practice of raising and processing animal livestock.

Q: Which of the following is correct according to the passage?
(a) Ancient cultures considered entomophagy taboo.
(b) Insect eating is increasingly lauded worldwide.
(c) A minority of societies currently eat insects.
(d) Entomophagy is being hailed as eco-friendly.

20. The second most valuable traded commodity in the world, behind oil, is coffee, with more than 50 countries involved in its production and sale. The commodity chain is extremely complex, with the majority of coffee originating on numerous small-scale farms of two hectares or less. The producers sell their unprocessed harvest to in-country brokers, who convey the intake to processing facilities and transact with exporters on the international market. Roasters in importer countries prepare coffee beans for consumption and then transport them to conglomerates like Kraft, Sara Lee, Proctor & Gamble, and Nestlé.

Q: Which of the following is correct about coffee according to the passage?
(a) Coffee's distribution and trade is broader that of oil.
(b) Large coffee farming companies operate in over 50 countries.
(c) A small number of growers sell to numerous processors.
(d) Middlemen move product between growers and big brands.

21. Egyptian-born Dorothy Hodgkin was a chemist who worked in the branch of chemistry dealing with the organization of atoms in solid materials. In her youth, she devoted herself to growing crystals, analyzing minerals, and conducting chemical analyses in a modest laboratory she set up in her attic. Interpreting the chemical structure of penicillin, using nothing more than images made by passing X-rays through crystals, was one of Hodgkin's greatest achievements. Later, using similar techniques, she elucidated the structure of vitamin B12 and insulin. For this work, she received the Nobel Prize for Chemistry in 1964.

Q: Which of the following is correct about Dorothy Hodgkin according to the passage?

(a) She became involved in the chemistry of liquids.
(b) She established a makeshift lab as a young girl.
(c) She showed how the body uses vitamin B12.
(d) She earned a Nobel Prize twice in her career.

22. The Four Causes are part of Aristotle's philosophy that attempts to explain the origin of things. Material cause is determined by an object's material. The existence of a statue, for example, is explained by the granite it comes from. Formal cause attributes an object's origin to the archetype on which it is based. In the case of a statue, that is the sculptor's internal vision. Moving cause is the manner by which an object came into being—by the endeavors of a sculptor. Final cause is the sake for which an object exists, such as a sculpture existing to be viewed by an audience.

Q: Which of the following is correct about Aristotle's Four Causes according to the passage?

(a) Formal cause and material cause are sometimes the same.
(b) Aristotle felt that material cause also had a spiritual aspect.
(c) An object's creator is the agent of its moving cause.
(d) The price of an object is what dictates its final cause.

23.

Dear Ms. Baez,

I can hardly express the delight I've derived listening to Kalia Mugeni's new album, *Fair Question*. Today's popular music, produced in an age when studio technology can digitize all the humanity out of vocalist, is depressingly homogenous. Rarely do you hear the honest rawness of an unprocessed human voice and the immediacy of the sound is tremendously uplifting. The direct sound of a talented vocalist has a powerful and irresistible effect that demands attention and respect. Congratulations to you, your team, and Kalia Mugeni on an unforgettable achievement.

Best regards,
Charlie Allen

Q: What can be inferred about Mr. Allen from the email?
(a) He is an ardent fan of modern musical styles.
(b) He feels there is no such thing as a perfect voice.
(c) He appreciates the innate quality of Mugeni's music.
(d) He is a music producer who has worked with Ms. Baez.

24. During his crusade to subjugate the territories of the Greek Empire, the Persian leader Xerxes commissioned an ambitious engineering project to span one of the straits at the boundary of Europe and Asia. This narrow body of water, now known as the Dardanelles, is little more than one kilometer wide at its narrowest. Xerxes envisioned shuttling his military forces across the gap on floating bridges and recruited a fleet of architects to design and build the pontoons. However, this first of two attempts was destroyed in a storm and all those involved were beheaded.

Q: What can be inferred from the passage?
(a) Xerxes was never able to conquer the Greek Empire.
(b) The Greek Empire fiercely defended the Dardanelles.
(c) Xerxes punished the architects for the bridge's destruction.
(d) The Persian troops eventually crossed the straits in boats.

25. Even today, the scope of women's experiences remains poorly represented in the New York art world. White men have dominated the art world in America, but to the extent their influence has ebbed, we have artists like Faith Ringgold to thank. In 1970, she helped organize a protest to challenge the Whitney Museum of American Art's discriminatory attitudes toward women. Today, as the president of a nonprofit organization to promote the canonical inclusion of artists of the African Diaspora, she continues to forge new opportunities for artists marginalized by their race or gender.

Q: What can be inferred about Faith Ringgold from the passage?

(a) She feels that white male artists are overrepresented.
(b) She has studied traditional techniques of African art.
(c) She gets her art displayed at major New York galleries.
(d) She has received unanimous support from male artists.

R

Part IV Questions 26—35

Read the passage, questions, and options. Then, based on the given information, choose the option that best answers each question.

Questions 26-27

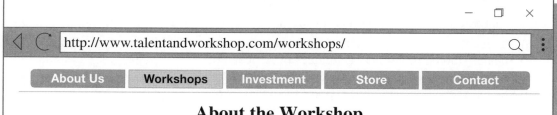

http://www.talentandworkshop.com/workshops/

| About Us | **Workshops** | Investment | Store | Contact |

About the Workshop

Have you ever thought you can turn buttons and tree leaves into pretty silver pieces? The truth is, you can! You can also transform other small objects into beautiful pieces of art. The secret is to learn how to use silver clay.

Sarah Campbell is a household name when it comes to making good use of silver clay, and we are delighted to invite her to host a workshop for creating silver clay pieces. She will teach you how to make beautiful silver clay jewelry, including rings and necklaces.

Did you know that silver clay pieces are green products? They are produced in an environmentally-friendly way. So, by learning how to create silver clay pieces, you can also learn how to strike a balance between creating quality products and helping to protect the environment.

Beginners' Class

· Price: $250.00 per person, including course materials
· Location: Silver Hall, Room 30, Ames Community Center
· Schedule: Every Monday and Wednesday 9:00 a.m. – 11:00 a.m.
      Every Tuesday and Thursday 1:00 p.m. – 3:00 p.m.
For more information, email cynthia.j@talentandworkshop.com.

26. Q: Which of the following is correct according to the webpage?

(a) Silver clay enthusiasts believe that Ms. Campbell is a washed-up artist.
(b) Producing silver clay pieces is not detrimental to the environment.
(c) Workshop participants must procure course materials from somewhere else.
(d) Ms. Campbell is a regular employee at Ames Community Center.

27. Q: How many hours per week do you attend the workshop if you register for beginners' class?

(a) 6 hours
(b) 8 hours
(c) 10 hours
(d) 12 hours

Questions 28-29

Not All Assassin Bugs Are Beneficial

Thanks to TV shows, most people know that assassin bugs are highly beneficial to humans. This is largely because these insects prey on flies, mosquitoes, and other harmful bugs. As a result, most gardeners welcome these predatory insects. Interestingly enough, they are called "assassin bugs" because they attack their prey surreptitiously just like assassins.

According to entomologists, there are approximately 7,000 species of assassin bugs in the world. Most of these species bring considerable benefits to humans, and yet some of them are very harmful. In particular, kissing bugs feed on the blood of vertebrates, and some medical scientists believe that these insects spread diseases among vertebrates.

Many people often confuse assassin bugs with wheel bugs because they look similar to each other. Both of them have relatively long heads, but, unlike wheel bugs, assassin bugs do not have crests. In addition, they show orange and black markings, whereas wheel bugs are gray in color. Finally, unlike wheel bugs, which prey on harmful insects, assassin bugs are not always beneficial to humans.

28. Q: Why does the article mention kissing bugs?
   (a) To explain that kissing bugs are benign to humans
   (b) To present a notable exception to the general fact about assassin bugs
   (c) To imply that kissing bugs share many similarities with wheel bugs
   (d) To suggest that the kissing bug is a representative species of the assassin bug

29. Q: Which of the following is correct according to the article?
   (a) The defense mechanisms of flies are more effective in warding off assassin bugs than those of mosquitoes.
   (b) Most species of assassin bugs are indigenous to North America.
   (c) Wheel bugs are widely known to prey on vertebrates.
   (d) Crests are one of the distinguishing features of wheel bugs.

R

POLITICS > NATIONAL *The Carolina Post*

The Dawn of the Conservative Era

The general election is around the corner, and more and more political pundits predict that the Conservative Party, led by Emily Smith, is poised to win the election. If their prediction is correct, the party will dramatically change the course of the nation. Some political commentators say that the Conservative Party's victory will mark the beginning of the conservative era.

Even a few months ago, no political pundits believed that the party would have any chance of winning the general election. As a result, when Ms. Smith became the leader of the Conservative Party in March, no commentators paid any attention. After all, she was a novice with no political experience, and the party was hopelessly incompetent.

Surprisingly, however, in a matter of months, the Conservative Party turned over a new leaf and attracted more and more voters. Most pundits agree that Ms. Smith's strong leadership and clear sense of direction made all these changes possible. According to them, once in power, the party will pursue conservative policies, such as balancing the federal budget and reinforcing defense capabilities, thus changing the course of nation.

30. Q: Which of the following is correct about Ms. Smith according to the article?

(a) When she became the leader of the Conservative Party, she had several years of political experience under her belt.
(b) She knows exactly what she wants to achieve in politics.
(c) She is the first female leader of the Conservative Party.
(d) She has recently changed her party affiliation to the Conservative Party.

31. Q: What can be inferred from the article?

(a) The Conservative Party will win the general election by a landslide.
(b) Most voters perceive Ms. Smith to be meek and mild.
(c) The current administration is running deficits in the federal budget.
(d) After the general election, the Conservative Party will expand the welfare state.

Many Different Explanations of Confirmation Bias

Almost everyone tends to process information in a way that reinforces his or her pre-existing opinions. As a result, people generally do not see things as they really are. There are many different ways to explain why this happens.

According to cognitive psychologists, confirmation bias occurs because people generally have a limited ability to deal with complicated tasks. In other words, people cannot effectively handle complex tasks, with the result that they try to simplify such tasks as much as possible. It may be possible that people can only carry out one task at a time.

Motivational psychologists present a different explanation of confirmation bias. According to them, people like pleasant ideas better than unpleasant ideas. As a result, they tend not to accept unpleasant ideas readily. When unpleasant ideas are presented to them, people have great difficulty understanding and processing such ideas.

Other psychologists, including evolutionary psychologists, have different ideas about why confirmation bias occurs. Each of these explanations may have an element of truth. Despite their differences, most psychologists agree that confirmation bias can lead to prejudice and poor decisions.

32. Q: What is the main topic of the passage?

(a) Various explanations of the reasons for prejudice and poor decisions
(b) Varied ideas on why a particular psychological phenomenon occurs
(c) How different physiologists approach confirmation bias in different ways
(d) Effective methods for remedying confirmation bias

33. Q: What can be inferred from the passage?

(a) Not many people are likely to face the reality as it is.
(b) Evolutionary psychology is a branch of cognitive psychology.
(c) Motivational psychology is concerned with motivating people to avoid having unpleasant experiences.
(d) The majority of psychologists agree that confirmation bias can result in genuine well-being.

◀ Peggy ☰

> Hi, Peggy. I do know that your relationship with your father is less than ideal. However, I must mention that it has been almost eleven years since you visited him in London. As far as I know, you haven't contacted him since then.
>
> Although I deeply respect your feelings, you might want to consider the fact that your father is in his late 90s. I don't imply anything, but at least a phone call to him can help you mend bridges with him.

me

> Hi, Julia. Your text messages always make me think about a lot of things in a different way, and this message is no exception. As a matter of fact, I've lately been thinking a lot about my relationship with my father. I think this may be a case of synchronicity.
>
> Anyway, I'm more than willing to listen to your advice. Perhaps, my father is not as insensitive as he used to be. I also hope that he is less stubborn than in the past. As you suggested, I'll call him soon. Thank you for being a thoughtful friend.

34. Q: Why did Julia send the message?

    (a) To consult with the recipient about how to maintain healthy relationships

    (b) To suggest a course of action before it is too late

    (c) To state that she is willing to become on good terms with the recipient

    (d) To invite the recipient to visit London in the near future

35. Q: What can be inferred from the chat messages?

    (a) Peggy usually feels affronted by Julia's text messages.

    (b) Peggy is likely to be responsive to Julia's suggestions.

    (c) Peggy does not believe in the concept of synchronicity.

    (d) Peggy has often persuaded Julia into changing her mind about many things.

You have reached the end of the Reading Comprehension section. Please remain seated until you are dismissed by the proctor. You are NOT allowed to turn to any other section of the test.

Listening
Comprehension

○ 정답 P 108

Part I   Questions 1—10

You will now hear ten individual spoken questions or statements, each followed by four spoken responses. Choose the most appropriate response for each item.

Part II   Questions 11—20

You will now hear ten short conversation fragments, each followed by four spoken responses. Choose the most appropriate response to complete each conversation.

Part III **Questions 21—30**

You will now hear ten complete conversations. For each conversation, you will be asked to answer a question. Before each conversation, you will hear a short description of the situation. After listening to the description and conversation once, you will hear a question and four options. Based on the given information, choose the option that best answers the question.

Part IV **Questions 31—36**

You will now hear six short talks. After each talk, you will be asked to answer a question. Each talk and its corresponding question will be read twice. Then you will hear four options which will be read only once. Based on the given information, choose the option that best answers the question.

Part V **Questions 37—40**

You will now hear two longer talks. After each talk, you will be asked to answer two questions. Each talk and its corresponding questions will be read twice. However, the four options for each question will be read only once. Based on the given information, choose the option that best answers each question.

L

Vocabulary & Grammar

DIRECTIONS

These two sections test your vocabulary and grammar knowledge. You will have 25 minutes to complete a total of 60 questions: 30 from the Vocabulary section and 30 from the Grammar section. Be sure to follow the directions given by the proctor.

Part I Questions 1—10

Choose the option that best completes each dialogue.

1. A: So, you were evicted without warning?
    B: Yeah, my landlord gave me no prior _____.
    (a) notice
    (b) report
    (c) news
    (d) form

2. A: You're not crazy about this abstract modern art, are you?
    B: It's true. I prefer art in a more _____ style.
    (a) conventional
    (b) abstruse
    (c) ambiguous
    (d) eclectic

3. A: Your parents must be proud of you for graduating.
    B: They are, but it's been difficult to _____ their high expectations.
    (a) take issue with
    (b) reach out to
    (c) get on with
    (d) live up to

4. A: You have no right to criticize my performance like that.
    B: OK, you don't have to get so _____ about it.
    (a) lavish
    (b) transient
    (c) infectious
    (d) defensive

5. A: You should confront Brett about his poor management style.
    B: I don't want to _____ the awkwardness between us.
    (a) subjugate
    (b) discipline
    (c) exacerbate
    (d) presume

6. A: Let's download the album from this file-sharing site.
    B: Sorry, I don't believe in _____ music.
    (a) curtailing
    (b) quashing
    (c) disarming
    (d) pirating

7. A: How about purchasing some better accounting software?
    B: That's _____ given the department's budget shortfall.
    (a) unfeasible
    (b) steadfast
    (c) impeccable
    (d) callous

8. A: I don't like working with Jeremy, nor he with me.
    B: Yes, I'm aware of your mutual _____.
    (a) enmity
    (b) secularism
    (c) aberration
    (d) mediocrity

9. A: Thanks for always talking with me about my problems.
    B: Hey, I enjoy being your _____.
    (a) apostle
    (b) confidant
    (c) consultant
    (d) malfeasance

10. A: Donna is always going on about how great yoga is.
    B: She acts as if it were a _____ for all ills.
    (a) panacea
    (b) zenith
    (c) candor
    (d) maxim

11. Unfortunately, the employees have lost faith in Mr. Walker's ability to _____ the company as CEO.

    (a) disparage
    (b) execute
    (c) oversee
    (d) elongate

12. When Alice Munro _____ the Nobel Prize in Literature in 2013, she became just the 13th woman to do so.

    (a) received
    (b) conceived
    (c) perceived
    (d) deceived

13. Mel delivered a _____ talk that obviously revealed his anxiety over speaking in public.

    (a) directed
    (b) polished
    (c) common
    (d) halting

14. The fact that water has been discovered on some asteroids _____ that life could exist outside of planets.

    (a) complies
    (b) signifies
    (c) maintains
    (d) derives

15. Most of the capital raised by the start-up firm was _____ on an extravagant office and loads of equipment.

    (a) pervaded
    (b) lamented
    (c) vindicated
    (d) squandered

16. It can be difficult to _____ the biodiversity of mammals especially compared to the dizzying variety in the insect world.

    (a) regard
    (b) appreciate
    (c) diagnose
    (d) predict

17. Professor Hopkins worries the physics text may be a bit too _____ for general readership.

    (a) esoteric
    (b) volatile
    (c) proprietary
    (d) incalculable

18. A recent study shows that the injuries suffered by soccer players when their team is ahead tend to be more _____.

    (a) grievous
    (b) oblique
    (c) irate
    (d) culpable

19. Author J. D. Salinger lived much of his life as a _____, refusing to meet with reporters or accept visitors.

    (a) shaman
    (b) vassal
    (c) tremor
    (d) recluse

20. San Antonio has undergone considerable _____ in recent decades, seeing once empty land transformed into suburbs.

    (a) drone
    (b) sprawl
    (c) plunge
    (d) beckoning

21. Sarah could not shake her _____ mood for a week after her favorite team lost the championship match.

    (a) affable
    (b) doleful
    (c) flagrant
    (d) sublime

22. Available in four different flavors, Sports Star Energy Drink is sure to _____ your thirst after a workout.

    (a) douse
    (b) wreck
    (c) moisten
    (d) quench

23. The investigator's accusation that the officer had been involved in wrongdoing was dismissed as _____.

    (a) conjecture
    (b) pedagogy
    (c) synchronous
    (d) cogitation

24. Under pressure from his accomplices, the suspect decided to _____ his confession implicating them in the robbery.

    (a) vex
    (b) recant
    (c) chide
    (d) parody

25. The health risks from receiving a vaccine via injection are _____ compared with the protection it offers.

    (a) lithe
    (b) flimsy
    (c) eminent
    (d) nominal

26. The Japanese whaling vessel was shadowed for three weeks by a boat operated by animal _____ seeking to save the whales.

    (a) bigots
    (b) partisans
    (c) advocates
    (d) exponents

27. The company's free speech policy does not cover verbal or written material that is needlessly _____ or otherwise offensive.

    (a) gaudy
    (b) vitriolic
    (c) complicit
    (d) prodigious

28. Mindy Thompson's vocals were so out of key that they created a jarring _____ with those of her backup singers.

    (a) dissonance
    (b) virtuoso
    (c) ellipsis
    (d) eddy

29. With Bolivia's currency _____ to that of the US, one dollar will always buy just under seven bolivianos.

    (a) quaffed
    (b) bandied
    (c) pegged
    (d) clogged

30. Some in his party lambasted the prime minister for _____ to the demands of the opposition.

    (a) dribbling
    (b) hobnobbing
    (c) pirouetting
    (d) kowtowing

You have finished the Vocabulary questions. Please continue on to the Grammar questions.

Part I   Questions 1—10

Choose the option that best completes each dialogue.

1. A: Hey, did you just join this gym?

    B: Actually, I _____ here for years.

    (a) come
    (b) had to come
    (c) will have come
    (d) have been coming

2. A: Have you ever seen such a colorful lizard?

    B: I saw _____ in the rainforest last year.

    (a) more colorful of a one
    (b) even more of a colorful
    (c) a colorful one even more
    (d) an even more colorful one

3. A: What do you think is wrong with my olive tree?

    B: Its growth is probably _____ as a result of the drought.

    (a) stunting
    (b) being stunted
    (c) been stunted
    (d) going to stunt

4. A: Thank goodness you got news of this secret sale.

    B: I _____ had it not been for my friend Sue.

    (a) haven't ever
    (b) would have never
    (c) never would have
    (d) wouldn't have ever

5. A: Why were you so late with your papers?

    B: I wasn't sure _____.

    (a) who reported to me to expect
    (b) I expected whom I reported
    (c) who expected me to report it
    (d) to whom I was expected to report

6. A: I'm still not sure why you're angry with me.

    B: Because you _____ have called me and said you'd be late.

    (a) may
    (b) would
    (c) must
    (d) should

7. A: I just tried to use the vending machine, but it's busted.

    B: I know. It's _____ early next week.

    (a) to be repaired
    (b) going to repair
    (c) been repaired
    (d) repairing

8. A: Why didn't you tell me you left my briefcase by the door?

    B: It wasn't _____.

    (a) put it where I thought
    (b) it where I thought I put
    (c) where I thought I put it
    (d) the thought I put it where

9. A: Thanks so much for visiting!

    B: And thank you for showing us _____ wonderful hospitality.

    (a) such
    (b) far
    (c) so
    (d) too

10. A: So that used car didn't turn out to be such a great deal.

    B: _____ will require thousands of dollars in repairs.

    (a) It was late that I too discovered
    (b) I too discovered that it lately
    (c) I discovered it that too late
    (d) Too late did I discover it

Choose the option that best completes each sentence.

11. _____ a message of reverie, the Blind Game's new song "Shout" has been a hit among listeners.

(a) Evoke
(b) It evokes
(c) To evoke
(d) Evoking

12. Employees from the firm Johnson & Davis _____ the company's annual retreat this coming weekend.

(a) have attended
(b) be attending
(c) will be attending
(d) will have attended

13. The authorities have mandated that residents _____ the area by Monday evening, before the hurricane hits.

(a) evacuate
(b) evacuated
(c) will evacuate
(d) have evacuated

14. Only _____ achieve a perfect attendance record during the semester will be eligible to forgo the final exam.

(a) those students
(b) students whom
(c) the students who
(d) of those students

15. This April 29 marks _____ the 65th birthday of racecar driver Dale Earnhardt, and his hometown of Kannapolis is celebrating.

(a) have to be
(b) what is it being
(c) would have been it
(d) what would have been

16. _____ in the 1880s greatly influenced the writings of Scottish author Robert Louis Stevenson.

(a) He sailed to the Pacific islands
(b) Which Pacific islands he sailed to
(c) Sailing to the Pacific islands which
(d) The Pacific islands to which he sailed

17. The tiny West African nation of Gambia withdrew from the Commonwealth of Nations in 2013 _____ for nearly 50 years.

(a) a member to hold after
(b) held membership after
(c) after holding membership
(d) holding after membership

18. At the time of his death, Mozart _____ a piece of music titled "Requiem Mass in D minor."

(a) composes
(b) was composing
(c) had to be composed
(d) will have been composed

19. Investigators maintain that the senator _____ the bribes his aides were accepting from lobbyists.

(a) must have known about
(b) would have been known
(c) knew to have about
(d) had about to know

20. The seismic event off the coast of Japan was _____ that tremors were felt as far away as Anchorage, Alaska.

(a) too powerful an earthquake
(b) an earthquake too powerful
(c) so powerful an earthquake
(d) so a powerful earthquake

21. The fact that Mr. Altern was fired from his job after 28 years of service _____.

(a) no end to his anger
(b) was an anger to him
(c) ended to him in anger
(d) angered him to no end

22. _____ such heights as it did following the three days of sustained rainfall last month.

(a) Had seldom reached the water level
(b) The water level reached seldom the
(c) Had the water level seldom reached
(d) Seldom had the water level reached

23. As soon as the person _____ signs for it, it is considered in his or her possession.

(a) the package was it delivered to that
(b) the agent delivers the package is who
(c) who the agent delivers to the package
(d) to whom the agent delivers the package

24. _____ of an outright victory in the primary, the candidate was forced to compete in a runoff election.

(a) To fall short
(b) He fell short
(c) Had fallen short
(d) Having fallen short

25. Beet sugar produced by the region's farmers never sold for the prices _____.

(a) they hoped to that command
(b) that to command they hoped it
(c) that they hoped it would command
(d) they hoped it would command that

G

Read each dialogue or passage carefully and identify the option that contains a grammatical error.

G

26. (a) A: I just adore this black trench coat I bought at the mall.
(b) B: I'm glad you got it. It's quite sophisticated look.
(c) A: Thanks, I agree. Too bad it has to be dry-cleaned, though.
(d) B: That's not as much of a hassle as you might think.

27. (a) A: Can you tell me how your company distributes bonus miles?
(b) B: Miles are earned by them flying more than 30 flights per year.
(c) A: Are those round-trip flights, or can they be one-way?
(d) B: Unfortunately only round-trip flights contribute towards miles.

28. (a) Due to their volcanic origins, Spain's Canary Islands riddle with old lava tubes, caves, and craters. (b) So the existence of Cueva de los Verdes, a massive, 6-kilometer-long lava tube on the island of Lanzarote, should come as no surprise. (c) Only, there is something unique about this particular lava tube, something that draws tourists from around the world. (d) Located in a cavernous space near the cave entrance is a functioning concert hall that can seat upwards of 500 people.

29. (a) The Marxist revolutionary Che Guevara helped overthrow a dictator in Cuba, led armed troops in the Congo, and fought in Bolivia. (b) But did you know that he was not from any of these places, but rather hailed from Argentina? (c) Guevara was born and grew up in the city of Rosario, enjoying a comfortable upbringing in an upper-middle-class family. (d) It was during this period that he developed a sympathy for the poor and leftist political leanings that would chart to come the course of his life.

30. (a) Everything about the Australian fungus known as Aseroe rubra, starting with its name, signifies our natural aversion to it. (b) The moniker of the red, star-shaped fungus comes from the Greek meaning "disgusting red juice." (c) In addition to its vibrant color, the name is a reference to the offensive odor given off by the fungus. (d) Having smelled strongly of carrion, its stench plays a vital role in attracting the flies that distribute its reproductive spores.

You have reached the end of the Vocabulary & Grammar sections. Do NOT move on to the Reading Comprehension section until instructed to do so. You are NOT allowed to turn to any other section of the test.

Reading
Comprehension

DIRECTIONS

This section tests your ability to comprehend reading passages. You will have 40 minutes to complete 35 questions. Be sure to follow the directions given by the proctor.

Part I **Questions 1—10**

Read the passage. Then choose the option that best completes the passage.

1. Tiraspol is the capital of Transnistria, a nation _____.
   It is a nation that seceded from Moldova by declaring independence in 1990, though
   the Republic of Moldova still does not officially recognize its autonomy. Rather, it is
   deemed a territory with special legal status, under Moldova's own jurisdiction. And yet,
   Transnistria has its own government, legislature, military, and currency. Nonetheless, as
   they live in an unrecognized nation, most citizens of Transnistria must hold Moldovan,
   Russian, or Ukrainian citizenship, or some combination of the three.

   (a) possessing a unique cultural heritage
   (b) with an unresolved regional sovereignty
   (c) whose citizens want to merge with Moldova
   (d) in danger of invasion from three different countries

2.
Science News

A team of researchers studying memory in mice managed to induce memories not
based on real events. After identifying cells associated with a specific memory stored
in a mouse's brain, scientists stimulated its retrieval by targeting it with light, a
technique that activates memory engram-bearing neurons in the brain. The scientists
then artificially stimulated the neurons while shocking the mouse's foot in a specific
contextual environment. Studying the mouse's subsequent behavior, they concluded
it was possible to implant a false memory of fear. As proof, they caused the mouse to

_____.

   (a) remember by deactivating engram neurons
   (b) lose its memory of the foot shock incident
   (c) exhibit a fearless response to harsh stimuli
   (d) anticipate foot shocks in a different context

3.

Dear Editors,

As an astronomer and a stickler for science factualness in popular media, I read your article "Comets Hit the Big Screen" (November *Skywatchers*) _____. This is because I believe it is the duty of publications like yours to challenge Hollywood's sensationalist depiction of near-Earth asteroids and comets. As your contributor pointed out, Hollywood's default strategy of blowing up any incoming asteroids is grievously misguided. The fragments would slam Earth's atmosphere with all the kinetic energy of the comet, causing potential explosions greater than all of our nuclear bombs put together!

Nicola Barletta

(a) in utter disbelief at the ignorance
(b) expecting a bit more on Hollywood
(c) still scratching my head about asteroids
(d) with personal satisfaction and gratitude

4. Spoken Prism is a symposium focused on the collaborative relationship between libraries, endangered language communities, and language revitalization advocates. Speakers of rare languages, librarians, and linguists will discuss their efforts to prevent fleeting cultural records from becoming lost artifacts. Since its founding, the State Library has built up an Indigenous Australian languages collection that makes linguistic materials accessible to the public. Selections from this collection will be on display during the symposium, sponsored by the Aboriginal Information and Resource Network. Through this and other events, the State Library _____.

(a) promotes learning of the world's major languages and cultures
(b) generates funds for this nationwide language-learning program
(c) aids librarians everywhere in the preservation of book collections
(d) continues to contribute to indigenous language revitalization

5. In his novel *Into the Wild*, Jon Krakauer traces the life and death of Christopher McCandless, a young man who renounced materialism and journeyed into the Alaskan wilderness alone to live off the land, eating what the environment provided. The author suggested that the cause of the protagonist's death was his consumption of *Hedysarum alpinum* seeds, which, Krakauer proposed, were toxic. Later biochemical analysis, however, invalidated this assumption, and the author was roundly criticized. Yet some now suspect that the author's original estimation may have been correct. The seeds in question _____.

   (a) are too small to contain a lethal dose of the poison
   (b) have been found growing throughout the state of Alaska
   (c) have recently been shown to contain a disabling neurotoxin
   (d) are biochemically similar to a species of seeds eaten by animals

6. The simplistic theological beliefs of some philosophers in classical civilizations fettered their _____. They proposed all manner of theories about the world that were fanciful and incorrect. Nonetheless, these ancient thinkers were at times led to correct conclusions by the direct observations they made, such as the presence of sea shells in inland mountains. From this, they interpreted rightly that the land had in the past been periodically covered and uncovered by the ocean. They also had a fairly solid conception of the hydrological cycle—evaporation, condensation, precipitation, and the draining of water from rivers into ocean basins.

   (a) accurate understanding of the Earth
   (b) research into an understanding of the water cycle
   (c) correctly ascertaining the nature of mountains
   (d) collaborations among scholars of different religions

7. Within the human brain, facial recognition is likely handled by a specialized cognitive domain, wherein mental processing occurs reflexively and in isolation from the rest of the brain. Functional neuroimaging studies of the healthy brain have localized a particular region only a few square millimeters in area that is strongly associated with face perception and processing. Scientists call this the fusiform face area. If there is damage to the facial recognition module, it is probably _____.

   (a) linked to the loss of control of one's facial muscles
   (b) going to cause malfunctioning of the person's reflexes also
   (c) localized and unrelated to cognitive impairment elsewhere
   (d) similar to patients who sustain other kinds of brain damage

8. Yes, there are flickers of genuine empathy and tenderness at the beginning of *The Little Anthem* that a small part of me finds satisfying. I thought the film might even be sympathetic to women's issues. But it takes a turn with insulting and stereotypical depictions of women, making it easy and entirely justifiable for me to completely dismiss *The Little Anthem* and its director. This project was filmmaker Roald Liu's opportunity to rebut audiences' criticism of his shortcomings in depicting female characters. But the director reminds me of the saying that a leopard cannot change its spots. *The Little Anthem* _____.

(a) exhibits none of the genius of Liu's earlier works
(b) shows very little remission of offense to women
(c) drags on too long in developing female characters
(d) falls short of the promises of all the advertising hype

9. Each anatomical feature of the human body corresponds to regions in the brain's primary motor cortex and primary somatosensory cortex. However, the proportion of the brain's resources allotted to each body part differs considerably from the body's actual proportions. The hands, for example, which are a relatively small feature of our physical form, take up a disproportionately large amount of brain space. This makes sense, as they are an indispensable means by which we interact with and manipulate objects in our environment. _____, they draw a lot of cortical processing power.

(a) Instead
(b) Otherwise
(c) Furthermore
(d) Consequently

10. Greek philosophers conjectured that four fundamental components—earth, air, fire, and water — inhabited the body as "humors." These were fluids they identified as black bile, blood, yellow bile, and phlegm, respectively. The second-century Roman physician Claudius Galen postulated that an imbalance of these humors might affect people's minds, and he devised a protocol for diagnosing psychological issues according to surfeits or deficits of specific humors. He was completely wrong. _____, others followed with atrociously flawed approaches to treating psychological problems, such as the letting of blood to ameliorate symptoms of egomania.

(a) As a matter of fact
(b) Despite this
(c) On the contrary
(d) Put another way

Read the passage and identify the option that does NOT belong.

R

11. Chemist Linus Pauling rose to prominence in the 1920s, early in his career. (a) His most groundbreaking work centered on the nature of chemical bonds, and for this research he received the 1954 Nobel Prize in Chemistry. (b) This prize had been awarded annually since 1901 to only the most prolific chemists. (c) During WWII, while other scientists of his caliber developed the first atomic bomb, Pauling became an activist for peace. (d) He advocated a ban on nuclear weapon testing, and in 1962 was the recipient of the Nobel Peace Prize.

12. In the 1980s, the Kenyan government undertook a study to determine the economic effects of commercial sugarcane production. (a) The results signaled that sugarcane producers have considerably higher incomes than other farmers. (b) The reason for this discrepancy stems from the government's pricing policy for sugarcane. (c) Its program effectively insulates local farmers from the fluctuating world price of sugar, protecting their incomes. (d) When sugar rates rise in the global marketplace, farmers' incomes follow suit, and vice versa.

Read the passage, question, and options. Then, based on the given information, choose the option that best answers each question.

R

13. The Bycreek Family Farm has been in operation for more than 70 years, a tradition kept alive by the accumulated knowledge of three generations of Bycreek farmers. Over the decades, we have cultivated strong ties with our local community, who have entrusted us with one of the most profoundly important roles a business can fulfill—that of nourishing their families. For that reason, we never use pesticides or hormones on our farm. We proudly deliver superior all-natural, pesticide-free produce to our customers. You can always trust that our products are grown according to safe and sustainable methods.

    Q: What is the main idea about Bycreek Family Farm in the advertisement?
    (a) It is a family-owned business with a long history.
    (b) Its products comply with government standards.
    (c) It promotes environmentalism through organic farming.
    (d) It is committed to safe and naturally grown produce.

14. A kitchen microwave oven uses oscillating electromagnetic waves, much like radio waves except that they move at a faster rate to cook food. Microwaves only affect certain types of molecules, those that have a positive side and a negative side, such as water. During operation, microwaves emitted by the device cause water molecules in your food to spin back and forth with the oscillations of the wave. This excites individual water molecules, which transfer their energy to other nearby molecules, resulting in quick heating of your food.

    Q: What is the passage mainly about?
    (a) The reason why molecules in food are heated uniformly
    (b) The physics underpinning the function of microwave ovens
    (c) How water reacts differently to electromagnetic than radio waves
    (d) A unique microwave oven that utilizes different waves of energy

15. The incidence of lightning striking planes is fairly common, occurring on average once annually per plane in the US commercial fleet. Evidence collected by researchers over the years has shown that, in fact, the presence of an airplane in a charged thunderhead can induce lightning strikes. For this reason, commercial jets are designed specifically to withstand the stress of an electrical strike, with all sensitive components shielded from the current. During a lightning strike, the electric current propagates from the point of initial contact through the plane's conductive outer shell and egresses through a terminal point such as the tail.

Q: What is the main topic of the passage?

(a) Reasons why airplanes avoid flying in storms
(b) The handling of lightning strikes by airplanes
(c) The dangers of lightning strikes on planes in flight
(d) The need for designing lightning-free aircraft

16. In Middle English, the word "discomfit" meant "defeat in battle," inherited from an Old French appropriation of the Latin prefix *dis-* (denoting negation) and root *conficere* (meaning "put together"). In modern usage, however, its meaning has converged with that of "discomfort," meaning "to make (someone) uneasy." Despite their similarity in spelling and pronunciation, the two words are etymologically different. *Discomfort* derives from the Old French verb *conforter*, meaning "to comfort." Yet there is a tendency in Standard American English to mate the two terms as a noun/verb pair, with *discomfort* as the noun and *discomfit* as the verb.

Q: What is the best title for the passage?

(a) The Loss of Word Meanings over Time
(b) Middle English Influences from Old French
(c) A Gradual Marriage of Two Discrete Words
(d) Why *Discomfort* and *Discomfit* Match Each Other

17. As many as 130 million domestic water buffalo are raised in agricultural settings throughout India and Southeast Asia. Broad hooves and foot joints allow them to maneuver in sodden wetlands and wallow in muddy pools without sinking too deeply into the silt. In addition to these adaptations, the animals possess extreme size and weight, standing up to 1.9 meters and weighing as much as 1,200 kilograms. Owing to such characteristics, water buffalo have long served as beasts of burden, helping farmers till rice fields in southern Asia for more than five millennia.

Q: Which of the following is correct about water buffalo according to the passage?

(a) Their numbers in Asia are in excess of 130 million.
(b) Their immense weight causes them to sink in mud.
(c) They were domesticated in Asia over 5,000 years ago.
(d) They sometimes reach a maximum height of 1.5 meters.

18. The Royal Navy mission called Operation Source was a clandestine maneuver involving six X-class midget submarines. Devised in 1943, its aim was to disable the German battleships *Tirpitz*, *Scharnhorst*, and *Lützow* stationed in northern Norway. Dispatching the Royal Navy's midget submarines to the battle site presented strategists a logistical challenge, since crewing the vessels for a long journey was not feasible. In such incommodious craft, two weeks' confinement was unendurable. Nor could the mini-subs be conveyed to northern Norway by surface vessels, as that would compromise the operation's secrecy. Instead, the X-class submersibles were towed up the Norwegian coast by six conventional submarines.

Q: Which of the following is correct according to the passage?

(a) Germany learned of the operation some time before 1943.
(b) Twelve submarines attacked and sank three German ships.
(c) Operation Source was conducted with Norway's knowledge.
(d) Large submarines were used to transport the smaller ones.

19. For the first time since the early twentieth century, a long-lost masterpiece by the Dutch artist Vincent Van Gogh has resurfaced. Sitting outside in a rocky field among small oaks, Van Gogh painted the landscape titled *Sunset at Montmajour* on July 4, 1888. The work was sold in 1901, after Van Gogh's death, by his brother. It changed hands again in 1908, when it was purchased by a Norwegian art collector. Assuming the work a forgery, the client deposited the painting in an attic, where it lay for more than a century, lost to the art world.

Q: Which of the following is correct about the painting according to the passage?

(a) It turned up in the estate of Van Gogh's brother.
(b) It was neglected under suspicion of being a fake.
(c) It depicted a sunset over a Norwegian landscape.
(d) It was painted by an artist after Van Gogh's death.

20. Painters have been practicing the technique known as glazing for as long as oil painting has been around. Essentially, it is the application of very thin translucent layers of color over a dry surface to alter the hue of the colors beneath it. As light passes through the overlying transparent layer and reflects off the surface below, it glows with an aura of the color of the glaze. Furthermore, by layering glazes of different colors, oil painters take advantage of an illusion wherein the pigments interact optically to fool the eye into perceiving a blended color that is not actually present.

Q: Which of the following is correct about glazing according to the passage?

(a) Its invention occurred long after that of oil painting.
(b) It was first employed to protect a painting's surface.
(c) Its color typically matches that of the painting.
(d) It manipulates light to produce novel colors.

21.

Revolutionize the Way You Work with Our Software!

Our latest cloud-based version of CaseBase software will change the way your law firm operates.

- With our in-context research system you can search the web's largest database of public records in real time.

- Automated time-tracking functionality makes billing simple, intuitive, and accurate.

- You can generate faultless invoices at the click of a button.

- Full-featured calendar software expedites collaboration and syncs with attorneys' mobile devices to ease deadline management.

- Collaborators can share case information, including contacts, documents, and correspondence, in a manner that minimizes data duplication.

- And CaseBase has the security of a financial institution, featuring 256-bit SSL encryption to protect sensitive client details.

Q: Which of the following is correct about CaseBase according to the advertisement?

(a) Its next version update will feature automated time-tracking.
(b) Comprehensive research resources are its primary offering.
(c) It facilitates collaboration between colleagues.
(d) Advanced security encryption is available at extra cost.

22. Compared to other taxa in the suborder Serpentes, the blind snakes that comprise the family *Typhlopidae* are relatively unevolved. Their tubular bodies and rounded terminal portions are reminiscent of worms, though they are unrelated. These snakes' heads almost indistinguishable from their blunt tails, one could be forgiven for speculating that *Typhlopidae* are two-headed animals. Their body plan is adapted for burrowing, plated with resilient scales that sheathe their interiors and reduce friction when they plow through loamy and sandy soils, which are their preferred habitat.

Q: Which of the following is correct according to the passage?

(a) The heads of blind snakes are slightly larger than their tails.
(b) Some *Typhlopidae* have tails with long tapered features.
(c) *Typhlopidae* snakes inhabit a subterranean environment.
(d) Blind snakes evolved from the newest branch of snakes.

23.

Education News

On Monday, the University of North Dakota drew one step closer to expanding its law school. The panel convened to commission an architecture firm to design the addition announced it has appointed Grand Forks-based Icon Architectural Group as the principal consultants on the $11.4 million project. Built in 1923, the law school has remained unmodified throughout the intervening years, excepting the construction of a library, and so it now scarcely accommodates the 250 students enrolled in the law program. As a result of this insufficiency, the Admissions Office has had to deny suitable candidates entrance into the program.

Q: What can be inferred from the report?

(a) The Icon Architectural Group built the law school's library.
(b) The addition will allow the acceptance of more law students.
(c) The academic reputation of the law school has steadily declined.
(d) The law school is one of the university's largest graduate programs.

24.

Neighbors:

I am writing in regards to my seven-month-old puppy. My hope is that a member of our community might possess information that will help me find my four-legged best friend. Yesterday, my beloved Staffordshire Bull Terrier, Oriole, went missing while she was outdoors unsupervised in my enclosed backyard. Though it grieves me to envision such a scenario, circumstances force me to confront the possibility of her abduction by a malicious passerby. If you witnessed a suspicious person in the vicinity of Gogh Avenue yesterday, please get in touch with me immediately.

Sincerely,
Mallory Chama

Q: What can be inferred about Ms. Chama from the notice?

(a) Her property is situated along a busy street.
(b) She doubts the dog could have escaped on its own.
(c) Her dog has previously gotten loose in the neighborhood.
(d) She seldom leaves her pets unsupervised for long periods of time.

25. *World Prospects* is an open-access journal serving the international community of economic scientists. Its activities are consonant with its charter to promote original academic research that redefines the understanding of the nature of global economic networks, as well as to publish exemplary scholarship. Whereas the majority of other journals within the field adhere to an antiquated publishing paradigm that impractically delays publication of pioneering research by many months, *World Prospects* has embraced a new, streamlined model of publishing. This enables us to make new work instantly and freely accessible after editorial review.

Q: What can be inferred about *World Prospects* from the passage?

(a) It is provided free of charge to professional economists.
(b) It sees itself as more progressive than other publishers.
(c) It awards large grants to young industry researchers.
(d) It fails to conduct thorough editorial oversight.

Part IV **Questions 26—35**

Read the passage, questions, and options. Then, based on the given information, choose the option that best answers each question.

R

Questions 26-27

http://www.simplyjobs.com/job-titles/collections-officers

| About Us | **Job Titles** | Locations | Overseas Jobs | Contact |

Part-Time Collections Officers for Capri Museum

Capri Museum is widely known as an "amazing place to learn about human history." As such, we have been devoted to collecting artifacts from different historic eras. We are currently seeking experienced collections officers who will help us accomplish our mission and keep history relevant to all community members.

■ Responsibilities
• To help our curatorial team collect artifacts from different historic periods
• To help our museum organize special exhibits for children
• To train and supervise museum interns
• To encourage community members to donate money or volunteer to the museum

■ Requirements
• A bachelor's degree in anthropology is required, but a master's degree in cultural anthropology is preferred.
• Candidates must have at least two years of experience working on curatorial projects.
• Candidates must be proficient in English and French.
• Candidates must have excellent interpersonal skills.
• Candidates must be willing to work on the weekends.

For further information, visit our website at www.caprimuseum.org or call us at 315-555-2500.

26. Q: What can be inferred from the webpage?

   (a) The museum focuses on collecting prehistoric artifacts.
   (b) The museum seems to believe that history can be pertinent to children.
   (c) The museum's internship program attracts large numbers of applicants.
   (d) Financial woes prevent the museum from hiring regular employees.

27. Q: Which of the following can be one of the requirements for the advertised position?

   (a) A master's degree in paleoecology
   (b) Bilingualism in English and French
   (c) Excellent performance under pressure
   (d) The ability to act on one's own initiative

BUSINESS >LOCAL *The Iowa Times*

Can Online Stores and Physical Stores Coexist?

All across the country, online stores are competing furiously with brick-and-mortar stores, and such competition can sometimes turn into enmity. Are there any ways to resolve such conflicts?

Sarah's Electronics, one of the oldest electronics stores in Iowa, suggests that there can be many different ways for online stores and physical stores to generate more profits by working together. Since last August, Sarah's Electronics has been collaborating with Harmonia, one of the largest electronic commerce companies in North America, and their partnership has helped them maximize their profits.

When a customer orders an electronics product on Harmonia, that order is processed by Sarah's Electronics, which ships the product to the customer. At the same time, Harmonia recommends similar products to that customer. If he or she places another order, the customer is entitled to receive a 15% discount. When a customer buys a product at Sarah's Electronics, the information about that purchase is shared with Harmonia. Again, the e-commerce company recommends similar products to the customer.

Both Harmonia and Sarah's Electronics are completely satisfied with their partnership, which suggests that online stores and brick-and-mortar stores can work together for greater good.

28. Q: What is the main topic of the article?

(a) The possibility of collaboration between two competing types of retailers
(b) Fierce competition between online stores and physical stores
(c) A long-standing feud between Harmonia and Sarah's Electronics
(d) A precarious partnership between an online store and a physical store

29. Q: What can be inferred from the article?

(a) Many online stores have their own physical stores.
(b) Sarah's Electronics used to cooperate with large numbers of online stores.
(c) Other physical stores might learn from the partnership between Harmonia and Sarah's Electronics.
(d) Competition between online stores and brick-and-mortar stores will become less and less intense.

R

Will Gene Therapy Be a Panacea?

As medical technology advances rapidly, more and more people are becoming interested in gene therapy. Some even believe that it will be a cure-all for every disease. Before examining that belief, we need to look at what gene therapy is.

Gene therapy is aimed at allowing abnormal genes to restore their functions by delivering "normal" genes to human cells. In many cases, abnormal genes contain faulty proteins, which can be fixed by gene therapy. If medical scientists insert genes directly into human cells, those genes do not usually work. Therefore, they often use modified viruses to deliver normal genes to human cells.

Two types of viruses are often used in gene therapy. Retroviruses add normal genes to the chromosomes of human cells, whereas adenoviruses insert normal genes into the nuclei of human cells. Whichever types of viruses are used, they can be directly injected into human tissues.

Gene therapy may become a panacea in a distant future. At present, however, medical scientists have too many obstacles to overcome. For instance, they have difficulty targeting "normal" genes to specific human cells. Until such obstacles are overcome, it is unlikely that gene therapy will effectively cure diseases.

30. Q: Which of the following is correct according to the passage?
   (a) Gene therapy is incapable of producing beneficial proteins.
   (b) Gene therapy is particularly effective in treating somatic symptom disorders.
   (c) Normal genes can be inserted into the chromosomes of human cells.
   (d) Adenoviruses cannot penetrate into the nuclei of human cells.

31. Q: What can be inferred from the passage?
   (a) The writer wants the reader to rest assured that gene therapy will cure every disease.
   (b) Proteins may affect the functioning of cells.
   (c) All retroviruses cause the abnormal growth of cells.
   (d) Adenoviruses are widely known to debilitate the immune system.

Distinguished for Humor?

For most Americans, including me, the Pulitzer Prize for Fiction means something serious, something profound, something inaccessible. Well, the winner of this year's prize for fiction may help shatter that perception.

Andrew Sean Greer's *Less* has received that prize, and this novel is remarkably funny. Strangely enough, Greer didn't originally want to write a funny novel. In fact, the theme of the novel is very serious. It deals with the transience of youth and the harsh realities of life.

Arthur Less, the novel's protagonist, travels around the world in an effort not to attend his ex-boyfriend's wedding. These trips teach him life lessons about the elusiveness of youth and the harsh realities facing ordinary people. What is remarkable about Less's travels is that they offer him a lot of chances to laugh at himself.

When Greer learned that he won this year's Pulitzer Prize for Fiction, he was stunned. That was largely because he knew that American literary critics tend to disregard comic novels. This year, those critics may have changed their minds, or they may have been impressed by Greer's sense of humor. Whatever the reason, the Pulitzer Prize for Fiction has finally recognized the distinction of having a great sense of humor.

---

32. Q: What is the main idea of the article?
  (a) The prestige of the Pulitzer Prize for Fiction is vastly overrated.
  (b) The Pulitzer Prize for Fiction will encourage a light-hearted approach to literature.
  (c) Greer's *Less* is the funniest novel recognized by American literary critics.
  (d) Greer's *Less* can change people's perception of a literary award.

33. Q: Which statement would the writer most likely agree with?
  (a) The Pulitzer Prize for Fiction remains something most Americans cannot relate to.
  (b) Being able to laugh at oneself is one of the qualities of a great novelist.
  (c) Greer's *Less* has succeeded in presenting a serious theme in a humorous manner.
  (d) Greer's *Less* will lead American literary critics to seriously compromise their standards.

From:	Alexandra Green <alexandra_g@jcconstruction.com>
To:	Jack Smith <j_smith@gaconstruction.com>
Date:	Fri, July 13 at 11:33 AM
Subject:	Project Procurement

Hi Jack,

As you may already know, the Government of South Australia introduced the State Procurement Act 2004, and they decided that "prescribed construction projects" worth more than $150,000 would not be regulated by the Act. Because the total value of our project is $180,000, we don't have to comply with the Act. However, we need to contact several government agencies to discuss technical matters.

When do you think you can visit me in Adelaide? Do you think Julia can accompany you? According to a government agency I contacted yesterday, both you and she need to visit the agency in person to settle several technical issues.

Please let me know when you will be available to come to Adelaide. I think you will have some time to go sightseeing after visiting the agency. I would be more than willing to be a tour guide for you.

I look forward to seeing you again soon. Take care and stay healthy.

Best wishes,
Alexandra Green

34. Q: What is the main purpose of the e-mail?
    (a) To inform the recipient that he needs to discuss technical matters with Julia
    (b) To ask the recipient to visit Adelaide and help procure a project
    (c) To invite the recipient to visit Adelaide for pleasure
    (d) To advise Jack and Julia to restore their strained relationships

35. Q: Which of the following is correct according to the e-mail?
    (a) Most construction companies must obey the State Procurement Act 2004.
    (b) Mr. Smith is highly likely to be familiar with technical matters.
    (c) Ms. Green and Mr. Smith work at the same construction company.
    (d) Ms. Green is a lifelong resident of Adelaide.

You have reached the end of the Reading Comprehension section. Please remain seated until you are dismissed by the proctor. You are NOT allowed to turn to any other section of the test.

Listening
Comprehension

DIRECTIONS

1. In the Listening Comprehension section, all content will be presented orally rather than in written form.

2. This section contains five parts. For each part, you will receive separate instructions. Listen to the instructions carefully, and choose the best answer from the options for each item.

MP3 바로 듣기
받아쓰기 테스트
모바일 단어장

Part I **Questions 1—10**

You will now hear ten individual spoken questions or statements, each followed by four spoken responses. Choose the most appropriate response for each item.

Part II **Questions 11—20**

You will now hear ten short conversation fragments, each followed by four spoken responses. Choose the most appropriate response to complete each conversation.

You will now hear ten complete conversations. For each conversation, you will be asked to answer a question. Before each conversation, you will hear a short description of the situation. After listening to the description and conversation once, you will hear a question and four options. Based on the given information, choose the option that best answers the question.

L

Part IV **Questions 31—36**

You will now hear six short talks. After each talk, you will be asked to answer a question. Each talk and its corresponding question will be read twice. Then you will hear four options which will be read only once. Based on the given information, choose the option that best answers the question.

Part V Questions 37—40

You will now hear two longer talks. After each talk, you will be asked to answer two questions. Each talk and its corresponding questions will be read twice. However, the four options for each question will be read only once. Based on the given information, choose the option that best answers each question.

Vocabulary & Grammar

DIRECTIONS

These two sections test your vocabulary and grammar knowledge. You will have 25 minutes to complete a total of 60 questions: 30 from the Vocabulary section and 30 from the Grammar section. Be sure to follow the directions given by the proctor.

Part I Questions 1—10

Choose the option that best completes each dialogue.

1. A: Were you able to convince Dan to go on a date with you?

   B: No, I'm afraid I _____ .

   (a) struck out
   (b) fell in
   (c) wound up
   (d) put down

2. A: I've never heard of the author of the book you're reading.

   B: Oh, he's just some _____ French writer from the 18th century.

   (a) rustic
   (b) stellar
   (c) obscure
   (d) potential

3. A: What do you think of the English cheese?

   B: It _____ the flavors of the wine well.

   (a) moistens
   (b) dilutes
   (c) irrigates
   (d) complements

4. A: What's your problem with Steven?

   B: I'm not sure, but he really _____ .

   (a) keeps my chin up
   (b) counts me among his friends
   (c) rubs me the wrong way
   (d) stops me in my tracks

5. A: One of my students continues to act up regardless of what I do.

   B: It may be time to pursue more serious _____ action.

   (a) flagrant
   (b) pejorative
   (c) disciplinary
   (d) subversive

6. A: I don't understand how hypnotherapy works.

   B: It's supposed to access memories you may have _____ .

   (a) repressed
   (b) undermined
   (c) blanketed
   (d) entombed

7. A: Has your boss agreed to increase your time off?

   B: No, he's refused to _____ at all.

   (a) compromise
   (b) assemble
   (c) segregate
   (d) rectify

8. A: I'm sure you were shocked at your poor test score.

   B: Shocked? I was absolutely _____ .

   (a) sidetracked
   (b) belittled
   (c) dumbfounded
   (d) heartfelt

9. A: Is obesity widespread in other countries as well?

   B: Actually, it's an even more _____ problem abroad.

   (a) extraneous
   (b) fluent
   (c) prevalent
   (d) ample

10. A: Tell me the reasons why you're unhappy with the product.

    B: I don't have time to _____ them all now.

    (a) proliferate
    (b) enumerate
    (c) condone
    (d) legitimize

Choose the option that best completes each sentence.

11. Those who _____ in the company earlier this year are reaping the rewards of its rising stock price.

    (a) positioned
    (b) invested
    (c) directed
    (d) thrived

12. Japanese cuisine connoisseurs on the _____ for a decent sushi restaurant in Middleton should visit the Umami Café.

    (a) seek
    (b) find
    (c) look
    (d) hunt

13. The United States underwent 13 years of Prohibition before the unsuccessful ban on alcohol was _____.

    (a) repealed
    (b) outdone
    (c) pursued
    (d) upended

14. Dogs _____ very specific behaviors when they are nervous or feel ill at ease in a situation.

    (a) conduct
    (b) organize
    (c) exhibit
    (d) regulate

15. The diner placed her napkin on top of her plate to signal the waiter that she was _____.

    (a) past
    (b) after
    (c) through
    (d) beyond

16. Chez Deni's _____ dish is braised lamb, for which it has earned international renown.

    (a) signature
    (b) identifiable
    (c) caricatured
    (d) indicative

17. Performing silent meditation for ten minutes a day can go a long way towards _____ stress.

    (a) fortifying
    (b) contradicting
    (c) embellishing
    (d) alleviating

18. The CEO _____ all options carefully before moving forward with the layoffs.

    (a) relayed
    (b) shifted
    (c) weighed
    (d) hefted

19. Although the _____ punishment for littering is a $500 fine, most violators are assessed less than $100.

    (a) redundant
    (b) sufficient
    (c) excessive
    (d) maximum

20. Myanmar has been exploited for decades by powerful neighbors who want a share of its natural _____.

    (a) articles
    (b) capabilities
    (c) resources
    (d) artifacts

21. Though the mayor was a lively speaker, his talks were rambling and often _____.

(a) stumped
(b) commendable
(c) languid
(d) incoherent

22. The narrow canyon was once famous for being the _____ of the train robber gang.

(a) blackout
(b) hideout
(c) lookout
(d) cutout

23. Professor Menken will not be teaching classes next semester while he is on _____.

(a) withdrawal
(b) virtuoso
(c) sabbatical
(d) purgatory

24. SymTech's tagging system is guaranteed to _____ seamlessly with whatever ad server you currently use.

(a) integrate
(b) attune
(c) embody
(d) mingle

25. Just before passage, the bill was _____ by the Senate to include greater relief funding for the unemployed.

(a) ascended
(b) amended
(c) attended
(d) appended

26. Many of Dickens' longer works were published in _____ form, meted out in weekly installments.

(a) lenient
(b) serial
(c) buoyant
(d) foregone

27. The Granny Smith apple hits the _____ with a tartness that is uncharacteristic of sweeter varieties.

(a) palate
(b) essence
(c) partition
(d) gulley

28. One must _____ the dough gently and by hand so as not to cause the final product to be too dense.

(a) buff
(b) knead
(c) ply
(d) scour

29. When astronomers first learned that our _____ contains over 300 billion stars, they reacted with incredulity.

(a) orbit
(b) nebula
(c) galaxy
(d) meteorite

30. In hindsight, the market crash of 2008 was _____ by the liquidity crisis of August 2007.

(a) presaged
(b) conveyed
(c) siphoned
(d) mediated

You have finished the Vocabulary questions. Please continue on to the Grammar questions.

Part I Questions 1—10

Choose the option that best completes each dialogue.

1. A: Why did you go with this light green paint color?
   B: My consultant told me it _____ with the orange well.
   (a) will have contrasted
   (b) would contrast
   (c) is to contrast
   (d) would have contrasted

2. A: We have about a half pound of pasta.
   B: I'm worried _____ enough for the recipe.
   (a) those aren't
   (b) they haven't
   (c) that isn't
   (d) it wasn't

3. A: How long have you been living in North Carolina?
   B: I _____ for eight years this coming August.
   (a) will have been here
   (b) will be here
   (c) was here
   (d) have been here

4. A: So, we're going to have to lay off some workers.
   B: Yes, _____ in order to balance the budget.
   (a) in conclusion it was necessary for us
   (b) it was necessary to conclude
   (c) we concluded it was necessary
   (d) we necessarily concluded it was

5. A: What was it like competing as a child athlete?
   B: The intense atmosphere during tournaments _____.
   (a) could be intimidating
   (b) is to intimidate
   (c) intimidated them
   (d) could be intimidated

6. A: You should really spend less time watching TV.
   B: That's just _____ last night.
   (a) that Lauren told
   (b) what Lauren told me
   (c) that Lauren was telling
   (d) what Lauren and I told

7. A: What are some of the requirements of the job?
   B: They want to find _____.
   (a) someone with social media familiar
   (b) a familiar one with social media
   (c) someone familiar with social media
   (d) a familiar social media one

8. A: Did you hear? Professor Merritt was awarded tenure!
   B: There's no doubt that he _____ without the support of his students.
   (a) did it
   (b) could have it
   (c) didn't do it
   (d) couldn't have done it

9. A: Are you still feeling upset with Camilla?
   B: _____ and she didn't even notice.
   (a) Such an effort I put for her forth
   (b) I put forth such an effort for her
   (c) An effort such as I put forth her
   (d) She put such effort for me forth

10. A: Brandon handles everything related to the neighborhood watch.
    B: If you could _____, that would be great.
    (a) touch to put me with him
    (b) touch me to put him with
    (c) put him to touch with me
    (d) put me in touch with him

Part II Questions 11—25

Choose the option that best completes each sentence.

11. _____, the Alamo Heights Dragons stand a good chance of winning.

 (a) They play whichever team
 (b) The team they play whichever
 (c) Whichever they play the team
 (d) Whichever team they play against

12. The wild animals, quite unsurprisingly, did not react calmly to _____ by the researchers.

 (a) being captured
 (b) capturing them
 (c) be captured
 (d) have captured

13. Mrs. Fletcher decided to sell _____ that she had inherited from her grandmother.

 (a) the all dining room furniture antiques
 (b) all the furniture of antique dining room
 (c) all the antique dining room furniture
 (d) the dining room all antique furniture

14. _____ you experience any delay during your travels, please notify the logistics officer immediately.

 (a) Could
 (b) Should
 (c) Might
 (d) Must

15. _____ at the airport than he realized he'd misread his ticket.

 (a) Had the passenger arrived no sooner
 (b) No sooner the passenger had arrived
 (c) The passenger had arrived no sooner
 (d) No sooner had the passenger arrived

16. The normally toxic chemical poses no harm to animal or plant life _____.

 (a) once it renders inert
 (b) it rendered inert
 (c) once rendered inert
 (d) rendering it inert

17. All lawmakers must make a pledge _____ the Constitution when they are sworn into office.

 (a) to uphold
 (b) having upheld
 (c) that upheld
 (d) in upholding

18. Retired NBA all-star Bill Russell played for the Boston Celtics and _____.

 (a) the team contributed his great success
 (b) greatly succeeded to contribute the team
 (c) contributed greatly to the team's success
 (d) successfully contributed a great team

19. _____ in the war, many soldiers found the return to civilian life largely unmanageable.

 (a) To have been traumatized
 (b) Having been traumatized
 (c) To be traumatized
 (d) Having traumatized

20. Carl had already agreed to cook dinner before _____ that it was a huge task.

 (a) it occurred to him
 (b) he occurred to it
 (c) it was occurred to him
 (d) he was to occur it

21. On Tuesday, the President seemed to distance himself from his earlier statement, which _____ by his opponents.

    (a) has to criticize since

    (b) was since to criticize

    (c) he has since criticized

    (d) had since been criticized

22. In a personal letter to the CEO, Mr. Whittaker expressed that he _____ alongside his ex-wife in the financial department.

    (a) rather than continue to work

    (b) would rather not continue working

    (c) hadn't rather continued working

    (d) was rather continuing to work

23. Who knows how public opinion of the Revolutionary War _____ had photography existed at the time.

    (a) had differed

    (b) would have been different

    (c) wouldn't have differed

    (d) was very different

24. At a press conference, a company spokesperson maintained _____ on account of gender or age.

    (a) that no employees were discriminated against

    (b) employees who were against discrimination

    (c) that employees weren't against discrimination

    (d) employees who wouldn't be discriminated against

25. Allegedly, Mr. Vaughn _____ as he was passing through the immigration checkpoint.

    (a) slipped the officer to a bill

    (b) billed and slipped the officer

    (c) slipped a bill to the officer

    (d) and the officer slipped a bill

Part III Questions 26–30

Read each dialogue or passage carefully and identify the option that contains a grammatical error.

26. (a) A: Hey, look what I picked up at the store: a new toaster!
    (b) B: Oh, you didn't need to do that. I was able to fix our old one.
    (c) A: You must have mentioned that to me before I bought a replacement.
    (d) B: Sorry, I wasn't aware that you were going to do that.

27. (a) A: I have you confirmed for the 5:30 flight to Bangalore.
    (b) B: Great, and can you tell me which seat am I in?
    (c) A: It looks like you've been assigned 15A, a window seat.
    (d) B: If possible, I'd like to change that to an aisle seat, please.

28. (a) Following his victory in the Second Civil War, Oliver Cromwell turned his attention to Ireland. (b) During his 1649-50 Irish Campaign, Cromwell led his forces against the Irish Catholics who have backed the defeated British king. (c) In what today would likely be considered acts of ethnic cleansing, Cromwell's troops massacred whole populations of civilians on multiple occasions. (d) Once the fighting was done, another 50,000 Irish were deported to England as indentured servants.

29. (a) The world's worst industrial disaster took place on December 2, 1984, in the city of Bhopal, India. (b) A gas leak at a Union Carbide pesticide plant exposed 500,000 people to toxic chemicals and led to the immediate death of at least 2,200. (c) The longer-term effects are harder to quantify, but government estimates suggest that more than half a million have been adversely affected. (d) Serious repercussions for the company and its employees have yet to feel.

30. (a) We often think of the Arctic as a relatively desolate region, supporting little life. (b) But some is the fact that 21,000 species of animals, plants, funguses, and microbes call the Arctic home. (c) And all of them are directly threatened by the environmental changes unfolding as a result of global warming. (d) Without urgent action on the part of humans, the biodiversity of an entire eco-zone may be all but annihilated.

You have reached the end of the Vocabulary & Grammar sections. Do NOT move on to the Reading Comprehension section until instructed to do so. You are NOT allowed to turn to any other section of the test.

Reading
Comprehension

DIRECTIONS

This section tests your ability to comprehend reading passages. You will have 40 minutes to complete 35 questions. Be sure to follow the directions given by the proctor.

Part I   Questions 1—10

Read the passage. Then choose the option that best completes the passage.

1. When tongue cancer cannot be mitigated by other methods, surgeons may perform a glossectomy, _____. This treatment may seem drastic, yet aggressive action is necessary because this form of cancer can swiftly proliferate to nearby lymph nodes. Depending on the size of the cancerous region to be extracted, a partial glossectomy may be feasible, in which case the surrounding tissue is sewn closed after the operation. In more severe cases, the tongue may be repaired with a graft excised from another part of the body.

   (a) using powerful anti-cancer drugs
   (b) the removal of the cancerous tumor
   (c) something that many patients may actually prefer
   (d) a procedure that removes part or all of the tongue

2. Lakeview's first annual Sounder's Festival will take place on Saturday, December 17th from 11:00 a.m. to midnight. In addition to serving up a healthy portion of local music, the purpose of the grant-sponsored event is to showcase underutilized performance spaces in South Lakeview. This is a district that remains stigmatized by a history of poverty, crime, and municipal neglect. By inviting festival-goers into South Lakeview's public spaces, engaging the public in community building, the organizers of Sounder's Festival _____.

   (a) are planning to feature only local musicians
   (b) anticipate a record showing for the event
   (c) hope to ameliorate the neighborhood's image
   (d) will raise funds for a new performance space

3. There is a strong positive correlation between _____.
   In 2015, mothers with a college education allocated an average of 4.5 more hours a week to the care of children than mothers with less education than a high school degree. Interestingly, this trend does not reflect a disparity in employment rates, since higher-educated mothers are more likely to be employed than mothers who never finished high school. The implication is that the observed difference in parental time allocation arises from differences in culturally constructed preferences rather than time availability outside of paid work hours.

   (a) income level and happiness of the family unit
   (b) parental education and time investment in children
   (c) success in high school and future employment
   (d) time spent in the home and parenting prowess

4.

Sports News

After just seven months, Watford City has opted to offload Irish fullback Antolin Overbeek, who was signed to bring some speed to Watford's backline. After receiving the news, Overbeek took to Twitter to criticize manager Chris Abdulla's decision to leave him off the squad, posting an inflammatory comment that he later abjured. Earlier this week, the notoriously fractious player stipulated that he would only commit his future to the club if assured a regular first-team spot. That and his disappointing performance in the first two games of the season

_____ .

(a) vindicated Watford City's decision to extend Overbeek's contract
(b) suggested that seven months was not enough time to judge the player
(c) combined to lead Abdulla to publicly censure Overbeek
(d) were cited as the reasons for his exclusion from the team

5. By February of 1864, the tide had already turned in the Union's favor in the U.S. Civil War. Yet it was during this month that the Northern forces fought what, in terms of percentages, became one of their bloodiest encounters. At the Battle of Olustee in northern Florida, 5,500 Union soldiers engaged 5,000 Confederates as the former pushed towards Tallahassee. Once the fighting was done, 203 Union troops lay dead, with 1,152 wounded and another 506 missing. Considering the casualty rate of 265 per 1,000 men,

_____ .

(a) the number of wounded was higher than usual
(b) reinforcements were quickly sent in to continue the fight
(c) both sides retreated from the battle with heavy losses
(d) Olustee went down as one of the worst Union defeats

6. Eastern Mountain Gear accepts returns on nearly all of its items, excepting products specifically debarred from our exchange policy due to liability concerns. Climbing gear, ski and snowboarding equipment, and bicycles _____.
Our return policy stipulates that items be unused and returned in their original packaging with tags attached. Returns must be received by Eastern Mountain Gear within a month of the purchase date, at which point the customer will be issued store credit equaling the amount of the purchase price. The cost of return shipping, however, will be deducted from this credit.

(a) constitute such unreturnable inventory
(b) are the specialty of our retail outlet
(c) always ship using an expedited service
(d) can be returned for a full cash refund

7. People generally conform to social norms, behaving in a way that is comprehensible and justifiable in the estimation of others. But at times, people act in ways that are unaccountably self-destructive, a type of behavior classified by those in psychiatry and psychology as "impulsivity." Impulse-driven people are more susceptible to addiction to substances like drugs, alcohol, and even food. Brain scientists have elucidated some of the neurochemical mechanisms underlying normal motivation and reward systems, pathways that in impulse-driven people appear to wield excessive control over behavior. Such research _____.

(a) may help doctors develop new interventions for destructive impulsivity
(b) implicates addiction as a common cause of impulse-driven behavior
(c) calls into question the notion that humans prefer to adhere to social norms
(d) could lead to the abandonment of traditional psychiatric practices

8.

Dear Editor,

Your article highlighting the historic diners around town certainly deserves a measure of approbation. However, the omission of my favorite joint, Bluebell's on 53rd and Howsen, is a mortifying blunder. As the oldest continuously operating diner in the city, patronized in its early days by local dignitaries like Harv Rodriguez and Dottie Brown, Bluebell's _____. With this letter, I hope to expiate your oversight and remind *Daily Press* readers of a legendary institution we should all cherish.

Sincerely,

Luke Alvarez

(a) is at long last closing its doors next month
(b) has been featured in many a publication
(c) merits top listing in an article such as this
(d) holds a special place in the editor's heart

9. The metamorphosis of a caterpillar transpires within a protective shell, called the chrysalis, revealed when the organism sloughs off its skin during its final molting stage. The dramatic change of form, from caterpillar to butterfly, that characterizes the pupal stage of its life cycle, occurs in the seclusion of this shell. Enzymes digest the caterpillar's former body, essentially reducing it to a slurry of rudimentary cells with the potential to develop new functionality. Some, _____, mature into wings, while others form the legs, antennae, and various organs. A butterfly will emerge from the chrysalis in 10 to 14 days, a miraculously transmuted organism.

(a) in any case
(b) however
(c) for example
(d) nevertheless

10. Water harvesting projects, including the collection of rainwater, are an important aspect of water-resource management in arid and semi-arid regions. Yet water-resource development must be carefully managed, because in affecting the hydrological balance of the natural habitat, water harvesting can have an outsized impact on ecology that relies on water. Disease-transmitting insects, in particular, are able to take advantage of collected water to proliferate. _____, this poses a public health hazard, as more of these disease vectors are present in the environment to spread devastating illnesses such as malaria and dengue fever.

(a) In fact
(b) Even so
(c) And yet
(d) In turn

Part II **Questions 11—12**

Read the passage and identify the option that does NOT belong.

11. Microbes have much to offer humankind. (a) One of their potential contributions is in the cleanup of industrial solvents at sites where toxic chemicals constitute considerable environmental and health hazards. (b) Former military installations also often exhibit the signs of improper disposal of potentially life-threatening materials. (c) After inoculating one such site with species of bacteria belonging to the *Dehalococcoides* genus, scientists obtained astonishing results. (d) Within a matter of months, the microbes had completely neutralized a refractory groundwater contaminant.

12. At Rain & Roots, our objective is to produce food in a conscientious way that has a low impact on our planet. (a) We have established a clear set of guidelines to assess the sustainability of our actions and steer our growth. (b) In this way, we have made considerable progress toward the lofty goals we set for ourselves. (c) While our critics may consider such goals unachievable, we beg to differ. (d) For example, last year we diverted more than 95% of our waste from landfills by using anaerobic digestion to manage our organic waste.

Part III **Questions 13—25**

Read the passage, question, and options. Then, based on the given information, choose the option that best answers each question.

R

13. What happens when a body is exposed to the vacuum of space? Science fiction movies portray an unrealistic drama, that of explosive decompression, wherein a person's body is turned inside out. However, human skin is actually durable enough to withstand the drop in pressure from normal atmospheric conditions to zero pressure. Of course, decompression is not the only hazard posed by space, for, in the absence of air, hypoxia, or the inadequate supply of oxygen to the brain, will quickly incapacitate a human being.

Q: What is the main idea of the passage?

(a) The human brain requires less oxygen in zero pressure.
(b) Instant decompression is more dangerous than hypoxia.
(c) Pop culture misrepresents the realities of outer space.
(d) Our skin is more durable than early researchers thought.

14. Black Cove Press is a printing workshop in Wichita, Kansas. It furnishes local artists, institutions, and publishers a state-of-the-art facility for the production of lithographs, woodcuts, and screen prints. Experienced printmakers have the option of renting time in the studio to run their own editions. Studio time can be booked hourly, daily, or weekly at a rate of ten dollars per hour. Those with limited printing experience are welcome to rent time in the studio but must arrange in advance to be assisted by a Black Cove Press member at all times.

Q: What is mainly being advertised?

(a) A publisher of art books
(b) A work of a local artist
(c) Art studio space for hire
(d) Top-of-the-line art tools

15. The mythology surrounding Lycaon is drenched in blood. That the figure's name appears to derive from the Greek word for wolf, *lykos*, hints at its gruesome theme, wolves having the disreputable distinction of being man-eaters in Greek mythology. According to the legend, Lycaon attempted to covertly serve Zeus a cannibalistic meal by incorporating human flesh into a dish served to the god at a feast. Enraged by Lycaon's effrontery, Zeus delivered a swift and vitriolic punishment, transforming Lycaon into a wolf and slaying the man's numerous offspring.

Q: What is the passage mainly about?

(a) The story of an ancient Greek legend
(b) Why wolves were seen as killers in ancient Greece
(c) A Greek myth involving a half-man, half-wolf
(d) How a certain Greek word evolved over time

16. The publishers wish to solicit the aid of readers in compiling a list of errors for the first printing of *Deux Mondes: The Language and Culture of France*. These errors will be rectified in the forthcoming second printing of the text. Below, please find a comprehensive list of corrections compiled to date. Should you notice any omissions from this compendium, please apprise our editors at ivy@unf.edu and martine@unf.edu. The publishers would like to express their gratitude to all of the readers who submit errata for the second printing.

Q: What is mainly being announced?

(a) An apology from a publisher for errors contained in its book
(b) A tentative release date for the second edition of a popular work
(c) An opportunity for the public to participate in the revising of a text
(d) A forum for readers to register complaints about erroneous claims

17. Climate change is having an effect on food security. In 2012, heat waves devastated crop production in North America's corn-producing regions. According to quantitative estimates, the thermal stress reduced harvests by more than 25% of the expected yield. Acute meteorological events such as these are projected to intensify under current models of climate change and could have a destabilizing effect on global food production systems. Even with a comparatively modest rise in mean temperature of about 1.7 degrees Celsius, the incidence of prolonged extreme high temperature events is forecast to triple.

Q: Which of the following is correct according to the passage?
(a) Worldwide food production depends on low summer temperatures.
(b) We can expect adverse weather conditions to affect agriculture.
(c) 2012 saw multiple record food shortages in North America.
(d) Higher temperatures will lead to 25% more heat waves.

18. Skylight is a cloud storage service that obviates the necessity of carrying a portable storage device to access important files across devices. Entry-level Skylight accounts offer five gigabytes of storage and seamless synching and integration among PCs, smartphones, and other Android, Linux, and iOS devices. This is the most popular option for the sharing of photos, music, and documents. Additional storage can be purchased at a rate of $5.00 a month for 100 gigabytes, or, for business applications, $16.00 a month for one terabyte.

Q: Which of the following is correct about Skylight according to the passage?
(a) A separate account is needed for each device.
(b) Businesses pay more per month per gigabyte than individuals.
(c) The files stored on its servers require a fee to access.
(d) Most of its clients use only five gigabytes of storage.

19. The dietary guidelines issued by the American Heart Association delineate the great significance of fruits, vegetables, and grains in attaining nutritional adequacy. It is recommended that consumers procure essential vitamins and minerals by integrating whole foods into their diet, as opposed to reliance upon dietary supplements like vitamin tablets. In addition, the guidelines urge against consumption of high-sugar foods like sweets, desserts, and soft drinks. These displace healthier calorie sources and are correlated with a decrease in essential nutrients.

Q: Which of the following is correct about the dietary guidelines according to the passage?

(a) They have recently been updated to address vitamin tablets.
(b) They discourage the consumption of artificial nutrient sources.
(c) They warn against the prevalence of high-calorie foods in society.
(d) They allow the inclusion of small amounts of high-sugar foods.

20.

Movie Review

Not even the eye-popping special effects could redeem *The Doctor*, a vapid retelling of a 1991 low-budget action film titled *Doctor, Doctor*. This reboot completely misses the mark. Absent are the subversive indictments of political corruption and the gleeful torpedoing of repressive gender roles that made *Doctor, Doctor* a cult favorite. Worst of all, the totalitarian cybernetic narcotics officer Captain Marilyn, veraciously played by Cassie Robicheaux in the original, has been recast as a mealy disciplinarian who lacks the magnetizing brutality of Robicheaux's impenitent anti-heroine.

Q: Which of the following is correct according to the review?

(a) The revision of one of the main roles is particularly unsuccessful.
(b) The two films are meant to be watched back to back.
(c) The themes in *Doctor, Doctor* are identical to *The Doctor*.
(d) The success of the earlier film paved the way for the later.

21. Wisława Szymborska was the recipient of the 1996 Nobel Prize in Literature. A Polish poet of international renown, she is regarded by literary critics as a luminary among the great poets of Poland. Early in her career, writing as World War II came to a close in Europe, she was rebuked for her impenetrable verse, deemed unreadable by the public. Though her first collection of poetry was finished in 1948, it would not be published for another four years, after Szymborska had rewritten the entirety.

Q: Which of the following is correct about Wisława Szymborska according to the passage?

(a) She writes about life in wartime Poland.
(b) She is not widely known among today's readers.
(c) She is held in high esteem by contemporary critics.
(d) She faced opposition to her work before World War II.

22.

Notice

Dear Resident,

Recovered Resources Coalition would like to remind you of the upcoming residential bulk collection scheduled for your neighborhood the week of March 15-22. During this biannual event, residents may discard cumbersome and weighty items normally barred from weekly curbside pickup.

- Admissible refuse includes appliances, auto parts, and furniture.

- Prohibited items include yard detritus, construction debris, and hazardous materials, which may be safely disposed of at our municipal hazardous household waste facility on Cunningham Road.

- Placing restricted items curbside for bulk pickup will preclude collection at the residence for the duration of the bulk collection period.

Thank you,
Recovered Resources Coalition

Q: Which of the following is correct according to the letter?

(a) Auto parts are something typically picked up weekly.
(b) Residents should place only permissible waste at the curb.
(c) The collection period runs for two weeks per neighborhood.
(d) All items must be transported to a special disposal facility.

23. In mid-February, the ancient Romans observed the festival of Lupercalia, a ritual intended to thwart evil spirits and restore vitality and fertility to the celebrants. Named in honor of the mythological figure Lupercus, a deity associated with shepherds, Lupercalia involved the ritual sacrifice of their wards: goats. Following these killings, the animals' hides were slashed into strips. Participants administered lashings with the skins, in the belief that flogging their friends and neighbors would improve their chances of conceiving children.

Q: What can be inferred about Lupercalia from the passage?

(a) It originated as a method of distributing meat within villages.
(b) It was thought to benefit those who wanted to start a family.
(c) It was held to curry favor with the god of livestock.
(d) It involved the sacrifice of different types of animals.

24. According to the Ohio Department of Natural Resources, the bobcat may be removed from the endangered species list. In a report to the Ohio Wildlife Council this month, the department cited a growing trend in bobcat sightings throughout the state as evidence of the population's resurgence. Wildlife specialists credit decades of habitat improvement efforts as the dynamic driving the endangered animal's rebound. Prior to World War II, the state was severely deforested. Now, while perhaps not replete with woodlands, the state's forest coverage hangs at about 31%, a marked improvement from the mid-20th century.

Q: What can be inferred about the bobcat from the passage?

(a) It faces continued threats from hunting.
(b) Its population peaked during WWII.
(c) It is an introduced species to Ohio.
(d) Its natural habitat is woodland.

25. After Representative Bower's drunk driving arrest, I refrained from contributing to the acrimony surrounding this unfortunate event. I did this in the misguided belief that justice would be served, and Bower would be removed from office. Hearing the court's verdict today, I can no longer hold my tongue. If the representative's actions truly pose no threat to the public interest, as addiction specialist Alana King asserted in her testimony on Thursday, then why was he endangering the lives of his constituents by driving while intoxicated? If such reckless conduct does not qualify as a threat to the public, then I don't know what would.

Q: What can be inferred from the passage?

(a) The court decided not to remove the representative from office.
(b) The public did not pay much attention to the proceedings.
(c) Representative Bower was found innocent of drunk driving charges.
(d) The writer has struggled with bouts of addiction in the past.

Part IV **Questions 26—35**

Read the passage, questions, and options. Then, based on the given information, choose the option that best answers each question.

Questions 26-27

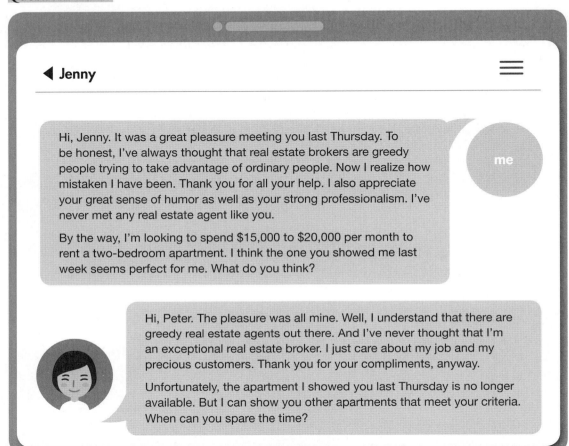

26. Q: Why did Peter send the message?

(a) To make an appointment to meet with Jenny to talk about an apartment
(b) To ask Jenny for her opinion about an apartment to rent
(c) To confess to having a grudge against real estate agents
(d) To thank Jenny for her compliment on his professionalism

27. Q: What can be inferred from the conversation?

(a) Peter's meeting with Jenny informed his perception of real estate brokers.
(b) Jenny is offended by Peter's condescending attitude toward real estate agents.
(c) Jenny is the funniest person Peter has ever met.
(d) Jenny does not take her job seriously enough to care about her customers.

214

Questions 28-29

   http://www.ukhistory.com/parliament

Love-Hate Relationships Between Kings and the Parliament of England

Prior to the English Civil War, the relationships between kings and the Parliament of England were complicated. On the surface, monarchs seemed to have absolute control over the parliament, in that they could dissolve it any time they wanted to. However, the Parliament of England had financial means to resist.

During those periods, the parliament was, in essence, an advisory committee which was set up according to a king's orders. Nevertheless, representing the interests of the aristocracy, the institution could thwart the monarch's attempts to collect taxes. When the parliament refused the king's requests to raise taxes, there was no way for him to force the institution to do so.

Consequently, monarchs needed the cooperation of the parliament, which was one of the reasons why they allowed the institution to make policy proposals. However, kings had the absolute discretion to accept such proposals. Such interdependent, yet potentially confrontational, relationships were one of the main forces that led to the outbreak of the English Civil War.

28. Q: What is the main topic of the article?

   (a) The complicated relationships between the aristocracy and the peasantry
   (b) Why tension existed between monarchs and the Parliament of England
   (c) Ideological factors contributing to the outbreak of the English Civil War
   (d) How a constitutional monarchy was established in the United Kingdom

29. Q: Which of the following is correct according to the article?

   (a) Many monarchs dissolved the Parliament of England on numerous occasions.
   (b) The Parliament of England tried to safeguard the interests of the gentry.
   (c) English kings sought to collect high taxes for the purpose of leading extravagant lifestyles.
   (d) The Parliament of England strove to radically reform British society.

R

Children's Mental Health Is Being Threatened

Surprisingly, mental health is a burning issue for large numbers of children in the nation. Hospital admissions of children with mental illness have been increasing dramatically for the past five years. Experts believe that the majority of cases of children with mental illness go unreported.

In many ways, school teachers are working on the frontline, dealing with large numbers of mentally ill students. Most of these students report cases of stress, depression, and eating disorders. Good teachers naturally want to help them cure such mental illnesses.

Both elementary and middle schools may offer mental health training programs for teachers, but such programs are generally too expensive to provide. Fortunately, however, there are a lot of things that conscientious teachers can do to help mentally ill students.

One of the most effective ways to help them is to create an environment where mental health issues can be discussed in a supportive manner. This simple step is also one of the more inexpensive ways to deal with mental health problems, compared with providing mental health training programs.

For information on other ways to help mentally ill children, refer to the attached article. You can also make suggestions by emailing us at suggestions@mentalhealth.org.

30. Q: What is the main purpose of the article?
   (a) To inform the reader that children's mental health is deteriorating at an alarming pace
   (b) To encourage teachers to report cases of children with mental illness to the authorities
   (c) To invite teachers to propose practical ways to help mentally ill children
   (d) To suggest effective ways to aid a particular group of children

31. Q: Why does the writer believe that creating a supportive environment is better than offering mental health training programs?
   (a) Because it involves fewer teachers than providing such programs.
   (b) Because most children are reluctant to discuss their mental health issues.
   (c) Because elementary and middle school students are not mature enough.
   (d) Because it is more cost-effective than providing such programs.

Is Coffee Break a Socially Irresponsible Company?

Coffee Break, based in Indianapolis, Indiana, is well-known among the locals as a socially responsible company which employs the disadvantaged. According to its website, the coffee house donates $360,000 for a worthy cause every year. That is why Coffee Break is one of the most respected businesses in the United States.

Last week, *INN News* reported that the coffee house had not paid any corporation tax since 2014. INN News reporters found out that Coffee Break had been involved in all kinds of tax avoidance "arrangements." According to several tax experts whom the reporters consulted with, some of those arrangements might be illegal.

Shocked by this devastating news about Coffee Break, several consumer groups in Indianapolis have threatened to boycott the coffee house as a protest at its attempts to avoid paying taxes. Industry experts agree that the corporate image of Coffee Break has been badly damaged regardless of whether or not those groups will actually carry out their threat.

Coffee Break has declined *The Indiana Times's* request for comment.

32. Q: Why is Coffee Break respected widely in the United States?
    (a) Because it conceived the concept of corporate social responsibility
    (b) Because it generates annual profits worth more than $360,000
    (c) Because it continues to pursue gender equality at work
    (d) Because it helps promote social values by offering financial support

33. Q: What can be inferred about Coffee Break from the article?
    (a) The actual amount of its donation has not been independently confirmed by *The Indiana Times*.
    (b) It has had strained relationships with INN News since 2014.
    (c) It consults with tax experts on a regular basis to make sure that it complies with tax laws.
    (d) It is highly likely to hold a press conference in the very near future.

R

The Geographic and Geomagnetic Poles of the Earth

Most people are familiar with the Earth's geographic poles: the North and South Poles. The North Pole is the Earth's most northern point, whereas the South Pole is the planet's southernmost point. However, not many people know that the Earth has geomagnetic poles as well.

In order to understand what the Earth's geomagnetic poles are, you need to understand that the Earth has a "dipole field." A dipole field is created when two different poles are separated in space. The Earth's geomagnetic poles are the poles of its dipole field. The axis of this field intersects the planet's surface at its geomagnetic poles.

Scientists had long believed that the Earth's geomagnetic poles remain the same. It was only in the 1920s when they observed that the planet's geomagnetic poles change. This is called a "geomagnetic reversal." In 1929, a Japanese geophysicist named Motonori Matuyama argued that a geomagnetic reversal occurred in the early Pleistocene.

Unfortunately, it took more than thirty years for the scientific community to take his ideas seriously and study geomagnetic reversals. Those studies will be covered in the next issue of *Geoscience Today*.

---

34. Q: Which of the following is correct according to the passage?

    (a) Most people mistakenly believe that the Earth's geomagnetic poles remain the same.

    (b) There is no relationship whatsoever between the geographic and geomagnetic poles of the Earth.

    (c) Separation between two different poles in space leads to the creation of a dipole field.

    (d) Geomagnetic reversals have occurred multiple times throughout history.

35. Q: What can be inferred about Matuyama from the passage?

    (a) He was the first geophysicist to discover the Earth's geomagnetic poles.

    (b) His ideas were seriously considered by the scientific community in the 1940s.

    (c) He collected basalt specimens in many parts of the world.

    (d) In 1929, his ideas were perceived to be unworthy of serious consideration.

You have reached the end of the Reading Comprehension section. Please remain seated until you are dismissed by the proctor. You are NOT allowed to turn to any other section of the test.

MEMO

MEMO

Actual Test
1~6

Listening Comprehension

Vocabulary

Grammar

Reading Comprehension

Actual Test 1

청해
Listening Comprehension

p. 27

1	(d)	2	(d)	3	(a)	4	(a)	5	(d)	6	(b)	7	(b)	8	(b)	9	(a)	10	(a)
11	(d)	12	(d)	13	(b)	14	(d)	15	(c)	16	(a)	17	(d)	18	(c)	19	(a)	20	(b)
21	(c)	22	(c)	23	(d)	24	(b)	25	(b)	26	(c)	27	(d)	28	(c)	29	(c)	30	(c)
31	(c)	32	(c)	33	(d)	34	(b)	35	(d)	36	(d)	37	(b)	38	(d)	39	(b)	40	(a)

어휘
Vocabulary

p. 33

1	(d)	2	(b)	3	(b)	4	(c)	5	(b)	6	(a)	7	(d)	8	(a)	9	(b)	10	(b)
11	(d)	12	(d)	13	(c)	14	(d)	15	(b)	16	(a)	17	(a)	18	(c)	19	(a)	20	(c)
21	(a)	22	(a)	23	(c)	24	(a)	25	(b)	26	(a)	27	(a)	28	(d)	29	(a)	30	(a)

문법
Grammar

p. 37

1	(c)	2	(b)	3	(a)	4	(a)	5	(d)	6	(b)	7	(b)	8	(c)	9	(a)	10	(b)
11	(d)	12	(b)	13	(d)	14	(d)	15	(d)	16	(b)	17	(d)	18	(b)	19	(d)	20	(a)
21	(b)	22	(b)	23	(b)	24	(a)	25	(c)	26	(d)	27	(b)	28	(d)	29	(d)	30	(c)

독해
Reading Comprehension

p. 41

1	(b)	2	(d)	3	(d)	4	(b)	5	(b)	6	(c)	7	(b)	8	(d)	9	(c)	10	(a)
11	(c)	12	(d)	13	(a)	14	(a)	15	(b)	16	(b)	17	(d)	18	(c)	19	(c)	20	(c)
21	(d)	22	(a)	23	(a)	24	(c)	25	(c)	26	(d)	27	(c)	28	(b)	29	(b)	30	(b)
31	(d)	32	(d)	33	(b)	34	(b)	35	(c)												

Part I

1

W It's been far too long since you took some time off.
M _____

(a) That's where I'm planning to go.
(b) I think they'll get there eventually.
(c) Wait a little longer because it's almost over.
(d) There's just been so much work coming in.

W 네가 휴가를 낸 지 너무 오래됐어.
M _____

(a) 거기가 내가 가려고 하는 곳이야.
(b) 그들이 결국은 거기에 도착할 것 같아.
(c) 거의 다 끝났으니까 조금만 더 기다려줘.
(d) 밀려 들어오는 일이 그렇게 많았어.

take time off 휴가를 내다   **eventually** 결국

2

M Who should I call about this leaky faucet?
W _____

(a) A friend of mine told me so.
(b) I was certain I'd turned it off.
(c) They just installed it last week.
(d) Check the directory for a plumber.

M 이렇게 수도꼭지가 새는 것에 관해서는 누구에게 전화해야 하나요?
W _____

(a) 제 친구가 그렇게 말했어요.
(b) 전 틀림없이 잠갔어요.
(c) 겨우 지난주에 설치했어요.
(d) 전화번호부에서 배관공을 찾아보세요.

leaky 새는   **faucet** 수도꼭지   **certain** 확신하는   **turn off** 잠그다, (전원을) 끄다   **install** 설치하다   **directory** 전화번호부   **plumber** 배관공

3

M Whatever became of Ms. Linn from marketing?
W _____

(a) That whole team was transferred to Dubai.
(b) As long as you ask her permission first.
(c) I don't really care much, either.
(d) It's the latest in online sales.

M 마케팅팀의 린 씨는 어떻게 된 거예요?
W _____

(a) 그 팀 전체가 두바이로 전근 갔어요.
(b) 먼저 그녀의 허락을 구하기만 하면요.
(c) 저도 실은 별로 상관없어요.
(d) 그건 가장 최근에 온라인 판매에 올라온 거예요.

transfer 옮기다, 전근시키다   **as long as** ～하기만 하면   **permission** 허락   **latest** 최신의

4

W How come I can never reach you on your cell phone?
M _____

(a) I forgot to say I changed my number.
(b) You should because I'll be there.
(c) Never mind. It's not a big deal.
(d) Here. Let me get it for you.

W 왜 네 휴대폰으로 전혀 연락되지 않는 거니?
M _____

(a) 깜박 잊고 번호를 바꿨다는 말을 안 했어.
(b) 내가 그곳에 갈 거니까 꼭 연락해.
(c) 신경 쓰지 마. 별거 아니야.
(d) 여기 있어. 내가 가져다줄게.

reach (연락이) 닿다   **never mind** 신경 쓰지 마   **It's not a big deal.** 별일 아니야.

5

M Do you know a reliable cure for a sore throat?
W _____

(a) I'm happy to hear you're on the mend.
(b) It's a bit pricey but it works wonders.
(c) The doctor will see you as soon as he can.
(d) Try drinking some hot tea and lying down.

M 목 아픈 데 확실한 치료법을 알고 있어?
W _____

(a) 회복 중이라니 기쁘다.
(b) 좀 비싸긴 하지만 효과는 엄청나.
(c) 의사가 가능한 한 빨리 널 진찰할 거야.
(d) 뜨거운 차를 마시고 누워 있도록 해 봐.

cure 치료(법)   **sore** 따끔거리는, 아픈   **on the mend** 회복 중인   **pricey** 비싼   **work wonders** 효과가 엄청나다   **lie down** 눕다

6

W I hope you've had a chance to go over the report I sent.
M _____

(a) I'll never assume that to be the case.

(b) To be honest, I haven't gotten to it yet.

(c) I'd rather not be on the receiving end.

(d) No, remember, I asked you for it before.

W 제가 보낸 보고서를 검토할 기회가 있으셨다면 좋겠군요.

M _____

(a) 저는 그럴 거라고는 전혀 짐작도 못할 거예요.

(b) 솔직히 말하자면, 아직 시작도 못했어요.

(c) 차라리 제가 받는 쪽이 아니었으면 좋겠군요.

(d) 아뇨, 기억해 보세요. 제가 전에 그것을 요청했잖아요.

go over 검토하다 **assume** 추정하다 **be the case** 사실이 그러하다 **get to** 시작하다, 착수하다 **be on the receiving end** 받는 쪽이다, 당하는 입장이다

7

W So, where is this Ronald I've been hearing so much about?

M _____

(a) I'll make sure to tell him.

(b) Stuck at the office again.

(c) Whenever he has the time.

(d) He also hasn't met any of us.

W 그래서, 그동안 그렇게 귀가 아프게 들어왔던 그 로널드는 어디 있어요?

M _____

(a) 틀림없이 그에게 말할게요.

(b) 또 사무실에 붙잡혀 있어요.

(c) 그가 시간이 날 때 언제라도요.

(d) 그 사람도 우리 중 누구를 만난 적은 없어요.

make sure 반드시 ~하다 **stuck** 갇힌, 꼼짝 못 하는

8

M I'm not sure why you're replacing a perfectly fine dishwasher.

W _____

(a) But I said you are a good dishwasher.

(b) New models are much more efficient.

(c) It sure is difficult to figure you out.

(d) Just leave it and I'll clean it.

M 네가 왜 완벽하게 성능이 뛰어난 식기 세척기를 교체하려고 하는지 모르겠어.

W _____

(a) 하지만 네가 설거지를 잘한다고 내가 말했잖아.

(b) 새로운 모델이 훨씬 효율적이야.

(c) 너를 이해하는 것이 분명 어렵네.

(d) 그냥 두면 내가 치울게.

replace 교체하다 **perfectly** 완벽하게 **dishwasher** 식기 세척기; 설거지 담당자 **efficient** 효율적인 **figure out** 이해하다, 알아내다

9

W You dance like you've been doing it your whole life!

M _____

(a) Well, I've been taking lessons.

(b) Sure, I'd love to accompany you.

(c) That's what I originally thought.

(d) I forget the name of this dance.

W 평생 춤을 춰온 사람처럼 춤을 추는구나!

M _____

(a) 그게, 강습을 받아왔거든.

(b) 물론, 너와 함께 한다면 정말 좋지.

(c) 나도 처음에 그렇게 생각했어.

(d) 이 춤의 이름을 잊어버렸어.

accompany 동반하다, 동행하다 **originally** 처음에

10

W I'm not sure I can handle a full course load this semester.

M _____

(a) There's always the part-time option.

(b) I meant to cancel our study session.

(c) Apply to as many colleges as possible.

(d) But I thought you got an A in that class.

W 이번 학기에 정규 강의를 감당할 수 있을지 모르겠어.

M _____

(a) 언제라도 시간제 수업을 선택할 수는 있어.

(b) 우리 스터디 모임을 취소할 생각이야.

(c) 가능한 한 많은 대학에 지원하도록 해.

(d) 하지만 네가 그 수업에서 A를 받았다고 생각했는데.

semester 학기 **part-time** 시간제의 **option** 선택권 **mean to** ~할 작정이다 **study session** 스터디 모임 **apply to** ~에 지원[신청]하다

Part II

11

W Hey, you work at Phillip Systems, right?

M That's right. Do I know you?

W We met at Paul Kendall's party last year.

M _____

(a) I hear they're hiring again.

(b) Oh, you must work there too.

(c) Sure, he's a good friend of ours.

(d) Of course! Now I recognize you.

W 저기요, 필립 시스템즈에서 일하시죠?
M 맞아요. 절 아세요?
W 작년에 폴 켄달의 파티에서 만났잖아요.
M _____

(a) 그들이 다시 채용할 거라고 하던데요.
(b) 아, 당신도 거기서 일하나 보군요.
(c) 물론이죠, 그는 우리의 좋은 친구예요.
(d) 그렇군요! 이제 알아보겠어요.

hire 채용하다   **recognize** 알아보다

12

W How's it looking for Saturday's picnic?
M The forecast is calling for thunderstorms.
W Oh, no. Should we risk it?
M _____

(a) There's no crime around there.
(b) Yes, I'm absolutely starving.
(c) Well, we brought umbrellas.
(d) I'd prefer to reschedule.

W 토요일 야유회는 어떻게 되고 있어요?
M 일기예보에서 뇌우를 예보하고 있어요.
W 아, 저런. 위험을 무릅쓰고 가야 할까요?
M _____

(a) 그 주변에는 범죄가 전혀 없어요.
(b) 네, 정말 배가 고파요.
(c) 저기, 우산 챙겨왔어요.
(d) 날짜를 변경하는 게 좋을 것 같아요.

forecast 일기예보   **thunderstorm** 뇌우   **risk** 위험을 무릅쓰고 하다
absolutely 절대로, 굉장히   **starve** 굶주리다   **reschedule** 일정을
변경하다

13

M Your passport please, ma'am.
W Here you go. And my customs form, too.
M Nothing to declare?
W _____

(a) I'll make a photocopy of it.
(b) No. I only bought a few trinkets.
(c) Please fill it out front and back.
(d) I'm waiting to renew my passport.

M 여권을 보여 주세요.
W 여기 있어요. 그리고 세관신고서도요.
M 신고하실 것이 있습니까?
W _____

(a) 제가 그걸 복사할게요.
(b) 아니요. 몇 가지 장신구밖에 사지 않았어요.
(c) 그걸 앞뒤로 전부 기입해 주세요.
(d) 여권을 갱신하기 위해 기다리고 있어요.

customs form 세관신고서   **declare** (세관에 과세 물품을) 신고하다
make a photocopy 복사하다   **trinket** 값싼 장신구   **fill out** (서식을)
채우다   **renew** 갱신하다

14

W Who sold you this auto insurance policy?
M I purchased it myself online.
W You have way too much coverage for your old car.
M _____

(a) I was advised to head for cover.
(b) Brenda's the one who sold it.
(c) Now it looks as good as new.
(d) I like to play it safe.

W 당신에게 이 자동차 보험을 판매한 사람이 누구예요?
M 온라인에서 제가 직접 구입했어요.
W 당신의 옛날 자동차에 비해 보장이 너무 과하네요.
M _____

(a) 안전한 곳으로 가라는 권유를 받았어요.
(b) 브렌다가 그것을 판매한 사람이에요.
(c) 이제 그건 새것처럼 보이네요.
(d) 저는 안전에 신경 쓰는 것을 선호하는 편이죠.

insurance policy 보험   **purchase** 구입하다   **coverage** (보험의)
보장 범위   **head for cover** (바·총알 등을 피해) 안전한 곳으로 가다
play it safe 안전을 기하다

15

M Here's a copy of the first-quarter report.
W Didn't I ask you for this last week?
M Yes, but we were having computer problems.
W _____

(a) OK, if you have to.
(b) Fine, but I need that report.
(c) Well, better late than never.
(d) Then, ask someone else to get it.

M 여기 1사분기 보고서 사본이에요.
W 제가 지난주에 이걸 요청하지 않았나요?
M 네, 하지만 컴퓨터에 문제가 있어서요.
W _____

(a) 좋아요, 꼭 그래야 한다면요.
(b) 좋아요, 하지만 저는 그 보고서가 필요해요.
(c) 그래요. 늦더라도 안 하는 것보다 나으니까요.
(d) 그렇다면, 다른 사람에게 그걸 가져오라고 부탁하세요.

copy 복사본   **quarter** 분기   **ask for** 요청하다

16

M Do you know how the novel ends?
W Yeah, I stayed up late last night to finish it.
M Well, don't spoil it for me.
W _____

(a) I'll just say there's a real twist at the end.
(b) It shouldn't come around again.
(c) In that case, here are the details.
(d) I'm just agreeing with the critics.

M 그 소설이 어떻게 끝나는지 알아?
W 응, 어젯밤 늦게까지 다 읽었어.
M 그럼, 나한테 말하지 마.
W _____

(a) 마지막에 진짜 반전이 있다는 것만 말할게.
(b) 그건 다시는 나오지 않을 거야.
(c) 그렇다면, 자세한 내용은 이래.
(d) 나도 평론가들의 의견에 동의해.

stay up late 늦게까지 자지 않고 깨어 있다 **spoil** 망치다, 발설하다
twist 반전 **come around** 나오다, 출시되다 **critic** 평론가

17

W Wait, where'd my car go?
M It looks like you parked it in a loading zone.
W Are you saying it was towed?
M _____

(a) I'll have them come tow it.
(b) You'd better watch out.
(c) Put it right over there.
(d) So it would appear.

W 잠깐만요, 제 차가 어디 갔죠?
M 적재 구역에 주차하신 것 같군요.
W 제 차가 견인되었단 말인가요?
M _____

(a) 제가 사람들을 불러서 그걸 견인시킬게요.
(b) 조심하시는 게 좋겠군요.
(c) 바로 저쪽에 놓아주세요.
(d) 그런 것 같군요.

loading zone 적재 구역(짐을 싣고 내리는 것만 허용되는 구역) **tow**
견인하다 **watch out** 조심하다

18

M Are you entering the cooking competition?
W I'm seriously considering it.
M Any idea which recipe you'll go with?
W _____

(a) I've been cooking since I was a kid.
(b) The ingredients are a family secret.
(c) Either the pork chili or my salmon.
(d) I'll aim for the 500-dollar prize.

M 요리 경연대회에 참가할 거예요?
W 심각하게 고려 중이에요.
M 어떤 조리법으로 할지 생각하는 게 있어요?
W _____

(a) 전 어릴 때부터 요리를 해왔어요.
(b) 재료는 집안 비밀이에요.
(c) 포크 칠리나 제 연어 조리법 중에 하나요.
(d) 500달러의 상금을 목표로 할 거예요.

enter ~에 참가하다 **competition** 시합, 대회 **seriously** 심각하게,
진지하게 **go with** 따르다, 받아들이다 **ingredient** (요리) 재료 **aim
for** ~을 목표로 하다

19

W Looks like the flight's been delayed again.
M And we've already been waiting for two hours!
W I wonder if it'd be better just to rebook.
M _____

(a) Not unless they cancel it.
(b) Another five hours is all.
(c) It's in my checked baggage.
(d) I was sure I booked for that time.

W 비행기가 또 지연되는 것 같군요.
M 그런데 우리는 이미 두 시간이나 기다리고 있잖아요!
W 그냥 다시 예약하는 게 낫지 않을까 싶어요.
M _____

(a) 비행이 취소되지 않는 한 안 돼요.
(b) 다섯 시간만 더 기다리면 돼요.
(c) 이미 수속을 마친 짐 속에 있어요.
(d) 그 시간에 예약한 게 확실했어요.

rebook 재예약하다 **check** (비행기를 탈 때 짐을) 부치다

20

M I heard Mr. Kim's diagnosis isn't good.
W Lung cancer or so rumor has it.
M That really is terribly sad.
W _____

(a) I'll remind him you said so.
(b) If anyone can beat it, he can.
(c) He just got over it last month.
(d) There's a rumor going around.

M 김 선생님의 검진 결과가 좋지 않다고 들었어.
W 폐암이라는 등의 소문이 있어.
M 정말 너무 안타깝다.
W _____

(a) 네가 그렇게 말했다고 그에게 알려 줄게.
(b) 그걸 이겨낼 수 있는 사람이 있다면, 바로 그 사람이야.
(c) 그는 지난달에서야 그것에서 회복했어.
(d) 소문이 돌고 있어.

diagnosis 진단 **lung cancer** 폐암 **rumor has it** ~라는 소문이
있다 **beat** 이기다 **get over** 극복하다, 회복하다 **go around**
돌아다니다

Part III

21

Listen to a conversation between a customer and an airline representative.

W Pacific Airways, how can I help you?
M Yes, I'm booked on the midnight flight from Los Angeles to Sydney.
W OK. Are you calling to confirm your reservation?
M Actually, I'm hoping to make a change.
W Certainly, sir. What would you like to do?
M I was wondering if there were any seats on the morning flight.

Q What is the man mainly doing?
(a) Seeking the status of a morning flight
(b) Purchasing a one-way ticket to Sydney
(c) Inquiring about getting on another flight
(d) Making sure his reservation is confirmed

고객과 항공사 직원의 대화를 들으시오.

W 퍼시픽 에어웨이즈입니다. 뭘 도와 드릴까요?
M 네, 로스앤젤레스에서 시드니까지 자정 비행기를 예약했습니다.
W 알겠습니다. 예약을 확인하시려고 전화하신 건가요?
M 실은 변경하고 싶어서요.
W 물론 가능합니다. 고객님. 어떻게 하시고 싶으십니까?
M 아침 비행기에 자리가 있는지 모르겠군요.

Q 남자가 주로 하고 있는 것은?
(a) 아침 비행기 상황을 알아보고 있다
(b) 시드니행 편도 표를 구입하고 있다
(c) 다른 비행기 탑승에 관해서 문의하고 있다.
(d) 예약이 제대로 되어 있는지 확인하고 있다

booked 예약된 **confirm** 확인하다 **status** 상태

22

Listen to a conversation between two friends.

W Jimmy, this furniture is absolutely marvelous!
M Oh, come on. You're just saying that.
W Not at all! Where did you learn to work with wood like that?
M I taught myself from books and online videos.
W Well, your woodwork is excellent. It's a beautiful cabinet.
M Thanks, Eve. I'm really glad you like it.

Q What is mainly being discussed?
(a) The woman's cabinet purchase
(b) The man's videos on woodworking
(c) The man's outstanding carpentry skills
(d) The woman's taste in wooden furniture

두 친구의 대화를 들으시오.

W 지미, 이 가구 정말로 멋져요!
M 아, 진정해요. 그냥 해보는 말이잖아요.
W 전혀 아니에요! 그렇게 나무로 작업하는 것은 어디서 배웠어요?
M 책이나 인터넷 동영상 보고 독학했어요.
W 당신의 목공예는 정말 탁월해요. 그건 아름다운 장식장이네요.
M 고마워요, 이브. 마음에 든다니 정말 기뻐요.

Q 주로 말하고 있는 것은?
(a) 여자의 장식장 구입
(b) 목공예에 관한 남자의 동영상
(c) 남자의 뛰어난 목공예술
(d) 목제 가구에 대한 여자의 취향

absolutely 절대적으로, 틀림없이 **marvelous** 놀라운, 훌륭한
You're just saying that. 그냥 해보는 말이죠. **teach oneself**
독학하다 **woodwork** 목공예 **cabinet** 보관장, 캐비닛 **purchase**
구매 **outstanding** 뛰어난, 탁월한 **carpentry** 목공예 **wooden**
나무로 된, 목재의 **taste** 취향

23

Listen to a conversation at a farmer's market.

M Excuse me, is your kale organically grown?
W All of our produce is certified organic.
M Really? Where do you grow it?
W My husband and I have a farm just west of town.
M And you truck it to this market each week?
W Yes, and we sell it to local grocery stores as well.

Q What is the conversation mainly about?
(a) The man's quest for organic certification
(b) The woman's method for growing organic kale
(c) The manner in which organic kale is sold
(d) The origins of the organic kale produce

농산물 직판장에서 이뤄지는 대화를 들으시오.

M 실례합니다. 당신의 케일은 유기농으로 재배한 겁니까?
W 우리 농산물은 모두 유기농 인증을 받은 것입니다.
M 정말요? 어디서 재배하세요?
W 남편과 저는 이 지역 서쪽에 농장을 갖고 있어요.
M 그러면 매주 이 시장으로 트럭에 싣고 오시나요?
W 네, 그리고 근처 식료품점에도 판매해요.

Q 대화의 주된 내용은?
(a) 유기농 인증을 받으려는 남자의 노력
(b) 유기농 케일을 재배하는 여자의 방법
(c) 유기농 케일이 판매되는 방식
(d) 유기농 케일 농산물의 공급원

organically grown 유기농으로 재배된 **produce** 농산물 **certified**
인증을 받은 **organic** 유기농의 **quest** 탐구, 노력 **certification**
인증 **manner** 방법

24

Listen to two classmates discuss their classes.

W Have you signed up for classes yet? I did.

M Sophomores can't register until Tuesday.

W Oh, right. Well, do you have your schedule planned out?

M Yes, but I have to take Organic Chemistry.

W Organic Chemistry isn't so bad. I took it last year and liked it.

M Really? I suppose I ought to look forward to it.

Q Which is correct according to the conversation?

(a) The man is worried he cannot register on Tuesday.

(b) The woman took the class the man will take.

(c) The woman has not signed up for any classes yet.

(d) The man is avoiding taking Organic Chemistry.

두 학급친구가 수업에 관해 말하는 것을 들으시오.

W 이제 수강 신청은 다 했니? 난 다 했는데.

M 2학년생은 화요일부터 할 수 있어.

W 아, 맞다. 시간표 계획은 자세히 세웠니?

M 응, 근데 유기 화학을 들어야 해.

W 유기 화학이 그렇게 골치 아프진 않아. 내가 작년에 들었는데 재미있었어.

M 정말? 그 수업 좋아하게 될 것 같은데.

Q 대화 내용과 일치하는 것은?

(a) 남자는 화요일에 수강 신청을 할 수 없어서 걱정하고 있다.

(b) 여자는 남자가 수강할 과목을 이미 들었다.

(c) 여자는 아직 이번 학기 수강 신청을 하지 않았다.

(d) 남자는 유기 화학 수강을 피하고 있다.

sign up for a class 수강 신청을 하다 **sophomore** 2학년생 **plan out** 세심히 계획을 세우다 **Organic Chemistry** 유기 화학

25

Listen to a conversation between two co-workers.

M You gave a great speech at the company meeting yesterday.

W Thanks. You have no idea how difficult that was.

M Seriously? You made it look pretty easy.

W The version I delivered was draft 13.

M Wow… I had no idea.

W Yeah, it'll be a while before I do something like that again.

Q Which draft did the woman deliver at the company meeting?

(a) The 3rd draft

(b) The 13th draft

(c) The 15th draft

(d) The 30th draft

두 직장동료의 대화를 들으시오.

M 어제 회사 회의에서 한 연설 정말 훌륭했어요.

W 고마워요. 얼마나 힘들었는지 모를 거예요.

M 정말요? 아주 쉬워 보였는데요.

W 제가 한 그 연설문이 13번째 원고였어요.

M 와… 전혀 몰랐어요.

W 네, 다시 그런 일을 하기까지는 시간이 꽤 걸릴 거예요.

Q 회사 회의에서 여자가 연설한 원고는?

(a) 3번째 원고

(b) 13번째 원고

(c) 15번째 원고

(d) 30번째 원고

give a speech 연설하다 **version** ~판, 버전 **deliver** (연설을) 하다 **draft** 원고, 초안

26

Listen to two friends discuss some music.

W This is some really cool electronic music.

M I like it. Who is it again?

W Vines. This is off their new album.

M Oh, right. They remind me of Litmus Project.

W You could say that. But Vines is more funk-inspired.

M That's true. You can hear it in the bass lines.

Q Which is correct according to the conversation?

(a) Litmus Project's music is more funk-based.

(b) The man recognized the music immediately.

(c) The couple is listening to the music of Vines.

(d) Vines is indistinguishable from Litmus Project.

두 친구가 음악에 관해 말하는 것을 들으시오.

W 이건 정말 멋진 전자 음악이네요.

M 좋네요. 누구라고요?

W 바인즈요. 그들의 새 앨범에 실린 거예요.

M 아, 맞아요. 그들은 리트머스 프로젝트를 떠오르게 해요.

W 그렇게 말할 만해요. 하지만 바인즈가 더 펑크적인 느낌이죠.

M 맞아요. 베이스라인에서 그걸 들을 수 있어요.

Q 대화에 따르면 다음 중 옳은 것은?

(a) 리트머스 프로젝트의 음악이 더 펑크에 기반하고 있다.

(b) 남자는 이 음악을 바로 알아차렸다.

(c) 두 사람은 바인즈의 음악을 듣고 있다.

(d) 바인즈는 리트머스 프로젝트와 구별하기 어렵다.

remind A of B A에게 B를 떠오르게 하다 **recognize** 알아차리다 **indistinguishable from** ~와 구별하기 어려운

27

Listen to a conversation between two friends.

M My finger is just throbbing with pain.
W You stubbed it during the basketball game, right?
M Yeah, catching a pass. Do you think it's broken?
W No, it's more than likely just sprained.
M I already took some painkillers, but they're not helping.
W I'd put an icepack on it and call the doctor.

Q Which is correct about the man?
(a) He stopped his finger from hurting.
(b) He broke his finger while playing sports.
(c) He has avoided taking pain medication.
(d) He is advised to seek medical attention.

두 친구의 대화를 들으시오.

M 손가락이 통증 때문에 욱신거려.
W 농구 시합 중에 부딪혔지?
M 응, 패스한 볼을 잡으려다가. 부러진 것 같아?
W 아니, 그보다는 그냥 삔 것 같아.
M 진통제는 이미 먹었는데, 효과가 없어.
W 얼음팩을 갖다 대고 의사를 부르는 게 좋겠다.

Q 남자에 대해서 옳은 것은?
(a) 손가락 아픈 것이 멈추었다.
(b) 운동을 하다가 손가락이 부러졌다.
(c) 진통제 복용을 피했다.
(d) 치료를 받으라는 충고를 받고 있다.

throb 욱신거리다   stub 찧다   sprained (손목, 발목이) 삔
painkiller 진통제   medication 약

28

Listen to a conversation between a couple.

W Those look like thunderclouds rolling in.
M Hmm… the weather report didn't say rain.
W Forget the report. It's about to start pouring.
M It sure looks it. And here we are in the park.
W Let's start walking back to the car.
M Yes, better safe than sorry.

Q Why will the speakers leave the park now?
(a) They are getting wet in the rain.
(b) They heard a forecast predict rain.
(c) They feel the weather is worsening.
(d) They want to check a weather forecast.

커플의 대화를 들으시오.

W 저기 뇌운이 몰려오는 것 같아.
M 일기예보에서는 비에 대한 말은 없었는데.
W 일기예보 같은 건 잊어버려. 금방이라도 쏟아지기 시작할 것 같아.
M 정말 그래 보인다. 그런데 우리는 여기 공원에 있고 말이야.
W 이제 차로 돌아가자.
M 그래. 나중에 후회하는 것보다 미리 조심하는 게 나으니까.

Q 화자들이 지금 공원을 떠나려는 이유는?
(a) 비에 젖어서
(b) 일기예보에서 비를 예보하는 것을 들어서
(c) 날씨가 나빠지고 있는 걸 느껴서
(d) 일기예보를 확인하고 싶어서

thundercloud 뇌운   roll in 밀려오다   be about to 막 ~하려는
참이다   pour 쏟다, 붓다   better safe than sorry 나중에 후회하는
것보다 미리 조심하는 게 낫다   predict 예측하다   worsen 악화되다

29

Listen to a conversation about a weekend plan.

W We're going hiking this Saturday, right?
M Oh, Sarah, I'm afraid I have to work this weekend.
W What? Are they going to pay you overtime?
M No, but it's expected that everyone work overtime.
W That's ridiculous, Fred. Why put up with that?
M If I want to keep my job, I have no choice.

Q What can be inferred about the man from the conversation?
(a) He is earning quite a high wage.
(b) He will start looking for a new job.
(c) He is going to be working Saturday.
(d) He will accompany the woman hiking.

주말 계획에 관한 대화를 들으시오.

W 우리 이번 토요일에 하이킹하러 갈 거지?
M 아, 사라. 난 이번 주말에 일해야 할 것 같아.
W 뭐라고? 회사에서 초과 근무 수당은 준대?
M 아니, 하지만 모두가 초과 근무를 하기로 되어 있어.
W 그건 말도 안 돼, 프레드. 왜 그런 걸 참고 있어?
M 일자리를 지키고 싶으면, 다른 도리가 없어.

Q 대화로부터 남자에 대해서 유추할 수 있는 것은?
(a) 꽤 높은 급여를 받고 있다.
(b) 새로운 일자리를 찾아보기 시작할 것이다.
(c) 토요일에 근무할 것이다.
(d) 여자와 함께 하이킹할 것이다.

overtime 초과 근무   ridiculous 말도 안 되는, 터무니없는   put up
with ~을 참다, 견디다   earn (돈을) 벌다   accompany 동행하다

30

Listen to a conversation between a couple.

M This place is rather spacious.

W Yes. What do you think?

M To be honest, it might be a lot bigger than we need.

W Oh, but we could do with extra space.

M Then we'll consider this a possibility.

W OK, let's go and see a few more rentals.

Q What can be inferred about the man and woman from the conversation?

(a) They have only ever lived in a large home.

(b) They are going to refurbish their apartment.

(c) They are looking for a new place to live in.

(d) They have just sold their apartment.

커플의 대화를 들으시오.

M 이 장소는 좀 널찍하다.

W 그래. 네 생각은 어때?

M 솔직히 말하면 우리가 필요한 것보다 너무 클 수도 있어.

W 아, 하지만 여유 공간이 필요할 수도 있잖아.

M 그렇다면 이곳도 가능성을 염두에 두자.

W 좋아, 세 들 곳을 몇 군데 더 보러 가자.

Q 대화로부터 남자와 여자에 대해서 유추할 수 있는 것은?

(a) 이제까지 쭉 큰 집에서만 살았다.

(b) 아파트를 새로 단장할 예정이다.

(c) 살 곳을 새로 알아보는 중이다.

(d) 그들 소유의 아파트를 막 팔았다.

spacious 널찍한 **to be honest** 솔직히 말하면 **possibility** 가능성 **rental** 임대(물) **refurbish** 새로 꾸미다

Part IV

31

Mice have a highly effective sense of smell that enables them to steer clear of predators. Specifically, their olfactory system is tuned in to the smell of urine of certain carnivores, like cats. Despite their acute sensitivity, this particular sense of smell is controlled by just one gene in a mouse's brain. Remove or "turn off" this gene and the mouse loses its ability to detect and avoid feline predators.

Q What is the main topic of the talk?

(a) Ways carnivores have evolved to hunt mice

(b) A gene that mice and cats have in common

(c) An inherent ability in mice to smell danger

(d) How complex a mouse's sense of smell is

쥐는 대단히 효과적인 후각을 가지고 있는데, 이 덕분에 포식자를 피할 수 있다. 특히, 그들의 후각 체계는 고양이처럼 특정 육식동물의 소변 냄새를 잘 알고 있다. 매우 발달한 예민한 감각에도 불구하고, 이처럼 특별한 후각은 쥐의 뇌에 있는 단 한 개의 유전자에 의해서 통제된다. 이 유전자를 제거하거나 '끄면' 쥐는 고양이과 포식자를 감지하고 피하는 능력을 잃어버린다.

Q 담화의 주제는?

(a) 육식동물이 쥐를 사냥하도록 진화한 방식

(b) 쥐와 고양이가 공통으로 지니고 있는 유전자

(c) 위험한 냄새를 맡는 쥐의 타고난 능력

(d) 쥐의 후각의 복잡한 정도

highly 매우, 대단히 **effective** 효과적인 **steer clear of** ~을 피하다, 가까이하지 않다 **predator** 포식자 **specifically** 특히 **olfactory** 후각의 **be tuned in to** ~을 잘 알고 있다, ~에 맞추어져 있다 **urine** 소변 **carnivore** 육식동물 **acute** 예민한 **sensitivity** 예민성 **particular** 특정한 **gene** 유전자 **detect** 탐지하다 **feline** 고양이과(의) **have … in common** 공통점이 있다 **inherent** 내재하는, 타고난 **complex** 복잡한

32

When Queen Beatrix of the Netherlands abdicated in April of 2013, she ended a 33-year reign. Despite this relatively lengthy tenure as the head of the Dutch monarchy, the queen's verbal legacy is limited. This is due in large part to an injunction issued shortly after her inauguration that prohibited the press from quoting her directly. She addressed the nation from Parliament every fall and delivered speeches on special occasions, but there are very few official records of her unscripted conversations.

Q What is mainly being discussed in the talk?

(a) Reasons for Queen Beatrix's abdication

(b) Accomplishments during Queen Beatrix's reign

(c) Restrictions in media reporting on the Queen

(d) Queen Beatrix's disagreements with the press

네덜란드의 베아트릭스 여왕은 2013년 4월에 퇴위할 때, 33년간의 통치를 끝냈다. 네덜란드 군주제의 수장으로서 이처럼 비교적 긴 재임 기간에도 불구하고, 여왕이 말로 남긴 유산은 한정되어 있다. 이는 주로 그녀의 즉위 직후에 공표된 명령 때문인데, 언론이 그녀의 말을 직접 인용하는 것을 금지한 것이었다. 그녀는 매년 가을에 의회에서 국민에게 연설을 했으며 특별한 행사 때도 연설을 했다. 하지만 원고 없이 진행된 대화의 공식적인 기록은 거의 없다.

Q 담화에서 주로 다루어지고 있는 것은?

(a) 베아트릭스 여왕이 퇴위한 이유

(b) 베아트릭스 여왕의 통치 동안 업적

(c) 베아트릭스 여왕에 대한 언론 보도의 제한

(d) 베아트릭스 여왕과 네덜란드 언론과의 의견 충돌

abdicate 퇴위하다 **reign** 통치 **tenure** 재임 기간 **monarchy** 군주제 **verbal** 말로 된, 구두의 **injunction** 명령 **issue** 발표하다, 공표하다 **shortly** 곧, 즉시 **inauguration** 즉위 **the press** 언론 **quote** 인용하다 **address** 연설하다 **parliament** 의회 **unscripted** 대본이 없는, 즉흥의 **accomplishment** 업적, 성취 **disagreement** 의견 충돌

33

Nature Photography Magazine is proud to announce its 25th annual Travel Photography Competition. For 25 years now, we've been attracting entries from some of the best photographers in the business. And this year, to celebrate the milestone, we're giving away some very special prizes. Two runners-up will receive a week-long, all-expense-paid trip to a European destination of their choice. And the photographer who takes the grand prize will go on a fully-paid *Nature Photography Magazine* expedition to Siberia and publish a photo essay in our fall issue!

Q What is being offered as the competition's top prize?

(a) A package tour of European cities

(b) Top-of-the-line photography equipment

(c) A two-year subscription to the magazine

(d) A trip and a professional assignment

〈네이처 포토그래피 매거진〉에서는 자부심을 가지고 제25회 연례 여행 사진전을 알려 드립니다. 지금까지 25년 동안, 저희는 업계 최고의 사진작가들로부터 출품작을 받아왔습니다. 그리고 올해, 이정표가 되는 해를 기념하기 위해 매우 특별한 상들을 수여하고자 합니다. 우수상 두 명에게는 각자 선택한 유럽의 여행지로 모든 경비가 지불된 일주일간의 여행이 주어집니다. 그리고 최우수 사진을 찍은 사진작가는 저희 부담으로 〈네이처 포토그래피 매거진〉의 시베리아 원정을 가서 가을 호에 포토 에세이를 출간하게 됩니다!

Q 대회의 1등 상품으로 제공되는 것은?

(a) 유럽 도시들로의 패키지여행

(b) 최고급 사진 장비

(c) 잡지의 2년 구독권

(d) 여행과 전문적인 임무

competition 경쟁, 경연 대회 **attract** 유치하다 **entry** 참가작 **milestone** 획기적인 사건, 이정표 **give away** 수여하다 **runner-up** 차점자, 2위 **grand prize** 최우수상 **expedition** 탐험, 원정 **top-of-the-line** 최고급의, 최신식의 **subscription** 구독

34

Ladies and gentlemen, Flight 471 is at the gate and is ready for boarding. However, we regret to inform you that this flight is overbooked. We're looking for two passengers with flexible travel plans to give up their seats and instead take the flight that leaves at 6:15 this evening. In return, the airline is offering each passenger a $500 voucher good on any domestic flight. Please approach the agent desk if you're interested. Thank you.

Q Which is correct according to the announcement?

(a) Passengers can move to first class for $500.

(b) Too many seats were sold for the flight.

(c) Two passengers have yet to check in.

(d) The flight has been delayed to 6:15.

여러분, 471 비행편이 게이트에 도착해서 탑승 준비가 되었습니다. 하지만 유감스럽게도 이 비행편이 초과 예약되었음을 알려 드립니다. 여행 계획에 여유가 있으셔서 좌석을 포기하시고 대신 오늘 저녁 6시 15분에 떠나는 비행편을 타실 승객 두 분을 찾고 있습니다. 보답으로, 항공사에서는 각각의 승객분들께 국내 어떤 항공편에서도 유효한 500달러 상당의 상품권을 드리겠습니다. 관심이 있으신 분은 직원이 있는 데스크로 와 주시기 바랍니다. 감사합니다.

Q 안내에 따르면 옳은 것은?

(a) 승객들은 500달러를 내고 일등석으로 옮길 수 있다.

(b) 비행편에 너무 많은 좌석이 판매되었다.

(c) 승객 두 명이 아직 탑승 수속을 하지 않았다.

(d) 비행편은 6시 15분으로 연기되었다.

overbooked 초과 예약된 **in return** 보답으로 **voucher** 상품권 **domestic** 국내의 **agent** 직원 **check in** 탑승 수속하다

35

The Battle of Chancellorsville, a major engagement in the US Civil War taking place in Virginia in 1863, was bittersweet for the Confederacy. On the one hand, a small Confederate force defeated a much larger contingent of Union troops. Yet it was during this battle that famed Lieutenant General "Stonewall" Jackson was mortally wounded. Even worse, Jackson died not from a Union musket ball but from friendly fire. This turned out to be a loss the Confederacy could ill afford.

Q Which is correct according to the lecture?

(a) The Confederates succumbed to Union troops.

(b) Jackson was wounded by a lieutenant general.

(c) The Union troops were significantly outnumbered.

(d) Jackson was shot accidentally in the battle.

챈슬러즈빌 전투는 미국 남북전쟁 때 버지니아에서 1863년 발발한 큰 교전으로, 남군에게는 달콤하면서도 씁쓸한 것이었습니다. 한편으로, 소규모 남군 병력이 훨씬 규모가 큰 북군 파견대를 무찔렀습니다. 하지만 이 전투에서 유명한 '스톤월' 잭슨 중장이 치명적인 부상을 입었습니다. 게다가, 잭슨은 북군의 소총이 아니라 아군의 포격으로 사망했던 것입니다. 이는 남군이 감당할 수 없는 손실로 드러났습니다.

Q 강의에 따르면 옳은 것은?

(a) 남군은 북군에게 항복했다.

(b) 잭슨은 중장에게 부상을 당했다.

(c) 북군은 수적으로 크게 열세였다.

(d) 잭슨은 전투에서 실수로 포격을 당했다.

engagement 교전 **US Civil War** 미국 남북전쟁 **bittersweet** 달콤 씁쓸한 **the Confederacy** (남북전쟁 때의) 남부 연합, 남군 **Confederate force** 남부 연합군 **contingent** 파견대 **Union** (남북전쟁 때의) 연합군, 북군 **famed** 유명한 **lieutenant general** 중장 **even worse** 설상가상으로 **musket ball** 머스킷총 포탄 **friendly fire** 아군의 포격 **turn out** ～으로 드러나다 **loss** 손실 **can ill afford** 감당할 여유가 없다 **succumb to** ～에게 굴복하다 **significantly** 상당히 **outnumber** 수적으로 우세하다

36

When a company is interested in procuring a commodity or service from an independent provider, it will sometimes distribute a request for proposal (RFP). A typical RFP outlines what the company is looking for and invites providers to submit proposals and bids. While this may seem to place the onus of action solely on providers, the RFP is a two-way street. The company creating the document must be as forthcoming about its requirements as those submitting bids must be in how they will meet them.

Q What can be inferred from the talk?
(a) RFPs are the responsibility of sales departments.
(b) The RFP is as legally binding as any business contract.
(c) A company has no control over who receives its RFP.
(d) Multiple providers may bid on a single RFP.

한 회사가 독립적인 공급업체로부터 물품이나 서비스를 얻는 데 관심이 있을 때, 그 회사에서는 때로 제안요청서(RFP)를 배포한다. 전형적인 RFP는 회사가 찾고 있는 것이 무엇인지를 주요 내용으로 하며 공급업체가 제안서와 입찰가를 제출할 것을 요청한다. 이것은 공급업체에만 행위의 책임을 지우는 것처럼 보일지 모르나, RFP는 쌍방향적인 것이다. 입찰가를 제출하는 쪽이 어떻게 그것을 충족시킬지를 기꺼이 밝혀야 하는 것과 마찬가지로, 서류를 작성하는 회사는 요건을 기꺼이 밝혀야 한다.

Q 담화로부터 유추할 수 있는 것은?
(a) RFP는 영업부의 업무이다.
(b) RFP는 어떤 사업 계약만큼 법적 구속력이 있다.
(c) 회사는 RFP를 누가 받는지를 통제할 수 없다.
(d) 다수의 공급업체가 단 하나의 RFP에 입찰할 수 있다.

procure 구하다, 입수하다 **commodity** 상품, 물품 **independent** 독립적인 **provider** 공급업자 **distribute** 분배하다 **proposal** 제안(서) **typical** 전형적인 **outline** 개요하다 **submit** 제출하다 **bid** 입찰(에 응하다) **place the onus on** ～에게 책임을 돌리다 **solely** 단지, 오직 **two-way street** 쌍방향적인 관계 **forthcoming** 기꺼이 말하는 **requirements** 요건 **meet** 충족시키다 **legally binding** 법적 구속력이 있는 **multiple** 다수의

Part V

37-38

This is the time of the year to watch a variety of birds! On our famous island, you can see 10 species of woodswallows, 26 species of plovers, 15 species of sandpipers, and 9 species of terns. Once called swallow-starlings, woodswallows fly smoothly with their large wings. Plovers can be easily distinguished from other birds because they have short bills. They can be found almost anywhere in the world. Sandpipers are well-known for their highly sensitive bills. Some of them are 26 inches long. Although they are found all over the world, terns are usually seen near wetlands. Come to our island to watch all these amazing birds. Unless you surprise them, they will welcome you warmly.

다양한 새들을 관찰해야 할 때가 왔습니다! 유명한 저희 섬에서는 10종(種)의 숲제비, 26종의 물떼새, 15종의 도요새, 그리고 9종의 제비갈매기를 볼 수 있어요. 한 때는 제비-찌르레기라고 불린 숲제비는 큰 날개로 매끄럽게 날아다녀요. 물떼새는 부리가 짧아서 다른 새들과 쉽게 구별됩니다. 물떼새는 세계의 거의 어디에서나 발견됩니다. 도요새는 부리가 대단히 예민한 것으로 잘 알려져 있어요. 도요새들 가운데 일부는 길이가 26인치입니다. 제비갈매기는 전 세계에서 발견되긴 하지만 대개 습지 가까이에서 볼 수 있어요. 저희 섬에 오셔서 이 모든 놀라운 새들을 관찰하세요. 놀라게 만들지 않는 한, 여러분을 따뜻하게 맞이할 거예요.

37 Q How many species of swallow-starlings live on the island?
(a) 9
(b) 10
(c) 11
(d) 12

Q 섬에는 몇 종의 제비-찌르레기가 살고 있는가?
(a) 9종
(b) 10종
(c) 11종
(d) 12종

해설 지문 초반에 섬에 숲제비가 10종이 있다고 했는데 이 숲제비는 제비-찌르레기라고도 불린다고 했으므로 정답은 (b)이다.

38 Q What can be inferred from the announcement?
(a) The wings of woodswallows are far larger than those of sandpipers.
(b) The bills of plovers are much longer than those of terns.
(c) There are only 26 species of plovers in the world.
(d) Plovers are likely to be found in Asia and Africa.

Q 안내로부터 추론할 수 있는 것은?
(a) 숲제비의 날개는 도요새의 날개보다 훨씬 더 크다.
(b) 물떼새의 부리는 제비갈매기의 부리보다 훨씬 더 길다.
(c) 세계에는 26종의 물떼새만이 존재한다.
(d) 물떼새는 아시아와 아프리카에서 발견될 가능성이 있다.

해설 고난도 문항이다. 안내에 나오는 새들의 특징을 모두 메모해 두어야만 정확하게 풀 수 있는 문항이기 때문이다. (a)는 주어진 내용만으로는 정확하게 알 수 없기 때문에 오답이다. 짧은 부리 때문에 다른 새들과 쉽게 구별된다고 말한 점을 감안할 때 (b)는 틀린 내용이므로 오답이다. (c)는 이 섬에 살고 있는 물떼새가 26종이라는 정보만으로 명확히 알 수 없는 내용이다. 따라서 정답은 주어진 내용으로부터 자연스럽게 추론할 수 있는 (d)이다.

a variety of 다양한 **woodswallow** 숲제비 **plover** 물떼새 **sandpiper** 도요새 **tern** 제비갈매기 **distinguish** 구별하다 **bill** 부리 **sensitive** 예민한, 민감한 **wetland** 습지

39-40

Although ice cream is one of the most popular foods in the world, its history is still shrouded in obscurity. For instance, we don't know for sure who really invented ice cream soda. Some historians believe that Robert Green invented it in 1874. Others disagree. Similarly, historians don't know who really invented the ice cream sundae. Nor do they know where it was first sold to the general public. Now, you may wonder who first brought ice cream to Europe. The answer is, as you may guess, that we don't know for sure. Some say that an Italian duchess made ice cream popular among Europeans. Again, others disagree, because there is no convincing evidence supporting that claim. Some historians believe that Charles I of England was the reason why ice cream was available only to royal families. Other historians don't accept that claim. Well, whatever its history, ice cream still tastes good, which matters to most of us.

세계에서 가장 인기 있는 식품이긴 하지만, 아이스크림의 역사는 여전히 모호함에 싸여 있습니다. 예컨대 누가 정말로 아이스크림소다를 만들어냈는지 확실히는 몰라요. 어떤 역사학자들은 로버트 그린이 1874년에 아이스크림소다를 발명했다고 생각합니다. 다른 역사학자들은 생각이 다릅니다. 마찬가지로 역사학자들은 누가 정말로 아이스크림선디를 만들어냈는지 모릅니다. 또한 처음으로 어디에서 일반 대중에게 판매되었는지도 모릅니다. 이제 누가 처음으로 아이스크림을 유럽에 가져왔는지가 궁금할지도 모릅니다. 짐작하듯이, 해답은 확실히 모른다는 것입니다. 어떤 이들은 이탈리아의 공작부인이 유럽인들 사이에서 아이스크림이 인기를 끌도록 만들었다고 말합니다. 역사나 다른 이들은 생각이 다른데요, 이는 그 주장을 뒷받침하는, 설득력 있는 증거가 없기 때문입니다. 어떤 역사학자들은 영국의 찰스 1세가 왕실만이 아이스크림을 먹을 수 있게 된 이유였다고 생각합니다. 다른 역사학자들은 그 주장을 받아들이지 않습니다. 글쎄요, 역사야 어떻든, 아이스크림은 여전히 맛있는데요, 그것이 우리 대부분에게 중요한 사실이죠.

39 Q What is the main point of the lecture?
(a) Not many historians are interested in elucidating the history of ice cream.
(b) The exact history of ice cream is still elusive.
(c) Green was the most influential figure in the history of ice cream.
(d) Ice cream is the most delicious food in the world.

Q 강의의 요점은?
(a) 아이스크림의 역사를 해명하는 데 관심을 갖는 역사학자들은 별로 없다.
(b) 아이스크림의 정확한 역사는 여전히 파악하기 어렵다.
(c) 그린은 아이스크림의 역사에서 가장 영향력이 있는 인물이었다.
(d) 아이스크림은 세계에서 가장 맛이 뛰어난 식품이다.

해설 주어진 강의는 아이스크림의 역사에 대해 분명하지 않은 점이 많다는 데 초점을 맞추고 있다. 따라서 정답은 (b)이다. (a)는 주어진 내용에서 서로 다른 주장을 하는 역사학자들이 많다는 점에서 정답이 아니다. (c)와 (d)는 모두 지나치게 세부적인 사항이기도 하면서, 주어진 내용으로부터 분명하게 알 수 없기 때문에 정답이 될 수 없다.

40 Q Which is correct according to the lecture?
(a) Ice cream soda mightn't have been invented in 1874.
(b) The ice cream sundae was first sold to the general public in Italy.
(c) An Italian duchess developed a variety of recipes for ice cream.
(d) During the nineteenth century, only royal families could afford to eat ice cream.

Q 강의에 따르면, 다음 중 옳은 것은?
(a) 아이스크림소다가 1874년에 발명되지 않았을지도 모른다.
(b) 아이스크림선디는 이탈리아에서 처음으로 일반 대중에게 팔렸다.
(c) 이탈리아의 공작부인이 아이스크림을 만드는 다양한 조리법을 개발했다.
(d) 19세기 동안 왕실만이 아이스크림을 먹을 수 있는 여유가 있었다.

해설 이 문항과 같은 세부 사항 유형은 강의를 들으면서, 출제가 예상되는 내용을 간단하게 메모하는 것이 주된 대비 전략이다. (b)는 정확하게 알 수 없다고 했기 때문에, (c)는 강의에서 언급한 내용이 아니기 때문에 오답이다. (d)는 찰스 1세 때문에 영국 왕실에서만 아이스크림을 먹을 수 있다는 내용은 있지만 찰스 1세가 19세기에 통치했다는 내용은 지문에서 알 수 없다는 점에서, 둘째 역사학자들에 따라 생각이 다르다는 점에서 오답이다. 따라서 정답은 (a)이다. 세부 사항 유형이나 추론 유형에서 might, could 등이 선택지에 쓰인 경우 정답일 가능성이 높음에 유의해야 한다.

shroud 뒤덮다, 가리다 **obscurity** 모호함; 무명 **invent** 발명하다 **disagree** 의견이 다르다 **the general public** 일반 대중 **duchess** 공작부인 **convincing** 설득력 있는 **evidence** 증거 **royal family** 왕실, 왕족 **elucidate** 해명하다 **elusive** 포착하기 어려운

Vocabulary

p.33

Part I

1 정답 (d)

A 피자 먹고 싶지 않니?

B 아니, 사양할게. 그런 기름진 음식류 모두가 내게 발진을 <u>일으키거든</u>.

grease 기름, 지방 **come to** ~이 되다 **settle down** 진정시키다 **move on** ~로 넘어가다, 이동하다 **break out** 발발하다, 발생하다

2 정답 (b)

A 지진 현장을 찍은 사진은 더는 못 보겠어.

B 맞아. 그런 <u>참사</u>는 비극이야.

earthquake 지진 **tragic** 비극적인 **condolence** 애도 **devastation** 대참사 **ambience** 분위기 **repression** 억압

3 정답 (b)

A 레베카의 건방이 신경에 거슬려.

B 나도 그래. 그 애는 정말 <u>쌀쌀맞기</u>까지 해.

haughtiness 건방짐, 오만 **get on one's nerves** 신경에 거슬리다, 짜증나게 하다 **modest** 겸손한 **aloof** 냉담한, 쌀쌀맞은 **noble** 고상한 **resolute** 단호한

4 정답 (c)

A 여기는 내가 이제까지 가본 호텔 로비 중에 가장 멋진 곳이야.

B 맞아, 선정한 디자인 하나하나가 <u>완벽한</u> 취향을 보여 주고 있어.

exhibit 보이다 **implacable** 확고한, 완강한 **insouciant** 무관심한, 태평한 **impeccable** 흠 잡을 데 없는 **indecorous** 보기 흉한

5 정답 (b)

A 보고서는 어떻게 돼 가요?

B 이 자료를 모두 <u>분류하는</u> 데 몇 시간이 더 걸려요.

How's A coming? A는 어떻게 돼 가? **round out** 마무리하다 **sort through** 분류하다 **watch over** 지키다 **glide about** 미끄러지듯 가다

6 정답 (a)

A 법원에서 오늘 세법 폐기 결정에 착수하는 것 같아요.

B 당신은 그 법의 <u>폐지</u>를 지지한다고 여겼는데요.

set to 시작하다 **strike down a law** 법률의 폐기를 결정하다 **tax law** 세법 **assume** 추정하다 **in support of** ~을 지지하여 **nullification** 무효화, 파기 **depredation** 약탈 **lucidity** 명석, 명쾌 **caprice** 변덕

7 정답 (d)

A 라켈이 게임에서 진 것 때문에 아직도 침울해하고 있는 것 같아.

B 맞아, 오늘은 특히나 <u>침울해</u> 보이네.

I take it ~인 것 같다 **mope** 맥이 빠져 있다, 침울해하다 **particularly** 특히 **grave** 근엄한, 의젓한 **dry** 재미없는, 딱딱한 **sedate** 차분한, 조용한 **glum** 침울한

8 정답 (a)

A 그 일을 하게 만들려고 제러드를 직접 대면했어요?

B 네, 하지만 <u>변명</u>만 더 늘어놓았을 뿐이에요.

confront 맞서다, 직면하다 **prevarication** 얼버무림, 핑계, 기만 **exorbitance** 과대, 엄청남 **attenuation** 약화, 감소 **improvidence** 경솔함

9 정답 (b)

A 당신 작업에 대한 비판을 받아들이나요?

B 건설적인 경우에만요. 노골적인 <u>모욕</u>은 참지 않아요.

criticism 비판, 비난 **constructive** 건설적인 **stand for** 참다, 그냥 넘어가다 **outright** 노골적인, 명백한 **indigence** 극빈, 극심한 곤궁 **denigration** 명예 훼손 **soliloquy** 독백 **emollient** 피부 연화 크림

10 정답 (b)

A 당신에게 어떤 해도 끼칠 의도가 없다는 것을 알아주셨으면 해요.

B 걱정하지 말아요. 당신에게는 어떤 <u>악감정</u>도 <u>갖고 있지 않아</u>요.

ill will 악감정 **regard** 간주하다 **harbor** (생각 등을) 품다 **board** 탑승하다 **remit** 송금하다, (처벌 등을) 면제해 주다

Part II

11 정답 (d)

판매가 계속 <u>부진하면</u>, 회사는 직원들의 급여 인상 요구를 거부할 것이다.

resist 반대하다, 저항하다 **call for** ~에 대한 요청 **pay raise** 급여 인상 **shirk** 회피하다, 게을리하다 **tick** (시계 등이) 째깍거리다 **rend** 찢다, 찢어발기다 **lag** 뒤처지다, 뒤떨어지다

12 정답 (d)

텍사스 중부의 몇몇 천연 대수층은 4년간의 가뭄 동안 위험할 정도로 <u>고갈되었다</u>.

aquifer 대수층(지하수를 품고 있는 지층) **drought** 가뭄 **repulse** 물리치다, 격퇴하다 **eradicate** 근절하다 **assert** 단언하다 **deplete** 고갈시키다

13 정답 (c)

일확천금을 하려는 꿈에 <u>이끌려</u> 많은 사람들이 복권을 사게 된다.

strike it rich 일확천금을 하다 **lottery ticket** 복권 **defect** (정당·국가 등을) 버리다, 떠나다 **exonerate** 해방하다, 면제하다 **beguile** 속이다, 현혹하다, 기만하다 **impugn** 비난 공격하다

14 정답 (d)

논픽션 작가들은 이야기를 윤색할 수는 있지만, 사건을 날조할 <u>권한</u>은 없다.

engage in ~에 관여[참여]하다 **embellishment** 꾸밈, 윤색 **fabricate** 날조하다 **diversion** 전환 **probate** 공증 **tribute** 헌사 **license** 면허, 허가

15 정답 (b)

<u>만성</u> 통증으로 고통받는 환자들은 진통제를 복용하기 전에 담당 의사와 상담해야 한다.

urge 촉구하다 **consult** 상담하다 **painkiller** 진통제 **timeless** 끝없는 **chronic** 만성의 **immortal** 불멸의 **abiding** 지속적인, 변치 않는

16 정답 (a)

판사는 사건을 검토한 후, 정부가 그 남자의 재산을 몰수한 것은 헌법에 위배된다고 판결했다.

rule 판결을 내리다 **property** 재산 **unconstitutional** 헌법에 위배되는 **seizure** 몰수, 압수 **deficiency** 결핍 **barrage** (질문) 공세 **liability** 법적 책임

17 정답 (a)

폭우와 뒤이은 산사태로 필리핀의 작은 섬에 20명이 넘는 사망자가 생겼다.

landslide 산사태 **ensuing** 다음의, 뒤이은 **vociferous** 소리 높여 외치는 **limpid** 맑은 **bludgeon** 때려눕히다, 억지로 시키다

18 정답 (c)

미국은 자국의 무역 정책을 모든 나라들에 동등하게 적용하지 않는다면 위선자로 낙인찍힐 위기에 처해 있다.

risk 위험을 무릅쓰다 **hypocrite** 위선자 **apply A to B** A를 B에 적용하다 **trade policy** 무역 정책 **equally** 동등하게 **assign** 할당하다 **redouble** 배가하다, 강화하다 **brand** 낙인을 찍다 **daub** 바르다

19 정답 (a)

만약 이 용액을 삼키거나 눈에 닿았을 경우에는 즉시 응급 서비스에 연락하십시오.

solution 용액 **ingest** 삼키다 **sterilize** 살균하다 **cultivate** 경작하다 **dispatch** 발송하다

20 정답 (c)

평론가들은 브로드웨이 연극에서 그 배우가 칠레의 독재자인 아우구스토 피노체트를 묘사한 것에 찬사를 보냈다.

critic 평론가 **applaud** 갈채[찬사]를 보내다 **dictator** 독재자 **play** 연극 **heresy** 이단 **proponent** 지지자 **portrayal** 묘사 **depletion** 고갈, 소모

21 정답 (a)

주류 문화가 날이 갈수록 점점 더 세속적이 되어 가고 있지만, 국민 대다수는 종교적 신념을 유지하고 있다.

mainstream 주류 **by the day** 날이 갈수록 **maintain** 유지하다 **religious faith** 종교적 신념 **secular** 세속적인 **didactic** 교훈적인 **meager** 메마른, 빈약한 **opaque** 불투명한

22 정답 (a)

투자자들은 어제의 불안정한 주가가 앞으로 몇 주 동안 추가적인 혼란의 전조가 될까 봐 걱정한다.

investor 투자자 **unstable** 불안정한 **stock** 주식 **turmoil** 혼란 **portend** 전조가 되다 **allay** 가라앉히다 **cajole** 회유하다 **weave** 엮다, 짜다

23 정답 (c)

옥수수 경작자들에게 주는 연방 보조금은 지원을 받지 못하는 다른 농부들에 비해 불공정한 시장 우위를 부여한다.

federal 연방의 **grower** 재배자 **unfair** 불공정한 **advantage** 우위, 이점 **unsupported** 지원받지 못하는 **accolade** 포상, 칭찬 **precinct** 구역, 선거구 **subsidy** 보조금 **snub** 모욕, 무시

24 정답 (a)

〈중급 웹 디자인〉은 전에 웹 디자인을 잠깐 해 본 적이 있지만, 본격적으로 기술을 발전시키고자 하는 사람들을 위한 교재이다.

intermediate 중급의; 중급자 **textbook** 교재 **previously** 전에 **advance** 발전시키다 **dabble** (취미 삼아) 잠깐 해 보다 **ogle** 추파를 던지다 **traverse** 가로지르다 **oust** 몰아내다

25 정답 (b)

현대적인 도로 포장 기법이 나오기 전에는, 미드웨스트에 있는 도로들은 조금만 비가 와도 통행할 수 없게 되곤 했다.

prior to ~이전에 **advent** 도래, 출현 **paving** 도로 포장 **destitute** 궁핍한 **impassable** 통행할 수 없는 **barren** 황폐한 **oblivious** 의식하지 못하는

26 정답 (a)

워런 버핏은 자신의 재산 대부분을 자선단체에 기부하기로 약속했으며 다른 재벌들에게도 선례를 따르도록 촉구한다.

pledge 약속하다 **donate** 기부하다 **majority** 과반, 대부분 **charity** 자선단체 **encourage** 장려하다, 촉구하다 **mogul** 재벌 **follow suit** 선례를 따르다

27 정답 (a)

대도시인 쿠알라룸푸르는 곰박 강과 클랑 강이 합류하는 곳에 위치해 있다.

metropolis 대도시 **be situated at** ~에 위치해 있다 **confluence** (두 강의) 합류 지점 **mishmash** 뒤죽박죽 **rejoinder** 응수, 답변 **assemblage** 조립, 회합

28 정답 (d)

이 씨의 초기 작품들은 참신하고 관습에 얽매이지 않은 글을 보여 주었지만, 최근 발표작들은 실망스럽게도 평범하다.

unconventional 관습에 얽매이지 않은 **prose** 산문(작품) **latest** 최근의 **offering** 제공된 것 **disappointingly** 실망스럽게도 **arcane** 신비로운, 불가사의한 **rampant** 만연하는 **choleric** 화를 잘 내는 **prosaic** 평범한, 진부한

29 정답 (a)

그 종류의 꽃은 일반적으로 연보라색과 청록색의 줄무늬가 번갈아 나타나는 얼룩덜룩한 꽃잎을 띠고 있다.

species (생물의) 종 **typically** 일반적으로 **display** 보이다 **petal** 꽃잎 **alternating** 교차의 **band** 띠, 줄무늬 **mauve** 연보라색 **cyan** 청록색 **variegated** 얼룩덜룩한 **temperate** 온화한 **nonplussed** 몹시 놀라 어쩔 줄 모르는 **laconic** 말수가 적은

30 정답 (a)

표절 스캔들이 있은 직후에, 마르티네즈 교수가 대학에 사직서를 제출했다는 소식이 들렸다.

on the heels of ~후 즉시, ~의 바로 뒤에 **plagiarism** 표절 **resignation** 사직(서) **tender** 제출하다 **substantiate** 입증하다 **underwrite** (비용 부담에) 동의하다 **divest** 벗기다, 박탈하다

Grammar

p.37

Part I

1 정답 (c)

A 과학 박람회에서 일등을 한 걸 축하해!

B 네가 없었더라면 난 해내지 못했을 거야.

해설 주절의 동사가 〈조동사의 과거형+have p.p.〉인 것으로 보아 가정법 과거완료 문장이다. if절의 가정법 과거완료 형태는 had p.p.이므로 (c)가 정답이다. if it hadn't been for는 '~이 없었더라면'이라는 뜻이다.

congratulations 축하해 **science fair** 과학 박람회

2 정답 (b)

A 휴가 때 파리에 가는 게 좋을까 아니면 상하이에 가는 게 좋을까?

B 어느 쪽을 선택하더라도 즐거운 시간이 될 거야.

해설 선택지 중에서 빈칸 앞의 no matter와 연결될 수 있는 것은 (b) which이다. 이 경우 no matter which는 '어느 것을 ~하더라도'라는 뜻으로 양보를 나타내는 부사절을 이끌며 whichever로 바꿔 쓸 수 있다.

have a great time 즐거운 시간을 보내다

3 정답 (a)

A 오늘 저녁에 당신에게 멋진 저녁 식사를 만들어 줄게요.

B 단지 저를 위해서라면 무리하지 마세요.

해설 선택지로 보아 빈칸에는 '무리하다, 애를 쓰다'라는 뜻의 put oneself out이라는 표현이 들어가야 알맞다. 명령문의 생략된 주어는 you인데, 목적어가 가리키는 대상이 주어와 동일하므로 재귀대명사인 yourself를 써야 한다. 또한 〈동사+부사〉로 이루어진 이어동사의 목적어로 대명사가 올 때는 동사와 부사 사이에 들어가야 하므로 (a)가 정답이다. 문법적인 접근보다 put oneself out이라는 표현을 통째로 알아두자.

fabulous 굉장히 멋진, 엄청나게 좋은

4 정답 (a)

A 저는 온종일 킴을 보지 못했어요, 당신은 봤어요?

B 그녀는 그 보고서를 끝내느라 아직도 사무실에 있어요.

해설 '~하느라, ~하면서'라는 뜻으로 동시동작을 나타내는 분사구문이 들어가야 알맞다. 현재분사로 시작하는 (a)가 정답이다.

all day 온종일

5 정답 (d)

A 어머님이 아직도 입원해 계시니? 꽤 오래되었는데.

B 응, 다음 달이면 입원하신 지 1년째가 돼.

해설 어떤 동작이 미래 특정 시점 이전에 시작되어 미래 특정 시점에 완료되는 경우에는 미래완료(will have p.p.) 시제를 사용하므로 (d)가 정답이다.

be in hospital 입원하다 **it's been a while** 시간이 꽤 지나다
hospitalize 입원시키다

6 정답 (b)

A 모두가 새로 나온 전쟁 영화에 관해서 얘기하는 것 같아.

B 그래. 하도 영화에 대해 대대적으로 광고를 해서 기대에 부응할 수 있을지 의심스러워.

해설 '매우 ~해서 …하다'라는 뜻으로 〈so[such] ~ that〉 구문이 되어야 알맞다. so 다음에는 부사나 형용사가 오고, such 다음에는 명사가 온다. hype라는 명사가 오므로 such를 쓴 (b)가 정답이다.

live up to expectations 기대에 부응하다 **hype** (대대적이고 과장된) 광고

7 정답 (b)

A 다이애나가 새로운 CEO가 될 거예요, 그렇죠?

B 이사회에서 공식적으로 발표하지는 않았지만, 그럴 것 같아요.

해설 어순에 관한 문제이다. 동사인 hasn't announced를 중심으로 부사인 officially는 조동사 다음에 오고 목적어인 it은 동사 뒤에 오는 (b)가 정답이다.

the board 이사회 **announce** 발표하다 **officially** 공식적으로

8 정답 (c)

A 오늘 회사 사무실 중 한 곳에서 파티가 있지 않나요?

B 네, 하지만 어디서 열리는지는 잊어버렸어요.

해설 빈칸에는 문맥상 '누구의 사무실에서'를 나타내는 표현이 들어가야 자연스러우므로 전치사 in과 '누구의 것'을 의미하는 의문사 whose가 있는 (c)가 정답이다.

firm 회사 **hold** 열다, 개최하다

9 정답 (a)

A 만약 피터가 네 노트북을 가져갔다는 것이 밝혀지면 어떻게 할 거니?

B 물론 당장 돌려달라고 요구해야지.

해설 요구, 주장, 제안 등을 나타내는 동사(demand, insist, suggest)의 목적어가 되는 that절에서는 주어 다음에 〈should+동사원형〉을 쓰는데 이때 should는 종종 생략하므로 (a)가 정답이다.

turn out ~인 것으로 밝혀지다 **demand** 요구하다 **at once** 당장

10 정답 (b)

A 정말로 그 고객의 계좌는 놓치지 않으면 했어요.

B 우리는 일어날 수도 있었던 일에 대해 걱정하면서 시간을 허비해서는 안 돼요.

해설 빈칸은 전치사 about의 목적어가 들어갈 자리이므로 '~하는 것'이란 뜻으로 선행사를 포함한 관계대명사 what이 이끄는 절이 들어가야 한다. 따라서 what으로 시작하는 (b)가 정답이다. could have p.p.는 '~할 수도 있었다'라는 뜻으로 과거에 하지 못한 것에 대한 아쉬움을 나타낸다.

client 고객 **account** 계좌 **worry about** ~에 대해 걱정하다

Part II

11 정답 (d)
범인은 몇 시간 후에 은행 건물 주변을 돌아다니다 붙잡혔다.

해설 문맥상 '돌아다니다가 들켰다'라는 뜻이 되어야 알맞다. '~하다가 들키다'라는 뜻으로 be caught –ing의 구문을 쓰므로 (d)가 정답이다.

criminal 범인 **premises** (한 사업체의 건물) 부지, 구내 **prowl** 돌아다니다

12 정답 (b)
골동품 인형 수집품은 미국 역사 학회의 신탁금에 의해 관리된다.

해설 태에 관한 문제이다. 문맥상 수집품은 '관리되는' 대상이므로 수동태가 되어야 알맞다. 선택지 중에서 수동태는 (b)뿐이다.

collection 수집(품) **antique** 골동품(의) **trust** 신탁(금) **maintain** 유지하다, 관리하다

13 정답 (d)
금융 위원회에 따르면, 정전 중에 체결된 전자 상거래가 하나도 기록되지 않았다.

해설 made부터 blackouts까지가 electronic trades를 수식하고 있으며, which were가 생략된 관계사절로 봐도 무방하다. 특정 기간을 나타내는 명사(blackouts)가 나왔으므로 빈칸에는 기간을 나타내는 전치사가 와야 한다. 그러므로 정답은 (d)이다. 참고로 blackout이 복수로 쓰인 것으로 보아, 정전이 수차례 연속적으로 일어났던 것으로 추정할 수 있다.

financial commission 금융 위원회 **electronic trade** 전자 거래 **power blackout** 정전

14 정답 (d)
칭기즈 칸이 이끈 군대는 전투 중에 적군에게 절대 자비를 보이지 않는 것이 관례였다.

해설 mercy 뒤에 다른 수식어가 없으므로 the를 쓸 이유가 없고, none은 대명사이므로 명사를 수식할 수 없으며, any는 부정문이나 의문문에 쓰이므로 역시 알맞지 않다. no가 들어가 부정의 의미를 이루는 것이 알맞으므로 (d)가 정답이다. '자비를 보이다'라고 할 때는 관사 없이 show mercy라고 한다.

customary 관례적인 **mercy** 자비 **battle** 전투

15 정답 (d)
오늘날 살아 있는 모든 척추동물은 수백만 년 전에 공통의 조상을 두었던 것으로 여겨진다.

해설 〈be believe[said/thought]+to부정사〉는 '~라고 여겨지다[말들하다/ 생각되다]'라는 뜻이다. 이때 to부정사가 주절보다 더 먼저 일어난 일일 경우, 완료 부정사(to have p.p.)를 쓴다. 척추동물이 공통의 조상에서 대를 내려온 것은 주절의 현재 시제(are believed)보다 앞선 과거의 일이므로 완료 부정사를 쓴 (d)가 정답이다.

vertebrate 척추동물 **alive** 살아 있는 **ancestor** 조상 **descend from** ~의 자손이다

16 정답 (b)
데이먼 씨는 횡령 사건에 연루되지 않았더라면, 지금쯤 근무조 관리자가 되었을 것이다.

해설 빈칸부터 새로운 절이 시작되고 있는데, 선택지에 접속사가 없는 것으로 보아 접속사를 생략하고 주어와 동사가 도치된 형태가 들어감을 알수 있다. 문맥상 가정법 종속절인데, 앞에 나온 주절은 현재에 대한 가정을 나타내지만, 뒤에 나올 조건절은 과거에 일어난 일에 대한 가정을 나타내므로 혼합가정법이다. 접속사 if를 생략하고 조동사 had가 주어 앞으로 나간 형태인 (b)가 정답이다. 가정법에서는 조동사가 앞으로 도치될 때 부정어 not이 나가지 않는다.

shift supervisor 근무조 관리자 **be involved in** ~와 관련되다 **embezzlement** 횡령

17 정답 (d)
실각한 정치인이 언론에 연설을 할 때, 마치 아무런 특별한 일도 일어나지 않은 것처럼 말했다.

해설 빈칸 뒤에 절이 나오므로 전치사구인 (a)는 정답에서 제외된다. 문맥상 '마치 ~인 것처럼'이라는 뜻의 (d) as if가 들어가야 자연스럽다. as if 다음에는 가정법을 쓴다는 점에 주의한다.

disgraced 망신을 당한, 실각한 **address** 연설하다 **untoward** (좋지 못한 방향으로) 뜻밖의, 별다른 **regardless of** ~와 상관없이

18 정답 (b)
투자자들은 지난 분기에 윌머 홀딩의 수익 증가가 매우 놀라운 사태 전환이라는 데 동의했다.

해설 agreed의 목적어가 되는 that절에서 빈칸에는 동사 was의 보어가 되는 명사구가 들어가야 한다. 이 경우에는 선택지를 하나하나 살펴보며 의미가 통하는 명사구를 선택해야 한다. '매우 놀라운 사태 전환'이라는 뜻을 이루는 (b)가 정답이다. most surprising이 최상급 의미라기보다 '매우(very)'라는 뜻일 때 앞에 정관사 the 대신 a를 붙이기도 한다.

investor 투자자 **revenue** 수익 **quarter** 분기 **turn of events** 사태 전환

19 정답 (d)
아부다비의 정부가 기금을 제공했는데, 그 기금이 없었더라면 건설 사업은 여전히 완공을 기다리고 있을지도 모른다.

해설 문맥상 빈칸에는 '그 기금이 없었더라면'이라는 뜻이 들어가야 알맞다. 반복되는 명사 funding을 선행사로 하는 계속적 용법의 관계대명사 which를 쓴 (d)가 정답이다.

funding 기금 **await** ~을 기다리다 **completion** 완공

20 정답 (a)
마라톤으로 지쳐서, 그 주자는 지역 병원으로 급히 옮겨졌다.

해설 선택지로 보아 접속사와 주어 없이 절이 이어지고 있으므로, 분사구문이 됨을 알 수 있다. 주절의 주어인 the runner가 분사구문의 주어가 되므로, 주어에 맞게 '지친'이라는 뜻이 되려면 Being exhausted가 되어야 한다. Being은 생략 가능하므로 (a)가 정답이다.

runner 주자 **exhausted** 지친, 기진맥진한

21 정답 (b)
판사는 몇몇 소비자 단체의 주장을 듣고 난 후, 소비세가 적정 금액 이상으로 인상되었음을 알게 되었다.

해설 빈칸 앞에 비교급 greater는 than과 호응하므로 (a)와 (b)가 정답 후보이다. 이때 than 뒤에는 반복되는 어구 amount가 생략되는데, 생략된 amount가 들어가 절이 완성될 수 있는 것은 (b)이다. 이 경우 than은 접속사와 생략된 주어 역할을 동시에 하는 일종의 관계대명사로 볼 수 있다.

judge 판사 argument 논쟁, 주장 excise tax 소비세 raise 인상하다 reasonable 합리적인, 적당한

22　정답 (b)

석유 유출로 인해 피해를 본 모든 개체는 시민이나 기업이나 똑같이 보상을 받을 권리가 있다.

해설 All entities ~ alike가 주어이고 are entitled가 동사이다. 따라서 빈칸은 주어를 수식하는 분사가 되어야 알맞다. 수식하는 명사 All entities ~ alike가 '불이익을 당한' 대상이므로 수동태를 나타내는 과거분사 (b)를 써야 한다.

entity 독립체, 개체 corporation 기업 alike 둘 다, 똑같이 as a result of ~의 결과로 oil spill (해상의) 석유 유출 be entitled to ~할 자격이[권리가] 있다 remuneration 보수, 보상 disadvantage 불이익을 주다

23　정답 (b)

교황 자신의 확신에 찬 메시지조차도 점점 거세지는 비난을 막지는 못했다.

해설 빈칸이 없어도 완전한 문장을 이루고 있다. 따라서 빈칸 앞의 Pope를 수식하여 '직접, 자기 자신의'라는 강조의 뜻을 나타내는 재귀대명사 (b)가 들어가야 알맞다.

reassurance 안심(시키는 말), 확신 Pope 교황 stem 막다, 저지하다 rising tide 밀물 accusation 혐의, 비난

24　정답 (a)

우리가 아는 한, 보조금 지급을 책임지고 있는 위원회는 누구의 제안을 받아들일지 아직 결정하지 못했다.

해설 빈칸에는 has yet과 함께 동사를 이루는 어구가 먼저 나와야 한다. have yet to do는 '아직 ~하지 못했다'라는 뜻이므로 to부정사가 나오는 (a)와 (c)가 정답 후보이다. 둘 중에서 decide의 목적어로 '누구의 제안을 받아들일지'라는 뜻을 바르게 나타낸 (a)가 정답이다.

as far as ~하는 한 committee 위원회 responsible for ~에 책임이 있는 award 수여하다, 지급하다 grant money 보조금

25　정답 (c)

면밀한 검사로는 눈에 보일지 몰라도, 그 그림의 붓 칠은 너무나 섬세해서 일반 관람객들은 알아차리지 못할 정도이다.

해설 뒤에 나오는 to note와 호응할 수 있는 것은 〈too … to부정사〉 구문을 이루는 (c)이다. 의미상으로도 '너무 섬세해서 알아차리지 못하다'라는 뜻이 되어야 자연스럽다. for the average viewer는 to부정사의 의미상 주어를 나타낸다.

visible 눈에 보이는 close inspection 면밀한 검사 brushstroke 붓 칠 note 주목하다, 알아차리다 fine 섬세한

Part III

26　정답 (d) do find → do

(a) A 전에 MRI 촬영을 해 본 적 있니?
(b) B 응, 작년에 무릎 인대가 찢어졌을 때.
(c) A 그 경험이 조금이라도 무섭게 여겨졌니?
(d) B 별로 안 그랬어, 하지만 어떤 사람들은 그렇다고 하더라.

해설 (d)에서 do find는 동사가 중복되어 어색하다. 질문과 중복되는 동사 find를 대동사 do로 받고 나머지 어구는 생략하는 것이 일반적이므로, find를 빼야 한다.

tear 찢다, 찢어지다 ligament 인대 frightening 무서운

27　정답 (b) will provide → was provided

(a) A 벌써 식사했니, 모니크?
(b) B 응, 오늘 점심은 콘퍼런스에서 무료로 제공되었거든.
(c) A 그래서 내가 만든 이 라자냐는 조금도 먹고 싶지 않다는 거구나?
(d) B 혹시 남으면 나중에 맛보고 싶어.

해설 (b)에서 점심(lunch)이 주어 자리에 왔는데 능동의 형태로 사용되었다. 문맥상 점심이 제공되는 것이지, 점심 스스로가 무언가를 제공하는 경우가 아니며, A의 두 번째 발언에서 '라자냐를 원하지 않겠네?'라고 하고 있으므로 과거에 제공되었음을 유추할 수 있다. 그러므로 will provide를 was provided로 수정해야 옳다.

for free 무료로 later 나중에

28　정답 (d) to trap → trapping

2013년 5월에, 지구 대기의 이산화탄소 농도는 400ppm으로 측정되었다. 그때가 처음으로 그러한 수준에 도달한 때로 산업혁명 이전에 측정된 기준치인 280ppm에서 우려할 정도의 증가를 기록하고 있다. 실제로, 일부 과학자들은 이것이 지난 2천 년에 걸쳐 최고 농도라고 여기고 있다. 대기의 이산화탄소는 태양열을 대기와 지구 표면에 가두어 기후 변화의 주된 원인으로 여겨지고 있다.

해설 (d)에서 to trap은 to부정사의 부사적 용법인 목적(~하기 위해서), 원인(~하니), 조건(~한다면) 중 어느 것에도 해당 사항이 없어 문맥상 어색하다. 부대상황을 나타내는 분사구문이 되어야 알맞으므로 trapping으로 고쳐야 한다.

atmospheric 대기의 concentration 농도 carbon dioxide 이산화탄소 measure 측정하다 part 배합 비율을 나타내는 단위 alarming 걱정스러운 baseline 기준치 pre-industrial 산업혁명 이전의 driver 추진 요인, 동인 climate change 기후 변화 trap 가두다

29　정답 (d) decades coming → decades to come

1400년대에, 중국의 해군 제독인 정화는 엄청난 규모의 해상 탐험을 연달아 명령했다. 일곱 차례의 이런 '보물 항해'를 하도록 만든 최초의 동기는 알려지지 않고 있지만, 그 결과에 대해서는 의심의 여지가 없다. 중국 함대는 수많은 이웃 왕국들을 그들의 군대와 정치적 통제 하에 둘 수 있게 되었다. 그 후에, 명 왕조의 통치자들은 향후 수십 년 동안 이 약소국가들에서 뽑아낸 부로부터 이득을 보았다.

해설 (d)에서 for decades coming은 '향후 수십 년 동안'이라는 뜻이다. 이때 '다가올'이란 뜻으로 decades를 수식하려면 coming 대신 to come을 써야 한다. to부정사가 기본적으로 앞으로의 일을 나타내는 속성이 있기 때문이다.

admiral 해군 제독 command 명령하다 a series of 일련의 maritime 바다의 expedition 탐험, 원정 tremendous 엄청난, 대단한 scope 범위 initial 초기의 impetus 자극, 추진력 outcome 결과 fleet 함대 dynasty 왕조 ruler 통치자 benefit from ~로부터 이익을 얻다 extract 뽑다, 추출하다 lesser power 약소국가

30 정답 (c) than → that

핵베리는 북아메리카 남부와 중부를 비롯한 북반구의 여러 지역이 원산지인 낙엽수의 일종이다. 이것은 예전에는 느릅나뭇과로 분류되었지만, 현재의 분류에서는 더 넓은 범위의 대마 종류로 분류된다. 핵베리를 성가신 존재로 여기는 이들이 있는데, 이 나무가 번식 성공률이 매우 높아서 잡초와 비슷한 정도의 끈질긴 성질로 퍼질 수 있기 때문이다. 하지만 건조한 지역에서는 내건성으로 유명해서, 그 목재는 가구 제작에 유용하다.

해설 (c)에서 비교급이 없는데 than이 쓰이고 있는 것이 어색하다. 앞에 있는 so와 호응할 수 있는 접속사 that이 되어야 알맞다. so ~ that은 '매우 ~해서 …하다'라는 뜻이다.

hackberry 핵베리 **genus** (생물 분류상의) 속 **deciduous tree** 낙엽수 **native to** ~에 고유한 **hemisphere** 반구 **including** ~을 포함해서 **categorize** 분류하다 **elm** 느릅나무 **family** (생물 분류상의) 과 **current** 현재의 **classification** 분류 **hemp** 삼, 대마 **nuisance** 골칫거리 **reproduce** 번식하다 **spread** 퍼지다 **tenacity** 집요함, 끈기 **weed** 잡초 **drought tolerance** 내건성 **cabinetry** 가구 제작

Reading Comprehension p.41

Part I

1

티모시 리어리는 대중의 찬사와 매도를 동시에 받았다. 하버드 대학의 심리학 교수이자 연구자인 리어리는 1960년에 환각제 실험을 시작했고 반체제적인 시각을 가졌다. 이 때문에 그는 1963년에 하버드 교수직에서 제명되었고, 그는 사회에서 도태된 도처의 학생들을 찾아다니는 것으로 알려졌다. 많은 미국인들이 리어리를 문화적 타락의 상징으로 여겼지만, 의견이 다른 사람들도 있었다. 그들은 그의 사회적 반란이 변화를 가져오기 위해 필요하다고 여겼다.

(a) 사회와 문화에 대한 그의 시각을 정통이 아니라고
(b) 사회적 반란이 변화를 가져오기 위해 필요하다고
(c) 행동이 건강한 사회에 심각한 위협이라고
(d) 감정 폭발이 진단되지 않은 정신질환의 징후라고

해설 Timothy Leary라는 심리학 교수에 대해 빈칸 앞에서 a symbol of cultural degeneration(문화적 타락의 상징)이라고 했는데, 빈칸은 이에 동의하지 않는(others disagreed) 사람들의 생각에 해당한다. 따라서 앞의 부정적인 내용과 대조적으로 긍정적인 내용을 담은 (b)가 어울린다.

revile 매도하다 **general public** 대중 **experiment** 실험하다 **psychedelic drug** 환각제 **adopt** 채택하다 **anti-establishment** 반체제의 **expulsion** 축출, 제명 **faculty** (대학) 교수진 **publicize** 알리다 **drop out of** ~에서 탈락하다 **regard A as B** A를 B로 간주하다 **degeneration** 타락, 퇴보 **disagree** 의견이 다르다 **unorthodox** 정통이 아닌 **rebellion** 반란, 반항 **bring about** 야기하다 **outburst** 감정의 폭발 **undiagnosed** 진단되지 않은

2

소설가 앤드류 콤베는 1995년에 그의 베스트셀러작인 〈분수의 도시〉로 우리의 상상력을 사로잡았다. 삼 년 후에, 속편인 〈산과 계곡〉은 그의 첫 번째 소설이 세운 높은 기준에는 미치지 못했지만, 그럼에도 여전히 독자들의 흥미를 끌었다. 하지만 그 이후로 콤베는 원래 분야였던 공상과학 이외 장르의 작품 창작을 꾀하면서 실패를 거듭했다. 그의 최신작인 〈굽이치는 개울을 따라서〉는 빅토리아 시대의 영국의 시골을 배경으로 한 지나치게 감상적인 러브스토리이다. 본 비평가의 생각에는, 콤베는 승리의 공식에서 벗어나지 말았어야 했다.

(a) 공상과학으로 되돌아가지 말았어야 했다
(b) 기본적으로 어떤 종류의 장르도 착수할 수 있다
(c) 논픽션을 고수했더라면 더 좋았을 것이다
(d) 승리의 공식에서 벗어나지 말았어야 했다

해설 한 소설가의 첫 작품부터 이후의 작품들까지를 개괄하고 있다. 첫 두 권이 성공한 것과 대조적으로 이후 실패를 거듭한 이유를 공상과학 이외의 장르를 썼다(as Combe has attempted to write in genres other than science fiction)는 것에서 찾을 수 있다. 따라서 잘하는 분야에 주력해야 한다는 (d)가 비평가의 의견이라고 보는 게 타당하다.

capture 사로잡다 **imagination** 상상력 **sequel** 속편 **high bar** 높은 기준 **nonetheless** 그럼에도 불구하고 **excite** 흥미를 끌다 **flop** 실패작 **one after another** 잇따라서 **latest** 최신의 **over-sentimentalized** 지나치게 감상적인 **reviewer** 검토자, 평가자 **basically** 기본적으로 **stick to** ~을 고수하다 **deviate from** ~에서 벗어나다 **winning formula** 승리의 공식

3

가끔 스코트족을 대영 제국의 큰 독립체 안에 있는 한 민족으로 보는 경우가 있다. 이는 결코 통일이라고 볼 수 없는 지역의 역사를 고려할 때 아이러니한 일이다. 900년 전에 지금은 스코틀랜드로 알려진 지역에 별개의 여러 부족들이 거주하고 있었다. 이들 중에 주요 집단이 픽트족이었는데, 로마인들은 영국 제도를 정복하려 군사 작전을 폈을 때 이들을 성공적으로 제압하지 못하였다. 부족 규모의 다른 민족에는 게일인과, 브리튼, 그리고 앵글로인들이 있었는데, 결과적으로 이들 모두가 합쳐져 오늘날의 스코트랜드인의 정체성을 형성하게 되었다.

(a) 대부분 고대 로마의 정복의 결과라는 점을
(b) 스코트족이 오래 전에 로마인들에 맞서 싸웠다는 것을
(c) 나라가 현재보다 더 통일되어야 한다는 것을
(d) 결코 통일이라고 볼 수 없는 지역의 역사를

해설 스코트족을 대영 제국에 속한 민족으로 보는 경우가 있는데 그것이 아이러니라고 하므로 빈칸에는 그에 반대되는 의견이 들어가는 것이 알맞다. 따라서 분리된 역사를 가지고 있다는 내용의 (d)가 적절하다

Scot 스코트족, 스코틀랜드 사람 **people** 국민 **ironic** 아이러니한 **inhabit** 살다 **distinct** 뚜렷이 다른, 별개의 **tribe** 부족 **grouping** 집단, 분류 **campaign** 군사 작전 **conquer** 정복하다 **tribal** 부족의, 종족의 **ethnicity** 민족성 **coalesce** 합치다 **identity** 정체성 **conquest** 정복 **unified** 통일된 **anything but** ~이 결코 아닌

4

전기어는 사냥이나 포식자에 대항하기 위해 피할 목적으로 독특하게도 그들 몸에서 나오는 전기장을 띠고 있다. 예를 들어, 전기뱀장어는 최대 600 볼트에 해당하는 충격을 방출하여 먹이를 꼼짝 못하게 하거나 죽인다. 그들의 기관에 있는 세포들에는 소량의 전위를 발생시키는 능력이 있으며, 이와 유사한 수십만 개의 다른 세포가 함께 전위를 방출될 때, 강력한 전기파를 생성한다. 반면에, 전기가 약한 물고기는 사냥보다는 감지를 위해서 전압이 낮은 전기장에 의존한다. 포식자가 그들의 전기장에 들어오면, 물고기는 장애물을 감지하고 포획을 피할 수 있다.

(a) 추위로부터 자신을 보호하기 위해서
(b) 사냥보다는 감지를 위해서
(c) 같은 종들 사이의 의사소통을 위해서
(d) 내부 장기를 보호하기 위해서

해설 On the other hand로 보아 앞부분과 다른 화제가 나올 것임을 알 수 있다. 이 경우 빈칸 다음에 나오는 문장을 통해 힌트를 찾을 수 있다. 낮은 전기장을 이용해서 장애물을 감지하여 위험을 피하는 경우를 들고 있으므로 (b)가 적절하다.

electric fish 전기어 **uniquely** 독특하게 **be equipped with** ~을 갖추다 **electric field** 전기장 **defend** 방어하다 **predator** 포식자 **electric eel** 전기뱀장어 **emit** 배출하다 **incapacitate** 꼼짝 못 하게 만들다, 무능력하게 만들다 **prey** 먹이 **generate** 발생시키다 **electrical potential** 전위(전기장 내의 전기에너지의 양) **discharge** 방출하다 **in unison with** ~와 협력하여 **electric pulse** 전기파 **weakly** 약하게 **perceive** 감지하다 **disturbance** 방해, 장애 **intra-species** 같은 생물종 내의 **insulate** 보호하다 **internal organ** 내부 장기

5

경제학은 소비자의 선택과 행동에 관한 연구가 주축이 된다. 하지만 경제학 분야는 점점 더 실제 사건에서 벗어난, 오직 통계 모델의 분석으로 절뚝거리고 있는 것처럼 보인다. 이러한 곤란함은 경제학에서 순수 이론만 경외되고 추상적인 생각에서 벗어난 어떤 것(예를 들어 응용 경제 이론)도 중요하게 다뤄져야 할 만큼 가치 있는 것으로 생각되지 않는 경제학의 흐름에서 비롯된다. 그래서 경제학자들은 인간의 의사결정에 대한 그들의 이론에서 점차 수학적 공식에 의존하게 된다. 결과적으로 그들의 계산은 현실적인 시장에는 전혀 기반을 두고 있지 않다.

(a) 다소 정확하게 소비자 경향을 따른다
(b) 현실적인 시장에는 전혀 기반을 두고 있지 않다
(c) 컴퓨터에 의해 수행되어야 한다
(d) 매우 적절한 것으로 여겨진다

해설 경제학자들이 현실을 등한시한 채 이론적인 연구에만 몰두한다는 우려의 글이다. 빈칸 앞 문장에서 인간의 의사 결정을 수학 공식에만 의존한다는 것을 지적하고 있으므로, 그렇게 도출해낸 계산 결과는 현실적인 시장에서는 기반이 없다는 (b)가 들어가야 알맞다.

revolve around ~을 중심으로 삼다, ~이 주축이 되다 **hobble** 방해하다 **predicament** 곤경, 궁지 **revered** 존경 받는 **abstract** 추상적인 **reliant on** ~에 의존하는 **formulae** 공식 **decision-making** 의사결정 **calculation** 계산 **carry out** 수행하다 **eminently** 대단히 **relevant** 적절한

6

> **알레르기가 있는 개들을 위한 최고의 사료**
>
> 여러분은 알레르기 유발 물질이 없는 식사를 만드는데, 여러분의 가장 친한 친구도 그만한 대접을 받을 자격이 있습니다. 여러분의 애완견을 위해 특별히 제조되어 여러분의 동물 친구의 건강을 증진할 것이 확실한 앨리슨의 개 알레르기용 사료를 소개합니다. 앨리슨 사료는 여러분이 기르는 개의 알레르기 내용에 기초하여 고객 맞춤으로 만든다는 점에서 특별합니다. www.alisonscacc.com에서 온라인으로 등록하여 담당 수의사가 시행한 알레르기 테스트 결과를 보내시기만 하면, 나머지는 저희가 알아서 처리하겠습니다. 여러분은 일주일에 한 번 7일간의 사료를 저희 주방에서 여러분의 강아지 접시까지 바로 배송받으시게 됩니다.

(a) 하지만 개는 알레르기를 겪지 않는 것으로 알려져 있습니다
(b) 반면에 다른 알레르기들은 집안에서 키우는 애완동물이 원인이 됩니다
(c) 그리고 여러분의 가장 친한 친구도 그만한 대접을 받을 자격이 있습니다
(d) 하지만 애완동물에게 남은 음식을 먹이지 않도록 주의하십시오

해설 알레르기가 있는 애완견을 위한 맞춤 사료를 제공하는 애완견 사료 업체의 광고이다. 사람이 자기가 가진 특정한 알레르기에 맞추어 음식을 만들듯이 애완견도 사람처럼 알레르기를 고려한 사료를 먹어야 한다는 내용이 알맞으므로 (c)가 적절하다.

allergen 알레르기 유발 물질 **canine** 개(의) **formulate** 만들어내다 **specifically** 특히 **guarantee** 보장하다 **custom-tailored** 고객 맞춤의 **veterinarian** 수의사 **shipment** 배송 **straight** 직접의 **scraps** 먹고 남은 음식

7

슬랙라인이 처음으로 고안되었을 때, 그것은 다소 재미없는 활동이었다. 이것은 반 인치 넓이의 가늘고 긴 끈을 땅 위의 낮은 두 지점 사이에 묶고, 사람이 그 사이를 걷는 것으로 이루어진다. 어떤 이들은 이것이 아마추어 줄타기에 지나지 않는다고 비웃음을 샀다. 그러나 곧, 점점 더 많은 전문 선수들이 줄 위에서 물구나무서기나 뒤공중제비돌기 같은 고난도 연기를 하기 시작했다. 차세대 혁신 주자는 '하이라인'으로, 두 절벽이 마주 보고 있는 사이에서 지상 수백 피트 상공에 매달린 슬랙라인이다. 구경꾼들은 대담한 모험가들이 안전 밧줄도 없이 줄 위를 걸을 때 입이 딱 벌어졌다.

(a) 아무도 그 디자인을 이해하지 못했다
(b) 그것은 다소 재미없는 활동이었다
(c) 그것은 너무 위험해서 인기를 끌 수 없는 것으로 증명되었다
(d) 선수들은 매우 대담하고 무모한 요소를 도입했다

해설 슬랙라인이 처음으로 소개되었을 당시의 반응이 어떠했을지 짐작해 본다. 세 번째 줄에서 아마추어 줄타기라고 비웃음을 샀다는 것으로 미루어 보아, 스포츠라고 보기에는 시시하게 보였음을 알 수 있으므로 (b)가 알맞다.

slackline 슬랙라인(스포츠의 일종인 줄타기) **conceive** 생각해내다, 고안하다 **consist of** ~으로 이루어지다 **strip** 길고 가느다란 조각 **fabric** 천, 섬유 **ridicule** 비웃다 **tightrope walking** 줄타기 **athletic practitioner** 전문 선수 **stunt** 스턴트, 고난도 연기 **handstand** 물구나무서기 **backflip** 뒤공중제비돌기 **onlooker** 구경꾼 **gape** (놀라서) 입이 딱 벌어지다 **daredevil** 무모한 모험을 하는 사람 **tame** 재미없는

8

원자폭탄의 폭발이 어떠한지는 상식적으로 잘 알려져 있지만, 방사능이 살아 있는 조직에 해를 끼치는 방식은 그렇지 아니하다. 우선, 문제가 되는 에너지의 종류는 감마선으로, 폭발과 거의 동시에 배출된다. 폭발로 인한 감마선은 살아 있는 세포에 침투하여 우리의 DNA를 둘러싸고 있는 물분자로부터 전자를 몰아낸다. 이들 물분자는 이제 전자쌍이 맞지 않은 불안정한 유리기 상태이며, DNA 분자로부터 원자를 끌어들이면서 그로 인해, DNA를 파괴하고 암과 기타 질병의 위험을 높이게 된다.

(a) 방사능이 확산될 수 있는 거리
(b) 가까이 있는 사람들이 실제로 어떻게 증발되는지
(c) 각기 다른 종류의 방사선이 왜 대기로 유입되는지
(d) 방사능이 살아 있는 조직에 해를 끼치는 방식

해설 잘 알려지지 않은 에너지 종류인 감마선이 인간을 비롯한 생명체에 해를 끼치는 방법에 대해 설명하는 글이므로 (d)가 적절하다.

atomic bomb 원자폭탄 **explosion** 폭발 **common knowledge** 상식 **first of all** 무엇보다, 우선 **gamma radiation[ray]** 감마선 **microsecond** 마이크로초(백만 분의 1초) **detonation** 폭발 **penetrate** 관통하다, 침투하다 **dislodge** 몰아내다, 제거하다 **electron** 전자 **molecule** 분자 **unstable** 불안정한 **free radical** 유리기 **co-opt** 끌어들이다 **radiation** 방사능 **proximity** 근접, 가까움 **vaporize** 증발시키다 **tissue** (세포) 조직

9

미리암 듀크 씨가 최고 투자 임원직을 사퇴한 후 곧바로 그녀를 대신할 사람을 찾는 것이 경영진의 의도였습니다. 하지만 이제 그녀가 떠난 지 한 달이 되었는데도, 우리는 아직 적당한 후임을 정하지 못했습니다. 현 시점에서, 우리는 외부 컨설턴트를 고용하여 다양한 능력과 전문성을 갖춘 모범적인 후보들 중에서 추려내는 것이 좋을 것 같습니다. 물론 컨설턴트를 고용하는 데에 들어가는 비용도 중요하므로, 이 제안이 이사회에서 승인되는 동안 지체가 되고 있습니다.

(a) 그 사이에
(b) 그러므로
(c) 하지만
(d) 마찬가지로

해설 빈칸 앞 문장에서 원래는 곧바로 후임을 찾는 것이라고 했는데, 빈칸 뒤에서는 한 달이 되었는데도 후임을 정하지 못했다고 하므로 대조와 역접을 나타내는 (c)가 들어가야 알맞다.

intention 의도, 목적 **abdication** 퇴위, 사직 **cull** 추려내다 **exemplary** 모범적인 **candidate** 후보 **have yet to** 아직 ~하지 못하다 **suitable** 적당한 **successor** 후임 **expense** 비용, 경비 **inconsequential** 중요하지 않은 **the board** 이사회

10

유한책임 회사(LLC)는 개인 기업과 주식회사 사이에 해당한다. 주식회사와 마찬가지로, LLC는 소유주에게 유한 책임을 준다. 즉, 회사를 상대로 소송이 제기될 경우에 소유주의 개인 재산 및 부동산은 보호를 받는다. 반면에, LLC는 또한 세제에 관해서는 개인 기업과 유사하다. 회사가 벌어들인 수익은 소유주 개인 소득으로 간주되어 개인 소득 수준으로 과세된다.

(a) 반면에
(b) 요컨대
(c) 게다가
(d) 그럼에도 불구하고

해설 유한책임 회사를 정의하면서 개인 기업(sole proprietorship)과 주식회사(corporation)와 비교하여 설명하고 있다. 빈칸 앞에서는 주식회사와의 유사성을, 빈칸 뒤에서는 개인 기업과의 유사성을 언급하고 있다. 따라서 화제를 대조하여 반전시키는 (a)가 알맞다.

limited liability 유한책임 **sole proprietorship** 개인 기업 **corporation** 법인, 주식회사 **suit** 소송 **when it comes to** ~에 관한 한 **tax** 세금을 부과하다 **subsequently** 그 뒤에, 나중에 **for all that** 그럼에도 불구하고

Part II

11

새벽부터 황혼까지, 아들러 도로에 위치한 〈마누카 카누와 카약〉은 여러분에게 바다에서의 최고의 시간을 선사하는 데 전념하고 있습니다. (a) 이번 주에 오시면, 여름이 온 것을 기념하여 저희의 모든 보트 대여료가 20% 할인됩니다. (b) 저희는 전통적인 카약과 카누에서부터 서서 타는 서프보드와 자전거 보트까지 다양한 보트를 구비하고 있습니다. (c) 또한, 올해부터 발효되는 새 안전 법령에 부합하도록 여러분의 장비를 새로 장착하는 것을 잊지 마세요. (d) 저희가 가지고 있는 모든 보트는 안전 인증이 되어 있고 귀하가 방해받지 않고 수상 스포츠를 즐길 수 있도록 평생 보증이 되는 제품들입니다.

해설 마누카 카누와 카약이라는 보트 대여 업체를 광고하고 있다. (a)에서는 가격 할인을, (b)에서는 구비하고 있는 다양한 종류의 보트를 광고하고, 마지막 (d)에서는 장비의 안전성을 보장하고 있다. (c)는 광고의 흐름과 상관 없이 안전 법령의 실시에 대해서 말하고 있다.

dawn 새벽 **dusk** 황혼 **be dedicated to** ~에 전념[헌신]하다 **maximum** 최고의 **stock** (상품을) 구비하다 **craft** 보트, 배 **stand-up paddleboard** 서서 타는 서프보드 **retrofit** 새로 장착하다 **marine** 바다의, 해양의 **comply with** 준수하다, 지키다 **ordinance** 법령, 조례 **effective** 유효한 **lifetime** 평생 **guarantee** 보증

12

1781년 가을에 노예선 '종'은 아프리카에서 카리브해로 442명의 노예를 싣고 대서양을 건너고 있었다. (a) 항해 오류로 인해, 배는 육지에 다다르기 전에 저장 식수를 다 써버리고 말았다. (b) 그래서 승무원들은 142명의 노예를 바다에 빠뜨려 살해하기로 결정을 내렸다. (c) 승무원 중 아무도 이 범죄에 대해 재판을 받지 않았지만, 이 사건은 유럽과 미국에서 노예폐지 운동을 촉발시켰다. (d) 미국의 노예폐지론자인 존 브라운은 거의 80년이 지나서 하퍼스 페리에 있는 연방 무기고를 습격했으나 실패했다.

해설 노예폐지 운동을 촉발시킨 한 사건에 대해 일관되게 서술하고 있는데, (d)는 노예제 폐지와 관련하지만 별개의 사건을 서술하고 있으므로 주제에서 벗어난다.

navigation 항해 **expend** 쓰다, 소비하다 **prior to** ~이전에 **landfall** 상륙 **crew** 승무원 **thereby** 그것 때문에 **drown** 익사시키다 **try** 심리[재판]하다 **incident** 사건 **spark** 촉발시키다 **abolitionist movement** 노예폐지 운동 **unsuccessful** 성공하지 못한 **raid** 습격 **armory** 무기고

Part III

13

> 린 씨께,
>
> 블레이크 미술관 및 진행 중인 모든 행사와 특별 전시에 관심을 가져 주신 데 대해 감사드립니다. 귀하의 질문에 답변 드리자면, 현재는 일반인들의 기부금을 받지 않고 있는데, 저희 기금 대부분은 국립 예술 학회로부터 기부금의 형태로 들어오기 때문입니다. 미술관의 회원이 되시면 확실히 저희를 후원하실 수 있습니다. 연간 회원권은 65달러부터 시작하며 저희 웹 사이트인 www.blake-art.org를 통해 구입하실 수 있습니다.
>
> 지원팀장
> 로라 버그 드림

Q 이메일의 주된 목적은?
(a) 기부에 대한 문의에 대답하는 것
(b) 미술관에 대한 국가 보조금을 요청하는 것
(c) 미술관에서 예정하고 있는 행사들을 홍보하는 것
(d) 고객에게 회원권을 갱신할 것을 장려하는 것

해설 In answer to your question에서 상대의 질문에 대답을 하기 위한 목적의 이메일임을 알 수 있다. 미술관의 기부금에 대해 안내하고 있으므로 (a)가 정답이다.

ongoing 진행 중인 **roster** 명단 **exhibit** 전시회 **currently** 현재 **monetary contribution** 금전적 기부 **funding** 기금 **endowment** 기부금 **certainly** 확실히 **outreach** 봉사[지원]활동 **solicit** 요청하다 **grant** 보조금 **promote** 홍보하다 **patron** 고객, 후원자

14

몇 달간 예상하는 소문이 떠돈 후에, 비디오게임 제작업체인 PRF 엔터테인먼트가 마침내 차세대 게임기 GEX-2를 공개할 예정이었다. 서둘러서 제품을 시장에 출시하면서, 회사는 올해 말로 예정된 레지놀드의 카잠 3.0의 출시에 앞서 시장을 장악하기를 바랐다. PRF의 제품 출시 행사에 참석한 업계 관계자들은 새로운 게임기와의 첫 대면을 기다리면서 자신들의 반응을 실시간으로 생방송 하였는데, 실제로 첫 대면은 없었다. 〈게이머 인사이더〉지의 한 기자는 "실제로 게임기를 보여주지도 않고 게임기를 공표한다고?"라고 비웃었고 "그것참 시시하다"고 하였다.

Q 지문의 주된 내용은?
(a) 새로운 제품을 공개하지 않은 한 회사
(b) 최고 게임기 업체 두 곳의 경쟁
(c) 과장 광고된 게임기의 부진한 초기 판매
(d) 게임 산업 행사에서의 언론의 열광적 관심

해설 한 게임 회사가 새 게임기 출시 행사를 하면서 실제로 게임기는 보여 주지 않아 사람들이 비웃었다는 내용이다. 업체가 제품 시연을 하지 못한 것을 다루는 기사이므로 (a)가 적절하다.

anticipatory buzz 예상하는 소문 **manufacturer** 제조업자 **unveil** 발표하다, 공개하다 **console** 게임기 **grab** 움켜쥐다 **ahead of** ~보다 앞서 **upcoming** 다가오는 **release** 출시, 공개 **slated for** ~로 예정된 **insider** 내부자 **attendance** 참석 **broadcast live** 생중계하다 **play-by-play** 실황 방송 **sneer** 비웃다, 조롱하다 **lame** 변변찮은, 시시한 **rivalry** 경쟁 **hyped** 과대 광고한 **frenzy** 열광, 광란

15

수력 발전은 움직이는 물 안에 담긴 에너지를 사용 가능한 형태로 전환하는 하나의 발전 방식이다. 전통적인 발전 방식은 댐을 갖춘 저수지 안에 담긴 위치 에너지를 활용한다. 물이 댐의 구멍을 통해 흐르면서 엄청나게 큰 터빈의 날개를 돌리면, 이것이 붙어 있는 중심축을 회전시킨다. 축의 반대쪽 끝에서는, 회전자라고 하는 부품이 터빈과 중심축과 함께 돌아간다. 회전자가 움직이면서 그 안에 있는 자석이 구리선을 감아 만든 고정된 고리를 지나면서 순환한다. 이것이 선에 있는 전자를 움직여서 전기가 흐르게 만드는 것이다.

Q 지문에서 주로 묘사하고 있는 것은?
(a) 다양한 수력 발전 방식
(b) 수력 발전 작동에 수반되는 기술
(c) 다른 에너지원을 뛰어넘는 수력 발전의 장점
(d) 수력 발전의 지속 가능성

해설 수력 발전이 무엇인지를 정의한 후 수력 발전이 물리적으로 작동되는 원리를 순서대로 설명하고 있다. 즉, 수력 발전의 작동 기술에 대해 설명하고 있으므로 (b)가 적절하다.

hydropower 수력 발전 **generation** 발생 **channel** 돌리다 **conventional** 전통적인 **capitalize on** ~을 활용하다 **dam** 댐을 건설하다 **reservoir** 저수지 **aperture** 작은 구멍 **massive** 거대한 **rotate** 회전시키다 **central shaft** 중심축 **be attached to** ~에 붙어 있다 **component** 부품 **rotor** 회전자 **spin** 돌다, 회전하다 **in unison with** ~와 함께 **magnet** 자석 **stationary** 정지된, 움직이지 않는 **copper wire** 구리선 **operation** 작동 **sustainability** 지속 가능성

16

네팔 중부의 랑탕 밸리 주변 지역에서는 뚜렷이 다른 별개의 두 문화 및 민족이 충돌하고 있다. 남쪽으로는 카트만두 밸리가 있는데, 고도가 더 낮은 지역으로 네팔의 수도이자 최대 도시인 카트만두가 있는 곳이다. 그곳은 주로 힌두교를 주요 종교로 하는 네팔 사람들이 사는 곳이다. 랑탕 밸리는 거리상으로는 가깝지만, 현저히 다른 민족이 사는데, 티벳 민족과 그들의 친족인 타망족으로 이루어져 있으며, 두 민족 모두 불교 신앙을 추종하는 이들이다.

Q 지문에 가장 적절한 제목은?
(a) 문화적 다양성에 대한 네팔의 접근
(b) 한 국가 안의 별개 문화들
(c) 종교와 민족의 모순
(d) 카트만두의 종교적 갈등

해설 첫 문장이 지문의 주제를 함축하고 있다. 네팔에서 종교적으로 갈린 두 문화(힌두교와 불교)가 충돌하고 있다는 내용이므로 한 국가 안에서의 다른 문화를 나타내는 (b)가 알맞다.

ethnicity 민족성 **collide** 충돌하다 **elevation** 고도 **capital** 수도 **proximate** 가까운, 인접한 **strikingly** 두드러지게, 굉장히 **adherent** 지지자 **paradox** 역설 **conflict** 갈등, 충돌

17

경제 뉴스

이번 주에, 영국의 파운드화가 2년 만에 달러 대비 최저 가치로 떨어져서, 파운드당 1달러 50.73센트에 거래되고 있다. 최근 몇 달간, 달러 대비 영국 통화 가치는 약 7퍼센트 감소했다. 또한, 영국 경제 전망이 어둡다는 경제 분석가들의 말을 고려하면, 달러 대비 파운드는 조만간은 오르지 않을 것으로 예상된다. 동시에 유로는 급등해서 올해에만 파운드 대비 가치가 상승했다.

Q 지문에 따르면 다음 중 옳은 것은?
(a) 영국의 파운드화는 여전히 달러보다 가치가 낮다.
(b) 달러는 파운드 대비 7퍼센트의 가치를 잃었다.
(c) 파운드는 최저 가치일 때 1.5073유로 정도였다.
(d) 유로와 달러는 올해에 파운드 대비 가치가 상승했다.

해설 첫 문장에서 달러 대비 파운드 가치는 하락했다고 했고, 마지막 문장에서 유로는 급등했다고 하므로, 결국 유로와 달러는 파운드에 비해 모두 가치가 상승한 것이므로 (d)가 정답이다.

trade 거래하다 **currency** 통화 **diminish** 감소하다 **given that** ~을 고려하면 **outlook** 전망 **dismal** 암울한 **make gains** 이윤을 내다 **skyrocket** 급등하다

18

대부분 사람들에게 이것은 가끔 즐기는 오락용 여가활동이지만, 인구의 약 2퍼센트에게 도박은 지속적인 해를 초래하는 병적인 충동을 나타낸다. 공식적으로 도박 중독이라는 정신적 질환으로 알려져 있지만, 이것은 대개 눈에 띄지 않는 질환으로, 우울증이나 불면증처럼 수반될 수 있는 다른 질병으로 가장하고 있다. 도박 중독에 대한 효과적인 치료법이 존재하는데, 어떤 점에서 병적인 도박을 치료하는 것은 약물 중독자를 재활 치료하는 것과 비슷하다. 하지만 물론, 도박 습관은 신체적 중독이 아니므로 약물 남용처럼 의학적으로 평가할 수는 없다.

Q 지문에 따르면 다음 중 옳은 것은?
(a) 도박은 정신 질환으로 인정되지 않는다.
(b) 도박자의 2퍼센트는 병적으로 도박을 한다.
(c) 도박 치료는 다른 중독에 대한 치료와 비슷하다.
(d) 도박 충동은 객관적인 의학적 테스트로 측정된다.

해설 병적인 도박을 치료하는 것은 대개 눈에 띄지 않는 질환으로 약물 중독자를 재활 치료하는 것과 비슷하다(treating pathological gambling is like rehabilitating substance abusers)고 하므로, 약물 중독을 other addictions로 바꿔 표현한 (c)가 정답이다.

recreational 오락의 **pastime** 소일거리, 여가활동 **from time to time** 가끔 **gambling** 도박 **pathological** 병적인 **impulse** 충동 **lasting** 지속적인 **officially** 공식적으로 **psychiatric** 정신의학의 **addiction** 중독 **disorder** 질환 **invisible** 눈에 보이지 않는 **disguised** 변장한 **affliction** 고통 **accompany** 수반하다 **depression** 우울증 **insomnia** 불면증 **effective** 효과적인 **treatment** 치료(법) **rehabilitate** 재활치료를 하다 **substance abuser** 약물 남용자 **medically** 의학적으로 **assess** 평가하다 **drug abuse** 약물 남용 **identify** 밝히다

19

이번 주 초에, 자동차 제조업체인 TL 모터스가 페어 스카이즈 에너지와 협력하여 자동차 구매자들에게 태양전지판 할인이라는 특별한 혜택을 제공할 것이라는 발표가 있었다. 다음 달부터, 소비자들은 TL 모터스에서 새로 전기 차량을 구입할 경우, 페어 스카이즈 에너지의 태양전지판 시스템을 200달러 할인 받을 수 있다. TL 모터스의 대변인은 할인 프로그램이 탄소 배출량을 줄이는 데 관심이 있는 소비자들을 유치하기 위해 마련된 것이라고 밝혔다. 페어 스카이즈 에너지는 자사 태양열 제품이 TL 모터스의 환경을 생각하는 고객층의 관심을 끌 것이라고 자신하고 있다.

Q 고객들이 전기 차량을 구입할 때 받게 되는 혜택은?
(a) 정부의 에너지 정책으로부터 200달러의 환불
(b) 가정 에너지 사용을 위한 무상 태양전지판 시스템
(c) 페어 스카이즈 에너지의 제품에 대한 할인
(d) TL 모터스의 보증 기한 연장

해설 TL 모터스의 전기 차량을 구입하는 고객은 페어 스카이즈 에너지의 태양전지판 시스템에 대해 200달러를 할인받을 수 있다고 하므로 (c)가 정답이다.

team up with ~와 팀을 이루다, ~와 협력하다 **solar panel** 태양전지판 **be eligible for** ~할 자격이 있다 **spokesperson** 대변인 **attract** 끌다, 유인하다 **carbon emission** 탄소 배출 **confident** 확신하는 **appeal to** 관심을 끌다 **environmentally conscious** 환경을 생각하는 **customer base** 고객층 **rebate** 환불 **initiative** 정책, 프로그램 **extended** 연장된 **warranty voucher** 보증서

20

전 세계에 흩어져 있는 유대인 공동체의 특정 파벌은 항상 이스라엘 땅으로의 복귀를 주장하는데, 이것은 일반적으로 1800년대 중반 무렵까지는 대다수의 의견이 아니었다. 그 무렵에 유럽에서 반유대주의 정서가 점점 거세지면서 점점 더 많은 유대인들이 함께하는 고국이 반드시 필요하다고 여기도록 만들었다. 시온주의라고 알려진 이 운동은 1917년 팔레스타인에서 유대 국가의 건설을 지지한 영국의 밸푸어 선언으로 대승을 거두었다. 불과 30년 후에, 시오니즘의 바람은 현실이 되었다.

Q 지문에 따르면 다음 중 옳은 것은?
(a) 고국에 대한 갈망이 유대인 역사의 긴 부분을 차지한다.
(b) 유대인들은 1800년대 중반 이후에는 반유대주의를 덜 겪었다.
(c) 차별 때문에 시온주의 국가에 대한 지지가 생겨났다.
(d) 밸푸어 선언은 이스라엘 건국을 기념했다.

해설 1800년대를 기점으로 반유대주의 정서 때문에 유대인들이 국가의 필요성을 느끼게 되었고 시온주의 운동이 시작되었다고 한다. anti-Semitic sentiment를 discrimination으로 표현한 (c)가 정답이다.

faction 파벌 **Jewish** 유대인의 **diaspora** 전 세계에 흩어져 살면서 유대교의 규범을 유지하는 유대인 공동체 **advocate for** ~을 지지하다 **viewpoint** 관점 **anti-Semitic** 반유대주의의 **sentiment** 정서, 감정 **prompt** 촉발하다 **necessity** 필요성, 필요한 것 **Zionism** 시온주의 (유대인들의 국가 건설을 위한 민족주의 운동) **declaration** 선언 **back** 지지하다 **creation** 창조, 창설 **yearning** 갈망 **discrimination** 차별 **advocacy** 지지 **founding** 창립

21

창립 이후 3년이 여기 커브 사의 디자이너와 웹 개발자로 이루어진 우리 팀에게는 엄청나게 빨리 지나갔습니다. 회사의 창립 이후, 우리는 디지털의 창조적인 표현의 한계를 시험하고 기술 혁신에 이르기 위해 분투해왔습니다. 사용자 경험을 최우선으로 하는 것이 우리 작업의 신조이자 우리가 절대 타협하지 않는 원칙입니다. 실제로 의뢰인들이 정기적으로 알려오는 바에 따르면, 연구를 통해 그들 고객의 요구에 맞는 서비스를 제공하는 우리의 성실함으로 혼자서라면 절대 이루지 못했던 참신하고 귀중한 통찰력을 제공했다고 합니다.

Q 커브 사에 대해서 다음 중 옳은 것은?
(a) 느리게 출발한 후에 성공을 거두고 있다.
(b) 기술 개발을 외부에 위탁한다.
(c) 고객과의 관계보다 기술에 중점을 둔다.
(d) 고객 연구를 수행해서 의뢰인들을 돕는다.

해설 마지막 문장에서 커브 사는 의뢰인들을 위해 그들의 고객층(customer base)을 연구하는 일을 한다는 것을 알 수 있으므로 (d)가 정답이다.

incredibly 엄청나게 **explore** 탐구하다 **boundary** 경계 **innovation** 혁신 **priority** 우선순위 **hallmark** (전형적인) 특징 **principle** 원칙 **compromise** 타협하다 **diligence** 근면, 성실 **yield** (수익을) 내다 **invaluable** 귀중한 **insight** 통찰력 **outsource** 외부에 위탁하다

22

깡충 거미의 가장 흥미로운 특징 중 하나는 뛰어난 시력으로, 이는 네 쌍의 눈에 의해 가능하다. 거미의 얼굴에 위치해 있는 두 쌍 중 한 쌍인 앞 가운데 눈은 모든 쌍 중 가장 크며 깡충 거미가 3차원의 시력을 갖추도록 해준다. 이 눈 덕분에 깡충 거미는 대단히 정확하게 먹이의 위치를 파악할 수 있으며, 그 결과 뛰어올라 가하는 공격은 매우 치명적이다. 거미의 시력은 전자기 스펙트럼의 작은 부분에 한정되어 있는 인간의 눈보다 훨씬 예민하다. 깡충 거미는 인간에게는 보이지 않는 스펙트럼 대의 색상인 자외선도 감지할 수 있다.

Q 깡충 거미에 대해서 다음 중 옳은 것은?
(a) 8개의 눈에서 절반은 얼굴에 위치해 있다.
(b) 거미의 3차원 시력은 주로 공격을 피하기 위함이다.
(c) 자외선 시력은 먹이를 감지할 때 주로 사용된다.
(d) 시력의 예리함이 인간과 비슷하다.

해설 얼굴에 위치한 두 쌍(의 눈) 중 한 쌍은 가장 크다고 했으므로 정답은 (a)로 볼 수 있다. 3차원 시력으로 방어를 한다는 언급이나 자외선을 이용해 먹이를 감지한다는 언급은 없으므로 (b)와 (c)는 맞지 않다.

characteristic 특징 **jumping spider** 깡충 거미 **vision** 시력 **anterior median eye** 앞 가운데 눈 **equip A with B** A에게 B를 갖추게 하다 **three-dimensional** 3차원의 **locate** 위치를 알아내다 **exceptional** 이례적일 정도로 우수한 **precision** 정확성 **as a consequence** 그 결과 **leap** 뛰어오르다 **deadly** 치명적인 **sensitive** 예리한, 민감한 **segment** 부분, 조각 **electromagnetic spectrum** 전자기 스펙트럼 **perceive** 인지하다 **ultraviolet light** 자외선 **acuity** 예리함

23

1938년에 라디오 청취자들은 뉴스에서 매우 놀라운 소식을 들었는데, 지구가 외계 생명체에 의해 정복당하고 있다는 소식이었다. 물론, 1938년 10월 30일에 그런 침공은 일어나고 있지 않았다. 그것은 H.G. 웰즈의 1898년도 고전 공상과학 소설인 〈우주 전쟁〉을 극화한 것일 뿐으로, 할로윈 특별 프로그램으로 한 극단에서 제작한 것이었다. 공연은 청취자들이 뉴스 보도에서 듣는 데 익숙한 보도 방식을 취했기 때문에, 많은 사람들이 공황 상태에 빠졌다. 실제로 존재하는 나치의 침공에 대해 고조된 불안감이 외계인 침공이라는 말을 믿게 하는 역할을 했다.

Q 지문으로부터 유추할 수 있는 것은?
(a) 원작 소설에는 독일의 침공을 암시하는 부분이 없었다.
(b) 공연에는 노련한 뉴스 기자가 등장했다.
(c) 라디오는 뉴스를 전파하는 새로운 수단이었다.
(d) 미국 정부는 라디오 제작을 경제적으로 지원했다.

해설 원작 소설은 방송일인 1938년보다 훨씬 이전의 것이므로, 독일 침공과는 아무런 관련이 없음을 알 수 있으므로 (a)가 정답이다. 공연이 뉴스 보도 방식을 취한 것일 뿐, 기자가 등장한 것은 아니므로 (b)는 맞지 않다.

astonishing 매우 놀라운 **alien life form** 외계 생명체 **invasion** 침공 **dramatize** 각색하다 **classic** 고전의 **performance** 공연, 연기 **emulate** 모방하다 **be accustomed to** ~에 익숙하다 **panic** 공황 상태에 빠지다 **heightened** 고조된 **anxiety** 걱정, 불안 **believability** 믿을 수 있음 **allude** 암시하다 **feature** ~을 주연으로 하다 **veteran** 노련한 **medium** 매개체, 수단

24

1609년에서 1610년으로 넘어가는 겨울은 역사학자들 사이에서는 영국 정착지인 버지니아 주 제임스타운의 "기아 시대"로 알려져 있다. 이 호칭은 그 시절 제임스타운을 휩쓴 재난의 진상을 분명코 축소한 것인데, 그때 주민의 80퍼센트가 죽었다. 상황은 너무나 끔찍해서 먹기 위해 무덤에서 시체를 파낼 정도였다. 2012년 법인류학자들은 썰고 자르는 데 쓰는 가정용 도구로 도려낸 두개골 조각에서 식인 풍습의 물리적 증거를 회수했는데, 이는 사망한 이웃을 먹는 식민지 주민들이 휘두른 것으로 보인다.

Q 제임스타운 정착지에 대해서 유추할 수 있는 것은?
(a) 엄청난 파괴를 가져온 대규모 사망에서 전혀 회복하지 못했다.
(b) 주민 일부가 식량 때문에 서로를 죽였다.
(c) 주민들은 그곳의 환경에 대처할 준비가 부족했다.
(d) 역사학자들은 영국 식민지들 중에서 이례적인 곳으로 간주한다.

해설 제임스타운 정착지는 인육을 먹을 정도로 심각한 기아에 시달렸다고 했으므로 새로운 환경을 고려한 식량 준비가 제대로 되지 않았기 때문이라고 볼 수 있으므로 (c)가 적절하다. "기아 시대" 이후에 대한 언급은 없으므로 (a)에 대해서는 알 수 없다.

historian 역사학자 **starving** 기아 **settlement** 정착(지) **appellation** 명칭, 호칭 **arguably** 거의 틀림없이 **downplay** 경시하다, 축소하다 **scope** 범위 **sweep** 휩쓸다 **perish** 죽다 **dire** 끔찍한, 대단히 심각한 **corpse** 시체 **forensic anthropologist** 법인류학자 **cannibalism** 식인 풍습 **skull** 두개골 **fragment** 조각 **gouge** 도려내다 **chop** 썰다 **utensil** 가정용 도구, 기구 **ostensibly** 표면상으로 **wield** (도구를) 휘두르다 **colonist** 식민지 주민 **deceased** 사망한 **peer** 동료, 친구 **devastating** 대단히 파괴적인 **die-off** 종의 급격한 소멸 **ill equipped** 장비[준비]가 부족한 **anomaly** 변칙, 이례

25

영화 리뷰

〈철의 에티켓〉으로 도나 모리슨 감독이 불운한 연인들이자 운명의 힘에 의해 좌절된 관계인 퀴린과 맬로리의 대서사시로 돌아온다. 모리슨은 청춘들만이 지닐 수 있는 달콤한 이상주의에 들뜬 사랑에 관한 첫 영화 〈제노아에서의 밤들〉을 감독한 것은 15년 전이다. 그 이후 그녀의 인생은 영화 감독으로서 더 깊은 통찰력 주었다. 새 영화에서 모리슨의 카메라는 다른 디테일에 초점을 맞추고 있는데, 주인공에 대한 의미 있는 시각과 생계를 유지하는 현실이다. 데뷔 작품에서 두드러졌던 대담한 열정은 로맨스에 대한 더 섬세한 묘사로 대체되었으며, 이는 더 잔잔하고 절제된 반면, 현실에 대해서는 훨씬 더 의미가 깊어졌다.

Q 평론으로부터 유추할 수 있는 것은?
(a) 〈제노아에서의 밤들〉은 평론가들로부터 엇갈린 평가를 받았다.
(b) 〈철의 에티켓〉은 모리슨의 이전 영화를 다시 보여주고 있다.
(c) 모리슨의 새로운 영화는 그녀의 개인적 성장에서 영향을 받았다.
(d) 〈제노아에서의 밤들〉의 속편은 15년이라는 기간을 담고 있다.

해설 Her life experience since then has earned her deeper insights as movie director. In her new film, Morrison's lens focuses on different details를 통해 모리슨 감독의 지난 15년간의 성장이 영화에 나타났다는 것을 알 수 있으므로 (c)가 적절하다.

director 감독 saga 대하소설 luckless 운 나쁜 stymie 방해하다 fate 운명 buoy 기분 좋게[들뜨게] 하다 possess 소유하다, 지니다 insight 통찰력 glance 흘끗 봄 protagonist 주인공 brazen 뻔뻔한 subtle 미묘한 portrayal 묘사 understated 절제된 mixed review 엇갈린 평가 retell 바꾸어 이야기하다 sequel 속편

Part IV

26-27

혈액형이 성격을 결정하는가?

일본과 한국의 많은 이들은 혈액형이 성격적 특성을 '좌우한다'는 확고한 믿음을 갖고 있다. 이 믿음은 과학적으로 인정할 만한 요소가 있는가? 아니면 그저 잘못된 통념인가?

흥미롭게도, 역사상 가장 위대한 생물학자 가운데 한 명이었던 아리스토텔레스조차도 혈액형이 조상이 성격적 특성을 물려주는 데 주된 역할을 맡는다고 생각했다. 그럼에도 불구하고, 대다수의 과학자들은 혈액형이 어떤 유의미한 방식으로든 성격에 영향을 미친다는 증거가 거의 없다는 데 동의한다.

마리 야마구치에 따르면, 이 '이론'은 나치가 유대인을 포함해서, 독일인이 아닌 이들을 차별하는 것을 정당화하기 위한 노력의 일환으로 이용되었다고 한다. 독일들 가운데는 A형과 O형이 흔한 데 반해, 유대인과 다른 민족 집단에는 B형이 꽤 흔하다. 나치는 그런 차이가 독일인들이 다른 국민들에 비해 우월하다는 증거라고 주장했다. 그렇지만 나치조차도 결국에는 너무 비과학적이어서 이 이론을 포기했다.

1970년대에 이 비과학적인 이론을 부활시켜서 대중화한 이는 바로 마사히코 노미였다. 그때 이래로, 이 잘못된 통념은 많은 면에서 일본과 한국에 부정적인 영향을 미쳐왔는데, 이는 「삶과 과학」의 다음 호에서 다룰 것이다.

26

Q 기사에 따르면, 다음 중 옳은 것은?
(a) 일본과 한국은 유대인의 민족적 특성에 대해 공통의 잘못된 통념을 공유한다.
(b) 아리스토텔레스의 성격적 특성에 대한 이론은 경험적 증거에 근거했다.
(c) 야마구치는 오랫동안 의학 분야에서 교육을 받았다.
(d) 과학적으로 인정할 만한 요소가 없어서 나치는 혈액형의 성격에 대한 영향 이론을 포기했다.

해설 (a)는 일본과 한국이 혈액형과 성격 사이의 관계에 대한 잘못된 통념을 공유하는 것이기 때문에 오답이다. (b)는 기사에서 언급하지 않은 내용이므로 정답이 아니다. (c)는 야마구치의 의학적 배경에 대한 언급이 없기 때문에 오답이다. 따라서 정답은 기사의 내용에 충실한 (d)이다.

27

Q 기사로부터 추론할 수 있는 것은?
(a) 성격적 특성이 혈액형에 의해 결정된다는 것은 과학적으로 입증되었다.
(b) 유전이라는 개념은 아리스토텔레스가 처음으로 제안했다.
(c) 나치는 독일인들이 열등한 국민들을 차별해도 된다고 믿었다.
(d) 노미는 나치의 극단적인 이념을 강력하게 지지했다.

해설 (a)는 기사의 내용에 어긋나기 때문에 오답이다. (b)는 그렇게 판단할 근거가 전혀 제시되어 있지 않기 때문에 반드시 오답으로 처리해야 한다. 설령 아리스토텔레스가 유전이라는 개념을 실제로 처음으로 제안했다고 하더라도, 기사에 그 내용이 없기 때문에 오답이다. (d)는 전형적인 비약인데, 노미는 부활시킨 것은 혈액형과 성격 사이의 관계에 대한 이론이므로 오답이다. 따라서 정답은 기사에서 자연스럽게 추론할 수 있는 (c)이다.

personality 성격, 개성 firmly 확고히, 단호히 dictate 좌우하다, 결정하다 trait 특성, 특징 merit 가치, 장점 myth 근거 없는 통념 pass down 물려주다 justify 정당화하다 ethnic 인종의, 민족의 people 국민, 민족; 사람들 abandon 버리다, 포기하다 revive 부활시키다 popularize 대중화하다 renounce 단념하다, 포기하다 heredity 유전

28-29

비즈니스 〉 지역   그린타임스

지역 경제단체들은 일관성을 요구한다

수요일에, 리치빌 상공회의소를 포함한 지역 경제단체들과 협회들은 시 정부가 리치빌시(市)에 영향을 미치는 중요한 정책을 일관되게 추구할 것을 요구했다. 특히 이 단체들은 외국인직접투자(FDI)에 대한 시 정부의 정책이 너무도 오랫동안 갈팡질팡했다고 우려를 표명했다.

리치빌 상공회의소에 따르면, 리치빌시는 전통적으로 FDI에 대해 개방적이었다고 한다. 그렇지만 2016년에 시 정부는 갑작스럽게 방향을 바꿔서 많은 FDI에 적대적인 정책들을 시행했다. 그때 이래로, 시 정부는 FDI에 대해 일관성이 없었다. 그 결과 많은 다국적 기업들이 리치빌시에 직접 투자를 꺼리고 있다. 또한 현재 너무도 많은 시민들이 FDI가 지역 경제에 해롭다고 생각한다.

리치빌 상공회의소는 이처럼 세계화된 세상에서 FDI가 리치빌시에 경제적 번영을 가져오는 주된 요인이라고 지적한다. 물론 지역 경제협회들은 시 정부가 그 사실을 인식할 것을 요구한다. 그렇지만 지금으로서는 시 정부의 정책이 FDI에 대해 최소한 일관성이 있었으면 좋겠다고 희망한다. 그렇게 일관성이 있다면, 모든 이해 당사자들이 잘 알고서 투자 결정을 내리는 데 도움이 될 것이다.

28 Q 경체단체들과 협회들이 시 정부에 대해 주로 바라는 것은?

(a) 보다 수익성이 있는 투자 결정을 내리는 것

(b) 관련된 모든 당사자들에게 분명한 메시지를 전하는 것

(c) 세계화된 세상에서 훨씬 더 경쟁력을 갖추는 것

(d) 경제단체들과 협회들이 해외 시장으로 진입하는 데 도움을 주기 위해 노력하는 것

해설 이처럼 전반적인 정보를 측정하는 유형은 제목이나 첫 단락의 첫 문장에 중요한 단서가 있다. 이 문항의 경우에도, 제목으로부터 경제단체들의 핵심 요구 사항이 정책의 일관성임을 알 수 있다. 따라서 정답은 (b)이다.

29 Q 지문으로부터 추론할 수 있는 것은?

(a) 리치빌의 시민들의 일부만이 대부분 FDI에 맹렬하게 반대한다.

(b) 리치빌 상공회의소는 다국적 기업들이 리치빌시에 직접 투자를 하기를 원할 수도 있다.

(c) 시 정부는 정치적 이득을 위해 리치빌시에 더 많은 FDI를 유치하기로 결정할 가능성이 높다.

(d) FDI가 경제성장을 가져오는 데 담당하는 역할은 대단히 과대평가되어 있다.

해설 (a)는 '너무도 많은 시민들'이 대부분의 시민들은 아닐 수 있기 때문에 오답이다. (c)는 현재 시 정부의 정책에 일관성이 없어서 이렇게 추론할 수 없기 때문에, 정답이 아니다. (d)는 과대평가되었다고 추론할 수 있는 근거가 없으므로 오답이다. 따라서 정답은 지문의 내용으로부터 자연스럽게 추론할 수 있는 (b)이다.

consistency 일관성 **association** 협회 **consistent** 일관된, 한결같은 **vacillate** 동요하다 **change course** 진로를 바꾸다 **implement** 시행하다 **inconsistent** 일관성이 없는 **multinational corporation** 다국적 기업 **detrimental** 해로운 **prosperity** 번영, 번성 **profitable** 수익성이 있는 **vehemently** 격렬하게, 맹렬히 **vastly** 엄청나게

30-31

주민 안내문

많은 이들에게, 블루힐빌리지는 편안한 생활의 이미지를 떠올리게 합니다. 그렇지만 저희가 주민들이 서로와 사교적으로 상호작용을 할 수 있는 기회를 충분히 제공한다는 사실을 알고 있는 이들은 많지 않습니다. 저희가 그만큼 사회적 상호작용을 중시하는 이유는 그것이 행복의 참된 비결이기 때문입니다. 저희는 주민들이 모두 진정으로 행복하기를 원합니다.

다음의 프로그램들은 주민들 사이의 사회적 상호작용을 증진할 의도로 기획되었습니다.

■ 영화 감상 모임: 현재 6개의 영화 감상 모임이 있으며, 어떤 모임에든 가입하실 수 있습니다.

■ 명상 모임: 현재로서는, 주민들이 8개의 명상 모임에 가입할 수 있습니다.

■ 종교 활동 모임: 15개의 종교 활동 모임이 영적인 것을 추구하는 어떤 이든 환영합니다.

■ 운동 모임: 체력이 강해지는 데 관심이 있는 누구든 9개의 운동 모임에 가입할 수 있습니다.

영적인 것을 추구하고 싶으시다면, melanie_j@bluehillvillage.com로 멜라니 존슨에게 연락하세요. 다른 것들을 추구하고 싶으시면, julia_b@bluehillvillage.com로 줄리아 블랙에게 연락하세요.

30 Q 누가 존슨에게 이메일을 보낼 가능성이 가장 높은가?

(a) 명상이 건강에 미치는 효과를 연구한 아만다

(b) 어린 시절 이래로 기독교에 관심이 있는 존

(c) 가장 좋아하는 영화 장르가 공포영화인 신시아

(d) 빈혈이 생긴 리처드

해설 안내문에서 영적인 것이 종교라고 밝혔기 때문에 정답은 (b)이다. 이 유형은 NEW TEPS로 전환되면서 새롭게 제시된 문제 유형인데, 지문 전체를 빨리 읽고 필요한 정보를 신속하게 찾는 연습을 통해 효과적으로 대비할 수 있는 문제 유형이다. 독해 파트 4에서 시간 부족을 호소하는 수험생이 의외로 많은데, 이와 같은 유형에서 문제를 푸는 시간을 줄여야 안정적으로 시간 관리가 가능함을 명심해야 한다.

31 Q 안내문으로부터 추론할 수 있는 것은?

(a) 블루힐빌리지는 헌신적인 의사들이 있는, 높이 평가되는 요양원이다.

(b) 근래에 운동 모임의 수가 급격히 증가하고 있다.

(c) 종교 활동 모임은 영화 감상 모임과 긴장된 관계를 맺어왔다.

(d) 거주민이 아닌 이들은 명상 모임에 가입할 자격이 없을지도 모른다.

해설 (a)와 (b)는 안내문의 내용만으로는 추론할 수 없는 사항이므로 오답이다. (c)는 일반적인 상식을 잘못 활용할 때 고를 수도 있는 오답이다. 안내문의 내용만으로는 그런 긴장된 관계를 생각할 수 없다. (d)는 명상 모임에 주민이 가입할 수 있다고 말한 내용으로부터 자연스럽게 추론할 수 있는 사항이므로 정답이다.

notice 공문문; 통지 **conjure up** 떠올리게 하다 **ample** 충분한 **socially** 사교적으로; 사회적으로 **value** 중요시하다 **genuine** 진정으로, 순수하게 **promote** 증진하다, 촉진하다 **meditation** 명상 **spirituality** 영성(靈性) **Christianity** 기독교 **anaemia** 빈혈 **nursing home** 요양원

32-33

http://www.Greenbaum-Pharmaceutical.com/our-heritage

핵심 가치 ∨ **우리의 유산** ∨ 제품 ∨ 연혁 ∨ 연락

우리의 유산

오늘날 그린바움제약은 세계에서 가장 존경을 받는 제약회사들 가운데 하나입니다. 매년 수십억 명의 소비자들이 저희를 전적으로 신뢰하기 때문에 저희의 의약품을 구매합니다. 저희는 결코 그 신뢰를 당연한 것으로 여긴 적이 없습니다.

1899년에 제니퍼 그린바움이 자매인 로라와 레베카와 함께 그린바움제약을 설립했을 때, 그린바움제약은 환자들의 건강상태를 향상시키는 데 헌신하는 작은 기업이었습니다. 현재 저희는 세계에서 가장 큰 제약회사들 가운데 하나입니다. 저희의 기적적인 성장은 소중한 고객들의 신뢰가 없었다면 불가능했을 것입니다.

그것이 저희의 가장 중요한 유산들 가운데 하나이며, 그에 대해 저희는 긍지를 갖고 있습니다. 조금의 주저함도 없이, 저희는 고객들이 항상 저희를 신뢰하실 수 있다고 확언할 수 있습니다. 그 신뢰를 결코 배반하지 않겠습니다.

32 Q 웹페이지에 따르면, 다음 중 옳은 것은?

(a) 회사의 핵심 가치에는 너그러움과 인내가 포함된다.

(b) 회사를 설립했을 때, 제니퍼는 레베카보다 훨씬 더 나이가 많았다.

(c) 회사는 세계에서 가장 오래된 제약회사들 가운데 하나이다.

(d) 회사는 가족 소유의 회사로 시작했다.

해설 세부 사항 유형이기 때문에, 주어진 내용을 하나하나씩 확인해야 한다. (a)는 우선 이 웹페이지가 회사의 핵심 가치를 나타내는 페이지도 아니며, 내용에도 없기 때문에 오답이다. (b)는 자매 관계에서 나이에 대한 정보가 제공되지 않았으므로 정답이 아니다. (c)는 가장 오래되었는지의 여부를 알 수 없다. 따라서 정답은 웹페이지의 내용에 충실한 (d)이다.

33 Q 웹페이지로부터 추론할 수 있는 것은?
(a) 회사는 수십억 계열의 의약제품들을 갖추고 있다.
(b) 회사에 단골 고객이 많은 가능성이 높다.
(c) 레베카가 회사의 현재 최고경영자일 가능성이 아주 높다.
(d) 회사의 본사는 본래 독일에 있었다.

해설 (a)는 의약품을 구입하는 고객 수가 수십억이라고 했지 제품군이 수십억이라고 하지 않았으므로 오답이다. (c)와 (d)는 웹페이지에 추론의 근거가 전혀 제시되어 있지 않으므로 정답이 아니다. 정답은 항상 주어진 내용에 근거해야 함을 명심해야 한다. 따라서 정답은 지문의 내용으로부터 자연스럽게 추론이 가능한 (b)이다.

heritage 유산 **pharmaceutical** 제약의 **medical** 의학의, 의료의 **take for granted** 당연시하다 **found** 설립하다 **dedicated** 헌신적인, 전념하는 **miraculous** 기적적인 **valued** 소중한, 귀중한 **take pride in** ~을 자랑스러워하다 **reservation** 의구심; 예약 **assure** 확약하다, 보증하다 **betray** 배신하다 **generosity** 후하게 베푸는 것 **perseverance** 인내 **line** (제품의) 종류

34-35

◁ 수잔

⟨나⟩
안녕, 수잔. 7월에 만나고 싶은 마음이 간절하구나. 또한 이 제임스라는 사람에게 의심이 간다고 말하지 않을 수 없구나. 왜 그가 너를 데리러 공항에 오려고 할까? 그는 심지어 너를 만난 적조차 없잖아.

물론, 인터넷상의 관계가 아름다운 것으로 성장할 수도 있어. 그렇지만 다른 누군가와 진정한 관계를 쌓는 데는 시간이 많이 필요하다는 사실을 명심해야 해. 정말로 제임스를 신뢰할 수 있는지 좀 더 기다려 보는 건 어떨까? 단지 네가 안전하길 바랄 뿐이야.

⟨수잔⟩
안녕, 잭. 너와 대화를 나누는 것은 언제나 기쁜 일이야. 친절한 말에 미소를 짓게 되는데, 그래서 아주 고마워. 물론 7월에 만나길 고대하고 있단다. 토론토에서 행복한 추억들을 많이 만들었는데, 도쿄에서도 그런 기회가 있기를 바란단다.

내 안전에 대해 신경을 써 줘서 고마워. 음, 제임스가 나쁜 사람이라고 생각하지는 않아. 그렇지만 격언에서 말하듯이, "후회하는 것보다는 조심하는 게 낫지." 대중교통을 이용하기로 결정했어. 다시 한 번, 올바른 충고를 해 줘서 고마워.

34 Q 잭은 왜 메시지를 보냈는가?
(a) 제임스가 납치할 것이라고 수잔에게 경고하기 위해서
(b) 수잔에게 안전한 행동 방침을 권하기 위해서
(c) 수잔에게 공항에 데리러 갈 것이라고 다시 알려 주기 위해서
(d) 인터넷상에서 사람을 만나지 말라고 수잔에게 충고하기 위해서

해설 (a)는 전형적인 비약에 해당하는 선택지이다. 잭이 제임스에 대해 의심을 갖고 있지만, 그것은 온라인을 통해서 알게 된 사이라는 이유 때문이다. (c)는 잭이 데리러 가는 것이 아니므로 오답이다. (d)는 잭이 하고 싶은 말은 진정한 관계를 쌓는 데 시간이 걸린다는 것으로, 꼭 온라인으로 사람을 만나지 말라는 것이 아니기 때문에 정답이 아니다. 따라서 정답은 잭의 의도를 정확히 말한 (b)이다.

35 Q 채팅 메시지로부터 추론할 수 있는 것은?
(a) 수잔은 인터넷상에서 굉장히 인기가 많다.
(b) 수잔은 제임스와 오랫동안 서신을 주고받았다.
(c) 수잔과 잭은 7월에 도쿄에서 만날 가능성이 높다.
(d) 수잔은 제임스에게 악랄한 동기가 있다고 확신한다.

해설 (a)는 지나친 비약이다. 주어진 메시지로부터 알 수 있는 내용은 수잔이 제임스와 온라인으로 만났다는 내용밖에 없다. (b)는 주어진 메시지로 봐서 '오랫동안' 서로를 아는 사이라고 할 수 없기 때문에 오답이다. (d)는 나쁜 사람이라고 생각하지 않는다고 말했으므로 정답이 아니다. 따라서 정답은 채팅 메시지에 충실한 (c)이다.

suspicious 의심하는 **appreciate** 감사하다; 가치가 오르다 **public transportation** 대중교통 **sound** 건전한 **kidnap** 납치하다 **correspond** 서신을 주고받다 **heinous** 극악무도한

Actual Test 2 — Answer Keys

청해 Listening Comprehension p.59

1 (c) 2 (d) 3 (a) 4 (d) 5 (c) 6 (d) 7 (c) 8 (a) 9 (c) 10 (a)
11 (b) 12 (c) 13 (a) 14 (b) 15 (d) 16 (c) 17 (d) 18 (d) 19 (c) 20 (b)
21 (c) 22 (d) 23 (b) 24 (c) 25 (c) 26 (c) 27 (c) 28 (d) 29 (d) 30 (d)
31 (b) 32 (d) 33 (a) 34 (d) 35 (b) 36 (a) 37 (b) 38 (c) 39 (d) 40 (b)

어휘 Vocabulary p.65

1 (a) 2 (b) 3 (d) 4 (a) 5 (a) 6 (c) 7 (b) 8 (a) 9 (b) 10 (d)
11 (b) 12 (d) 13 (d) 14 (d) 15 (c) 16 (c) 17 (c) 18 (d) 19 (b) 20 (a)
21 (d) 22 (d) 23 (a) 24 (b) 25 (d) 26 (a) 27 (a) 28 (b) 29 (c) 30 (c)

문법 Grammar p.69

1 (d) 2 (a) 3 (d) 4 (b) 5 (b) 6 (d) 7 (a) 8 (a) 9 (c) 10 (c)
11 (b) 12 (a) 13 (b) 14 (c) 15 (b) 16 (b) 17 (a) 18 (c) 19 (d) 20 (c)
21 (c) 22 (c) 23 (a) 24 (b) 25 (a) 26 (b) 27 (b) 28 (a) 29 (b) 30 (b)

독해 Reading Comprehension p.73

1 (d) 2 (a) 3 (b) 4 (c) 5 (a) 6 (c) 7 (d) 8 (a) 9 (a) 10 (c)
11 (b) 12 (a) 13 (d) 14 (b) 15 (a) 16 (c) 17 (c) 18 (d) 19 (d) 20 (d)
21 (d) 22 (c) 23 (c) 24 (b) 25 (c) 26 (c) 27 (d) 28 (b) 29 (c) 30 (d)
31 (b) 32 (b) 33 (b) 34 (a) 35 (d)

Part I

1

M When can I expect to see you again?

W _____

(a) Four weeks ago tomorrow.
(b) It's been quite a while.
(c) I'll stop by before long.
(d) Not as often as I'd like.

M 당신을 언제 다시 볼 수 있을까요?

W _____

(a) 4주 전 내일이요.
(b) 꽤 오랜만이군요.
(c) 머지않아 들를게요.
(d) 내가 원하는 것만큼 자주는 못 봐요.

It's been quite a while. 꽤 오랜만이다. **stop by** 들르다 **before long** 머지않아

2

W Any word on our product shipment?

M _____

(a) It's supposedly made by hand.
(b) Used merchandise is cheaper.
(c) I'd be happy to bring it back.
(d) I'm sure it'll be here in no time.

W 저희 상품 배송에 대해 하실 말씀이라도 있나요?

M _____

(a) 아마 수제품일 거예요.
(b) 중고품이 더 저렴해요.
(c) 그걸 돌려주시면 좋겠네요.
(d) 분명히 금방 도착할 거라고 믿어요.

shipment 배송 **supposedly** 아마 **used merchandise** 중고품 **in no time** 즉시

3

M Miranda, how did you ever find this cozy café?

W _____

(a) I just happened on it one day.
(b) I'm not quite ready to order yet.
(c) I'm glad you feel the same way.
(d) I still prefer your other coffee brand.

M 미란다, 이 아늑한 카페를 도대체 어떻게 알게 됐니?

W _____

(a) 어느 날 그냥 우연히 발견했어.
(b) 아직 주문할 준비가 안 됐어.
(c) 같은 생각이라서 기뻐.
(d) 여전히 너의 다른 커피 브랜드가 더 좋아.

cozy 아늑한 **happen on** 우연히 발견하다 **feel the same way** 동감이다

4

W We exceeded our sales target last quarter.

M _____

(a) Each sale gets a commission.
(b) I'll take ten at the discount.
(c) Right, and they did it again.
(d) By quite a bit, I hear.

W 지난 분기에 판매 목표를 초과했어요.

M _____

(a) 판매할 때마다 수수료가 붙어요.
(b) 할인할 때 10개를 살게요.
(c) 맞아요, 그래서 그들이 또 한 번 해냈어요.
(d) 그것도 꽤 많이라고 들었어요.

exceed 초과하다 **commission** 수수료 **quite a bit** 상당량

5

W Who oversees building maintenance here?

M _____

(a) Dr. Park will be overseeing your case.
(b) We all help out with the housework.
(c) You want Mr. Hendrick on floor 2.
(d) It's an owner-occupied home.

W 이곳 건물 관리를 감독하는 분이 누구시죠?

M _____

(a) 닥터 박이 당신의 증상을 살필 거예요.
(b) 우리 모두 집안일을 도와요.
(c) 2층에 계시는 헨드릭 씨예요.
(d) 이 집에는 집주인이 직접 살고 있어요.

oversee 감독하다 **maintenance** 관리, 정비 **help out** 도와주다 **housework** 집안일 **owner-occupied** 집주인 자신이 살고 있는

6

M Where is the janitorial staff going?

W _____

(a) I'll find someone to clean it up.
(b) The talk was about their benefits.
(c) They're based out of Philadelphia.
(d) A meeting with the boss was called.

M 청소부원이 어디로 가고 있나요?
W _____

(a) 청소할 사람을 찾겠습니다.
(b) 회의에서 그들의 수당에 관한 말이 오고 갔어요.
(c) 그들은 필라델피아에 기반을 두고 있어요.
(d) 사장님이 참석하는 회의가 소집되었거든요.

janitorial 수위의, 잡역부의   **benefit** 수당, 혜택   **be based out of**
~에 기지가 있다, ~에 기반을 두다   **call** 소집하다

7

W Won't your bike get stolen if you leave it unlocked?
M _____

(a) No, I bought this bike fair and square.
(b) You can file a report with the police.
(c) It'll only be unattended for a moment.
(d) Yes, I prefer walking over driving.

W 자전거를 잠그지 않고 두면 도난당하지 않을까?
M _____

(a) 아니, 이 자전거는 돈 내고 정직하게 구입한 거야.
(b) 경찰에 신고해도 좋아.
(c) 잠시만 내버려둘 거야.
(d) 응, 운전하는 것보다 걷는 게 더 좋아.

fair and square 정직하게   **file a report** 신고하다   **unattended**
방치된, 지켜보는 사람이 없는

8

M Why must the air conditioner be set so low?
W _____

(a) I can turn it up if you're still hot.
(b) We're going to save a lot on heating.
(c) Open a window and feel the cold air.
(d) It's one of the latest models out there.

M 에어컨을 그렇게 약하게 설정해 둬야 하는 이유가 뭐죠?
W _____

(a) 아직도 덥다면 세기를 높여 드릴 수 있어요.
(b) 난방비가 많이 절약될 거예요.
(c) 창문을 열어 시원한 바람을 쐬세요.
(d) 이것은 최신 모델 중의 하나예요.

latest (가장) 최근의, 최신의

9

W What department are you from again?
M _____

(a) Sure, let's meet there at 3.
(b) No, not the sales department.
(c) Oh, I don't actually work here.
(d) Well, my passion is in finance.

W 어느 부서에서 오셨다고요?
M _____

(a) 좋아요, 3시에 그곳에서 만납시다.
(b) 아니요, 영업부가 아니에요.
(c) 실은 이 회사에서 일하지 않아요.
(d) 저는 금융 부문에 열정을 갖고 있어요.

department 부서   **passion** 열정   **finance** 금융

10

W You said you had some urgent news for me.
M _____

(a) You'd better brace yourself.
(b) I get my news from the radio.
(c) It'll be ready by the end of the week.
(d) My job is my number-one priority.

W 나에게 긴급히 전할 소식이 있다며?
M _____

(a) 마음의 준비를 단단히 하는 게 좋을 거야.
(b) 나는 라디오를 통해 뉴스를 알게 돼.
(c) 그건 이번 주 끝 무렵에 준비될 거야.
(d) 직장이 나의 최우선 사항이야.

urgent 긴급한   **brace oneself** 마음의 준비를 다하다   **number-**
one priority 최우선 사항[과제, 목표]

Part II

11

W Did the new guy take inventory yesterday?
M Yes, I showed him the ropes.
W Well, he filled out the stock form all wrong.
M _____

(a) I'll fill his order right away.
(b) Maybe I wasn't clear enough.
(c) Let me train him on inventory.
(d) It's him you should be mad at.

W 새로 온 사람이 어제 재고 조사를 했나요?
M 네, 제가 요령을 가르쳐 주었어요.
W 재고 양식을 모두 잘못 작성했던데요.
M _____

(a) 즉시 그의 주문대로 이행할게요.
(b) 아마도 제 말이 똑바로 전달되지 않은 것 같군요.
(c) 그에게 재고 교육을 할게요.
(d) 당신이 화내야 할 사람은 그예요.

take inventory 재고 조사를 하다   **rope** 요령   **fill out** 작성하다
stock 재고   **form** 양식   **fill an order** 주문에 응하다

12

W Mason, what's the rush?
M I have a class in Arnold Hall in two minutes.
W You'll never make it on time!
M _____

(a) But I promise I'll be punctual.
(b) Right, so I'd better call ahead.
(c) Don't worry, I know a shortcut.
(d) I have two weeks to finish the essay.

W 메이슨, 뭐가 그리 급해?
M 2분 후에 아놀드 홀에서 수업이 있어.
W 정각에 절대로 도착하지 못할 걸!
M _____

(a) 하지만 앞으로 시간을 엄수하겠다고 약속할게.
(b) 맞아, 그래서 미리 전화하는 편이 낫겠어.
(c) 걱정하지 마, 지름길을 알고 있거든.
(d) 2주 동안 보고서를 끝내야 해.

What's the rush? 뭐가 그렇게 바쁜 거야? **make it** 시간 맞춰 가다
punctual 시간을 잘 지키는 **shortcut** 지름길

13

M Where did you get this copper figurine?
W On a recent trip to Bali.
M The craftsmanship is exquisite.
W _____

(a) It cost me a small fortune.
(b) The artist wouldn't tell me.
(c) I'd like to go there myself.
(d) The store is just down the road.

M 구리로 된 이 작은 조각상을 어디서 구했어?
W 최근에 발리 여행을 갔다가 구했어.
M 솜씨가 정교한데.
W _____

(a) 돈이 꽤 들었지.
(b) 예술가가 나에게 말해 주려고 하지 않아.
(c) 나도 그곳에 가보고 싶어.
(d) 가게는 이 길 따라가면 있어.

copper 구리 **figurine** 작은 조각상 **craftsmanship** 손재주, 솜씨
exquisite 정교한 **small fortune** 상당한 돈

14

M Hi, United Bank? I misplaced my credit card last night.
W Would you like for me to put a hold on the account?
M Yes, it might have been stolen.
W _____

(a) That's a shame. We'll hold onto it then.
(b) Alright. Your card is on hold now.
(c) Sure thing. We can hold it over there.
(d) Then could you please re-activate it soon?

M 안녕하세요, 유나이티드 은행이죠? 어젯밤에 신용 카드를 어디에 뒀는지 모르겠어요.
W 계좌를 정지시키겠습니까?
M 네, 도난당했는지도 모르거든요.
W _____

(a) 유감입니다. 그렇다면 그 카드를 유지하겠습니다.
(b) 알겠습니다. 귀하의 카드는 이제 정지되었습니다.
(c) 당연하죠. 우리가 저기서 정지할 수 있어요.
(d) 그럼 곧 그 카드의 효력을 다시 발생시키실 수 있나요?

misplace 제자리에 두지 않다 **activate** 작동시키다

15

M Check out this shirt I just bought.
W Hey, that looks really sharp.
M You don't think it's too formal, do you?
W _____

(a) I'm not a fan of green.
(b) Try the three-piece suit.
(c) If they have it in my size.
(d) Just undo the top button.

M 방금 산 이 셔츠 좀 봐 주세요.
W 꽤 맵시 있어 보이는데요.
M 너무 격식을 차린 것 같지는 않죠?
W _____

(a) 나는 초록색을 그다지 좋아하지 않아요.
(b) 스리피스 슈트를 입어 보세요.
(c) 내게 맞는 크기의 셔츠를 갖고 있다면요.
(d) 맨 위 단추를 한번 풀어 보세요.

sharp 멋진, 맵시 있는 **three-piece suit** 세 가지가 갖추어진 한 벌의
양복(상의, 조끼, 바지) **undo** 풀다

16

W How much was your tax rebate this year?
M Actually, I didn't get a rebate.
W What? Weren't you entitled to one?
M _____

(a) Yes, but I already received it last year.
(b) No, I'm happy with my salary.
(c) Not according to my accountant.
(d) Apparently I'm getting money back.

W 올해 세금 환급액이 얼마였어요?
M 실은 환급을 받지 않았어요.
W 뭐라고요? 받을 자격이 안 되었나요?
M _____

(a) 맞아요, 하지만 작년에 이미 수령했어요.
(b) 아니요, 급여에 만족해요.
(c) 회계사의 말에 의하면 그렇대요.
(d) 분명히 돈을 돌려받을 거예요.

tax rebate 세금 환급 **be entitled to** ~을 받을 자격이 있다
accountant 회계사 **apparently** 분명히

17

M What wild weather you have here.
W It's not always this windy, if that's what you mean.
M I was worried a hurricane was blowing in.
W _____

(a) This is the norm during the summer.
(b) It seems to happen about once a week.
(c) We usually make sure to stay indoors.
(d) It's just a freak thunderstorm.

M 날씨가 사납군요.
W 바람이 많이 불어서 그런 표현을 쓴 것 같은데, 항상 이렇지는 않아요.
M 허리케인이 아닌지 걱정했어요.
W _____

(a) 여름에는 늘 이렇습니다.
(b) 일주일에 한 번은 발생하는 것 같아요.
(c) 보통 우리는 실내에 있으려 하죠.
(d) 그냥 돌발적인 뇌우예요.

windy 바람이 많이 부는 **freak** 돌발적인 **thunderstorm** 뇌우

18

W I hear our hiring committee is still deliberating.
M There must have been a lot of qualified candidates.
W Or a bunch of poorly qualified ones.
M _____

(a) I'm sure it wasn't intentional.
(b) He's just trying to do his job.
(c) I'll put in a good word for you.
(d) You sound a little pessimistic.

W 인사 위원회에서 여전히 심의 중이라고 하던데요.
M 자질이 있는 후보가 많은 게 틀림없어요.
W 아니면 별 자질이 없는 후보가 많은지도 모르죠.
M _____

(a) 고의가 아닌 게 확실해요.
(b) 그는 본분을 다하려고 노력할 뿐이에요.
(c) 제가 잘 말씀드리겠습니다.
(d) 다소 비관적으로 말씀하시네요.

hiring committee 인사[채용] 위원회 **deliberate** 심의하다
qualified 자격[자질]이 있는 **candidate** 후보 **a bunch of** 다수의
intentional 고의적인 **do one's job** 본분을 다하다 **put in a
good word for** ~을 지지하는 말을 해주다 **pessimistic** 비관적인,
염세적인

19

M Who's responsible for all the layoffs?
W The CEO made the cuts himself.
M I'd like to give him a piece of my mind.
W _____

(a) But twenty percent of the staff was fired.
(b) Mr. Tim Takaro has been nominated.
(c) You'll probably have to get in line.
(d) It might be bad news instead.

M 이 모든 해고 사태의 책임자가 누구죠?
W 최고경영자가 직접 잘랐어요.
M 그에게 따끔하게 한마디 해 줘야겠어요.
W _____

(a) 하지만 직원 20퍼센트가 해고됐어요.
(b) 팀 타카로 씨가 임명되었어요.
(c) 당신도 아마 해고당하는 줄에 서게 될지도 몰라요.
(d) 오히려 나쁜 소식일 수 있어요.

layoff 일시 해고 **give a piece of one's mind** 따끔하게 한마디 하다
nominate 임명하다 **get in line** 줄에 들어가 서다

20

W Sir, we're going to fit your arm with a cast.
M How long will I have to wear it?
W It's up to the doctor, but probably around six weeks.
M _____

(a) He doesn't have the best bedside manner.
(b) I guess it takes that long for bone to heal.
(c) I'm glad that I can freely move my arms.
(d) Here's a pen to sign my cast with.

W 우리가 선생님 팔을 깁스로 고정할 거예요.
M 그걸 얼마나 하고 있어야 하나요?
W 의사한테 달렸지만 아마도 6주간은 해야 할 거예요.
M _____

(a) 환자를 대하는 그의 태도가 썩 좋지는 않던데요.
(b) 뼈가 나으려면 그 정도는 걸릴 거예요.
(c) 팔을 자유롭게 움직일 수 있어서 다행이에요.
(d) 여기 깁스에 서명할 펜이 있어요.

fit 맞게 달다[설치하다] **cast** 깁스 **up to** ~의 책임인 **bedside
manner** 환자를 대하는 의사의 태도 **heal** 낫다

Part III

21

Listen to a conversation between two friends.

> W Did your company employ a social media manager yet?
> M Not that I'm aware of. Are you interested?
> W No, but my niece Wendy has loads of experience.
> M Get her to contact me and I'll refer her.
> W That would be fantastic.
> M Here, take my card and give it to her.

Q What is mainly taking place in the conversation?
(a) The speakers are assessing job applicants.
(b) The speakers are discussing social media issues.
(c) The woman is recommending a relative for a job.
(d) The man is offering the woman his business card.

두 친구의 대화를 들으시오.

> W 너희 회사에서 이미 소셜 미디어 책임자를 뽑았니?
> M 아직 안 뽑은 걸로 알고 있어. 관심 있니?
> W 아니, 하지만 내 조카딸 웬디가 그쪽으로 경험이 많아.
> M 내게 연락하라고 해. 그러면 내가 주선할게.
> W 그렇게 되면 정말 좋겠다.
> M 여기, 내 명함이야. 그녀에게 전해줘.

Q 주로 일어나고 있는 일은?
(a) 화자들이 취업 지원자들을 평가하고 있다.
(b) 화자들이 소셜 미디어 문제에 대해 논의하고 있다.
(c) 여자가 취직자리에 친척을 추천하고 있다.
(d) 남자가 여자에게 명함을 주고 있다.

social media 소셜 미디어 **Not that I'm aware of.** 내가 알기에는 아냐. **niece** 조카딸 **loads of** 많은 **refer** 맡기다, 회부하다 **card** 명함(business card) **assess** 평가하다 **applicant** 지원자 **relative** 친척

22

Listen to a conversation in a workplace.

> M Have you picked up a company ID badge yet?
> W Yes, I did that first thing this morning.
> M Great. Now you'll need to stop by Human Resources.
> W To choose a benefits plan? Already done.
> M Good! Have you been assigned an office desk yet?
> W No, I'm waiting to hear back from the department head.

Q What is mainly being discussed in the conversation?
(a) A problem with the woman's identification
(b) A change in the woman's benefits package
(c) The transfer of the woman's equipment
(d) The woman's starting out at a new place

직장에서 이뤄지는 대화를 들으시오.

> M 회사 배지를 찾아왔나요?
> W 네, 오늘 아침에 그걸 제일 먼저 했어요.
> M 좋아요. 그럼 이제 인사부에 들르셔야 할 거예요.
> W 복리후생 제도를 고르는 것 때문에요? 그것도 이미 했어요.
> M 좋습니다! 사무실 책상은 배정받았나요?
> W 아니요, 부서장의 지시를 기다리고 있어요.

Q 주로 논의되고 있는 것은?
(a) 여자의 신원 문제
(b) 여자의 복리후생 제도에 생긴 변화
(c) 여자의 비품 운반
(d) 여자가 새 직장에서 일을 시작하는 것

pick up 찾다 **Human Resources** 인사부 **benefits plan** 복리후생 제도 **assign** 배정하다 **department head** 부서장 **identification** 신원 **transfer** 운반

23

Listen to a conversation between a couple.

> M Have you seen our waiter?
> W Not in a while. Do you want to order another drink?
> M No. Take a look at this steak.
> W Oh, it's practically raw.
> M Right, and I ordered it medium.
> W They missed the mark on that one.

Q What is mainly being discussed in the conversation?
(a) How the waiter was being rude
(b) The man's undercooked dish
(c) The drink the man will order
(d) How the menu is a little confusing

커플의 대화를 들으시오.

> M 웨이터 봤니?
> W 아니, 한동안 못 봤어. 음료 한 잔 더 시키려고?
> M 아니, 이 스테이크 좀 봐.
> W 오, 거의 안 익었네.
> M 맞아, 난 중간 정도로 익혀 달라고 주문했거든.
> W 완전히 실패작이군.

Q 주로 논의되고 있는 것은?
(a) 웨이터가 어떻게 불손했는지
(b) 남자의 설익은 음식
(c) 남자가 주문할 음료
(d) 메뉴가 어떤 면에서 다소 혼란스러운지

take a look at ~을 보다 **practically** 거의 **raw** 날것의 **miss the mark** 과녁을 벗어나다 **undercooked** 설익은 **confusing** 혼란스러운

24

Listen to a conversation about a place to stay.

W Where are you staying during your trip to Thailand?

M I've booked a room at the Fairmont Hotel.

W Really? I thought you were a hostel kind of guy.

M I was, but I'm just too old for hostels now.

W Sounds like you're prioritizing comfort over price.

M That about sums it up.

Q Which is correct about the man according to the conversation?

(a) He prefers not to make advanced lodging arrangements.

(b) He stays at the Fairmont every time he visits Thailand.

(c) He does not mind spending more on accommodation.

(d) He values the low cost of hostels above all.

숙소에 관한 대화를 들으시오.

W 태국 여행 가서 어디에 묵을 거예요?

M 페어몬트 호텔에 방을 예약했어요.

W 정말이에요? 호스텔을 애용하는 줄 알았는데요.

M 옛날에는 그랬지만 지금은 호스텔을 이용하기에는 나이가 너무 많아요.

W 이제 돈보다는 편안함을 우선시하는 것 같군요.

M 그런 셈이죠.

Q 남자에 대해 대화 내용과 일치하는 것은?

(a) 숙박을 예약하는 것을 좋아하지 않는다.

(b) 태국을 방문할 때마다 페어몬트에 묵는다.

(c) 숙박 시설에 돈을 더 많이 쓰는 것을 개의치 않는다.

(d) 무엇보다도 호스텔의 저비용을 중시한다.

book 예약하다   **hostel** 호스텔(청소년 여행용 저가 숙소)   **kind** 특별한 성질의 사람   **prioritize** 우선시하다   **that (about) sums it up** 그 말이 (얼추) 맞다   **make advanced arrangement** 예약하다   **lodging** 숙박   **accommodation** 숙박 시설

25

Listen to a conversation between two classmates.

M See you in Professor Wang's class tomorrow.

W Didn't I tell you? I had to change out of that class.

M Oh no! But I was looking forward to being your study partner.

W You still can be. I switched to the afternoon class.

M I didn't know there was a second one.

W Yes, it meets Tuesdays and Thursdays at 3:30.

Q Which is correct about the speakers according to the conversation?

(a) They are seeking a tutor for tomorrow's class.

(b) They have a study date on Thursday at 3:30.

(c) They have the same class at different times.

(d) They both switched to an afternoon class.

두 학급친구의 대화를 들으시오.

M 내일 왕 교수님 수업에서 보자.

W 내가 말 안 했던가. 반을 바꾸기로 한 것 말이야.

M 이런! 난 꼭 너의 스터디 파트너가 되고 싶었는데.

W 그건 아직도 유효해. 난 단지 오후반으로 바꾼 거든.

M 반이 또 있는 줄 몰랐어.

W 응, 수업 시간이 화요일과 목요일 3시 반이야.

Q 화자들에 대해 대화 내용과 일치하는 것은?

(a) 내일 수업을 위해 개인 지도 교사를 찾고 있다.

(b) 목요일 3시 반에 스터디 약속이 있다.

(c) 같은 수업을 다른 시간대에 듣는다.

(d) 둘 다 오후반으로 옮겼다.

switch 바꾸다   **tutor** 개인 지도 교사

26

Listen to a conversation between two friends.

W Check out my brand-new mountain bike!

M Wow, it's gorgeous! Do you have plans to use it?

W I thought I'd take it to Mount Taylor this weekend.

M Hmm, wouldn't Darrow Hill be better to start on?

W That's way too tame. I enjoy the challenge of Taylor.

M Oh, I didn't realize you already had riding experience.

Q Which is correct according to the conversation?

(a) The woman bought a second hand bike.

(b) The man wants to try the bike on Mount Taylor.

(c) The woman is planning to bike on the weekend.

(d) The man does not recommend Darrow Hills for biking.

두 친구의 대화를 들으시오.

W 나의 새 산악자전거 좀 봐.

M 와, 멋진데! 그것은 언제 사용할 계획이 있니?

W 이번 주말에 테일러 산에서 탈 생각이야.

M 음, 처음 시작하기에는 대로우 힐이 더 좋지 않을까?

W 거긴 너무 단조로워. 난 테일러에 도전하는 게 즐거워.

M 오, 네가 벌써 라이딩 경험이 있는 줄 몰랐어.

Q 대화 내용과 일치하는 것은?

(a) 여자는 중고 자전거를 샀다.

(b) 남자는 테일러 산에서 자전거를 타보고 싶어 한다.

(c) 여자는 주말에 자전거를 탈 계획이다.

(d) 남자는 자전거 탈 장소로 대로우 힐을 권하지 않는다.

brand-new 신제품인   **gorgeous** 멋진   **way** (부사·전치사 강조) 훨씬, 아주   **tame** 단조로운   **second hand** 중고의

27

Listen to a conversation about donations.

M Good morning. I'm collecting donations for the Save the Earth Foundation.

W I'm afraid I won't be able to contribute.

M I'm sorry to hear that. Do you know about our cause?

W I do, but I donate to other environmental groups.

M Let me leave you this flyer in case you change your mind.

W OK, I'll look it over.

Q Why will the woman not make a donation?

(a) She disagrees with the group's mission.

(b) She will contribute to the foundation soon.

(c) She already supports a different organization.

(d) She has no interest in going through a flyer.

기부에 관한 대화를 들으시오.

M 안녕하세요. 세이브 디 어스 재단을 위한 기부금을 모으고 있어요.

W 기부할 수 없을 것 같은데요.

M 유감이군요. 저희의 뜻을 알고 계시나요?

W 물론 알죠. 하지만 전 다른 환경 단체에 기부하고 있어요.

M 혹시 마음이 바뀔지도 모르니까 이 전단을 드리고 갈게요.

W 네. 검토해 볼게요.

Q 여자가 기부하지 않으려는 이유는?

(a) 이 단체가 하는 일에 반대한다.

(b) 곧 이 재단에 기부할 것이다.

(c) 이미 다른 단체를 돕는다.

(d) 전단을 검토하는 데 전혀 관심이 없다.

donation 기부 **foundation** 재단 **contribute** 기부하다 **cause** 신조, 대의 **flyer** 전단 **in case** 만약 ~인 경우에는 **look over** 검토하다 **go through** 자세히 검토하다

28

Listen to two friends discuss a movie.

W I saw *Wounded Honor* last night—amazing.

M I thought it wasn't playing here in town.

W It was at the independent theater. Last night was the final showing.

M Oh, I wish you'd invited me!

W I had no idea you liked art house movies.

M I guess I'll try to catch it on DVD.

Q Which is correct according to the conversation?

(a) The woman thought the movie was too art house.

(b) The film is to be screened in town tomorrow.

(c) The speakers only enjoy blockbuster films.

(d) The man plans to rent the movie.

두 친구가 영화에 관해 말하는 것을 들으시오.

W 어젯밤 〈상처 입은 영광〉을 봤는데 아주 재미있었어.

M 이 도시에선 상연하지 않을 줄 알았는데.

W 독립 영화관에서 했지. 어젯밤이 마지막 상연이었어.

M 이런, 나도 부르지 그랬어!

W 예술 영화를 좋아하는지 몰랐어.

M 나중에 DVD로 봐야겠군.

Q 대화 내용과 일치하는 것은?

(a) 여자는 영화가 너무 예술적이라고 생각했다.

(b) 영화가 내일 이 도시에서 상연될 예정이다.

(c) 화자들은 블록버스터 영화만 즐긴다.

(d) 남자는 영화를 빌려 볼 생각이다.

wounded 상처 입은 **independent theater** 독립 영화관 **art house** 예술영화관; 예술적인 **screen** (영화를) 상영[방영]하다 **blockbuster cinema** 막대한 돈을 들인 영화

29

Listen to a conversation in a museum.

M Welcome. Are you a member of the art museum?

W This is my first time visiting, actually.

M Oh, did you know that members enjoy free museum access?

W Well, I'm just here specifically to research a class assignment.

M Great. With your student discount, admission is only 4 dollars.

W Here you are. And I'd like a building map, please.

Q What can be inferred from the conversation?

(a) The museum is preparing to raise its prices.

(b) The woman is ineligible for membership.

(c) Maps are complimentary only for members.

(d) The woman is enrolled in a class.

박물관에서 이뤄지는 대화를 들으시오.

M 어서 오세요. 미술관 회원이신가요?

W 사실은 첫 번째 방문이에요.

M 오, 회원은 미술관을 무료로 이용할 수 있다는 걸 몰랐나요?

W 음. 그냥 저는 특별히 숙제를 조사하기 위해 온 거예요.

M 알겠어요. 학생은 할인되니까 입장료가 4달러예요.

W 여기 있어요. 그리고 건물 지도 한 장 주세요.

Q 대화로부터 추론할 수 있는 것은?

(a) 미술관은 입장료 인상을 준비하고 있다.

(b) 여자는 회원 자격이 없다.

(c) 지도는 회원들에게만 무료이다.

(d) 여자는 수업에 등록되어 있다.

art museum 미술관 **access** 이용, 접근 **specifically** 특별히 **assignment** 과제, 숙제 **discount** 할인 **admission** 입장료 **ineligible** 자격이 없는 **complimentary** 무료의 **enroll** 등록하다

30

Listen to a conversation in a bookstore.

W Hello, I'd like to return this textbook I bought yesterday.

M I'm sorry, but all returns are processed at customer service.

W But I was told I could do it at any register.

M No, whoever told you that was wrong.

W I guess I stood in line for nothing.

M I apologize for the inconvenience.

Q What can be inferred about the woman from the conversation?

(a) She does not know where customer service is.

(b) She feels she overpaid for the textbook.

(c) She has no time to stand in line again.

(d) She is upset about being misled.

서점에서 이뤄지는 대화를 들으시오.

W 안녕하세요, 어제 샀던 이 교재를 반품하고 싶은데요.

M 죄송하지만 모든 반품은 고객 서비스실에서 처리해요.

W 하지만 모든 등록기에서 반품할 수 있다고 들었는데요.

M 아니요, 누가 그런 말을 했는지는 몰라도 그건 틀린 말이에요.

W 헛되이 줄 서 있었던 것 같군요.

M 불편을 끼쳐서 죄송합니다.

Q 여자에 대해 추론할 수 있는 것은?

(a) 고객 서비스실이 어디에 있는지 모른다.

(b) 교재값을 너무 비싸게 줬다고 생각한다.

(c) 다시 줄 설 시간이 없다.

(d) 잘못 안내를 받아서 속상하다.

process 처리하다 **register** 등록기 **stand in line** 줄 서다 **for nothing** 헛되이 **inconvenience** 불편 **overpay** 과다 지급하다 **mislead** 잘못 인도하다

Part IV

31

Here we are at the Mueller Botanical Gardens. Please remember that we have limited time to spend here today, and that you should be back on the tour bus no later than 3:15. Any later and we won't have enough time to fit in our final stop, which is the magnificent Parliament Building. I won't be joining you in the gardens, so if you have any questions inside, please inquire at the visitor's information booth.

Q What is the speaker mainly doing?

(a) Explaining a safety precaution for a site visit

(b) Outlining the protocol for a tour

(c) Giving the history of a tourist attraction

(d) Reviewing the entire itinerary of a tour

이제 뮬러 식물원에 도착했습니다. 오늘 우리가 이곳에서 보낼 시간은 제한되어 있으니 늦어도 3시 15분까지는 관광버스로 돌아와야 한다는 점을 꼭 기억해 두시기 바랍니다. 조금이라도 늦으면 우리의 마지막 여정인 웅장한 국회의사당을 구경할 시간을 충분히 갖지 못할 것입니다. 식물원에는 제가 같이 안 갈 것이므로 만약 그 안에서 질문 사항이 있으시면 방문객 안내소에 물어보시기 바랍니다.

Q 화자가 주로 하고 있는 것은?

(a) 현장 방문에 대비한 안전 예방책 설명하기

(b) 관광에서 지켜야할 규칙 약술하기

(c) 관광 명소의 역사 알리기

(d) 여행의 전체 일정 검토하기

botanical garden 식물원 **no later than** 늦어도 ~까지는 **fit in** 끼우다, (예정 등을) 맞추다 **magnificent** 웅장한 **precaution** 예방책 **outline** 약술하다 **protocol** 규칙 **current** 현재의 **tourist attraction** 관광 명소 **itinerary** 여행 일정표, 여정

32

Any vegetable you are familiar with might be just one among many types belonging to the same species. Consider the potato. There are an astounding 4,000 different varieties of this root vegetable, and it comes in a wondrous range of sizes, shapes, colors, and tastes. Have you heard of the blue potato, for example? It's a small specimen compared to the common baking potato, and once cooked, its flesh takes on a deep purple color.

Q What is mainly being discussed in the lecture?

(a) Innovations in the world of potato growing

(b) Varieties of potatoes that are only now available

(c) Potatoes as an example of selective breeding

(d) Vegetable diversity as shown by the potato

여러분이 잘 알고 있는 채소가 같은 종에 속하는 많은 품종 중 하나에 불과할지도 모릅니다. 감자를 생각해 보십시오. 놀랍게도 이 뿌리채소의 품종은 4천 가지나 되며, 매우 다양한 크기와 모양과 색깔과 맛으로 나옵니다. 가령, 푸른 감자에 대해 들어보신 적이 있나요? 이는 일반적인 구이용 감자에 비교해 작은 편에 들며, 일단 조리하면 짙은 자주색을 띱니다.

Q 주로 논의되고 있는 것은?

(a) 감자 재배 분야에서의 혁신

(b) 지금만 구할 수 있는 감자 품종

(c) 선별적 재배 작물의 실례로 든 감자

(d) 감자로 살펴본 채소의 다품종성

species 종 **astounding** 놀라운 **variety** 품종 **root vegetable** 뿌리채소 **a wondrous range of** 놀라울 정도로 다양한 **specimen** 견본, 표본 **flesh** 과육 **take on** (양상·색채 등을) 띠다 **diversity** 다양성

33

In a surprise move this morning, Gail Altman, public relations manager for the tech firm InTotal, announced the relocation of the company's production facilities. For the past 15 years, the firm has been doing the bulk of its manufacturing in Shenzhen, China. Now, in what's being described by analysts as a vote of confidence for domestic manufacturing, InTotal is coming home. By this time next year, 95% of their production lines will be located in the US.

Q Which is correct about InTotal according to the report?
(a) It had previously manufactured its products abroad.
(b) It will keep a majority of production lines abroad.
(c) It started domestic manufacturing 15 years ago.
(d) It has decided to relocate to Shenzhen, China.

오늘 오전, 기술 회사 인토탈의 홍보 책임자인 게일 앨트먼이 자사의 생산 시설을 이전한다는 놀라운 조치를 발표했습니다. 지난 15년 동안 이 회사는 중국의 선전에서 대부분의 생산 작업을 해왔습니다. 이제, 분석가들에 의해 국내 생산에 대한 신임 투표로 묘사되고 있는 가운데, 인토탈이 고국으로 돌아오고 있습니다. 내년 이맘때는 생산 라인의 95%가 미국에 설치될 것입니다.

Q 인토탈 사에 대해 보도 내용과 일치하는 것은?
(a) 이전에는 제품을 외국에서 생산했다.
(b) 생산 라인의 대부분을 해외에 둘 것이다.
(c) 15년 전에 국내 생산을 시작했다.
(d) 중국 선전으로 이전하기로 했다.

move 조치 public relations 홍보 relocation 이전 production facilities 생산 시설 bulk 대부분 manufacturing 제조, 생산 analyst (증권가 등의) 분석가 a vote of confidence 신임 투표, 지지 previously 이전에

34

British novelist Zadie Smith was a literary celebrity even before she became a published author. On the strength of some early short stories written while she was a student at Cambridge, a publisher signed a contract with her for a novel. In 1997, she presented an unfinished manuscript for *White Teeth*. Though still a work in progress, it earned her accolades from the wider literary world, and when the book was finally published in 2000, it was an instant success. It was even adapted for television by Channel 4 in England.

Q Which is correct about Zadie Smith according to the talk?
(a) She was an actress before becoming a novelist.
(b) She finished her first novel while at Cambridge.
(c) She never completed the *White Teeth* manuscript.
(d) She gained literary fame while in university.

영국 소설가 제이디 스미스는 책을 내기도 전에 이미 문단의 명사였다. 그녀가 케임브리지 대학 시절에 쓴 몇몇 초기 단편 소설들 덕분에 한 출판사가 그녀의 소설을 출간하기로 계약을 맺었다. 1997년에 그녀는 〈하얀 치아〉라는 제목의 미완성 원고를 건네줬다. 비록 여전히 진행 중인 작품이었음에도 불구하고 이것은 더 광범위한 문학계로부터 찬사를 받았고, 마침내 책이 2000년에 출판되자마자 날개 돋친 듯이 팔려나갔다. 심지어 이 작품은 영국의 채널4가 TV용으로 각색하기도 했다.

Q 제이디 스미스에 대해 바르게 말한 것은?
(a) 소설가가 되기 전에 배우로 활동했다.
(b) 케임브리지 대학을 다니는 동안 첫 번째 소설을 완성했다.
(c) 〈하얀 치아〉의 원고를 결국 완성하지 못했다.
(d) 대학 시절 문학적 명성을 얻었다.

novelist 소설가 literary 문학의 celebrity 명사 published author 책을 낸 적이 있는 작가 on the strength of ~덕분에, ~에 입각하여 publisher 출판사 manuscript 원고 in progress 진행 중인 accolade 찬사 instant 즉각적인 adapt 각색하다 fame 명성

35

Young stars are characteristically surrounded by a disk of gas and dust that can coalesce to form planets. That's what appears to be happening around TW Hydrae, a star observed at 176 light-years from Earth in the constellation of Hydra. Except that the star's one planet is forming at a distance of 7.5 billion miles away from it. For perspective, that's twice the radius of Pluto's orbit around the sun. Scientists are uncertain how an aggregation of gas and dust could be occurring so far from the influence of the star's gravity.

Q How far away from Earth is TW Hydrae observed?
(a) 76 light-years
(b) 176 light-years
(c) 7.5 billion miles
(d) 17.5 billion miles

젊은 별은 원반 모양의 가스와 먼지로 둘러싸여 있는 것이 특징인데, 이것들이 합쳐져서 행성을 형성할 수 있습니다. 이것이 바다뱀자리에 있는, 지구에서 176광년 떨어진 곳에서 관측되는 별인 TW 히드라 주변에서 일어나고 있는 현상처럼 보입니다. 이것 외에, 이 별에서 75억 마일 떨어진 곳에서 하나의 행성이 형성되고 있습니다. 이 거리는 태양 주위를 도는 명왕성의 궤도 반경의 두 배라고 말하면 원근감이 느껴질 것입니다. 과학자들은 이 별의 중력의 영향을 받지 않는 곳에서 어떻게 가스와 먼지가 뭉쳐지는 현상이 일어날 수 있는지 확신을 못하고 있습니다.

Q TW 히드라가 지구에서 관측되는 거리는?
(a) 76광년
(b) 176광년
(c) 75억 마일
(d) 175억 마일

characteristically 특징으로서 disk 원반 coalesce (더 큰 덩어리로) 합치다 planet 행성 light-year 광년 constellation of Hydra 바다뱀자리 perspective 원근감 radius 반경 Pluto 명왕성 orbit 궤도 aggregation 집합, 집성 gravity 중력

36

Up until May of 2012, Hawadax Island in the western Aleutian Islands was officially known as Rat Island. The name was a reference to the invasive population of brown rats that had overrun the island following a Japanese shipwreck in the 18th century. Thanks to an eradication campaign managed by the US Fish and Wildlife Service, the island was declared "rat free" in 2009. To recognize this important achievement, the new moniker of Hawadax, meaning "entry" or "welcome" in Aleut, was bestowed.

Q What can be inferred about Hawadax Island from the talk?

(a) The brown rats arrived there from a Japanese ship.
(b) It is still referred to as Rat Island among islanders.
(c) The US invested in commercial developments there.
(d) Its indigenous rat species was eradicated in 2012.

서부 알류산 열도에 속하는 하와다 섬은 2012년 5월까지만 해도 공식적으로 쥐섬으로 알려져 있었다. 쥐섬이란 이름은 18세기에 한 일본 선박이 침몰하면서 섬에 급속히 퍼진 갈색쥐가 섬을 침범한 모습을 빗대어 표현한 것이었다. 미국 어류 및 야생동물 보호국에 의해 실시된 박멸 운동 덕분에 섬은 2009년에 '쥐 없는 곳'으로 선포되었다. 이 중요한 성과를 잊지 않기 위해 알류트어로 '입장' 혹은 '환영'을 뜻하는 하와다라는 새로운 이름이 부여되었다.

Q 하와다 섬에 대해 추론할 수 있는 것은?
(a) 갈색쥐들이 일본 선박에 타고 있다가 이곳에 상륙했다.
(b) 섬 주민들은 여전히 쥐섬이라고 부른다.
(c) 미국은 상업적인 개발을 위해 이곳에 자금을 투입했다.
(d) 2012년에 토착 쥐들이 박멸되었다.

up until ~까지 **reference** 언급 **invasive** 급속히 퍼지는, 침습성의 **overrun** ~에 들끓다 **shipwreck** 난파(선) **eradication** 박멸 **achievement** 업적 **moniker** 이름 **bestow** 부여하다 **islander** 섬의 주민 **commercial** 상업의 **indigenous** 토착의

Part V

37-38

Artificial intelligence (AI) has been affecting every aspect of our lives, and most of us wonder how it will change our future. Fortunately, we can get definite answers from Dr. Susan Brown. She is a very familiar name for those interested in AI. Since the 1990s, Dr. Brown has been involved in 29 AI development projects and published 19 papers on AI. She is currently writing a book about how AI will change the future of the human race. By now you will understand why we have invited her to present a special lecture on what kinds of changes AI will bring about. No prior knowledge is required. Just bring your intellectual curiosity to the Brown Library Auditorium next Tuesday at 6:00 p.m. Admission to the lecture is free!

인공지능이 우리 삶의 모든 측면에 영향을 미치고 있어서, 우리들 대부분은 인공지능이 우리의 미래를 어떻게 바꿔놓을지 궁금해 합니다. 다행스럽게도 수잔 브라운 박사에게서 확실한 대답을 얻을 수 있습니다. 브라운 박사는 인공지능에 관심이 있는 이들에게는 아주 익숙한 이름입니다. 1990년대 이래로, 브라운 박사는 29건의 인공지능 개발 프로젝트에 관여했고, 인공지능에 대한 19편의 논문을 발표했습니다. 현재 인공지능이 어떻게 인류의 미래를 바꿔놓을지에 대한 책을 쓰고 있습니다. 이제 여러분은 인공지능이 가져올 변화에 대해 특별 강연을 부탁하기 위해 왜 그녀를 초대했는지 이해하시겠죠. 어떤 사전 지식도 필요하지 않습니다. 다음 주 화요일 오후 6시에 브라운도서관 강당으로 지적 호기심만 갖고 오십시오. 강연회 입장은 무료입니다!

37 Q Why has Dr. Brown been invited to deliver a special lecture next Tuesday?

(a) Because she has published numerous books on artificial intelligence
(b) Because she is highly qualified to field the questions that most people ask about artificial intelligence
(c) Because she is the most renowned pioneer of artificial intelligence
(d) Because she has the highest level of intellectual curiosity

Q 브라운 박사가 다음 주 화요일에 특별 강연을 하도록 초청을 받은 이유는?
(a) 인공지능에 대한 수많은 책을 출간했기 때문에
(b) 대부분의 사람들이 인공지능에 대해 갖는 질문에 답할 자격이 충분하기 때문에
(c) 가장 저명한 인공지능 개척자이기 때문에
(d) 가장 높은 수준의 지적 호기심이 있기 때문에

해설 고난도 문항이다. 지문에서 박사가 참여한 인공지능 프로젝트와 관련 논문을 언급하면서 인공지능이 가져올 미래 변화에 대해 강연을 부탁하기 위해 초대했다고 언급하고 있다. 이 내용을 가장 잘 옮긴 보기는 (b)이다.

38 Q Which is correct according to the announcement?

(a) Artificial intelligence was explored and developed in the 1990s.

(b) Dr. Brown has participated in 19 AI development projects.

(c) Even those without background knowledge of AI can attend the lecture.

(d) The Brown Library Auditorium was built at the behest of Dr. Brown.

Q 안내에 따르면, 다음 중 옳은 것은?

(a) 인공지능은 1990년대에 탐구되어 개발되었다.

(b) 브라운 박사는 19건의 인공지능 개발 프로젝트에 참가했다.

(c) 인공지능에 대한 배경지식이 없는 이들조차도 강연에 참석할 수 있다.

(d) 브라운도서관 강당은 브라운 박사의 요청으로 건립되었다.

해설 (a)는 주어진 내용만으로는 정확하게 알 수 없는 사항이므로 오답이다. (b)는 19건이 아니라 29건이어야 정답이 될 수 있다. (d)는 그런 근거가 전혀 제시되어 있지 않기 때문에 오답이다. 따라서 정답은 주어진 내용에 충실한 (c)이다.

artificial intelligence 인공지능 **affect** 영향을 미치다 **aspect** 측면 **definite** 확고한, 분명한 **familiar** 익숙한, 친숙한 **paper** 논문; 신문 **currently** 현재, 지금 **bring about** 초래하다 **prior** 사전의 **intellectual** 지적인 **auditorium** 대강당 **admission** 입장, 입회 **numerous** 수없이 많은 **field** (질문을) 재치 있게 받아넘기다 **renowned** 유명한 **pioneer** 개척자, 선구자 **at the behest of** ~의 요청[명령]으로

39-40

A lot of people believe that hormones are identical to neurotransmitters. There's a grain of truth in that belief because both of them are chemicals. In addition, both can affect bodily functions. However, there are several differences between these two. To begin with, hormones need to enter the blood stream in order to influence bodily functions. On the other hand, neurotransmitters need to pass through the neurons in the brain in order to affect behaviors as well as bodily functions. Further, traveling through the blood stream, hormones contact the receptors of target cells, which can lead to specific bodily functions such as sleep. In contrast, when penetrating the neurons in the brain, neurotransmitters change into electrical impulses, which regulate behaviors and bodily functions.

많은 이들은 호르몬이 신경전달물질과 똑같다고 생각합니다. 그런 생각에는 맞는 부분도 있는데요, 호르몬과 신경전달물질이 둘 다 화학물질이기 때문입니다. 또한 둘 다 신체 기능에 영향을 미칠 수 있습니다. 그렇지만 이 둘 사이에는 몇 가지 차이가 있습니다. 우선 첫째로, 호르몬은 신체 기능에 영향을 미치기 위해서 혈류에 들어가야 합니다. 반면 신경전달물질은 신체 기능뿐만 아니라 행동에 영향을 미치기 위해서 두뇌의 신경 세포를 통과해야 합니다. 더욱이 혈류를 통해 이동하면서, 호르몬은 목표 세포의 수용기에 접촉하는데, 이는 수면과 같은 특정한 신체 기능으로 귀결될 수 있습니다. 이와는 대조적으로, 두뇌의 신경세포를 관통할 때, 신경전달물질은 전기 임펄스로 바뀌는데, 이 전기 임펄스가 행동과 신체 기능을 통제합니다.

39 Q What is the main point of the lecture?

(a) The similarities between hormones and neurotransmitters are overwhelming.

(b) Both hormones and neurotransmitters can influence behaviors and bodily functions.

(c) Both hormones and neurotransmitters originate from the neurons in the brain.

(d) Despite some similarities, hormones differ from neurotransmitters in some ways

Q 강의의 요점은?

(a) 호르몬과 신경전달물질 사이의 유사성은 압도적이다.

(b) 호르몬과 신경전달물질이 둘 다 행동과 신체 기능에 영향을 미칠 수 있다.

(c) 호르몬과 신경전달물질이 둘 다 두뇌의 신경세포에서 유래한다.

(d) 몇 가지 유사성에도 불구하고, 호르몬은 몇몇 측면에서 신경전달물질과 다르다.

해설 이처럼 전반적인 정보를 측정하는 유형은 세부적인 내용이 아니라 전체적인 내용의 흐름에 유의해야 정답을 제대로 찾아낼 수 있다. (a)는 유사성이 있지만 다른 점이 많다는 것이 요지이므로 오답이다. (b)는 주어진 내용만으로 판단하면, 행동에 영향을 미칠 수 있는 것은 신경전달물질이다. 게다가 지나치게 세부적인 내용이므로 요점으로 부적절하다. 그리고 (c)는 전혀 알 수 없는 사항이므로 오답이다. 따라서 정답은 (d)이다.

40 Q What can be inferred from the lecture?

(a) All hormones are secreted by endocrine glands.

(b) Hormones may not pass through the neurons in the brain.

(c) Neurotransmitters travel to every part of the body to affect bodily functions.

(d) Electrical impulses are the original forms of hormones.

Q 강의로부터 추론할 수 있는 것은?

(a) 모든 호르몬은 내분비샘에서 분비된다.

(b) 호르몬은 두뇌의 신경세포를 통과하지 않을 수도 있다.

(c) 신경전달물질은 신체 기능에 영향을 미치기 위해서 신체의 모든 부분으로 이동한다.

(d) 전기 임펄스가 호르몬의 본래 형태이다.

해설 뉴텝스의 추론 유형에서도 세부 사항 유형과 마찬가지로, 주어진 내용으로부터 분명하게 알 수 있는 선택지만이 정답이 될 수 있음을 꼭 기억해야 한다. 선택지 (a), (c), (d)는 설령 올바른 내용이라고 하더라도, 주어진 강의에서 분명하게 밝히지 않았기 때문에 정답이 아니다. 따라서 정답은 (b)이다. 신경전달물질이 두뇌의 신경세포를 통과해야 하는 데 반해, 호르몬은 혈류에 들어가야 한다고 했기 때문에 추론하기에 올바른 내용이다.

identical 동일한 **neurotransmitter** 신경전달물질 **chemical** 화학물질; 화학적인 **bodily** 신체의 **function** 기능 **blood stream** 혈류 **receptor** 수용기, 감각기 **specific** 구체적인, 특정한 **impulse** 충격, 임펄스 **penetrate** 관통하다 **regulate** 통제하다 **overwhelming** 압도적인 **secrete** 분비하다 **endocrine gland** 내분비샘

Vocabulary

p.65

Part I

1 정답 (a)
A 네 동생 새 여자 친구는 어때?
B 솔직히 말해서 내 기대에 못 <u>미쳐</u>.

measure up to ~에 부응하다 **expectation** 기대 **commit** (죄 · 과실 등을) 저지르다 **impress** 깊은 인상을 주다 **feature** 특징을 이루다

2 정답 (b)
A 노스이스트 항공사가 불법 행위로 고소당했다는 뉴스를 들었어요.
B 그런 일이 <u>폭로되면</u> 회사가 문 닫을 수도 있어요.

sue 고소하다 **malfeasance** 불법[부정] 행위 **alternative** 대안 **exposure** 폭로, (언론을 통해) 알려짐 **regimen** 식이 요법 **collision** 충돌

3 정답 (d)
A 에드워즈 씨가 제게 또 일찍 나오라고 하더군요.
B 그 사람 요구에 <u>따를</u> 필요 없어요.

demand 요구 **come across** 우연히 발견하다 **switch up** 바꾸다 **cover for** 대신하다, 보호하다 **submit to** ~에 복종하다

4 정답 (a)
A 이봐, 카페 저쪽에 빈자리가 있어.
B 하지만 먹고 난 식기를 아직 <u>치우지</u> 않았는걸.

free 사용 중이 아닌 **bus** 먹고 난 식기를 치우다 **rake** 긁어모으다 **cast** 주조하다 **lube** ~에 윤활유를 치다

5 정답 (a)
A 선생님, 이 알약을 복용했는데도 요통이 낫질 않아요.
B <u>복용량</u>을 두 배로 늘리도록 합시다.

pill 알약 **backache** 요통 **double** 두 배로 하다 **dosage** 투여량, 복용량 **malady** 병, 병폐 **symptom** 증상 **placebo** 위약

6 정답 (c)
A All the Way Around라는 노래를 좋아할 줄 알았어요.
B 농담하지 마세요. 그 노래는 <u>질색이에요</u>.

Are you kidding? 농담하지 마. **taunt** 비웃다 **uphold** 지키다, 따르다 **loathe** 몹시 싫어하다 **embroil** (분쟁 · 전쟁 등에) 끌어들이다

7 정답 (b)
A 벌써 퇴근할 시간인가요?
B 네, 하던 일을 <u>마무리하세요</u>.

win over 이겨내다 **wrap up** 마무리하다 **stick out** (물체 · 신체의 일부분을) 내밀다 **keep down** 진압하다

8 정답 (a)
A 사만사가 이번 주말에 우리랑 산악자전거를 타러 갈까?
B 아직 발목 부상에서 <u>회복</u> 중인 것 같아.

recuperate 회복하다 **badger** 난처하게 만들다 **accrue** 누적되다 **endorse** 지지하다

9 정답 (b)
A 노사가 어떻게 합의에 이르렀나요?
B 제3자에게 <u>중재</u>를 요청했어요.

workers and management 노동자와 경영진 **come to an agreement** 합의에 이르다 **enlist** 협력을 요청하다 **a third party** 제3자 **conduct** (특정한 활동을) 하다 **debility** 쇠약, 중증 장애 **arbitration** 중재 **concision** 간결 **polemic** 논쟁, 반론

10 정답 (d)
A 팀이 내게 시간당 겨우 8달러를 번다고 하던데.
B 그렇게 적은 돈을 받고 왜 일하려고 하는지 <u>이해가</u> 안 가는군.

enthrall 마음을 사로잡다 **digress** 주제에서 벗어나다 **resign** 사퇴하다 **fathom** (의미 등을) 헤아리다[가늠하다]

Part II

11 정답 (b)
중국어는 서로 다른 <u>방언</u>으로 이루어져 있다고 주장하는 언어학자들이 있는 반면, 사실상 별개의 언어라고 주장하는 언어학자들도 있다.

linguist 언어학자 **be made up of** ~로 구성되다 **claim** 주장하다 **distinct** 뚜렷이 구별되는, 별개의 **associate** 동료 **dialect** 방언 **synonym** 동의어 **homophone** 동음이의어

12 정답 (d)
폴란드를 <u>합병</u>하려는 나치 독일의 움직임이 유럽 국가들을 2차 세계대전에 끌어들였다.

ascertain 확인하다 **apprehend** 체포하다 **adjourn** 연기하다 **annex** 합병하다

13 정답 (d)
비록 지금은 의구심이 일고 있지만, 옥수수를 원료로 한 에탄올이 석유를 대체할 친환경 에너지로 오랫동안 <u>홍보</u>되어왔다.

environmentally friendly 환경친화적인 **petroleum** 석유 **raise doubts** 의구심을 일으키다 **bear** (아이를) 낳다 **surge** 끓어오르게 하다 **loft** 높이 쳐올리다 **tout** 광고[홍보]하다

14 정답 (d)
범죄의 세부 사항이 너무나 <u>악랄</u>해서 보통은 그것을 보도하는 뉴스에 포함되지 않았다.

details 자세한 이야기, 세부 사항 **typically** 일반적으로, 보통 **cover** 취재[보도]하다 **deferential** 경의를 표하는 **assiduous** 근면 성실한 **cloistered** 세속으로부터 격리된 **heinous** 악랄한, 극악무도한

15 정답 (c)
19세기에는 지금보다 현금이 훨씬 부족했기 때문에, 잡화점에서 고객들이 <u>외상</u>으로 물건을 사는 것이 허용될 때가 많았다.

general store 잡화점 **make a purchase** 구매하다 **scarce** 부족한 **on demand** 요구가 있는 즉시 **on term** 정기적인 **on credit** 외상으로 **on leave** 휴가 중인

16 정답 (c)
막대한 재원을 공동 출자함으로써 <u>협력단</u> 구성원들은 쓰러져가는 기업을 되살릴 수 있었다.

pool 공동 출자하다 vast 막대한 financial resources 재원
prop up 지원하다, 받쳐주다 ailing 비틀거리는, 병약한 divestment
주식 매각 matrimony 결혼 consortium 협회, 합작 기업
accumulation 축적, 누적

17 정답 (c)
시장은 고아원 프로젝트에 대한 지원이 순수하다고 주장했지만, 그를 폄하하는 사람들은 그에게 속셈이 있다는 뜻을 비쳤다.

orphanage 고아원, 보육원 genuine 진실된 detractor 중상을
일삼는 사람 exterior 외부의 anterior 앞의 ulterior 겉으로 드러나지
않은 posterior 뒤의

18 정답 (d)
중서부에 거주하는 아미쉬파의 가구 세공은 공을 들여 세세히 신경 쓰는
것으로 유명하다.

craftsmanship 솜씨, 세공 Amish 아미쉬파(현대 기술 문명을 거부하고
소박한 농경 생활을 하는 미국의 한 종교 집단) engendering 야기하는
groundbreaking 획기적인 vituperative 독설을 퍼붓는
painstaking 공들인

19 정답 (b)
대부분의 TV 방송국들이 재방송에 의존하는 여름 시즌은 보통의 TV 시청
자에게 침울한 시간이 될 수 있다.

turn to ~에 의지하다 rerun 재방송 quarry 채석장 doldrums
우울, 침울 tyranny 압제, 폭압 catalyst 촉매

20 정답 (a)
정부가 보조금과 세금 우대 조치로 대기업들을 계속 애지중지하는 한, 시
위는 끊이지 않을 것이다.

subsidy 보조금 tax break 세금 우대 조치 coddle 애지중지하다
saddle (의무 등을) 부과하다 meddle 간섭하다 riddle 수수께끼를 내다

21 정답 (d)
총격 피해자들을 받게 된 긴급 의료원들이 가장 먼저 해야 할 일은 출혈을
멈추게 하는 것이다.

paramedic 긴급 의료원, 응급 구조원 presented with ~이 주어진
gunshot 총에 맞은 deign 거들먹거리다 loll 축 처지게 하다 tamp
채워 누르다 stanch (출혈을) 멈추게 하다

22 정답 (d)
사제는 자신의 소명에 대해 너무나도 강한 의혹이 일었던 믿음의 위기를
겪은 후 교회를 떠났다.

faith 신념, 신앙 overwhelming 너무나도 강력한 calling 소명 (의식)
priest 사제, 신부 plight 역경 disaster 재난 trauma 정신적 외상
crisis 위기

23 정답 (a)
회사 원장에서 자신의 개인 계좌로 수년간 자금을 빼돌린 의장이 마침내
횡령 혐의로 유죄 판결을 받았다.

corporate 회사의 ledger (사업체 등에서 거래 내역을 적은) 원장
account 계좌 chairwoman 여자 의장[회장] be convicted of
~로 유죄 판결을 받다 embezzlement 횡령 siphon (돈을) 빼돌리다
slather 낭비하다 subvert 전복시키다 scuttle 무산시키다

24 정답 (b)
국가의 역사 기록물을 자세히 조사하던 연구자는 이 나라 초창기의, 그리
고 가장 존경받던 지도자 중 한 명에 대해 뜻밖의 사실을 발견했다.

comb 자세히 조사하다 revered 존경받는 dirge 장송곡 annals
연보, 기록물 mallet 나무망치 sinew 힘줄

25 정답 (d)
많은 아메리카 인디언 부족들의 이동해 다니는 생활방식과 전통은 유럽인들
로 하여금 그들이 정착해서 농경 생활을 했다는 주장을 하지 못하게 했다.

tribe 부족 preclude 막다, 불가능하게 하다 insistence 주장
practice agriculture 농사를 짓다 clandestine 비밀의 arable
농작 가능한 felicitous 적절한 peripatetic (일을 하러) 이동해 다니는

26 정답 (a)
대기 오염을 줄이기 위해 화물 배달 트럭을 주차장에서 공회전하는 채로
내버려두는 것을 금지하는 법령이 통과되었다.

cut down on 줄이다 ordinance 법령, 조례 prohibit ~ from
-ing ~가 …하는 것을 금지하다 delivery truck 화물 배달 트럭
idle (기계가) 헛돌다, 공회전하다 draft 초안을 작성하다 flock 모이다
sap 약화시키다

27 정답 (a)
토머스 에디슨은 유년 시절에, 단 3개월 만에 초등학교를 중퇴하고 여러
가지 잡다한 일을 하게 되는 비교적 무기력한 삶을 살았다.

relatively 비교적 drop out of school 학교를 중퇴하다 take
on (일을) 떠맡다 odd jobs 잡다한 일 feckless 무기력한, 무책임한
puissant 권력 있는 meretricious 저속한, 음란한 canonical
규범적인

28 정답 (b)
재무장관이 상원 의원들 앞에서 증언하는 자리에서, 경기 침체에 대한 처
리 방식을 놓고 빗발치는 질문 공세를 받았다.

secretary of finance 재무장관 testify 증언하다 concerning ~
에 관하여 handling 취급, 처리 downturn (경기) 하강, 침체
gambit 우세를 확보하려는 수 fusillade 연속 사격, 빗발치는 것
platitude 상투어, 진부 umbrage 불쾌, 화

29 정답 (c)
홍보 책임자는 회사의 기록적인 이윤과 전례 없는 시장 지배에 대한 이야
기로 방문하는 잠재 투자자들을 즐겁게 해 주었다.

public relations 홍보 potential 잠재적인 record-setting
기록적인 profit margin 이윤 unprecedented 전례 없는
domination 지배, 우세 efface 지우다, 없애다 besmirch 더럽히다
regale 즐겁게 하다 abate 약화시키다

30 정답 (c)
초식 공룡의 특징을 천천히 움직이는 거대한 짐승으로 묘사한 것은 그 동물
의 관절이 외관상 빠른 동작을 하게끔 만들어져 있다는 사실과 모순된다.

characteristic 특징적인 depiction 묘사 herbivorous 초식성의
behemoth 거대한 짐승 belie ~이 거짓임을 보여 주다, ~과 모순되다
joint 관절 arresting 주의를 끄는 embossed 돋을새김의
plodding 천천히 움직이는, 터벅터벅 걷는 abraded (살갗이) 벗겨진

Part I

1　정답 (d)

A 어떻게 그렇게 건강해?

B 공원에서 축구를 하거든.

해설 현재의 습관을 나타낼 때는 현재 시제를 사용하므로 (d)가 정답이다.

keep in good shape 건강을 유지하다

2　정답 (a)

A 그럼 이 글을 써서 날 도와줄 거지?

B 내가 말한 '도움'은 정확히 그런 뜻이 아니야.

해설 알맞은 관계대명사를 고르는 문제이다. 문맥상 빈칸에는 선행사를 포함한 관계대명사 (a) what(= the thing which)이 적절하다. (b)는 선행사가 없고, (c)는 선행사도 없을 뿐 아니라 that 앞에 전치사가 올 수 없으므로 오답이다.

essay 보고서, 논문　**exactly** 정확히

3　정답 (d)

A 민디가 정말로 컴퓨터 파일을 훔쳤다고 생각해?

B 훔치고 싶었어도 그렇게 할 수 없었을 거야.

해설 과거 사실에 반대되는 일을 가정하고 있으므로 가정법 과거완료 (If+주어+had p.p. ~, 주어+조동사의 과거형+have p.p. ~)를 써야 한다. 따라서 정답은 (d)이며, (c)의 must not have p.p.는 '~했을 리가 없다'란 뜻이다.

steal 훔치다　**even if** ~할지라도

4　정답 (b)

A 레몬 라임 소다가 어땠어?

B 지금 네가 갖고 있다면 한 병 더 마시고 싶을 거야.

해설 another는 '또 하나의 것[사람]'이란 뜻으로 불특정한 것을 나타낼 때 쓰므로 (b)가 정답이다. (a) others는 '다른 것들[사람들]', (d) the others는 '다른 나머지 것들[사람들]'이란 뜻이다.

lemon-lime soda 레몬 라임 소다(레몬 맛이 나는 탄산음료)

5　정답 (b)

A 그 남자가 정말로 범죄 현장을 떠났나요?

B 네. 공공의 안전을 그렇게 무시하는 건 처음 봐요.

해설 선택지 모두 강조어로 쓰이지만, 이 중에서 명사(disregard)를 수식할 수 있는 것은 형용사인 (b) such이다. 나머지는 모두 부사이다.

the scene of the crime 범죄 현장　**disregard** 무시　**public safety** 공공의 안전

6　정답 (d)

A 일자리 지원한 곳에서 무슨 연락이라도 왔니?

B 아직. 하지만 다음 주 이맘때까지는 통보가 올 거야.

해설 미래 특정 시점 이전에 시작되어 미래 특정 시점에 완료되는 동작은 미래완료(will have p.p.) 시제를 사용하므로 (d)가 정답이다.

apply for 지원하다　**notify** 통보하다

7　정답 (a)

A 네 모형 비행기를 부숴서 정말 미안해.

B 이제 그걸 가지고 뭘 어떻게 할 수 있는 게 별로 없네.

해설 that 관계절이 '부서진 모형 비행기에 할 수 있는'이라는 의미의 형용사절이다. 그리고 그 앞에 유도부사 there절의 부정문이 오고 있으므로 '없다'거나 '많지 않다' 정도의 의미가 연결됨이 적절하다. 그러므로 (a)의 a lot이 정답이다.

model 모형

8　정답 (a)

A 독후감은 금요일에 제출하기로 되어 있어.

B 불행히도 아직 읽을 책도 고르지 않았는걸.

해설 의문사절의 주어가 주절의 주어와 같은 경우, 의문사절의 주어를 생략하고 〈의문사+to부정사〉 형태로 줄여 쓸 수 있는데, 이 문제는 그 용법을 알고 있는지를 묻는 문제이다. 즉 I have yet to select which book I should read에서 I should read가 to read로 바뀌므로 정답은 (a)가 된다.

book report 독후감　**be supposed to** ~하기로 되어 있다　**turn in** 제출하다　**have yet to** 아직 ~하지 않다　**select** 고르다

9　정답 (c)

A 새 스카프가 당신한테 무척 잘 어울리는데요.

B 그렇게 말씀해 주시다니 정말로 친절하세요, 감사합니다.

해설 'how 감탄문'의 올바른 어순을 묻는 문제이다. how 다음에는 형용사가 와야 하므로 (a)와 (d)는 일단 제외한다. to부정사의 의미상의 주어는 kind와 같이 사람의 성질을 나타내는 형용사가 앞에 있을 경우에는 〈of+목적격〉을 사용하므로 to tell 앞에 of you가 와야 한다. 따라서 정답은 (c)이다. 이 문장은 it's very kind of you to tell me that을 감탄문으로 고쳤다고 생각하면 쉽게 이해할 수 있다.

becoming on ~에게 어울리는

10　정답 (c)

A 해외여행은 여러모로 끔찍한 것 같아요.

B 사람들은 종종 자신이 전혀 알지 못하는 것에 대해 두려움을 갖죠.

해설 두 문장을 연결해 주는 말이 필요하므로 빈칸에는 접속사나 관계대명사가 와야 한다. (a), (b), (d)는 전치사 about의 목적어가 없으므로 일단 문법적으로 맞지 않다. 따라서 선행사 that과 목적격 관계대명사 which를 쓴 (c)가 정답이다.

terrifying 끔찍한, 무섭게 하는　**in a lot of ways** 여러모로

Part II

11　정답 (b)

환경 고문은 양심상 채광 작업을 진행하는 것을 용납할 수 없었다.

해설 동사 condone은 목적어로 동사가 올 때는 동명사 형태를 취하므로 일단 (c)와 (d)는 제외한다. 단순형 동명사(-ing)는 술어동사와 같은 시제 또는 그 이후의 시제를 나타내며, 완료형 동명사(having -ing)는 본동사 이전의 시제를 나타낸다. 여기서는 전자에 해당하므로 (b)가 정답이다.

in good conscience 양심상　**condone** 용납하다　**move forward with** ~을 진행하다　**mining operation** 채광 작업

12 정답 (a)

쓰나미 희생자 중에는 당시 그곳에서 마침 휴가를 보내던 미국인이 몇 명 있었다.

해설 vacation은 '휴가를 보내다'라는 뜻인데 여기서는 '휴가를 보내고 있던' 미국인이라고 해야 맞으므로 진행형이 되어야 한다. 따라서 정답은 happen to 다음에 be vacationing이 따라온 (a)이다.

victim 희생자 **tsunami** 쓰나미 **vacation** 휴가를 보내다

13 정답 (b)

최근에 빈발했던 학교 총기 사건을 고려하여, 해머라인 초등학교는 경비원을 추가로 고용하고 있다.

해설 전치사 given(~을 고려해 볼 때, ~을 감안하면)을 알고 있는지 묻는 문제이다. (a)는 그 앞에 주어가 없으며, (c)와 (d) 역시 '주다'라는 뜻으로는 말이 되지 않는다.

spate 대량, 빈발 **school shootings** 학교 총기 사건 **elementary** 초등학교(elementary school) **security guard** 경비원

14 정답 (c)

전 세계에는 무화과나무라고 더 알려진 약 850종의 피커스가 자라고 있다.

해설 일단 refer to A as B(A를 B라고 부르다)를 수동태로 바꾸면 A is referred to as B가 된다. A (which is) referred to as B에서 referred를 수식하는 부사 more commonly는 그 앞에 위치한다.

species 종 **fig tree** 무화과나무 **refer to A as B** A를 B라고 부르다

15 정답 (b)

범죄자와 그를 도왔던 사람들 모두 최대한 연방법의 적용을 받는다.

해설 both A and B에서 A가 명사(criminal)이므로 B도 명사이어야 하고 동시에 본동사 are의 주어가 되어야 한다. 명사가 절(aided him)을 이끌려면 그 앞에 관계사가 필요하므로 (b)가 정답이다.

criminal 범죄자 **subject to** ~의 지배를 받는 **full measure** 부족함이 없는 양

16 정답 (b)

암으로 사망하기 전에 우고 차베스는 자신을 계승할 니콜라스 마두로를 당 대표로 지명했다.

해설 동사가 앞에 있는 명사를 수식하는 형용사 역할을 하려면 to부정사 형태를 취해야 하므로 (b)가 정답이다.

prior to ~에 앞서 **nominate** 지명[임명]하다 **succeed** 계승하다

17 정답 (a)

공세에 시달리는 국회의원은 많은 보수 단체의 지지를 잃자 사퇴하는 것 외에는 달리 방도가 없음을 느꼈다.

해설 모든 선택지에 접속사가 없는 걸로 보아 빈칸에는 절과 절을 연결해 주는 분사구문이 올 자리이다. 물론 to부정사도 올 수 있지만 (c)는 의미상 말이 되지 않는다. 보수 단체의 지지를 잃은 것이 사퇴할 수밖에 없음을 느낀 것보다 앞선 시제이므로 빈칸에는 완료형 분사구문인 (a)가 적절하다.

conservative 보수적인 **embattled** 공세에 시달리는 **congressman** 국회의원 **have no choice but to** ~하지 않을 수 없다

18 정답 (c)

찰스 휴즈는 캘리포니아 주민 몇 천 명만 더 윌슨이 아니라 그에게 표를 던졌더라면 제29대 미국 대통령이 되었을 것이다.

해설 가정법 과거완료 구문으로 의미상 '~했을 것이다'가 되어야 하므로 (b)나 (c) 중에 답이 있다. 여기서 very well은 might have been을 강조하는 부사구인데, 이럴 경우 might와 have been 사이에 위치하므로 (c)가 정답이다. 만약 very well이 might have been 뒤에 온다면 마치 보어처럼 느껴져서 문장이 이상해짐을 금방 알 수 있을 것이다.

vote for ~에 찬성표를 던지다 **might have p.p.** ~했을 것이다

19 정답 (d)

눈과 쿤은 히말라야 산들인데, 그것의 고지대로부터 9마일 길이의 샤파트 빙하가 흐른다.

해설 알맞은 관계대명사를 고르는 문제이다. Nun and Kun are the Himalayan mountains와 the 9-mile-long Shafat Glacier flows from Nun and Kun's heights를 합치면 중복되는 Nun and Kun이 선행사가 되고 두 번째 문장의 from Nun and Kun's heights가 from whose heights로 바뀌어 앞으로 나가므로 정답은 (d)이다.

height 고지, 정상 **glacier** 빙하

20 정답 (c)

A⁺ Dogs의 훈련 과정은 애완동물의 요구를 하나하나 틀림없이 만족시켜 주는 다양한 훈련 기술을 제공한다.

해설 두 가지 동사의 올바른 어순을 묻는 문제이다. 문맥상 먼저 be guaranteed to do(반드시 ~하다)라는 숙어에서 be가 빠진 과거분사가 앞의 techniques를 수식하는 형태가 되어야 하고, 그다음에 needs를 목적어로 취하는 동사 suit가 따라온 (c)가 정답이다. techniques 다음에 which are를 넣어보면 쉽게 이해가 될 것이다.

a range of 다양한 **individual** 각각의 **needs** 필요, 요구 **be guaranteed to** 반드시 ~하다 **suit** 만족시키다

21 정답 (c)

지난 몇 십 년 동안 그리스는 서유럽 탐험가들이 국경 너머로 탈취해간 수백 점의 공예품을 반환해 달라고 요구했다.

해설 물질·추상·고유명사는 원칙적으로 정관사를 사용할 수 없으나 수식어구로 한정될 경우에는 정관사 the를 붙여야 한다. 여기서는 추상명사 return이 of hundreds of artifacts의 제한을 받으므로 그 앞에 the가 붙은 (c)가 정답이다.

artifact 공예품 **explorer** 탐험가

22 정답 (c)

그 소설가는 북미에서 검열의 위협에 직면하기보다는 유럽에서 작품을 출간하기로 작정했다.

해설 문맥상 빈칸에는 '~보다는, ~대신에'라는 말이 와야 자연스러우므로 (c)가 정답이다.

censorship 검열 **novelist** 소설가 **rather than** ~보다는

23 정답 (a)

그 거대 기술 회사는 만약 경쟁자가 소송에 승리한다면 두바이 공장을 어쩔 수 없이 폐쇄해야 할 것이다.

해설 알맞은 시제를 고르는 문제이다. 시간·조건의 부사절에서는 현재 시제가 미래 시제를 대신하므로 (a)가 정답이다. if 이하가 미래의 일이라고 해서 (b)를 고르지 않도록 유의하자.

be forced to ~하지 않을 수 없다 shut down 폐쇄하다
competitor 경쟁자 lawsuit 소송

24 정답 (b)

한때 꽤 귀에 거슬리는 소리를 냈던 자동차 엔진이 제대로 정비를 하자 칙칙 거리는 소리조차 나지 않았다.

해설 not so much as(~조차 않다)라는 숙어를 알면 쉽게 풀수 있는 문제이지만, 설령 몰랐다 해도 우급 비교를 부정할 때는 〈not+as[so]+형용사[부사]+as〉와 같이 표현하므로 (b)를 정답으로 어렵지 않게 고를 수 있을 것이다.

cacophonous 귀에 거슬리는 let out (소리를) 내다 splutter 일련의 짧은 폭발음 같은 소리, 칙칙 거리는 소리 tune 정비하다

25 정답 (a)

흙으로 된 제방은 대규모 홍수 때 비록 쉽게 붕괴되긴 하지만 주변 지역이 침수되는 것을 예방하기 위해 널리 쓰인다.

해설 양보의 뜻을 가진 〈형용사+as+주어+동사〉 구문을 묻는 문제이므로 (a)가 정답이다. 참고로, 형용사 자리에 부사나 무관사 명사도 올 수 있으며 이때의 as는 though의 뜻이다.

earthen 흙으로 된 levee 제방 collapse 붕괴하다 inundation 침수 prone to ~하기[당하기] 쉬운

Part III

26 정답 (b) which to pay with → with which to pay

(a) A 이 식당은 신용 카드는 받지 않는 것 같군요.
(b) B 하지만 지불할 현금이 없는걸요.
(c) A 괜찮아요. 이번엔 제가 낼 테니까 다음에 갚으면 돼요.
(d) B 아, 고마워요. 다음번 점심은 제가 살게요.

해설 〈전치사+관계대명사+to부정사〉 구문을 묻는 문제이다. 원래 이 문장은 I have no cash which I can pay with. 혹은 I have no cash with which I can pay.였는데, 주절의 주어와 관계대명사절의 주어가 같은 경우 주어와 can을 생략하고 그 자리에 to부정사의 to를 넣을 수 있다. 이 경우 전치사는 반드시 관계대명사 앞에 위치시켜야 하므로 (b)가 정답이다. 참고로 which를 생략하고 to부정사가 바로 수식하여 to pay with로 고쳐도 무방하다.

cover (요금·비용 등을) 감당하다 next lunch will be on me 다음 점심은 제가 살게요

27 정답 (b) wouldn't support → hadn't supported

(a) A 접수 일을 보던 때가 기억나세요?
(b) B 당신이 저의 승진을 돕지 않았더라면 지금도 그곳에서 일하고 있을 거예요.
(c) A 음, 전 당신이 영업부에 꼭 맞을 거로 생각했죠.
(d) B 네, 저에게 잘 맞아서 일을 신 나게 하고 있어요.

해설 B는 혼합 가정법이다. 즉 주절은 현재 사실에 반대되는 '가정법 과거' 문장이고, 종속절은 의미상 과거 사실에 반대되는 '가정법 과거완료(if+주어+had p.p. ~)' 구문이 되어야 하므로 wouldn't support를 hadn't supported로 고쳐야 한다.

promotion 승진 fit in ~에 꼭 맞다 sales department 영업부 suit 맞다, 편리하다

28 정답 (a) even most accomplished → even the most accomplished

(a) 연설이 초래하는 압박감에 대처하는 방식은 사람마다 다 다르며, 이런 압박감은 심지어 가장 능숙한 연설자라도 어느 정도는 경험하게 된다. (b) 어떤 사람은 연설하기 몇 분 전에 정신을 맑게 하려고 호흡에 집중하며 명상을 한다. (c) 또 어떤 사람은 긴장한 것에 대해 신경을 쓰지 않기 위해 사람들과 교류하고 대화를 나누는 것이 필요하다. (d) 또한, 자신이 말할 내용과 그것을 말할 방법을 정확히 마음에 골똘히 그려보는 시각화 기법에 의존하는 사람도 있다.

해설 3음절 이상 형용사의 최상급을 표기할 때는 그 앞에 the most를 붙이므로 (a)의 even most accomplished를 even the most accomplished로 고쳐야 한다.

cope with ~에 대처하다 bring on 야기하다 public speaking 대중 연설 to some degree 어느 정도는 accomplished 숙달된, 노련한 orator 웅변가, 연설자 meditation 명상 clear 맑게 하다 interaction 상호작용 take one's attention off ~에서 눈을 돌리다 at hand 당면한 swear by ~을 깊이 신뢰하다 visualization 눈 앞에 없는 물체의 영상을 마음속에 그리기 intently 집중하여, 골똘히 picture 마음에 그리다

29 정답 (b) So close to stepping → Stepping so close to

(a) 세계가 1962년 쿠바 미사일 위기 때보다 핵 폐지에 더 근접한 적은 한 번도 없었다. (b) 결정적 국면에 거의 다가가면서 대립하던 양쪽의 두 강대국, 즉 미국과 구소련이 변화하는 듯 보였다. (c) 실제로, 양국은 불과 몇 달 후에 모스크바-워싱턴 '핫라인'을 개설했다. (d) 이는, 원칙적으로는 장래에 위기가 닥치면 교섭과 갈등 해결을 용이하게 해 줄 직접적인 의사소통 라인이었다.

해설 (b)는 동사(seemed)는 있지만 주어가 없다. 그러므로 동명사 stepping을 주어로 내세운 다음, 이를 수식하는 so close와 접근 대상인 to the brink를 차례로 붙이면 주어부가 완성된다. 따라서 So close to stepping을 Stepping so close to로 바꾸어야 한다.

annihilation 소멸 brink 고비, 결정적 국면 superpower 초강대국 confrontation 대치, 대립 USSR 소련(Union of Soviet Socialist Republics) establish 개설하다 hotline (정부 간의) 직통 전화 in theory 원칙적으로는 facilitate 용이하게 하다 negotiation 교섭 conflict 갈등 resolution 해결

30 정답 (b) have decimated → had decimated

(a) 유럽인들이 도착하기 이전의 미주리 주는 삼림이 울창하고 많은 흑곰들이 서식하던 곳이었다. (b) 하지만 1920년대 무렵, 사냥에 대한 규제가 없고 서식지가 파괴되면서 이곳의 흑곰이 대량으로 죽었다. (c) 50년대와 60년대에, 다른 지역에서 미주리 남부의 오자크 숲으로 곰을 운송해오는 재도입 캠페인이 개시되었다. (d) 이제, 생물학자들은 수백만 마리의 곰들이 다시 미주리 주를 보금자리로 여기는 것으로 추정하고 있다.

해설 (b)는 by the 1920s가 있으므로 '유럽인들이 도착한 후부터 1920년대까지' 벌어진 일을 나타내는 시제를 써야 한다. 따라서 have decimated를 대과거인 had decimated로 고쳐야 옳다.

prior to ~이전에 forested 숲으로 뒤덮인 healthy 많은, 큰 unregulated 규제되지 않은 habitat 서식지 destruction 파괴 decimate 대량으로 죽이다 reintroduction 재도입 initiate 개시하다 transport 운송하다 biologist 생물학자 estimate 추정하다 call 여기다

Part I

1

미국의 많은 지역이 계속 경제난을 겪고 있는 반면, 한때 버려진 작은 지역들이 급속히 발전하고 있다. 여기에는 노스다코타 주 마이넛과 윌리스턴 주변의 평원 지대와 텍사스 주의 남부 평야 지대가 들어간다. 이 두 지역에서 사람을 결속시키는 특징은 대규모 석유 및 천연가스 지층이 지하 깊숙한 곳에 자리하고 있다는 점이다. 최근에 수압 파쇄 기법이 상업화되면서 이와 같은 손대지 않은 매장 층으로의 접근이 가능해졌다. 그리하여 두 지역에는 <u>막대한 자본과 노동이 유입</u>되었다.

(a) 기초 산업의 호전
(b) 다른 지역들보다 낮은 유류세율
(c) 경제적 다각화의 부진
(d) 막대한 자본과 노동의 유입

해설 한때 버림받은 곳이었지만 대규모 석유 및 천연가스 지층이 있어 경제난 속에서도 급속히 발전하고 있는 두 지역을 소개하고 있다. 따라서 새롭게 경제적 호황을 기대할 수 있는 이 지역들에 어울리는 현상으로 (d)가 적절하다.

struggle 어려움을 겪다 **forsaken** 버려진 **pocket** (작은) 지역 **plains** 평원 지대(flats) **unifying** 통합시키는 **characteristic** 특징 **existence** 존재 **formation** 지층 **commercialization** 상업화 **hydraulic fracturing** 수압 파쇄 기법 **accessing** 이용, 접근 **hitherto** 지금까지 **untapped** 손대지 않은 **deposit** 매장 층 **upturn** 상승, 호전 **grassroots** 기초 **fuel tax rate** 유류세율 **stagnation** 부진 **diversification** 다각화 **infusion** 주입 **capital** 자본

2

테로네티 더플 백

<u>한정된 예산으로 일체형 제품을 가질</u> 수 없다고 누가 말하던가요? 현대의 여행자에게 짐 문제를 혁신적으로 해결해 주는 테로네티 더플 팩을 소개합니다. 80리터들이 메인 칸에 튼튼한 상단 손잡이가 두 개 달린 이 상품은 가격이 저렴한 최고의 더플 백입니다. 하지만 이게 끝이 아닙니다. 손잡이 양쪽 끝에 있는 찍찍이가 끈을 풀고, 그것을 완전히 펴면 더플 백이 이제 편리한 배낭이 됩니다! 다루기가 편리한 더플을 원하든, 손을 쓸 필요가 없는 배낭 방식을 원하든 간에 테로네티 더플 팩은 귀하를 위한 가방입니다.

(a) 한정된 예산으로 일체형 제품을 가질
(b) 찍찍이의 힘을 믿을
(c) 어른일 때 배낭여행을 갈
(d) 더플을 여행 가방으로 변환시킬

해설 가격이 저렴하고 일반 가방도 되고 배낭도 되어 편리한 일체형 더플 백을 광고하고 있으므로 (a)가 정답이다.

duffel bag 더플 백 **innovative** 혁신적인 **luggage** 짐 **solution** 해결 **compartment** 칸, 격실 **sturdy** 튼튼한 **ultimate** 최고의 **affordable** (가격이) 알맞은 **undo** 풀다 **Velcro** 벨크로, 찍찍이 **strap** 끈 **extend** 펴다 **backpack** 배낭 **hands-free** 손을 쓸 필요가 없는 **all in one** 모두 하나로 된; 하나로 모든 것을 겸한 제품 **on a budget** 한정된 예산으로 **go backpacking** 배낭여행을 가다 **convert** 변환시키다

3

표트르 대제라고도 알려진 표트르 1세는 1682년부터 1725년까지 러시아를 통치했다. 그는, 대부분이 프랑스와 같은 서유럽 국가 출신인 참모들의 끈질긴 요청을 받고 다양한 문화적 변화를 단행했다. 여기에는 의무적으로 턱수염을 깎게 하거나, 귀족들로 하여금 프랑스 패션을 받아들이게 하는 것 등이 포함되었다. 또한 그는 서구 열강의 군대를 따라 하고자 군부를 개편했으며, 대대적인 함선 건조 사업을 시작했다. 러시아의 많은 사람들은 이런 상의하달식 변화에 크게 분개했다. 하지만 이를 통해 러시아는 <u>중세의 전통을 버리고 근대 유럽인이 되는</u> 결과를 맞게 되었다.

(a) 표트르는 마음 내키지 않았지만 많은 중대한 변화를 겪는
(b) 중세의 전통을 버리고 근대 유럽인이 되는
(c) 서구의 패션과 경쟁하기 위해 독자적인 패션을 개발하는
(d) 모두가 인정하는 프랑스의 이전 식민지들의 지배자가 되는

해설 러시아의 표트르 1세가 단행한 개혁에 관한 글이다. 빈칸에는 개혁의 결과가 올 자리로, however로 시작하는 것으로 보아 앞의 내용에 상반되는 긍정적인 내용임을 알 수 있다. 개혁의 핵심이 근대 서구 열강의 모습을 따르는 것이므로 (b)가 적절하다.

czar 황제 **behest** 끈질긴 요청 **advisor** 참모 **hail from** ~ 출신이다 **implement** 시행하다 **mandatory** 의무적인 **beard** 턱수염 **adoption** 채택 **nobleman** 귀족 **reorganize** 개편하다 **initiate** 개시하다 **navy** 함선 **enterprise** 사업 **resent** ~에 분개하다 **top-down** 상의하달식의 **undergo** 겪다 **significant** 중대한 **hesitancy** 망설임 **medieval** 중세의 **undisputed** 모두가 인정하는 **overlord** 지배자, 권력자

4

일기 예보

오늘 오후 이른 시각부터 헨더슨 지역 전체에 폭우가 지속적으로 내리고 있는 가운데, 일부 구역은 1인치가 넘는 강우량을 기록했습니다. 이 폭풍우는 밤새 계속 될 것으로 예상되며, 더불어 기온이 하강하면서 영하로 이어질 가능성이 크겠습니다. 이에 따라 얼어붙은 도로를 매우 위험한 상태로 분류하오니, 모든 주민들은 절대적으로 필요한 경우가 아니면 오늘밤 실내에 머물러 주시기 바랍니다. 이런 기후 상태가 내일 아침을 거쳐 더 지속될 가능성이 있다는 점을 고려해, <u>학교가 내일 모든 학생들의 편의를 위해 휴교합니다</u>.

(a) 평상시 하던 야외 활동은 지속되어야 합니다.
(b) 눈이 누그러지지 않고 계속 내릴 것으로 예상됩니다
(c) 학교가 내일 모든 학생들의 편의를 위해 휴교합니다
(d) 시장이 운전 금지령을 해제했습니다

해설 마지막 문장의 these conditions는 비가 계속되면서 기온이 영하로 떨어지고 도로 상태가 나쁜 상황을 가리킨다. 이런 상황을 고려하여 벌어질 수 있는 일로는 (c)가 적절하다.

heavy rain 폭우 steadily 지속적으로 neighborhood 지역 accompany 동반하다 temperature 기온 freezing 영하의 resultant 결과로서 생기는, 그에 따른 icy 얼어붙은 categorize 분류하다 extremely hazardous 매우 위험한 be encouraged to ~하도록 권고되다 in light of ~에 비추어, ~을 고려하여 sustain 지속시키다 unabated 약해지지 않는 suspend 일시 정지하다 ban 금지령 lift 해제하다 mayor 시장

5

우리가 예술에 얼마나 관심이 있든 간에, 우리는 저마다 내면의 창조성을 표출할 출구를 필요로 합니다. 이것이 바로 뭔가 새로운 창조적인 일을 발견하려는 개인과 그것을 공유할 사람들을 돕는 온라인 커뮤니티 '미트-크리에이트'의 설립 원칙입니다. 커뮤니티 회원들은 회화, 편물, 목공 등, 공통적으로 관심을 갖는 활동에 기초해 그룹을 형성합니다. 각 그룹 내에서는 강좌가 개설되고, 프로젝트의 설정 및 공유가 이루어지며, 적극적인 지원책이 제공됩니다. 어떤 경우에는 도시권에서의 실제 만남이 기획됩니다. 오늘 미트-크리에이트에 가입하셔서, 같은 생각을 가진 분들의 도움을 받아 여러분의 창조성에 활기를 불어넣으세요.

(a) 같은 생각을 가진 분들의 도움을 받아 여러분의 창조성에 활기를 불어넣으세요
(b) 여러분의 인근 지역 사회에 거주하는 성공한 예술가들을 만나 보세요
(c) 할인된 가격으로 첫 미술용품을 배송받으세요
(d) 또한 그림 그리는 법에 주력하고자 하는 분들을 만나 보세요

해설 회원들의 예술성 발휘를 돕는 온라인 커뮤니티를 광고하고 있다. 마지막 문장이 Join Meet-Create today로 시작하고 있으므로, 빈칸에는 이 커뮤니티에 가입함으로써 얻게 되는 이점을 드러내며 광고 내용과 일맥상통하는 (a)가 정답이다.

regardless of ~와 상관없이 outlet 출구 creativity 창조성 founding 설립 principle 원칙 pursuit 추구 knitting 편물 woodworking 목공 available 이용할 수 있는 real-life 실제의 meet-up 만남 organize 기획하다 metropolitan area 도시권 jumpstart ~에 활기를 불어넣다 like-minded 같은 생각을 가진 accomplished 재주가 많은 shipment 배송 art supplies 미술용품 reduced 할인된 focus on ~에 주력하다

6

서양에서 달력을 본다면 그것은 그레고리력일 가능성이 높다. 이는 중요한 종교적 행사, 특히 다른 어느 행사보다 더욱 한결같이 매년 동일한 태양일을 고수하고 있는 부활절을 지키기 위한 목적으로 1582년에 제작되었다. 율리우스 카이사르에 의해 도입된 율리우스력은 이보다 더 이전의 것이었고 더 원시적인 역법 체계였는데, 이 역법이 윤년을 단순화해서 사용하다 보니 실제 태양일에 비교하여 역일이 점점 '표류'하는 결과가 빚어졌다. 새로운 그레고리력은 100으로 나눠지는 해에서 이들 윤년을 쳐내는 식으로 계산법을 개선하였고, 이에 따라 그레고리력이 확실히 태양년의 길이를 더욱 정확하게 반영하게 되었다.

(a) 하지와 동지, 춘분과 추분을 이용해 보정하다 보니
(b) 이 역법이 하루의 길이를 마찬가지로 잘못 인식하다 보니
(c) 이 역법이 윤년을 단순화해서 사용하다 보니
(d) 이 역법이 그레고리력의 디자인에 끼친 영향으로

해설 그레고리력의 탄생 배경을 설명하는 글이다. 그 이전의 역법인 율리우스력에 따르면 세월이 흐를수록 실제 태양일과 역일의 오차가 점점 벌어지게 되는데, 이는 율리우스력이 1년의 길이를 365.25일로 생각하고(실제로는 365.2422일임) 무조건 4년마다 윤년을 두었기 때문이다. 즉, 율리우스력이 윤년을 너무 단순화해서 사용했기 때문에 오차가 벌어지는 일이 생긴 것으로 빈칸에는 (c)가 적절하다.

chances are ~할 가능성이 충분하다 Gregorian calendar 그레고리력 Easter 부활절 consistently 한결같이 solar day 태양일(태양이 자오선을 통과하여 다음에 다시 통과할 때까지의 시간) Julian calendar 율리우스력 initiate 착수시키다 result in ~라는 결과를 낳다 gradual 점진적인 drift 표류 calendar day 역일 compared to ~와 비교하여 refine 개선하다 calculation 계산 trim 다듬다, 잘라내다 leap year 윤년 divisible 나누어떨어지는 ensure 확실하게 하다 solar year 태양년 solstice 하지점과 동지점 equinox 춘분과 추분 calibration 보정 측정 misconception 오해 simplified 간소화한 employment 이용

7

지구에서 관찰되는 대부분의 혜성은 멀리 떨어져 있으며, 태양을 도는 그것의 궤도에 따라서 예정된 시간에 나타나고 또 나타나기를 반복하는 반면, 렉셀 혜성은 그러한 두 가지 사항에 대해서 특이한 모습을 보였다. 1770년 6월 14일에 천문학자 샤를 메시에가 처음 관측한 이 혜성은 궤도를 도는 동안에 우리 행성(지구)에 너무나 가깝게 근접하는 것으로 밝혀졌다. 이 혜성이 지구에 가장 근접했을 때 지구와의 거리가 140만 마일이었는데, 이는 지구와 달 사이 거리의 6배밖에 되지 않는 수치이다. 하지만 이 이후로 아무도 렉셀 혜성을 관찰하지 못했다. 알 수 없는 이유로 1770년 후에 그것의 궤도가 수정되었고, 이제는 사라진 것으로 여겨지고 있다.

(a) 규칙적으로 일관성 없는 궤도를 보인다
(b) 혜성 구성 이론이 틀렸음을 입증한다
(c) 어느 한순간에 지구와 거의 충돌할 뻔했다
(d) 그러한 두 가지 사항에 대해서 특이한 모습을 보였다

해설 일반 혜성이 지구에서 멀리 떨어져 있고 일정하게 나타나는 특성이 있는데, 빈칸 이후로 렉셀 혜성이 지구에 너무 근접했고 1770년 이후로 볼 수 없었다고 하므로 일반 혜성과 다른 모습을 보였다는 요점을 나타내는 (d)가 적절하다.

comet 혜성 visible 관찰되는 prescribed 예정된 orbit 궤도 astronomer 천문학자 trajectory 궤도 shockingly 극단적으로, 매우 planet 행성 alter 바꾸다 inconsistent 일관성 없는 disprove ~이 틀렸음을 입증하다 composition 구성 collide with ~와 충돌하다 anomalous 이례적인, 변칙의 count 사항

8

식물 병원체인 감자 역병균은 1840년대 아일랜드의 감자 기근 사태를 촉발시킨 것으로 가장 잘 알려져 있지만, 이 파괴적인 균류는 오늘날에도 여전히 문제를 일으키고 있다. 실제로, 감자 역병균으로 인해 농작물 손실과 계속 진행되는 근절 노력에 드는 비용이 전 세계적으로 매년 60억 달러가 넘는 것으로 추정되고 있다. 가장 문제가 되는 것은 현대에 등장한 종이 악명 높은 이전 것보다 훨씬 더 치명적이라는 사실이다. 이렇게 된 것은 아마도 전염병에 잘 견디는 감자 품종을 재배하려는 인간의 노력이 원인인 것 같다. 이 모든 것은 또 한 번 대규모 감자 흉작이 발생할 수 있다는 공포감을 불러일으킨다.

(a) 또 한 번 대규모 감자 흉작이 발생할 수 있다는
(b) 그 해로운 균류가 더 많은 유전학적 돌연변이를 일으킬 거라는
(c) 다른 미지의 식물 병원체들이 공격할 태세를 갖추고 있을지도 모른다는
(d) 감자가 어느 날 더 이상 주식이 되지 못할 거라는

해설 감자 역병균이 역사적으로 큰 문제였던 적이 있지만 오늘날에도 여전히 골칫거리라는 내용이며, 이 문제가 점점 치명적으로 되어 또 한 번 안 좋은 결과를 가져올 수 있다는 결론으로 이어지는 것이 적절하다.

pathogen 병원체 Phytophthora infestans 감자 역병균
precipitate 촉발시키다 famine 기근 devastating 파괴적인
fungus 균류 cause trouble 문제를 일으키다 estimate 추정하다
crop 농작물 ongoing 진행 중인 eradication 근절, 박멸
manifestation 나타남 species 종 virulent 치명적인 infamous
악명 높은 predecessor 이전 것 transformation 변화 breed
재배하다 strain 변종, 품종 resist 잘 견디다 infection 전염병
raise 불러일으키다 realm 영역 genetic mutation 유전학적 돌연변이
be poised to ~할 만반의 태세를 갖추다 strike 공격하다 cease
멈추다 dietary staple 주식

9

아주까리 씨앗, 즉 아주까리 열매를 수 세기 동안 생산 및 가공해 온 것은
그것의 독특한 기름 때문이었다. 피마자기름은 치료 약에서부터 공업용 윤
활유, 식품 보존제까지 안 쓰이는 데가 없었다. 그와 동시에, 살아있는 종
자에서 발견되는 화합물 리신의 독성 수준은 건강에 심각한 위험 요소가
된다. 4~8개의 씨앗 섭취는 치사량으로 여겨진다. 그리하여 이 식물은 사
람에게 유용할 수도 있고 해로울 수도 있는 이중성을 지니고 있다는 면에
서 독특하다 하겠다.

(a) 그와 동시에
(b) 결과적으로
(c) 그러므로
(d) 결국

해설 유용할 수도 있고 해로울 수도 있는 아주까리의 이중성을 설명하고
있다. 빈칸을 중심으로 앞에서는 유용성에 대해 말하고 있고, 뒤에서는 위
험성에 대해 이야기하고 있다. 따라서 두 가지 상반된 사실을 한 번에 설
명할 때 적절한 (a)가 정답이다.

castor bean 피마자, 아주까리 process 가공하다 put to use
사용하다 medicinal 의약의 healing 치유, 치료 industrial 공업의
lubrication 윤활 food preservation 식품 보존 toxic 유독성의
compound 화합물 ingest 섭취하다 lethal dose 치사량 duality
이중성 simultaneously 동시에 consequently 그 결과로서
wherefore 그러므로 inevitably 불가피하게, 결국

10

아기가 어떤 식으로든 말을 할 수 있으려면 1년이 걸릴지도 모르는데, 그
사이에 부모가 아기의 생각과 느낌을 이해하기란 힘들 것이다. 반대로, 아
이들 스스로는 다른 아이들의 정서적 상태를 정확하게 식별할 수 있을지
도 모른다. 이는 생후 5개월쯤 된 아기가 다른 유아가 표현하고 있는 감정
을 식별해서 그대로 따라 할 수 있다는 사실을 발견한 새로운 발달 심리학
연구에 따른 결론이다. 생후 6개월이 되면 아기는 친숙한 어른에 대해서도
그렇게 할 수가 있는데, 이는 부모가 아기를 이해하는 것보다 아기가 부모
를 더 잘 이해할지도 모른다는 것을 의미한다.

(a) 다시 말해서
(b) 게다가
(c) 반대로
(d) 요컨대

해설 빈칸을 중심으로 앞에서는 부모가 아기의 생각과 느낌을 이해하기
어려운 반면 뒤 문장에서는 아기들이 다른 아기들의 정서적 상태를 알 수
있을지도 모른다는 상반된 내용을 말하고 있으므로 (c)가 적절하다.

capacity 능력 comprehend 이해하다 precisely 정확히
identify 식별하다 developmental psychology 발달 심리학
mimic 흉내 내다 obtain 얻다

Part II

11

지금까지 발견되지 않은 동물은 가장 깊숙한 열대 우림이나 가장 외딴 사
막 고유의 종임이 틀림없다고 생각하는 경향이 있다. (a) 당연히, 어떤 지
역에서 인간과 공존하고 있는 생물은 분명히 수 세기 전에 목격되어 목록
에 올라와 있을 것으로 여겨진다. (b) 예를 들면, 오늘 현재 목록에 올라와
있는 존재가 인정된 새의 종은 전 세계적으로 만 개가 넘는다. (c) 이런 생
각은 2013년에 캄보디아 재봉새가 학술지에 추가됨으로써 틀렸음이 증
명되었다. (d) 2009년에 처음으로 주목받고 4년 후 별개의 종으로 확정된
이 새는 캄보디아의 수도이자 최대 도시인 프놈펜에서 확연히 잘 보이는
곳에서 살아왔다.

heretofore 지금까지 species 종 endemic 고유의 rainforest
열대 우림 remote 외딴 assume 당연한 것으로 여기다 cohabit
동거하다 catalogue 목록을 작성하다 as of today 오늘 현재로
Cambodian Tailorbird 캄보디아 재봉새 refute 반박하다, 논박하다
notion 개념, 생각 ascertain 확정하다 in plain sight 앞이 잘 보여
capital 수도

해설 인간과 가까운 곳에서 살고 있는 동물은 이미 수세기 전에 발견되어
목록에 올라와 있을 것으로 생각하지만, 2009년에 대도시에서 신종 조류
가 발견됨으로써 이러한 생각이 잘못됐음을 지적하는 글이다. 따라서 목
록에 올라와 있는 새의 종류가 몇 개인가 하는 것은 이 글의 주제에서 완
전히 벗어나 있다.

12

캐나다 횡단 고속도로를 타고 밴프 국립공원을 관통하는 운전자들은 몇몇
특이한 광경을 기대할 것이다. (a) 밴프는 실제로 캐나다에서 최초로 생긴
국립공원이며, 세계에서 사람들이 가장 많이 찾는 공원 중의 하나이다. (b)
공원 구역 내에는 두 개의 아치형 고가도로가 식물로 덮여 있는데, 사람들
의 통행을 위한 것이 아니다. (c) 이는 차들이 쌩쌩 달리는 4차선 도로 위
를 동물들이 안전하게 지나다닐 수 있도록 특별히 제작된, 그리고 감시를
받고 있는 야생 생물용 고가로이다. (d) 야생 생물을 건너다니게 하기 위해
캐나다 횡단 고속도로 밑에 설치한 22개의 길도 고가로보다 덜 눈에 띄지
만, 효과적인 것은 마찬가지다.

해설 캐나다 밴프 국립공원을 관통하는 고속도로를 야생 동물이 지나
다닐 수 있도록 공원 측이 설치한 overpass(고속도로 위 고가 도로)와
underpass(고속도로 아래를 통과하는 길)를 설명하는 글이다. 밴프 국립
공원 자체에 관한 내용인 (a)는 이 주제와 전혀 관계없다.

Trans-Canada Highway 캐나다 횡단 고속도로 limit 구역, 경계
arched 아치형의 overpass 고가로, 육교 vegetation 식물
wildlife 야생 생물 speeding 과속하는 noticeable 눈에 띄는
underpass (다른 도로·철도의) 아래쪽 도로

Part III

심리학자들이 개체군에 대한 연구를 할 때, 그들은 자기들이 목격하는 행동이 그 개체들이 일상생활에서 보여주는 행동의 전형이라고 가정한다. 하지만 호손 효과는 이러한 가정에 이의를 제기한다. 호손 효과는 작업 공간의 조명을 밝게 하면 생산성이 증대하는지를 알아보기 위해 호손 웍스 전기 공장에서 행해진 실험에서 관찰되었다. 연구자들은 일부 근로자의 생산성이 높아진 것을 발견했지만, 그것은 더 밝아진 조명 때문이 아니었다. 그들은 근로자들이 평상시대로 행동하지 않은 것은 자신이 실험에 참가하고 있다는 사실을 알고 있었기 때문이라는 결론을 내렸다.

Q 지문의 주제는?
(a) 직원으로부터 생산성을 끌어내기 위한 전략
(b) 사회적 행동을 연구하는 사람들에 대한 영향
(c) 작업 관례에 대한 심리학적 연구의 필요성
(d) 실험하는 동안 행동이 변화하여 발생한 왜곡된 결과

해설 '호손 효과(Hawthorne Effect)'를 설명하는 글로, 이는 누군가 자신을 지켜보고 있다는 사실을 의식해서 본래의 모습과 다른 행동을 취한다는 이론이다. 따라서 실험 대상의 변화된 행동으로 인한 잘못된 결과를 나타내는 (d)가 주제로 적절하다.

psychologist 심리학자 **group of individuals** 개체군 **assume** 가정하다 **representative** 대표하는, 전형적인 **call ~ into question** ~에 이의를 제기하다 **experiment** 실험 **determine** 알아내다 **productivity** 생산성 **alter** 바꾸다 **participate in** ~에 참가하다 **engender** 발생시키다 **research on** ~에 대한 연구 **skew** 왜곡하다

14

커피콩 생산은 지구상에서 가장 착취적인 산업 중의 하나일 수 있지만, 또한 경제적으로 가장 많은 힘을 실어주는 산업 중의 하나가 될 수 있는 잠재력을 갖고 있습니다. 이것이 바로, 모든 커피콩을 지속 가능 경영과 윤리 경영을 하는 커피 농장으로부터 공급받는 브라이트 로스터즈의 인도적 신념입니다. 저희와 제휴한 중미와 동남아시아의 농부들은 엄격한 환경 기준을 따르고, 근로자들을 공정하게 대우하며, 그들에게 공정한 대가를 치르는 데 헌신하고 있습니다. 바로 이 때문에 여러분이 카페에서 브라이트 로스터즈에서 만든 라테를 주문하면 여러분의 돈이 공정한 작업장 관행을 후원하게 됨을 확신하셔도 됩니다.

Q 주로 광고되고 있는 것은?
(a) 착취에 반대하는 인권 단체
(b) 윤리적으로 신뢰할 수 있는 커피콩 소매업자
(c) 브라이트 로스터즈 커피를 판매하는 현지 카페
(d) 환경 친화적인 커피 농장을 운영하는 회사

해설 노동 착취 없이 근로자들을 공정하게 대하는 윤리 경영을 하는 커피 농장으로부터 커피콩을 공급받는 공정 무역 커피인 자사 제품을 이용해 달라는 커피콩 소매업체의 광고이다. 따라서 정답은 (b)이다.

coffee bean 커피콩 **exploitative** 착취적인 **potential** 가능성, 잠재력 **empower** 힘을 부여하다 **source** 공급받다 **sustainably** 지속 가능하게, 환경 파괴 없이 지속될 수 있게 **ethically** 윤리적으로 **plantation** 농장 **dedicated to** ~에 헌신하는 **stringent** 엄격한 **latte** 뜨거운 우유를 탄 에스프레소 커피 **rest assured** ~을 확신해도 [믿어도] 된다 **workplace** 작업장 **responsible** 신뢰할 수 있는 **retailer** 소매업자 **ecofriendly** 환경친화적인

15

> 편집자에게,
>
> 귀사의 7월 5일 화요일 자 신문에 '권위주의를 옹호하며: 경제적인 관점에서 칠레의 피노체트 지지'라는 제목의 의견 기사가 실렸습니다. 이 기사는 독재자 아우구스토 피노체트 정권 때 실시된 권위주의적 경제 개혁의 결과로 칠레 국민들이 오늘날 사실상 더 유복해졌음을 보여 주려는 취지로 쓰였습니다. 칠레 출신의 여성으로서 저는 필자가 그 문제를 냉담하고 무례하게 취급한 것에 대해 분노했습니다. 수십 년간 자행된 인권 남용을 진부한 경제 분석 몇 줄로 축소하는 것은 비양심적인 처사이며, 따라서 저는 귀사의 간행물 구독을 중단했습니다.
>
> 재닛 알바레즈

Q 편지에서 알바레즈 씨가 주로 하고 있는 것은?
(a) 매체의 한 견해에 대한 반감 표현하기
(b) 신문 기자의 잘못된 보도를 정정하기
(c) 구독을 취소한 이유 문의하기
(d) 칠레의 경제적 성공 원인을 다른 관점에서 주장하기

해설 칠레의 독재자인 아우구스토 피노체트를 경제적인 결과 측면에서 두둔하는 신문 기사에 대해 피노체트가 저지른 인권 남용을 축소하고 있다며 항의하는 편지이다.

edition 판 **entitled** ~라는 제목의 **authoritarianism** 권위주의, 독재주의 **argument for** ~에 찬성함 **op-ed** (신문의 사설 반대쪽 페이지로 칼럼, 특별기고 등 논평 기사가 실리는) 기명 논평 페이지 **purport** 취지로 하다 **better off** 부유한 **institute** 시행하다 **dictator** 독재자 **descent** 혈통, 가문 **outrage** 격분하게 하다 **callous** 냉담한 **irreverent** 무례한 **human rights abuse** 인권 남용 **platitudinous** 진부한 **unconscionable** 비양심적인, 불합리한 **suspend** 중단하다 **subscription** 구독 **publication** 간행물 **disapproval** 반감, 못마땅함 **erroneous** 잘못된 **inquire into** 조사하다 **assert** 주장하다 **alternative** 대신하는

16

미시시피 강은 아마도 북미에서 가장 유명한 수역으로, 수많은 노래와 이야기, 기타 문화적 시금석의 주제이자 배경이 되어왔다. 하지만 몇 가지 중요한 점에서, 이 강의 주요 지류 중 하나가 실제로 미시시피 강을 무색하게 만든다. 미주리 강은 몬타나에서 발원하여 세인트루이스의 합류점에서 미시시피 강과 하나로 합치는데, 더 유명한 강인 미시시피보다 실제로는 더 길다. 게다가 미주리 강은 유역 면적에서도 미시시피 강에 비해 앞선다.

Q 지문의 요지는?
(a) 미주리 강물의 대부분이 미시시피 강으로 흐른다.
(b) 미시시피 강은 미국인들이 강에 대해 생각하는 방식을 구체화시켰다.
(c) 미주리 강은 지리학적 넓이에서 미시시피 강을 대적한다.
(d) 미시시피 강의 지류는 미주리 강의 그것보다 그 수가 많다.

해설 미주리 강은 북미의 가장 유명한 강인 미시시피 강의 지류이지만, 지리학적으로 미시시피 강보다 더 길며, 유역 면적도 더 넓다는 내용이므로 (c)가 정답이다.

celebrated 유명한 **a body of water** 수역, 물줄기 **setting** 배경 **touchstone** 시금석 **respect** 점, 측면 **outshine** ~보다 뛰어나다 **tributary** 지류 **confluence** 합류(점) **counterpart** 대응 관계에 있는 사람[것] **basin** 유역 **geographic** 지리학의 **vastness** 광대함, 광대한 넓이 **outnumber** 수에서 우위를 점하다

17

노인 황반변성, 즉 AMD는 노년기의 시력 상실을 초래하는 비교적 흔한 질병이다. 병이 진행되면서 흐릿하게 보이는 증상은 병이 악화됨에 따라 시력에 악영향을 주게 되는데, 불행히도 이는 콘택트렌즈만으로는 치료되지 않는다. 하지만 연구원들이 최근에 새로운 유형의 콘택트렌즈, 즉 멀리까지 볼 수 있는 기능을 제공하여 AMD 환자에게 나타나는 망막 손상의 악영향을 바로잡을 수 있는 렌즈를 제작하는 데 성공한 것이다. 이 렌즈는 이중 거울 면을 담고 있음에도 불구하고 두께가 1밀리미터밖에 안돼서 매일 사용해도 편안하고 편리할 수 있다는 것이 입증될 것이다.

Q 보고서 내용과 일치하는 것은?
(a) AMD 환자에게 고통을 주는 실명은 노소를 가리지 않는다.
(b) AMD 환자를 돕는 특수 안경이 여전히 사용된다.
(c) 특수 콘택트렌즈가 AMD 환자의 시야를 개선할 수 있다.
(d) AMD 교정용 콘택트렌즈는 아직 다소 크다.

해설 노인황반변성(AMD) 치료에 도움이 되는 콘택트렌즈가 개발되었다는 내용이다. 새로 발명된 콘택트렌즈가 멀리까지 볼 수 있는 기능을 제공한다고 하므로 AMD 환자의 시야를 개선한다는 (c)가 일치한다.

age-related macular degeneration 노인 황반변성(신체의 노화에 따라 망막의 황반 기능이 저하됨으로써 시력이 떨어지거나 상실되는 질병) **condition** 질병 **lead to** 초래하다 **progressive** 진행성의 **blurriness** 흐릿함 **untreatable** 치료할 수 없는 **fabricate** 제작하다 **telescopic** 멀리까지 보이는 **functionality** 기능 **retinal** 망막의 **dual** 이중의 **afflict** 괴롭히다 **bulky** 부피가 큰

18

엘리자베스 여왕 시대에 윌리엄 셰익스피어가 오랫동안 일한 극단으로 잘 알려진 로드 챔벌린스 맨은 1599년에 최초의 글로브 극장을 건립했다. 14년 동안 이 극장은 셰익스피어의 몇몇 희곡들을 공연하는 최고의 무대가 되었다. 불행히도 1613년 6월에 극장이 화재로 소실되었다. 당시의 기록으로는, 셰익스피어의 작품인 〈헨리 8세〉가 공연되는 동안 극적인 효과를 위해 대포를 발사했다가 구조물의 나무와 짚 부분에 불이 붙었다고 한다. 이듬해 두 번째 글로브 극장이 세워져서 거의 30년간 활동을 하다가 1642년에 폐쇄되었다.

Q 지문 내용과 일치하는 것은?
(a) 최초의 글로브 극장은 셰익스피어의 모든 희곡을 상연했다.
(b) 셰익스피어의 동료들이 글로브에 불이 난 것을 그의 탓으로 돌렸다.
(c) 셰익스피어가 글로브 극장의 건립을 의뢰했다.
(d) 두 번째 글로브 극장은 처음 것보다 더 오래 지속되었다.

해설 셰익스피어의 몇몇 명작들이 공연되었던 글로브 극장의 역사를 설명하는 글이다. 첫 번째 글로브 극장은 14년간 운영되었고, 화재 후 재건된 두 번째 글로브 극장은 30년 동안 운영되었다고 하므로 (d)가 정답이다.

Elizabethan 엘리자베스 시대의 **drama company** 극단 **serve as** ~의 역할을 하다 **premier** 최고의 **staging** 상연 **venue** 장소 **performance** 공연 **celebrated** 유명한 **contemporary accounts** 당시의 기록 **firing** 발사 **cannon** 대포 **ignite** 불을 붙이다 **thatch** (지붕을 이는 데 쓰는) 짚 **component** 구성 요소, 부분 **iteration** 반복, 신판 **shutter** ~을 덧문으로 닫다, 폐쇄하다 **colleague** 동료 **blame A for B** B에 대한 책임을 A에게 지우다 **commission** 의뢰하다

19

미국에서 입법 활동은 대의 민주제의 형태를 통해 수행된다. 즉 시민들이 자기들을 대표하는 국회의원을 선출하면, 선출된 의원은 자기 선거구민들의 요구에 기초한 법안을 발의하고 가결하는 책임을 진다. 이는 개개의 시민이 직접 법안을 발의하고 가결하는 직접 민주제에 반대된다. 미국 창건자들은 직접 민주제를 의심의 눈초리로 바라봤는데, 다수가 소수에게 자신의 의지를 전제적으로 강요하는 것을 경계했다. 아직도 미국의 일부 주에서는 국민투표를 통해 직접 민주제를 시행하고 있는데, 거기서는 시민들이 표결을 통해 법률을 폐기하거나 지지할 수 있다.

Q 지문 내용과 일치하는 것은?
(a) 미국 의회가 맡은 일은 경제 로비스트들의 요청대로 하는 것이다.
(b) 직접 민주제가 대의 민주제보다 우수한 것으로 여겨졌다.
(c) 미국 창건자들은 소수는 그들의 생각대로 해야 한다고 보았다.
(d) 일부 주는 특정 법률에 대해 결정할 때 직접 민주제를 허용한다.

해설 미국의 대의 민주제와 직접 민주제를 설명하는 글이다. 마지막 문장에서 아직도 미국의 일부 주에서는 시민들이 표결을 통해 법률을 폐기하거나 지지하는 직접 민주제를 시행하고 있다고 하므로 (d)가 정답이다.

lawmaking 입법 **representative democracy** 대의 민주제 **member of Congress** 국회의원 **be charged with** ~을 책임지고 있다 **constituent** 선거 구민 **counter to** ~에 반대되는 **direct democracy** 직접 민주제 **vote on** 가결하다 **founder** 창건자 **wary of** ~을 경계하는 **tyrannically** 전제적으로, 포학하게 **impose** 강요하다 **referendum** 국민투표 **annul** 폐기하다 **uphold** 지지하다 **do the bidding of** ~의 요청[명령]대로 하다 **have one's way** 제멋대로 하다, 자기 생각대로 하다

20

음악 〉 재즈   엔터테인먼트 투데이

핫 퓨전의 새 앨범

3인조 재즈 밴드 핫 퓨전이 최신 앨범 〈Some Like It Hot〉을 발매하면서 밴드의 뿌리였던 비밥으로의 성공적인 복귀를 보여주고 있다. 이 밴드는 지난 십 년간 애시드 재즈와 기타 비전통적 장르들을 실험하면서 많은 팬들을 당황하게 했는데, 이번 앨범으로 팬들이 커다란 안도감을 얻을 것 같다. 핫 퓨전이 마지막으로 내놓았던 세 곡은 비록 비평가들로부터 호평을 받기는 했지만, 매출 면에서는 완전히 실패로 끝났는데, 그룹이 원점으로 돌아가게 된 것은 바로 이 때문이라는 소문이 있다. 트럼펫 주자인 맥스 말로니는 "저희가 비밥을 다시 연주하고 있기는 하지만 새로운 방식으로 그것에 접근하고 있습니다"라고 말했다.

Q 핫 퓨전의 최신 앨범에 대해 기사 내용과 일치하는 것은?
(a) 십 년간 활동이 없다가 복귀의 신호가 되었다.
(b) 애시드 재즈 단계에 속하는 것으로 여겨졌다.
(c) 아마도 판매 수치에 대해서는 무관심 할 것이다.
(d) 밴드의 예전 앨범 스타일에서 벗어났다.

해설 밴드는 처음에 비밥으로 시작했다가 중간에 애시드 재즈와 기타 비전통적 장르들을 실험했고, 다시 비밥으로 돌아온 것이므로 이전의 앨범에서 떠났다는 (d)가 내용과 일치한다.

trio 3인조 **demonstrate** 보여주다 **triumphant** 성공한 **bebop** 비밥(재즈의 일종) **release** 음반 발매 **perturb** 당황하게 하다 **acid jazz** 애시드 재즈(1970년대 펑크와 디스코에 힙합과 라틴 장르가 뒤섞인 댄스 음악) **offering** 제공된 것 **critically acclaimed** 비평가들의 극찬을 받은 **fall flat** 실패로 끝나다 **reportedly** 소문에 의하면 **impetus** 자극 **get back to basics** 기본[원점]으로 돌아가다 **conceive** 생각하다

21

오늘날 복잡한 부동산 시장을 대하는 보통의 소비자는 해답을 아는 것보다는 의문점이 더 많을 것 같습니다. 지금이 집을 매매하기 가장 좋은 때일까? 집을 소유하는 것과 임차하는 것의 장점은 무엇일까? 누구에게 도움을 구해야 하는가? 저희는 업계 선도자로서 이런 질문에 너무나 익숙해 있는데, 바로 이 때문에 저희가 부동산 시장의 베일을 벗기는 데 전력을 다하는 계간지 〈주택 경기〉를 창간하기로 결정하게 되었습니다. 지금 구독하시면 할인된 요금 20달러로 1년 치를 받아보실 수 있습니다.

Q 〈주택 경기〉에 대해서 광고 내용과 일치하는 것은?
(a) 주택 매매에 관해 주로 다룬다.
(b) 일단의 평범한 집 소유자들을 위해 그리고 그들에 의해 제작된다.
(c) 업계에서 일하는 사람들에게 조언해 준다.
(d) 정기 구독을 하면 한 부당 5달러에 제공된다.

해설 부동산 관련 정기 간행물의 창간을 알리는 광고이다. 계간지의 1년 구독료가 20달러이므로 한 부는 5달러가 된다. 따라서 (d)가 정답이다. 부동산 시장의 모든 의문점을 다루고 있고, 일반 소비자를 대상으로 한 책이므로 나머지 선택지들은 일치하지 않는다.

complexity 복잡함 **real estate** 부동산 **homeownership** 자택 소유 **renting** 임차 **turn to** ~에 의지하다 **familiar with** ~에 익숙한 **launch** 출간하다 **quarterly publication** 계간지(1년에 4회 발간) **dedicated to** ~에 전념하는 **lift the veil** 베일을 벗기다, 진상을 밝히다 **property market** 부동산 시장

22

소중한 사용자님,

맵뷰는 사람들, 특히 저희 사용자분들을 대할 때 항상 투명성의 원칙을 지켜왔습니다. 바로 이 점 때문에 맵뷰가 지구상의 어떤 곳이라도 그 장소의 지도를 자신의 기호에 맞출 수 있는, 최고의 무료 소셜 미디어 지도 제작 사이트가 되었다고 생각합니다. 저희는 최근의 기술 발전 덕분에 서비스 약관을 갱신할 수 있게 되었는데, 이는 업계 전체에 걸쳐 바뀐 개인정보 규정을 수용하게 됨에 따른 것입니다. 귀하는 수정 사항 목록을 보고, 아래의 "상세 읽기" 링크를 클릭하면 개정된 서비스 약관을 전부 읽을 수 있습니다. 언제나 그렇듯이, 저희는 귀하의 의견을 존중하며 귀하의 조언을 환영합니다.

맵뷰 팀

Q 회사에 대해 이메일 내용과 일치하는 것은?
(a) 이제부터 개인용 지도에 대한 요금을 청구할 것이다.
(b) 사용자 의견에 기반을 둬 약관을 수정하고 있다.
(c) 새로운 사용자 개인정보 규범에 따른다.
(d) 요청을 하면 서비스 약관(TOS)을 보여 줄 것이다.

해설 무료 지도 제작 사이트를 운영하는 업체가 사용자에게 보내는 이메일로, 바뀐 개인 정보 규정에 따라 서비스 약관을 갱신했다는 사실을 알리고 있으므로 (c)가 정답이다.

uphold 지키다, 지지하다 **principle** 원칙 **transparency** 투명 **mapping** 지도 제작 **personalize** ~을 각 개인의 기호에 맞추다 **terms of service** 서비스 약관 **accommodate** 수용하다 **industry-wide** 업계 전반에 걸쳐 **privacy** 개인정보 **modification** 수정 **charge** 요금을 청구하다 **feedback** 반응, 의견 **conform to** (관습에) 따르다 **request** 요청

23

신문 인쇄는 1884년에 오트마르 머건탈러가 자동 주조 식자기를 발명하면서 영구히 달라졌다. 이전에는 인쇄업자들이 수 세기 동안 내려온, 글자를 하나하나 조판하는 기술을 사용했다. 즉 이전 기술로는 금속 활자와 구두점을 미리 주조한 다음 그것들을 하나하나 모아야만 원고 한 행이 만들어졌다. 자동 주조 식자기는 원고를 자판에 입력한 후, 그 원고를 담은 단일의 금속 덩어리, 즉 슬러그를 맞춤 주조함으로써 일제히 전 행을 만드는 것을 가능하게 했다. 이는 신문을 인쇄하는 방편에 혁명을 일으켰고, 전 세계적으로 신문 면수와 신문 발행 횟수를 증가시켰다.

Q 자동 주조 식자기에 대해 추론할 수 있는 것은?
(a) 타자기의 발명을 낳았다.
(b) 몇몇 종류의 신문 인쇄용으로 아직도 사용되고 있다.
(c) 우리가 오늘날 알고 있는 신문으로 이끄는 데 조력하였다.
(d) 결과물이 미적인 면에서 전통적인 조판보다 못했다.

해설 한 자씩 조판하는 기존의 방법과 달리, 원고를 단일 금속판에 조판할 수 있었던 라이노타이프의 발명이 신문 인쇄술에 혁명을 가져왔다는 내용이다. 이것의 발명으로 신문 인쇄가 영구히 달라졌다(changed forever)는 첫 번째 문장에서 (c)를 추론할 수 있다.

printing 인쇄 **linotype** 라이노타이프, 자동 주조 식자기 **previously** 이전에는 **printer** 인쇄업자 **employ** 사용하다 **typesetting** 식자, 조판 **pre-cast** 미리 주조된 **punctuation mark** 구두점 **assemble** 조립하다, 모으다 **input** 입력하다 **custom-cast** 맞춤 주조하다 **slug** (라이노타이프의) 한 행분이 하나로 주조된 활자의 행 **revolutionize** 혁명을 일으키다 **frequency** 빈도 **give rise to** ~을 낳다, 일으키다 **typewriter** 타자기

24

스페인 거장 프란시스코 고야의 '검은 회화' 연작은 그것을 그려낸 표현 수단이 독특하다. 고야는 말년에 자신의 마드리드 집 내부의 회반죽 바른 벽에 그것들을 직접 그렸다. 제목이 전혀 붙어 있지 않은 채 총 14점으로 되어 있는 이 작품들은 죽음과 폭력, 고독의 어둡고 좀처럼 잊을 수 없는 장면들을 그리고 있다. 고야가 이 그림들에 대해 아무에게도 말하거나 글을 쓴 적이 없었다는 사실에서, 우리는 그가 검은 회화를 전시할 생각이 전혀 없었음을 짐작할 수 있다. 그가 사망한 지 46년이 지난 후, 그 그림들은 회반죽에서 떼어져 캔버스로 옮겨졌고 마드리드의 한 미술관으로 보내졌다.

Q 검은 회화에 대해서 추론할 수 있는 것은?
(a) 고야의 사망 전에 일반에 공개되었다.
(b) 다루고 있는 주제로 그 이름이 불린다.
(c) 고야가 완성한 가장 값이 많이 나가는 작품 중에 속했다.
(d) 초창기 회반죽 회화의 대표적인 예이다.

해설 프란시스코 고야의 '검은 회화'라는 연작에 관한 내용으로, 죽음과 폭력, 고독의 어둡고 잊을 수 없는 장면들을 그리고 있다(the works portray dark, haunting scenes of death, violence, and loneliness)고 하므로 이름이 그 주제를 드러내는 것으로 추론할 수 있다.

master 거장 **medium** 표현 수단[기법] **plaster** 회반죽 **bear** (이름 · 직함 · 성질 등을) 가지다 **portray** 묘사하다 **haunting** 좀처럼 잊히지 않는 **loneliness** 고독 **assume** 추정하다 **transfer** 옮기다 **name** 이름을 짓다 **address** 다루다 **lucrative** 수지맞는

25

수십 년 동안 우리는, 생명체의 기본 구성요소인 DNA가 환경적인 요인들의 영향을 전혀 받지 않고 혈통을 통해 전해지는 것으로 생각해왔다. 하지만 새로운 조사 결과는 환경적 요인이 연이은 세대에 영향을 주는 식으로 우리의 유전자를 형성할 수 있음을 암시하고 있다. 오랫동안 겪은 영양실조와 같이, 젊었을 때 심한 스트레스를 경험한 사람은 스트레스에 더 민감한 자식을 낳는 것으로 드러났다. 또한 일부 데이터는 상관관계를 증명하기에는 너무 제한적이긴 하지만, 이러한 취약성이 2세대, 즉 원 피험자의 손주에서 분명히 나타날 수 있음을 입증하고 있다.

Q 지문으로부터 추론할 수 있는 것은?
(a) 건강한 DNA는 환경적 스트레스를 막는 타고난 방어 기제를 가지고 있다.
(b) 극심한 스트레스를 겪는 사람들은 아이를 낳을 수 없다.
(c) 세대 간의 연관성에 대한 증거는 아직 완전하지 않다.
(d) 인생 초기에 유전자가 손상되는 것은 훗날 손상되는 것보다 더 해롭다.

해설 환경적 요인에 의해 사람의 유전자에 영향을 줄 수 있다는 요지이다. 젊었을 때 심한 스트레스를 겪은 사람은 더 민감한 자식을 낳고 손주도 그런 취약성이 나타날 수 있다는 것이다. 하지만 그 상관관계를 증명하기에는 제한적이라는 말을 덧붙인 걸로 보아 아직 이러한 세대적인 연관성에 관한 증명이 완결되지 않았다는 (c)를 추론할 수 있다.

building block 건축용 블록, 구성요소 **pass down** 물려주다, 전해주다 **family line** 혈통 **more or less** (부정문에서) 전혀 ~않다 **factor** 요인 **gene** 유전자 **reverberate** 반향하다, 영향을 주다 **generation** 세대 **severe** 심한 **prolonged** 장기의 **malnutrition** 영양실조 **produce** 낳다 **offspring** 자식 **susceptible to** ~에 민감한[영향을 받기 쉬운] **correlation** 상관관계 **vulnerability** 취약성 **subject** 피험자 **defense** 방어 기제(defense mechanism) **transmittance** 전송 **pending** 미정의, 미완의

Part IV

26-27

http://www.NLF.org/our-programs/microloans
우리의 사명 ∨ **우리의 프로그램** ∨ 온라인 서비스 ∨ 기부 ∨ 문의

소규모 자영업자를 위한 소액 융자

■ 목적
1992년에 설립된 이래로, 새로운삶재단(NLF)은 소규모 자영업자들의 삶을 향상시키기 위해 힘껏 노력해왔습니다. 그들이 말 그대로 우리 사회의 근간이라고 확신합니다. 그들이 끊임없이 재정적 문제에 얽매인다면, 우리 사회의 안정성은 심하게 약화될 것입니다. 그 때문에 NLF 소액 융자 프로그램을 운영하고 있습니다. 이 수상 경력이 있는 프로그램은 소규모 자영업자들이 우리 사회의 안정과 번영에 기여하도록 생존하고 번영하는 데 도움을 줄 것입니다.

■ 자격 요건
NLF 소액 융자 프로그램을 신청하기 위해서는, 다음 요건을 충족해야만 합니다.
· 신용 기록이 수용 가능한 수준이어야만 합니다.
· 어떤 대출에 대해서도 채무 불이행 기록이 없어야만 합니다.
· 소규모 자영업을 최소한 2년 동안 운용한 경력이 있어야만 합니다.
· 저희의 혁신 경영 과정을 이수해야만 합니다.
· 최소한 6개월 동안 멘토와 함께 일할 각오가 되어 있어야 합니다.

26

Q 웹페이지에 따르면, NLF 소액 융자 프로그램에 대해 올바른 설명은?
(a) NLF가 프로그램을 운용한 지가 30년이 넘었다.
(b) 일반대중들이 탐탁하게 여긴 적이 없다.
(c) NLF는 그 프로그램이 사회적 안정성을 뒷받침하는 데 도움이 된다고 생각한다.
(d) 프로그램은 본래 여러 명의 소규모 자영업자에 의해 제안되었다.

해설 (a)는 소액 융자 프로그램을 언제부터 운용했는지를 명시적으로 밝히지 않았기 때문에 오답이다. (b)는 수상 경력이 있다는 점에서 일반대중이 긍정적으로 생각함을 알 수 있으므로 정답이 아니다. (d)는 그렇게 판단할 수 있는 근거가 없다. 따라서 정답은 웹페이지의 내용에 충실한 (c)이다.

27

Q 다음 가운데 NLF 소액 융자 프로그램의 신청 자격 요건이 될 수 있는 것은?
(a) 약간 의심스러운 신용 내력
(b) 2년까지 소규모 자영업을 운영한 경력
(c) 6년 동안 동기 사업주로부터 기꺼이 배우려는 마음가짐
(d) 채무 상환 능력

해설 NEW TEPS로 전환되면서, 새롭게 제시되는 유형이다. 문제에서 요구하는 정보가 있는 부분을 찾아 중요 정보 위주로 정확히 판단해야 한다. (a)는 수용 가능한 수준이어야 한다고 했기 때문에 오답이다. (b)는 최소한 2년이라고 했는데, '2년까지'라고 하면 1년도 포함될 수 있기 때문에 정답이 아니다. 기간과 관련해서 흔히 제시하는 오답 유형이다. (c)는 멘토가 반드시 '동기 사업주'는 아닐 수가 있기 때문에 오답이다. 따라서 정답은 (d)이다.

microloan 소액 융자 **establishment** 설립; 기득권층 **literally** 말 그대로 **backbone** 근간, 등뼈 **woe** 문제, 고민 **stability** 안정, 안정성 **undermine** 약화시키다 **thrive** 번성하다, 번창하다 **eligibility** 자격, 적격 **acceptable** 받아들일 수 있는 **credit history** 신용 내력 **delinquent** 체납의 **innovative** 혁신적인 **willing** 기꺼이 ~하려는 **approve of** 좋다고 인정하다 **buttress** 지지하다 **dubious** 의심스러운 **solvent** 상환 능력이 있는

28-29

정치 > 지역 　　　　　　　　　　　　패서디나 투데이

패서디나시(市)의 정체성 위기

2017년에 시장으로 선출된 이래로, 리처드 밀러는 많은 논란을 불러일으킨 정치인이다. 사실 그를 비판하는 이들 가운데 일부는 밀러 시장이 패서디나시(市)의 최악의 적이라고까지 주장한다. 그들에 따르면, 밀러가 시장으로 선출된 이래로, 패서디나시는 끊임없이 정체성 위기에 직면해왔다고 한다.
밀러 시장을 강력히 비판하는 인물들 가운데 한 명인 사라 포스터는 패서디나시가 예전에는 자유와 정의와 같은 미국의 이상의 불빛이었다고 말한다. 거리 시위의 금지를 포함한, 시장의 퇴행적인 정책들 때문에, 패서디나시는 독재 정치에 의해 지배되는 것 같다. 설상가상으로, 서로 다른 인종 집단들 사이의 긴장은 역대 최고에 이르렀다.
포스터에 따르면, 밀러 시장은 과거에 패서디나시를 정의했던 이상들을 계속해서 공격할 것이라고 한다. 이 정체성 위기를 해결하기 위해서는, 모든 시민들이 당파 관계를 초월하여 패서디나시가 미국의 이상의 원동력으로 재정립될 수 있도록 모든 노력을 다해야만 한다.

28 Q 기사에 따르면, 밀러 시장에 대해 다음 중 올바른 설명은?

(a) 그는 민주적인 개혁을 시행함으로써 미국의 이상들을 구현하기 위해 분투해왔다.

(b) 그의 정책들이 패서디나시의 인종 갈등을 악화시키고 있을 수 있다.

(c) 그는 2016년 이래로 정체성 위기를 겪고 있다.

(d) 그의 정책들은 자유와 정의라는 가치를 옹호하는 것을 목표로 삼는다.

해설 (a)는 기사의 내용에 정면으로 어긋나므로 오답이다. (c)는 밀러 시장이 아니라 패서디나시가 정체성 위기를 겪는 것이므로 정답이 아니다. (d)는 정반대의 내용이므로 오답이다. 따라서 기사의 내용에 충실한 (b)이다. 특히, 세부 사항 유형의 선택지에 may나 might이 있는 경우에는 정답일 가능성이 높음에 유의해야 한다.

29 Q 다음 중 포스터가 가장 동의할 것 같은 진술은?

(a) 밀러 시장을 탄핵하는 절차가 즉시 개시되어야만 한다.

(b) 시 정부의 진보적인 정책들이 시장에 대한 반발을 초래했다.

(c) 패서디나시의 자유와 정의를 지키기 위해서는 사람들의 힘이 필요하다.

(d) 패서디나가 미국의 이상의 수호자로서의 지위를 양도해야 할 때이다.

해설 (a)는 전형적인 비약에 해당하는 선택지이다. 포스터가 (a)에 대해 밝힌 내용이 없기 때문에 반드시 오답으로 처리해야 한다. (b)는 정반대로 생각해야 하므로 정답이 아니다. (d)는 포스터의 성향을 생각할 때, 오히려 반대로 말해야 하므로 오답이다. 따라서 정답은 (c)이다. 이와 같은 소거법은 특히 고난도 문항에서 효과적으로 활용할 수 있는 풀이 기법이다.

controversial 논란이 많은 enemy 적대자, 원수 prominent 중요한, 두드러진 detractor 비방하는 사람 beacon 불빛; 지침이 되는 것 regressive 퇴행하는, 퇴보하는 demonstration 시위; 시연 dictatorship 독재 정치 tension 긴장, 갈등 attack 공격하다; 비난하다 resolve 해결하다, 해소하다 transcend 초월하다 party affiliation 당파 관계 driving force 원동력, 추진력 embody 구현하다 uphold 옹호하다, 지지하다 impeach 탄핵하다 backlash 반발 relinquish 양도하다, 내주다

30-31

성요한초는 플라시보인가 진짜 약품인가?

세계의 많은 지역에서, 성요한초는 약효가 있는 것으로 생각되어왔다. 미국에서는 많은 이들이 성요한초라는 약초를 우울증을 치료하는 효과적인 수단으로 여긴다. 그렇지만 미국 국립정신건강연구소를 포함한 많은 기관들은 대중에게 성요한초의 효과성이 과학적으로 입증되지 않았다고 경고한다.

흥미롭게도, 몇몇 연구들은 성요한초가 경미한 우울증의 치료에 항우울제만큼이나 효과가 있다는 사실을 밝혔다. 그럼에도 불구하고, 꽤 심각한 우울증의 치료에, 성요한초나 항우울제는 모두 유의미한 정도로 효과가 있지 않다. 더욱이 국립정신건강연구소는 대중이 두 의약품을 혼합하지 않기를 권한다.

그러면 성요한초는 플라시보인가, 아니면 진짜 약품인가? 글쎄, 어쩌면 둘 다일지도 모른다. 성요한초의 부작용이라는 또 다른 것도 고려해야 한다. 『당신의 건강』 다음 호에서 이 중요한 주제를 다루겠다.

30 Q 기사의 주제는?

(a) 경미한 우울증의 치료에 대해 성요한초가 갖는 효능

(b) 성요한초를 항우울제와 혼합하는 방법

(c) 성요한초가 플라시보보다 효과가 있는 이유

(d) 어떤 정신질환의 치료에 대해 성요한초가 나타내는 효능

해설 (a)가 특히 매력적인 오답임에 유의해야 한다. 기사는 경미한 우울증뿐만 아니라 꽤 심각한 우울증에 대해서도 말하고 있기 때문에 (a)는 정답이 아니다. (b)는 국립정신건강연구소에서 반대하는 내용이기도 하고, 지나치게 세부적인 사항이어서 오답이다. (c)는 성요한초와 플라시보의 효과에 대한 비교 내용이 없기 때문에 정답이 아니다. 따라서 정답은 (d)이다.

31 Q 기사에 따르면, 다음 중 옳은 것은?

(a) 성요한초는 수백 년 동안 약품으로 사용되어왔다.

(b) 성요한초에 대한 일반 미국인들의 인식은 잘못된 것일지도 모른다.

(c) 심한 우울증의 치료에는 항우울제가 성요한초보다 훨씬 더 효과가 있다.

(d) 치료용으로 쓰일 때, 성요한초에는 알려진 부작용이 없다.

해설 성요한초가 얼마나 오랫동안 약품으로 사용되었는지에 대한 정보가 없으므로 (a)는 오답이다. (c)는 심한 우울증 치료의 경우 두 가지가 모두 효과가 없다고 말했으므로 정답이 아니다. (d)는 다음 호에서 부작용을 다룬다고 했으므로 오답이다. 따라서 정답은 주어진 내용에 충실한 (b)이다.

placebo 플라시보 medicinal 약효가 있는 property 속성; 부동산 herbal medicine 약초로 만든 약; 약초학 antidepressant 항우울제 moderately 꽤; 적정하게 erroneous 잘못된 therapeutically 치료적으로

32-33

소음 민원을 해결하는 방법

로랜드 시의회의 권고 사항

요즘 많은 시민들이 소음 방해 행위에 대해 불만을 제기합니다. 그렇지만 많은 경우에, 소음이 방해 행위에 해당하는지를 결정하는 것은 쉽지 않습니다. 그런 결정을 내리는 데는 고려해야 할 요인들이 아주 많습니다.

따라서 '소음'을 내기 전에 이웃과 상의하는 것이 항상 좋은 아이디어입니다. 어떤 문제든 이웃과 의논하세요. 놀랍게도, 시민들은 대부분 생각보다 훨씬 더 이해심이 많습니다. 결국엔 그들도 소음을 내는 것을 피할 수가 없으니까요.

그렇지만 어떤 경우에는 이웃이 소음에 대한 민원을 제기합니다. 로랜드 시의회는 대개 그런 문제를 경고장 발부나 과태료 부과로 처리합니다. 시의회가 소음이 소음 법규 위반이라고 결정하면, 그 문제는 환경부에서 다루게 됩니다. 환경부에는 기소를 권할 수 있는 권한이 있습니다.

보다 자세한 정보를 원하시면, http://www.lowlandcitycouncil. gov/에 방문해 주세요.

32 Q 소음이 소음 법규 위반이라고 결정하면, 시의회가 취할 가능성이 가장 높은 행위는?

(a) 환경부의 규제를 회피하려고 할 것이다.

(b) 문제를 해당 부서에 회부할 것이다.

(c) 검사에게 직접 연락을 취할 것이다.

(d) 이웃에게 엄중한 경고장을 발부할 것이다.

해설 NEW TEPS의 새로운 유형에 해당하므로 꼼꼼하게 익혀둘 필요가 있다. 주어진 내용에서 소음 법규 위반일 때는 환경부에서 다루게 된다고 했으므로, 정답은 (b)이다. 이 선택지에서처럼 '환경부'라고 하지 않고 '해당 부서'라고 말하는 정답 유형에 숙달될 필요가 있다. 이런 정답 유형은 문제의 난이도를 높이려는 데 목적이 있기 때문에, 앞으로도 흔히 접하게 될 정답 유형이다.

33 Q 지문으로부터 추론할 수 있는 것은?
(a) 소음 공해가 공중보건에 심한 피해를 주고 있다.
(b) 모든 소음이 시의회에 의해 방해 행위라고 여겨지지는 않는다.
(c) 로랜드의 주민들은 항상 서로에게 예의가 바르다.
(d) 환경부는 벌금을 부과할 권한이 없다.

해설 소음 공해에 대한 직접적인 언급이 없으므로 (a)는 정답이 아니다.
(c)는 전형적인 비약에 해당한다. 이 유형은 흔히 always나 never와 같
은 말이 있으면 오답일 확률이 높다는 규칙을 따르는 유형이다. (d)는 지
문의 내용만으로는 추론할 수 없는 내용이다. 따라서 정답은 (b)이다.
NEW TEPS에서도 추론 유형과 세부사항 유형의 경계가 다소 모호할 때
가 있음에 유의해야 한다.

complaint 불평, 불만 **advise** 권고하다; 통지하다 **nuisance** 방해;
불쾌한 것 **constitute** 구성하다 **factor** 요인 **take into account**
고려하다 **consult** 상의하다 **understanding** 이해심 있는
inevitably 불가피하게, 필연적으로 **warning** 경고 **issue** 발부하다
impose 부과하다 **penalty** 벌금, 과태료 **offense** 법률 위반
prosecution 기소 **circumvent** 회피하다; 법률 등을 빠져나갈 방도를
찾다 **refer** 회부하다 **prosecuting attorney** 검사 **stern** 엄중한
take a toll on 〜에 피해[타격]을 주다

34-35

발신: 줄리아 스미스 박사 〈jsmith@bremser.edu〉
수신: 신시아 스펜서 〈c_spencer@cmail.com〉
일자: 5월 5일 토요일 오전 9:33
주제: 통찰력이 있군요

스펜서 씨에게

저는 줄리아 스미스 박사이고요. 저희 『생물학 연구 저널』에 통찰력이
엿보이는 논문을 응모해 줘서 감사합니다. 이미 아시다시피, 이 학술지
는 브렘저대학교와 영국생물학자협회가 공동으로 발간합니다. 저희는
생물학 교수들과 생물학 전공 대학원생들로부터 원고 투고를 받습니다.
당신은 논문에서 종(種)의 개념에 근거하여 찰스 다윈의 진화론을 비
판합니다. 또한 지구의 역사가 다윈적 진화가 일어나기에는 너무 짧다
고 지적합니다.
당신은 주류인 진화론에 대해 잘 알고 있는 것 같습니다. 그렇지만 그
이론은 여전히 '이론'일 뿐입니다. 주류 이론의 타당성을 존중하지만,
저는 또한 대학원생들에게 기존 이론을 자유롭게 탐구하고 반박하도
록 장려합니다. 그래야만 진리를 발견할 수 있습니다.
통찰력이 돋보이는 논문을 응모한 데 대해 다시 한 번 감사드립니다.
응모한 논문과 관련해서 앞으로 20일 이내에 통지를 받을 거예요.

줄리아 스미스 박사

---

34 Q 이메일의 주된 목적은?
(a) 스펜서가 생물학의 어떤 주류 이론을 비판하려고 시도한 데 대해 감사
를 표하는 것
(b) 수취인에게 제출한 논문이 학술지에 게재될 것이라고 통지하는 것
(c) 수취인에게 법칙과 이론을 구별하라고 조언하는 것
(d) 스펜서가 영국생물학자협회에 가입할 것을 권장하는 것

해설 (b)는 게재 여부가 아직 결정되지 않았기 때문에 오답이다. (c)는 법
칙과 이론의 차이가 이메일에 제시되어 있지 않기 때문에 정답이 아니다. (d)
는 직접적으로 권하는 내용이 없으므로 오답이다. 따라서 정답은 (a)이다.

35 Q 이메일로부터 스펜서에 대해 추론할 수 있는 것은?
(a) 브렘저대학교의 생물학 교수이다.
(b) 진화론을 충분히 이해하지 못했다.
(c) 화학과 지질학을 전공하고 있다.
(d) 대학원생일 가능성이 아주 높다.

해설 (a)가 정답이라면 스펜서의 이메일 주소가 @bremser.edu로 끝나
야 하는 것이 보통이다. 그런데 그렇지 않으므로 정답이 아니다. (b)는 스
미스 박사의 언급으로 보아 반대일 가능성이 높다. 생물학 전공 대학원생
일 것이므로 (c)는 오답이고, (d)가 정답이다. 스펜서가 교수라고 추론할
수 있는 근거가 전혀 없음에 유의해야 한다.

insightful 통찰력이 있는 **submit** 제출하다 **article** (소)논문; 기사
jointly 공동으로 **association** 협회 **theory of evolution** 진화론
assume 추정하다, 상정하다 **mainstream** 주류의 **wisdom** 타당성;
지혜 **existing** 기존의 **notify** 통지하다, 알리다

Actual Test 3

청해 Listening *Comprehension*

p.91

1 (a)	2 (b)	3 (c)	4 (c)	5 (a)	6 (d)	7 (a)	8 (d)	9 (d)	10 (a)
11 (a)	12 (c)	13 (d)	14 (a)	15 (d)	16 (b)	17 (c)	18 (c)	19 (b)	20 (d)
21 (d)	22 (d)	23 (b)	24 (b)	25 (a)	26 (a)	27 (a)	28 (c)	29 (c)	30 (a)
31 (c)	32 (d)	33 (b)	34 (b)	35 (a)	36 (d)	37 (b)	38 (d)	39 (b)	40 (c)

어휘 Vocabulary

p.97

1 (a)	2 (b)	3 (c)	4 (d)	5 (d)	6 (d)	7 (a)	8 (a)	9 (a)	10 (c)
11 (d)	12 (a)	13 (d)	14 (a)	15 (a)	16 (d)	17 (c)	18 (d)	19 (b)	20 (d)
21 (d)	22 (c)	23 (d)	24 (c)	25 (b)	26 (c)	27 (d)	28 (c)	29 (d)	30 (b)

문법 Grammar

p.101

1 (d)	2 (c)	3 (d)	4 (c)	5 (b)	6 (d)	7 (c)	8 (c)	9 (c)	10 (c)
11 (d)	12 (d)	13 (a)	14 (b)	15 (b)	16 (c)	17 (c)	18 (b)	19 (d)	20 (d)
21 (d)	22 (b)	23 (b)	24 (d)	25 (d)	26 (d)	27 (c)	28 (a)	29 (c)	30 (d)

독해 Reading *Comprehension*

p.105

1 (d)	2 (c)	3 (d)	4 (d)	5 (d)	6 (c)	7 (c)	8 (b)	9 (d)	10 (c)
11 (d)	12 (c)	13 (b)	14 (b)	15 (d)	16 (d)	17 (c)	18 (c)	19 (d)	20 (b)
21 (b)	22 (b)	23 (c)	24 (d)	25 (b)	26 (d)	27 (b)	28 (d)	29 (b)	30 (b)
31 (c)	32 (a)	33 (b)	34 (b)	35 (b)					

Listening Comprehension p.91

Part I

1

W Can you join us for dinner today?
M _____

(a) Count me out.
(b) Let's set a date.
(c) Jeff's also invited.
(d) I'm not picky with food.

W 오늘 저희랑 저녁 식사 함께하실 수 있나요?
M _____

(a) 저는 빼주세요.
(b) 날짜를 정합시다.
(c) 제프도 초대받았어요.
(d) 전 식성이 까다롭지 않아요.

count ~ out ~을 빼다   **set a date** 날짜를 잡다   **picky** 까다로운

2

W I'll do what I can to help you find your daughter.
M _____

(a) Hang in there a little longer.
(b) I can't thank you enough.
(c) She was the love of my life.
(d) I'll never let that happen again.

W 최선을 다해 따님 찾으시는 일을 도와 드리겠습니다.
M _____

(a) 조금만 더 힘내세요.
(b) 뭐라고 감사를 드려야 할지 모르겠네요.
(c) 내 생에서 사랑한 사람은 바로 그녀였습니다.
(d) 다시는 그런 일이 일어나지 않도록 하겠습니다.

hang in there 꿋꿋이 버티다

3

W Don't slouch in your chair.
M _____

(a) I'll get a better chair.
(b) I'll take a nap on my couch.
(c) Alright, I'll sit up straight.
(d) Actually, I haven't been dozing.

W 구부정하게 의자에 앉지 마세요.
M _____

(a) 좀 더 좋은 의자를 구입할게요.
(b) 소파에서 낮잠을 잘 거예요.
(c) 알았어요, 똑바로 앉을게요.
(d) 사실은 졸지 않았어요.

slouch 앞으로 구부리다   **take a nap** 잠깐[낮잠] 자다   **sit up straight** 똑바로 앉다   **doze** 졸다

4

W I'm sure our son is strong enough to pull through the operation.
M _____

(a) I'll go along with their opinion.
(b) He's in the intensive care unit.
(c) He'll make it without a hitch.
(d) Now you're in on it.

W 우리 아들은 아주 건강해서 수술을 끝까지 견뎌 낼 수 있을 거라고 확신해요.
M _____

(a) 그들의 의견에 따를 거예요.
(b) 그는 중환자실에 있어요.
(c) 그는 쉽게 이겨 낼 거예요.
(d) 이제 당신은 그 일에 개입되었어요.

pull through 이겨[견뎌] 내다   **operation** 수술   **go along with** ~에 동의하다   **intensive care unit** 중환자실   **make it** 이겨[버텨] 내다   **without a hitch** 아무 문제없이, 술술   **be in on** ~에 참개[관계]하다

5

M I asked for medium-rare, but this steak is well-done.
W _____

(a) There must've been a mix-up.
(b) I'll go and check when it'll be ready.
(c) Your order will be taken care of shortly.
(d) The new gas stove is not working well.

M 스테이크를 보통보다 조금 덜 익혀 달라고 했는데 바짝 익혀 왔네요.
W _____

(a) 착오가 있었던 게 분명해요.
(b) 그것이 언제 준비될지 가서 확인해 볼게요.
(c) 주문을 금방 처리해 드리겠습니다.
(d) 새 가스레인지가 잘 작동하지 않는데요.

medium-rare 보통보다 조금 덜 익힌 것   **mix-up** (특히 실수로 인한) 혼동   **take care of** 처리하다   **shortly** 곧   **gas stove** 가스레인지   **work** 작동하다

6

W Why has my credit card been revoked?
M _____

(a) My credit has been ruined in the process.
(b) You need to consent to have it revoked.
(c) I'll use my debit card from now on.
(d) You have a large outstanding bill.

W 제 신용 카드가 왜 취소되었나요?
M _____

(a) 그 과정에서 제 신용이 바닥으로 떨어졌어요.
(b) 그것을 철회하는 데 동의가 필요해요.
(c) 이제부터는 직불카드를 사용하겠어요.
(d) 지불되지 않은 요금이 많아서요.

revoke 취소[철회]하다   **consent** 동의하다   **debit card** 직불카드
from now on 이제부터   **outstanding** 미결제의   **bill** 청구서

7

M When can I possibly have a discussion with you?
W _____

(a) I'll pencil you in for 3 on Monday.
(b) The matter can be discussed openly.
(c) I don't think I can possibly defer that.
(d) I'll look forward to seeing you again.

M 당신과 언제 논의를 할 수 있을까요?
W _____

(a) 월요일 3시로 일단 잡아놓을게요.
(b) 그 문제는 공개적으로 논의될 수 있어요.
(c) 그것을 연기할 수 없을 것 같아요.
(d) 다시 뵙기를 고대하겠습니다.

have a discussion with ~와 토론하다   **pencil in** 일단 예정에 넣다
defer 연기하다

8

W Business is so slow. I might have to close my store.
M _____

(a) You'll get the hang of it soon.
(b) You've been taking on too much.
(c) Slow down and relax a little more.
(d) It'd be best to persevere if you can.

W 경기가 너무 부진해요. 가게 문을 닫아야겠어요.
M _____

(a) 곧 요령을 터득하시게 될 거예요.
(b) 너무 흥분하셨어요.
(c) 속도를 늦추고 좀 더 느긋해지세요.
(d) 할 수 있다면 버티는 것이 최선인 것 같아요.

get the hang of it 요령을 터득하다   **take on** 흥분하다, 이성을 잃다
persevere 인내하다

9

W I'd like the hem of the skirt to be let out.
M _____

(a) The skirt can be tailor-made.
(b) I'll have the skirt ironed in no time.
(c) The skirt is made of hand-made fabric.
(d) The alteration can be done in 10 minutes.

W 치마 단을 내어 길게 해 주세요.
M _____

(a) 치마는 맞출 수 있어요.
(b) 당장 치마를 다림질할게요.
(c) 치마는 수제 직물로 만들어졌어요.
(d) 수선은 10분 내로 가능합니다.

hem (천·옷의) 단   **let out** (부분적으로 고쳐) 크게[길게] 하다   **tailor-made** 맞춤의   **iron** 다림질하다   **in no time** 당장에   **fabric** 직물
alteration 수선

10

M We're late. Let's use the Self Check-In machine.
W _____

(a) I'd prefer to do it the regular way.
(b) Thank goodness we don't fly today.
(c) The check-out line is exceptionally long.
(d) I wish there were a money exchange here.

M 늦었어요. 자동 발권 기계를 사용합시다.
W _____

(a) 일반적인 방식대로 하고 싶은데요.
(b) 오늘 비행기를 안 타서 다행이에요.
(c) 체크아웃 줄이 대단히 길군요.
(d) 이곳에 환전소가 있으면 좋을 텐데요.

Self Check-In machine (공항 내의) 자동 발권 기계, 자동 체크인기
thank goodness ~해서 다행이다   **fly** 비행기를 타다   **exceptionally**
대단히   **money exchange** 환전소

Part II

11

M Oh, no. Look at the mess!
W Someone must've broken in.
M It's going to take forever to clean.
W _____

(a) At least no one got hurt.
(b) That's how things get stolen.
(c) Let's make a list of broken items.
(d) All the windows must've been locked.

M 오, 이런. 이 어질러진 것 좀 봐요!

W 누군가 침입한 게 틀림없어요.

M 정돈하려면 시간이 엄청나게 걸리겠군요.

W _____

(a) 적어도 아무도 다치지는 않았어요.

(b) 바로 이런 식으로 물건이 도난당한 거예요.

(c) 파손된 물품 리스트를 만듭시다.

(d) 틀림없이 모든 창문이 잠겨 있었을 거예요.

mess 엉망인 상태 **break in** 침입하다 **take forever** 엄청난 시간이 걸리다 **lock** 잠그다

12

W Do you know if a new tenant moved in upstairs?

M Not directly above us, no.

W But I heard loud noises coming from above.

M _____

(a) People should be more considerate of others.

(b) I'd better ask why they complained about it.

(c) It might be from the next floor above.

(d) I'll be more cautious from now on.

W 위층에 새로운 세입자가 들어왔는지 아세요?

M 우리 바로 윗집에는 들어오지 않았어요.

W 하지만 위에서 시끄러운 소리가 나는 걸 들었는걸요.

M _____

(a) 사람들은 타인을 좀 더 배려해줘야 해요.

(b) 그들이 그것에 대해 불평하는 이유를 물어보는 게 좋겠어요.

(c) 아마도 위층 그 윗집에서 나는 소리였을 거예요.

(d) 이제부터는 좀 더 신중해질게요.

tenant 세입자 **move in** 이사 오다 **considerate of** ~을 배려하는 **complain** 불평하다 **cautious** 신중한

13

W My term deposit will expire tomorrow.

M Do you have any plans as to what to do with it?

W Well, I was thinking of investing it in a mutual fund.

M _____

(a) They are classified by their principal investments.

(b) Investing in a fund required lots of research.

(c) I learned investors pay the fund's expenses.

(d) I've heard you can lose money in those.

W 저의 정기예금이 내일 만기예요.

M 그걸로 뭘 할지 무슨 계획이라도 있나요?

W 글쎄요. 뮤추얼 펀드에 투자할까 생각 중이에요.

M _____

(a) 그것들은 주요 투자 대상에 따라 분류되어 있어요.

(b) 펀드 투자는 많은 조사가 필요했어요.

(c) 투자자들이 펀드 비용을 지불한다고 알고 있었어요.

(d) 그런 것에 넣으면 돈을 잃을 수도 있다고 들었어요.

term deposit 정기예금 **expire** 만기가 되다 **as to** ~에 관해서는 **classify** 분류하다 **principal** 주요한 **investment** 투자 대상 **require** 필요로 하다

14

M What are you looking for?

W The liquid fertilizer I bought last week for our plants.

M Where did you leave it last?

W _____

(a) I think it was you who put it away.

(b) I bought it from a nearby flower shop.

(c) I searched everywhere for the fertilizer.

(d) I should water the plants more regularly.

M 뭘 찾고 있나요?

W 지난주에 식물 주려고 샀던 액비요.

M 마지막에 그걸 어디다 뒀지요?

W _____

(a) 그걸 치운 사람은 당신이었던 것 같은데요.

(b) 인근 꽃집에서 샀어요.

(c) 비료를 찾으려고 안 뒤진 데가 없어요.

(d) 식물에 물을 좀 더 규칙적으로 주는 게 좋겠어요.

liquid 액체의 **fertilizer** 비료 **put away** 치우다 **water** 물을 주다

15

M How about coming to my new apartment for dinner?

W Sure. Is it a kind of housewarming party?

M You could put it that way, but there'll be only you and me.

W _____

(a) I'll catch you later.

(b) Let's make it potluck.

(c) The more the merrier, then.

(d) I wouldn't miss it for the world.

M 제 새 아파트에 저녁 먹으러 오지 않을래요?

W 좋지요. 일종의 집들이인가요?

M 그렇게 말해도 좋지만 참석자는 당신과 나뿐이에요.

W _____

(a) 나중에 봐요.

(b) 각자 음식을 가져와서 나눠 먹는 걸로 합시다.

(c) 그렇다면 사람이 많을수록 더 즐겁지요.

(d) 꼭 가야죠.

housewarming party 집들이 **put it that way** 그런 식으로 말하다 **catch you later** 다음에 보자, 안녕 **potluck** 참가자 각자가 음식을 가져와서 나눠 먹는 식사 **The more, the merrier.** 많을수록 더 즐겁다. **not ~ for the world** 무슨 일이 있어도 ~하지 않겠다

16

W I came to talk about this winter coat I had dry-cleaned here.

M Yes, is there something wrong with it?

W Look at all the creases.

M _____

(a) I owe you one, in that case.

(b) Sorry. I'll have it ironed again.

(c) You know this isn't the first time.

(d) Sure, there'll be no extra charge for that.

W 여기서 드라이클리닝을 한 이 겨울 코트에 대해서 말할 게 있어요.

M 네, 뭐가 잘못됐나요?

W 이 주름들을 보세요.

M _____

(a) 그렇다면 제가 신세 한번 진 거네요.

(b) 죄송합니다. 다시 다려드릴게요.

(c) 이번이 처음이 아닌 건 아시잖아요.

(d) 좋아요, 추가 요금은 더 없을 겁니다.

crease 주름, 접은 자국 **I owe you one.** 신세 한번 졌군요. **in that case** 그렇다면 **iron** 다림질을 하다 **extra charge** 추가 요금

17

M Hello, this is Brian Anderson. Could I speak to Amy Miller?

W Sorry, but she just stepped out.

M Oh, no. I need to speak with her right away.

W _____

(a) I'm afraid it's bad timing.

(b) She didn't leave any message.

(c) Maybe you can try her cell phone.

(d) Please hold and I'll put her through.

M 여보세요. 저는 브라이언 앤더슨인데요, 에이미 밀러 좀 바꿔 주실 수 있나요?

W 죄송하지만, 방금 나갔어요.

M 이런. 그녀와 지금 당장 통화해야 하는데요.

W _____

(a) 가는 날이 장날이군요.

(b) 아무 메시지도 남기지 않았는데요.

(c) 휴대전화에 걸어보세요.

(d) 연결해 드릴 테니 끊지 말고 기다리세요.

step out 나가다 **hold** (전화를) 끊지 말고 기다리다 **put through** (전화를) 연결하다

18

W Why the long face?

M My father embarrassed me in front of everyone at the family gathering!

W Don't get too upset. You know his character.

M _____

(a) You're right. There's no way out.

(b) That compensates for my humiliation.

(c) I've had just about enough of it already.

(d) Well, he's known for his idiosyncratic character.

W 왜 우울한 표정을 하고 계세요?

M 아버지께서 가족 모임에서 모든 사람이 보는 앞에서 절 당혹스럽게 했어요.

W 너무 언짢아하지 마세요. 그분의 성격을 알잖아요.

M _____

(a) 당신 말이 맞아요. 탈출구가 없어요.

(b) 그건 제가 당한 창피를 보상해 주네요.

(c) 저는 이미 당할 만큼 당했어요.

(d) 그분은 특이한 성격으로 유명하죠.

long face 우울한 얼굴, 슬픈 표정 **family gathering** 가족 모임 **upset** 화난 **way out** 탈출구 **compensate for** ~에 대해 보상하다 **humiliation** 굴욕 **I've had enough.** 지긋지긋해요, 더 이상 못 참겠어요. **be known for** ~로 유명하다 **idiosyncratic** 특이한

19

M Amy, what brings you here tonight?

W Oh, hi, Tom. Jeff invited me to this party.

M Really? I thought you two weren't getting along well.

W _____

(a) We barely get by as it is.

(b) Well, we've settled our differences.

(c) Can't complain at this stage.

(d) You will never be on good terms with him.

M 에이미, 오늘밤 여긴 어쩐 일이야?

W 안녕, 톰. 제프가 이 파티에 날 초대했어.

M 정말? 난 너희 두 사람이 잘 지내지 못하는 걸로 알았는데.

W _____

(a) 우린 그냥 근근이 살아가고 있어.

(b) 우린 화해했어.

(c) 현 단계에서는 불만이 없어.

(d) 너는 결코 그와 잘 지내지 못할 거야.

What brings you here? 여기는 어쩐 일이야? **get along well** 마음이 맞다 **barely get by** 근근이 살아가다 **as it is** 그냥, 있는 그대로 **settle differences** 화해하다, 차이를 해결하다 **can't complain** 불만이 없다, 더 바랄 게 없다 **at this stage** 현 단계에서는 **be on good terms with** ~와 잘 지내다

20

W Hi, my name's Iris, and I came to pick up the dish set I ordered.

M I'm afraid it hasn't been delivered to the store yet.

W But it's been a week since I ordered.

M _____

(a) I'll definitely order two right now.

(b) I'm afraid a refund is not possible.

(c) The order was processed immediately.

(d) I'll be sure to call you when it arrives.

W 안녕하세요, 저는 아이리스이고, 주문한 그릇 세트를 찾으러 왔어요.

M 유감이지만 아직 가게로 배달 오지 않았는데요.

W 하지만 주문한 지 일주일이나 됐는걸요.

M _____

(a) 지금 바로 두 개를 틀림없이 주문할게요.

(b) 유감스럽지만 환불은 불가능해요.

(c) 주문이 즉시 처리되었어요.

(d) 물건이 도착하면 꼭 전화를 드릴게요.

pick up 찾다 **refund** 환불 **process** 처리하다

Part III

21

Listen to a conversation between two friends.

W Why are you limping?

M I sprained my ankle today.

W Oh, no. How did that happen?

M I missed a step when I got off the bus this morning.

W Oh, I'm so sorry to hear that.

M Yes, it was pretty bad.

Q What is the main topic of the conversation?

(a) Why the man got off the bus where he did

(b) Why the man has cared for his ankle

(c) How the man stepped onto the bus

(d) How the man injured his ankle

두 친구의 대화를 들으시오.

W 발을 왜 절고 있나요?

M 오늘 발목을 삐었어요.

W 저런. 어쩌다가 그랬나요?

M 오늘 아침 버스에서 내리다가 발을 헛디뎠어요.

W 그렇군요, 그런 일이 있었다니 유감이에요.

M 네, 매우 안 좋았어요.

Q 대화의 주제는?

(a) 남자가 그곳에서 버스를 내린 이유

(b) 남자가 발목을 돌본 이유

(c) 남자가 버스에 올라탔던 방법

(d) 남자가 발목을 다친 경위

limp 절뚝거리다 **sprain one's ankle** 발목을 삐다 **miss a step** 헛디디다 **get off a bus** 버스에서 내리다 **care for** ~을 돌보다 **step onto a bus** 버스에 올라타다

22

Listen to a conversation between two acquaintances.

W Why did you retire but then get a job?

M I found out I'm happiest when I work.

W Didn't you find being at home very peaceful?

M Well, too peaceful. I missed the challenge of work.

W I can understand that. But there's also the stress.

M Well, you're never stress-free wherever you are!

Q What is the conversation mainly about?

(a) How stressed the man had been without work

(b) How different being retired and working is

(c) Why the woman finds being at home better

(d) Why the man decided to return to work

두 지인의 대화를 들으시오.

W 왜 은퇴하고서 다시 직장을 구했습니까?

M 일할 때 가장 행복하다는 걸 깨달았거든요.

W 집에 있는 것이 아주 평화로웠을 텐데요.

M 글쎄요, 너무 평화로웠죠. 일의 도전을 받을 때가 그리웠어요.

W 이해가 돼요. 하지만 스트레스도 있잖아요.

M 우리가 어디에 있든 스트레스에서 벗어날 수는 없는 법이죠!

Q 대화의 주된 내용은?

(a) 일이 없어서 남자가 얼마나 스트레스를 받았는지

(b) 은퇴 생활과 직장 생활이 얼마나 다른지

(c) 집에 있는 것이 더 낫다고 여자가 느끼는 이유

(d) 남자가 직장 생활을 다시 하겠다고 결정한 이유

retire 은퇴하다 **stress-free** 스트레스 없는

23

Listen to a conversation in a company.

M Hi. I'd like to apply here for a job interview.

W Okay, sir. Have you filled out an application form?

M I was going to fill one out now if you have one.

W Alright. You'll also need to enclose a photo.

M Oh, right, I think I have one. Will this be adequate?

W I'm afraid it'll have to be more formal than this.

Q What is the woman mainly doing in the conversation?

(a) She is administrating an interview with the man.

(b) She is assisting the man with a job query.

(c) She is selecting the people for interviews.

(d) She is pinpointing which photo to enclose.

회사에서 이뤄지는 대화를 들으시오.

M 안녕하세요. 이곳의 채용 면접에 지원하고 싶어요.
W 좋아요, 지원서 작성은 마치셨나요?
M 지원서 양식을 한 부 주시면 작성하겠습니다.
W 좋아요. 사진도 첨부해야 해요.
M 아, 제가 한 장 가지고 있는 것 같아요. 이 사진 괜찮겠죠?
W 이 사진보다 더 격식을 차린 것이어야 할 것 같아요.

Q 여자가 주로 하는 것은?
(a) 남자의 면접을 시행하고 있다.
(b) 남자의 구직 관련 의문점을 도와주고 있다.
(c) 면접을 위한 인원을 고르고 있다.
(d) 어떤 사진을 첨부해야 할지 골라주고 있다.

application form 지원서   enclose 첨부하다   adequate 적절한
formal 격식을 차린   administrate 집행하다   query 문의, 의문점
pinpoint 정확히 지적하다

24
Listen to two friends discuss a restaurant.

W Where should we go for dinner?
M How about trying a place for brunch?
W Isn't it too late for brunch now?
M No. I know a restaurant that serves brunch at all hours.
W So, you've eaten there before?
M Lots of time. It's one of my favorite places.

Q Which is correct according to the conversation?
(a) The woman wants to go somewhere for lunch.
(b) The brunch menu can be ordered anytime.
(c) The woman is dubious about a restaurant.
(d) The man planned to have a full dinner.

두 친구가 식당에 관해 말하는 것을 들으시오.

W 저녁 먹으러 어디로 갈까?
M 브런치 식당은 어때?
W 지금 브런치 먹기에는 너무 늦지 않아?
M 아냐. 언제든지 브런치를 제공하는 식당을 내가 알고 있어.
W 그럼 전에도 거기서 식사한 적이 있어?
M 많이 했지. 내가 아주 좋아하는 장소 중의 하나야.

Q 대화 내용과 일치하는 것은?
(a) 여자는 점심 먹으러 가고 싶은 장소가 있다.
(b) 브런치 메뉴를 언제든지 주문할 수 있다.
(c) 여자는 식당에 대해서 반신반의한다.
(d) 남자는 정찬을 먹을 계획이었다.

brunch 아침 겸 점심으로 하는 식사   be limited to ∼에 제한되다
dubious 반신반의하는

25
Listen to a conversation between a man and a woman.

M Excuse me, but have we ever met before?
W No, I don't think so.
M Haven't you ever worked as a nurse?
W Nurse? No, I've been a singer all my life.
M I'm sure I met you at North Shore Hospital 5 years ago.
W I believe you're mistaking me for someone else.

Q Why did the man start the conversation with the woman?
(a) He believes he has seen her somewhere before.
(b) He needs immediate medical care.
(c) He wants to work at a hospital as a nurse.
(d) He hopes to take her to a hospital.

남자와 여자의 대화를 들으시오.

M 실례합니다만, 전에 우리 어디서 만나지 않았나요?
W 아닌 것 같은데요.
M 간호사로 일한 적이 없나요?
W 간호사요? 아뇨, 저는 평생 노래만 했어요.
M 분명히 5년 전에 당신을 노스 쇼어 병원에서 만났어요.
W 다른 사람으로 착각하고 계신 것 같네요.

Q 왜 남자는 여자에게 말을 걸었는가?
(a) 그는 그녀를 전에 어디선가 본 적이 있다고 믿는다.
(b) 그는 즉각적인 치료가 필요하다.
(c) 그는 병원에서 간호사로 일하기를 원한다.
(d) 그는 그녀를 병원으로 데리고 가기를 바란다.

Have we ever met before? 우리 전에 만난 적이 있죠?   mistake A for B A를 B로 착각하다   immediate 즉각적인   medical care 치료

26
Listen to a conversation about an e-mail message.

W Is that spam mail?
M No, it's a notice to file a tax return.
W Oh, that's a very convenient reminder.
M Well, once I forgot I received such a notice.
W So, what happened?
M I had to pay the penalty for a late filing.

Q Which is correct according to the conversation?
(a) The man is being reminded to file a tax return.
(b) The man is receiving a notice of a late fee.
(c) The tax return notice for the man was a spam mail.
(d) The notice is the first of its kind sent to the man.

이메일 메시지에 관한 대화를 들으시오.

W 스팸 메일인가요?
M 아니오, 세금 신고를 하라는 안내문이에요.
W 오, 참 간편하게 상기시켜 주네요.
M 예전에는 내가 심지어 그런 안내문을 받았다는 것을 잊어버린 적도 있어요.
W 그래서 어떻게 됐는데요?
M 늦게 신고하는 바람에 벌금을 물어야 했죠.

Q 대화 내용과 일치하는 것은?
(a) 남자는 세금 신고를 하도록 연락받고 있다.
(b) 남자는 연체료 통지서를 받고 있다.
(c) 남자에게 온 세금 신고 안내문은 스팸 메일이었다.
(d) 안내문은 그런 종류로서는 남자에게 처음 보내졌다.

notice 안내문 **file a tax return** 연말 정산을 하다, 세금 신고를 하다
reminder 상기시키는 것 **penalty** 처벌, 벌금 **late fee** 연체료

27
Listen to a conversation about a teller.

M A teller near my home really infuriates me.
W Why? Aren't bank people usually nice?
M Not this one. He was so nosy when I went to close an account.
W How do you mean?
M He wanted to know how I would use the money.
W If I were you, I wouldn't go back there.

Q Which is correct according to the conversation?
(a) The man is exasperated by a teller.
(b) The teller speaks in a very loud voice.
(c) The teller gave advice on spending money.
(d) The woman recommends going to her bank.

은행 직원에 관한 대화를 들으시오.

M 집 근처 은행 직원이 날 화나게 해요.
W 왜요? 은행원들은 대체로 친절하지 않나요?
M 이 사람은 그렇지 않아요. 계좌를 해지하러 갔을 때 참견이 심했어요.
W 무슨 말이에요?
M 내가 그 돈을 어떻게 사용할 건지 알고 싶어 했죠.
W 내가 당신이라면 다시는 가지 않겠어요.

Q 대화 내용과 일치하는 것은?
(a) 남자는 은행원 때문에 화가 나 있다.
(b) 그 은행원은 매우 큰소리로 말한다.
(c) 은행원이 돈 쓰는 것에 대해 조언을 했다.
(d) 여자는 자신이 거래하는 은행에 갈 것을 권한다.

teller 은행 직원 **infuriate** 격분시키다 **nosy** 참견하기 좋아하는,
꼬치꼬치 캐묻는 **close an account** 계좌를 해지하다 **exasperate**
분개시키다 **recommend** 권하다

28
Listen to a conversation between two friends.

W I received a call from Tom after Sunny crashed her car.
M Why did he call you?
W He knew Sunny and I are friends.
M Was he actually with her at the time?
W No, she was in the car alone. She wasn't badly hurt.
M That's good. At least she walked away from it okay.

Q Which is correct according to the conversation?
(a) Tom crashed Sunny's car by accident.
(b) Sunny was in a car accident with Tom.
(c) Sunny had no major injuries in an accident.
(d) Tom called the woman about Sunny's friends.

두 친구의 대화를 들으시오.

W 써니가 자동차 충돌 사고를 낸 후 톰이 내게 전화했더라고.
M 네게 왜 전화한 거야?
W 그는 내가 써니와 친구란 걸 알고 있었거든.
M 톰이 사고 당시 그녀와 함께 있었니?
W 아니, 그녀만 차에 있었는데 부상이 심하진 않았어.
M 적어도 무사히 넘어갔다니 다행이네.

Q 대화 내용과 일치하는 것은?
(a) 톰은 사고로 써니의 차를 들이받았다.
(b) 써니는 톰과 함께 자동차 사고를 당했다.
(c) 써니는 사고로 큰 부상을 입지 않았다.
(d) 톰은 써니의 친구들 건으로 여자에게 전화했다.

crash 부딪히다, 박살 내다 **badly** 심하게 **major injury** 중상

29
Listen to a conversation about a man's order.

W Hi, I'm calling about the order you made on April 20.
M Oh, the aftershave lotion set?
W Yes, I'm afraid it's not in stock right now.
M Then, I'd like to cancel it.
W OK, the coupon you used will be put back onto your account, sir.
M That's great. I didn't know that was possible.

Q What can be inferred from the conversation?
(a) The man gets the same aftershave every time.
(b) The man checked the availability of the lotion.
(c) The man will be able to use the coupon later.
(d) The man is extremely upset about the cancellation.

남자의 주문에 관한 대화를 들으시오.

W 안녕하세요, 4월 20일 자 고객님의 주문과 관련해 전화드렸습니다.
M 애프터 쉐이브 로션 세트요?
W 네, 유감이지만 그게 지금 저희 재고에 없어서요.
M 그럼 취소할게요.
W 사용하신 쿠폰은 고객님의 계정에 다시 넣어질 것입니다.
M 그게 가능한지 몰랐는데, 잘됐네요.

Q 대화에서 추론할 수 있는 것은?
(a) 남자는 매번 똑같은 애프터 쉐이브 로션을 구입한다.
(b) 남자는 로션의 재고 여부를 확인했다.
(c) 남자는 쿠폰을 나중에 사용할 수 있을 것이다.
(d) 남자는 취소 건으로 매우 화가 난 상태다.

make an order 주문하다 **in stock** 재고 **account** 계정
availability 입수 가능성 **extremely** 매우 **cancellation** 취소

30

Listen to a conversation between two friends.

M Aren't you going to answer your cell phone?
W No, I can see it's the Internet provider saleswoman again.
M Has she been bothering you?
W Oh, yes. She's been pressing me to change to her company.
M So, why don't you? She probably offered a good deal, right?
W The service from my current company is fine.

Q What can be inferred about the woman from the conversation?
(a) She recognizes the number of the caller.
(b) She was bothered by a woman the man met.
(c) She is weighing which Internet company to pick.
(d) She was offered a deal with the man's company.

두 친구의 대화를 들으시오.

M 휴대전화 안 받니?
W 안 받을 거야. 또 인터넷 회사 여직원이 전화하는 거거든.
M 그 여자가 널 성가시게 하니?
W 응. 자기 회사로 옮기라고 계속 강요해.
M 그럼 옮기지 그래? 아마도 좋은 거래 조건을 제의했을 거 아냐?
W 현재 거래하고 있는 회사 서비스가 좋아.

Q 여자에 대해 추론할 수 있는 것은?
(a) 전화 건 사람의 번호를 알고 있다.
(b) 남자가 만났던 어떤 여자가 자기를 성가시게 했다.
(c) 어떤 인터넷 회사를 선택해야 할지 신중히 고려하고 있다.
(d) 남자가 이용하는 회사와의 거래를 제의받았다.

internet provider 인터넷 서비스 공급자 **saleswoman** 영업여사원
bother 성가시게 하다 **press** 강요하다 **deal** 거래 **current** 현재의
recognize 알아보다 **weigh** 신중히 고려하다

Part IV

31

Attention, everyone. There will be no electricity in this apartment complex for three hours from 10 am till 1 pm this coming Wednesday. This is due to the repair work on an old power circuit. Please make arrangements so that you will not be inconvenienced during those hours. Also, there will be no water during that time, so make sure you fill a container with enough water for the duration. We apologize for the inconvenience and we will finish the repairs as quickly as possible. Thank you.

Q What is the announcement mainly about?
(a) A sudden cut in the power supply
(b) What to do in case of a blackout
(c) An impending blackout and water shut-off
(d) How long electricity and water will be reduced

모든 입주자 여러분, 주목해 주십시오. 오는 수요일 이 아파트 단지에 오전 10시부터 오후 1시까지 3시간 동안 낡은 전력 회로에 대한 수리 작업으로 인해 전기가 들어오지 않을 것입니다. 이 시간 동안 불편을 겪지 않도록 준비를 해 두시기 바랍니다. 또한, 작업 동안에 급수가 되지 않사오니 반드시 통에 물을 충분히 채워 두십시오. 불편을 끼쳐서 죄송하며 가능한 한 빨리 수리 작업을 끝내도록 하겠습니다. 감사합니다.

Q 주된 공지 내용은?
(a) 갑작스러운 전원 차단
(b) 정전 시 해야 할 일
(c) 곧 닥칠 정전과 단수
(d) 전기와 수도가 제한 공급되는 기간

electricity 전기 **apartment complex** 아파트 단지
power circuit 전력 회로 **make arrangements** 준비하다
inconvenience 불편을 끼치다 **container** 통, 용기 **apologize for** ~에 대해 사과하다 **power supply** 전원 **in case of** ~의 경우에
blackout 정전 **impending** 임박한 **shut-off** 차단, 정지

32

Tim Anderson, the Miami man charged with mailing letters laced with poison to US government officials, was released on bond Wednesday. Attorney General Bradley Curtis announced the discharge to the Associated Press. But he also stated that he was not at liberty to discuss the full conditions for the release. It is believed that the FBI is now carrying out an investigation on whether Mr. Anderson had been framed.

Q What is the main topic of the news report?
(a) The alleged framing of a suspect by the FBI
(b) The reason why Tim Anderson was set free
(c) The arrest of a man who sent dangerous letters
(d) The release from custody of a crime suspect

마이애미에 거주하는 남자, 팀 앤더슨이 미국 정부의 관료들에게 독극물이 묻은 편지를 우송한 혐의로 기소되었다가 수요일 보석금을 내고 풀려났습니다. 법무장관 브래들리 커티스는 AP 통신에게 앤더슨의 방면을 확인해 주었습니다. 하지만 그는 이번 석방에 어떤 조건이 있었는지는 밝힐 수 없다고 말했습니다. FBI는 현재 앤더슨이 누명을 쓴 것인지에 대한 수사를 진행하고 있는 것으로 여겨집니다.

Q 뉴스 보도의 주제는?
(a) FBI의 용의자 범행 조작 혐의
(b) 팀 앤더슨이 석방된 이유
(c) 위험한 편지를 보낸 남자의 검거
(d) 구금된 범죄 용의자의 석방

charged with ~로 기소된 release 방면하다 on bond 보석금을 내고 Attorney General 법무장관 discharge 석방, 방면 Associated Press 연합통신사 state 공표하다 carry out 수행하다 investigation 수사 alleged 주장된, 의심스러운 frame 죄를 뒤집어씌우다 suspect 용의자 set free 석방하다 custody 유치, 구류

33

Eating problems often begin because of poor body image. About 35% of 9-year-old and 38% of 10-year-old girls are dissatisfied with their bodies. If your child is more preoccupied with dieting and increasingly limiting their food intake, it may indicate an eating disorder. Eating disorders, including bulimia nervosa and anorexia nervosa are serious, potentially life-threatening illnesses. So parents need to take such behavior seriously. They can play a pivotal role in preventing their child's dieting from turning into a serious condition requiring medical and psychological attention.

Q Which is correct according to the lecture?
(a) Half of all 9-year-olds are dissatisfied with their looks.
(b) A poor body image tends to lead to eating disorders.
(c) Parents can do little to prevent teen eating problems.
(d) Eating disorders rarely need medical intervention.

식이 장애는 종종 잘못된 신체상에서 비롯됩니다. 9세 여아의 약 35퍼센트, 그리고 10세 여아의 약 38퍼센트가 자신의 신체에 불만을 느낍니다. 만약 여러분의 자녀가 다이어트에 사로잡혀서 점점 음식 섭취를 제한한다면 이는 식이 장애의 징후일 수 있습니다. 폭식증, 거식증 등의 식이 장애는 심각한 병이며 생명을 위협할 수도 있습니다. 그러므로 부모들은 그런 행동을 심각하게 여길 필요가 있습니다. 부모는 자녀의 다이어트가 의료 및 심리 치료가 필요한 심각한 병으로 발전하지 않도록 막는 데 중요한 역할을 할 수 있습니다.

Q 강의 내용과 일치하는 것은?
(a) 전체 9세 아동의 절반은 자신의 외모에 만족하지 않는다.
(b) 잘못된 신체상이 식이 장애를 초래하기 쉽다.
(c) 부모는 10대의 식이 장애를 방지하는 데 별 역할을 하지 못한다.
(d) 식이 장애는 의학적인 개입이 거의 필요치 않다.

eating problem 식이 장애(eating disorder) body image 신체상 be dissatisfied with ~을 불만스럽게 여기다 be preoccupied with (생각·걱정에) 사로잡히다 intake 섭취 indicate ~의 징후이다 bulimia nervosa 폭식증 anorexia nervosa 거식증 potentially 가능성 있게, 어쩌면 life-threatening 생명을 위협하는 play a pivotal role in ~에서 중추적인 역할을 하다 turn into ~이 되다, ~으로 변하다 medical attention 의학적인 치료 psychological 심리[정신]적인

34

Archaeologists have discovered a collection of pottery inside the recently uncovered remains of a massive Iron Age building at Tel Motza in Israel. The collection included not only embellished cups and pedestals but also many tiny figurines in both human and animal form. These presumably religious artifacts found inside the temple was particularly surprising since places for rituals outside the capital city of Jerusalem were unknown in the late Iron Age. Religious rituals were thought to be carried out only at the Temple of Jerusalem.

Q Why was the discovery of the pottery surprising?
(a) It included cups made in the Iron Age.
(b) It served ritual purposes at an unlikely site.
(c) It had both animal and human forms on it.
(d) It showed that rituals occurred only in Jerusalem.

고고학자들이 이스라엘 텔 모짜의 최근에 발굴된 거대한 철기 시대 건축물의 유적 내부에서 도기 더미를 발견했다. 이 더미에는 장식이 있는 컵과 받침대뿐만 아니라 인간과 동물 형상을 한 수많은 작은 조각상들이 포함되어 있었다. 이 신전 내부에서 종교적인 것으로 추정되는 물건들을 발견한 된 것이 특히 놀라운 일이었는데, 왜냐하면 후기 철기 시대에, 수도를 벗어난 제사 장소가 알려지지 않았기 때문이다. 당시 종교 의식은 예루살렘에 있는 신전에서만 거행된 것으로 생각됐었다.

Q 도기의 발견이 놀라웠던 이유는?
(a) 철기 시대에 만들어진 컵을 포함하였다.
(b) 생각지도 못한 장소에서 종교적 목적에 사용되었다.
(c) 도기에 동물 및 인간의 형태가 담겨 있었다.
(d) 예루살렘에서만 있었던 종교 의식을 보여줬다.

archaeologist 고고학자 pottery 도기 uncover 발견[발굴]하다 remains 유적 massive 거대한 Iron Age 철기 시대 embellish 장식하다 pedestal 받침대 tiny 작은 figurine 작은 조각상 presumably 추정하건대, 짐작건대 artifact 인공물, 가공품 temple 신전 ritual 제사 capital city 수도 unlikely 생각지도 못할 rite 의식

35

Today's lecture will be on mosquitoes. Of all the insects that attack man and animals, they stand out as being the only carriers of malaria, yellow fever, and dengue fever for man. They also transmit viral encephalitis in horses and heartworms in dogs. There are more than 2,500 species of mosquitoes worldwide. Because of their blood-feeding activity, they are not only disease carriers but also major nuisances. Only the females suck blood, while the males are nectar feeders. The females need the protein in blood to produce viable eggs.

Q Which is correct according to the lecture?
(a) One can contract malaria from mosquitoes.
(b) Animals are immune to mosquito carried diseases.
(c) Female mosquitoes feed on male ones.
(d) There are over 25,000 mosquito species worldwide.

오늘의 강의 주제는 모기입니다. 사람과 동물을 공격하는 모든 곤충 중에서 오직 모기만이 사람에게 말라리아, 황열병, 뎅기열을 매개한다는 점에서 두드러집니다. 이것은 또한 말에게는 바이러스성 뇌염을, 개에게는 심장사상충을 전염시킵니다. 모기의 종은 전 세계적으로 2천 5백 개가 넘습니다. 이들의 흡혈 활동 때문에 모기는 단지 질병 매개체일 뿐만 아니라 대단히 성가신 존재이기도 합니다. 암컷만이 피를 빨아 먹는 반면 수컷은 과일즙을 먹습니다. 암컷은 독자 생존 가능한 알을 낳기 위해 피 속에 든 단백질이 필요합니다.

Q 강의 내용과 일치하는 것은?
(a) 사람은 모기에 의해 말라리아에 걸릴 수 있다.
(b) 동물은 병균을 옮기는 모기가 물어도 영향을 받지 않는다.
(c) 암컷 모기는 수컷을 먹고 산다.
(d) 전 세계적으로 모기가 25,000종이 넘는다.

mosquito 모기 **insect** 곤충 **stand out** 두드러지다 **carrier** (병원체의) 매개체 **yellow fever** 황열병 **dengue fever** 뎅기열 **transmit** 전염시키다 **viral encephalitis** 바이러스성 뇌염 **heartworm** 심장사상충 **species** 종 **nuisance** 골칫거리 **nectar** 과일즙 **feeder** ~을 먹는 동물 **protein** 단백질 **viable** 독자 생존 가능한 **immune to** ~에 면역성이 있는 **feed on** ~을 먹고 살다

36

Have you ever seen a painting of rows and rows of Campbell's soup cans? That art was created by Andy Warhol. Warhol is famous for turning mundane images into ironic art. His first drawing lesson began when he contracted a rare disease of the nervous system and was bedridden for several months, and drawing soon became his favorite childhood pastime. He was also an avid fan of the movies and took up photography at the age of 9, developing film in a makeshift darkroom in his home's basement.

Q What can be inferred about Andy Warhol from the lecture?
(a) He also preferred to draw in bed as an adult.
(b) He never cured his nervous system impairment.
(c) He was talented in depicting objects in fine detail.
(d) He was attracted to artistic hobbies at a young age.

당신은 길게 늘어선 캠벨 수프 깡통 그림을 본 적이 있으신가요? 그것은 앤디 워홀의 창작물입니다. 워홀은 일상적인 이미지를 역설적인 예술로 바꿔 놓기로 유명합니다. 그의 첫 그림 교습은 그가 신경계 희귀병에 걸려 몇 달 동안 침대에 누워 있었을 때 시작되었고, 그림은 곧 자신이 가장 좋아하는 어린 시절 소일거리가 되었습니다. 그는 또한 영화를 열렬히 좋아했으며, 9살에는 사진 찍기를 시작했는데 집의 지하실에 임시변통으로 만든 암실에서 필름을 현상했습니다.

Q 앤디 워홀에 대해서 추론할 수 있는 것은?
(a) 성인이 되어서도 침대에서 그림 그리는 것을 좋아했다.
(b) 신경계 장애를 결코 치유하지 못했다.
(c) 물체를 섬세하게 묘사하는 데 재능이 있었다.
(d) 어린 나이에 여러 예술적인 취미 활동에 매료되었다.

rows and rows of 길게 이어진 **mundane** 일상적인 **drawing** (색칠을 하지 않은) 그림, 데생 **contract** (병에) 걸리다 **rare disease** 희귀병 **nervous** 신경의 **bedridden** 아파서 누워 있는 **pastime** 취미, 소일거리 **avid** 열렬한 **take up** (취미·일을) 시작하다 **photography** 사진 촬영 **develop** 현상하다 **makeshift** 임시변통의 **darkroom** 암실 **basement** 지하실 **cure** 치유하다 **impairment** 장애 **depict** 묘사하다 **object** 물체 **in fine detail** 섬세하게 **be attracted to** ~에 매료되다

Part V

37-38

Do you think you can change your life by entering a writing contest? If you write well, you can! The 15th Annual Creative Writing Contest will offer cash prizes to 15 winners, some of whom will receive as much as $500,000! There are three age categories: people under the age of 18, people between the ages of 18 and 60, and people over the age of 60. Cash prizes will be offered to the top five winners in each age category. First place winners will receive $500,000! This year's prompt asks a timeless question: What is the meaning of life? You can answer this important question with a poem, a short story, or a novel. All entries should be emailed to ericaj@creativewriting.org no later than 11:00 p.m. on June 27th. Winners will be announced on July 28th. Enter this contest and change your life!

글쓰기 대회에 참가해서 인생 역전을 이룰 수 있다고 생각하시나요? 글을 잘 쓰신다면, 가능합니다! 제15회 연례 창작 글쓰기 대회는 15명의 입상자에게 상금을 수여하는데요, 입상자 가운데 일부는 50만 달러나 되는 상금을 받습니다. 연령대는 18세 미만, 18세에서 60세까지, 60세 이상의 세 가지로 분류합니다. 상금은 각 연령대마다 상위 입상자 5명에게 수여합니다. 1위 입상자는 50만 달러를 받습니다! 올해의 창작 주제는 삶의 의미는 무엇인가라는 영원한 문제입니다. 이 중요한 질문에 대한 답은 시, 단편소설, 또는 소설로 제시할 수 있습니다. 모든 출품작은 6월 27일 오후 11시까지 ericaj@creativewriting.org로 이메일로 보내셔야 합니다. 입상자는 7월 28일에 발표됩니다. 이 대회에서 응모하셔서 인생 역전을 이루세요!

37 Q When is the deadline for submitting an entry for the contest?

(a) June 7th

(b) June 27th

(c) July 8th

(d) July 28th

Q 대회에 출품작을 제출하는 기한은 언제인가?

(a) 6월 7일

(b) 6월 27일

(c) 7월 8일

(d) 7월 28일

해설 특히 청해의 파트4와 파트5에서 숫자 정보가 나올 때는 반드시 메모하는 습관을 가져야 한다. 숫자 정보는 중요한 평가 대상이기 때문이다. 이 문항의 경우에도 제출 기한을 묻고 있는데, 제출 기한은 6월 27일이기 때문에 정답은 (b)이다. (d)는 입상작 발표일이기 때문에 오답이다.

38 Q Which is correct according to the announcement?

(a) This year's contest will award cash prizes to 50 winners.

(b) People over the age of 60 aren't allowed to enter the contest.

(c) Three second place winners will receive $300,000.

(d) All entries should be electronically submitted to the person in charge.

Q 안내에 따르면, 다음 중 옳은 것은?

(a) 올해의 대회에서는 50명의 입상자들이 상금을 받을 것이다.

(b) 60세가 넘는 사람들은 대회에 응모할 수 없다.

(c) 세 명의 2위 입상자들은 30만 달러를 받을 것이다.

(d) 모든 출품작들은 담당자에게 인터넷으로 제출되어야 한다.

해설 (a)는 50명이 아니라 15명이기 때문에 오답이다. 영어에서는 두 숫자가 비슷하게 들릴 수 있기 때문에, 주의해서 들어야 한다. (b)는 60세가 넘는 사람도 응모할 수 있어서 오답이다. (c)는 전혀 제시되지 않은 정보이므로, 반드시 오답으로 처리해야 한다. 따라서 정답은 주어진 내용에 충실한 (d)이다.

contest 대회; 겨루다 **annual** 연례의 **creative** 창의적인 **cash prize** 상금 **category** 범주 **prompt** 길잡이; 자극하는 것 **timeless** 시간을 초월한, 영원한 **entry** 출품작, 응모작

39-40

In recent years, astrophysics has progressed at a phenomenal rate. Nevertheless, there are so many questions to which astrophysicists do not know the answers. One of them is concerned with antimatter. It is widely known that matter and antimatter annihilate each other. Many scientists believe that when the Big Bang occurred, the amount of matter was the same as that of antimatter. If that had been the case, however, matter and antimatter would have annihilated each other completely. Then, the universe would be empty now. But the universe is full of planets, stars, and galaxies. How can we unravel this mystery? One possible answer to this mystery is that matter and antimatter happened to drift apart, escaping from each other's fatal grasp. Somewhere in the universe, the antimatter world may exist with a safe distance from the matter world.

근래에 천체물리학은 경이적인 속도로 발전했습니다. 그럼에도 불구하고, 천체물리학자들이 해답을 알지 못하는 질문들이 너무도 많습니다. 그런 질문들 가운데 하나는 반물질(反物質)에 관한 것입니다. 물질과 반물질이 서로를 쌍(雙)소멸시킨다는 것은 널리 알려져 있습니다. 많은 과학자들은 빅뱅이 일어났을 때 물질의 양이 반물질의 양과 같았다고 생각합니다. 그렇지만 그것이 맞았다고 한다면, 물질과 반물질은 서로를 완전히 쌍(雙)소멸시켰을 것입니다. 그렇다면 우주에는 현재 아무것도 존재하지 않을 것입니다. 그렇지만 우주는 행성, 항성, 그리고 은하계로 가득합니다. 이 수수께끼를 어떻게 풀 수 있을까요? 이 수수께끼에 대한 한 가지 가능한 답은 물질과 반물질이 표류하다가 서로 멀리 떨어져 서로의 위험한 영향권을 벗어났다는 것입니다. 우주 어딘가에 물질계의 영향력과 안전한 거리를 두고 반물질계가 존재할지도 모른다는 것입니다.

39 Q What is the lecture mainly about?

(a) A kind of symmetry between matter and antimatter

(b) A question that continues to puzzle astrophysicists

(c) The amount of antimatter during the Big Bang

(d) The mysterious characteristics of antimatter

Q 강의는 주로 무엇에 관한 것인가?

(a) 물질과 반물질 사이의 일종의 대칭

(b) 천체물리학자들을 계속해서 곤혹스럽게 만드는 질문

(c) 빅뱅 동안의 반물질의 양

(d) 반물질의 불가사의한 특성들

해설 강의에서 전반적으로 다루는 사항을 정답으로 골라야 한다. (a)는 주어진 강의에서 언급하지 않았으므로 오답이다. (c)는 반물질의 양뿐만 아니라 물질의 양도 함께 언급되어야 하기 때문에 정답이 아니다. (d)는 강의에서 반물질의 여러 특성들이 언급되지 않았기 때문에 오답이다. 따라서 정답은 (b)이다. 이처럼 직접적이지 않은 방식으로 정답을 제시하는 선택지 유형에 익숙해질 필요가 있다.

40 Q What can be inferred from the lecture?

(a) During the Big Bang, the amount of matter might have been larger than that of antimatter.

(b) During the Big Bang, matter and antimatter must have destroyed each other completely.

(c) The antimatter world, if exists, is not nearby.

(d) Astrophysicists have recently been successful in creating antimatter.

Q 강의로부터 추론할 수 있는 것은?

(a) 빅뱅 동안에, 물질의 양이 반물질의 양보다 컸을지도 모른다.

(b) 빅뱅 동안에, 물질과 반물질은 서로를 완전히 파괴했음에 틀림없다.

(c) 반물질계가 존재한다면 가까이 있지 않다.

(d) 천체물리학자들이 최근에 반물질을 만들어내는 데 성공했다.

해설 (b)는 강의에서 틀렸다고 설명했기 때문에 오답이다. (a)와 (d)는 주어진 강의에서 전혀 말하지 않았기 때문에, 알 수 없는 내용이다. 따라서 반드시 오답으로 처리해야 한다. 이처럼 분명히 말하지 않은 내용을 오답으로 처리하는 것은 세부 사항 유형과 추론 유형에 공통으로 활용되는 중요 기법이다. 지문 마지막 내용을 고려할 때 정답은 (c)이다.

astrophysics 천체물리학 **progress** 발전하다 **phenomenal** 경이적인 **antimatter** 반물질 **annihilate** 쌍(雙)소멸시키다 **empty** 비어 있는, 공허한 **galaxy** 은하계 **unravel** 풀다; 해명하다 **mystery** 미스터리, 수수께끼 **symmetry** 대칭 **puzzle** 곤혹케 하다 **mysterious** 불가사의한 **observable** 관측할 수 있는

Vocabulary   p.97

Part I

1   정답 (a)

A 맘에 드는 남자만 만나면 얼어붙어요.

B 당신은 과묵하지 말고 거리낌 없이 말할 필요가 있어요.

freeze (두려움 등으로 몸이) 얼어붙다 **speak up** 거리낌 없이 말하다 **reticent** 과묵한, 신중한 **audacious** 대담한 **clamorous** 시끄러운, 떠들썩한 **impertinent** 무례한

2   정답 (b)

A 피터가 나보다 먼저 승진됐다니 믿을 수가 없어요!

B 글쎄요, 그의 기술이 당신 기술보다 훨씬 우수해요.

get promoted 승진되다 **far** 훨씬 **amend** 개정하다 **surpass** ~보다 낫다 **validate** 유효하게 하다 **endorse** 지지하다

3   정답 (c)

A 내일 마라톤 시합에 차 태워 드릴까요?

B 오전 7시 정각에 시청 앞 광장에 모일 거니까 태워주면 대단히 고맙죠.

ride (탈것 등을) 타기 **City Hall** 시청 **square** 광장 **sharp** 정각 **appreciate** 고맙게 여기다 **disperse** 해산하다 **convolute** 서로 얽히다 **congregate** 모이다 **disseminate** 퍼뜨리다

4   정답 (d)

A 오늘밤 콘서트가 즐거웠는지 모르겠군요.

B 오, 완벽한 공연에 무척 감동 받았어요.

impressed 감동 받는 **performance** 공연 **culpable** 과실이 있는 **expedient** 편리한 **delinquent** 비행의, 죄를 범한 **impeccable** 나무랄 데 없는

5   정답 (d)

A 이번에는 어떤 치욕도 참지 않을 거야!

B 진정해. 흥분해봤자 아무런 도움이 안 돼.

put up with ~을 참다 **humiliation** 치욕, 굴욕 **hot temper** 다혈질, 급한 성격 **act up** 못되게 굴다 **chip in** 끼어들다 **tag along** 따라가다 **simmer down** 진정하다, 화를 가라앉히다

6   정답 (d)

A 내가 산 스포츠카 좀 봐!

B 거기에 돈을 낭비하지 말았어야 했어.

scatter 뿌리다 **devour** 게걸스럽게 먹다 **deplete** 고갈시키다 **squander** 낭비하다

7   정답 (a)

A 이 문제에 대해서 당신을 믿어도 될까요?

B 물론이에요, 당신 비밀을 누구에게도 절대로 누설하지 않겠다고 약속하겠어요.

matter 문제 **divulge** 누설하다 **protest** 항의하다 **construe** 이해[해석]하다 **manifest** 나타내다

8   정답 (a)

A 어떻게 결국 여배우가 되었나요?

B 톰이 절 구슬려서 자기가 연출하던 극의 배역을 맡게 했어요.

end up -ing 결국 ~이 되다 **do a part** 배역을 맡다 **direct** 연출하다 **cajole A into -ing** A를 부추겨서 ~하게 하다 **reproach** 비난하다 **commend** 명하다 **reprimand** 꾸짖다

9   정답 (a)

A 냉장고에 이 먹다 남은 음식 좀 봐요! 곰팡이가 피었어요.

B 알아요. 게다가 나쁜 냄새도 나요.

leftover 먹다 남은 **fridge** 냉장고 **mold** 곰팡이 **give off** (냄새를) 풍기다 **odor** 냄새, 악취 **foul** 나쁜, 악취가 나는 **rough** 거친 **bland** 자극이 없는 **cruel** 잔인한

10   정답 (c)

A 당신 아버님을 어떤 사람으로 묘사하시겠어요?

B 안 된다는 대답은 듣지 않겠다는 매우 고집 센 유형이에요.

not take no for an answer 안 된다[싫다]는 대답을 거부하다 **colossal** 거대한 **obedient** 순종적인 **tenacious** 집요한, 고집 센 **meticulous** 꼼꼼한, 세심한

Part II

11 정답 (d)

그 단체는 건강 보조 식품 공장을 검열<u>했다</u>.

inspection 점검, 검사 **health-supplement** 건강 보조제 **escort** 호위하다 **deliver** 배달하다 **regulate** 단속하다 **conduct** (특정한 행동을) 하다

12 정답 (a)

이 와이파이 리피터는 당신의 기존 라우터 신호를 더 먼 거리까지 확장시킴으로써 네트워크 연결이 안 되는 지역을 <u>제거해</u> 줄 것이다.

Wi-Fi repeater 와이파이 신호를 강하게 만들어주는 기기 **dead spot** 미작동[불통] 지역 **extend** 확장하다 **existing** 기존의 **router** 근거리 통신망에서 데이터 패킷의 최적 경로를 선택하는 장치 **eliminate** 제거하다 **disband** 해체하다 **hinder** 방해하다 **omit** 생략하다

13 정답 (d)

<u>가혹한</u> 비평을 받은 후 그 소설가는 작가로서의 경력을 거의 포기했다.

critique 비평 **novelist** 소설가 **sympathetic** 공감하는 **banish** 추방하다 **amiable** 상냥한 **harsh** 가혹한, 냉엄한

14 정답 (a)

어떤 것이건 섬유로 된 물질이면 엉켜서 쓰레기 처리 설비를 <u>고장 나게</u> 할 수 있다.

fibrous 섬유로 된 **material** 물질 **tangle** 엉키다 **garbage** 쓰레기 **disposal** 처리 **jam** 못 움직이게 하다, 고장 나게 하다 **dump** 버리다 **loosen** 느슨하게 하다 **merge** 합치다

15 정답 (a)

안전 조치로서 관광객들에게 큰 무리를 지어 다니고 위험 지역은 가지 않도록 <u>강력히 권고하고</u> 있다.

safety measure 안전 조치 **in a group** 무리를 지어 **urge** 강력히 권고하다, 촉구하다 **entice** 유혹하다 **dissect** 해부하다 **promote** 촉진하다

16 정답 (d)

창문을 발포 비닐 포장으로 <u>단열 처리를</u> 하면 창문의 열 손실을 절반으로 줄일 수 있다.

bubble wrap 발포 비닐 포장 **invest** 투자하다 **insert** 삽입하다 **inscribe** 새기다 **insulate** 단열 처리를 하다

17 정답 (c)

사람들은 때때로 너무 지나친 <u>조롱</u>을 해서 깊은 수치심을 줄지도 모른다는 생각을 하지 않고 다른 사람들을 놀린다.

poke fun at ~을 놀리다 **overdo** ~을 지나치게 하다 **cause** 유발하다 **humiliation** 치욕, 수치심 **parody** 서투른 모방 **mimicry** 흉내 **mockery** 조롱 **pretense** 가식, 시늉

18 정답 (d)

이 세제는 찬물에서도 효과적으로 <u>얼룩</u>을 지우고 기름기를 없애고 때를 제거해준다.

detergent 세제 **effective** 효과적인 **get out** 지우다, 제거하다 **cut through** 없애다 **grease** (끈적끈적한) 기름 **lift** 제거하다 **grime** 때 **blemish** 티, 흠 **smirch** (명성 등의) 흠, 오점 **stigma** 낙인 **stain** 얼룩

19 정답 (b)

재판은 하루 <u>휴정한</u> 후 재개될 것이다.

trial 재판 **resume** 재개하다 **retreat** 후퇴하다 **adjourn** 휴정하다 **withdraw** 철회하다 **progress** 나아가다

20 정답 (d)

연구자들은 엄마가 <u>오염된</u> 물고기를 섭취하면 태아가 해를 입을 수 있다는 것을 발견했다.

fetus 태아 **consume** 먹다 **tarnished** 변색된 **distorted** 왜곡된 **loathsome** 혐오스러운 **contaminated** 오염된

21 정답 (d)

아이의 행동은 <u>매우 불쾌했지만</u>, 더 나쁜 것은 부모가 그것을 허용했다는 것이다.

behavior 행동 **brisk** 활발한 **decrepit** 노후한 **pungent** 신랄한, 자극적인 **obnoxious** 매우 불쾌한

22 정답 (c)

프리랜서로 일하는 것은 만약 당신이 적절한 시기에 적절한 장소에 있다면 회사에 다니는 것보다 더 많은 돈을 벌어서 <u>수지맞을</u> 수 있다.

freelancing 프리랜서로 일하는 것 **earn money** 돈을 벌다 **lousy** 불결한 **crappy** 쓰레기 같은 **lucrative** 수지맞는, 돈벌이가 되는 **partial** 부분적인, 불완전한

23 정답 (d)

<u>불경기</u> 때문에 일부 60대들이 은퇴 밑천을 다시 마련하고자 어쩔 수 없이 계속 일하고 있다.

force A to 강제로 A에게 ~하게 하다 **retirement** 은퇴 **nest-egg** 밑천, 비상금 **sturdy** 견고한 **astute** 약삭빠른 **ardent** 열렬한 **sluggish** 부진한

24 정답 (c)

아트센터는 수십 년 동안 그 지역 최고의 순수예술을 위한 <u>장소</u>였다.

premier 최고의 **fine arts** 미술 **zone** 지대, 지역 **niche** 적소, (시장의) 틈새 **venue** 장소 **abode** 거주지

25 정답 (b)

맹렬한 <u>눈보라</u>가 약 2~3피트의 눈을 뿌릴 것으로 예상되므로 모든 야외 활동을 삼가는 것이 좋다.

fierce 사나운, 맹렬한 **outdoor activity** 야외 활동 **discourage** 막다, 단념시키다 **tornado** 회오리바람, 토네이도 **blizzard** 눈보라 **drizzle** 가랑비 **frost** 서리

26 정답 (c)

시장이 붕괴되고 불황이 뒤따르면서 취업률이 <u>급락했다</u>.

employment rate 취업률 **in the wake of** ~의 결과로, ~의 뒤를 좇아 **market crash** 시장 붕괴 **subsequent** 그 이후의 **recession** 불황 **recuperate** 회복하다 **skyrocket** 급등하다 **plummet** 급락하다 **intervene** 개입하다

27 정답 (d)

'가정'이라는 용어는 성장하면서 고통과 정신적 외상을 겪은 이들에게는 나쁜 <u>의미</u>로 다가올 수 있다.

term 용어 **trauma** 정신적 외상 **grow up** 성장하다 **rendition** 연주, 번역 **elucidation** 설명, 해명 **denotation** 명시적 의미 **connotation** 함축, 언외의 의미

28 정답 (c)

복부 지방은 심장병, 고혈압, 심지어 알츠하이머병과 같은 몇 가지 건강 문제의 <u>전조</u>가 될 수 있다.

abdominal 복부의 **fat** 지방 **heart disease** 심장병 **high blood pressure** 고혈압 **Alzheimer's** 알츠하이머병 **integrate** 통합시키다 **compound** 악화시키다 **foreshadow** 전조가 되다 **accommodate** 수용하다

29 정답 (d)

경매를 통해 모은 전 <u>수익금</u>은 교회 복원 프로젝트를 후원할 것이다.

raise (자금을) 모으다 **auction** 경매 **restoration** 복원, 복구 **perks** 비금전적 혜택, 특전 **stakes** 내깃돈 **capital** 자본금 **proceeds** 수익금

30 정답 (b)

미합중국의 1960년대는 정치 및 사회적 <u>격변</u>으로 특징지어지는 격동의 시기였다.

tumultuous 격동의 **characterized by** ~이 특징인 **apathy** 무관심 **upheaval** 격변, 대변동 **tranquility** 평온 **stagnation** 침체, 정체

Grammar

p.101

Part I

1 정답 (d)

A 이 조그만 아파트에서 사는 것에 정말 질려버렸어요.
B 걱정 마세요. 우린 충분히 저축해서 내년쯤에는 더 큰 아파트로 가게 될 거예요.

해설 미래 특정 시점 이전에 시작되어 미래 특정 시점에 완료되는 동작은 미래완료(will have p.p.) 시제를 사용하므로 (d)가 정답이다.

be sick and tired of ~에 진절머리가 나다

2 정답 (c)

A 어머님이 치수를 어떻게 입으세요?
B 저만큼 호리호리해서 55를 입으세요.

해설 원급 비교의 올바른 어순을 묻는 문제이다. 즉 〈as+형용사[부사] 원급+as〉가 되어야 하므로 (c)가 정답이다.

wear 입다 **slim** 호리호리한

3 정답 (d)

A 은퇴 후에 인생이 너무 재미없어요.
B 뭔가 흥미로운 것을 찾으세요.

해설 3형식 문장 〈주어+동사+목적어〉의 올바른 순서와 목적어 something을 수식하는 형용사의 위치를 묻는 문제이다. 형용사는 명사 앞에 오는 것이 원칙이지만 -thing으로 끝나는 대명사를 꾸며줄 때는 그 뒤에 위치하므로 something exciting이 올바르다. 따라서 정답은 (d)이다.

mundane 재미없는 **retirement** 은퇴

4 정답 (c)

A 케이크 한 조각 드실래요?
B 죄송하지만 단것은 먹지 않기로 했어요.

해설 〈make+가목적어(it)+목적보어+진목적어(to부정사)〉 구문의 올바른 어순을 묻는 문제이다. 또한, to부정사를 부정할 때는 그 앞에 부정어를 두므로 (c)가 정답이다.

sweet 단 것 **make it a rule to** ~하기로 정하다, ~을 습관으로 하다

5 정답 (b)

A 회사의 구인란에 관리직이 나와 있나요?
B 지금은 아니지만, 앞으로 실릴 거예요.

해설 빈칸에 들어갈 어구에서 생략되는 것은 질문과 반복되는 어구이다. 완전한 문장은 it(= the managerial position) will be listed on the company's job openings page이므로 listed 이하의 반복되는 어구를 생략한 (b)가 정답이다.

managerial position 관리직 **listed** 실려 있는 **job opening** (직장의) 빈자리, 공석 **at the moment** 지금 당장, 현재

6 정답 (d)

A 파멜라의 피부 질환에 대해서 그녀에게 어떻게 하라고 말했니?
B 진찰을 받아보라고 했어.

해설 제안, 명령, 요구, 주장 등을 나타내는 동사의 목적어로 that절이 올 때, that절의 동사는 〈should+동사원형〉 혹은 should를 생략하고 동사원형을 써야 한다. 따라서 정답은 (d)이다. she가 3인칭 단수여서 sees를 고르지 않도록 유의해야 한다.

skin problem 피부 질환 **recommend** 권하다

7 정답 (c)

A TV에 출연하는 걸 승낙했나요?
B 아니요, 그러지 않기로 했어요.

해설 to부정사의 동사가 이미 언급된 것이면 중복을 피하기 위해 생략하고 대부정사 to만 쓰며, to부정사의 부정은 그 앞에 부정어를 붙이므로 (c)가 정답이다.

agree to ~하기를 승낙하다 **appear** 출연하다

8 정답(c)

A 새 규정에 대해서 아무것도 모르고 있어서는 안 됩니다.
B 그래요, 그것들에 대해서 알고 있어야 합니다.

해설 important(중요한), imperative(필수의), essential(절대 필요한), necessary(필요한), urgent(긴급한), desirable(바람직한) 등, 이성적 판단이나 필요성을 나타내는 형용사가 나오는 문장의 that절에서는 should가 생략되어 동사원형만 남는다. 문맥상 주어는 동사의 행위자가 아닌 대상이므로 수동태를 써야 옳다. 그러므로 (c)가 정답이다.

in the dark 알지 못하고   policy 정책, 규정   imperative 필수의, 의무적인   be informed of ~에 대해서 알고 있다

9   정답 (c)

A 짐이 승진되었나요?
B 회사에 큰 손실을 입혔기 때문에 사실은 강등되었어요.

해설 As he had caused a big loss to the company, he actually got demoted에서 종속절의 As he had caused ~를 분사구문으로 고치면 Having caused ~가 되므로 (c)가 정답이다.

get promoted 승진되다   get demoted 강등되다   cause 야기하다

10   정답 (c)

A 아버님 사업이 실패한 후에 꽤 어려웠지요?
B 네, 제 가족이 그전에는 그런 재정적 어려움을 겪은 적이 한 번도 없었어요.

해설 강조하기 위해 부사(never)를 문장 앞으로 내면 〈부사+조동사(조동사가 없으면 do)+주어+동사〉의 어순이 되므로 (c)가 정답이다. 원래 문장은 my family had never experienced이다.

collapse 무너지다, 실패하다   financial 재정상의

Part II

11   정답 (d)

작년 여름에 대홍수를 겪었기 때문에 시는 올해 대규모 댐을 건설할 계획을 갖고 있다.

해설 알맞은 분사구문을 고르는 문제이다. 분사구문이 나타내는 시간이 주절의 술부 동사보다 앞선 시제를 나타낼 때는 완료분사구문(having p.p.)을 쓰므로 (d)가 정답이다.

severe 극심한   flood 대홍수

12   정답 (d)

영화 내내 역사적 사건들에 대한 언급이 있었다.

알맞은 전치사를 고르는 문제이다. 문맥상 빈칸에는 '~동안 내내, ~의 처음부터 끝까지'란 뜻의 (d)가 적절하다.

reference to ~에 관한 언급

13   정답 (a)

사람은 나이를 먹음에 따라 삶의 질에 영향을 미치는 만성 질환에 걸리기 쉽다.

해설 알맞은 접속사를 고르는 문제이다. 문맥상 빈칸에는 '~함에 따라'라는 뜻이 필요하므로 (a)가 정답이다.

tend to ~하기 쉽다   develop (병·문제가) 생기다   chronic condition 만성 질환

14   정답 (b)

가수의 낭만적인 바리톤 목소리가 청중을 즐겁게 했다.

해설 먼저 amuse는 '즐겁게 하다'라는 타동사이다. 〈동사(keep)+목적어(audience)+목적보어〉에서 목적어인 청중이 즐거워하는 것이므로 수동형인 (b) amused가 정답이다.

baritone 바리톤   audience 청중   amuse 즐겁게 하다

15   정답 (b)

연사는 교육 및 간호직에 흑인 여성이 계속 과도하게 몰리고 있다고 덧붙였다.

해설 뜻은 없지만 주어와 같은 구실을 하는 there가 포함된 문장의 올바른 어순을 묻는 문제이다. 주어 역할을 하는 there가 맨 먼저 와야 하므로 (a)와 (c)는 일단 제외한다. 주어 다음에 본동사가 온 (b)가 정답이고, (d)는 동사 continue 스스로가 진행의 의미를 가지므로 진행형으로 쓰이지 않는다.

concentration 집중, 집결   continuation 계속

16   정답 (c)

일류 학교에 입학한 자들은 매일 일정 시간을 자신이 배웠던 내용을 복습하는 데 보냈다고 말했다.

해설 〈spend time (in) -ing(~하는 데 시간을 보내다)〉라는 관용 표현을 알고 있다면 쉽게 풀 수 있는 문제이다. 따라서 정답은 (c) reviewing이다.

material 자료, 내용   review 복습하다

17   정답 (c)

믹서를 자주 교체하는 것에 진저리가 난다면 수년간 당신을 위해 작동할 이 제품에 기대를 걸어봐도 좋습니다.

해설 product를 수식하는 어구의 올바른 순서를 묻는 문제이다. 동사 last는 '특정 기간 사용할 수 있도록 충분히 오래가다'란 뜻으로 〈last+사람+시간〉의 형태로 쓰인다. 따라서 product를 꾸며주는 형용사적 용법의 to부정사인 to last 다음에 사람과 시간이 따라온 (c)가 정답이다.

be sick of ~에 질리다   replace 교체하다   blender 믹서   rely on ~에 의지하다   last 충분히 오래가다

18   정답 (b)

온라인 학위 프로그램에 성공하기 위해서는 학습 과제를 완수하기 위한 시간을 일정 확보하는 데 철저해야 한다.

해설 time은 기간을 표현할 때는 가산명사로 쓰이며, 온라인 강의는 1회성 수업이 아닐 것이므로 '수차례에 걸친 어느 정도의 시간들'을 의미하는 (b)가 정답이다.

succeed in ~에 성공하다   degree 학위   strict 엄격한, 철저한   set aside 챙겨두다, 확보하다

19   정답 (d)

경매는 최저 경매 가격에 도달한 호가가 전혀 없었기 때문에 취소되었는데, 최저 경매 가격의 수준은 여느 때처럼 비밀에 부쳐졌다.

해설 알맞은 관계대명사를 고르는 문제이다. no bids reached the reserve price와 the level of the reserve price was as usual undisclosed를 합치면 중복되는 the reserve price가 선행사가 되고 두 번째 문장의 of the reserve price가 of which로 바뀌므로 정답은 (d)이다.

auction 경매   bid 호가   reserve price 최저 경매 가격   as usual 여느 때처럼   undisclosed 비밀에 부쳐진

20 정답 (d)

탄수화물을 너무 많이 섭취하면 실제로 지방 섭취를 줄이는 것보다 더 살찌게 된다.

해설 동명사가 주어인 문장의 올바른 어순을 묻는 문제로, 동명사 eating을 쓴 다음 eat의 목적어인 carbohydrates가 따라오고 부사가 동사를 그 뒤에서 수식한(too much) (d)가 정답이다.

carbohydrate 탄수화물 fat intake 지방 섭취

21 정답 (d)

전문가들은 불행히도 거의 그 어떤 것도 지난 금요일에 발생한 폭풍 피해를 막지 못했을 것이라고 말했다.

해설 unfortunately로 보아 다음 문장은 안 좋은 일이 벌어졌음을 알 수 있으므로 (d)가 정답이다.

expert 전문가 prevent 막다 storm 폭풍

22 정답 (b)

그 사회복지사는 직장에서 온종일 전화를 받았기 때문에 집에 도착했을 무렵에 녹초가 되었다.

해설 전화를 받은 것은 집에 돌아온 것(과거)보다 앞선 일이므로 대과거(had p.p.)를 쓴 (b)가 정답이다.

social worker 사회복지사 exhausted 기진맥진한

23 정답 (b)

제프는 아내가 그의 교육 경력에 대해 조롱을 하자 그녀와 거리를 두기 시작했다.

해설 두 문장을 연결하기 위해서는 접속사가 필요한데 접속사가 없는 것으로 보아 빈칸에는 분사구문이 와야 함을 알 수 있다. 따라서 주어인 Jeff가 조롱당한 것이므로 수동의 의미를 지닌 과거분사를 맨 앞에 둔 (b)가 정답이다. 원래는 Being mocked by his wife about ~이지만 과거분사 앞의 being은 생략 가능하므로 mocked만 남은 것이다.

aloof from ~와 거리를 두는 mock 놀리다

24 정답 (d)

격분한 소수 집단은 미래에 개선될 거라는 약속을 받을지라도 진정되지 않을 것이다.

해설 조동사가 있는 문장의 부정문은 〈주어+조동사+not+동사원형〉의 어순이며, 주어(minority groups)가 진정되는(be appeased) 것이므로 수동태를 쓴 (d)가 정답이다.

outraged 격분한 minority group 소수 집단[민족] improvement 개선 appease 달래다

25 정답 (d)

서식 가능한 미소 서식처의 수의 변화는 그에 상응하는 물고기 개체 수 규모에서의 변화를 낳을 것이다.

해설 서식처의 수에 변화가 있으면 서식처마다 물고기 개체 수의 규모도 달라질 것이므로 복수형을 사용한 (d)가 정답이다.

microhabitat 미소 서식처(미생물·곤충 등의 서식에 적합한 곳) result in ~을 낳다[야기하다] corresponding 상응하는

Part III

26 정답 (d) should → must

(a) A 동창회에 갈 거니?
(b) B 무슨 동창회? 금시초문인데.
(c) A 이상하군. 난 한 달 전에 통보받았는데.
(d) B 틀림없이 내게 통보하는 걸 잊어버렸을 거야.

해설 과거의 강한 추측은 must have p.p.(~했음이 틀림없다)로 표현하므로 (d)의 should를 must로 고쳐야 한다.

school reunion 동창회 notify 알리다, 통지하다(inform)

27 정답 (c) had been boiled → was boiling/had boiled

(a) A 이런. 수프 베이스를 다시 만들어야겠어.
(b) B 뭐가 잘못됐어?
(c) A 고추를 너무 많이 넣고 끓였다는 걸 방금 깨달았어.
(d) B 오, 그럼 수프를 새로 만들어야 할 것 같은데.

해설 (c)에서 목적어 it이 있으므로 boil(~을 끓이다)은 수동이 아니라 능동 형태가 되어야 한다. 따라서 had been boiled를 was boiling 또는 had boiled로 고쳐야 한다.

boil 끓이다 chili 고추, 칠리 afresh 새로

28 정답 (a) was tumbled → tumbled

(a) 직업을 갖고 있거나 구하고 있는 사람들의 수가 3월에 49만 8천 명 정도 크게 감소했다. (b) 이 때문에 노동 인구 비율이 노동 가능 인구의 63.3퍼센트로 하락했다. (c) 노동 인구의 이러한 감소에서 55세 이상은 12만 명이다. (d) 또한, 현역 노동 인구로 간주되는 65세 이상 사람의 수는 2월에 7만 2천 명 상승한 데 이어 실제로 2만 7천 명 증가했다.

해설 (a)의 tumble은 '폭락하다, 크게 추락하다'란 뜻의 자동사로 쓰이므로 was tumbled를 tumbled로 고쳐야 한다.

tumble 크게 추락하다 labor force 노동 인구 regarded as ~로 여겨지는

29 정답 (c) a little more expensive something → something a little more expensive

(a) 인간의 심리는 가격과 수요 간의 관계에서 중대한 역할을 한다. (b) 소비자들은 일반적으로 가장 값싼 제품은 품질이 나쁘다는 생각을 아무 의심 없이 받아들인다. (c) 예를 들어, 소비자는 가장 저렴한 와인을 사기 보다는 좀 더 비싼 것을 고름으로써 자신이 좀 더 품질이 좋은 와인을 사고 있다고 생각할 것이다. (d) 하지만 소비자가 모든 구입 결정을 가격에만 기준을 둔다면 비양심적인 판매자로부터 바가지를 쉽게 당할 수 있다.

해설 형용사는 명사 앞에 오는 것이 원칙이지만 something, anything, nothing 등과 같이 −thing으로 끝나는 대명사를 수식할 때는 그 뒤에 위치한다. 따라서 (c)의 a little more expensive something은 something a little more expensive로 고쳐야 한다.

psychology 심리 play a big part in ~에서 중요한 역할을 하다 unquestioned 아무 의심 없이 받아들여지는 of poor quality 질이 안 좋은 base A on B A의 기초를 B에 두다 purchase 구입 dupe 속이다 unscrupulous 비양심적인 overpriced 값이 너무 비싸게 매겨진

30 정답 (d) were associated → was associated

(a) 한 가정환경이 가지고 있는 가치관의 종류가 행복에 대한 전반적인 생각에 얼마나 영향을 미치는지에 대한 연구가 실시되었다. (b) 엄마와 사춘기 자녀가 세 가지 본질적인 가치와 세 가지 외적인 가치에 대해 어떻게 생각하는지가 조사되었다. (c) 그 결과 대체적으로 엄마는 자녀들보다 외적인 것보다 본질적인 가치를 더 강조한 것으로 드러났다. (d) 재미있는 것은 사춘기 자녀와 엄마의 행복 둘 다 그들이 외적인 가치보다 본질적인 가치를 우선시킨 정도에 따라 달라졌다는 점이다.

해설 (d)의 주어는 단수인 the happiness index이므로 동사는 were가 아니라 was가 되어야 한다.

degree 정도 environment 환경 well-being 행복 adolescent 청소년 survey 조사하다 intrinsic 본질적인, 내재한 extrinsic 외적인, 외부의 index 지수, 지표 be associated with ~와 관련되다 prioritize 우선순위를 매기다

Reading Comprehension p.105

Part I

1

워커 씨에게,

윌리엄스 에이전시의 일자리에 대해서 귀하와 정말 즐겁게 이야기를 나누었습니다. 그 자리는 바로 제가 찾던 것이었습니다. 귀하가 보여 주셨던 고객 관리에 대한 조직적 접근법은 제가 귀사에서 일하고 싶은 욕망을 확인시켜주었습니다. 제가 만약 그 자리에 가게 된다면 부서원들과의 협력은 물론 탁월한 글솜씨를 발휘하고 일에 대한 열정을 보여주는 등, 팀에서 없어서는 안 될 일원이 되기 위해 최선을 다할 것입니다. 이 자리에 대해서 귀하로부터 소식 듣기를 고대하겠습니다.

테렌스 존스

(a) 업무 회의를 위해 귀사를 방문하기를
(b) 비어 있는 자리에 대해서 곧 귀하와 이야기를 나누기를
(c) 다른 일원들에게 귀하를 소개하기를
(d) 이 자리에 대해서 귀하로부터 소식을 듣기를

해설 면접을 보았던 지원자가 담당자에게 면접 소감과 취직이 될 경우의 각오를 전하는 편지이다. 이런 편지의 마지막에는 대개 회사의 연락(입사 통보)을 기다리겠다는 말을 붙이므로 (d)가 적절하다.

structured 구조가 있는, 조직적인 approach 접근법 account management 고객 관리 illustrate (실례·도해 등으로) 설명하다 confirm 확인해주다 do one's very best 최선[전력]을 다하다 essential 없어서는 안 될 writing skill 문장력 enthusiasm 열정 cooperative 협력하는 department 부서 vacancy 공석 hear from ~로부터 연락을 받다

2

건강한 아침 식사를 먹는 것이 체중 감량에 도움이 되는 중요 인자로 밝혀져 왔다. 5년여에 걸쳐 15킬로를 감량한 이들은 그들이 먹은 아침 식사 종류 덕분에 그렇게 할 수 있었다. 그들은 당분이 많은 시리얼이나 패스트리보다는 달걀과 견과류 같은 단백질이 풍부한 식품을 먹었는데, 당분이 많은 시리얼이나 패스트리는 혈당 농도를 올렸다가 떨어뜨릴 수 있다. 과일 또한 도움이 되는데, 왜냐하면 그 안의 섬유질이 당분의 흡수를 늦추기 때문이다. 이런 건강식을 하루를 시작하면서 먹는 것은 신진대사량을 늘리고 칼로리를 연소한다.

(a) 당분이 많은 간식을 피하는 것이
(b) 매일 일찍 일어나는 것이
(c) 건강한 아침 식사를 먹는 것이
(d) 탄수화물보다 단백질을 좋아하는 것이

해설 체중 감량에 도움이 되는 중요 요소에 관한 글로, 아침 식사로 단백질이 풍부한 음식과 과일을 먹는 것이 도움이 된다고 한다. 따라서 빈칸에는 (c)가 적절하다. (d)는 체중 감량의 요소 중 일부만을 언급하고 있다.

component 요소 lose weight 체중 감량하다 protein-rich 단백질 함량이 높은 spike 급등시키다 dip 내려가게 하다 blood sugar level 혈당 수치 fiber 섬유질 content 내용물 absorption 흡수 wholesome 건강에 좋은 metabolism 신진대사 carbohydrate 탄수화물

3

영화 리뷰

베스트셀러 소설을 원작으로 한 이 영화는 인도네시아에 사는 한 소년을 중심으로 벌어지는 신비한 모험 이야기이다. 군데군데 멋진 특수효과를 보여줌으로써 3D로 놀라운 시각적 경험을 할 수 있고, 이 때문에 확실히 극장을 찾아갈 만하다. 나의 유일한 불만은 실질 내용이 부족하다는 점이다. 이 영화는 주로 효과를 쫓아가고 있다. 따라서 영화는 놀라운 모험물이지만 정서적으로는 실패작이다. 그래도, 추천할 수 있을 만큼 좋은 영화이다.

(a) 어린아이들이 보기에 좋지 않다
(b) 가족 모두에게 감동적인 이야기이다
(c) 감정의 기복이 심하다
(d) 추천할 수 있을 만큼 좋은 영화이다

해설 특수 효과가 두드러지는 한 모험 영화에 대한 글이다. 실질적인 내용은 부족하지만 시각적인 즐거움을 경험할 수 있어서 극장에 가서 볼 만하다(which makes it definitely worth a trip to the cinema)는 입장이므로 빈칸에는 (d)가 적절하다.

novel 소설 magical 신비한 adventure 모험 center on ~에 집중하다 awesome 경탄할만한 special effect 특수효과 extraordinary 기이한, 놀라운 visual 시각의 3D 삼차원, 입체 definitely 확실히 complaint 불만 lack 부족하다 substance 실질 내용 largely 주로 fizzle 흐지부지되다, 실패하다 emotional 정서적인 touching 감동적인 rollercoaster 기복이 심한

4

학습을 위해 전문화된 환경으로서 <u>언어 교실은 몇 가지 단점을 가지고 있</u><u>다</u>. 첫째, 그것은 실제 세계를 대신하지 못한다. 문화 간 의사소통과 경험적인 문화 학습은 책상과 종이 위에서만 모의 실험된다. 둘째, 교과 과정이 대체로 연역적인 추론과 규율에 의해 통제되는 교수법을 권장하도록 설계되어 있다. 마지막으로, 그것의 규격화된 성격은 '자연적인 주입'을 거의 제공하지 못하며, 언어 체득이 아닌 전통적 언어 학습에 전념한다.

(a) 현실적 적용이 교사들에 의해 지도되어야 한다
(b) 학교는 상대적으로 안전한 연습 장소를 제공한다
(c) 언어 교사는 또래 학습을 조장해야 한다
(d) 언어 교실은 몇 가지 단점을 가지고 있다

해설 언어 습득이 아닌 언어 학습에 전념하는 언어 교실(language classroom)이 갖고 있는 단점 세 가지를 열거하고 있으므로 첫 문장에 나올 수 있는 말로 (d)가 적절하다.

specialized 전문화된 **context** 맥락, 배경 **substitute** 대신하는 것 **intercultural** (이종) 문화 간의 **experiential** 경험에 의한, 경험적인 **simulate** 모의 실험하다 **curriculum** 교육과정 **be designed to** ~하도록 설계되다 **encourage** 조장하다 **deductive** 연역적인 **pedagogy** 교육(학) **institutional** 규격화된, 기관의 **be dedicated to** ~에 전념하다 **acquisition** 습득 **application** 적용 **relatively** 상대적으로 **peer** 동료 **demerit** 단점

5

존 덱스터의 신간 소설은 사람들이 스스로 운명을 선택하는지 아니면 운명이 그전부터 결정되어 있는지에 대한 생각을 탐색한다. 본질적으로 그 소설은 자유 의지 대 운명 예정설을 다루고 있다. 이들 두 대조적인 철학은 전쟁과 관련해서, 그리고 남녀들이 전쟁 상황에서 내리는 결정에 기초를 두고 고찰된다. 그들이 통제할 수 있고 없는 것 사이에는 부단한 갈등이 존재한다. 따라서 이 소설은 <u>서로 상반되는 자유 의지와 운명이라는 개</u><u>념</u>에 관심 있는 사람들에게 가장 매력적으로 다가올 것이다.

(a) 전쟁 소설과 대하 역사 소설류
(b) 전시에 하게 되는 올바른 선택의 중요성
(c) 우리가 취하는 모든 행동의 철학적 의미
(d) 서로 상반되는 자유 의지와 운명이라는 개념

해설 자유 의지 대 운명 예정설(the freedom of one's will versus pre-destination)을 다루고 있는 신간 소설을 소개하는 글로, 소설에 끌리는 사람들은 소설의 소재에 관심이 있는 독자들일 것이므로 (d)가 적절하다.

explore 탐구하다 **make a choice** 선택하다 **destiny** 운명 **essentially** 본질적으로 **versus** ~대 **pre-destination** 운명 예정설 **contrasting** 대조적인 **examine** 고찰하다 **in relation to** ~에 관련해서 **in terms of** ~의 측면에서, ~에 기초를 두고 **be caught up in** ~에 휘말리다 **constant** 부단한 **tension** 갈등 **wartime** 전시 **novelization** 소설화 **implication** 영향, 함축, 암시 **notion** 개념 **freewill** 자유 의지 **fatalism** 운명

6

리스 극장에서 공연된 크리스 콕스의 새로운 역사물은 <u>등장인물의 사실</u><u>적인 재현을 통해 도덕적 드라마를 만듦</u>으로써 역사에 생동감을 불어넣는다. 평범한 남자로서 사무엘은 생존에 대한 염려 때문에 이기적이고 표리부동한 인물이 된다. 하지만 자리에 대한 욕심에 윤리적인 면은 거의 거들떠보지도 않고 제멋대로 하는 정치인 리처드만큼 죄가 있는 것은 아니다. 리처드의 부패한 정치적 거래는 모르간의 이상주의와 함께 위기에 빠진다. 하지만 모르간이 그의 가치관을 끝까지 유지하는 반면 겁쟁이 나단은 협박에 굴복한다. 20세기 초반의 대호황 시대가 극의 시간적인 배경이지만, 극에서 제기되는 윤리적인 갈등과 쟁점들은 세월과 상관없이 오늘날의 우리에게도 공명을 준다.

(a) 누구나 최악의 악행을 저지를 수 있다는 점을 보여 줌
(b) 대호황 시대에 만연한 부정부패에 대해 자세히 말함
(c) 등장인물의 사실적인 재현을 통해 도덕적 드라마를 만듦
(d) 현대의 사건을 암시하는 정치적 스릴러를 무대에 올림

해설 연극을 비평하는 글로, 대호황 시대를 배경으로 다양한 성격의 등장인물들 간의 윤리적 갈등에 대해 이야기하고 있다. 이 작품의 내용과 성격을 표현한 것으로 (c)가 가장 적절하다.

production 작품 **enliven** 생동감 있게 만들다 **everyman** 전형적인 사람, 보통 사람 **concern** 걱정 **selfish** 이기적인 **duplicitous** 표리부동의 **culpable** 과실이 있는, 비난할 만한 **pampered** 방자한, 제멋대로 하는 **craving for** ~을 갈망하는 **tolerate** 용인하다, 참다 **virtue** 도덕, 윤리 **come to a head** 위기에 빠지다, 정점에 이르다 **cowardly** 비겁한, 겁이 많은 **cave into** ~에 굴복하다 **time frame** 시간, 기간 **ethical** 윤리적인 **resonant** 공명하는 **heinous** 악랄한 **detail** 자세히 말하다 **rife** 만연한 **stage** 무대에 올리다 **allusion** 암시 **contemporary** 현대의

7

유럽은 <u>줄어드는 노동 인구로 늘어나는 연금수령자를 부양하는</u> 중대한 문제에 직면해 있다. 일부 국가의 인구는 정체 상태이거나 이미 감소하고 있는데, 이는 미래의 노동력을 감소시킬 것이며 지속적인 경제 성장을 막을 것이다. 어느 곳에서나 근로자의 나이가 많아지고 있으며 이들을 대신할 노동력이 충분하지 않은 상태에서 은퇴를 앞두고 있다. 게다가 은퇴하는 인구가 늘어감에 따라 의료 혜택과 연금을 지불해야 하는 부담이 커지고 있다. 유럽의 국가들은 평균적으로 연금수령자 한 명당 노동자의 비율이 1:4이다. 이 비율이 2050년까지 1:2로 떨어질 것이다.

(a) 출산율 저하를 만회하기 위해 이민자를 필요로 하는
(b) 늦어지는 은퇴와 결부된 높은 실업률의
(c) 줄어드는 노동 인구로 늘어나는 연금수령자를 부양하는
(d) 노동 시장에서 근로자를 대체하는 자동화의

해설 인구 감소로 인한 노동력 감소, 그로 인한 경제적 여파에 관한 글이다. 은퇴 인구가 늘어나면서 이들을 부양해야 하는 노동자의 비율이 낮아질 것이라는 문제를 요약한 것은 (c)이다. 이민 노동자나 실업률, 인력을 대체하는 자동화 시스템에 대한 언급은 없다.

grave 중대한 **stagnant** 정체된 **dwindle** 줄어들다 **hinder** 방해하다 **head for** ~로 치닫다 **furthermore** 게다가 **retiree** 은퇴자 **burden** 부담, 짐 **pension** 연금 **on average** 평균적으로 **pensioner** 연금 수급자 **ratio** 비율 **supplement** 보충하다 **fertility rate** 출산율 **support** 부양하다 **automation** 자동화

8

모든 사람이 외국어를 같은 방법으로 배우는 것은 아니다. 어떤 사람의 성격, 동기 부여, 학습 방식이 다른 결과를 낳을 수 있다. 내성적인 사람은 터놓고 이야기하는 언어 학습 환경에서는 거리낌 없이 말하기를 주저하는 경향이 있다. 반면 외향적인 사람은 연습할 수 있는 좋은 기회를 최대한 활용할 것이다. 전체론적인 학습자는 세부 사항에 주의하지 않는 반면, 분석적인 학습자는 세부 사항에 많은 집중을 한다. 일부는 특정 활동에 의해 고무 받는 반면, 어떤 사람들은 그렇지 않을 수 있다. 가장 도움이 되는 학습 환경과 효율적인 학습 전략을 제공하기 위해서, 교사들이 <u>개개인의 이러한 차이점들을 이상적으로 맞추려 하는 것은</u> 당연하다.

(a) 그들 스스로의 가르치는 방식을 분석하여 득을 보는 것은
(b) 개개인의 이러한 차이점들을 이상적으로 맞추려 하는 것은
(c) 게으른 언어 학습자들에 협조하는 것을 피해야 하는 것은
(d) 모든 수업마다 주의 깊게 짠 수업 계획이 필요한 것은

해설 외국어 학습은 사람의 성격과, 동기 부여, 학습 방식에 따라 방법과 결과가 다를 수 있다는 내용으로, 학습 효과를 높이기 위해 교사가 하는 역할을 나타낸 것은 (b)이다.

personality 성격   **motivation** 동기 부여   **introvert** 내성적인 사람   **reluctant** 주저하는   **speak up** 거리낌 없이 말하다   **communicative** 터놓고 이야기하는   **extrovert** 외향적인 사람   **make most use of** ~을 최대한 활용하다   **ample opportunity** 충분한[좋은] 기회   **holistic** 전체론의   **heed** 주의하다   **analytical** 분석적인   **inspire** 고무하다   **stand to reason** 당연하다. 합리적이다   **conducive** 도움이 되는   **analyze** 분석하다   **cater to** ~의 구미에 맞추다. 충족시키다   **accommodate** 부응하다. 협조하다

9

체중을 감량하는 신뢰할 만한 방법은 단 한 가지, 더 적게 먹고 더 많이 운동하는 것이다. 하지만 많은 사람들은 유행 다이어트나 속성 다이어트를 지지하여 이런 유효성이 증명된 방법을 거부하는데, 이런 다이어트들은 너무 지독하거나 힘들고 엄격해서 어느 기간을 두고 따르기 어렵기 때문에 효과가 없다. 비록 이런 다이어트들이 처음에는 성공하는 것처럼 보일지는 몰라도 감량은 대부분 일시적일 뿐이다. 종종 서로 다른 다이어트를 잇달아 시도하기도 하는데, 이는 매번 이전의 것보다 더 어려운 시도로 살이 빠졌다가 다시 찌는 패턴을 반복하는 것으로 끝난다. 이러한 체중 오르내림은 또한 심장 질환의 위험성을 증가시킬 수 있다.

(a) 이런 이유로
(b) ~하기 때문에
(c) ~일 경우를 대비해서
(d) 비록 ~이지만

해설 사람들이 살을 빼기 위해 이미 증명된 다이어트 방법을 거부하고 유행 다이어트나 속성 다이어트를 하는 것은 효과가 일시적일 뿐만 아니라 건강상의 문제를 초래할 수 있다고 경고하고 있다. 빈칸이 있는 문장은 종속절과 주절이 상반되는 내용이므로 빈칸에는 역접을 나타내는 종속 접속사인 (d)가 적절하다.

reliable 신뢰할 만한   **reject** 거부하다   **tried-and-true** 유효성이 증명된   **in favor of** ~을 지지하여   **fad diet** 유행 다이어트(반짝 유행하는 다이어트)   **crash diet** 속성 다이어트   **work** 효과가 있다   **temporary** 일시적인   **a succession of** 일련의   **attempt** 시도하다   **regain weight** 살이 다시 찌다   **fluctuation** 변동, 오르내림

10

경기 후퇴는 경제가 전반적으로 여러 분기에 걸쳐 위축되는 기간이다. 이 기간은 투자하는 돈이 줄어들고, 실업률이 높아지며 개개인의 소득과 기업의 이윤이 줄어드는 등의 거시 경제 지표 등에 의해 종종 드러난다. <u>하지만</u> 이 시기는 정부가 성장 위주의 지출 정책을 시행하고 통화 정책을 미세하게 조정할 수 있는 최적의 시기이기도 하다. 그러므로 경기 불황이 기업과 근로자들을 옥죌 때, 정부의 지원 형태로 이러한 어려움을 만회할 대책들과 세금을 줄여달라는 요구가 있다.

(a) 게다가
(b) 마찬가지로
(c) 하지만
(d) 게다가

해설 경기 후퇴의 의미와 장단점에 대한 글이다. 빈칸을 기준으로 앞에서는 경기 후퇴의 부정적인 면을, 뒤에서는 긍정적인 면을 언급하고 있으므로 빈칸에는 역접을 나타내는 (c)가 적절하다.

recession 경기 후퇴   **contract** 위축하다   **quarter** 4분기   **be marked by** ~이 특징이다   **macroeconomic** 거시 경제의   **indicator** 지표   **investment** 투자   **unemployment** 실업   **implement** 시행하다   **expansionary** 확장성의   **fine-tune** 미세 조정을 하다   **monetary** 통화[화폐]의   **compensatory** 보상의, 벌충하는   **measure** 조치, 정책

Part II

11

노샘프턴셔의 수제화 전통은 그곳의 피혁 신발류 제작에 사용되는 원재료로서의 참나무 숲과 가죽과 함께 수 세기 전에 시작되었다. (a) 이 지역은 제2차 세계대전 이후에 영국 근대 제화 산업의 중심지 역할을 계속하였다. (b) 그러고 나서 더 저렴한 해외 제품들이 들어왔고 다수의 지역 공장들이 개인 주택으로 개조되었다. (c) 자국 내의 수요는 가라앉은 채로 변화가 없지만, 숙련된 솜씨의 유산은 전 세계적으로 불고 있는 명품 유행의 흐름을 한참 타고 있는 중이다. <u>(d) 전설 속의 인물 로빈 후드와 영화 속 인물 제임스 본드를 고객으로 하고 있다는 점에서 그 명성이 강화되었다.</u>

해설 영국의 한 지역의 전통 있는 수제화 산업에 관한 글이다. 시대의 변화에 따라 수제화 전통의 시작과 영국 근대 제화 산업의 중심지가 되었던 것, 이후 저렴한 제품들로 인해 내수는 가라앉았지만 현재 세계적으로는 명품으로 인정받고 있다는 흐름이다. (d)는 맥락에서 벗어나 있다.

raw material 원료, 자재   **leather** 가죽, 피혁   **handcrafted** 수제의   **heritage** 유산, 전통문화   **craftsmanship** 손재주, 솜씨, 기능   **bolster** 지지하다, 보강하다   **legendary** 전설의

12

중매결혼에 대한 통계에 의하면 중매결혼이 연애결혼보다 더 어려움을 잘 견딘다고 한다. (a) 미국에서는 연애결혼이 절반 가까이 이혼으로 끝나는데, 중매결혼의 경우 4%만이 결별한다. (b) 이러한 차이의 이유는 처음에 중매결혼이 구성된 방식에 있는 것 같다. <u>(c) 예를 들어, 타협이라는 중요한 관습을 유지하는 것은 분명히 화목한 관계의 일부이다.</u> (d) 중매결혼에서는 부모가 맞선을 주선하기 때문에 가치관이나 교육, 재정적인 상태 등이 서로 맞는 집안의 상대방이 아마도 미리 선별될 것이다.

해설 중매결혼이 연애결혼보다 어려움을 더 잘 견딘다고 하며, (a)는 이혼 통계를 들고 있고, (b)와 (d)는 그러한 이유를 미리 선별된 만남이라는 데에서 찾고 있다. 하지만 (c)는 결혼의 유형에 관계없이 화목한 관계를 위해서는 타협이 중요하다는 것으로 흐름에 어긋난다.

statistics 통계   arranged marriage 중매결혼   resilient 회복력 있는, 탄력 있는   love marriage 연애결혼   result in 결과적으로 ~이 되다   get separated 헤어지다   harmonious 조화로운 practice 관습   compromise 타협   presumably 짐작건대, 아마도

Part III

13

일부 사람들은 직장에서 울어도 괜찮다고 주장하는데, 예민한 이들 사이에서 감정이 고조될 수 있는 창조적인 영역에서 특히 더 그러하다고 한다. 하지만 그런 가끔 있는 정신적 붕괴가 용납될 수 있다는 의견에 모든 사람이 찬성하는 것은 아니다. 어떤 사람이 직장에서 흐느끼기 시작하면 전 사무실을 마비시킬 수 있다. 이것에 신경 쓰지 않기란 힘든 일이다. 뿐만 아니라, 직장에서 우는 것은 흠으로 여겨져 왔고 특히 남성들에게 더 그러하였다. 연구자들이 알아낸 바에 의하면, 여성은 41퍼센트가 직장에서 울었던 반면 남성은 약 9퍼센트만 그렇게 했다.

Q 지문의 주된 내용은?
(a) 여성은 정서적으로 울어야 할 필요성이 있음을 설명하기
(b) 직장에서 우는 문제에 대한 서로 다른 의견
(c) 직장에서 우는 사람이 미치는 영향
(d) 창조적인 영역에 종사하는 이들의 감정적 과잉 반응

해설 직장에서 우는 것에 대한 찬성 의견과 반대 의견을 말하고 있으므로 (b)가 정답이다. (c)에 대한 언급도 있지만 이것이 글의 주된 내용은 아니다.

occasional 가끔의   meltdown 정신적 붕괴   acceptable 용인되는 sob 흐느끼다   bring to a stop ~을 정지시키다   notice 주목하다 in contrast to ~와 반대로   necessity 필요성   differing 다른 workplace 직장   overreacting 과잉 반응

14

스미스 이사님께,

수년 전에 떠난 제 자리로 다시 복귀해달라는 제안에 정말로 많이 기뻤다는 것을 인정합니다. 저는 제가 그곳, 콜드웰에서 일할 때 직원들과 있었던 좋은 일만 기억이 납니다. 그리고 이사님의 제안을 얼마간 생각해 보았고, 그리고 그 문제를 제 아내와도 상의해 보았습니다만, 지금은 제안을 수락할 수 없는 걸로 결정했습니다. 시간이 많이 흘렀고, 건강을 고려해 볼 때에 예전에 제 전성기의 수준으로 업무를 더는 돌볼 수 없습니다. 이 편지를 귀하의 친절함에 대한 감사의 표시로 받아주시고, 그 업무를 잘 수행할 수 있는 훌륭한 누군가를 찾기를 진심으로 기원합니다.

귀하에게 평안과 안녕이 있기를 기원합니다.

크리스 잰스

Q 편지를 쓴 사람의 요지는?
(a) 예전의 업무로 복귀하기에는 아직 너무 아프다.
(b) 이전 직장으로 돌아가지 않기로 했다.
(c) 직장 복귀 요청을 받아서 영광이다.
(d) 회사에서 승진하기를 원한다.

해설 이전 직장에서 복귀 요청을 받았지만 고민 끝에 거절하는 뜻을 전하는 편지이므로 (b)가 적절하다.

flattered 기쁜, 으쓱한, 영광인   post 지위, 직   nothing but 그저 ~일 뿐인   consideration 고려   appreciation 감사   previous 예전의

15

선크림 사용은 암을 유발하는 인자로 알려진 자외선의 해로운 영향을 막는다. 연구에 의하면 선크림 사용은 비타민 D 결핍을 일으키지 않으며 태양 노출로 인한 편평상피암과 조기 노화를 방지해 준다고 한다. 그럼에도 선크림에 사용되는 옥시벤존 화합물의 해로움에 대한 우려가 존재한다. 몇몇 연구에 의하면 이 성분이 높은 것이 저체중 출산과 관련이 있다. 산화아연과 이산화티탄의 나노 입자 또한 피부에 쉽게 흡수되고 유리기 형성을 일으킬 수 있는 것으로 보인다.

Q 지문의 주제는?
(a) 선크림 제제의 무해함 입증
(b) 암을 유발하는 자외선 노출의 위험성
(c) 선크림이 피부암 방지에 미치는 영향
(d) 선크림의 안전성에 관한 연구 결과

해설 선크림 사용에 관한 여러 가지 연구 결과들에 대해 이야기하고 있다. 비타민 D 결핍을 일으키지 않고, 피부 질환 등으로부터 보호해 주지만, 다른 연구에 의하면 저체중 출산과 관련된 해로운 성분도 있다는 내용이므로 이를 포괄하는 주제로 (d)가 적절하다.

sunscreen 선크림, 자외선 차단제   radiation 방사선   agent (특정 효과를 일으키는) 물질, 요인   deficiency 결핍   carcinoma 상피성 암 premature 조숙한   exposure 노출   chemical 화합물   absorb 흡수하다   free radical formation 유리기 형성

16

십 대들의 문자 보내는 행동에 대한 연구에 의하면 보통의 십 대들이 잠자리에 들어서까지도 약 35통의 문자를 보낸다고 한다. 십 대들은 모든 태그와 업데이트, 멘트, 문자에 답해야 한다는 의무감을 느낀다. 다른 이들과 문자 메시지를 통해 연락하려는 이러한 충동은 이들의 마음을 온통 다 빼앗으며, 시공간에 있는 개인 간의 경계선의 규범을 벗어나고 있다. 문자 보내기는 통제가 안 되는 중독으로 이들의 정신적, 육체적 건강에 나쁜 영향을 줄 수 있다. 밤늦은 시간에 문자를 보내는 것은 수면 부족 및 감염 위험의 증가, 체중 증가, 불안, 우울증 등과 같은 수면 관련 건강 문제에 영향을 미치는 것으로 보인다.

Q 지문의 주된 내용은?
(a) 십 대의 문자 보내기가 소중한 공부 시간을 방해하는 이유
(b) 문자 보내기의 습관이 중독이 되는 것을 방지하기
(c) 십 대들이 밤늦게 문자 보내기에 소모하는 시간
(d) 십 대들의 심야 시간 문자 보내기와 그 영향

해설 십 대들이 심야 시간에 문자를 보내는 행위는 심각한 중독 현상으로, 그들의 정신과 육체 건강에 악영향을 미친다는 내용이므로 (d)가 정답이다. 문제를 제기할 뿐 어떤 해결책을 제시하고 있는 것은 아니므로 (b)는 옳지 않다.

texting 문자 보내기   average 평균의, 보통의   feel obliged 의무감을 느끼다   urge 열망, 충동   all-consuming 온통 마음을 다 빼앗는   via ~을 통하여   transcend 넘어서다   norm 표준, 규범   boundary 경계 addiction 중독   contribute 기여하다   deprivation 부족   anxiety 불안   depression 우울증

17

알츠하이머병의 조기 진단은 이제 자기공명영상(MRI) 기술을 사용함으로써 가능한데, 이 기술은 사람이 이 질병과 관련이 있는 뇌의 구성 성분 글루타싸이온(GSH)을 추적할 수 있다. 85명을 실험한 결과, 전체 평균 GSH 함유량이 남성보다는 건강한 젊은 여성에서 더 높은 것으로 밝혀졌다. 알츠하이머병의 진행을 저지하는 데 도움을 주는 치료도 가능해졌는데, 어떠한 약물이든지 GSH 수치를 관찰함으로써 그것의 유효성을 확인할 수 있기 때문이다. 이 신기술은 심신을 쇠약하게 만드는 이 질병이 광범위한 뇌 손상 단계에 도달하는 것을 방지하는 것을 도울 수 있다.

Q 지문 내용과 일치하는 것은?
(a) GSH 추적 기술은 알츠하이머병에서의 회복을 돕는다.
(b) 건강한 남성에게서 더 많은 GSH 함유량이 발견되었다.
(c) 치료법의 효과는 GSH 추적으로 측정될 수 있다.
(d) 알츠하이머병 환자의 GSH는 일부만 관찰될 수 있다.

해설 알츠하이머병의 조기 진단이 MRI 기술 덕분에 가능해졌다는 내용으로, 어떠한 약물이든지 GSH 수치를 관찰함으로써 그것의 유효성을 확인할 수 있다(the efficacy of any medication can be checked by monitoring GSH level)고 했으므로 (c)가 일치한다. 이 기술로 알츠하이머병의 진행을 저지할 수는 있어도(helps deter the progression of Alzheimer's), 병을 낫게 해준다는 언급은 없으므로 (a)는 오답이다.

diagnosis 진단 **Alzheimer's disease** 알츠하이머병 **Magnetic Resonance Imaging** 자기공명영상 **track** 추적하다 **component** 성분, 요소 **subject** 실험 대상 **overall mean** 전체 평균 **content** 함유량 **treatment** 치료 **deter** 저지하다 **progression** 진행 **efficacy** 유효성 **medication** 약물 **debilitating** 심신을 쇠약하게 만드는 **widespread** 광범위한 **impairment** 손상 **detect** 발견하다 **effectiveness** 유효

18

최근에 발견되어 리처드 3세(1452-1485)의 유해로 확인된 해골은 청소년기 발병 특발성 척추측만증 징후를 보인다. 1400년대에 이 질병은 소위 체액의 불균형이 원인인 것으로 여겨졌다. 당시의 치료법에는 연고, 마사지가 있었고 아마도 목재나 금속으로 된 척추 견인기 또는 교정기도 포함되었을 것이다. 만약 그가 이 질병을 앓았다면 이것이 그의 폐활량을 제한했을 것이다. 그가 치료를 받았을 것으로 추측되지만 그러한 치료의 어떤 조짐도 뼈에서 발견되지 않았다.

Q 리처드 3세에 대해 지문 내용과 일치하는 것은?
(a) 그의 병은 어려서부터 발병한 것으로 여겨진다.
(b) 그의 치료 방법은 연고로 제한되었다.
(c) 그는 아마도 호흡 제한을 겪었을 것이다.
(d) 질병에 대해 등 부목을 댔다.

해설 리처드 3세의 유골에서 척추측만증 흔적이 발견됐는데, 그가 이 질병을 앓았다면 폐활량이 제한되었을 것(it would have restricted his lung capacity)이라는 점에서 (c)가 일치하는 내용임을 알 수 있다. 그의 병은 청소년기에 발병했고, 당시의 치료 방법들의 흔적이 발견되지 않았다고 하므로 나머지는 오답이다.

skeleton 해골 **ascertain** 확인하다 **remains** 유해, 유골 **idiopathic** 특발성의 **adolescent-onset** 청소년기 발병 **scoliosis** 척추측만증 **imbalance** 불균형 **humor** (중세 생리학에서의) 체액 **treatment** 치료 **ointment** 연고 **traction** 견인기 **back brace** 등 부목 **metal** 금속 **condition** 질병 **restrict** 제한하다 **lung capacity** 폐활량 **speculate** 추측하다 **back brace** 부목

19

절대로 조리용 지방이나 지방을 부엌 싱크대에 버려서는 안 되는데, 이것이 싱크대 배관을 막기 때문이다. 끓는 물을 붓는다거나 음식 찌꺼기 처리기를 사용해 지방 찌꺼기를 잘게 부수어도 소용없을 것이다. 사실, 음식 찌꺼기 처리기 사용도 어찌 되었건 최소화되어야 할 것이다. 이렇게 하면 하수 배관이 막힐 가능성을 줄일 뿐만 아니라 유지 보수 비용 또한 줄일 것이다. 일부 지방 자치 단체는 새 거주지와 식당에서 음식 쓰레기 처리기의 사용을 금지하기까지 하고 있다. 심지어 이들은 집을 소유하고 있는 이가 변경되거나 집의 주요 구조를 변경할 때, 음식물 쓰레기 처리기를 제거할 것을 법으로 요구하기까지 한다.

Q 지문 내용과 일치하는 것은?
(a) 뜨거운 물은 지방질 음식 쓰레기를 분해하는 데 효과적이다.
(b) 음식물 분쇄기는 음식 찌꺼기를 없애는 데 실용적이다.
(c) 어떤 지역은 가정에 음식 찌꺼기 처리기 설치를 장려한다.
(d) 과거에 사용하던 쓰레기 처리기의 제거가 종종 강제화되기도 한다.

해설 일부 지역에서는 새 주거지와 식당에 음식 찌꺼기 처리기 설치를 금지하며, 리모델링을 할 때에도 법적으로 제거를 요구한다고 했으므로 (d)가 일치한다.

quantity 양 **grease** 기름 **clog** 막다, 막히다 **boiling water** 끓는 물 **mince** 갈아 부수다 **fatty** 지방의 **scraps** 먹다 남은 음식, 찌꺼기 **garbage disposal** 음식 찌꺼기 처리기(garbage disposal unit) **sewer** 하수관 **municipality** 지방 자치 단체 **district** 지역, 구역 **ban** 금하다 **removal** 제거 **ownership** 소유권 **get rid of** 제거하다 **leftover** 음식 쓰레기 **mandate** 명령하다, 지시하다

20

화산 폭발 안전 지침

화산 폭발로부터 당신을 보호할 수 있는 많은 것들이 있다. 용암과 이류, 날아다니는 돌, 파편 등을 피할 수 있도록 당국의 지시대로만 따라 대피하라. 하천 지역과 저지대를 피하라. 긴 팔 셔츠와 긴 바지로 갈아입어라. 콘택트렌즈는 피하고 고글이나 안경을 사용하라. 비상 마스크를 쓰거나 얼굴 위에 축축한 천을 대라. 실내에 있다면 창문과 문을 닫고 굴뚝을 막아라. 지붕 위를 과도하게 누를지도 모르는 화산재를 지붕에서 쓸어낼 필요가 있다는 점을 인식하라. 또한, 화산재는 엔진과 금속 부분에 손상을 입힐 수 있으므로 운전을 피하라.

Q 화산 폭발이 일어날 경우에 권고되는 것은?
(a) 물과 안전을 위해 하천 지역을 찾아라.
(b) 반드시 얼굴을 적절하게 보호하라.
(c) 화산재를 제거하기 위해 지붕 위에 오르는 것을 피하라.
(d) 폭발이 끝난 후에 운전하는 것은 괜찮다.

해설 화산 폭발 시의 대처 방법을 알리는 글이다. 비상 마스크를 쓰거나 얼굴 위에 축축한 천을 대라고(Wear an emergency mask or hold a damp cloth over your face.) 했으므로 (b)가 일치하는 내용이다. 하천 지역을 피하고, 지붕 위의 화산재를 쓸어낼 필요가 있으며, 운전을 피하라고 했으므로 나머지는 오답이다.

volcanic eruption 화산 폭발 **evacuate** 대피하다 **direct** 지시하다 **authority** 당국 **stay clear of** ~을 피하다 **lava** 용암 **mud flow** 이류 **debris** 잔해 **avoid** 피하다 **low-lying** 저지의 **emergency** 비상 **damp** 축축한 **air-borne** 하늘에 떠 있는 **ash** 화산재 **sweep away** 쓸어내다 **metal** 금속 **seek out** 찾아내다 **ensure** 반드시 ~하게 하다 **adequately** 적절하게 **clear away** 제거하다

21

자폐증을 가진 아이가 복부 세균과 싸우는 것을 도울 새로운 백신이 개발되고 있는데, 이는 또한 일부 자폐증 증상을 통제하는 데 도움이 될지도 모른다. 기본적으로 탄수화물로 되어 있는 이 백신은, 위장 장애의 한 원인인 것으로 알려져 있고 왠지는 모르겠지만, 종종 자폐증 아이들에서 더 많이 나타나는 장내 세균에 맞서 싸운다. 자폐증을 가진 아이의 90퍼센트 이상은 만성적인 위장 장애를 앓으며, 이들 90퍼센트 중 75퍼센트는 설사로 고통받는다. 불행히도, 백신의 임상 및 인체 실험은 10년 이상 걸릴지도 모른다.

Q 연구 내용과 일치하는 것은?
(a) 자폐증의 모든 증상이 새로운 백신에 의해 치유될 수 있다.
(b) 장내 세균이 자폐증 아이에서 더 자주 나타나는 이유는 불분명하다.
(c) 자폐증 아이의 약 75퍼센트는 설사로 고통받는다.
(d) 백신이 임상 및 인체 실험을 통과하는 데 10년이 걸렸다.

해설 장내 세균이 '왠지는 모르겠지만(somehow)' 자폐증 아이들에서 더 많이 나타난다고 했으므로 (b)가 일치하는 내용이다. 자폐증 아이 중 위장 장애를 앓는 아이가 90퍼센트 이상이며, 그중 75퍼센트가 설사로 고통을 받는다고 하므로 (c)는 맞지 않다.

autism 자폐증 regulate 통제하다 symptom 증상 carb 탄수화물 intestinal bacteria 장내 세균 gastrointestinal disorder 위장 장애 somehow 왜 그런지 모르겠지만 show up 나타나다 suffer from ~으로 고통받다 diarrhea 설사 clinical trial 임상 실험

22

미국인의 약 1퍼센트는 자기애성 인격 장애 특성을 가진 것으로 알려져 있다. 이들은 자신의 능력에 대해 과장된 시각을 갖고 있으며, 오만하고 도도하며 끊임없는 칭찬과 관심을 갈구한다. 또한, 모든 형태의 비난에 매우 민감한데, 그것을 주로 인신공격으로 여기기 때문이다. 불행히도, 이런 사람들은 대개 자신의 병을 인정하는 것을 꺼리기 때문에 치료하려고 하지 않는다. 만약 치료를 시작한다면 가족의 촉구에 의해서나 이 병의 통제 불가능한 증상을 치유하기 위해서이다.

Q 자기도취자에 대해 지문 내용과 일치하는 것은?
(a) 종종 기술 능력을 과장하곤 한다.
(b) 자신의 행동을 타인이 인정해 주는 것을 좋아한다.
(c) 타인에 대한 비판을 철회하는 것을 꺼린다.
(d) 치료가 필요한 가족이 있는 경우가 많다.

해설 자기애성 인격 장애자의 특성을 설명하는 글이다. 이들은 오만하고 도도하며 끊임없이 자신에 대한 칭찬과 관심을 갈구한다고 하므로 (b)가 일치한다.

possess 보유하다 characteristic 특성 narcissistic personality disorder 자기애성 인격 장애 exaggerated 과장된 arrogant 오만한 conceited 자만하는, 도도한 crave 갈망한다 constant 끊임없는 praise 칭찬 sensitive 민감한 reproach 비난 be regarded as ~로 간주되다 personal attack 인신공격 seek out 찾다 treatment 치료 unwilling 꺼리는 acknowledge 인정하다 therapy 치료 urging 촉구 out-of-control 통제불능의 symptom 증상 narcissist 자기도취자 heighten 고조되다, 고조시키다 validate 인정하다 retract 철회하다 criticism 비판

23

직장을 그만둔 지 1년이 지났다. 은퇴하기에는 다소 이른 나이라서 사람들이 다른 직장을 언제 구하기 시작할 거냐고 계속 묻는다. 그들은 내가 은퇴 이후의 시기에 돈을 어떻게 쓸 것인지를 걱정하는 듯하다. 나는 한 회사에서 20년 동안 일해 왔으며, 기업 세계의 부산함으로 다시 돌아가기가 망설여진다. 나는 남은 인생 동안 진실로 하고 싶은 일을 찾고 싶다. 그런 의미에서, 나는 내 관심사와 선택 사항들을 탐색하고, 친구와 가족들과 이러한 점들에 대해 상의해 볼 계획이며, 그러고 나서 앞으로 갈 길을 결정할 것이다.

Q 필자에 대해 추론할 수 있는 것은?
(a) 자신의 능력에 대한 자신감이 없다.
(b) 아마도 어디론가 긴 여행을 떠날 것이다.
(c) 다시는 회사 생활을 하지 않을 것 같다.
(d) 그는 취미생활을 할 수 있기를 평생 꿈꿔왔다.

해설 직장에서 은퇴한 사람이 다음에 할 일을 모색하겠다는 글이다. 기업 세계의 부산함으로 다시 돌아가기가 망설여지고, 남은 인생 동안 진실로 하고 싶은 일을 찾고 싶다고 하므로 (c)를 추론할 수 있다.

hesitant 주저하는 hustle and bustle 혼잡, 부산함 corporate 기업의 would rather ~하고 싶다 be unlikely to ~할 것 같지 않다

24

도처에 곤란의 징후들이 있다. 매장 공실률은 5퍼센트에서 15퍼센트로 증가했고, 주택 매매는 50퍼센트나 급락했다. 하지만 이런 수치들은 이전과 마찬가지의 삶을 계속 영위하는 대부분 사람들에게 통계에 불과할 뿐이다. 오늘날의 침체는 대체로 이전 정점으로부터의 생산량 하락에 의해서라기보다는 성장 부진 때문으로 평가된다. 다른 관점에서 보면, 우리는 1990년대 초반 이후 개인의 가처분 소득이 약 70퍼센트 상승했음을 발견한다. 경제 성장의 부재에도 많은 이들이 20년 전보다 더 높은 생활 수준을 누리고 있다.

Q 지문으로부터 추론할 수 있는 것은?
(a) 경기 침체로 인해 사람들이 씀씀이에 검소해지고 있다.
(b) 경기 하락의 정도가 부적절하게 측정되었다.
(c) 부자들은 더 부자가 되고 있지만, 국가 전체적으로는 더 가난하다.
(d) 현재의 불경기는 생활 수준에 거의 영향을 주지 않았다.

해설 지문 마지막에서 경기 침체에도 불구하고 개인 가처분 소득이 늘어나고 20년 전보다 더 높은 생활 수준을 누린다고 했으므로 정답은 (d)이다.

vacancy rate 공실률 plummet 급락하다 statistics 통계 carry on with ~을 계속하다 downturn 하강, 침체 assess 평가하다 output 생산량 previous 이전의 lack of growth 성장 부진 perspective 관점 disposable income 가처분 소득 standard of living 생활수준 economic slump 경기 침체 frugal 검소한 extent 정도 decline 하락 improperly 부적절하게 gauge 측정하다 impact 영향을 주다

25

문화 변용은 일련의 문화 집단이 다른 문화 집단의 신념과 관행을 들여올 때 발생한다. 일본은 국민들을 현대화하면서 서양의 문화에 성공적으로 동화되었고 봉건적 농본주의에서 산업적 자본주의로 옮겨갔다. 특히 그 국민들의 식생활이 서구화 되어서 일본인들 사이에서는 심혈관 질환이 많이 발생하는 것이 공중 보건의 문제가 될 지경이다. 서구 방식으로의 문화 변용은 정신 질환과 약물 남용이 더 많이 발생하는 것과도 관련이 있고, 성별에 따라 달리 나타난다.

Q 문화 변용에 대해 추론할 수 있는 것은?
(a) 전체 인구 중에서 자유분방한 이들에 가장 큰 영향을 미친다.
(b) 각 개인의 삶의 방식에 뿌리 깊은 영향을 준다.
(c) 문제점들이 있음에도 전반적으로는 한 문화에 이익이 된다.
(d) 전 연령대와 성별 구별 없이 똑같은 방식으로 영향을 준다.

해설 서로 다른 문화가 직접적, 지속적으로 접촉하여 그 한쪽 또는 양쪽이 원래의 문화 유형에 변화를 일으키는 현상인 문화 변용(acculturation)에 관한 글이다. 일본의 경우, 근대에 서구 문화를 받아들임으로써 심장혈관계 질환자가 늘어났고, 정신 질환과 약물 남용 사례가 더 많아졌다는 점에서 개인의 삶의 방식에 큰 영향을 준다는 (b)를 추론할 수 있다.

acculturation 문화 변용 **adopt** 채택하다 **transition** 이행[변천]하다 **feudal** 봉건의 **agrarianism** 농본주의 **to the extent** ~정도까지 **be linked with** ~와 연관되다 **instance** 사례, 경우 **cardiovascular disease** 심장 혈관계 질환 **drug abuse** 마약 남용 **liberal** 진보적인 **segment** 부분 **repercussion** 영향

Part IV

26-27

https://www.awesome.com/events/contest
뉴스 ∨ **사진** ∨ 행사 ∨ 회사 소개 ∨ 연락

제15회 연례 멋있는(Awesome) 사진 경연대회

일상생활에서 익살맞은 순간들을 포착하는 데 열정을 느끼시나요? 전세계 수백만 명의 사람들에게 웃음을 선사하는 데 열정을 느끼시나요? 예술의 한 형태로 사진술을 제시하는 데 열정을 느끼시나요? 그렇다면 올해의 멋있는 사진 경연대회에 참가해 보세요. 스스로 미소를 짓게 될지도 몰라요!
대회는 아동부, 청소년부, 성인부의 세 가지 부문으로 나눠 진행됩니다. 출품작 심사에 대해서는 저희가 아주 진지합니다. 사실 저희는 심사 절차의 엄정함으로 널리 알려져 있는데요, 심사 절차는 훌륭한 사진작가들이 진행합니다. 그러니 저희의 심사 절차를 웃음거리로 삼지 마세요!
■ 응모 사진은 다음의 요건을 충족해야만 합니다.
• 응모작의 해상도를 변경해서는 안 됩니다.
• 응모작의 크기를 늘리려고 해서는 안 됩니다.
• 응모작에 효과를 적용하려고 해서는 안 됩니다.
• 응모작은 JPEG 파일 형식으로 제출되어야 합니다. 응모작의 최대 파일 크기는 50MB입니다.
• 모든 응모작은 늦어도 7월 7일까지 amy.g@awesome.com로 이메일로 제출되어야 합니다.

26 Q 웹페이지에 따르면, 다음 중 옳은 것은?
(a) 사진 경연대회는 3개월마다 한 번씩 개최된다.
(b) 응모 사진들은 보는 사람이 심란함을 느끼도록 만들 가능성이 높다.
(c) 65세가 넘는 성인은 대회에 응모작을 제출하는 것이 금지된다.
(d) 심사 절차는 공정성이 아주 높을 것이다.

해설 (a)는 연례행사라고 했기 때문에 3개월마다 한 번이 아니라, 1년마다 한 번으로 수정해야 한다. (b)는 웃음을 자아낼 가능성이 높기 때문에 오답이다. (c)는 성인부에 속할 것으로 이해하는 것이 자연스럽기 때문에 정답이 아니다. 따라서 정답은 본문에서 강조한 (d)이다. 보통은 지문에서 내용을 제시하는 순서와 선택지의 배열순서가 일치된다는 규칙을 활용하는 것도 좋은 대비 전략이다.

27 Q 다음 중 어느 것이 대회의 응모작으로 받아들여질 수 있는가?
(a) 크기를 늘린, 웃음을 자아내는 사진
(b) 7월 5일에 amy.g@awesome.com로 이메일로 보낸 즐거운 상황을 담은 사진
(c) PDF 형식의 사진 파일
(d) 크기가 5GB인 사진 파일

해설 (a)는 크기를 늘리는 것을 금지하므로 오답이다. (c)는 JPEG 파일 형식으로만 제시했기 때문에 정답이 될 수 없다. (d)는 최대 파일 크기가 50MB이기 때문에 오답이다. 따라서 응모 기한과 응모 담당자의 이메일 주소, 응모작의 내용이 올바르게 설명된 (b)이다.

passionate 열정적인 **capture** 포착하다 **comic** 익살맞은 **photography** 사진술 **end up -ing** 결국 ~하게 되다 **category** 범주 **young adult** 청소년 **entry** 출품작, 응모작 **rigorous** 엄격한 **reputable** 평판이 좋은 **resolution** 해상도; 결심 **format** 형식 **distraught** 심란한 **fair** 공정한

28-29

생태학 〉 최근 뉴스   네이처 타임스

부활 생태학은 인류의 구원자인가?

'부활 생태학'이라는 용어가 일반인들에게 익숙하진 않지만, 부활 생태학의 아이디어는 꽤 간단하다. 부활 생태학은 고대의 동물과 식물, 그리고 미생물의 종(種)들을 '부활시킴'으로써 생물이 어떻게 진화하는지를 이해하는 것을 목표로 한다. 과학자들은 그 고대의 종들이 지구의 다양한 생물의 과거와 미래를 이해하는 데 도움을 줄 수 있다고 생각한다.

2012년 이래로, 고대의 많은 종들이 부활 생태학자들에 의해 부활되어 왔다. 그런 종들 가운데 일부는 700년밖에 되지 않은 데 반해, 다른 종들은 대략 3만년이 되었다. 과학자들을 가장 놀라게 만든 것은 어떤 박테리아인데, 이 박테리아는 대략 8백만 년이나 된 것으로 생각된다.

그렇게 부활된 동물과 미생물이 인류를 위협할 수 있는가? 부활 생태학자들은 그렇게 생각하지 않는다. 이들은 부활된 종들 대부분이 완전히 무해하다고 지적한다. 더욱이 지구온난화가 이미 여러 고대의 종들을 부활시켰기 때문에, 과학자들이 비슷한 종들을 부활시켜서 그 종들이 오늘날의 지구에 미치는 영향을 연구하는 것이 훨씬 더 나을 것이다.

부활 생태학이 인류에게 참으로 유익할지는 시간이 지나야만 알 수 있을 것이다.

28 Q 기사에 따르면, 부활된 고대의 종들에 대해 다음 중 올바른 설명은?
(a) 2012년 이래로, 생태 관련 단체들은 과학자들이 그 종들을 부활시키도록 압박했다.
(b) 그 종들 가운데 3만년이 넘는 것은 없는 것으로 생각된다.
(c) 대부분의 과학자들은 미생물들이 생태계를 황폐화시킬 것을 두려워하여 부활시키는 것을 피한다.
(d) 그 종들은 과학자들이 생물의 진화 과정을 이해하는 데 도움이 될 것으로 생각된다.

해설 세부 사항 유형이므로, 해당하는 정보가 있는 부분을 찾아서 측정하는 사항을 정확히 확인해야 한다. (a)는 생태 관련 단체에 대한 언급이 없기 때문에 오답이다. (b)는 8백만 년이 넘는 것이 있는 것으로 생각된다고 했기 때문에 정답이 아니다. (c)는 오히려 반대이기 때문에 오답이다. 따라서 정답은 기사의 내용에 충실한 (d)이다.

29 Q 부활 생태학자들이 가장 동의할 것 같은 진술은?
(a) 고대 동물의 종을 부활시키는 것은 인류에게 어떤 위험도 주지 않는다.
(b) 생물이 지구에서 진화한 것에 대한 지식은 인류에게 혜택을 줄 것이다.
(c) 고대의 식물 종들을 부활시키는 것은 거의 불가능하다.
(d) 지구온난화 때문에 더 많은 동물의 종들이 부활될 가능성은 높지 않다.

해설 고난도 문항이다. (a)는 세 번째 단락에서 부활될 종들 대부분이라는 제한 조건이 있기 때문에 정답이 아니다. 따라서 약간의 위험이 존재할 가능성이 있기 때문이다. (c)는 정확하게 추론할 수 있는 근거가 없기 때문에 반드시 오답으로 처리해야 한다. (d)는 지문의 내용에 어긋난다. 따라서 정답은 자연스럽게 추론할 수 있는 (b)이다.

resurrection 부활 ecology 생태학 savior 구세주 organism 유기체, 생물 microorganism 미생물 revive 부활시키다, 소생시키다 jeopardize 위태롭게 하다 harmless 무해한 beneficial 이로운, 유익한 wreak havoc on ~에 커다란 피해를 입히다 all but 거의

30-31

음악 혁명가 이고르 스트라빈스키

발레 뤼스를 위해 세 편의 발레곡을 작곡해 달라는 세르게이 디아길레프의 의뢰를 받았을 때, 이고르 스트라빈스키는 거의 '미숙한' 작곡가였다. 그럼에도 불구하고, 스트라빈스키가 디아길레프를 위해 작곡한 세 편의 발레는 많은 점에서 혁명적이었다. 특히, 그 발레곡의 마지막 작품인 「봄의 제전」은 여전히 많은 음악 사학자들로부터 높이 평가를 받고 있다.

많은 평론가들은 「봄의 제전」의 음악이 '째는 듯한 소리'와 '으르렁거리는 소리'와 같은, 독특한 소리로 구성되어 있다고 평한다. 반면에, 줄리어스 해리슨과 같은, 스트라빈스키를 비난하는 이들은 그 소리들이 단지 '흉측하다'고 주장한다.

그렇지만 심지어 그런 비평가들도 복조(複調)의 수준을 높였다는 데에는 동의한다. 발레 뤼스를 위해 작곡한 다른 두 발레곡도 복조를 실험하기는 했지만, 「봄의 제전」은 그 기법을 가장 높은 수준으로 정교화해서, 스트라빈스키가 전위적인 음악가로서 명성을 얻는 데 크게 기여했다.

30 Q 지문의 요점은?
(a) 「봄의 제전」은 음악 평론가들 사이에서 대단한 논란을 촉발했다.
(b) 「봄의 제전」은 스트라빈스키가 급진적인 음악가로서 명성을 확립하는 데 도움을 주었다.
(c) 스트라빈스키의 음악 경력은 복조를 정교화하려는 끊임없는 노력으로 정의되었다.
(d) 모든 음악 사학자들이 스트라빈스키의 실험적인 발레곡에 좋은 인상을 받지는 않았다.

해설 고난도 문항이다. 이처럼 지문의 요점을 묻는 문항의 경우는, 지문의 전반적인 흐름을 정확히 포착해야 한다. 이런 유형의 경우에, 마지막 문장이 정답의 단서를 제공하는 경우가 많다는 점에 유의할 필요가 있다. 정답은 (b)이다. 마지막 단락의 마지막 문장이 지문의 전반적인 내용을 요약했기 때문이다. 다른 선택지는 글의 초점에서 벗어나 있기 때문에 오답이다.

31 Q 지문으로부터 스트라빈스키에 대해 추론할 수 있는 것은?
(a) 혁명적인 발레 댄서로서 디아길레프의 잠재력을 알아봤다.
(b) 발레 뤼스를 위해 발레곡을 작곡해 달라는 디아길레프로의 의뢰를 받았을 때 20대 초반이었다.
(c) 복조에 대한 접근 방식이 다른 작곡가들의 방식과 상당히 달랐을 수도 있다.
(d) 작곡가로서 활동한 기간 내내 해리슨과 껄끄러운 관계를 유지했다.

해설 (a)는 추론할 수 있는 근거가 전혀 없으므로, 반드시 오답으로 처리해야 한다. (b)는 '미숙한' 작곡가가 반드시 20대 초반이라고 볼 근거가 없으므로 정답이 아니다. (d)는 스트라빈스키가 해리슨과 동시대의 인물인지도 알 수 없기 때문에 오답이다. 따라서 정답은 지문의 내용으로부터 분명하게 추론할 수 있는 (c)이다. '혁명적'이라든가 '전위적인'과 같은 말은 다른 작곡가들과 같은 방식을 취할 때 쓸 수 없는 말이기 때문이다.

revolutionary 혁명가; 혁명적인 commission 의뢰하다 inexperienced 경험이 부족한, 미숙한 ballet 발레; 발레곡 distinctive 독특한 shriek 째는 듯한 소리 snarl 으르렁거리는 소리 hideous 흉측한 bitonality 복조(複調) avant-garde 전위적인 radical 급진적인, 과격한 strained 껄끄러운, 긴장된 career 경력, 직업

32-33

발신: 신시아 테일러 〈cynthia_t@leadership.com〉
수신: 잭 하퍼 〈jack_h@jmail.com〉
일자: 6월 8일 금요일 오후 2:33
주제: 제13회 국제리더십회의

7월 13일부터 15일까지 개최 예정인, 제13회 국제리더십회의에 참석하시기를 기쁜 마음으로 초청합니다. 올해 회의는 온타리오주(州) 토론토의 메트로 토론토 컨벤션센터에서 치러질 예정입니다.

이 회의에 참석함으로써, 리더십의 참된 본질에 대한 통찰을 확실히 얻게 될 것입니다. 기조연설자들 가운데 한 명인 케이트 포터에 따르면, 리더십은 사람들을 이끄는 것이 본질이 아니라고 합니다. 대신에, 리더십은 잠재력을 온전히 실현할 수 있도록 다른 사람들을 섬기는 것이 본질이라고 합니다. 흥미롭게도 다른 연설자들은 리더십에 대해 다른 견해를 제시할 것입니다.

늘 그렇듯이, 질의/응답 시간과 대화식 토론이 있을 예정입니다. 다음 링크를 방문해서 회의 참석을 신청할 수 있습니다.

http://www.international-leadership-conference.com

질문이나 제안 사항이 있으시면, 자유롭게 cynthia_t@leadership.com로 제게 이메일을 주십시오.

국제리더십회의 진행 책임자
신시아 테일러 올림

32 Q 이메일의 주된 목적은?
(a) 수취인에게 국제 행사에 참석할 것을 요청하는 것
(b) 수취인이 국제리더십회의를 향상시키는 방법에 대해 제안하도록 초청하는 것
(c) 수취인에게 질의/응답 시간을 주재하도록 요청하는 것
(d) 테일러 씨에게 이메일을 보냄으로써 국제회의에 등록하도록 제안하는 것

해설 중요한 출제 유형이기 때문에, 꼼꼼하게 익혀두어야 한다. 특히, (b)와 같은 오답 유형은 흔히 활용되는 오답 유형이기 때문에, 정답과의 차이를 분명히 익혀야 한다. 이와 같은 오답 유형은 지문에 나온 표현을 그대로 쓰는 오답 유형이다. NEW TEPS의 도입을 전후해서 이와 같은 오답 유형이 많이 제시되었다. 정답은 이메일의 취지에 맞는 (a)이다.

33 Q 이메일로부터 포터 씨에 대해 추론할 수 있는 것은?

(a) 자신의 연설에서, 섬김의 리더십이 갖는 약점을 비판할 가능성이 높다.

(b) 섬김의 리더십이 참된 형태의 리더십이라고 생각할 수도 있다.

(c) 7월 15일에 기조연설을 할 예정이다.

(d) 발표를 하고 나서, 하퍼 씨가 묻는 질문에 답할 것이다.

해설 (a)는 정반대일 가능성이 높다. (c)는 기조연설이 행사의 마지막 날에 있을 것이라는 정보가 없기 때문에 오답이다. (d)는 하퍼 씨의 참석 여부가 정해지지도 않았기 때문에 정답이 아니다. 또한 하퍼 씨가 반드시 포터 씨에게 질문할 것이라고 추론할 수도 없다. 따라서 정답은 자연스럽게 추론할 수 있는 (b)이다.

slate (일정을) 계획하다   **definitely** 확실히, 분명히   **nature** 본성; 자연
keynote speaker 기조연설자   **potential** 잠재력; 잠재적인
register 등록하다   **coordinator** 진행자, 조정자   **preside** 주재하다

34-35

주관성이 개체성을 결정한다

쇠렌 키르케고르에 따르면, '단일한 개인'은 오랫동안 전통적인 철학에서 간과되었는데, 이는 전통적인 철학이 객관성과 보편성을 중시하기 때문이다. 키르케고르는 그런 개념들이 단일한 개인의 참된 의미를 드러내는 데 도움이 되지 않는다고 평한다.

키르케고르는 종교적 신념이 보편적인 윤리와 상충할 때 개인이 '개별적으로' 의미를 갖게 되는 기회가 생긴다고 지적한다. 그는 아브라함의 예를 드는데, 아브라함은 신으로부터 아들을 희생하라는 명령을 받는다.

아브라함이 보편적인 윤리를 따라서 신의 명령을 따르기를 거부한다면, 그의 존재는 '보편적으로' 의미를 갖게 되는데, 이는 그의 의도가 보편적으로 적용될 수 있는 윤리에 따라 좌우되기 때문이다. 그렇지만 아브라함이 신의 명령을 따르면, 그의 존재는 '개별적으로' 의미를 갖게 된다. 이것은 주로 그의 의도가 개인적인 신념에 의해 특유하게 지배되기 때문이다.

이 때문에, 키르케고르는 객관성이 아니라 주관성이 단일한 개인을 정의하는 데 기여할 수 있다고 생각한다. 이 덴마크 철학자에게는 주관성이 개체성을 의미한다.

34 Q 지문의 요점은?

(a) 키르케고르는 주관성과 개체성 사이에 강한 유의미한 관계가 없다고 생각한다.

(b) 키르케고르는 단일한 개인의 의미가 주관성에 의해 드러날 수 있다고 주장한다.

(c) 키르케고르는 전통적인 철학이 개체성의 발현을 오랫동안 저해했다고 주장한다.

(d) 키르케고르는 종교적 신념이 필연적으로 보편적인 윤리와 양립할 수 없다고 이해한다.

해설 NEW TEPS에서 주요 유형으로 출제될 가능성이 높은 철학 관련 지문이다. 키르케고르는 실존주의 철학자로 분류되는데, 기본적인 배경지식을 갖추어야 실전에서 당황하지 않을 수 있다. (a)는 지문 내용과 정반대된다. (c)는 개체성을 발현을 저해한 것이 아니라, 경시한 것이므로 정답이 아니다. 키르케고르가 둘 사이를 반드시 양립 불가라고 보는지는 정확히 알 수 없다. 따라서 정답은 (b)이다.

35 Q 키르케고르가 아브라함의 예를 든 이유는?

(a) 종교적인 신념이 끊임없이 보편적으로 적용할 수 있는 윤리를 거부한다고 단언하기 위해

(b) 종교적 신념이 개체성을 정의하는 데 어떻게 기여하는가를 예증하기 위해서

(c) 신의 명령은 어떤 희생을 치르더라도 반드시 따라야 한다고 주장하기 위해서

(d) 아브라함의 믿음이 진실에 대한 무지로 귀결된다고 설명하기 위해서

해설 (a)를 정답으로 고르지 않도록 특히 유의해야 한다. 키르케고르는 종교적인 신념이 보편적인 윤리와 상충할 때가 있다고 생각한 것이지, 반드시 상충한다고 생각한 것은 아니다. (c)와 (d)는 글의 흐름에도 어울리지 않는 선택지이다. 따라서 정답은 (b)이다. 이 지문의 제목에도 유의할 필요가 있다. 제목이 글의 전반적인 흐름을 결정할 때가 많기 때문이다.

subjectivity 주관성   **individuality** 개체성, 개성   **overlook** 간과하다
value 소중하게 여기다   **universality** 보편성, 일반성   **conflict**
상충하다   **divinely** 신의 힘으로   **intention** 의도   **ethics** 윤리; 윤리학
applicable 적용되는

Actual Test 4

Listening *Comprehension*

p.123

1	(d)	2	(a)	3	(c)	4	(d)	5	(a)	6	(d)	7	(c)	8	(d)	9	(c)	10	(c)
11	(a)	12	(b)	13	(d)	14	(c)	15	(d)	16	(d)	17	(d)	18	(c)	19	(b)	20	(b)
21	(a)	22	(c)	23	(c)	24	(d)	25	(d)	26	(d)	27	(b)	28	(b)	29	(a)	30	(a)
31	(c)	32	(b)	33	(d)	34	(d)	35	(b)	36	(a)	37	(b)	38	(b)	39	(c)	40	(c)

Vocabulary

p.129

1	(c)	2	(b)	3	(d)	4	(d)	5	(b)	6	(c)	7	(b)	8	(d)	9	(b)	10	(b)
11	(b)	12	(b)	13	(a)	14	(b)	15	(a)	16	(a)	17	(a)	18	(b)	19	(a)	20	(a)
21	(b)	22	(d)	23	(d)	24	(a)	25	(c)	26	(b)	27	(a)	28	(d)	29	(a)	30	(a)

Grammar

p.133

1	(d)	2	(c)	3	(c)	4	(b)	5	(c)	6	(b)	7	(d)	8	(c)	9	(c)	10	(d)
11	(b)	12	(b)	13	(b)	14	(a)	15	(d)	16	(d)	17	(d)	18	(d)	19	(d)	20	(c)
21	(c)	22	(b)	23	(d)	24	(d)	25	(d)	26	(b)	27	(c)	28	(c)	29	(c)	30	(d)

Reading *Comprehension*

p.137

1	(b)	2	(a)	3	(d)	4	(c)	5	(a)	6	(a)	7	(a)	8	(b)	9	(b)	10	(d)
11	(b)	12	(a)	13	(b)	14	(d)	15	(d)	16	(a)	17	(d)	18	(d)	19	(d)	20	(d)
21	(b)	22	(c)	23	(c)	24	(c)	25	(a)	26	(b)	27	(b)	28	(b)	29	(d)	30	(b)
31	(c)	32	(b)	33	(a)	34	(b)	35	(b)												

Part I

1

W Could you help me write a report?
M _____

(a) I was glad I could write it.
(b) It was very helpful to me.
(c) I look forward to reading it.
(d) I'm really backed up right now.

W 제가 보고서 쓰는 걸 도와줄 수 있나요?
M _____

(a) 제가 쓸 수 있어서 기뻤어요.
(b) 그건 저에게 정말 도움이 되었어요.
(c) 빨리 그걸 읽어보고 싶어요.
(d) 제가 지금 일이 정말 밀려 있어서요.

helpful 도움이 되는 **look forward to -ing** ~할 것을 고대하다 **be backed up** (일이) 밀려 있다

2

M Hi, I'm calling about your ad for a used pickup truck.
W _____

(a) Sorry, but it's been sold.
(b) Yes, I just got my license.
(c) Sure, just drop me off here.
(d) No, it's probably false advertising.

M 안녕하세요, 중고 픽업트럭에 관한 광고 때문에 전화 걸었는데요.
W _____

(a) 미안하지만, 이미 팔렸어요.
(b) 네, 전 막 면허증을 받았어요.
(c) 물론이죠, 그냥 여기에 내려주시면 돼요.
(d) 아뇨, 그건 거짓 광고인가 봐요.

ad 광고 **used** 중고의 **pickup truck** 짐칸의 덮개가 없는 소형 트럭
license 면허증 **drop off** ~을 내려주다 **false advertising** 거짓
광고, 허위 광고

3

W Mark, you need to step up your performance.
M _____

(a) It performed well on the day.
(c) Thanks for your confidence.
(c) But I thought I was doing well.
(d) I don't have time for exercise.

W 마크, 실적을 더 올려야겠네요.
M _____

(a) 그날은 작동을 잘했어요.
(b) 믿어주셔서 감사합니다.
(c) 하지만 잘하고 있었다고 생각했는데요.
(d) 연습할 시간이 없어요.

step up 늘리다, 높이다 **performance** 실적, 성과 **perform** 행하다,
작동하다 **confidence** 신뢰, 확신

4

W My baby is due in just four weeks.
M _____

(a) Sure, I can babysit tonight.
(b) Yes, he has eyes like you.
(c) Only eight months to go!
(d) You must be so excited!

W 4주만 있으면 제 출산 예정일이에요.
M _____

(a) 그럼요, 오늘밤에 아기를 봐줄 수 있어요.
(b) 네, 아기 눈이 당신과 닮았네요.
(c) 앞으로 8개월만 힘을 내요!
(d) 정말 흥분되겠네요.

due ~하기로 되어 있는, 예정된 **babysit** 아기를 돌봐주다

5

W Who do I call to request a day off?
M _____

(a) You don't need permission for that.
(b) One of the clients asked for you.
(c) I heard it started last week.
(d) I'll plan on seeing you there.

W 하루 휴가를 신청하려면 누구에게 전화를 걸어야 하죠?
M _____

(a) 그건 허락을 받을 필요가 없어요.
(b) 고객 한 명이 당신을 요청했어요.
(c) 그건 지난주에 시작했다고 들었어요.
(d) 그곳에서 당신을 만날 계획이에요.

request 요청하다 **day off** (근무를) 쉬는 날, 휴가 **permission** 허락

6

M Let's try that new Vietnamese restaurant on Wilson Avenue.
W _____

(a) It's pretty conveniently located, though.
(b) I think we're finally going to get served.
(c) The Asian store next to the restaurant.
(d) I ate there yesterday with Kimberly.

M 윌슨 가에 새로 생긴 그 베트남 식당에 한번 가봅시다.

W _____

(a) 하지만 그건 위치는 정말 편리해요.
(b) 마침내 우리에게 주문을 받으러 오는 것 같군요.
(c) 식당 옆에 있는 아시아 상점이요.
(d) 저는 어제 킴벌리와 거기서 식사를 했어요.

conveniently located 위치가 편리한   **get served** (종업원의)
서빙을 받다

7

W Which do you want to bring to the party, ice or
dessert?

M _____

(a) If it's not too much trouble.
(b) That sounds like a fun idea.
(c) I'll be responsible for the ice.
(d) I'm afraid I've already had dessert.

W 얼음과 디저트 중에서 파티에 뭘 가져올래?

M _____

(a) 그게 너무 번거롭지 않다면.
(b) 그거 재미있는 생각 같다.
(c) 난 얼음을 담당할게.
(d) 아쉽게도 난 벌써 디저트를 먹었어.

trouble 수고, 번거로움   **be responsible for** ~을 책임지다, 담당하다

8

W How do you feel about this wallpaper design?

M _____

(a) Honestly, I think I'm getting a cold.
(b) You choose it, and I'll buy.
(c) Yes, let's start remodeling.
(d) It's unusual, but I like it.

W 이 벽지 디자인에 대해 어떻게 생각해?

M _____

(a) 솔직히 말하자면, 나 감기에 걸린 것 같아.
(b) 네가 그걸 고르면, 내가 살게.
(c) 맞아, 리모델링을 시작하자.
(d) 독특한데, 마음에 들어.

wallpaper 벽지   **honestly** 솔직히   **get a cold** 감기에 걸리다

9

W It's high time for this carpet to go.

M _____

(a) I agree it is a softer one.
(b) It'll be here any minute now.
(c) Let's start pricing replacements.
(d) The installers did a wonderful job.

W 이 카펫을 버릴 때가 됐어요.

M _____

(a) 그게 더 부드럽다는 데 동의해요.
(b) 그것은 금세 여기에 도착할 거예요..
(c) 교체할 카펫의 가격을 비교해 봐요.
(d) 설치기사들이 일을 잘했군요.

It's high time ~할 때가 되다   **any minute now** 금방이라도, 곧
price 가격을 비교하다   **replacement** 교체, 대체물   **installer**
설치하는 사람

10

M Wouldn't you rather skip your school reunion?

W _____

(a) I can't believe we're hosting this thing.
(b) All of my old friends were there.
(c) I wouldn't dream of missing it.
(d) See you at the next one, then.

M 동창회에 안 나가고 싶지 않아?

W _____

(a) 우리가 이 일을 주최하고 있다는 게 믿어지지 않아.
(b) 예전 내 친구들 모두 그곳에 있었어.
(c) 거기에 빠지는 건 생각지도 못할 일이야.
(d) 그럼 다음번에 보자.

would rather (오히려) ~하고 싶다   **reunion** 모임, 동창회   **host**
주최하다

Part II

11

M How's the new minivan working out?
W So far so good!
M It looks incredibly spacious.
W _____

(a) Not only that, it gets good mileage.
(b) I can recommend one, if you'd like.
(c) Go ahead and stretch out a little more.
(d) I'll drive you to the dealership myself.

M 새 미니밴은 성능이 어떠니?
W 아직은 매우 좋아!
M 엄청 널찍해 보이던데.
W _____

(a) 그뿐만 아니라, 연비도 좋아.
(b) 네가 원한다면, 내가 하나 추천해 줄 수 있어.
(c) 어서 스트레칭을 좀 더 해.
(d) 내가 직접 대리점까지 태워줄게.

work out 잘 되다, 성공적이다   **incredibly** 엄청나게, 매우
spacious 널찍한   **mileage** 연료 소비율, 연비   **stretch out** 몸을 쭉
뻗다, 스트레칭하다   **dealership** 대리점

12

W How disappointing that the play is sold out.
M We can get tickets for the next performance.
W But when is that?
M _____

(a) It should last about two hours.
(b) I'll check at the box office.
(c) Let's meet at the theater.
(d) As soon as I'm able to.

W 연극이 매진되어서 정말 실망이야.
M 다음 공연 표는 구할 수 있어.
W 하지만 그게 언젠데?
M _____

(a) 약 2시간은 걸릴 거야.
(b) 매표소에서 확인해 볼게.
(c) 극장에서 만나자.
(d) 내가 할 수 있는 한 조만간.

disappointing 실망스러운 **sold out** 매진된 **performance** 공연 **last** 지속되다 **box office** 매표소

13

W I've renewed my passport, but do I need a visa too?
M You do in order to enter Russia.
W Where can I get one of those?
M _____

(a) Just hand over your passport.
(b) They'll collect your ticket here.
(c) At the bottom of your suitcase.
(d) Apply at the consulate downtown.

W 여권을 갱신했는데, 비자도 필요하나요?
M 러시아에 입국하려면 필요합니다.
W 그건 어디서 받을 수 있죠?
M _____

(a) 여권만 주시면 됩니다.
(b) 여기서 표를 수거할 겁니다.
(c) 여행 가방 맨 밑에요.
(d) 시내에 있는 영사관에서 신청하세요.

renew 갱신하다 **in order to** ~하기 위해서 **hand over** 건네주다 **consulate** 영사관 **downtown** 시내에

14

M So, you're throwing a party tomorrow evening?
W I hope you can come despite the short notice.
M I'm pretty sure I can make it.
W _____

(a) Let me double check and tell you.
(b) I'm happy to lend a hand at it.
(c) You're not going to regret it.
(d) I wish you'd told me earlier.

M 그래서, 내일 저녁에 파티를 연다고?
W 갑작스럽게 알리는 거지만 네가 올 수 있으면 좋겠다.
M 꼭 갈게.
W _____

(a) 다시 한 번 확인하고 말해 줄게.
(b) 그것을 도와줄 수 있어서 기뻐.
(c) 후회하지 않을 거야.
(d) 좀 더 일찍 말해주었더라면 좋았을 걸.

throw a party 파티를 열다 **short notice** 갑작스러운 통고 **make it** (모임 등에) 가다 **double check** 다시 한 번 확인하다 **lend a hand** 도와주다

15

M Ma'am, is this the book you wanted?
W Yes, but I'm looking for it in paperback.
M It hasn't been released in that format yet.
W _____

(a) A couple sheets of scrap paper will do.
(b) OK, thanks for autographing my copy.
(c) Please let me know when you locate it.
(d) Then, sorry, I can't afford the hardcover.

M 손님, 이게 원하셨던 책인가요?
W 네, 하지만 전 페이퍼백을 찾고 있는데요.
M 그 판형으로는 아직 발간되지 않았습니다.
W _____

(a) 이면지 몇 장이면 충분할 거예요.
(b) 알겠습니다. 제 책에 사인을 해 주셔서 감사합니다.
(c) 그것의 위치를 알아내면 제게 알려주세요.
(d) 그럼 미안하지만, 전 양장본은 살 여유가 없어서요.

paperback 페이퍼백(책 표지를 종이 한 장으로 장정한 포켓판 도서) **release** 출시하다, 발간하다 **format** 판형, 서식 **sheet** (종이) 한 장 **scrap paper** 이면지 **autograph** (유명인이) 사인하다 **locate** 위치를 알아내다 **afford** ~을 살 여유가 있다 **hardcover** 양장본(딱딱한 표지로 제본한 책)

16

W Will you be at the convention this weekend?
M I wish I could go, but I'm doing shift work.
W Won't one of your coworkers switch shifts?
M _____

(a) That was so nice of you.
(b) As long as I get to attend.
(c) I'll see you there tomorrow.
(d) They've all turned me down.

W 이번 주말에 총회에 참석할 거예요?
M 갔으면 좋겠지만, 교대 근무를 해야 해요.
W 동료가 근무를 바꿔주지 않을까요?
M _____

(a) 당신은 정말 친절했어요.
(b) 제가 참석할 수 있는 한은요.
(c) 내일 거기서 봐요.
(d) 모두 제 부탁을 거절했어요.

convention 총회 **shift work** 교대근무 **coworker** 동료 **switch** 바꾸다 **as long as** ~하는 한 **turn down** 거절하다

17

M I still haven't been given a new office.
W Really? I moved into mine yesterday.
M Oh, which wing of the building are you in?
W _____

(a) Come by my office later on.
(b) I'll let you know when I find out.
(c) I'm hoping to be assigned to sales.
(d) The one with the conference room.

M 전 아직 새 사무실을 배정받지 못했어요.
W 정말요? 전 어제 제 사무실로 옮겼는데요.
M 아, 건물 어느 관에 계시죠?
W _____

(a) 나중에 제 사무실에 들르세요.
(b) 제가 찾으면 알려 드릴게요.
(c) 영업부로 배정되기를 바라고 있어요.
(d) 회의실이 있는 건물이요.

wing (건물의) 동, 별관 **come by** 들르다 **later on** 나중에

18

W My email account is practically unusable.
M Because of all the spam in your inbox?
W That's right. Just look at all of this!
M _____

(a) You should have checked before sending it.
(b) Remind me of your email address again.
(c) Maybe you need a better email service.
(d) That's what I mistook for the spam.

W 제 이메일 계정은 사실상 사용할 수가 없어요.
M 수신함에 있는 그 많은 스팸 메일들 때문에요?
W 맞아요. 이것들 좀 보세요!
M _____

(a) 그것을 보내기 전에 확인했어야죠.
(b) 당신 이메일 주소를 다시 한 번 알려주세요.
(c) 더 나은 이메일 서비스가 필요하겠네요.
(d) 그것이 제가 스팸 메일로 착각했던 거예요.

email account 이메일 계정 **practically** 사실상 **unusable** 사용할 수 없는 **spam** 스팸 메일 **inbox** 수신함 **remind A of B** A에게 B를 일깨워주다 **mistake A for B** A를 B로 오해하다

19

W Wow, that horror movie was just fabulous.
M You and I have very different tastes in movies.
W You didn't see it as entertaining?
M _____

(a) Thanks, but I really don't have time.
(b) Actually, I found it quite disturbing.
(c) Yes, that's the film I'm referring to.
(d) No, I'm as keen on it as you are.

W 와, 그 공포영화는 정말 멋졌어.
M 너와 나는 영화에 대한 취향이 아주 다르구나.
W 너는 그게 재미있지 않았어?
M _____

(a) 고마워. 하지만 난 정말 시간이 없어.
(b) 실은, 몹시 거슬렸어.
(c) 응, 그게 내가 말하는 영화야.
(d) 아니, 나도 너만큼 그것을 좋아해.

fabulous 환상적인, 멋진 **taste** 취향 **entertaining** 재미있는 **disturbing** 거슬리는 **refer to** 언급하다 **keen on** ~을 매우 좋아하는, ~에 관심이 많은

20

M Sandra Williamson was hired as interim CEO.
W I know, everyone's talking about it.
M What have you heard about her?
W _____

(a) It'll only be a little while.
(b) Just that she's notoriously strict.
(c) She'll start as a marketing associate.
(d) That I probably wouldn't get the job.

M 산드라 윌리엄슨이 임시 CEO로 채용되었어요.
W 알아요, 모두가 그 얘기를 하고 있어요.
M 그녀에 대해 무슨 얘기를 들었어요?
W _____

(a) 잠시 동안만일 거예요.
(b) 그녀가 엄격하기로 악명 높다는 것만요.
(c) 그녀는 마케팅부서 사원으로 시작할 거예요.
(d) 제가 그 일자리를 얻을 수 없을 거라는 거요.

hire 채용하다 **interim** 임시의, 중간의 **notoriously** 악명 높게 **associate** 사원

Part III

21

Listen to a conversation between a couple.

> W Anything notable happening this weekend?
> M I was planning on staying in. Why?
> W I thought I might head to the coast.
> M That sounds fun. Will you spend the night?
> W No. I'll drive down Sunday morning and return at night.
> M Sounds like fun but I'd rather relax at home.

Q What is the couple mainly doing in the conversation?
(a) Sharing plans for the weekend
(b) Debating about driving to the coast
(c) Choosing a time for the woman's trip
(d) Making arrangements to visit the coast

커플의 대화를 들으시오.

W 이번 주말에 뭐 중요한 일 있어?
M 집에 있으려고 하는데. 왜?
W 바닷가에 갈 수도 있을 것 같아서.
M 그거 재미있겠다. 밤을 보내고 올 거야?
W 아니. 일요일 아침에 운전해 가서 밤에 돌아올 거야.
M 재미있을 것 같긴 한데 난 집에서 쉬고 싶어.

Q 두 사람이 대화에서 주로 하고 있는 것은?
(a) 주말 계획 공유하기
(b) 바닷가까지 운전하는 것에 관해 상의하기
(c) 여자의 여행 시간 선택하기
(d) 바닷가에 갈 약속 정하기

notable 주목할 만한, 중요한　**stay in** 나가지 않고 집에 있다　**head to** ~에 가다　**relax** 쉬다　**share** 공유하다　**debate** 논의하다　**make arrangements** 약속을 정하다, 준비하다

22

Listen to a conversation on the street.

> W Oh, no! Look at this huge scratch on my car!
> M Wasn't that there before?
> W No! It must have happened while we were in the café.
> M It looks like another car bumped into yours.
> W Yes, and they didn't leave a note or anything.
> M We should ask around in case anyone saw something.

Q What is the main topic of the conversation?
(a) An accident while driving a car
(b) How the man bumped into a car
(c) The damage done to the woman's car
(d) How no one saw who scratched the car

거리에서 이뤄지는 대화를 들으시오.

W 아, 저런! 내 차에 난 이 커다란 흠집 좀 봐!
M 그거 전에 있던 거 아니야?
W 아니! 우리가 카페에 있을 때 생긴 게 분명해.
M 다른 차가 네 차를 들이박은 것 같아.
W 맞아, 그리고 메모 같은 것도 남기지 않았어.
M 뭔가 본 사람이 있을지도 모르니 주변에 물어보자.

Q 대화의 주제는?
(a) 운전 중 사고
(b) 남자가 어떻게 차를 들이박았는가
(c) 여자의 차에 생긴 손상
(d) 어떻게 아무도 누가 차에 흠집을 냈는지를 보지 못했는가

scratch 긁힌 자국, 흠집; 긁다　**bump into** ~에 부딪치다　**note** 메모, 쪽지

23

Listen to a conversation between two friends.

> W I'm going to vote on Saturday morning. How about you?
> M Haven't you heard? You can't vote early anymore.
> W What? What are you talking about?
> M They passed a law that did away with the early voting period.
> W So now we can only vote on the day of the election?
> M Right. There's no other option.

Q What are the man and woman mainly discussing?
(a) Who they plan to vote for
(b) Places where they can vote
(c) A change in voting protocol
(d) A convenient time for voting

두 친구의 대화를 들으시오.

W 난 토요일 아침에 투표할 거야. 너는?
M 못 들었어? 더 이상은 사전 투표를 할 수 없어.
W 뭐라고? 무슨 말이야?
M 사전 투표 기간을 폐지하는 법이 통과되었어.
W 그래서 이제 우리는 선거 당일에만 투표할 수 있다고?
M 맞아. 다른 선택권이 없어.

Q 남자와 여자가 주로 말하고 있는 내용은?
(a) 누구에게 투표할지
(b) 투표할 수 있는 장소
(c) 투표 규정 변경
(d) 투표하기 편리한 시간

vote 투표하다　**do away with** ~을 없애다, 폐지하다　**early voting** 사전 투표제　**protocol** 의례, 규약

24

Listen to a conversation about a book and a workshop.

M Ms. Blake, your workshop was excellent.
W Good, I'm glad you found it helpful.
M The writing techniques you shared were very innovative.
W You know, I describe them in more detail in my book.
M Yes, I am considering buying it.
W The bookstore should have a copy.

Q Which is correct about the woman according to the conversation?
(a) She can give the man her book.
(b) She has never held a workshop.
(c) She spoke on book publishing.
(d) She is a published author.

책과 워크숍에 관한 대화를 들으시오

M 블레이크 씨, 당신의 워크숍은 훌륭했어요.
W 잘됐네요. 당신이 도움 되었다고 느꼈다니 저도 기뻐요.
M 당신이 알려 주신 작문 기법은 정말 혁신적이었어요.
W 아시겠지만, 제 책에서 더 자세히 설명해놓고 있어요.
M 네, 그걸 살까 생각 중이에요.
W 분명 서점에 그 책이 있을 거예요.

Q 대화에 따르면 여자에 대해서 옳은 것은?
(a) 여자는 남자에게 그녀의 책을 줄 수 있다.
(b) 한 번도 워크숍을 개최해 본 적이 없다.
(c) 출판에 관해서 이야기했다.
(d) 책을 출판한 저자이다.

innovative 혁신적인 **in detail** 자세히 **book publishing** 출판

25

Listen to a conversation between a passenger and a flight attendant.

W Sir, your seat at 15A is in the emergency exit row.
M Yes, is there a problem?
W No, but you will need to assist with the door in an emergency.
M Oh, I'm not sure I can do that.
W Well, if you have any doubts, I can reseat you.
M You'd better do that, thanks.

Q Why does the man want the woman to reseat him?
(a) Because he has a problem with another passenger
(b) Because he wants to help flight attendants
(c) Because he prefers a window seat
(d) Because he won't be able to assist in an emergency

승객과 승무원의 대화를 들으시오.

W 손님, 손님의 자리인 15A는 비상탈출구 줄에 있습니다.
M 네, 무슨 문제 있나요?
W 아뇨, 하지만 비상 시 탈출구 문 개폐를 도우셔야 합니다.
M 아, 제가 그 일을 할 수 있을지 모르겠군요.
W 저, 확신이 없으시다면, 새로운 자리를 마련해 드릴 수도 있습니다.
M 그래 주시면 좋겠어요, 감사합니다.

Q 남자가 여자가 자신의 좌석을 재지정해주길 바라는 이유는?
(a) 다른 승객과 문제가 있기 때문에
(b) 승무원들을 도우려고 하기 때문에
(c) 창가 자리를 선호하기 때문에
(d) 비상시 도울 수 없기 때문에

emergency exit 비상탈출구 **reseat** 새로운 자리를 마련하다

26

Listen to a conversation between a couple.

M My boss is sending me to a conference next month.
W Another one? It seems like you're gone all the time.
M Well, this one's abroad, in Italy.
W Oh, that sounds like fun.
M Yes, so why not come with me and we'll have a vacation.
W Hey, that's not a bad idea.

Q Which is correct according to the conversation?
(a) The man was denied time to go to a conference.
(b) The woman would prefer to bypass Italy.
(c) The man is getting transferred abroad.
(d) The woman approves of the man's plan.

커플의 대화를 들으시오

M 상사가 다음 달에 있는 콘퍼런스에 나를 보내려고 해.
W 또야? 당신은 항상 출장을 가는 것 같아.
M 그게, 이번에는 해외야, 이탈리아로.
W 아, 그건 재미있겠다.
M 그래, 그럼 나랑 같이 가서 휴가를 보내지 않을래?
W 야, 그거 괜찮은 생각인데.

Q 대화에 따르면 옳은 것은?
(a) 남자는 콘퍼런스에 갈 기회가 거부되었다.
(b) 여자는 이탈리아를 우회하는 쪽을 더 좋아할 것이다.
(c) 남자는 해외로 전근될 것이다.
(d) 여자는 남자의 계획에 찬성하고 있다.

deny 거부하다 **bypass** 우회하다 **transfer** 옮기다, 전근 가다

27

Listen to a couple discuss what to do for lunch.

> W I'm starving. What are we doing for lunch?
> M How about having some Chinese delivered?
> W No, let's go out. Is the deli OK?
> M I ate there yesterday, actually.
> W OK, let's go down to the taco stand, then.
> M That's fine with me.

Q Which is correct according to the conversation?
(a) The woman wants to skip lunch.
(b) The man ate at the deli yesterday.
(c) The woman will get food delivered.
(d) The man doesn't want to eat tacos.

커플이 점심 때 할 일에 관해 말하는 것을 들으시오.

W 배고파 죽겠어. 우리 점심을 어떻게 할까?
M 중국음식을 배달시키는 거 어때?
W 아니, 밖에 나가자. 델리 식당 괜찮아?
M 실은 어제 거기서 먹었거든.
W 알았어, 그럼 타코 가판대에 가자.
M 그게 좋겠다.

Q 대화에 따르면 옳은 것은?
(a) 여자는 점심을 건너뛰기를 원한다.
(b) 남자는 어제 델리 식당에서 식사를 했다.
(c) 여자는 음식을 배달시킬 것이다.
(d) 남자는 타코를 먹고 싶어 하지 않는다.

starving 몹시 배가 고픈 **stand** 노점, 가판대

28

Listen to a conversation between a passenger and a bus driver.

> M Is this the bus to Boston?
> W It is. I just need to see your ticket.
> M Uh-oh… where is it?
> W You have to have a ticket to board the bus.
> M Oh no, I must have lost it somewhere!
> W If you hurry, you can buy another before we depart.

Q Which is correct according to the conversation?
(a) The bus is leaving from Boston.
(b) The man did not have his ticket with him.
(c) The man can buy a ticket from the driver.
(d) There are no more bus tickets available.

승객과 버스운전사의 대화를 들으시오.

M 이게 보스턴행 버스인가요?
W 맞습니다. 표를 보여주셔야 합니다.
M 어어… 어디 있지?
W 버스에 승차하시려면 표가 있어야 합니다.
M 아 이런, 어딘가에서 잃어버렸나 봐요!
W 서두르시면, 출발하기 전에 표를 다시 사실 수 있습니다.

Q 대화에 따르면 옳은 것은?
(a) 버스는 보스턴에서 출발한다.
(b) 남자는 표를 소지하고 있지 않았다.
(c) 남자는 운전기사에게서 표를 살 수 있다.
(d) 더는 남아 있는 버스표가 없다.

board 승채[탑승]하다 **depart** 출발하다

29

Listen to a conversation in a restaurant.

> W Hi, Bill. Are you having your usual today?
> M Actually, no, I think I'll have chocolate cake and a coffee.
> W I'm afraid we're out of cake right now.
> M All right, then, the usual will be fine.
> W A slice of apple pie it is. Still want the coffee?
> M Yes, that'd be great. Thanks.

Q What can be inferred from the conversation?
(a) The man regularly eats apple pie.
(b) The restaurant only serves desserts.
(c) The woman is a relative of the man.
(d) The restaurant is known for its pies.

식당에서 이뤄지는 대화를 들으시오.

W 안녕하세요, 빌리. 오늘도 늘 먹던 걸로 할 거예요?
M 아뇨, 초콜릿 케이크와 커피를 먹을까 해요.
W 안타깝게도 지금 케이크가 다 떨어졌어요.
M 좋아요. 그럼 늘 먹던 것도 괜찮을 것 같네요.
W 애플파이 한 조각이요. 커피도 드려요?
M 네, 그럼 좋겠네요. 고마워요.

Q 대화로부터 추론할 수 있는 것은?
(a) 남자는 애플파이를 자주 먹는다.
(b) 이 식당은 디저트만 취급한다.
(c) 여자는 남자의 친척이다.
(d) 이 식당은 파이로 유명하다.

be out of ~이 다 떨어지고 없다 **the usual** 늘 먹던[마시던] 것
regularly 정기적으로, 자주 **serve** 제공하다 **dessert** 후식, 디저트
relative 친척 **be known for** ~로 잘 알려져 있다

30

Listen to a conversation in a workplace.

> M Jane, I need to speak with you.
> W Yes, Mr. Chan. Is there a problem?
> M It's about your sales numbers this past month.
> W I know. I've been off my game lately.
> M Well, do you think you can recover it soon?
> W I think so. I have a good feeling about this month.

Q What can be inferred from the conversation?

(a) The woman's recent performance has been poor.

(b) The woman has broken company regulations.

(c) The man thinks the woman is recovering fast.

(d) The man is going to fire the woman.

직장에서 이뤄지는 대화를 들으시오.

M 제인, 얘기를 좀 해야겠어요.

W 네, 챈 씨. 무슨 문제 있나요?

M 지난달 제인 씨의 영업 실적에 관해서요.

W 알고 있습니다. 최근에 제 실적이 부진했어요.

M 음, 조만간 원상태로 회복될 수 있을까요?

W 그럴 겁니다. 이번 달에는 분위기가 좋아요.

Q 대화로부터 추론할 수 있는 것은?

(a) 여자의 최근 실적이 저조했다.

(b) 여자가 회사 규정을 어겼다.

(c) 남자는 여자가 빠르게 회복하고 있다고 생각한다.

(d) 남자는 여자를 해고할 것이다.

off one's game 평소보다 못한, 부진한 **lately** 최근에 **recent** 최근의
performance 실적, 성과 **regulation** 규정 **fire** 해고하다

Part IV

31

Discoveries of new insect and plant species are announced quite often, and scientists estimate that there are likely to be many more to discover. To uncover a unique species of mammal, on the other hand, is quite rare. But that's just what happened in August of 2013 when the olinguito was unveiled to the world. This tiny relative of the raccoon has been living high in the trees of tropical forests in Colombia and Ecuador completely unknown to science.

Q What is mainly being discussed in the report?

(a) How new insects and plants are often found

(b) How tropical forests have unknown species

(c) A noteworthy discovery of a rare mammal

(d) The difficulty of discovering new species

새로운 종의 곤충 및 식물의 발견은 꽤 자주 알려지고 있으며, 과학자들은 아직도 발견할 것들이 더 많이 있는 것으로 추정하고 있다. 반면에 특이한 종의 포유류를 발견하는 것은 매우 드물다. 그런데 2013년 8월에 올링귀토가 세상에 공개되면서 바로 그런 일이 일어났다. 미국 너구리 과에 속하는 이 작은 동물은 과학계에 전혀 알려지지 않은 채 콜롬비아와 에콰도르에 있는 열대 숲의 나무 꼭대기에서 살아왔다.

Q 보도에서 주로 다루어지고 있는 것은?

(a) 어떻게 새로운 곤충 및 식물이 자주 발견되는가

(b) 어떻게 열대 숲에 알려져 있지 않은 생물 종들이 존재하는가

(c) 주목할 만한 희귀한 포유류의 발견

(d) 새로운 생물 종 발견의 어려움

estimate 추정하다 **uncover** 알아내다, 밝혀내다 **mammal** 포유류
rare 희귀한 **unveil** 공개하다, 밝히다 **tiny** 작은 **relative** 동족
raccoon 미국 너구리 **completely** 완전히, 전혀 **noteworthy**
주목할 만한

32

For café-quality flavor, there's just no substitute for a burr grinder. Unlike traditional blade grinders, which are often sold for grinding spices, a burr grinder renders maximum flavor from your coffee beans. Its multitude of incising surfaces also ensures an even consistency, so you get a perfect espresso grind every time. While burr grinders can be expensive, MarkTen's XL11 model is currently on sale for just $149. Try one today and taste the difference.

Q What is mainly being advertised?

(a) A gourmet espresso machine on sale

(b) An upscale grinder for coffee beans

(c) A café that sells grinders for spices and coffee

(d) A brand of instant coffee with café-quality flavor

카페 수준의 향을 위해서는, 버 그라인더만 한 것이 없습니다. 주로 향신료를 분쇄하는 용도로 판매되는 전통적인 블레이드 그라인더와 달리, 버 그라인더는 원두로부터 최대의 향을 냅니다. 여러 개의 톱날 면은 또한 고르고 일정하도록 해 주어, 항상 최상의 에스프레소 가루를 얻을 수 있습니다. 버 그라인더는 비쌀 수 있지만, MarkTen's XL11 모델은 현재 세일해서 불과 149달러입니다. 오늘 경험해 보시고 그 차이를 느껴보세요.

Q 주로 광고하고 있는 것은?

(a) 세일 중인 최고급 에스프레소 기계

(b) 고급 원두 분쇄기

(c) 향신료와 원두를 위한 분쇄기를 판매하는 카페

(d) 카페 수준의 향을 가진 인스턴트커피 상품

flavor 풍미, 향 **substitute** 대체물, 대용물 **grinder** 분쇄기 **spice**
향신료 **render** 주다 **maximum** 최대의 **multitude** 다수 **incise**
새기다 **even** 고른, 일정한 **consistency** 일관성 **currently** 현재
gourmet 최고급의 **upscale** 평균 이상의, 상류 계급의

33

The Centers for Disease Control and Prevention records an average of 30,000 cases of Lyme disease annually in the United States. But studies suggest that the true number of individuals afflicted with the illness is most likely 10 times higher. If this is true, Lyme disease represents one of the foremost health concerns in the nation and deserves intensified attention. Programs must be instituted to control the proliferation of the black-legged ticks which serve as carriers of Lyme disease.

Q According to the studies, how many cases of Lyme disease are most likely to occur each year?

(a) 30,000 cases

(b) 100,000 cases

(c) 130,000 cases

(d) 300,000 cases

질병 통제 및 예방 센터에는 미국에서 해마다 평균 3만 건의 라임병이 기록된다. 그러나 조사에 따르면 이 질병에 걸린 사람들의 실제 숫자는 10배가 넘을 것이라고 한다. 만약 이것이 사실이라면, 라임병은 미국에서 가장 큰 건강상 문제 중 하나로서 심층적인 관심을 기울여야 마땅하다. 라임병의 매개체인 라임 진드기의 확산을 통제하기 위한 정책이 도입되어야 한다.

Q 조사에 따르면, 매년 몇 건의 라임병이 발생할 가능성이 가장 높은가?

(a) 3만 건

(b) 10만 건

(c) 13만 건

(d) 30만 건

prevention 예방 **Lyme disease** 라임병(진드기가 옮기는 세균성 감염증) **annually** 해마다 **afflicted with** ~으로 고통받는 **represent** 대표하다 **foremost** 가장 앞선 **intensified** 심층적인 **institute** 도입하다 **proliferation** 급증, 확산 **black-legged tick** 라임 진드기 **carrier** 보균자, 매개체

34

At the western end of Winnemucca Lake, in a dry lakebed in the state of Nevada, lie several boulders decorated with ancient petroglyphs, or rock engravings. Some are relatively simple, composed of straight lines and swirls, while others appear to depict flowers, trees, and leaves. At around 10,000 years old, they are known as the oldest such carvings found to date in North America. Other ancient findings in the area include a mummified body in a cave and other human artifacts, including textiles, at nearby sites.

Q Which is correct about the petroglyphs according to the lecture?

(a) They were the only artifacts discovered in the area.

(b) They show complex scenes of people and nature.

(c) They are located beneath the surface of a lake.

(d) They are most notable because of their age.

네바다주의 말라붙은 호수바닥에 있는 위네뮤카 호수의 서쪽 끝에는, 고대 암각화로 장식된 바위들이 몇 개 있다. 일부는 비교적 단순하게, 직선과 소용돌이무늬로 이루어져 있는 반면, 꽃이나 나무, 나뭇잎들을 그린 것으로 보이는 것들도 있다. 약 1만 년 정도 된 것으로, 그것들은 북아메리카에서 발견된 조각 중에서는 연대가 가장 오래된 것으로 알려져 있다. 그 지역의 다른 고대 발견물 중에는 동굴에 있는 인간의 미라가 있고, 근처 유적지에서 직물을 비롯한 기타 인간이 만든 공예품들이 있다.

Q 강의에 따르면 암각화에 대해서 옳은 것은?

(a) 그 지역에서 발견된 유일한 공예품들이다.

(b) 사람과 자연의 복잡한 장면들을 보여 주고 있다.

(c) 호수 표면 아래에 있다.

(d) 연대 때문에 가장 주목을 받는다.

lakebed 호수 바닥 **lie** 놓여 있다 **boulder** 바위 **petroglyph** 암각화 **engraving** 조각 **relatively** 비교적 **composed of** ~로 이루어진 **straight line** 직선 **swirl** 소용돌이무늬 **depict** 묘사하다 **carving** 조각품 **date** 연대를 추정하다 **findings** 〈복수형으로〉 발견물 **mummify** 미라로 만들다 **artifact** 공예품 **textile** 직물 **notable** 주목할 만한

35

Are you looking for someone to bankroll your next travel adventure? Then, enter the Adventure Digest Competition! The Australian Tourism Board and *Expedition Magazine* are looking to fund a team of explorers for a month of travel on the continent. Anyone can enter and entrants should submit examples of past writing or photography work, along with a proposed travel itinerary. Finalists will be chosen by popular vote, and then the senior editor of *Expedition Magazine* will select the winning team. Enter today!

Q Which is correct according to the announcement?

(a) Only professional writers and photographers need apply.

(b) Applicants must come up with their own travel plans.

(c) *Expedition Magazine*'s editor will select all finalists.

(d) Explorers will be financed for several months.

여러분의 다음 모험 여행에 자금을 지원해 줄 누군가를 찾고 계십니까? 그렇다면 어드벤처 다이제스트 대회에 참가하십시오! 호주 관광청과 〈익스피디션 매거진〉에서는 한 팀의 탐험가들에게 한 달 동안의 호주 여행 경비를 지원하고자 합니다. 누구나 참가할 수 있으며 참가자들은 예전의 글이나 사진 작품 샘플과 함께 여행 일정 제안서를 제출해야 합니다. 결승 진출자들은 대중의 투표로 선정되며, 그 후 〈익스피디션 매거진〉의 편집장이 우승팀을 선정합니다. 오늘 참가하세요!

Q 안내방송에 따르면 옳은 것은?

(a) 전문 작가 및 사진작가만이 지원할 수 있다.

(b) 지원자들은 자신의 여행 계획을 세워야 한다.

(c) 〈익스피디션 매거진〉의 편집장이 결승 진출자 전원을 선발한다.

(d) 탐험가들은 몇 달 동안 재정 지원을 받게 된다.

bankroll 재정을 지원하다, 돈을 대다(= fund) **explorer** 탐험가 **continent** 대륙 **entrant** 참가자 **submit** 제출하다 **itinerary** 여행 일정표 **finalist** 결승 진출자 **senior editor** 편집장 **applicant** 지원자, 신청자 **come up with** ~을 생각해내다

36

Everything about newly discovered Kepler 78b, a planet 700 light-years from Earth, is extreme. Its orbital radius, the distance from the center of the planet to the center of its star, is only three times the radius of the star itself. Given this proximity, temperatures at the planet's surface are likely to be in the neighborhood of 5,000 degrees Fahrenheit. And its orbital path is so short that it completes a full orbit around its star in only 8.5 hours.

Q What can be inferred about Kepler 78b from the talk?

(a) A quick orbit is expected given its orbital radius.

(b) Kepler 78b is unusually hot despite its location.

(c) Its star is relatively small in comparison to its planet.

(d) Detailed analysis of it is impossible due to distance.

지구로부터 700광년 떨어진 행성인, 새로 발견된 케플러 78b에 대한 모든 것은 극단적이다. 행성의 중심부에서 모성(태양)의 중심부까지의 거리인 궤도 반경은 행성 자체의 반경의 세 배밖에 되지 않는다. 이렇게 가깝다는 것을 고려하면, 행성 표면의 온도는 화씨 5,000도 근처가 될 것으로 보인다. 또한, 궤도가 너무 짧아서 8.5시간이면 모성 주위의 궤도를 완전히 돌 수 있다.

Q 강의로부터 케플러 78b에 대해서 추론할 수 있는 것은?

(a) 그것의 궤도 반경을 고려할 때 짧은 궤도 주기가 예상된다.

(b) 케플러 78b는 위치와 맞지 않게 특이하게 뜨겁다.

(c) 행성과 비교했을 때 모성이 상대적으로 작다.

(d) 그것은 멀리 떨어져 있어서 자세한 분석이 불가능하다.

light-year 광년 **extreme** 극단적인 **orbital** 궤도의 **radius** 반지름, 반경 **distance** 거리 **proximity** 가까움

Part V

37-38

Did you know that only 30% of mentally ill children in our community receive adequate treatments? All children are the future of our society, and we must do something about this serious problem. That's why we've set the goal of raising at least $300,000 by September 19th. Donate any amount of money and help us support all these precious children. Every donor will be automatically entered into our drawing to win a variety of prizes. These prizes include a trip for three people to Toronto with Green Airlines, a two-year subscription to *Children's Health Magazine*, and lunch with one of the celebrities living in our community. Making a donation is as easy as calling us at 760-555-7798. Make a phone call today and save our children.

우리 지역사회에서, 정신 질환이 있는 아동들 가운데 30%만이 충분한 치료를 받는다는 사실을 아셨나요? 아동들은 모두 우리 사회의 미래이기 때문에, 이 심각한 문제에 대해 뭔가를 해야만 합니다. 그래서 저희는 9월 19일까지 30만 달러를 모금하는 목표를 세웠습니다. 액수가 얼마이든 기부하셔서, 저희가 이 모든 귀중한 아동들을 지원하는 데 도움을 주십시오. 기부자들은 모두 다양한 상을 받을 수 있는 추첨에 자동으로 응모됩니다. 이 상에는 그린항공사를 이용해서 3명이 토론토로 여행하는 것, 「아동 건강 잡지」 2년 구독권, 그리고 우리 지역 사회에 살고 있는 유명인과의 점심 식사가 포함됩니다. 기부는 760-555-7798로 전화하는 것만큼이나 간편합니다. 오늘 전화하셔서 우리의 아이들을 구해 주세요.

37 Q Which of the following is included in the prizes of the drawing?

(a) An overseas trip for two people for three weeks

(b) A meal with a resident of the community

(c) A two-month subscription to a health magazine

(d) A $300,000 cash prize

Q 다음 중 추첨의 상에 포함되어 있는 것은?

(a) 2명이 3주 동안 해외 여행하는 것

(b) 지역 사회 주민과의 식사

(c) 건강 관련 잡지의 2개월 구독권

(d) 30만 달러의 상금

해설 NEW TEPS의 중요 출제 유형이기 때문에, 꼼꼼하게 익혀두어야 한다. (a)는 인원이 3명이고, 기간은 나와 있지 않기 때문에 오답이다. (c)는 구독 기간이 2년이기 때문에 정답이 아니다. (d)는 30만 달러가 상금이 아니라, 모금 목표액이기 때문에 오답이다. 따라서 정답은 주어진 내용과 일치하는 (b)이다.

38 Q Which is correct according to the announcement?

(a) 30% of the children in the community are mentally ill.

(b) The majority of mentally ill children in the community don't get adequate medical attention.

(c) The charitable organization wants to raise $700,000 by the end of September.

(d) In order to enter into the drawing, donors need to make at least two phone calls to the organization.

Q 안내에 따르면, 다음 중 옳은 것은?

(a) 지역사회 아동들의 30%가 정신 질환이 있다.

(b) 지역사회에서 정신 질환이 있는 아동들의 대다수는 충분한 의학적 치료를 받지 못한다.

(c) 이 자선 단체는 9월 말까지 70만 달러를 모으고자 한다.

(d) 추첨에 응모하기 위해서 기부자는 단체에 최소한 두 번 전화를 걸어야 한다.

해설 (a)는 중요한 오답 유형이기 때문에 꼼꼼하게 익혀두어야 한다. 지역 사회 아동들의 30%가 정신 질환을 앓고 있는 것이 아니라, 정신 질환을 앓고 있는 아동들 가운데 30%만이 충분한 치료를 받는 것이다. (c)는 목표 금액과 기간이 모두 틀렸기 때문에 오답이다. (d)는 한 번으로 충분하기 때문에 정답이 아니다. 따라서 정답은 (b)이다. TEPS에서 말하는 the majority는 보통 50%가 넘는 것을 가리킨다는 사실도 기억해 두어야 한다.

mentally 정신적으로 **adequate** 충분한 **goal** 목표 **donate** 기부하다 **donor** 기부자 **drawing** 추첨 **subscription** 구독; 구독료 **celebrity** 유명 인사 **resident** 주민, 거주자 **medical** 의학의, 의료의 **charitable organization** 자선 단체

The history of the microwave oven began in 1939, when the British physicist Sir John Randall and Dr. H.A. Boot invented the magnetron, which was used to enhance radar systems. Since then, numerous companies have been involved in inventing and popularizing the microwave oven. Raytheon was an American company which produced magnetrons, and an employee named Percy L. Spencer found out that the microwaves from magnetrons could be used to cook food. In 1947, the first microwave oven was invented by Spencer and his co-workers. In 1955, the first home microwave oven was developed by Tappan. In 1967, the first home countertop microwave oven was invented by Amana, which had been acquired by Raytheon in 1965. Later, Japanese companies including Sanyo and Korean companies such as Samsung helped popularize the microwave oven.

전자레인지의 역사는 1939년에 시작되었는데, 이 해에 영국의 물리학자 존 랜덜 경(卿)과 H.A. 부트 박사가 마그네트론을 발명했으며, 마그네트론은 레이더 시스템을 향상시키기 위해 쓰였습니다. 그 해 이래로, 수없이 많은 기업들이 전자레인지를 발명하고 대중화하는 데 관여했습니다. 레이시언은 마그네트론을 생산하는 미국 회사였는데요, 퍼시 L. 스펜서라는 직원이 마그네트론에서 나오는 극초단파가 음식을 요리하는 데 쓰일 수 있다는 사실을 알아냈습니다. 1947년에 최초의 전자레인지가 스펜서와 동료들에 의해 발명되었어요. 1955년에 최초의 가정용 전자레인지가 태편에 의해 개발되었어요. 1967년에는 최초의 가정용 주방용 조리대에 놓는 전자레인지가 아마나에 의해 발명되었는데요, 아마나는 1965년에 레이시언에 인수된 회사였습니다. 이후에 산요를 포함한 일본 업체들, 그리고 삼성과 같은 한국 회사들이 전자레인지를 대중화하는 데 기여했습니다.

39 Q What is the main purpose of the lecture?

(a) To clarify what the original function of the magnetron was

(b) To elucidate the reason why Japanese companies competed with Korean ones in popularizing the microwave oven

(c) To explain how some companies helped to make the microwave oven available and popular

(d) To emphasize the need to render the microwave oven more user-friendly

Q 강의의 주된 목적은?

(a) 마그네트론의 본래 기능이 무엇이었는지를 분명하게 하는 것

(b) 전자레인지를 대중화하는 데 일본 업체들이 한국 업체들과 경쟁했던 이유를 설명하는 것

(c) 어떻게 몇몇 업체들이 전자레인지를 이용 가능하게 만들어서 인기를 끌게 했는지를 설명하는 것

(d) 전자레인지를 보다 사용자 친화적으로 만들어야 하는 필요를 강조하는 것

해설 강의의 전반적인 흐름에 유의해서 풀어야 하는 문항이다. 대체로 강의의 초반부에 정답이 제시되는데, 때로는 두 번째 문장에 정답이 있기도 하다는 점에 유의해야 한다. 강의의 주된 초점은 전자레인지의 대중화를 이끌어낸 업체들에 있기 때문에 정답은 (c)이다.

40 Q What can be inferred from the lecture?

(a) Raytheon was a company which was founded to mass-produce microwave ovens.

(b) Raytheon decided to acquire Amana for religious reasons.

(c) The first microwave oven might not have been convenient for home use.

(d) Tappan was an American company that mass-produced magnetrons.

Q 강의로부터 추론할 수 있는 것은?

(a) 레이시언은 전자레인지를 대량 생산하기 위해 창립된 회사였다.

(b) 레이시언은 종교적 이유에서 아마나를 인수하기로 결정했다.

(c) 최초의 전자레인지는 가정에서 사용하기에 편리하지 않았을 수 있다.

(d) 태편은 마그네트론을 대량 생산하는 미국 회사였다.

해설 (a)는 전자레인지가 아니라 마그네트론이라고 하면 정답이 될 수도 있다. 이처럼 부분적으로 틀린 정보를 제시하는 오답 유형은 중요한 오답 유형이다. (b)는 강의에서 전혀 말하지 않았기 때문에 추론할 수 없는 내용이다. (d)는 레이시언에 대한 추론으로 가능할 수 있지만, 태편에 대한 추론은 아니다. 태편이 최초의 전자레인지를 개발한 후 아마나에서 주방 조리대에 두고 쓸 수 있는 가정용 제품이 개발되었다고 했으므로 정답은 (c)이다.

microwave oven 전자레인지 **physicist** 물리학자 **magnetron** 마그네트론 **enhance** 향상시키다 **numerous** 수없이 많은 **popularize** 대중화하다 **microwave** 극초단파 **co-worker** 동료 **countertop** 주방용 조리대 **clarify** 명확하게 하다 **elucidate** 해명하다, 설명하다 **render** 만들다 **mass-produce** 대량 생산하다

Vocabulary

p.129

Part I

1 정답 (c)
A 주디에게서 네가 어젯밤에 어디에 있었는지 알아냈어.
B 네가 내 일에 그만 좀 <u>참견</u>했으면 좋겠어.

find out 알아내다 **affair** 일 **serve** 접대하다 **wade** 헤치고 나아가다
intrude 참견하다 **conform** 따르다

2 정답 (b)
A 여보세요, 911이죠? 방금 친구가 사다리에서 떨어져서 머리를 심하게
다쳤어요.
B 침착하세요, 구급차를 <u>보낼게요</u>.

fall off ~에서 떨어지다 **ladder** 사다리 **calm** 침착한 **forward**
전달하다 **send** 보내다 **label** 라벨을 붙이다 **ship** 운송하다

3 정답 (d)
A 너는 공원을 걷는 것을 왜 좋아하니?
B 그게 하루의 긴 근무를 마친 후에 <u>활력을 주는</u> 것 같아.

workday 근무일 **heed** 주의를 기울이다 **accord** 일치하다
obfuscate 애매하게 만들다 **revitalize** 새로운 활력을 주다

4 정답 (d)
A 제 글에 대한 솔직한 의견에 감사드립니다.
B 내가 정말로 어떻게 생각하는지를 너에게 말하지 않는다면 내 일을 <u>태
만히</u> 하는 게 되는 거지.

appreciate 감사히 여기다 **feedback** 의견, 피드백 **pragmatic**
실용적인 **gallant** 용감한 **devoid** 결여된, 없는 **remiss** 태만한

5 정답 (b)
A 제 일을 개선하기 위한 어떤 제안 사항 있습니까?
B 아뇨, 당신이 해온 대로 제가 <u>계속할게요</u>.

suggestion 제안 **improve** 개선하다 **think through** 충분히
생각하다 **carry on** 계속하다 **spin out** 오래 끌다 **tune in** 채널을
맞추다

6 정답 (c)
A 새로 복용하는 약에 부작용이 있습니까?
B 아침에 좀 <u>무기력하게</u> 만드는 경향이 있어요.

side effect 부작용 **medication** 약 **tend to** ~하는 경향이 있다
courteous 정중한 **insolent** 무례한 **lethargic** 무기력한 **suspect**
의심스러운

7 정답 (b)
A 저 밴의 운전사가 우리 차를 거의 뒤에서 들이받을 뻔했어!
B 그건 <u>의도치 않은</u> 실수인 게 확실해.

nearly 거의 **rear-end** 후미를 들이받다 **expedite** 촉진하다
inadvertent 고의가 아닌 **conspicuous** 눈에 잘 띄는, 튀는
magnanimous 도량이 넓은

8 정답 (d)
A 셰릴은 확실히 스포츠에서 이기는 것을 좋아해.
B 그건 삶에 대한 그녀의 전반적인 태도를 <u>전형적으로 보여 주는</u> 거지.

certainly 확실히 **in general** 전반적으로 **partake** 차지하다, 참가하다
divert 우회시키다 **subordinate** 경시하다 **exemplify** 전형적인
예가 되다

9 정답 (b)
A 얼굴에 무슨 일이야?
B 어젯밤에 농구 경기를 한 후에 약간의 <u>실랑이</u>가 있었어.

dribble 드리블 **scuffle** 실랑이, 난투 **mettle** 패기 **bobble** 털실
방울

10 정답 (b)
A 술집에서 담배 피울 수 있던 때가 그리워.
B 정부에서 그 금지법을 <u>폐지하리라고</u> 기대하지 마.

miss 그리워하다 **bar** 술집 **ban** 금지(법) **make way for** ~에게
양보하다 **do away with** ~을 폐지하다 **miss out on** ~을 놓치다
fall back on ~에 의지하다

Part II

11 정답 (b)
무대 연극은 영국의 엘리자베스 여왕 시대에 일반 대중들 사이에서 인기
있는 <u>소일거리</u>였다.

live theater 무대 연극 **general public** 일반 대중 **mission** 임무
pastime 소일거리, 여가활동 **relief** 안도, 안심 **station** 역; 방송국

12 정답 (b)
부유함만으로는 의미 있는 삶을 <u>보장하기</u>에 충분하지 않다.

wealth 부 **meaningful** 의미 있는 **coax** 구슬리다 **ensure**
보장하다 **fulfill** 충족시키다 **submit** 제출하다

13 정답 (a)
팀 주치의에 따르면, 그 풀백 선수는 부상에서 <u>회복하는</u> 데 꼬박 석 달이
필요할 거라고 한다.

physician 의사 **fullback** (축구, 하키, 럭비에서) 풀백 선수 **injury**
부상 **recover** 회복하다 **deepen** 악화시키다 **wander** 거닐다,
헤매다 **shelter** 피하다

14 정답 (b)
호텔 전 직원은 손님이 머무시는 내내 손님이 필요로 하는 모든 것을 확실
히 <u>보살펴 드릴</u> 것입니다.

staff (전체) 직원 **duration** (지속되는) 기간 **count** (수를) 세다
attend to ~을 처리하다[돌보다] **remark** 발언하다 **conduct** 행하다

15 정답 (a)
새로운 인사관리 서비스의 <u>실행</u>은 전 직원이 교육을 마칠 때까지 미뤄야
할 것이다.

human resource 인력, 인사관리 **complete** 완료하다
implementation 이행, 시행 **accommodation** 숙소
embarkation 탑승, 착수 **divination** 점(치기)

16 정답 (a)

남자는 자신의 언사가 단지 <u>반어적인</u> 표현일 뿐이었다는 주장으로 화난 친구를 납득시킬 수 없었다.

convince 납득시키다 **indignant** 분개한 **claim** 주장 **remark** 언급 **attempt at** ~하려는 시도 **ironic** 반어적인 **abusive** 모욕적인, 학대하는 **succinct** 간결한 **trivial** 사소한

17 정답 (a)

많은 미국 원주민 문화에서는 바위나 나무 같은 자연물에 특정한 초자연적인 속성을 <u>부여하였다</u>.

supernatural 초자연적인 **attribute** 속성 **object** 물건 **ascribe** 부여하다 **describe** 묘사하다 **subscribe** 구독하다 **inscribe** 쓰다, 새기다

18 정답 (b)

수년간 투표권을 위한 캠페인을 펼친 후에, 미국 여성들은 1920년에 <u>투표권</u>을 인정받았다.

campaign (사회·정치적 목적을 위한 조직적인) 운동[활동] **vote** 투표하다 **grant** 승인하다 **surveillance** 감시 **suffrage** 투표권, 참정권 **clemency** 관대한 처분 **constitution** 헌법

19 정답 (a)

교장은 교사 휴게실 바로 밖에서 <u>엿듣고 있는</u> 학생들 중 한 명을 붙잡았다.

principal 교장 **lounge** 휴게실 **eavesdrop** 엿듣다 **undervalue** 과소평가하다 **instigate** 선동하다 **collate** 수집 분석하다

20 정답 (a)

당연히 이사회 의장은 자신의 권력이 동료 이사들에 의해 약화되는 것에 <u>적대적이었다</u>.

not surprisingly 당연히 **chairman** 의장 **board** 이사회 **authority** 권력, 권위 **undermine** 약화시키다 **inimical** 적대적인 **apocryphal** 저작자가 미심쩍은, 외경의 **mercurial** 변덕스러운 **diabolical** 끔찍한, 악마 같은

21 정답 (b)

폭풍으로 전기가 나가게 될 경우, <u>보조</u> 전력시스템이 자동으로 작동을 시작하게 된다.

knock out 나가떨어지다 **automatically** 자동으로 **engage** (작동을) 시작하다 **burrow** 파묻다 **auxiliary** 보조의 **streamlined** 유선형의 **entrepreneurial** 기업가의

22 정답 (d)

뉴턴은 태양광선이 프리즘에 의해 <u>굴절된</u> 후에 두 번째 프리즘에 의해 재구성될 수 있음을 보여주었다.

beam 빛줄기 **prism** 프리즘 **reconstitute** 재구성하다 **impair** 손상하다 **extend** 연장하다 **demolish** 무너뜨리다 **refract** 굴절시키다

23 정답 (d)

카렌은 어릴 때 가지고 놀던 장난감을 바라보자 <u>향수</u>가 밀려왔다.

be beset by ~으로 시달리다, 괴로움을 당하다 **austerity** 궁핍, 금욕 **limbo** 불확실한 상태 **disparity** (불공평한) 차이 **nostalgia** 향수

24 정답 (a)

스페인의 '황소들의 질주' 동안 매년 참가자 몇 명은 <u>뿔로 들이받히며</u>, 또 다른 이들은 덜 심각한 부상을 입는다.

a handful of 소수의 **severe** 심각한, 중한 **gore** 뿔로 들이받다 **embalm** (시체에) 방부 처리를 하다 **peck** 쪼다 **garble** 왜곡하다

25 정답 (c)

전기 충격기와 후추 스프레이 같은 도구 덕분에 경찰은 장기적인 신체 손상을 유발하지 않고 용의자를 <u>꼼짝 못하게 할</u> 수 있다.

taser 테이저건, 전기충격기 **pepper spray** 후추 스프레이(호신용 분사 액체) **suspect** 용의자 **long-term** 장기간의 **physical** 신체적인 **pursue** 추구하다 **maim** 불구로 만들다 **incapacitate** 무능력하게 하다 **demote** 강등시키다

26 정답 (b)

법원은 오염이 된 부동산에 대한 <u>보상</u>으로 그 가족에게 38,500달러를 지불해야 한다는 판결을 내렸다.

rule 판결을 내리다 **corporation** 기업 **contaminate** 오염시키다 **munificence** 아낌없이 줌, 후함 **restitution** 배상, 보상 **stipend** 봉급 **bastion** 수호자, 보루

27 정답 (a)

상원의원을 구석으로 몰아붙인 후, 시위자들은 그녀가 세제 개혁안에 반대한 것에 대해 계속하여 <u>열변을 토했다</u>.

corner 궁지에 몰아넣다 **senator** 상원의원 **protester** 시위자 **oppose** 반대하다 **proceed** 계속해서 ~하다 **tax reform** 세제 개혁 **bill** 법안 **harangue** 열변을 토하다 **subject** 지배하에 두다 **waive** 면제해주다 **subpoena** (증인으로) 소환하다

28 정답 (d)

낙관적인 추정치가 발표되었음에도 불구하고, 회사 매출은 4사 분기에 <u>감소한</u> 것으로 나타났다.

quarter 분기 **despite** ~에도 불구하고 **optimistic** 낙관적인 **estimate** 추정(치) **forecast** 예상하다 **goad** 못살게 굴다 **belittle** 하찮게 만들다 **egress** 밖으로 나가다 **slacken** 감소하다

29 정답 (a)

종교적 체험으로 알려진 일을 경험한 후에, 그 범죄자는 자신의 <u>방탕한</u> 방식을 버리고 다른 사람들에게 봉사하는 데 헌신했다.

undergo 겪다 **purported** (사실이 아닐지도 모르지만) ~라고 알려진 **criminal** 범죄자 **give up** 포기하다 **dedicate oneself to** ~에 헌신하다 **heinous** 악랄한, 극악무도한 **rancorous** 악의에 불타는 **dexterous** 능수능란한 **solicitous** 세심히 배려하는

30 정답 (a)

절대 빙빙 <u>돌려 말하는</u> 사람이 아닌 매니저는 느려터진 직원에게 자신이 그를 어떻게 생각하는지를 정확히 말했다.

laggard 느림보[굼벵이] **exactly** 정확히 **mince** 완곡히 말하다 **castrate** 거세하다 **pique** 불쾌하게 하다 **grit** (이를) 갈다

Grammar

p.133

Part I

1 정답 (d)
A 영업 회의에서 늦게 나왔어요?
B 네, 그게 그렇게 오래 걸릴 줄 전혀 예상 못했어요.

해설 expect는 목적어로 that절, 또는 〈(목적어)+to부정사〉를 취한다. sales meeting을 목적어인 it으로 받고 목적보어로 to부정사를 쓴 (d)가 정답이다. 절의 형태를 취한 (a)는 takes 대신 would take를 쓰면 정답이 될 수 있다.

get out of ~에서 떠나다, 나가다

2 정답 (c)
A 유감스럽게도, 손님의 성함으로 예약된 사항이 없습니다.
B 하지만 제 예약은 거의 두 달 전에 한 건데요.

해설 태에 관한 문제이다. 주어인 reservation은 '이루어지는' 대상이므로 수동태가 되어야 한다. 선택지 중에서 수동태를 나타내는 동사는 (c)이다. make a reservation(예약을 하다)라는 표현을 수동태로 나타낸 것이다.

unfortunately 불행하게도   booking 예약

3 정답 (c)
A 버트가 자유롭게 우리 축구팀에 들어올 수 있을까요?
B 그가 들어올 수 있게 되든지, 아니면 다른 사람을 찾아야죠.

해설 빈칸 뒤에 or를 보고 바로 either A or B(A와 B 둘 중 하나인)라는 상관접속사를 떠올릴 수 있어야 한다. either 뒤의 어순이 맞게 쓰인 (c)가 정답이다. neither는 nor와 짝을 이루어 '둘 다 아닌'이라는 뜻으로 쓰인다.

join 합류하다

4 정답 (b)
A 요즘 일이 정말 바쁜가 봐요.
B 네, 그렇게 빡빡한 일정을 갖는 것이 어떤 것이었는지 잊고 있었네요.

해설 어순을 묻는 문제이다. What is A like?는 'A는 어떠냐?'라는 뜻으로 이때 주어인 A 자리에 to부정사나 동명사가 올 때는 가주어 it을 쓰고 to부정사나 동명사를 문장 뒤에 둔다. forgot의 목적어가 되는 간접의문문의 어순은 〈의문사+주어+동사〉이므로 (b)가 정답이다.

demanding 힘든, 빡빡한

5 정답 (c)
A 네가 이번에 절대로 승진을 못 할 것 같아.
B 이제 그건 분명한 사실이야.

해설 빈칸 앞에 has는 현재완료 시제를 이루는 조동사이므로 바로 다음에는 과거분사가 와야 하며 부정어 never나 not은 조동사와 과거분사 사이에 오므로 (c)가 정답이다. 직역하면 '그 사실이 지금보다 더 분명했던 적은 없어'라는 뜻으로 이제 정말로 분명한 사실이 되었다는 뜻이다.

promotion 승진   clear 분명한, 확실한

6 정답 (b)
A 당신이 전화 회의에 빠졌다니 믿을 수가 없네요.
B 그게, 저에게 다시 알려 주셨다면 안 그랬을 텐데요.

해설 주절에 wouldn't have (missed)로 보아 가정법 과거완료 구문임을 알 수 있다. 가정법 과거완료에서 if절에는 had p.p.를 쓰므로 (b)가 정답이다.

conference call 전화 회의   remind 상기시키다

7 정답 (d)
A 선택하셨어요?
B 네, 갈색 가죽 지갑 세 개 모두 살게요.

해설 명사를 수식하는 형용사의 어순을 묻는 문제이다. all은 모든 형용사 및 관사 앞에 위치하고, 일반적인 형용사의 어순은 수량-성질-색깔-재료 순서이다. 따라서 all three(수량) brown(색깔) leather(재료)의 순서인 (d)가 정답이다.

make a selection 선택하다   purse (여성용) 지갑

8 정답 (c)
A 그래서, 에어컨이 너에게 너무 세니?
B 응, 난 그렇게 낮은 온도에는 익숙하지 않아서.

해설 be accustomed to(~에 익숙하다)라는 표현을 알면 쉽게 답을 고를 수 있는 문제이다. 이때 to는 전치사이므로 다음에 명사나 동명사가 나온다는 것에 주의한다. such는 관사와 형용사 앞에 위치한다는 점도 함께 알아둔다.

temperature 온도

9 정답 (c)
A 여기를 방문하면 기억나는 게 있나요?
B 아, 내가 기억하는 그대로예요.

해설 빈칸에는 '내가 기억하는 그대로'라는 뜻이 들어가야 하는데, 이때 '~대로, ~처럼'이라는 뜻의 as를 쓴다. as 뒤에 주어와 동사의 어순이 올바른 (c)가 정답이다. 이때 as는 일종의 관계대명사로서 as 뒤에는 주어, 보어, 목적어가 빠진 불완전한 문장이 오는데, 여기서는 to be의 보어가 빠져 있다.

bring back memories 기억을 되살리다

10 정답 (d)
A 이 매운 칠리를 하나 먹을 수 있으면 먹어 봐.
B 네가 먼저 하나를 먹으면 나도 먹을게.

해설 I dare you to do는 '~해 보라고 부추기다, 즉 해 볼 테면 해 봐'라는 뜻이다. A의 말을 받아 B는 네가 먼저 먹으면 나도 먹겠다는 뜻이다. if 절에 현재 시제가 쓰였으므로 단순 조건을 의미하며, 조건이 성립되었을 때 벌어질 미래를 나타내야 하므로 (d)가 정답이다.

dare 부추기다, 해 보라고 하다

Part II

11 정답 (b)
여론조사에서 관심을 얻지 못해서 그 정치인은 예비 선거에 기권했다.

해설 선택지로 보아 접속사와 주어 없이, 콤마 뒤의 절과 이어지고 있으므로 분사구문이 들어가야 한다. 생략된 분사구문의 주어는 주절의 주어인 the politician으로 fail의 주체가 되므로 능동태를 쓴 (b)가 정답이다.

gain 얻다   traction 견인(력)   poll 여론조사   withdraw 철회하다, 기권하다   primary race 예비 선거

Actual Test 4

Actual Test 4

12 정답 (b)

유럽은 대부분 학생들이 해외 여행할 기회가 주어진다면 방문하겠다고 하는 지역이다.

해설 시제와 태를 묻는 문제이다. 앞에 조동사의 과거형인 would가 있는 것으로 보아 가정법 구문이므로 과거 동사를 쓴 (b)와 (c)가 시제상으로는 맞다. 빈칸 앞의 주어 they가 가리키는 것은 students로, 학생들에게 기회가 '주어지는' 것이므로 수동태인 (b)가 정답이다.

region 지역

13 정답 (b)

개를 찾았다는 소식에 엄청나게 걱정했던 주인은 안도하게 되었다.

해설 relief는 '안도, 안심'이라는 뜻의 추상명사이므로 관사를 붙이거나 복수형으로 쓰지 않는 것이 원칙이다. 하지만 구체적인 행위나 경험을 나타낼 때는 부정관사를 붙이므로 (b)가 정답이다.

relief 안도, 안심 **be worried sick** 엄청나게 걱정하다

14 정답 (a)

그 연구 결과는 확인되면, 우주생물학 분야에서 지대한 결과를 가져오게 될 것이다.

해설 빈칸 앞에 접속사 if가 있으므로 원래는 〈주어+동사〉로 이루어진 절이 나와야 맞다. 하지만 형태상으로 옳은 것처럼 보이는 (c)에서 they는 The study's findings를 가리키므로 수동태가 되어야 맞다. if they are confirmed에서 주어와 be동사를 생략한 형태인 (a)가 정답이다.

far-reaching 지대한 영향을 가져올 **consequence** 결과
astrobiology 우주생물학

15 정답 (d)

유감스럽게도, 회사는 역사상 최악의 분기를 겪고 나서 직원들을 정리 해고할 수밖에 없었다.

해설 선택지로 보아 부정어를 이중으로 사용하는 이중부정 구문이 들어감을 알 수 있다. 문맥상 '유감스럽지 않은 것은 아니지만'이라는 뜻이 되므로, without regret 앞에 not을 붙인다. 접속사 though(비록 ~이지만) 뒤에 주어와 be동사가 생략되어 있다.

regret 유감, 후회 **be forced to** ~할 수밖에 없다 **lay off**
정리해고하다

16 정답 (d)

기자가 정보를 받은 이상한 액센트를 쓰는 남자는 외국 스파이인 것으로 밝혀졌다.

해설 문장의 주어는 The man (with the strange accent)이고 동사는 turned out이므로 그 사이는 주어를 수식하는 관계대명사절임을 알 수 있다. 선행사가 주어인 The man이므로 관계대명사 whom을 써야 하고, 문맥상 '그 남자로부터' 정보를 받았다는 뜻이 되어야 하므로 전치사 from을 붙인 (d)가 정답이다.

tip 조언, 정보 **turn out** ~인 것으로 드러나다

17 정답 (d)

자신의 죄에 답변하기 위해서 법정에 소환되자, 용의자는 나라를 떠나 그 이후로 지금까지 모습을 보이지 않았다.

해설 분사구문이다. 분사구문의 주어인 the suspect가 '소환되는' 대상이므로 수동태가 되어야 하므로 (d)가 정답이다. 소환된 것은 나라를 떠난 것보다 먼저 일어난 일이므로 having been p.p.라는 완료형을 쓴다.

court 법정 **suspect** 용의자 **summon** 소환하다

18 정답 (d)

변덕스러운 이사회에 의해 연이어 CEO가 해고된 것은 창 씨가 떠난 후 채 일 년도 되기 전이었다.

해설 빈칸에는 접속사와 주어가 필요하다. 접속사 before와 주어인 another CEO의 어순에 yet의 위치를 정하는 것이 관건이다. yet another가 '잇따라, 또 하나의' 뜻이므로 (d)가 정답이다.

departure 출발, 떠남 **dismiss** 해고하다 **volatile** 변덕스러운
board 이사회 **yet another** 잇따라, 또 하나의

19 정답 (d)

과학자들이 효소에서 추출한 세포 샘플은 추출 절차 후에 바로 시들었다.

해설 주어가 The cell sample이고 동사는 withered이므로, 그 사이는 주어를 수식하는 관계절이 되어야 한다. 문맥상 '세포 표본으로 부터 효소를 추출하다(extracted the enzyme from the cell sample)'라는 뜻이므로, 선행사인 The cell sample을 받는 관계대명사 which 앞에 전치사 from을 쓴 (d)가 정답이다.

cell 세포 **enzyme** 효소 **wither** 시들다, 말라 죽다 **procedure** 절차
extract 추출하다

20 정답 (c)

일부 아동 전문가들은 어린아이들이 4살 생일이 될 때까지 유치원을 벗어나 있는 것이 좋다고 제안한다.

해설 조동사 문제이다. 문맥상 '~하는 것이 좋다'라는 뜻으로 should나 ought to가 가능한데, 이때 keep은 '두다, 유지하다'라는 뜻으로 young children을 주어로 하면 수동태가 되어야 한다. 따라서 (c)가 정답이다.

childcare 보육 **specialist** 전문가 **recommend** 추천하다, 제안하다
preschool 유치원

21 정답 (c)

시즌 전반기 동안, 볼티모어 오리올스는 거의 기록에 가까운 속도로 경기에서 승리를 거두고 있었다.

해설 어순 문제이다. 관사인 a가 맨 앞에 나오고 명사인 pace가 맨 뒤에 위치해야 한다. record가 '기록'을 뜻하므로, 기록에 가깝다는 뜻으로 앞에 near를 붙인 (c)가 올바른 어순이다.

record 기록 **pace** 속도

22 정답 (b)

시험을 치르는 동안 연필이 부러질 경우, 감독관에게 알리면 연필 한 자루를 더 줄 것이다.

해설 빈칸에 들어갈 대명사는 부러진 연필 말고 다른 연필, 즉 '연필 한 자루 더'를 뜻한다. 따라서 '또 하나의 (것), 추가의 (것)'이라는 뜻의 (b) another를 써야 한다.

notify 알리다 **proctor** 시험 감독관

23 정답 (d)

록히드 C-130 헤라클레스는 화물과 군대를 필요로 하는 곳으로 수송하는 데 주로 사용되는 거대한 4기통 항공기이다.

해설 빈칸 앞이 완전한 문장을 이루므로 빈칸 이하는 수식어가 되어야 한다. 문맥상 앞에 있는 명사 aircraft를 수식하여 '~하는 데 사용되는'이라는 뜻으로 〈used to부정사〉 형태의 분사가 들어가야 알맞다. 분사를 수식하는 부사 often은 분사 앞에 와야 하므로 (d)가 정답이다.

massive 거대한 **cargo** 화물 **troop** 군대 **transport** 수송[운송]하다

24 정답 (d)

예정된 비행으로부터 48시간 이내에 요청되는 어떤 변경에 대해서도 20 달러의 추가 요금이 부과됩니다.

해설 will be levied가 문장의 동사이므로 준동사 형태인 (b)와 (d)가 가능하다. 앞에 있는 명사 changes를 수식하는 분사가 들어가야 하는데, 변경이 '요청되는' 것으로 수동의 관계에 있으므로 과거분사를 쓴 (d)가 정답이다.

surcharge 추가 요금 **levy** 부과하다, 징수하다

25 정답 (d)

이주민 문제는 복잡할 수도 있지만, 그래서 그것들을 정면으로 다루는 것이 그토록 중요하다.

해설 that is why(그래서 ~하다, 그것이 ~한 이유다)라는 구문과 〈it is 형용사 that절〉 구문이 올바로 결합된 문장을 찾아야 한다. (d)가 정답으로, 이때 that은 앞 문장 전체를 가리킨다. it은 빈칸 뒤에 나오는 that절을 대신하는 가주어이다.

immigration 이주, 이민 **complex** 복잡한 **tackle** (문제를) 다루다 **head on** 정면으로, 똑바로

Part III

26 정답 (b) have been having → had been having

(a) A 어젯밤에 왜 그렇게 맥주를 많이 마셨니?
(b) B 그게, 정말 힘든 하루였거든, 알겠어?
(c) A 알아, 하지만 더는 술을 마시지 않겠다고 약속했잖아.
(d) B 지금부터는 더 잘할게, 약속해.

해설 (a)가 어젯밤에 과음한 것에 대해 따지고 있으므로, (b)가 힘든 하루였다고 말한 것은 어제를 가리킨다는 것을 알 수 있다. 따라서 어젯밤이라는 과거의 특정 시점까지의 계속을 나타내는 과거완료 진행으로 had been -ing를 써야 한다.

a tough day 힘든 하루 **from now on** 지금부터

27 정답 (c) Hasn't it → Had it not

(a) A 어젯밤에 못 가서 정말 미안해.
(b) B 괜찮아, 어쨌든 나는 즐거운 시간을 보냈어.
(c) A 눈이 그렇게 심하게 오지 않았더라면, 갈 수 있었을 텐데.
(d) B 정말로, 신경 쓰지 마. 나는 클럽에 가서 밤새 춤췄거든!

해설 (c)는 주절에 〈조동사의 과거형+have p.p.〉가 나오는 것으로 보아 가정법 과거완료 구문이다. 조건절에 if가 없으므로 접속사를 생략하고 주어와 조동사가 도치된 형태이다. 가정법 과거완료 조건절에는 had p.p.를 쓰며, 부정어 not은 조동사와 함께 도치되지 않으므로, Had it not been이 되어야 한다.

make it (약속 장소에) 가다 **end up -ing** 결국 ~하게 되다

28 정답 (c) developed → developing

지구에서 발견된 고대 화성의 운석과 화성에서 발견된 암석의 비교 연구에서 놀라운 발견이 나왔다. 발견된 것들에 기초해서, 과학자들은 약 40억 년 전에 화성에 산소가 풍부한 대기가 존재했다고 여기고 있다. 이것은 지구에서 똑같은 환경이 발전하기 딱 15억 년 전이다. 이는 우리 지구에서는 아직도 매우 발생 초기 단계일 동안 화성에서는 복잡한 생명체가 진화했다 소멸했을 수도 있음을 시사한다.

해설 (c)에서 developed는 앞에 있는 명사인 conditions를 수식하는 분사이다. conditions가 develop의 주체로 능동의 관계에 있기 때문에 현재분사인 developing을 써야 한다.

comparative study 비교 연구 **Martian** 화성의 **meteorite** 운석 **yield** (결과, 수익을) 내다 **astounding** 믿기 어려운, 놀라운 **atmosphere** 대기 **exist** 존재하다 **prior to** ~이전에 **implication** 함축, 암시 **evolve** 진화하다 **perish** 죽다, 소멸되다 **nascent** 발생기의, 초기의

29 정답 (c) that high → so high

다람쥐는 정원을 망치고 단열재를 파괴하며 심지어 전선을 씹어서 화재를 일으키기도 하여 주택 소유주들에게는 정말로 해로운 동물일 수 있습니다. 안심하시려면, 첨단 기술의 초음파 해충박멸기, '다람쥐 퇴치제 5000'을 사용해 보십시오. 이 작은 금속 상자 안에는 여러분이 들을 수 없을 정도로 아주 높은 주파수를 발생시키는 무선 송신기가 들어 있습니다. 하지만 다람쥐는 확실히 들을 수 있으며 그들에게는 이 소리가 매우 커서, 그것들을 여러분의 집 근처에 얼씬도 못하게 합니다.

해설 (c)에서 '너무 ~해서 …할 수 없을 정도로'라는 뜻으로는 so ~ can't 구문을 쓴다. 따라서 that high가 아닌 so high라고 해야 한다.

squirrel 다람쥐 **pest** 해충, 해로운 동물 **ruin** 망치다 **insulation** 단열재 **chew** 씹다 **electrical line** 전선 **put one's minds at ease** ~을 안심[진정]시키다 **high-tech** 최신 기술의 **ultrasonic** 초음파의 **pest repellent** 해충 박멸제 **contain** 담다 **radio transmitter** 무선 송신기 **emit** 방출하다 **frequency** 주파수 **loud** 시끄러운, 소리가 큰 **stay (well) away from** ~에서 (상당히) 떨어져 있다

30 정답 (d) A warning let this be → Let this be a warning

유명 메탈 밴드인 화이트 앵커는 큰 기대를 갖고 지난가을 소위 '리바이벌 투어'를 시작했다. 그들에게는 애석하게도, 예전 그 밴드의 대규모 팬들이 공지를 받지 못한 것으로 보인다. 동북부의 최대 공연장 여덟 군데에서 공연한 콘서트의 참석률은 매우 참담했다. 이것은 마술처럼 과거를 부활시킬 수 있다고 생각하는 예전에 큰 명성을 얻은 다른 이들에게 경고가 될 만하다.

해설 (d)는 문맥상 '이것(화이트 앵커의 실패 사례)이 경고가 되게 하라'는 뜻이 되어야 알맞다. 동사 let으로 시작하는 명령문으로 목적어는 this, 목적보어로 동사원형인 be를 쓰고 be동사의 보어로 a warning이 나오는 것이 올바른 어순이다.

famed 저명한 **so-called** 소위 **unfortunately** 불행하게도 **legion** 부대, 많은 사람들 **attendance** 참석(률) **arena** 경기장, 공연장 **absolutely** 절대적으로, 매우 **pitiful** 측은한, 한심한 **warning** 경고 **former** 예전의 **great** 위대한 인물 **magically** 마술처럼 **resurrect** 부활시키다

Part I

1

투명성을 위하여, 다음은 <u>저희 서비스를 이용하는 조건</u>에 대한 간추린 내용입니다. 스푼풀 계정에 등록하시면, 귀하의 IP 주소와 모바일 네트워크, 주소, 운영체계를 비롯한 개인 정보에 대한 습득 및 보유를 허가하게 됩니다. 스푼풀은 전체 통신량과 사용 경향을 감사하여 서비스 개선에 도움을 받기 위해 귀하의 하드디스크에 작은 데이터 파일을 심어둘 수도 있습니다. 우리 서비스를 이용하시면, 여기 명시된 개인 정보의 수집에 동의하시게 됩니다.

(a) 귀하의 자료를 추적하고 마케팅하는 것
(b) 저희 서비스를 이용하는 조건
(c) 개인정보 정책에 대한 귀하의 동의
(d) 귀하의 자료를 이용하는 저희를 어떻게 감시하는지

해설 회원 가입을 한 사이트에서 개인 정보 사용에 대한 규정을 공지하는 내용이다. 스푼풀이라는 사이트에서 개인 정보를 어떻게 얻고 이용하는지 밝히고 있다. 따라서 간추린 내용에 해당하는 것은 (b)이다.

transparency 투명성 **outline** 간추리다 **authorize** 인가하다 **acquisition** 습득 **retention** 보유 **audit** 회계 감사하다 **aggregate** 총액(의) **enhance** 보강하다 **consent to** ~에 동의하다 **track** 추적하다 **monitor** 감시하다

2

20세기 초에, 영국의 HMS '드레드노트'는 조선 공학에서 중요한 기술 발전을 대표하는 것이었다. 그 존재로 인해 다른 국가들은 위협을 느껴 세계 무대에서 해군의 존재를 유지하기 위해 낡은 선박을 폐기하고 새로운 선박을 건설하게 되었다. 남아메리카 국가들의 경우에 특히 더 그러했는데, 브라질은 한 척이 아니라 드레드노트급의 전함을 세 척이나 건설하기 시작했다. 뒤지지 않기 위해서, 아르헨티나와 칠레도 각자 '드레드노트' 두 척씩을 수주하였다. 그들은 조치를 취하고 <u>해군 강국으로 영국과 보조를 맞출</u> 수밖에 없었다.

(a) 해군 강국으로 영국과 보조를 맞출
(b) 군사 지출이 그들의 관심사가 아니라는 것을 보여 줄
(c) 드레드노트가 위협이 되는 것을 막을
(d) 해양 패권을 위해 지역 분쟁을 일으킬

해설 영국의 조선 공학 발전에 위협을 느껴 특히 남아메리카의 국가들이 새로운 선박을 건조하기 시작했다는 내용이다. 이런 조치들은 영국과 맞설 해군력을 강화하기 위해서는 (a)가 들어가야 알맞다.

naval engineering 조선 공학 **presence** 존재 **intimidate A into -ing** A를 위협하여 ~을 하게 하다 **scrap** 폐기하다 **maintain** 유지하다 **warship** 전함 **outdo** 능가하다 **commission** 의뢰[주문]하다 **take action** 조치를 취하다 **keep pace with** 보조를 맞추다 **expenditure** 지출, 비용 **prevent A from -ing** A가 ~하지 못하도록 하다 **clash** 분쟁 **maritime** 해양의 **supremacy** 패권

3

영화 리뷰

올여름 대대적으로 광고되었던 블록버스터 〈랭커 오브 트루스〉가 8월에 개봉했다. 가진 자와 못가진 자로 나뉘어 있는 미래의 디스토피아를 다루면서 영화는 우리 자신의 시대를 반영할 수 있는 가능성을 가지고 있었다. 하지만 카티아 네코프 감독은 이 문제는 피상적으로 건드리고, 대신에 영화 가득히 늘 등장하는 총 싸움과 길거리와 차량에서의 현란한 추격신을 채워놓았다. 결국, 영화를 보고 난 관객들이 받은 인상은 <u>액션은 가득하지만, 더 심오한 의미는 빠져 있다는</u> 것이다.

(a) 고난도 액션으로 가득하면서도 사회적 메시지를 담은
(b) 폭력이 우리 사회를 형성하는 방식에 대해 비판적인
(c) 점점 커져가는 세계 부의 차이를 돌아보는
(d) 액션은 가득하지만, 더 심오한 의미는 빠져 있다는

해설 한 블록버스터 영화를 리뷰하는 글로, 마지막 문장에서 결론을 내리고 있다. 주제는 피상적으로(superficially) 건드리고 볼거리만 채워 놓았다는 것으로 보아 (d)가 적절하다.

much-hyped 대대적으로 광고되는 **debut** 첫선을 보이다 **dystopia** 디스토피아, 반이상향 **potential** 가능성, 잠재력 **delve** 뒤지다 **superficially** 피상적으로 **load up** 싣다 **obligatory** 의무적인 **dazzle** 눈부시게 하다 **stunt** 스턴트, 고난도 액션 **critical** 비판적인 **packed** 가득 찬 **bereft of** ~이 전무한, 상실한

4

화이트 씨께,

계좌를 해지해 달라고 이메일을 통해 제출하신 귀하의 요청을 10월 12일 자로 수령했습니다. 유감스럽게도, 개설 시 동의하신 계약서에 명시된 대로, 귀하의 계좌 계약기간은 24개월이며 그 기간이 끝나기 전에 해지하시면 130달러의 위약금이 발생하게 됩니다. 이 위약금이 전액 납부될 때까지는 해지 절차를 진행할 수 없습니다. 뒷면에 나와 있는 주소로 수표나 우편환을 통해 송금해 주시기 바랍니다. 그렇지 않으면, 귀하의 24개월 계약기간이 끝나는 2월 2일까지 계좌를 끝까지 유지하십시오. 그 후에는, <u>전혀 비용 없이 계좌를 해지할 수 있습니다.</u>

계좌업무 지원부서
덕 월러스

(a) 갱신할 수 있습니다
(b) 위약금이 전액 지급될 것입니다
(c) 전혀 비용 없이 계좌를 해지할 수 있습니다
(d) 납부액이 전액 환급될 것입니다

해설 계약 기간 이전에 계좌를 해지할 경우 위약금이 부과되니 송금하라는 통지이다. 빈칸 앞 문장에서 위약금을 내지 않으려면 명시한 날짜까지 계좌를 유지하라고 했으므로, 그 날짜 이후에는 위약금을 내지 않고 계좌를 해지할 수 있다는 안내가 나올 수 있다.

termination 종료 **via** ~을 통해 **stipulate** 명시하다 **outset** 착수, 시작 **term** 기간 **prior to** ~이전의 **incur** 발생시키다, 초래하다 **penalty** 벌금 **remit** 송금하다 **money order** 우편환 **on the reverse** 뒷면에 **alternatively** 그 대신에, 그렇지 않으면 **in good standing** 조건을 모두 충족한, 완불한 **be eligible for** ~의 자격이 있다 **renewal** 갱신 **refund** 환급해주다

5

19세기에, 스웨덴의 열기구 조종사인 살로몬 앙드레는 <u>열기구로 고립된 곳에 도달하는</u> 생각에 매력을 느꼈다. 특히 아직 탐사가 되지 않은 극지방에는 거부할 수 없는 매력이 있었다. 스웨덴의 왕이 앙드레의 북극 원정에 자금을 지원했고, 계획을 세운 지 3년 후인 1897년 7월에 원정이 시작되었다. 하지만 원정 대원들은 실종되었고, 구조대도 결실을 거두지 못했다. 대기권 상층의 바람 패턴에 대한 이해가 부족하여, 아무도 수색의 초점을 어디에 두어야 할지를 몰랐기 때문이었다.

(a) 열기구로 고립된 곳에 도달하는
(b) 80일간 열기구를 타고 세계를 탐험하는
(c) 북극까지 최초로 도보 여행을 하는
(d) 열기구가 바람 패턴에 어떻게 반응하는지 측정하는

해설 살로몬 앙드레가 아직 탐사되지 않은 극지방에 매력을 느껴 자금을 지원받아 열기구로 원정을 시작했지만 결실을 거두지 못했다고 한다. 앙드레가 매력을 느낀 것은 극지방처럼 고립된 지역에 열기구를 타고 가는 것이라고 볼 수 있으므로 (a)가 적절하다.

balloonist 열기구 조종사 **enamored** 매혹된 **in particular** 특히 **polar region** 극지방 **irresistible** 거부할 수 없는 **allure** 매력 **finance** 자금을 대다 **North Pole** 북극 **expedition** 탐험, 원정 **rescue mission** 구조대 **futile** 헛된, 소용없는 **isolated** 고립된 **trek** 도보 여행하다 **measure** 측정하다

6

커내버럴 팬이라면 모두 알다시피, 이슬비 내리는 가을밤은 팰머스 경기장에서의 저녁을 추운 행사로 만들 수 있습니다. 커내버럴 로거헤즈의 공식 사계절 담요와 함께 추위로부터 당신을 보호하십시오. 담요는 두 겹의 플리스 소재로 만들어졌고 방수가 되는 외부 커버를 특별히 포함하고 있어서, 나일론 천의 방수 기능과 전통 플리스 소재의 부드러움, 편안함을 결합하였습니다. 95%의 바람을 막아내지만 통기성이 있으며 부하게 보이지 않으면서도 보온을 해 줍니다. 로거헤즈 선수들만큼 억세서 <u>대자연이 무엇을 던지더라도 견뎌낼 수 있습니다.</u>

(a) 대자연이 무엇을 던지더라도 견뎌낼 수 있습니다
(b) 사계절 내내 스포츠 장비를 청소하는 데 이상적입니다
(c) 어떤 계절에서든 반가운 동반자가 될 것입니다
(d) 여러분이 좋아하는 모든 스포츠팀의 로고가 자랑스럽게 새겨져 있습니다

해설 커내버럴 로거헤즈 제품의 사계절 담요를 광고하고 있다. 빈칸 앞에서 튼튼하다(tough)는 언급이 있으므로, 어떤 날씨도 견딜 수 있다는 의미의 (a)가 적절하다.

drizzly 이슬비 내리는 **chilly** 추운 **safeguard** 보호하다 **two-ply** 두 겹의 **fleece** 플리스(직물의 일종) **water-repellant** 방수의 **external** 외부의 **combine A with B** A와 B를 결합하다 **fabric** 천 **breathable** 통기성 있는 **insulate** 단열하다, 보온하다 **bulky** 부피가 큰 **bear** 견디다; 지니고 있다 **equipment** 장비 **proudly** 자랑스럽게

7

그린란드의 대부분을 덮고 있는 것과 같은 빙상은 실은 대륙의 기반암에 얹혀 있는 것으로, 그곳은 지형 구조가 균일하게 편평한 얼음이 시사하는 것보다 훨씬 더 복잡할 수 있다. 예를 들어, 그린란드의 얼음 밑에는 애리조나에 있는 그랜드 캐니언보다 더 오래되고 그만큼이나 깊은 거대한 협곡이 놓여 있다. 연구자들은 수백만 년 전에 이 섬이 얼기 전에, 그 협곡에 큰 하천계가 있었을 것으로 생각한다. 최근의 이 발견이 시사하는 바에 의하면 <u>우리는 우리가 생각하는 것만큼 지표면을 알지 못하는 것일 수도 있다.</u>

(a) 우리는 우리가 생각하는 것만큼 지표면을 알지 못하는 것일 수도 있다
(b) 지구온난화가 그린란드에 영향을 끼치고 있음이 분명하다
(c) 빙상은 담수가 흐르는 곳에 형성되는 경향이 있다
(d) 그랜드 캐니언은 한때 거대한 빙상으로 덮여 있었다

해설 우리 눈에 보이는 그린란드의 편평한 얼음 밑에 실은 거대한 협곡이 놓여 있다고 한다. 이런 발견이 시사하는 바는 우리가 생각보다 지구의 본모습을 잘 알지 못하고 있다는 것이다.

ice sheet 빙상 **rest on** ~에 얹혀 있다 **continental** 대륙의 **bedrock** 기반암 **terrain** 지형, 지역 **flatness** 편평함 **beneath** ~의 아래에 **massive** 거대한 **canyon** 협곡

8

푸에블로족의 고대 상형문자는 사막 큰뿔양이 <u>이전에는 아메리카 대륙의 남서부에 널리 존재했음을</u> 증명한다. 이 토종 양의 개체는 19세기 중반에 급격하게 감소했는데, 이때 문명이 서쪽으로 팽창한 것이 이 동물을 거의 멸종으로 몰아갔다. 현재, 사막 큰뿔양은 원래 살던 영역의 약 3분의 1 정도에만 퍼져 있으며 개체들은 불안정하고 취약한 상태이다. 이는 1991년에 생태학자들의 재착생 운동과 같은 보존 노력이 있었음에도 그러하다. 이들은 유타와 다코타를 가로지르는 보호 서식지에 독자 생존이 가능한 큰뿔양 개체수를 재건하려는 희망에서 고립된 이들을 포획하고 이전시키고자 하였다.

(a) 힘든 환경적 압박을 맞이한 상황에서 회복력
(b) 이전에는 아메리카 대륙의 남서부에 널리 존재했음
(c) 아메리카 원주민들에게 희귀성과 가치
(d) 불과 몇 천 년에 걸쳐 급속한 생태학적 진화

해설 사막 큰뿔양과 관련해서 빈칸에 들어갈 말은 뒤에 이어지는 내용과 관련이 있어야 한다. 사막 큰뿔양이 급격히 감소해서 거의 멸종 위기에 처했다고 하므로, 빈칸에는 상형문자를 통해 고대에 이 종이 많았던 것을 알 수 있다는 내용인 (b)가 알맞다.

pictograph 상형문자 **attest to** ~을 증명하다 **desert bighorn (sheep)** 사막 큰뿔양 **decline** 감소하다 **drastically** 급격하게 **westward** 서쪽으로 **expansion** 팽창, 확대 **extinction** 멸종 **range** 범위가 ~에 이르다 **territory** 영토, 영역 **unstable** 불안정한 **vulnerable** 취약한 **conservation** 보호, 보존 **recolonization** 재착생 **ecologist** 생태학자 **capture** 포획하다 **relocate** 이전시키다 **viable** 독자 생존이 가능한 **habitat** 서식지 **resilience** 회복력 **abundance** 풍부 **rapid** 급속한 **evolution** 진화

9

많은 이들의 마음속에서 휴가라는 생각은 수정처럼 맑은 물이 찰싹거리는 열대지방의 모래사장을 떠오르게 한다. <u>그렇긴 하지만,</u> 여름에 즐거움을 찾는 사람들은 점점 더 바닷가 휴가의 나른한 속도를 거부하고 더 자극적인 도시에서의 휴가를 선호하고 있다. 도시 휴가는 제한적인 일정과 한정된 예산을 가진 사람들에게 재정적으로 더 합리적이다. 바닷가 휴가지보다 접근성이 좋아, 도시를 방문하는 것은 여행 시간을 실질적으로 줄일 수 있고 항공료로 들어갈 돈이 줄어든다.

(a) 게다가
(b) 그렇긴 하지만
(c) 그렇지 않으면
(d) 다시 말하자면

해설 빈칸 앞에서는 자연에서 보내는 휴가를 언급했지만 뒤에서는 이와 상반되는 도시에서의 휴가를 선호하는 경향에 대해 언급하고 있다. 따라서 앞에서 말한 내용을 부분적으로 수정하면서 내용을 보충할 때 쓰는 연결사로 '그렇긴 하지만'이란 뜻의 (b)가 알맞다.

conjure 불러일으키다, 떠올리게 하다　**sandy** 모래로 뒤덮인　**shoreline** 해안가　**lap** 찰싹거리다　**crystal clear** 수정같이 맑은　**merrymaker** 흥청거리는 사람　**reject** 거부하다　**stultifying** 멍청하게 만드는　**in favor of** ~을 좋아하여　**getaway** 휴가(지)　**fiscal** 재정의　**restrictive** 제한적인　**finite** 한정된　**accessible** 접근 가능한

10

인위적이거나 인간이 초래한 기후 변화에 관한 논의는 이산화탄소가 기후 변화에 미치는 영향력에 중점을 두는 경향이 있다. 그것이 인간이 내뿜는 온실가스의 주요한 형태이기는 하지만, 결코 유일한 것은 아니며, 나아가 가장 치명적인 것도 아니다. 메탄은 농업의 온실가스 부산물인데 분자당 무게가 이산화탄소의 25배에 달한다. 마찬가지로, 아산화질소는 오존층을 감소시키는 기체로 제조업과 농사를 통해 배출되며 분자당 열을 잡아두는 능력이 이산화탄소와 비교할 때 300배 이상이다.

(a) 아직도
(b) 개의치 않고
(c) 결과적으로
(d) 마찬가지로

해설 기후 변화의 가장 주된 원인에 대해 이산화탄소보다 더 유해한 것으로 메탄을 언급했고, 빈칸 뒤에서도 역시 아산화질소도 이산화탄소보다 더 유해하다는 내용이 이어진다. 따라서 유사한 예를 들고 있으므로 '마찬가지로'라는 뜻의 (d)가 알맞다.

anthropogenic 인위적인　**alter** 바꾸다　**predominant** 우세한, 두드러진　**emit** 배출하다　**by no means** 결코 ~이 아닌　**pernicious** 치명적인　**methane** 메탄　**byproduct** 부산물　**molecule** 분자　**nitrous oxide** 아산화질소　**deplete** 고갈시키다

Part II

11

고대부터 서아프리카 문화에서 알려진, 콜라나무 열매는 나이지리아에서 문화적 및 종교적 의미를 띠고 있다. (a) 나이지리아의 한 민족 집단인 이그보족에게, 콜라나무 열매는 사회적 상호작용에 있어서 특정한 상징적 관련성을 가지고 있다. (b) 또한, 이그보족이 재배하는 참마도 그들 문화에서는 매우 중요한 의미를 두고 있다. (c) 이 콜라 열매는 속담이나 조상에게 비는 기도, 공동체 구성원들을 위한 중재를 전달할 때 사람들에게 돌려진다. (d) 그렇게 한 후, 조각으로 나누어져 개인의 지위에 따라 분배된다.

해설 첫 문장의 콜라나무 열매가 이 글의 소재이며, 이 열매가 나이지리아에서 특정한 사회적 의미를 띤다는 것이 주제이다. (b)는 참마라는 다른 소재를 언급하고 있으므로 맥락에서 벗어난다.

religious 종교적인　**significance** 의미, 중요성　**ethnic** 민족의　**symbolic** 상징적인　**relevance** 관련성　**additionally** 게다가　**yam** 얌, 참마　**accord** 부여하다　**pass around** 돌리다　**proverb** 속담　**invocation** 기도, 탄원　**intercession** 중재, 간청　**status** 위치

12

트로전이라고 알려진 태양계의 천체는 행성과 같은 궤도에 상주하는 소행성이다. (a) 천문학에서는 이런 소행성 중에서 가장 큰 것들을 트로전 위성으로 분류하는데, 이론상으로는 트로전 행성도 있을 수 있다. (b) 그들은 라그랑주 점이라고 하는 안정된 위치에 있는 궤도를 따라 행성의 뒤를 쫓거나 행성의 앞에 간다. (c) 이 소행성들은 너비가 최대 수백 킬로미터에 이르며, 기본적으로 중력에 의해 제자리를 유지하고 있다. (d) 하지만 그들이 영원히 제자리에 고정된 것은 아닌데, 지역에 따른 중력의 미세한 변화로 떨어져 나가 행성과의 조화를 잃어버릴 수 있기 때문이다.

해설 트로전이라는 소행성의 궤도의 특성에 관한 글로, (a)는 소행성의 규모에 관한 내용이다.

solar system 태양계　**object** 천체　**asteroid** 소행성　**inhabit** 거주하다　**orbit** 궤도　**astronomy** 천문학　**trail** 추적하다　**stable** 안정적인　**width** 너비　**basically** 기본적으로　**in place** 제자리에　**gravity** 중력　**subtle** 미묘한　**shift** 변화　**regional** 지역의　**out of sync** 동시에 이루어지지 않는, 조화를 이루지 못하는

Part III

13

명상이 생산성을 향상시킨다는 것을 보여 주는 증거에 자극을 받아, 직원들에게 명상 수업을 제공하려는 직장의 경향이 기업의 수익을 향상시킬 것 같다. 하지만 명상 전문가들은 개인의 성장을 지향하는 명상의 목적과 명상을 장려하는 기업의 이익을 추구하는 계산 사이의 불편한 간극을 부정할 수 없다. 그래서 명상을 가르치는 사람들은 자신이 혼란스러운 타협으로 내몰리는 것을 느낀다. 물질적 소유로부터 사심을 버리고 무심함을 가르치는 정신적인 전통에 대한 그들의 교육은 자본주의의 중심적인 교리인 '이익 지상주의'와 극명한 대조를 이룬다.

Q 지문에 가장 적절한 제목은?
(a) 명상 강사들은 수강료를 받을 자격이 없다
(b) 기업의 명상과 그 역설적인 목표
(c) 자본주의자들은 정신적인 명상을 이용해 돈을 번다
(d) 직장 명상의 효험에 대한 회의

해설 기업에서 생산성 향상을 위해 제공하는 명상 수업은 개인의 성장을 지향하는 명상의 본래 목적과 매우 대조적이라는 내용이다. 불편한 간극(the uncomfortable gulf), 혼란스러운 타협(discomfiting compromise), 극명한 대조(stark contrast) 등의 어구에서 기업체에서 행해지는 명상은 명상의 본래 의미를 퇴색시킨다는 (b)가 적절하다.

spur 박차를 가하다, 자극하다　**meditation** 명상　**productivity** 생산성　**boost** 향상시키다　**return** 수익　**practitioner** 전문적인 일을 하는 사람　**gulf** 격차　**objective** 목적, 목표　**profit-motivated** 이익 추구의　**calculation** 계산　**promote** 장려하다　**discomfit** 혼란스럽게 하다　**compromise** 타협　**spiritual** 정신적인　**selflessness** 사심이 없음　**detachment** 무심함　**material possession** 물질적 소유　**stand in stark contrast to** ~와 (극명한) 대조를 이루다　**capitalism** 자본주의　**tenet** 주의, 교리　**corporate** 기업의　**paradoxical** 자기모순의, 역설의　**make money off** ~을 이용해 돈을 벌다　**efficacy** 효험

14

Q 이메일의 주된 내용은?
(a) 독특한 사용자 이름과 비밀번호 선택하기
(b) 여행업계 회사에서 일자리 지원하기
(c) 여행 콘퍼런스의 장소에 대해 투표하기
(d) 온라인 포럼을 통해 여행 관련 네트워크 쌓기

해설 콘퍼런스 참석자들에게 사용자 이름과 비밀번호를 알려주며 콘퍼런스 전용 온라인 플랫폼에 접속할 것을 권하고 있다. 이 플랫폼에 접속하여 동료 여행 블로거나 여행지 홍보 기구들과 연락하라는 내용이므로 (d)가 적절하다.

dedicated 전용의 **fellow** 동료의 **in-person** 직접의
representative 대표 **in attendance** 참석한 **fill up** 채워지다

15

Q 안내문의 요지는?
(a) 스키를 타는 사람들은 종종 고산병에 시달리기 쉽다.
(b) 관광객들은 리프트가 언제라도 멈출 수 있다는 점을 알아야 한다.
(c) 기상 상황이 안 좋지만, 날씨는 앞으로 좋아질 것이다.
(d) 리프트는 운행되지만, 안전을 위해 주의해야 한다.

해설 날씨 예보와 함께 리프트가 예정대로 운행된다는 것을 알리고, 탑승권 구입 시에는 개인의 안전을 스스로 책임질 것을 당부하고 있다. 따라서 이 두 가지를 모두 포함한 (d)가 적절하다.

forecast 예보하다 **pristine** 아주 깨끗한 **unlimited** 무제한의
visibility 시계, 가시성 **chairlift** 리프트 **forewarn** 경고하다
altitude 고도 **fluctuate** 변동을 거듭하다 **precipitously** 급작스럽게
wind gust 돌풍 **cease** 중단되다 **assume** 맡다 **liability** 법적 책임
hazard 위험 **incidental to** ~에 따르기 마련인 **facility** 시설

16

Q 지문의 요지는?
(a) 빵의 여러 특성들에 기여하는 글루텐의 역할
(b) 여러 가지 밀가루로 만든 여러 가지 글루텐
(c) 빵에 들어있는 클루텐으로 인한 화학적 반응
(d) 다양한 빵을 만드는 데에 이스트의 중요성

해설 빵을 만드는 과정에서 글루텐의 역할에 대해 설명하고 있다. 빵의 탄성과 쫄깃함, 부풀어 오르게 하는 작용 등이 글루텐의 역할이다.

flour 밀가루 **complex** 복합체 **substance** 물질 **confer** 부여하다
elasticity 탄성 **chewiness** 씹힘성, 쫄깃쫄깃함 **mechanical**
기계적인 **knead** (반죽을) 치대다 **align** 일직선으로 하다 **dough**
밀가루 반죽 **scaffold** 골격(을 세우다) **hold together** 뭉치게 하다
yeast 이스트 **porous** 다공성의 **customary** 관례적인 **attribute**
속성, 특성 **yield** 내다, 산출하다

17

Q 지문에 따르면 알리샤 알론소에 대해서 다음 중 옳은 것은?
(a) 1930년대에 한 〈지젤〉 공연에 등장했다.
(b) 일생 대부분 동안 시력이 안 좋아 고생했다.
(c) 그녀의 회복은 종종 무용 연습을 수반했다.
(d) 그녀의 1943년에 무대로의 복귀는 호평을 받았다.

해설 마지막 문장에서 알리샤 알론소가 1943년 〈지젤〉로 무대에 복귀하여 찬사를 받았다(earning acclaim)고 하므로 (d)가 일치한다. 시력이 안 좋아 장기간의 요양을 필요로 하기는 했지만 회복해서 다시 무대로 복귀했으므로 (b)는 오답이다.

venerate 존경하다 **figure** 인물 **establish** (명성을) 확고히 하다
reputation 명성 **obligate** 강요하다 **suspend** 중단하다
surgery 수술 **necessitate** ~을 필요하게 만들다 **bed rest** 안정,
요양 **engage in** ~에 관여[참여]하다 **rehearsal** 리허설 **visualize**
상상하다 **archetypal** 전형적인 **lead** 주인공, 주연 **recuperate**
회복하다 **fill in for** ~을 대신하다 **earn acclaim** 찬사를 받다
unparalleled 비할 데 없는, 유례없는 **interpretation** 해석
production 상연, 제작 **well received** 호평을 받은

18

원형요새는 철기시대에 아일랜드 전역에서 건설된 돌이나 흙으로 만든 요새였다. 무려 50,000개나 존재한다고 여겨지고 있으며 다른 것들은 수세기에 걸쳐 파괴되었을 수도 있다. 이 고대 요새의 용도에 대해서 다양한 설명이 제기되어 왔지만, 어떤 것도 확실하지 않다. 어떤 것들은 그저 가축을 위한 우리였던 것으로밖에 보이지 않는 반면, 더 규모가 큰 원형요새는 산업과 무역의 중심지로서 경제적 역할에 충실했었을 수도 있다. 방어적 목적을 추정하는 다른 이론들도 있는데, 습격을 받을 때 방어용 제방으로 사용되었을 수도 있기 때문이다.

Q 지문에 따르면 다음 중 옳은 것은?
(a) 아일랜드는 청동기 시대에 50,000개의 원형요새의 본거지였다.
(b) 아일랜드의 원형요새 유적은 아일랜드 북부에만 위치해 있다.
(c) 원형요새는 가축을 가두는 데 사용되었다는 것이 증명되었다.
(d) 전문가들은 원형요새가 어떤 구체적인 기능을 수행했는지 확신하지 못한다.

해설 고대 요새의 용도에 대해서 다양한 설명이 제기되어 왔지만, 어떤 것도 확정적이지 않다(Various explanations as to the purpose of these ancient outposts have been proposed, though none are definitive)고 하므로 (d)가 일치한다.

earthwork 흙을 쌓아 만든 보루 **fortification** 방어시설, 요새 **outpost** 전초기지 **propose** 제안하다 **definitive** 확정적인 **no more than** ~일 뿐(= only) **enclosure** 울타리로 둘러싼 장소 **livestock** 가축 **fulfill** 충족시키다 **trading** 거래, 무역 **hub** 중심지 **postulate** 추정하다 **defensive** 방어의 **protective** 보호하는 **embankment** 둑, 제방 **raid** 습격 **remains** (복수형으로) 유적 **confine** 가두다 **specific** 구체적인, 명확한

19

식충 관습, 즉 곤충이나 거미류를 먹는 것과 인간과의 관계는 복잡하다. 벌레는 많은 고대 문화권에서 자양분을 얻는 원천으로 섭취되었고, 실제로, 전 세계 수백만 명의 사람들은 아직도 그것들을 먹고 있다. 하지만 특히 선진국 사회 안에서는 식충성은 금기되었는데, 벌레는 주로 '역겨운' 것으로 여겨지기 때문이다. 하지만 이는 조만간 바뀔 수도 있는데, 많은 전문가들이 동물 가축을 기르고 가공 처리하는 관습에 대해 환경적으로 건전한 대안으로 식충성의 채택을 요구하고 있기 때문이다.

Q 지문에 따르면 다음 중 옳은 것은?
(a) 고대 문화들은 식충성을 금기시켰다.
(b) 곤충을 먹는 것은 전 세계적으로 점점 칭찬받고 있다.
(c) 소수의 사회만이 현재 곤충을 먹는다.
(d) 식충성은 환경친화적인 것으로 일컬어지고 있다.

해설 지문 마지막에서 식충은 동물 가축을 기르고 가공하는 것보다 환경적으로 건전한 대안이 될 수 있다고 했으므로 정답은 (d)이다.

relationship 관계 **entomophagy** 식충성(곤충을 식용으로 먹는 것) **arachnid** 거미류 **consume** 소비하다, 먹다 **sustenance** 자양물 **developed nation** 선진국 **taboo** 금기 **primarily** 주로 **gross** 역겨운 **call for** ~을 요구하다 **adoption** 채택 **sound** 건전한 **livestock** 가축 **laud** 칭찬하다 **minority** 소수 **hail** 묘사하다, 일컫다

20

석유 다음으로, 세계에서 두 번째로 가장 귀중한 무역품은 커피로서, 50여 국가가 커피의 생산과 판매에 관여하고 있다. 이 상품 사슬은 대단히 복잡하여, 대부분의 커피는 2헥타르 이하의 수많은 소규모 농가에서 나온다. 생산자는 국내 중개인에게 가공하지 않은 수확물을 판매하고, 중개인은 받아들인 물품을 가공 시설로 전달하여 국제 시장에서 수출업자와 거래한다. 수입국에서 커피를 볶는 사람은 원두를 소비할 수 있도록 준비한 다음 크래프트나 사라리, 프록터 앤 갬블, 네슬레 같은 대기업으로 운송한다.

Q 지문에 따르면 커피에 대하여 다음 중 옳은 것은?
(a) 커피의 유통 및 거래는 석유보다 더 넓다.
(b) 50개가 넘는 국가에서 대규모 커피 재배 회사들이 운영된다.
(c) 소수의 재배자들이 수많은 가공업자들에게 판매한다.
(d) 중개인이 재배자와 대기업 사이에서 상품을 나른다.

해설 중개인(broker)이 생산자에게서 물품을 사서 가공 시설을 거쳐 수출업자에게 판매한 후 결국 대기업(conglomerate)으로 운송된다고 하므로 (d)가 정답이다. 대부분의 커피는 수많은 소규모 농가(numerous small-scale farms)에서 나온다고 했으므로 (b)와 (c)는 오답이다.

valuable 귀중한 **commodity** 상품, 물품 **extremely** 극도로, 굉장히 **majority** 다수 **originate** 유래하다 **numerous** 수많은 **producer** 생산자 **unprocessed** 가공되지 않은 **harvest** 수확(물) **broker** 중개인 **convey** 전달하다 **intake** 받아들임 **transact** 거래하다 **exporter** 수출업자 **roaster** 굽는[볶는] 사람 **importer** 수입업자 **transport** 운송하다 **conglomerate** 대기업 **distribution** 분배, 유통 **middleman** 중간 상인, 중개인

21

이집트에서 태어난 도로시 호지킨은 고체의 원자 구조를 다루는 화학 분야에서 일한 화학자였다. 젊은 시절, 그녀는 자신의 다락방에 세운 초라한 실험실에서 크리스털을 재배하고 광물을 분석하고 화학 분석을 하는 데 전념했다. 엑스레이를 크리스털을 통과시킴으로써 만들어진 것에 지나지 않는 영상을 이용하여 페니실린의 화학 구조를 해석한 것은 호지킨의 가장 큰 업적 중 하나였다. 그 후에, 유사한 기법을 이용하여, 그녀는 비타민 B12와 인슐린의 구조를 밝혀냈다. 이러한 공로로, 그녀는 1964년에 노벨 화학상을 받았다.

Q 지문에 따르면 도로시 호지킨에 대하여 다음 중 옳은 것은?
(a) 액상 화학 분야에 관여하게 되었다.
(b) 젊었을 때, 임시변통으로 실험실을 만들었다.
(c) 신체가 비타민 B12를 어떻게 사용하는지를 보여주었다.
(d) 경력에서 노벨상을 두 번 받았다.

해설 도로시 호지킨이 다락방에 초라한 실험실을 세웠다(modest laboratory she set up in her attic)고 했는데, 이것을 makeshift lab(임시변통의 실험실)으로 표현할 수 있다. 첫 문장에서 고체(solid materials)를 연구했다고 했고, 비타민 B12의 구조를 밝혀냈다고 했으므로 (a)와 (c)는 오답이다.

chemist 화학자 **deal with** ~을 다루다 **organization** 구조, 구성 **atom** 원자 **solid material** 고체 **devote oneself to** ~에 헌신[전념]하다 **modest** 평범한, 초라한 **set up** 설치하다 **attic** 다락방 **achievement** 업적, 성과 **elucidate** 설명하다, 자세히 밝히다 **makeshift** 임시변통의

22

4원인은 사물의 기원을 설명하려고 시도하는 아리스토텔레스 철학의 일부이다. 질료인은 사물의 재료에 의해 결정된다. 예를 들어, 조각상의 존재는 그것이 만들어진 화강암에 의해 설명된다. 형상인은 사물의 기원을 그것이 기초하고 있는 원형에서 찾는다. 조각상의 경우에, 그것은 조각가 내부의 심상이다. 동력인은 사물이 생겨난 방식으로, 즉 조각가의 노력에 의한 것이다. 마지막 원인은 사물이 존재하는 목적으로, 조각이 관람객들에게 보이기 위해 존재하는 것 같은 경우이다.

Q 지문에 따르면 아리스토텔레스의 4원인들에 대해서 다음 중 옳은 것은?
(a) 형상인과 질료인은 때로 똑같은 것이다.
(b) 아리스토텔레스는 질료인이 영적인 측면도 가진다고 생각했다.
(c) 사물의 창조자는 그 동력인의 주요 동인이다.
(d) 사물의 가격은 마지막 원인을 좌우하는 것이다.

해설 동력인은 사물이 생겨나게 된 방식이라고 했는데, 이는 곧 사물의 창조자에 해당한다(Moving cause is the manner by which an object came into being—by the endeavors of a sculptor.)고 하므로 (c)가 일치한다.

attempt 시도하다 **origin** 기원 **material** 재료 **existence** 존재
statue 조각상 **granite** 화강암 **attribute A to B** A의 원인을 B에 두다 **archetype** 원형 **be based on** ~에 기초하다 **sculptor** 조각가 **manner** 방법 **come into being** 생성되다 **endeavor** 노력, 시도 **sake** 목적 **sculpture** 조각 **dictate** 영향을 주다, 좌우하다

23

바에즈 씨께,

저는 칼리아 무제니의 새 앨범인 〈페어 퀘스천〉을 듣고 얼마나 기쁜지 표현을 할 수 없을 정도입니다. 오늘날의 대중음악은 녹음실 기술로 보컬리스트로부터 모든 인간적인 부분을 디지털화 하여 맥 빠질 정도로 천편일률적입니다. 날 것 그대로 정직한, 가공하지 않은 인간의 목소리는 거의 들을 기회가 없기에, 바로 듣는 것 같은 그 소리는 엄청나게 기분 좋게 만드는 것입니다. 재능 있는 보컬리스트의 직접적인 표현은 관심과 존경을 요구할 정도로 거부할 수 없는 강력한 영향력을 가지고 있습니다. 바에즈 씨를 비롯한 팀원들과 칼리아 무제니 씨에게 잊을 수 없는 성과를 축하합니다.

찰리 알렌 드림

Q 이메일로부터 알렌 씨에 대해 추론할 수 있는 것은?
(a) 현대의 음악 스타일을 열렬히 지지한다.
(b) 완전한 목소리 같은 것은 없다고 생각한다.
(c) 무제니의 음악에 내재된 특성을 높이 평가한다.
(d) 바에즈 씨와 일한 적이 있는 음악 프로듀서이다.

해설 알렌 씨는 녹음실에서 다듬은 소리에 대해 부정적이며, 무제니의 앨범처럼 가공하지 않은 자연 그대로의 목소리(the honest rawness of an unprocessed human voice)를 높이 평가하고 있다.

delight 기쁨 **derive** 끌어내다, 얻다 **vocalist** 보컬리스트, 가수
depressingly 맥 빠지게, 울적하게 **homogenous** 동종의
rawness 날 것 **immediacy** 직접성 **tremendously** 엄청나게
uplifting 기분 좋게 하는 **talented** 재능 있는 **ardent** 열렬한
appreciate 높이 평가하다

24

그리스 제국의 영토를 복속시키려는 성전을 치르는 동안, 페르시아의 지도자인 크세르크세스는 유럽과 아시아의 경계에 놓인 해협 중 하나를 가로지르는 야심 찬 토목 공사를 발주했다. 현재 다르다넬스 해협이라고 알려진 이 좁은 수역은 가장 좁은 곳의 너비가 1킬로 남짓밖에 되지 않는다. 크세르크세스는 이 간격을 가로질러 부교 위로 군대를 실어 나르는 것을 머릿속에 그리고 부교를 설계하고 건설할 건축가 집단을 모집했다. 하지만 이러한 처음 두 번의 시도는 폭풍우로 파괴되었고, 관련된 이들은 모두 참수를 당했다.

Q 지문으로부터 추론할 수 있는 것은?
(a) 크세르크세스는 그리스 제국을 결코 정복하지 못했다.
(b) 그리스 제국은 맹렬하게 다르다넬스 해협을 방어했다.
(c) 크세르크세스는 다리 파괴의 책임을 물어 건축가들을 처벌하였다.
(d) 페르시아 군대는 결국 배로 해협을 건넜다.

해설 마지막 문장에서 다리가 파괴된 후 관련된 이들을 모두 참수했다고 했는데, 관련된 이들이라면 건설에 참여한 건축가들일 것이다.

span 가로지르다 **strait** 해협 **boundary** 경계 **envision** 상상하다
shuttle (정기적으로) 실어 나르다 **floating bridge** 부교 **recruit**
모집하다 **fleet** 무리 **behead** 목을 베다, 참수하다 **fiercely** 맹렬하게

25

오늘날에도, 뉴욕의 예술계에서 여성의 활동 범위는 여전히 빈약하게 나타나고 있다. 백인 남성이 미국의 예술계를 주도해왔지만, 어느 정도 그들의 영향력이 줄어들기까지 페이스 링골드 같은 예술가들에게 감사해야 한다. 1970년에, 그녀는 휘트니 미술관의 여성에 대한 차별적인 태도에 반기를 드는 항의를 주최하는 데 조력했다. 오늘날, 흑인 예술가들을 기본적으로 포함하는 것을 촉구하는 비영리단체의 회장으로서, 그녀는 인종이나 성에 의해 소외된 예술가들에게 새로운 기회를 만들어주는 일을 계속하고 있다.

Q 지문으로부터 페이스 링골드에 대해서 추론할 수 있는 것은?
(a) 백인 남성 예술가들이 지나치게 많다고 여긴다.
(b) 아프리카 예술의 전통 기법을 연구했다.
(c) 뉴욕의 주요 화랑들에서 자신의 미술작품을 전시한다.
(d) 남성 예술가들로부터 만장일치의 지지를 받았다.

해설 두 번째 문장에서 예술계를 주도해 온 백인 남성의 영향력이 줄어든데 대해 페이스 링골드에게 감사를 해야 한다는 것과, 이어지는 문장에서 여성에 대한 차별적인 태도에 반기를 들었다는 점에서 그녀가 백인 남성들이 예술계를 독식한다고 여겼음을 추론할 수 있다.

scope 기회, 범위 **dominate** 주도하다 **ebb** 서서히 약해지다
organize 주최하다, 조직하다 **discriminatory** 차별의 **nonprofit**
organization 비영리단체 **canonical** 표준이 되는 **inclusion** 포함
diaspora 이주민 공동체 **forge** 구축하다 **marginalize** 소외시키다
gender 성, 성별 **overrepresented** 대표가 지나치게 많은
unanimous 만장일치의

Part IV

26-27

http://www.talentandworkshop.com/workshops/

소개 ∨ **워크숍** ∨ 투자 ∨ 가게 ∨ 연락

워크숍에 대해

단추나 나뭇잎을 예쁜 은제품으로 바꿀 수 있다고 생각해 본 적이 있나요? 진실은 바꿀 수 있다는 것입니다! 다른 작은 물체들도 또한 아름다운 미술품으로 변형할 수 있어요. 비결은 은점토를 다루는 법을 배우는 것입니다.

사라 캠벨은 은점토의 능숙한 이용과 관련해서 누구나 아는 이름인데요, 은점토 작품 창작을 위한 워크숍을 개최하도록 기쁜 마음으로 초빙했습니다. 캠벨은 반지와 목걸이를 포함해서, 아름다운 은점토 장신구를 만드는 방법을 가르칠 거예요.

은점토 작품이 친환경 제품이라는 사실을 아셨나요? 은점토 작품은 친환경적인 방식으로 제작됩니다. 따라서 은점토 작품을 만드는 방법을 배움으로써, 우수한 제품을 만드는 것과 환경 보호에 도움을 주는 것 사이에 균형을 맞추는 방법도 배울 수 있습니다.

초급자 강좌
- 수강료: 교재비를 포함하여 1인당 250달러
- 장소: 에임스 문화센터 실버홀 30호
- 일정: 월요일/수요일 오전 9시~오전 11시
  화요일/목요일 오후 1시~오후 3시

보다 많은 정보를 원하시면, cynthia.j@talentandworkshop.com 으로 이메일을 보내주세요.

26 Q 웹페이지에 따르면, 다음 중 옳은 것은?
(a) 은점토 애호가들은 캠벨 씨가 완전히 망한 미술가라고 생각한다.
(b) 은점토 작품 제작은 환경에 해롭지 않다.
(c) 워크숍 참가자들은 교재를 다른 곳에서 구해야만 한다.
(d) 캠벨 씨는 에임스 문화센터의 정규 직원이다.

해설 이와 같은 세부 사항 유형에서는 내용이 지문에 제시된 순서에 따라 선택지의 내용이 배열되는 것이 일반적임도 기억해 두자. 물론 순서가 약간씩 바뀔 수도 있다. (a)는 누구나 알 정도로 유명함을 알 수 있으므로 오답이다. (c)는 안내에서 교재비가 포함되어 있음을 밝혔으므로 정답이 아니다. (d)는 초빙했다고 말했으므로 오답이다. 따라서 정답은 웹페이지의 설명에 충실한 (b)이다.

27 Q 초급자 강좌에 등록하면, 1주일에 몇 시간을 워크숍에 참석하는가?
(a) 6시간
(b) 8시간
(c) 10시간
(d) 12시간

해설 NEW TEPS로 바뀌면서 새롭게 제시된 유형인데, 세부적인 정보를 측정하는 유형으로 요구하는 정보가 있는 부분을 찾아서 정확한 정보를 확인하는 능력을 길러야 효과적으로 대비할 수 있다. 1주일에 월요일부터 목요일까지 매일 2시간씩이므로 정답은 (b)이다. 독해 파트4와 관련해서 문제를 풀 수 있는 시간이 너무 부족하다고 호소하는 수험생들이 많은데, 이와 같은 유형에서 문제 풀이 시간을 줄여야, 다른 문항을 풀 수 있는 시간을 더 많이 확보할 수 있음을 기억하자.

transform 변형시키다 **object** 물체; 목표 **secret** 비결; 비밀 **clay** 점토 **household** 귀에 익은; 가구(家口) **jewelry** 장신구 **necklace** 목걸이 **environmentally-friendly** 환경 친화적인 **strike a balance** 균형을 맞추다 **enthusiast** 열광자 **washed-up** 완전히 실패한 **detrimental** 해로운 **procure** 입수하다, 조달하다

28-29

모든 침노린재가 이롭지는 않다

TV 프로그램 덕택에, 사람들은 대부분 침노린재가 인간에게 아주 이롭다는 사실을 알고 있다. 이것은 주로 이 곤충이 파리, 모기, 그리고 다른 해로운 벌레를 먹이로 삼기 때문이다. 그래서 대부분의 정원사들은 이 포식성 곤충을 환영한다. 흥미롭게도, 마치 자객처럼 먹잇감을 몰래 공격하기 때문에 '자객 벌레'라고 불린다.

곤충학자들에 따르면, 세계에는 대략 7천 종의 침노린재가 있다고 한다. 이 종(種)들은 대부분 인간에게 상당한 이득을 가져다주지만, 일부는 매우 해롭다. 특히, 흡혈성 침노린재는 척추동물의 피를 먹고 사는데, 일부 의학자들은 이 곤충이 척추동물 사이에 질병을 퍼뜨린다고 생각한다.

많은 이들이 서로 비슷하게 생겨서 침노린재를 왕침노린재와 종종 혼동한다. 둘 다 상대적으로 머리가 길지만, 왕침노린재와 달리 침노린재는 돌기가 없다. 또한 침노린재는 주황색과 검은색 반점이 있지만, 왕침노린재는 색깔이 회색이다. 마지막으로 해로운 곤충을 먹이로 삼는 왕침노린재와 달리, 침노린재가 항상 인간에 이롭지는 않다.

28 Q 기사는 왜 흡혈성 침노린재를 언급하는가?
(a) 흡혈성 침노린재가 인간에게 유순하다고 설명하기 위해
(b) 침노린재에 대한 일반적 사실의, 주목할 만한 예외를 제시하기 위해
(c) 흡혈성 침노린재가 왕침노린재와 많은 유사성을 공유한다고 함의하기 위해
(d) 흡혈성 침노린재가 대표적인 침노린재 종(種)이라고 암시하기 위해

해설 NEW TEPS에서도 특이한 동식물에 대한 지문이 꾸준하게 출제되고 있음에 유의해야 한다. 기사에서는 침노린재가 보통 사람에게 이롭지만, 일부가 해롭다는 예외를 말하고 있고, 그 예로서 흡혈성 침노린재를 제시했다. 따라서 정답은 (b)이다. 단순하게 생각하면, 흡혈성 침노린재가 인간에게 해롭다는 정보를 제공하기 위함이라고 이해할 수 있지만, 실전에서는 이와 같이 보다 일반화한 선택지를 제시함에 유의해야 한다.

29 Q 기사에 따르면, 다음 중 옳은 것은?
(a) 파리의 방어기제가 모기의 방어기제보다 침노린재를 물리치는 데 보다 효과적이다.
(b) 대부분의 침노린재 종들은 북아메리카가 원산지이다.
(c) 왕침노린재는 척추동물을 잡아먹고 사는 것으로 널리 알려져 있다.
(d) 돌기가 왕침노린재의 두드러진 특징이다.

해설 (a)는 기사에서 전혀 말하지 않은 내용이므로 오답이다. (b)는 세계에 분포하고 있는 종의 수만 밝혔기 때문에 알 수 없는 사항이다. (c)는 왕침노린재에 대한 설명이 아니라, 흡혈성 침노린재와 관련될 수 있는 설명이다. 물론 흡혈성 침노린재가 척추동물을 잡아먹는 것은 아니다. 정답은 (d)로 기사에서 설명한 내용과 일치한다.

beneficial 이로운, 유익한 **prey on** ~을 먹이로 삼다 **predatory** 포식성의 **surreptitiously** 몰래 **entomologist** 곤충학자 **vertebrate** 척추동물 **crest** (물건의) 꼭대기 **marking** 무늬, 반점 **benign** 유순한 **notable** 눈에 띄는 **ward off** 물리치다 **indigenous** 토착의, 원산의 **distinguishing** 특징적인

30-31

정치 〉 전국　　　　　　　　　　　　　캐롤라이나 포스트

보수 시대의 조짐

총선이 임박했는데, 점점 더 많은 정치 전문가들이 에밀리 스미스가 이끄는 보수당이 선거에서 승리할 태세를 갖추었다고 예측한다. 이들의 예측이 맞다면, 보수당은 국정의 진로를 극적으로 바꿀 것이다. 일부 정치 평론가들은 보수당의 승리가 보수 시대가 시작된다는 전조일 것이라고 말한다.

몇 개월 전만 해도, 보수당이 총선에서 승리할 가능성이 있다고 생각하는 정치 전문가는 없었다. 그래서 3월에 스미스 씨가 보수당의 총수가 되었을 때, 주의를 기울인 평론가는 없었다. 스미스 씨는 정치 경력이 전무한 신출내기였고, 보수당은 절망적으로 무능했기 때문이었.

그렇지만 놀랍게도, 몇 달 만에, 보수당은 환골탈태하여 점점 더 많은 유권자를 끌어들였다. 대부분의 전문가들은 스미스 씨의 강력한 지도력과 명확한 방향 감각 때문에 이 모든 변화가 가능했다는 데 동의한다. 이들에 따르면, 일단 권력을 잡게 되면, 보수당이 연방 정부 예산의 균형을 맞추고 방위력을 강화하는 것과 같은 보수적인 정책을 추구하여 국정의 진로를 변경할 것이라고 한다.

30 Q 기사에 따르면, 스미스 씨에 대해 다음 중 옳은 것은?
(a) 보수당의 총수가 되었을 때, 여러 해 동안의 정치 경력을 갖추고 있었다.
(b) 정치에서 정확히 무엇을 성취하기를 원하는지 알고 있다.
(c) 보수당 최초의 여성 총수이다.
(d) 최근에 소속 정당을 보수당으로 바꿨다.

해설 NEW TEPS로 전환되면서, 정치와 경제, 사회와 문화에 관련된 신문·잡지의 기사 문항의 비중이 높아졌음에 유의하자. (a)는 신출내기라고 했으므로 오답이다. (c)와 (d)는 기사의 내용만으로는 정확히 알 수 없는 정보이므로 반드시 오답으로 처리해야 한다. (b)는 기사에서 '명확한 방향 감각'이라는 말을 통해 알 수 있는 정보이므로 정답이다.

31 Q 기사로부터 추론할 수 있는 것은?
(a) 보수당은 총선에서 압승할 것이다.
(b) 대부분의 유권자들은 스미스 씨가 유순하다고 인식한다.
(c) 현 행정부는 연방 예산에서 재정 적자에 빠져 있다.
(d) 총선 이후에, 보수당은 사회복지를 확대할 것이다.

해설 (a)는 전형적인 비약에 해당한다. 선거에서 승리할 것으로 예측되지만, 압승의 여부는 알 수 없다. (b)는 강력한 지도력의 소유자라고 했기 때문에 오답이다. (d)는 일반적으로 보수 정치의 특징이 아니다. 그런데 이런 배경 지식이 없다고 하더라도, 연방 정부 예산의 균형을 맞추겠다는 말에서 현재 재정 적자임을 알 수 있기 때문에 정답은 (c)이다. 물론 (d)의 내용이 기사에서 예로 제시되지 않았기 때문에 오답이라고 생각할 수도 있다.

dawn 시작, 발단; 여명　**general election** 총선거　**pundit** 전문가
poised 태세를 갖춘　**commentator** 논객, 평론가　**mark** (새로운 일의) 전조이다　**novice** 신출내기　**turn over a new leaf** 거듭나다
defense capability 방위력　**under one's belt** 소유하여, 경험하여
landslide 압도적인 승리

32-33

확증 편향에 대한 다양한 설명

거의 모든 이들은 기존의 견해를 강화하는 방식으로 정보를 처리하는 경향이 있다. 따라서 사람들은 일반적으로 상황을 있는 그대로 이해하지 않는다. 이런 일이 왜 일어나는지를 설명하는 다양한 방식들이 있다.

인지심리학자들에 따르면, 확증 편향은 사람들이 일반적으로 복잡한 과제를 다루는 능력이 제한되어 있기 때문에 발생한다. 바꾸어 말하면, 사람들은 복잡한 과제를 효과적으로 다루지 못해서 그런 과제를 가능한 한 단순화하려고 노력한다. 사람들이 한 번에 하나의 과제만을 수행할 수 있을지도 모른다.

동기심리학자들은 확증 편향에 대해 다른 설명을 제시한다. 이들에 따르면, 사람들은 불쾌한 생각보다 유쾌한 생각을 더 좋아한다. 따라서 불쾌한 생각을 선뜻 받아들이지 않는 경향이 있다. 불쾌한 생각이 제시될 때, 사람들은 그런 생각을 이해하고 처리하는 데 큰 어려움을 겪는다.

진화심리학자들을 포함한, 다른 심리학자들은 확증 편향이 발생하는 이유에 대해 생각이 다르다. 이런 설명들 각각에는 약간의 진실이 들어 있을지도 모른다. 서로 다른 입장에도 불구하고, 대부분의 심리학자들은 확증 편향이 편견과 형편없는 결정으로 귀결될 수 있다는 데 동의한다.

32 Q 지문의 주제는?
(a) 편견과 형편없는 결정의 이유들에 대한 다양한 설명들
(b) 특정한 심리 현상이 발생하는 이유에 대한 다양한 생각들
(c) 생리학자들마다 확증 편향에 다르게 접근하는 방식들
(d) 확증 편향을 바로잡은 효과적인 방법들

해설 NEW TEPS에서도 심리학과 관련된 내용의 출제 비중이 높음에 유의해야 한다. 정답은 (b)인데, '확증 편향'이라는 용어를 쓰지 않았음에 주목해야 한다. NEW TEPS의 시행을 전후하여, 이처럼 지문의 구체적인 용어가 아니라, 보다 일반화한 용어를 쓴 선택지가 정답으로 제시되는 경우가 늘었다. (c)는 매력적인 오답인데, '생리학자'가 아니라 '심리학자'라고 해야 정답이 될 수 있다. (d)는 지문에서 다루고 있지 않다.

33 Q 지문으로부터 추론할 수 있는 것은?
(a) 현실을 있는 그대로 직시할 가능성이 있는 사람은 많지 않다.
(b) 진화심리학은 인지심리학의 한 분과이다.
(c) 동기심리학은 사람들이 불쾌한 경험을 피하도록 동기를 부여하는 것과 관련된다.
(d) 대부분의 심리학자들은 확증 편향이 진정한 행복으로 귀결될 수 있다는 데 동의한다.

해설 (b)는 지문의 내용으로부터 추론할 수 없는 사항이므로, 반드시 오답으로 처리해야 한다. (c)는 실제로 그럴 수 있을지도 모르지만, 지문의 내용만으로는 알 수 없다. 이런 선택지도 반드시 오답으로 처리해야 함을 명심해야 한다. (d)는 지문의 내용에 어긋난다. 따라서 정답은 자연스럽게 추론할 수 있는 (a)이다.

confirmation bias 확증 편향　**process** 처리하다; 과정　**reinforce** 강화하다　**pre-existing** 기존의　**complicated** 복잡한　**readily** 선뜻, 기꺼이　**prejudice** 편견　**physiologist** 생리학자　**remedy** 교정하다, 바로잡다　**well-being** 행복

34-35

◁ 페기

〈나〉

안녕, 페기. 아버지와의 관계가 결코 이상적이지 않다는 사실을 잘 알고 있어. 하지만 네가 아버지를 방문하러 런던에 간 지가 거의 11년이 되었다는 사실을 말해야겠다. 내가 알기로는, 그때 이래로 아버지와 연락을 하지 않았어.

네 감정을 아주 존중하지만, 아버지가 90대 후반이시라는 사실을 생각해 봤으면 해. 어떤 것도 암시하는 건 아니지만, 적어도 아버지께 전화를 드리는 것이 관계를 개선하는 데 도움이 될 수 있을 거야.

〈페기〉

안녕, 줄리아. 네 문자 메시지는 늘 다양한 것들에 대해 다른 방식으로 생각해 보도록 만드는데, 이 메시지도 예외가 아니야. 사실 근래에 아버지와의 관계에 대해서 생각을 많이 하고 있어. 이것이 어쩌면 동시성의 사례가 아닐까 싶구나.

어떻든, 기꺼이 네 충고를 받아들이려고 해. 아버지가 어쩌면 예전만큼 무신경하시진 않을지도 모르겠어. 또 과거보다는 덜 완고하시길 바라고 있어. 제안한 대로, 곧 전화를 드릴 생각이야. 생각이 깊은 친구가 되어 줘서 고마워.

34 Q 줄리아는 왜 메시지를 보냈는가?

(a) 건강한 관계를 유지하는 방법에 대해 수취인과 상의하기 위해

(b) 너무 늦기 전에 어떤 행동 방침을 제안하기 위해

(c) 수취인과 좋은 관계를 회복하기를 바란다고 말하기 위해

(d) 가까운 장래에 수취인이 런던을 방문해달라고 초청하기 위해

해설 (a)는 줄리아가 오히려 충고를 하는 입장이므로 오답이다. (c)는 줄리아와 수취인과의 관계가 아니라, 수취인과 수취인의 아버지 사이의 관계에 대해 말하기 때문에 정답이 아니다. (d)는 메시지에서 밝힌 내용이 아니다. 따라서 정답은 (b)이다. 수취인의 아버지가 90대 후반이라고 했다는 점을 고려할 때 지체할 시간이 많지 않음을 알 수 있다.

35 Q 채팅 메시지로부터 추론할 수 있는 것은?

(a) 페기는 대개 줄리아의 문자 메시지에 대해 모욕을 느낀다.

(b) 페기는 줄리아의 제안에 즉각 반응할 가능성이 높다.

(c) 페기는 동시성이라는 개념을 믿지 않는다.

(d) 페기는 종종 줄리아로 하여금 많은 것에 대한 생각을 바꾸도록 설득해 왔다.

해설 (a)는 정반대로 말했기 때문에 오답이다. (c)는 페기가 동시성의 개념을 믿고 있음을 확인할 수 있기 때문에 정답이 아니다. (d)는 중요한 오답 유형인데, 동작의 주체가 거꾸로 제시되었다. 따라서 정답은 자연스럽게 추론이 가능한 (b)이다. NEW TEPS에서도 추론 유형이 세부 사항 유형과 상당히 유사하게 출제되는 경우가 종종 있음에 주목해야 한다. 이는 TEPS의 추론 유형이 지문의 내용에 대단히 충실할 것을 요구하기 때문이다. 바꾸어 말해서, 절대로 비약해서는 안 되며, 추론의 정도가 다소 약한 정도에 머물러야 한다.

ideal 이상적인 **imply** 함축하다, 시사하다 **synchronicity** 동시성 **insensitive** 냉담한, 무신경한 **stubborn** 완고한 **affront** 모욕하다 **responsive** 즉각 반응하는

Actual Test 5

청해 Listening *Comprehension*

p.155

1	(c)	2	(c)	3	(c)	4	(b)	5	(c)	6	(d)	7	(c)	8	(c)	9	(a)	10	(d)
11	(c)	12	(d)	13	(a)	14	(d)	15	(a)	16	(c)	17	(d)	18	(a)	19	(d)	20	(b)
21	(d)	22	(b)	23	(b)	24	(b)	25	(d)	26	(c)	27	(d)	28	(c)	29	(c)	30	(c)
31	(a)	32	(a)	33	(d)	34	(c)	35	(a)	36	(b)	37	(d)	38	(b)	39	(c)	40	(b)

어휘 Vocabulary

p.161

1	(a)	2	(a)	3	(d)	4	(d)	5	(c)	6	(d)	7	(a)	8	(a)	9	(b)	10	(a)
11	(c)	12	(a)	13	(d)	14	(b)	15	(d)	16	(b)	17	(a)	18	(a)	19	(d)	20	(b)
21	(b)	22	(d)	23	(a)	24	(b)	25	(d)	26	(c)	27	(b)	28	(a)	29	(c)	30	(d)

문법 Grammar

p.165

1	(d)	2	(d)	3	(b)	4	(c)	5	(d)	6	(d)	7	(a)	8	(c)	9	(a)	10	(d)
11	(d)	12	(c)	13	(a)	14	(c)	15	(d)	16	(d)	17	(c)	18	(b)	19	(a)	20	(c)
21	(d)	22	(d)	23	(d)	24	(d)	25	(c)	26	(b)	27	(b)	28	(a)	29	(d)	30	(d)

독해 Reading *Comprehension*

p.169

1	(b)	2	(d)	3	(d)	4	(d)	5	(c)	6	(a)	7	(c)	8	(b)	9	(d)	10	(b)
11	(b)	12	(d)	13	(d)	14	(b)	15	(b)	16	(c)	17	(c)	18	(d)	19	(b)	20	(d)
21	(c)	22	(c)	23	(b)	24	(b)	25	(b)	26	(b)	27	(b)	28	(a)	29	(c)	30	(c)
31	(b)	32	(d)	33	(c)	34	(b)	35	(b)												

Part I

1

M Several questions on the exam had me stumped.
W _____

(a) Sorry, I don't have time for any questions.
(b) Actually, I didn't think they were.
(c) Still, I'm certain you did well.
(d) No, I haven't taken the exam yet.

M 몇몇 시험 문제가 날 당황스럽게 했어.
W _____

(a) 미안해, 어떤 문제든 풀 시간이 전혀 없어.
(b) 사실은 문제들이 그렇다고 생각하지 않았어.
(c) 그래도 넌 분명히 잘했을 거야.
(d) 아니, 아직 시험을 안 쳤어.

stump 난처[당황]하게 하다 **take an exam** 시험을 치르다

2

M Catherine just told me there were cookies in the break room.
W _____

(a) I probably won't take a break today.
(b) Thanks for bringing the snacks.
(c) Yes, but there won't be for long.
(d) Oh, no, I didn't make them.

M 휴게실에 과자가 있다고 캐서린이 방금 알려줬어요.
W _____

(a) 오늘 저는 아마 휴식을 취하지 않을 거예요.
(b) 과자를 갖다 줘서 고마워요.
(c) 네, 하지만 금방 없어질 거예요.
(d) 오, 아니에요, 내가 만들지 않았어요.

break room 휴게실 **take a break** 휴식을 취하다

3

M I didn't see you in the audience. Where were you sitting?
W _____

(a) The tickets were already sold out.
(b) It was hard to see what was going on.
(c) My seat was near the back of the theater.
(d) I've been waiting here for about 20 minutes.

M 관객들 속에서 네가 안 보이던데, 어디에 앉아 있었니?
W _____

(a) 표가 이미 매진됐어.
(b) 무슨 일이 일어나고 있는지 알기 힘들었어.
(c) 극장 뒤쪽 부근에 앉아 있었어.
(d) 이곳에서 기다린 지 20분쯤 됐어.

sold out (표가) 매진된

4

M Do you know how long Keisha has been working here?
W _____

(a) Things have worked out like I hoped.
(b) Since her first semester of college.
(c) I'm sure I saw her here earlier.
(d) She sure is fitting in here nicely.

M 케이샤가 이곳에서 얼마 동안 근무해왔는지 아세요?
W _____

(a) 내가 바란 대로 일이 잘되고 있어요.
(b) 그녀가 대학을 다니던 첫 학기 때부터요.
(c) 나는 그녀를 예전에 이곳에서 봤다고 확신해요.
(d) 그녀는 분명 여기에 잘 적응할 겁니다.

work out (일이) 잘되어가다 **semester** 학기

5

M Who should I ask for assistance, Keith or May?
W _____

(a) Remind Keith not to be late.
(b) That would be very thoughtful.
(c) Neither will be able to help you.
(d) I'd recommend seeking some aid.

M 키쓰와 메이 중에 누구에게 도움을 청해야 할까요?
W _____

(a) 지각하지 말라고 키쓰에게 다시 한 번 말해 주세요.
(b) 그건 매우 사려 깊은 처사일 거예요.
(c) 둘 다 당신을 도울 수 없을 거예요.
(d) 도움을 구할 것을 권합니다.

ask for 요청하다 **assistance** 도움 **thoughtful** 사려 깊은

6

W Do you want whipped cream on your hot chocolate?
M _____

(a) No, I didn't until it was too late.
(b) Oh, I heard something about that.
(c) Don't worry, I told them to hold the cream.
(d) I'd better not, as I'm watching my weight.

W 핫초코에 거품 크림 원하세요?
M _____

(a) 아니요, 제가 원했을 때는 이미 너무 늦었어요.
(b) 오, 그것에 관해 들은 바가 있어요.
(c) 걱정하지 마세요, 크림은 빼달라고 했어요.
(d) 체중 관리를 하고 있어서 안 넣는 게 좋겠어요.

whipped cream 거품 크림(생크림에 거품이 일게 한 것) **hold** ~을
빼다[넣지 말다] **watch one's weight** 체중 관리를 하다

7

M I forgot about the report you asked me to proofread!
W _____

(a) I wouldn't have if I knew you wanted to.
(b) I'll keep that in mind and let you know.
(c) I'm disappointed that you let me down.
(d) I wish I had read it so I could do that for you.

M 당신이 교정 봐 달라고 했던 보고서를 깜박 잊고 있었어요.
W _____

(a) 당신이 원한다는 걸 알았다면 그러지 않았을 텐데요.
(b) 명심해 두었다가 알려 드릴게요.
(c) 당신은 날 실망시켰어요.
(d) 당신을 대신해서 그 전에 그것을 읽었다면 좋았을 텐데.

proofread 교정 보다 **disappointed** 실망한 **let down** 실망시키다,
기대를 저버리다

8

W May I speak with the manager about my application?
M _____

(a) That's what the manager will take care of.
(b) Please submit your application first.
(c) Could you please call back in an hour?
(d) You didn't get my documentation.

W 저의 지원서 건에 대해서 책임자와 통화할 수 있을까요?
M _____

(a) 그게 바로 책임자가 관리할 일이에요.
(b) 먼저 지원서를 제출해 주세요.
(c) 한 시간 뒤에 다시 전화 주시겠어요?.
(d) 제 증빙 서류를 받지 못했군요.

application 지원(서) **submit** 제출하다 **documentation** (증빙) 서류

9

W What's wrong? You seem preoccupied.
M _____

(a) It's just that my presentation is today.
(b) Nothing, I've got some spare time.
(c) Of course I'm trying to correct it.
(d) I am, but not until after lunch.

W 무슨 일 있어요? 무슨 생각을 그렇게 골똘히 하세요?
M _____

(a) 오늘 프레젠테이션을 해야 하거든요.
(b) 아무것도 아니에요, 짬이 좀 났어요.
(c) 물론 그걸 바로잡으려고 노력하고 있죠.
(d) 맞아요, 하지만 점심시간이 지나서야 그럴 거예요.

preoccupied 몰두한, 정신이 팔린 **spare time** 여가, 짬 **correct**
고치다, 바로잡다

10

M Are you worried about the cutbacks in your
  department?
W _____

(a) Many more than we ever expected.
(b) The end of last month saw some cuts.
(c) I couldn't believe it was already done.
(d) I earn a lot of revenue so I think I'm safe.

M 당신 부서의 인원 감축 때문에 걱정 되세요?
W _____

(a) 우리가 예상했던 것보다 훨씬 많군요.
(b) 지난달 말에 약간의 인원 감축이 있었어요.
(c) 이미 끝났다니 믿을 수가 없었어요.
(d) 전 큰 수입을 올리고 있어서 문제없을 거예요.

cutback (인원·생산 등의) 감축 **department** 부서 **revenue** 수입,
수익

Part II

11

W Are these slacks too wrinkled to wear to dinner?
M Honestly, they could do with a quick press.
W That's what I figured. Could you iron them while I
  shower?
M _____

(a) Don't forget to press them quickly.
(b) I thought you were done with them.
(c) Hand them over and I'll take care of it.
(d) Thanks, but I'll just wear them as they are.

W 이 바지는 주름이 너무 많아서 정찬에 입고 갈 수 없겠죠?
M 사실, 빠르게 다리미질 하면 괜찮을 것 같은데요.
W 내 생각도 바로 그거예요. 제가 샤워하는 동안 좀 다려 주실래요?
M _____

(a) 잊지 말고 빨리 다려 주세요.
(b) 저는 당신이 바지를 다 다린 줄 알았어요.
(c) 이리 주세요. 제가 해 놓을게요.
(d) 고맙지만, 그냥 그대로 입을게요.

slacks (정장용이 아닌) 바지 **wrinkled** 주름이 있는 **do** 괜찮다, 잘되다
press 다리미질(을 하다) **iron** 다리미질을 하다 **hand over** 넘겨주다

12

W Can I help you find anything?
M Actually, yes. I need eight ounces of roasted barley.
W All our grains are weighed in pounds.
M _____

(a) Sure, I'll go get that for you.
(b) OK, that'll be ninety-five cents.
(c) I only have a couple pounds left.
(d) In that case, give me a half pound.

W 찾으시는 물건이 있으면 도와 드릴까요?
M 네. 볶은 보리 8온스가 필요해요.
W 저희 곡물은 모두 파운드 단위로 중량을 재요.
M _____

(a) 물론이죠, 그걸 가져다 드릴게요.
(b) 좋습니다, 그럼 95센트 되겠습니다.
(c) 남은 건 2파운드밖에 없어요.
(d) 그럼 반 파운드 주세요.

roasted barley 볶은 보리   **grain** 곡물

13

M Hi, Skylark Lounge. Johan speaking.
W Hello, do you have any live music scheduled for tonight?
M Sure do. Which branch are you interested in?
W _____

(a) Oh, I didn't realize there was more than one.
(b) No problem, I just wanted to know the schedule.
(c) That's alright, because I'll think about it.
(d) I would if it were a free show tonight.

M 안녕하세요, 스카이락 라운지의 요한입니다.
W 안녕하세요, 오늘밤 일정에 라이브 음악도 포함되어 있나요?
M 물론이죠. 어느 분점을 원하시나요?
W _____

(a) 오, 스카이락이 다른 곳에도 있는 줄 몰랐어요.
(b) 괜찮아요, 그냥 일정을 알고 싶었을 뿐이에요.
(c) 괜찮습니다, 왜냐하면 그것에 대해 생각해 볼 거니까요.
(d) 오늘밤 쇼가 무료라면 그럴게요.

Sure do. 물론이지, 두말하면 잔소리지.   **branch** 지점, 분점

14

W You look like Johnny Depp in those horn-rimmed glasses.
M Thanks, but I'm not sure I want to buy them.
W Well, how much are they?
M _____

(a) I still think they're worth it.
(b) Actually, that's a good price.
(c) You could ask the clerk for a discount.
(d) A hundred dollars more than I can afford.

W 그 뿔테 안경을 쓰니까 조니 뎁 같군요.
M 고마워요, 하지만 사야 할지 말아야 할지 잘 모르겠어요.
W 음, 얼만데요?
M _____

(a) 그래도 그만한 가치가 있다고 생각해요.
(b) 사실, 좋은 가격이에요.
(c) 점원에게 할인해 달라고 요구해 보세요.
(d) 제가 지불할 수 있는 것보다 100달러 더 비싸요.

horn-rimmed 뿔테의   **clerk** 점원, 판매원   **afford** ~을 지불할 수 있다

15

W We'd better hurry or we won't make the plane.
M Yes, and unfortunately, our gate's over in Terminal B.
W When do they close the boarding door?
M _____

(a) About fifteen minutes from now.
(b) Departing at 5:10 on flight 292.
(c) I must have forgotten the tickets.
(d) We're in Terminal A at the moment.

W 서두르지 않으면 비행기를 놓칠 거야.
M 응, 근데 불행히도 우리 탑승구가 터미널 B 쪽에 있어.
W 탑승구가 언제 닫히지?
M _____

(a) 약 15분 후에.
(b) 292편으로 5시 10분에 출발해.
(c) 표를 두고 온 게 틀림없어.
(d) 우린 지금 터미널 A에 있어.

make (탈것·모임 등의) 시간 안에 가다   **gate** 탑승구   **depart** 출발하다
at the moment 지금

16

M Guess what tomorrow is, Dena.
W I know. It's your moving day, and you need my help.
M Wow, you read my mind! So, will you lend a hand?
W _____

(a) Because you told me about it last weekend.
(b) Thanks for the offer, but there's no need.
(c) Only if you buy me pizza after.
(d) Well, my cousin's helping me.

M 디나, 내일이 무슨 날인지 맞춰봐.
W 알아. 네 이삿날이잖아. 그래서 내 도움이 필요한 거고.
M 와, 내 맘을 읽었구나! 그럼 도와주겠니?
W _____

(a) 지난 주말에 그 일에 대해 내게 말했기 때문이지.
(b) 제의는 고맙지만 그럴 필요 없어.
(c) 끝난 후에 피자를 사주기만 한다면야.
(d) 음, 내 사촌이 날 도울 거야.

moving day 이삿날 **lend a hand** 도와주다 **offer** 제의
only if ~해야만

17

W Dad, what are you still doing up?
M Waiting for you to get home. You had an 11 o'clock
   curfew.
W Come on, it's only quarter after 11.
M _____

(a) Oh, let me set the alarm clock then.
(b) No, I was waiting right up until 11.
(c) That's why I was going to sleep.
(d) When I said 11, I meant it.

W 아빠, 아직도 안 주무시고 뭐 하세요?
M 네가 집에 도착하기를 기다리고 있지. 11시까지 들어오라고 했잖아.
W 에구. 11시에서 겨우 15분 지났는걸요.
M _____

(a) 오, 그럼 내가 자명종을 맞춰 놓을게.
(b) 아니, 11시까지 꼬박 기다리고 있었어.
(c) 그 때문에 내가 잠자려고 한 거야.
(d) 내가 11시라고 했을 때는 그냥 하는 소리가 아니었어.

up 깨어 있는 **curfew** (부모가 자녀에게 부과하는) 귀가 시간
alarm clock 자명종 **I mean it.** 진심이야, 농담이 아니야.

18

W Sorry, we've had to cancel the final day of Rock City
   Fest.
M But I paid fifty dollars for my ticket!
W We'll refund a third of the ticket price.
M _____

(a) That's better than nothing, I guess.
(b) No, we can't, as they're sold out.
(c) Thanks, I'll pay you back later.
(d) No, I said I paid full ticket price.

W 유감스럽게도 우린 마지막 날 록 시티 페스티벌을 취소해야만 해요.
M 하지만 50달러 주고 표를 이미 샀는걸요!
W 표 값의 3분의 1을 환불해 드릴게요.
M _____

(a) 아무것도 안 받는 것보다는 낫겠군요.
(b) 아니요, 표가 매진돼서 그럴 수 없어요.
(c) 고마워요, 나중에 갚을게요.
(d) 안 돼요, 표 값을 전액 지불했다고 했잖아요.

cancel 취소하다 **refund** 환불하다 **sold out** (표가) 매진된

19

M Do you know where Bus 33-22 stops around here?
W Near the construction site on Vale Street.
M But wasn't the bus stop relocated?
W _____

(a) Renovations have been underway since spring.
(b) You can pay when you get on the bus.
(c) I used to live along Vale Street.
(d) That would be news to me.

M 33-22번 버스가 이 근처 어디에 서는지 아세요?
W 베일 가에 있는 건설 현장 부근에 서요.
M 근데 버스 정류장이 다른 곳으로 이전 안 됐나요?
W _____

(a) 봄철부터 보수 작업을 해오고 있어요.
(b) 버스를 탈 때 요금을 내면 돼요.
(c) 예전에 베일 가에 살았어요.
(d) 처음 듣는 소리인데요.

construction site 건설 현장 **relocate** 이전하다 **renovation**
수리, 보수 **be underway** 진행[진척] 중이다

20

W Oh, no. They took the peanut butter smoothie off the
   menu.
M But, look, there's one listed right here.
W That one has bananas in it. Yuck.
M _____

(a) I'm afraid they're out of that flavor.
(b) Maybe you'd like it if you tried it.
(c) I thought you wanted a sandwich.
(d) Just ask for a takeout smoothie.

W 오, 이런. 메뉴에서 땅콩버터 스무디가 빠졌어요.
M 아니요, 보세요, 여기 그 메뉴가 있잖아요.
W 그건 바나나가 든 거잖아요. 윽.
M _____

(a) 안타깝게도 그 양념은 빠진 것 같아요.
(b) 맛을 보면 좋아하게 될지 몰라요.
(c) 나는 당신이 샌드위치를 원하는 줄 알았어요.
(d) 그냥 사서 들고 갈 수 있는 스무디를 달라고 해 보세요.

smoothie 스무디(음료의 일종) **yuck** 윽, 우왝(역겨울 때 내는 소리)
flavor 향료, 양념 **takeout** 사서 들고 갈 수 있는

Actual Test 5

Part III

21

Listen to a conversation between two acquaintances.

> W I hear you're going to Iceland next month.
> M That's right. My wife and I will spend 10 days there.
> W But January in Iceland is brutally cold.
> M Yes, cold and dark. But I want to see the Northern Lights.
> W Is winter the best time to see them?
> M Yes, at least according to what I've read.

Q What is the main topic of the conversation?
(a) The woman's harsh experiences in Iceland
(b) What Iceland is best for in winter months
(c) What time to see the Northern Lights
(d) The man's upcoming Icelandic trip

두 지인의 대화를 들으시오.

> W 다음 달에 아이슬란드에 가신다면서요.
> M 네. 아내와 함께 그곳에서 열흘간 지낼 거예요.
> W 하지만 아이슬란드의 1월은 지독하게 추운데요.
> M 네, 춥고 어둡죠. 하지만 북극광을 보고 싶어요.
> W 그걸 구경하는 데 겨울이 최적기인가요?
> M 네, 적어도 제가 읽은 바로는 그래요.

Q 대화의 주제는?
(a) 여자의 혹독했던 아이슬란드 경험
(b) 아이슬란드가 겨울철에 가장 좋은 것
(c) 북극광을 봐야 할 때
(d) 남자의 다가오는 아이슬란드 여행

brutally 무지막지하게   **Northern Lights** 북극광   **harsh** 가혹한
upcoming 다가오는   **Icelandic** 아이슬란드의

22

Listen to a conversation in a gym.

> W Our trainers set high standards for all our customers.
> M What exactly does that mean?
> W Our goal is to have people bench press one and a half times their body weight.
> M But I'm nowhere near that goal right now.
> W Don't worry, we understand it's a long-term goal.
> M I guess I'll work up to it over time.

Q What is the woman mainly doing in this conversation?
(a) Inviting the man to start work as a trainer
(b) Explaining the target trainers aim for
(c) Discouraging the man from working out too hard
(d) Questioning the man's commitment to training

헬스클럽에서 이뤄지는 대화를 들으시오.

> W 저희 트레이너들은 모든 고객들에게 목표를 높이 정해줘요.
> M 그게 정확하게 무슨 뜻이지요?
> W 고객이 자기 체중의 1.5배의 벤치 프레스를 할 수 있기를 기대하고 있죠.
> M 하지만 저로선 그 목표에 도달하려면 아직 한참 멀었어요.
> W 걱정하지 마세요. 우린 그게 장기 목표란 걸 알고 있으니까요.
> M 시간이 지나면 저도 그렇게 될 수 있을 거예요.

Q 여자가 주로 하고 있는 것은?
(a) 남자에게 트레이너로서의 업무를 시작하도록 부탁하기
(b) 트레이너들이 지향하는 목표에 대해 설명하기
(c) 남자에게 너무 강도 높게 운동하지 못하게 하기
(d) 남자가 훈련에 너무 열중하는 것을 문제 삼기

set a standard 기준을 정하다   **bench press** 벤치 프레스(벤치 같은 데 누워 역기를 들어 올리는 운동)를 하다   **body weight** 체중   **nowhere near** ~은 당치도 않다   **long-term** 장기의   **work up to** ~에 달하다   **discourage A from -ing** A가 ~하는 것을 막다   **work out** 운동하다   **question** 문제 삼다   **commitment** 몰두

23

Listen to a conversation between a patient and a receptionist.

> M Hello, this is Tavis at Dr. Khan's office.
> W Can I please speak with Dr. Khan?
> M I'm sorry, she's with a patient right now. Can I take a message?
> W This is Sonia Swaden. I'm asking for the results of my blood test.
> M Certainly. I'll let Dr. Khan know you called.
> W Thank you. Hope to hear back from her soon.

Q What is the conversation mainly about?
(a) What to expect during an upcoming appointment
(b) A patient's inquiry to her doctor about a test
(c) The final results of the woman's blood test
(d) Why Dr. Khan is currently too busy to talk

환자와 접수원의 대화를 들으시오.

> M 안녕하세요, 칸 병원의 타비스입니다.
> W 칸 선생님과 통화할 수 있을까요?
> M 죄송하지만, 지금 환자를 보고 계십니다. 메모 남기시겠어요?
> W 제 이름은 소냐 스와덴이고요, 제 혈액 검사 결과를 알고 싶어요.
> M 알겠습니다. 전화 왔었다고 칸 선생님께 전해 드릴게요.
> W 감사합니다. 그녀로부터 연락이 빨리 왔으면 좋겠군요.

Q 대화의 주된 내용은?
(a) 곧 있을 약속 시간 동안 기대할 내용
(b) 환자가 검사 건으로 의사에게 문의하기
(c) 여자의 혈액 검사에 대한 최종 결과
(d) 칸 선생님이 현재 대화를 할 수 없을 정도로 바쁜 이유

patient 환자   **inquiry** 정보를 구함, 문의   **currently** 현재

24

Listen to two friends discuss concert tickets.

M Daniela, do you still have those concert tickets?

W Oh, sorry. I gave them to Steve because you didn't want them.

M Oh, no. I wish I'd taken them now.

W Really? Well, you can always ask Steve to take you.

M No, I know he's going to take Stephanie.

W Yeah, you're probably right.

Q Which is correct according to the conversation?

(a) The woman sold concert tickets to Steve.

(b) The man regrets refusing the woman's offer.

(c) The man will ask Steve for a concert ticket.

(d) The woman is going to the concert with Steve.

두 친구가 콘서트 표에 관해 말하는 것을 들으시오.

M 다니엘라, 아직도 그 콘서트 표 갖고 있니?

W 아, 미안해. 네가 원하지 않는다고 해서 스티브에게 줬어.

M 아, 저런. 지금은 그 표가 있었으면 좋겠는데.

W 정말? 그럼, 언제라도 스티브에게 너를 데려가 달라고 하면 될 거야.

M 아냐, 그가 스테파니를 데려갈 게 뻔하잖아.

W 응, 네 말이 맞는 것 같다.

Q 대화에 따르면 다음 중 옳은 것은?

(a) 여자는 스티브에게 콘서트 표를 팔았다.

(b) 남자는 여자의 제안을 거절한 것을 후회한다.

(c) 남자는 스티브에게 콘서트 표를 달라고 부탁할 것이다.

(d) 여자는 스티브와 함께 콘서트에 갈 것이다.

regret 후회하다   **refuse** 거절하다

25

Listen to a conversation in a restaurant.

W After closing, we have to wash the dishes.

M OK, that shouldn't be a problem.

W Fill the basin with hot water and add powdered sanitizer.

M That's a new procedure. What's it for?

W To kill bacteria. Once you've washed the dishes, dip them into it.

M OK, but watch to make sure I'm doing it right.

Q Why is the new procedure implemented?

(a) To find a better way to wash the dishes

(b) To determine if powdered sanitizer is better than soap

(c) To make sure that the man works faster

(d) To get rid of potentially harmful microbes

식당에서 이뤄지는 대화를 들으시오.

W 문을 닫은 후에 우린 설거지를 해야 해요.

M 좋아요, 그건 별 문제 안 돼요.

W 대야에 뜨거운 물을 채운 후 가루 살균제를 넣으세요.

M 그건 새로운 방식이군요. 그걸 넣는 이유가 뭐죠?

W 세균을 죽이기 위해서예요. 일단 식기를 씻고 나면 그릇을 담그세요.

M 알았어요, 하지만 제가 제대로 하고 있는지 지켜봐 주세요.

Q 새로운 절차가 시행되는 이유는?

(a) 설거지를 하는 더 나은 방법을 찾기 위해서

(b) 가루 살균제가 비누보다 나은지 결정하기 위해서

(c) 남자가 더 빨리 일하도록 확실하게 하기 위해서

(d) 잠재적으로 해로운 미생물을 제거하기 위해서

basin 대야   **powdered** 가루로 된   **sanitizer** 살균제   **procedure** 방식   **dip** 담그다   **determine** 결정하다   **potentially** 잠재적으로

26

Listen to a conversation about a woman's contact lenses.

M How do the new contact lenses feel?

W They're comfortable enough, but my left eye is still blurry.

M That's normal. The lenses will move into place soon.

W Is there any way to speed it up?

M If you blink your eye a few times, that might help.

W That fixed it. I can see much more clearly now.

Q Which is correct according to the conversation?

(a) The woman needs a new pair of contact lenses.

(b) Most contact lenses are uncomfortable at first.

(c) The woman adjusted her lenses by blinking.

(d) The man is unsure how to fix the woman's vision problem.

여자의 콘택트 렌즈에 관한 대화를 들으시오.

M 이 새 콘택트렌즈를 끼니까 어때요?

W 그런대로 편안하지만, 왼쪽 눈은 여전히 흐릿해요.

M 그게 정상이에요. 곧 렌즈가 움직여서 제자리를 찾을 거예요.

W 그것을 좀 빨리 되게 하는 방법은 없나요?

M 눈을 몇 차례 깜박이면 도움이 될 거예요.

W 아, 되네요. 이제 훨씬 더 뚜렷하게 볼 수 있어요.

Q 대화 내용과 일치하는 것은?

(a) 여자는 새 콘택트렌즈가 필요하다.

(b) 대부분의 콘택트렌즈는 처음에 불편함을 느낀다.

(c) 여자는 눈을 깜박여 콘택트렌즈가 제자리에 오게 했다.

(d) 남자는 여자의 시력 문제를 어떻게 고칠지 확실히 알지 못한다.

blurry 흐릿한   **speed up** 속도를 높이다   **blink** 눈을 깜박이다   **fix** 고치다

27

Listen to a conversation about a kayaking trip.

> W We might have to put off our kayaking trip tomorrow.
> M You mean because of the forecast? I think we'll be fine.
> W I don't know about that. They're predicting severe storms.
> M That's in the evening. We'll be off the water long before that.
> W Even so, it seems there's a chance we'll get soaked.
> M The risk of rain adds to the adventure!

Q Which is correct about the speakers according to the conversation?

(a) They intend to avoid any risk of getting rained on.
(b) Their kayaking trip tomorrow has been canceled.
(c) They doubt the accuracy of the weather forecast.
(d) Their outing will take place before the evening.

카약 여행에 관한 대화를 들으시오.

W 내일 카약 여행을 연기해야 할지도 몰라요.
M 일기 예보 때문인가요? 전 괜찮을 거라고 생각하는데요.
W 과연 그럴까요? 예보에 의하면 대규모 폭풍이 올 거라는데요.
M 그건 저녁때예요. 우린 그보다 훨씬 이전에 물에서 나올 거예요.
W 그렇다 하더라도 우린 비에 흠뻑 젖을 가능성이 없지 않아요.
M 비를 맞을 위험성 때문에 더욱더 신나는 모험이 될 수 있다고요!

Q 화자들에 대해 바르게 말한 것은?
(a) 비 맞을 위험성을 피하고자 한다.
(b) 내일 카약 여행이 취소되었다.
(c) 일기 예보의 정확성을 믿지 않고 있다.
(d) 야외 활동은 저녁이 되기 전에 이루어질 것이다.

put off 연기하다　**forecast** (일기) 예보　**predict** 전망하다　**get soaked** 흠뻑 젖다　**get rained on** 비를 맞다　**accuracy** 정확성　**outing** 여행, 소풍　**take place** 발생하다

28

Listen to a conversation on the street.

> M Excuse me. Have you seen a small, white dog around?
> W Sorry, I'm afraid not.
> M Oh. He escaped from my yard when a delivery man came.
> W I'm sorry to hear that. Is your house nearby?
> M Yes, I'm at 144 Cooley Lane.
> W Well, if I find your dog I'll take him there.

Q Which is correct according to the conversation?

(a) The delivery man has yet to arrive.
(b) The woman is in search of a lost dog.
(c) The man's house is not far from the woman's.
(d) The dog was seen by the woman on Cooley Lane.

거리에서 이뤄지는 대화를 들으시오.

M 실례지만, 주위에서 작은 흰색 개를 못 봤나요?
W 유감스럽지만, 못 봤는데요.
M 오, 배달원이 집에 왔을 때 개가 마당을 빠져나갔지 뭐예요.
W 어쩌면 좋아요. 집이 근처세요?
M 네, 쿨리로 144번지예요.
W 음, 제가 만약 댁의 개를 찾으면 거기로 데려갈게요.

Q 대화 내용과 일치하는 것은?
(a) 배달원이 아직 도착하지 않았다.
(b) 여자가 잃어버린 개를 찾고 있다.
(c) 남자의 집은 여자의 집에서 멀지 않다.
(d) 여자가 쿨리로에서 개를 보았다.

delivery man 배달원　**have yet to** 아직 ~하지 않았다　**in search of** ~을 찾아서

29

Listen to a conversation about a man's tennis ability.

> W You're steadily improving at tennis.
> M But I can't seem to hit the ball with much power.
> W Try loosening your grip on the racquet.
> M Don't I need a strong grip to hit the ball hard?
> W Power comes from swinging your wrist, not the grip.
> M OK, I'll try that. Thanks for the tip.

Q What can be inferred from the conversation?

(a) The man has never played tennis before.
(b) The woman is tired from playing tennis.
(c) The woman is more experienced in tennis than the man.
(d) The man needs to get a better tennis racquet.

남자의 테니스 실력에 관한 대화를 들으시오.

W 테니스 실력이 꾸준히 늘고 있군요.
M 하지만 공을 세게 치지는 못하는 것 같아요.
W 라켓을 느슨하게 쥐어 보세요.
M 공을 세게 치려면 꽉 쥐어야 하지 않나요?
W 힘은 라켓을 잡는 힘이 아니라 손목을 돌리는 것에서 나와요.
M 좋아요. 그렇게 해 볼게요. 조언 고마워요.

Q 대화로부터 추론할 수 있는 것은?
(a) 남자는 전에 테니스를 해 본 적이 없다.
(b) 여자는 테니스를 하느라 지쳐 있다.
(c) 여자는 남자보다 테니스 경험이 많다.
(d) 남자는 더 좋은 테니스 라켓이 필요하다.

steadily 꾸준히　**loosen** 느슨하게 하다　**grip** 단단히 쥠　**wrist** 손목　**racquet** 라켓

30

Listen to a conversation between two alumni.

W May I please speak with Armin Mohsen?

M This is Armin. May I ask who's calling?

W It's Leila. We went to Astley High School together. Do you remember?

M Of course, Leila Cunningham from the drama club!

W Actually, it's Leila McGrane now.

M Great to hear from you, Leila! How did you find me?

Q What can be inferred about the woman from the conversation?

(a) She was upset the man mispronounced her name.

(b) She only recently graduated from high school.

(c) She has not spoken with the man in years.

(d) She wants to arrange a drama club reunion.

두 졸업생 사이의 대화를 들으시오.

W 아르민 모흐센 좀 바꿔 주실래요?

M 제가 아르민인데요, 누구시죠?

W 레일라야. 우리가 애스틀리 고등학교를 함께 다녔잖아. 기억나니?

M 물론이지. 연극 동아리를 했던 레일라 커닝햄!

W 사실 지금 이름은 레일라 맥그레인이야.

M 레일라, 네게서 연락을 받다니 무척 기뻐! 날 어떻게 찾아냈니?

Q 여자에 대해 추론할 수 있는 것은?

(a) 그녀는 남자가 자기 이름을 잘못 발음해서 속상했다.

(b) 그녀는 최근에야 고등학교를 졸업했다.

(c) 그녀는 오랫동안 남자와 이야기하지 못했다.

(d) 그녀는 연극 동아리 동창회를 열고 싶어 한다.

hear from ~로부터 연락이 오다(직접적인 연락) **upset** 속상한
mispronounce 잘못 발음하다 **graduate from** ~을 졸업하다
reunion 모임, 동창회

Part IV

31

The Battle of Stalingrad, a huge German offensive in World War II, began in August of 1942 and turned into a month-long siege. In the early days, German aerial forces overpowered Stalingrad's skies and crippled the Soviet military, leaving little to defend the city from advancing enemy tanks. The women of the 1077th Anti-Aircraft Regiment were one of the last bulwarks against the German onslaught. With only 37 anti-aircraft guns, they resisted a division of German tanks until they were finally overrun.

Q What is mainly being discussed about the Battle of Stalingrad in the lecture?

(a) A Soviet regiment's defense of the city

(b) German aerial dominance of Soviet land forces

(c) The role of German tanks during the battle

(d) The losses suffered by the militaries on both sides

제2차 세계대전에서 독일의 엄청난 공격이었던 스탈린그라드 전투는 1942년 8월에 시작되어 점점 한 달에 걸친 포위전 양상을 띠게 되었다. 초기에는 독일 공군이 스탈린그라드의 하늘을 제압해 소련군에게 심각한 타격을 주었는데, 그 결과 진격하는 적의 탱크로부터 도시를 방어할 수단이라곤 거의 남아 있지 않게 되었다. 제1077 대공포 연대의 여성들은 독일의 맹습에 대항한 최후의 보루 중 하나였다. 그들은 불과 37개의 대공 화기로 독일 기갑 사단에 저항하다가 결국 괴멸되었다.

Q 강의에서 스탈린그라드 전투에 대해서 중점적으로 말해지고 있는 것은?

(a) 소비에트 연대의 도시 방어

(b) 소련 탱크를 제압한 독일 항공기

(c) 전투 기간 동안 독일 탱크 부대의 역할

(d) 양쪽 군대가 입은 손실

huge 엄청난 **offensive** (군사적) 공격 **siege** 포위 공격 **aerial** 항공기의 **overpower** 제압[압도]하다 **cripple** 심각한 손상을 주다 **advance** 전진하다 **anti-aircraft** 대공의 **regiment** 연대 **bulwark** 방어물, 보루 **onslaught** 맹공격, 맹습 **division** 사단 **overrun** 격파하다, 괴멸시키다 **dominance** 지배, 우세

32

In the animal world, the term "coprophagy" describes the practice of feeding on excrement. For insects, the feces of other animals are a source of food that they can digest and extract additional nutrients from. Among humans, coprophagy is rare because of the potential for transferring disease. However, certain therapeutic treatments involve the introduction of beneficial bacteria to the intestines of a human patient by administering a dose of fecal matter from a healthy donor.

Q What is mainly being discussed in the talk?

(a) The uses of excrement by insects and humans

(b) The reasons for coprophagy among humans

(c) The niche of coprophagy in insect evolution

(d) The role of intestinal bacteria in digestive function

동물 세계에서 '식분증'이란 배설물을 먹고 사는 행위를 묘사하는 용어이다. 곤충들에게 다른 동물의 배설물은 그들이 소화하여 영양물을 추가로 얻어낼 수 있는 식량 자원이다. 인간의 식분증은 전염병을 옮길 수 있기 때문에 드문 일이다. 하지만 건강한 기증자의 대변을 투여해 유익한 세균을 환자의 장내에 주입하는 특정 치료법도 있다.

Q 담화문에서 주로 논의되고 있는 것은?

(a) 곤충과 인간의 배설물 이용

(b) 사람에게서 식분증이 있는 이유

(c) 식분증이 곤충 진화에서 한 역할

(d) 장내 세균이 정상적인 소화 기능에서 담당하는 역할

coprophagy 식분증, 대변먹기증   feed on ~을 먹고   excrement 배설물, 대변   feces 똥, 배설물   extract 뽑아내다   nutrient 영양물   potential 가능성   transfer 옮기다   therapeutic treatment 치료법, 치료적 처우   intestine 장, 창자   patient 환자   administer a dose 투약하다   fecal matter 대변   donor 제공자, 기증자   niche 아주 편한 자리, 역할   ingestion 섭취   digestive function 소화 기능

33

We're looking forward to seeing the creativity and talent of our members. That said, affiliation with the Ceres Fiction Workshop is not a requisite for entry into the logo design competition. Designs will be judged by a panel of independent jurors convened for this task. The winning design will be adopted as our official logo and will appear on promotional materials for the organization, including online media, print materials, and merchandise.

Q Who will judge the design competition?
(a) The organizers of the Ceres Fiction Workshop
(b) The workshop's director of online media
(c) A panel formed from earlier design winners
(d) Judges unaffiliated with the workshop

우리는 우리 회원들의 독창성과 재능을 보기를 고대하고 있습니다. 그렇다 하더라도, 세레스 픽션 워크숍에 소속되어야만 로고 디자인 대회에 참가할 수 있는 것은 아닙니다. 디자인들에 대한 평가는 이 임무를 수행하기 위해 소집된 독립 심사원들로 구성된 패널에 의해 내려질 것입니다. 일등을 한 디자인은 우리의 공식 로고로 채택될 것이며, 온라인 매체, 인쇄물, 그리고 상품 등 저희 단체의 홍보 자료에 게재될 것입니다.

Q 누가 디자인 경쟁을 심사할 것인가?
(a) 세레스 픽션 워크숍의 주최 측
(b) 워크숍의 온라인 매체 책임자
(c) 전 디자인 우승자들로 구성된 패널
(d) 워크숍에 무관한 이들로 구성된 심사위원들

that said 그렇긴 하지만   affiliation 소속, 가맹   requisite 필요한, 불가결한   juror 심사원   convene 소집하다   adopt 채택하다   promotional 홍보의   merchandise 제품   unaffiliated (기관 등에) 소속되어 있지 않은

34

One of the effects of depression on the brain is the impairment of a brain region associated with memory making. In particular, depression negatively impacts a person's ability to separate patterns, a mechanism that enables the brain to organize components of memories into amalgamated representations that it can then more easily differentiate. Because of the inhibition of the brain's pattern-separation faculty, individuals suffering from depression have a diminished ability to distinguish between similar but distinct memories.

Q Which is correct about pattern separation according to the lecture?
(a) It creates more emotionally positive memories.
(b) Multiple brain mechanisms are involved in it.
(c) It helps distinguish between similar memories.
(d) It is heightened in persons suffering depression.

우울증이 두뇌에 미치는 영향 중 하나는 기억 생성과 연관된 뇌 부위의 손상이다. 특히 우울증은 형태를 구별하는 능력, 즉 두뇌로 하여금 기억의 구성 요소들을 융합된 표상으로 조직할 수 있게 해주는—그렇게 되면 두뇌는 융합된 표상들을 더 쉽게 구별해낼 수 있다—메커니즘에 부정적인 영향을 준다. 두뇌의 형태 구별 능력이 억제되기 때문에, 우울증을 앓는 사람은 유사하지만, 명백히 다른 기억들을 서로 구별해낼 수 있는 능력이 떨어지게 된다.

Q 형태 구별에 대해 강연 내용과 일치하는 것은?
(a) 감성적으로 더 긍정적인 기억을 창조해낸다.
(b) 다양한 두뇌 메커니즘이 그것에 관여한다.
(c) 유사한 기억들을 구별하는 것을 돕는다.
(d) 우울증을 겪는 이들에게 강화된다.

depression 우울증   impairment 해침, 손상   associated with ~와 연관된   separate 분리[구분]하다   component 구성 요소   amalgamate 혼합[융합]시키다   representation 표상, 심상   differentiate 구분 짓다   inhibition 억제, 방해   faculty 능력   diminished 감소한   distinct 뚜렷이 다른   be involved in ~와 관련되다

35

In the quest for the Eastern League Championship, Newton Heath has qualified for one of the last remaining berths, thanks to a magnificent comeback by goalkeeper Enzo Lial. Lial reigned in the goal area, rebuffing every one of Catlin City's charges with graceful swats and swipes, like a lion fending off bothersome gnats. Gone was the feeble and tentative goaltending that jeopardized his squad's shot at the championship in Wilshire Stadium in October. Last night, Lial was on top of his game.

Q Which is correct according to the report?
(a) Newton Heath's goaltender had a good game.
(b) Catlin City dominated the match against Newton Heath.
(c) Enzo Lial made his team lose the championship.
(d) The Eastern League Championship was held in Wilshire Stadium.

동부 리그 선수권 대회에 출전하기를 꿈꾸는 뉴턴 히스는 골키퍼 엔조 리알의 화려한 복귀 덕분에 마지막 남은 자리 중 하나를 차지하게 되었습니다. 리알은 골문 지역을 장악했는데, 마치 성가신 모기의 공격을 막아내는 사자처럼 캐틀린 시티의 공격을 멋진 쳐내기 동작으로 모조리 막아냈습니다. 10월에 윌셔 스타디움에서 열릴 선수권 대회에 팀의 출전 가능성을 위태롭게 한 부진하고 자신 없는 골문 수비는 사라졌습니다. 어젯밤 리알은 경기를 지배했습니다.

Q 보도 내용과 일치하는 것은?
(a) 뉴턴 히스의 골키퍼가 좋은 경기력을 보여줬다.
(b) 캐틀린 시티가 뉴턴 히스와의 경기를 지배했다.
(c) 엔조 리알 탓에 팀이 선수권을 잃었다.
(d) 동부 리그 선수권 대회가 윌셔 스타디움에서 개최되었다.

quest 추구, 탐구 **qualify for** ~의 자격을 얻다 **berth** 토너먼트에서 경기할 기회 **magnificent** 최고의, 훌륭한 **reign** 군림하다 **rebuff** 저지하다 **charge** 공격 **swat** (파리 등을 잡기 위해 손바닥이나 파리채 등으로) 찰싹 때리기 **swipe** (공격 대상을 향해 팔 등을) 휘둘러 치기 **fend off** ~의 공격을 막아내다[피하다] **gnat** 각다귀, 모기 **feeble** 약한, 부진한 **tentative** 머뭇거리는, 자신 없는 **goaltending** 골문 수비 **jeopardize** 위태롭게 하다 **squad** 팀 **shot** 기회, 가능성 **on top of** ~을 지배하여 **dominate** 지배하다

36

Debate over the usage of the serial, or Oxford comma has raged for decades. This is the comma placed immediately before the coordinating conjunction in a list. For example, "I ordered a burger *comma* fries *Oxford comma* and a drink." Those in favor of including the Oxford comma maintain that it helps avoid ambiguity in meaning. Those opposed argue it is redundant and wastes space. Regardless of your personal opinion, in your writing you should follow whichever style guideline is stipulated by your professor.

Q What can be inferred from the talk?
(a) The speaker favors using the Oxford comma.
(b) Opinions in the debate vary with the individual.
(c) The Oxford comma is archaic and can be abolished.
(d) Students are encouraged to do as they choose.

시리얼 콤마, 즉 옥스퍼드 콤마의 사용을 놓고 수십 년 동안 맹렬한 논쟁이 벌어져 왔다. 이것은 리스트의 등위접속사 바로 앞에 붙이는 콤마로, 가령 '나는 버거, 프라이, 그리고 음료를 주문했다'와 같은 문장을 들 수 있다. 옥스퍼드 콤마의 삽입을 지지하는 사람들은 그것이 의미의 모호함을 피하는 데 도움이 된다고 주장한다. 반대자들은 그것이 쓸데없이 중복되고 공간을 낭비한다고 주장한다. 여러분은 자신의 개인적인 의견에 상관없이, 글쓰기를 할 때 담당 교수가 규정하는 표기법이라면 무엇이 됐든 그것을 따르는 것이 좋다.

Q 담화문에서 추론할 수 있는 것은?
(a) 화자는 옥스퍼드 콤마의 사용을 지지한다.
(b) 콤마 논쟁에서의 의견은 개인별로 각기 다르다.
(c) 옥스퍼드 콤마는 구식이며 철폐될 수 있다.
(d) 학생들은 그들이 원하는 대로 콤마를 사용하도록 권장된다.

serial[Oxford] comma 여러 대상을 나열할 때 마지막에 오는 등위접속사 앞에 붙이는 콤마 **rage** 맹렬히 계속되다 **coordinating conjunction** 등위접속사 **in favor of** ~을 지지하여 **ambiguity** 모호성 **redundant** 쓸데없이 중복되는 **regardless of** ~에 상관없이 **style** 표기법 **stipulate** 규정하다 **vary** 다르다 **archaic** 구식의 **abolish** 폐지하다

Part V

37-38

For the past 25 years, Dr. Erica Lawrence has been an inspiration for tens of thousands of students at Richville University. At the same time, she has been a thoughtful friend to her colleagues and a passionate lover of molecular biology. Now she is retiring and will be missed by all of us. Please join us to honor her as she leaves Richville University after 25 years of excellent service. Dr. Lawrence's retirement party will be held from 2:00 p.m. through 5:00 p.m. on July 7th, in the Moore Room, Roberts Hall. Please contact Julia Smith at the Office of Human Resources if you want to deliver a speech at her party. Please contact Richard Green at the President's Office if you want to make a donation to her. Again, come join us to celebrate Dr. Lawrence's retirement!

지난 25년 동안, 에리카 로렌스 박사는 리치빌대학교의 수만 명의 학생들에게 영감을 주었습니다. 또한 동료들에게는 사려 깊은 친구이면서, 분자생물학에 열렬한 애정을 가진 인물이었습니다. 이제 로렌스 박사가 퇴임하게 되어, 우리 모두가 그리워할 것입니다. 25년 동안의 탁월했던 근무를 마치고 리치빌대학교를 떠나는 박사를 예우하는 자리에 함께 해 주십시오. 로렌스 박사의 퇴임 기념 파티는 7월 7일 오후 2시부터 5시까지 로버츠 강당의 무어실(室)에서 개최됩니다. 퇴임 기념 파티에서 연설을 하시고 싶으시면 인사과의 줄리아 스미스에게 연락하십시오. 박사에게 기부금을 전하고 싶으시면 총장실의 리처드 그린에게 연락하십시오. 다시 한 번 말씀드리오니, 로렌스 박사의 퇴임을 저희와 함께 경축해 주십시오.

37 Q Why would someone try to contact Ms. Smith?
(a) To visit Roberts Hall on July 17th.
(b) To pledge to support Dr. Lawrence financially
(c) To have flowers delivered to the retirement party
(d) To deliver an address at the retirement party

Q 왜 누군가가 스미스 씨에게 연락을 취할 것인가?
(a) 7월 17일에 로버츠 강당에 방문하기 위해서
(b) 로렌스 박사에 대한 재정적 지원을 약속하기 위해서
(c) 퇴임 기념 파티에 꽃을 배송시키기 위해서
(d) 퇴임 기념 파티에서 연설하기 위해서

해설 세부 사항 유형이기 때문에, 안내를 들으면서 출제가 예상되는 정보를 간단히 메모해 두는 것이 매우 효과적인 대응 전략이다. 우선 (a)는 날짜가 7월 7일이 되어야 정답으로 고려될 수 있기 때문에 오답이다. 그리고 (c)는 전혀 제시되어 있지 않은 사항이므로 반드시 오답으로 처리해야 한다. 정답은 주어진 내용에 충실한 (d)이다.

38 Q What can be inferred from the announcement?

(a) Dr. Lawrence has been teaching molecular biology in the Moore Room.

(b) Dr. Lawrence may receive a donation from a party participant.

(c) Around 25,000 students graduate from Richville University each year.

(d) Mr. Green is in charge of handling donations from biology associations.

Q 안내로부터 추론할 수 있는 것은?

(a) 로렌스 박사는 무어실(室)에서 분자생물학을 가르쳐왔다.

(b) 로렌스 박사는 파티 참가자로부터 기부를 받을지도 모른다.

(c) 대략 2만 5천 명의 학생들이 매년 리치빌대학교를 졸업한다.

(d) 그린 씨는 생물학 협회들로부터의 기부를 담당하고 있다.

해설 NEW TEPS의 추론 유형에서도 정답은 반드시 주어진 내용에 근거가 있어야 한다는 원칙을 명심해야 한다. (a)와 (c)는 그렇게 추론할 수 있는 근거가 전혀 제시되어 있지 않다. (d)는 그린 씨가 로렌스 박사의 퇴임 기념 파티와 관련해서 기부를 담당하는 것은 맞지만, 생물학 협회들로부터의 기부를 담당한다고 추론할 수 있는 근거가 없다. 따라서 정답은 (b)이다. 세부 사항이나 추론 유형에서 may, might, could가 포함된 선택지는 정답일 가능성이 높다는 사실도 기억해 두어야 한다.

inspiration 영감, 창조적 자극 **colleague** 동료 **passionate** 열정적인, 열렬한 **molecular biology** 분자생물학 **honor** 예우하다; 명예 **speech** 연설; 말 **president** (대학교) 총장; 대통령 **celebrate** 경축하다 **pledge** 약속하다, 맹세하다 **address** 연설 **association** 협회

39-40

In 1989, David Strachan published an important article in the *British Medical Journal*. In this article, he observed that eczema and hay fever were more common in only children than in children with siblings. According to Strachan, children with siblings had more exposure to infectious agents, which could result in the development of stronger immune systems. Conversely, less exposure to infectious agents could lead to weaker immune systems. This is called the hygiene hypothesis, and epidemiologists have extensively tested its truth. They have concluded that living with siblings helps children develop strong immune systems. On the other hand, mere exposure to infectious agents such as the measles virus does not necessarily lead to strong immune systems.

1989년에, 데이비드 스트라찬은 『영국의학저널』에 중요한 논문을 발표했습니다. 이 논문에서 그는 습진과 고초열이 형제자매가 있는 아동들보다 외동인 아동에게 보다 흔하다는 의견을 제시했어요. 스트라찬에 따르면, 형제자매가 있는 아동들은 감염원에 보다 많이 노출되는데, 이에 따라 보다 튼튼한 면역 체계가 발달될 수 있다고 합니다. 역으로, 감염원에 덜 노출되면 면역 체계가 약해질 수 있습니다. 이것은 위생 가설로 불리는데, 전염병학자들이 그 진실성을 광범위하게 검증했습니다. 이들은 형제자매와 함께 살면 아동이 강한 면역 체계를 갖는 데 도움이 된다고 결론을 내렸습니다. 반면에, 홍역바이러스와 같은 감염원에 단순히 노출된다고 해서 반드시 면역 체계가 강해지지는 않습니다.

39 Q What is the main purpose of the lecture?

(a) To completely refute the hygiene hypothesis

(b) To recommend early exposure to the measles virus

(c) To analyze a hypothesis in medicine

(d) To explain why epidemiologists have become interested in infectious agents

Q 강의의 주된 목적은?

(a) 위생 가설을 완전히 반박하는 것

(b) 이른 나이에 홍역바이러스에 노출되는 것을 권장하는 것

(c) 의학 분야의 어떤 가설을 분석하는 것

(d) 전염병학자들이 감염원에 대해 관심을 갖게 된 이유를 설명하는 것

해설 (a)는 매력적인 오답이다. 그런데 강의의 내용을 잘 들어 보면, 완전히 반박하는 것이 아니라 부분적으로 인정하고 있음을 알 수 있다. (b)는 이 강의가 구체적인 행동을 권장하는 것은 아니기 때문에, (d)는 강의에서 분명하게 제시한 내용이 아니기 때문에 오답이다. 따라서 정답은 (c)인데, 이처럼 '위생 가설'을 '의학 분야의 어떤 가설'과 같이 패러프레이징된 선택지에 익숙해져야만 고득점이 가능하다.

40 Q Which of the following can lead to strong immune systems?

(a) Spending your childhood away from your siblings

(b) Growing up in a family with many children

(c) Early exposure to varicella zoster virus

(d) Having minimal contact with farm animals

Q 다음 중 강한 면역 체계로 귀결될 수 있는 것은?

(a) 어린 시절을 형제자매와 떨어져서 지내는 것

(b) 아이들이 많은 가정에서 자라는 것

(c) 이른 나이에 수두대상포진 바이러스에 노출되는 것

(d) 가축과 접촉을 최소화하는 것

해설 (a)는 떨어져서 지내는 것이 아니라 함께 살아야 하는 것이므로 오답이다. (c)에서 말한 수두대상포진 바이러스는 지문에서 언급되지 않았기 때문에 정답이 아니다. (d)는 주어진 내용만으로는 알 수 없기 때문에 오답이다. 따라서 정답은 주어진 내용에 충실한 (b)이다.

article (소)논문; 기사 **observe** 평하다, 말하다 **eczema** 습진 **hay fever** 고초열 **only child** 외동 **sibling** 형제자매 **exposure** 노출 **infectious agent** 감염원 **immune system** 면역 체계 **conversely** 거꾸로, 역으로 **hygiene** 위생 **hypothesis** 가설 **epidemiologist** 전염병학자 **extensively** 광범위하게 **conclude** 결론을 내리다 **measles** 홍역 **necessarily** 필연적으로 **refute** 반박하다 **analyze** 분석하다 **minimal** 최소의

Vocabulary

p.161

Part I

1 정답 (a)
A 그럼 통보도 없이 쫓겨난 거예요?
B 네, 집주인이 전혀 사전 통보를 하지 않았어요.

evict 퇴거시키다, 쫓아내다 **warning** 통보, 통고 **landlord**
(집·건물 등의) 주인 **prior notice** 사전 통보 **report** 보도 **news**
소식 **form** 종류

2 정답 (a)
A 이 현대 추상 미술에 푹 빠진 건 아니겠지, 그렇니?
B 그럼. 난 보다 전통적인 양식의 작품을 좋아해.

abstract 추상적인 **conventional** 전통적인 **abstruse** 난해한
ambiguous 모호한 **eclectic** 절충주의의

3 정답 (d)
A 네가 졸업을 해서 부모님이 자랑스러워하시겠구나.
B 응, 하지만 부모님의 높은 기대에 부응하기가 힘들었어.

take issue with ~에 반대하다, 이의를 제기하다 **reach out to** ~에
접근하다 **get on with** (특히 중단했다가) ~을 계속하다 **live up to**
(기대·명성 등에) 부응하다, ~에 따라 생활하다

4 정답 (d)
A 당신은 내가 한 일을 그런 식으로 비난할 권리가 없어요.
B 알았어요, 그렇게 방어적인 태도를 보일 필요 없어요.

criticize 비난하다 **performance** 실적, 성과 **lavish** 풍성한, 호화로운
transient 일시적인, 순간적인 **infectious** 전염성의 **defensive**
방어적인

5 정답 (c)
A 그의 허술한 관리 방식을 놓고 브렛에게 맞서야 해요.
B 그와 나 사이의 거북한 관계를 악화시키고 싶지 않아요.

confront 맞서다, 대항하다 **awkwardness** 거북함 **subjugate**
복종시키다 **discipline** 징계하다 **exacerbate** 악화시키다
presume 추정하다

6 정답 (d)
A 이 파일 공유 사이트에서 음악 앨범을 내려받아.
B 미안하지만 난 음악을 불법 복제하는 건 옳지 않다고 생각해.

album (음악) 앨범 **file-sharing site** 파일 공유 사이트 **believe in**
~을 좋다고[옳다고] 생각하다 **curtail** 단축하다, 삭감하다 **quash**
무효로 하다, 취소하다 **disarm** 무장 해제시키다 **pirate** 저작권을
침해하다, 불법 복제하다

7 정답 (a)
A 좀 더 나은 회계 소프트웨어를 구입하는 게 어때요?
B 부서의 예산 부족을 생각하면 그건 실행 불가능한 일이에요.

accounting 회계 **given** ~을 고려해볼 때 **shortfall** 부족
unfeasible 실행[달성]할 수 없는 **steadfast** 확고한, 부동의
impeccable 나무랄 데 없는 **callous** 냉담한, 무정한

8 정답 (a)
A 난 제레미와 같이 일하는 게 싫고, 그도 나와 일하는 걸 싫어해요.
B 네, 두 분이 서로 적의를 품고 있다는 걸 알고 있어요.

mutual 상호 간의 **enmity** 증오, 원한 **secularism** 세속주의
aberration 일탈 **mediocrity** 평범, 보통

9 정답 (b)
A 내 문제에 대해서 항상 의논해줘서 고마워.
B 이봐, 난 너의 절친한 친구로 있는 게 즐거워.

apostle 사도, 주창자 **confidant** (속을 터놓고 대화할 수 있는) 절친한
친구 **consultant** 컨설턴트, 상담역 **malfeasance** 부정[위법]행위

10 정답 (a)
A 도나는 요가가 얼마나 좋은지에 대해서 늘 떠벌리고 있어.
B 그녀는 그것이 마치 만병통치약인 것처럼 굴어.

go on about ~에 대하여 말을 늘어놓다 **panacea** 만병통치약
zenith 절정, 극치 **candor** 정직, 솔직 **maxim** 격언, 금언

Part II

11 정답 (c)
유감스럽게도 직원들은 최고경영자로서 회사를 감독하는 워커 씨의 능력
을 신뢰하는 마음을 잃었다.

CEO 최고경영자(chief executive officer) **disparage** ~의 신용을
떨어뜨리다, 비난하다 **execute** 실행하다 **oversee** (작업·활동이 제대로
이뤄지는지) 감독하다 **elongate** 연장하다, 길게 하다

12 정답 (a)
앨리스 먼로가 2013년에 노벨 문학상을 받았을 때, 역대 수상자 중 여성
작가로는 13번째에 불과했다.

literature 문학 **receive** 받다 **conceive** 상상하다 **perceive**
인지하다 **deceive** 속이다

13 정답 (d)
멜은 말을 더듬거려 대중 앞에서 연설하는 것에 대한 불안감을 명백히 드
러냈다.

deliver (연설·강연 등을) 하다 **obviously** 명백히 **directed** 지시된
polished 세련된 **common** 흔한 **halting** (말이) 자꾸 끊어지는,
더듬거리는

14 정답 (b)
일부 소행성에서 물이 발견되었다는 사실은 행성 밖에도 생명체가 존재할
수 있다는 것을 의미한다.

asteroid 소행성 **planet** 행성 **comply** 따르다, 응하다 **signify**
나타내다, 의미하다 **maintain** 유지하다 **derive** 이끌어내다, 유래하다

15 정답 (d)
그 신생 기업에 의해 모금된 자금 대부분이 사치스러운 사무실과 많은 장
비에 낭비되었다.

Actual Test 5

Vocabulary • 119

capital 자금, 자본 start-up 신진의 extravagant 사치스러운,
낭비하는 pervade 널리 퍼지다, 스며들다 lament 한탄하다
vindicate ~의 정당성을 입증하다 squander 낭비하다

16 정답 (b)
포유류의 생물 다양성은 특히 서로 아찔하게 다양한 곤충 세계에 비교할
때 제대로 인식하는 것이 힘들 수 있다.

biodiversity 생물의 다양성 mammal 포유동물 regard ~으로
평가하다 appreciate 충분히[제대로] 인식하다 diagnose 진단하다
predict 예측하다 envision 마음속에 그리다

17 정답 (a)
홉킨스 교수는 물리학 교재가 일반 독자층에게 좀 너무 난해할지도 모른
다는 점을 우려하고 있다.

readership 독자(층) esoteric 난해한, 소수만 이해하는 volatile
휘발성의, 불안정한 proprietary 소유자의, 전매특허의 incalculable
헤아릴 수 없는, 막대한

18 정답 (a)
최근 조사 결과에 의하면 축구 선수가 자기 팀이 이기고 있을 때 입는 부
상은 좀 더 아프게 느껴지는 경향이 있다고 한다.

grievous (상처 등이) 몹시 아픈, (고통이) 심한 oblique 기울어진
irate 성난 culpable 과실이 있는, 비난받을 만한

19 정답 (d)
작가 J. D. 샐린저는 기자를 만나거나 방문객을 들이는 것을 거부하며 인
생의 대부분을 은둔자로 살았다.

shaman 주술사 vassal (봉건 시대의) 봉신, 가신 tremor 떨림, 전율
recluse 은둔자

20 정답 (b)
샌 안토니오는 한때 비어 있던 땅이 교외로 바뀌는 것을 보면서, 최근 수십
년 사이에 도시가 외곽으로 무질서하게 확산되는 현상을 상당히 겪었다.

considerable 상당한 transform 바꾸어 놓다 suburbs 교외
drone 낮게 윙윙거리는 소리, 단조로운 저음 sprawl (도시의) 스프롤
현상 plunge 돌진, 급락 beckoning 손짓하여 부르기

21 정답 (b)
사라는 자신이 좋아하는 팀이 챔피언 결정전 시합에서 패배하자 일주일
동안 우울한 기분을 떨쳐버릴 수가 없었다.

shake 떨쳐내다 affable 상냥한 doleful 슬픔에 잠긴, 우울한
flagrant 파렴치한 sublime 숭고한

22 정답 (d)
서로 다른 네 가지 맛으로 나오는 스포츠 스타 에너지 드링크는 운동 후
당신의 갈증을 확실히 풀어 줍니다.

available 이용할 수 있는 workout 운동 douse (불을) 급히 끄다,
물에 처넣다 wreck 난파시키다, 파괴하다 moisten 축축하게 하다
quench (갈증을) 가라앉히다

23 정답 (a)
그 관리가 부정행위에 개입했다는 수사관의 혐의 제기는 추측일 뿐이라며
일축되었다.

investigator 수사관 accusation 혐의 제기, 고발 be involved
in ~에 개입되다 wrongdoing 범법 행위 dismiss 묵살[일축]하다
conjecture 추측, 억측 pedagogy 교육 synchronous 동시에
일어나는 cogitation 심사숙고

24 정답 (b)
용의자는 공범들로부터 압력을 받고 그들이 이 강도 사건에 연루되었음을
나타내는 자백을 부인했다.

accomplice 공범 suspect 용의자 confession 고백, 자백
implicate 관련되었음을 나타내다 vex 짜증 나게 하다 recant (진술
등을) 철회[부인]하다 chide 꾸짖다 parody 풍자적으로 모방하다

25 정답 (d)
주사를 통해 백신을 접종할 때 생길 수 있는 건강상의 위험은 백신이 주는
보호에 비교하면 매우 적다.

via ~에 의해 injection 주사 compared with ~에 비교하면
lithe 나긋나긋한, 유연한 flimsy 부서지기 쉬운, 무른 eminent
저명한, 걸출한 nominal 아주 적은

26 정답 (c)
고래를 구하려는 동물 권익 보호론자들이 운행하는 배 한 척이 3주 동안
일본 포경선을 미행했다.

whaling vessel 포경선 shadow 미행하다 bigot 편협한 사람,
광신자 partisan 동지, 신봉자 advocate 지지자, 옹호자
exponent (사상·학설 등의) 주창자

27 정답 (b)
회사의 자유 발언 정책은 불필요하게 신랄하든지 아니면 공격적인 구두
혹은 문서 자료를 포함하지 않는다.

verbal 구두의 offensive 공격적인, 모욕적인 gaudy 화려하고 속된
vitriolic 신랄한 complicit 공모한, 공범의 prodigious 거대한, 막대한

28 정답 (a)
민디 톰슨의 보컬은 가락이 맞지 않아 코러스들의 노래와 어울리지 않는
불협화음을 냈다.

out of key 가락이 맞지 않아 jarring 괴리감이 있는 dissonance
불협화음 virtuoso 거장, 명인 ellipsis 생략 eddy 소용돌이

29 정답 (c)
볼리비아의 화폐가 미국의 화폐에 고정되어 있어서, 1달러는 항상 7볼리
비아노에 조금 못 미치는 정도가 될 것이다.

currency 화폐 buy (돈이) ~에 상당하다 boliviano 볼리비아노
(볼리비아의 화폐 단위) quaff 벌컥벌컥 마시다 bandy (언쟁 따위를)
주고받다 peg (가격·임금 등의 수준을) 고정하다 clog (배수구 등을)
막히게 하다

30 정답 (d)
수상이 야당의 요구에 굽실거렸기 때문에 그의 당원 중 일부가 그를 호되
게 비난하였다.

lambast 엄하게 꾸짖다, 호되게 비난하다 opposition party 야당
dribble (물 등이) 똑똑 떨어지다 hobnob 친하게 사귀다 pirouette
발끝으로 돌다 kowtow 굽실거리다, 아첨하다

Grammar

p.165

Part I

1 정답 (d)

A 이봐요, 이 헬스클럽에 갓 들어왔나요?

B 실은 여기 가입한 지 수년이 지났어요.

해설 어떤 동작이 과거에 시작되어 현재에도 계속될 때는 현재완료진행형 (have+been+-ing)을 사용한다. 현재완료진행형은 계속의 의미를 지니므로 주로 for나 since와 함께 쓰인다는 것도 알아두자.

gym 헬스클럽

2 정답 (d)

A 이토록 색상이 화려한 도마뱀을 본 적 있나요?

B 작년에 열대 우림에서 그보다 훨씬 더 화려한 도마뱀을 봤어요.

해설 어순 문제이다. 일단 부정대명사 one을 포함한 어구는 〈a[an]+형용사+one〉의 어순을 취하며, 비교급을 만드는 부사인 more는 형용사 바로 앞에, 비교급을 강조하는 부사 even은 비교급 앞에 붙이므로 (d)가 알맞다.

lizard 도마뱀   **rainforest** 열대 우림

3 정답 (b)

A 내 올리브 나무에 뭐가 문제인 것 같아?

B 아마도 가뭄 때문에 성장이 저해되는 것 같아.

해설 stunt는 '(성장을) 방해하다'란 뜻의 타동사이다. 여기서는 '성장 (growth)'이 주어 자리에 왔으므로 술부는 수동태가 되어야 의미상 적절한데, 방해받는 것은 지속적인 상황이므로 수동태 진행형을 쓴 (b)가 정답이다. (c)의 〈be동사+been+p.p.〉는 영어에는 없는 형태이다.

drought 가뭄   **stunt** (성장을) 방해하다

4 정답 (c)

A 당신이 이런 은밀한 판매에 대한 정보를 얻다니 정말 다행이에요.

B 내 친구 수가 아니었다면 절대로 불가능했을 거예요.

해설 종속절이 had it not been for ~이고, 그 앞이 주절인 가정법 과거완료 문장이다. 선택지를 보면 일단 주절은 p.p. 이하가 생략된 부정문 형태임을 알 수 있는데, 부정어 never는 보통 be동사·조동사 뒤, 일반동사 앞에 놓이지만, 이 문제에서처럼 본동사가 생략된 경우에는 조동사 앞에 놓이므로 (c)가 알맞은 어순이다. (d)가 답이 되려면 have와 ever의 어순이 바뀌어야 한다.

thank goodness 정말 다행이다   **had it not been for** ~이 아니었다면

5 정답 (d)

A 과제 제출이 왜 그렇게 늦었니?

B 내가 누구에게 보고해야 하는지 잘 몰랐어.

해설 빈칸은 문장의 목적절이 되는 간접의문문이 들어갈 자리로, 〈의문사+주어+동사〉의 어순이 되어야 한다. 따라서 (b)는 구조상 답이 될 수 없으며, 의미상 (d)가 적절하다.

appointment 약속

6 정답 (d)

A 네가 왜 나에게 화가 나 있는지 아직도 잘 모르겠어.

B 내게 전화해서 늦을 거라고 말해주지 않았기 때문이야.

해설 '~해야 했는데 그렇지 못했다', 즉 과거의 하지 못한 일에 대한 유감을 나타낼 때는 should have p.p.를 쓰므로 (d)가 정답이다. (a) may have p.p.는 '~했을지도 모른다(과거에 대한 약한 추측)', (c) must have p.p.는 '~했음에 틀림없다(과거에 대한 강한 추측)'의 뜻이다.

7 정답 (a)

A 방금 자동판매기를 사용하려고 했는데 고장이 나 있었어.

B 알아. 다음 주 초에 수리할 거야.

해설 주어가 it(= the vending machine)이므로 빈칸에는 '수리되다', 즉 수동태가 와야 한다. 따라서 (b)와 (d)는 일단 제외한다. (c)는 현재완료 (has been repaired)이므로 early next week와 시제가 맞지 않다. 정답은 〈be동사+to부정사〉로 '예정'을 나타낸 (a)이다.

vending machine 자동판매기   **busted** 고장 난

8 정답 (c)

A 왜 문 옆에 내 가방을 두고 왔다고 말하지 않았니?

B 그곳에 내가 가방을 두지 않은 것 같았거든.

해설 선행사가 생략된 관계부사절의 올바른 어순을 고르는 문제이다. 먼저 장소를 나타내는 관계부사 where 다음에 절이 와야 하므로 where I put it(가방을 두었던 장소)이 기본 뼈대가 된다. 그리고 삽입절 I thought은 where와 I 사이에 두므로 (c)가 정답이다.

briefcase 서류 가방

9 정답 (a)

A 방문해 주셔서 대단히 감사합니다.

B 크게 환대해 주셔서 저희야말로 감사합니다.

해설 알맞은 강조어를 고르는 문제이다. such는 〈such+(a[an])+형용사+명사〉, so와 too는 〈so/too+형용사+a[an]+명사〉, 그리고 far는 형용사의 비교급을 강조하므로 정답은 (a)가 된다. 여기서, 〈so/too+형용사+a[an]+명사〉의 경우는 부정관사가 반드시 있어야 한다는 점에 주의하자.

hospitality 환대

10 정답 (d)

A 그럼 그 중고차는 저렴하게 잘 산 게 아닌 것이 되었군요.

B 수리비로 수천 달러가 들 거라는 걸 너무 늦게 알게 된 거죠.

해설 어순 문제이다. 문맥상 'that 이하를 너무 늦게(too late) 발견했다'가 되어야 하므로 I discovered too late that ~이지만 강조를 위해 too late를 주어 앞으로 보내면 (d)와 같이 된다. 여기서 that 다음의 it은 that used car를 가리키며 that절의 주어이다.

used car 중고차   **turn out** ~로 판명되다

Part II

11 정답 (d)

몽상과 환희의 메시지를 자아내는 블라인드 게임의 신곡 〈외침〉이 청취자들 사이에 큰 인기를 끌었다.

해설 빈칸에는 이유를 나타내는 부사절 As it evokes나 분사구문 Evoking이 와야 문장이 성립되므로 (d)가 정답이다.

reverie 환상, 몽상   **evoke** 불러일으키다

12 정답 (c)

존슨 앤 데이비스 사의 종업원들은 다가오는 주말에 회사 연례 수련회에 참석하고 있을 것이다.

해설 this coming weekend와 어울리는 시제는 미래이므로 (a)와 (b)는 일단 제외한다. 미래완료는 미래의 특정 시점까지 계속되거나 완료되는 동작이나 상태를 표현하므로 정답은 미래진행형을 쓴 (c)이다.

firm 회사 **retreat** 수련회

13 정답 (a)

당국은 주민들에게 허리케인이 강타하기 전에 월요일 저녁까지 그 지역에서 대피하도록 지시했다.

해설 제안, 명령, 요구, 주장 등을 나타내는 동사의 목적어로 that절이 올 때, that절의 동사는 〈should+동사원형〉을 써야 하는데, 이때 should는 생략할 수 있다. 따라서 정답은 동사원형만 남은 (a) evacuate이다.

mandate 명령[지시]하다 **resident** 주민 **evacuate** (위험한 장소를) 떠나다, 피난하다

14 정답 (c)

학기 동안 출석률 100퍼센트를 달성한 학생들만 기말시험을 면제받을 것이다.

해설 빈칸에는 동사 will be의 주어가 필요하므로 (d)는 일단 제외한다. 나머지 선택지들을 보면 students가 주어이고 achieve 이하 semester까지가 students를 수식하는 관계사절이어야 문장이 성립됨을 알 수 있다. 관계대명사 자리 다음에 주어가 빠져 있으므로 주격 관계대명사 who를 쓴 (c)가 정답이다.

attendance 출석 **semester** 학기 **eligible** 자격이 있는, 가능한 **forgo** 포기하다, ~없이 지내다

15 정답 (d)

오는 4월 29일은 (사망한) 카레이서 데일 언하르트의 65번째 생일이 되는 날이라, 그의 고향 마을인 카나폴리스에서 기념행사가 열릴 예정이다.

해설 빈칸은 동사 marks의 목적어가 올 자리이므로 선행사를 포함한 관계대명사 what을 사용한 (d)가 알맞다. (b)도 what으로 시작하지만, 문법적으로 맞지 않는 어구이다.

mark 표시하다, 기념하다

16 정답 (d)

스코틀랜드 작가 로버트 루이스 스티븐슨이 1880년대에 직접 배를 타고 도달한 태평양 신탁 통치 제도는 그의 작품에 지대한 영향을 끼쳤다.

해설 빈칸은 동사 influenced의 주어가 올 자리이므로 (a)와 (b)는 일단 제외한다. 문맥상 정답은 관계절 to which he sailed가 주어인 the Pacific islands를 수식하는 형태의 (d)이다.

influence 영향을 미치다 **Pacific islands** 태평양 신탁 통치 제도 (미국의 신탁 통치령이었던 Marshall, Mariana, Caroline 군도)

17 정답 (c)

아프리카 서부의 소국 감비아는 거의 50년 동안 영연방의 회원국으로 있다가 2013년에 탈퇴했다.

해설 빈칸 앞까지가 완전한 문장으로 되어 있어 빈칸 이하는 부사구(전치사구 포함)나 부사절 또는 수식어구가 올 것임을 예상할 수 있다. 따라서 정답은 전치사 after 다음에 목적어로 holding membership(회원 자격을 갖다)을 취한 전치사구 (c)이다.

withdraw 탈퇴하다 **Commonwealth of Nations** 영국연방

18 정답 (b)

죽음을 앞두고 모차르트는 '진혼곡 D단조'라는 제목의 음악 작품을 작곡하고 있었다.

해설 빈칸 다음에 compose의 목적어 a piece of music이 있으므로 빈칸에는 능동태가 와야 하고, 과거의 일을 말하고 있으므로 시제는 과거이어야 한다.

a piece of music 하나의 음악 작품 **requiem** 진혼곡 **mass** 미사 **minor** 단조 **compose** 작곡하다

19 정답 (a)

수사관들은 상원의원이 자신의 측근이 로비스트로부터 받고 있었던 뇌물에 대해서 분명히 알고 있었을 것이라고 주장한다.

해설 선택지들을 문법적으로만 파악해도 정답을 고를 수 있는 문제이다. 즉 (b)는 수동태인 점이 틀렸고, (c)는 동사 know의 목적어로 to부정사가 올 수 없을 뿐 아니라 have의 목적어가 없으며, (d)는 had의 목적어도 없고, about의 목적어로 to부정사가 올 수 없으므로 틀렸다. 따라서 정답은 과거나 현재 사실에 대한 강한 추정을 나타내는 조동사 must 다음에 know about(~에 대해서 알다)을 붙인 (a)이다.

investigator 수사관 **maintain** 주장하다 **senator** 상원의원 **bribe** 뇌물 **aide** 보좌관

20 정답 (c)

일본 연해에서 발생한 지진이 너무나 강력해 알래스카의 앵커리지까지 진동이 느껴졌다.

해설 강조부사 so와 too는 〈so/too+형용사+a[an]+명사〉의 어순이므로 (b)와 (d)는 일단 제외한다. 이 문장은 의미상 so ~ that…(너무 ~해서 …하다) 구문이 적절하므로 (c)가 정답이다.

seismic 지진의 **tremor** 떨림 **far away** 멀리

21 정답 (d)

알턴 씨는 28년 근무 후 직장에서 해고된 사실에 화를 멈출 수 없었다.

해설 빈칸에는 우선 전체 문장의 주어 the fact에 이어지는 동사가 와야 한다. 따라서 정답은 〈동사+목적어+부사구〉로 된 (d)이다. (b)도 정답처럼 보이지만 anger가 불가산명사이므로 그 앞에 부정관사를 붙일 수 없다.

service 근무 **to no end** 매우

22 정답 (d)

수위가 지난달 3일간 계속 비가 내린 후에 도달했던 높이까지 다다른 적이 거의 없었다.

해설 빈칸은 빈도부사 seldom(거의 ~않다)이 포함된 주절이 올 자리이다. seldom은 일반동사 바로 앞, be동사·조동사 바로 뒤에 두므로 The water level had seldom reached가 올바른 어순이며, seldom을 강조해 문장 앞으로 위치시키면 주어와 동사가 도치되어 (d)와 같이 된다.

sustain 지속하다

23 정답 (d)

대리인에 의해 배달된 소포를 받은 사람이 그것에 서명하는 즉시 그 물건은 그 사람 것으로 간주한다.

해설 선행사 the person을 수식하는 관계사절의 올바른 어순을 고르는 문제이다. the agent delivers the package to the person에서 the person이 선행사가 되면 전치사 to의 목적격 관계대명사 whom이 필요하고, 이것이 to와 함께 앞으로 나가면 (d)와 같이 된다.

possession 소유 **agent** 직원, 대리인 **package** 소포

24 정답 (d)

예비 선거에서 완전한 승리를 거두지 못했기 때문에 그 후보는 결선 투표에서 경쟁할 수밖에 없었다.

해설 빈칸에는 이유를 나타내는 부사절 As he had fallen short나 분사구문 Having fallen short가 와야 문장이 완성되므로 (d)가 정답이다. 여기서, 완료형 분사구문을 쓴 것은 분사구문의 동사가 주절의 동사보다 한 시제 앞서기 때문이다.

outright 완전한 candidate 후보 be forced to ~하지 않을 수 없다 runoff election 결선 투표 fall short of ~에 불충분하다, 부족하다

25 정답 (c)

그 지역 농부들이 생산한 첨채당은 그들이 합당하다고 생각하는 가격에 절대 팔리지 않았다.

해설 선행사 the prices를 수식하는 관계사절의 알맞은 어순을 고르는 문제이다. they hoped it would command the prices(그들은 그것이 그 가격에 팔리기를 원했다)에서 the prices가 선행사가 되면 동사 command의 목적격 관계대명사 which나 that이 필요하고, 이것이 앞으로 나가면 (c)와 같이 된다.

beet sugar 첨채당(사탕무로 만든 설탕) command (응당 받아야 할 것을) 받다

Part III

26 정답 (b) quite sophisticated look
→ quite a sophisticated look

(a) A 쇼핑몰에서 구입한 이 검은색 트렌치코트가 정말 맘에 들어요.
(b) B 당신이 그걸 사서 다행이에요. 꽤 세련돼 보이네요.
(c) A 나도 그렇게 생각해요. 고마워요. 하지만 드라이클리닝을 해야 한다는 게 유감이에요.
(d) B 그건 당신이 생각하는 것만큼 번거로운 일이 아니에요.

해설 quite(꽤)가 〈형용사+단수가산명사〉를 수식할 때는 such와 마찬가지로 〈quite/such+a[an]+형용사+명사〉의 어순을 취하는데, 이때 부정관사를 빼지 않도록 유의해야 한다.

adore 아주 좋아하다 trench coat 트렌치코트(레인 코트) sophisticated 세련된 hassle 번거로운 일

27 정답 (b) them flying → those who fly

(a) A 귀사에서는 보너스 마일을 어떻게 지급하는지 말씀해 주시겠어요?
(b) B 연간 30차례 이상 비행을 하시는 분만 마일리지를 얻게 돼요.
(c) A 왕복 비행을 말하는 건가요, 아니면 편도 비행도 가능한가요?
(d) B 안타깝게도, 왕복 비행만 마일리지 혜택을 줍니다.

해설 '~한 사람들'은 관계대명사를 써서 those who ~로 표현한다. 따라서 (b)의 them flying을 those who fly로 고쳐야 맞다.

distribute 분배하다 round-trip 왕복의 one-way 편도의 contribute toward ~에 기여하다

28 정답 (a) riddle → are riddled

(a) 스페인의 카나리아 제도는 원래 화산 지대이어서 오래된 용암굴, 동굴, 분화구들로 가득하다. (b) 그리하여 란자로테 섬에 6킬로미터 길이의 거대한 용암굴인 쿠에바 데 로스 베르데스가 있는 것은 새삼스러운 일도 아니다. (c) 이 특별한 용암굴에는 독특한 것, 전 세계 관광객을 끌어들이는 뭔가가 있다. (d) 500석 이상의 좌석을 갖추고 있는 연주회장이 동굴 입구 근처의 해면체 공간에 위치해 있다.

해설 riddle은 be riddled with의 형태로 '~투성이다, ~로 (벌집처럼) 구멍투성이가 되다'란 뜻으로 쓰인다.

volcanic 화산의 be riddled with ~ 투성이다 lava tube 용암굴 crater 분화구 massive 거대한, 대규모의 come as no surprise 새삼스러운 일이 아니다 cavernous space 해면체 공간 seat ~ 명의 좌석을 가지다 upwards of ~의 이상

29 정답 (d) would chart to come → would come to chart

(a) 마르크스주의 혁명가 체 게바라는 쿠바에서 독재자를 타도하는 데 일조했고, 콩고에서 무장 군대를 이끌었으며, 볼리비아에서 투쟁하였습니다. (b) 하지만 여러분은 그가 이런 곳들이 아니라 아르헨티나 출신이라는 걸 알고 계셨나요? (c) 게바라는 로자리오 시에서 태어나 중상류층 가문에서 안락한 생활을 누리며 성장했습니다. (d) 그가 자신의 인생행로를 결정하게 될, 빈곤한 자와 좌익 사상에 대한 공감대를 발전시키게 되는 것은 이 시기 동안이었습니다.

해설 (d)의 that would chart to come the course of his life는 선행사 a sympathy for the poor and leftist political leanings를 수식하는 관계대명사절로 문맥상 '그의 인생행로를 결정하게 될'이란 뜻이 되어야 한다. '~하게 되다'는 come to, '결정하다'는 chart, '그의 인생행로'는 the course of his life이므로 would chart to come이 would come to chart로 바뀌어야 한다.

Marxist 마르크스주의의 revolutionary 혁명가 overthrow 타도하다 dictator 독재자 hail from ~출신이다 upbringing 양육, 교육 sympathy 공감 leftist 좌익의 leaning 경향 chart 정하다, 계획을 세우다

30 정답 (d) Having smelled → Smelling

(a) 그 이름부터 시작해 '아세로에 루브라'로 알려진 호주 균류에 대한 모든 것은 우리가 그것을 원래부터 혐오할 수밖에 없게 만든다. (b) 붉은 별 모양의 이 균류의 이름은 '구역질 나는 붉은 주스'를 의미하는 그리스어에서 유래한다. (c) 그 이름은 그것의 강렬한 색깔 외에도 호주 균류가 발산하는 불쾌한 냄새를 언급한 것이다. (d) 썩은 고기 냄새가 강하게 나는 악취는 이 균류의 생식 포자를 퍼뜨릴 파리를 유인하는 데 중요한 역할을 한다.

해설 완료형 분사구문은 분사구문의 시제가 주절의 시제보다 앞설 때 쓴다. 하지만 (d)는 의미상 분사구문과 주절의 시제가 같으므로 완료형 분사구문 Having smelled가 아니라 단순 분사구문인 Smelling이 되어야 맞다.

fungus 균류 signify 나타내다 aversion 혐오 moniker 이름 disgusting 구역질 나는 vibrant (색이) 강렬한 offensive 불쾌한 give off 발산하다 carrion (짐승의) 썩은 고기 stench 악취 vital 매우 중요한 reproductive 생식의 spore 포자

Part I

1

티라스폴은 <u>지역 주권 문제가 미해결된</u> 국가인 트란스니스트리아의 수도이다. 트란스니스트리아는 1990년에 독립을 선언함으로써 몰도바에서 탈퇴한 나라이지만, 몰도바 공화국은 아직도 자치권을 공식적으로 인정하지 않고 있다. 오히려, 몰도바의 관할 하에서 특별한 법적 지위를 가진 영토로 여겨지고 있다. 하지만 트란스니스트리아는 자신만의 정부와 입법 기관, 군대, 화폐를 가지고 있다. 그럼에도 불구하고 미승인 국가에서 살고 있기 때문에 대부분의 트란스니스트리아 시민들은 몰도바나 러시아, 우크라이나의 시민권을, 혹은 그 세 나라 중 이중이나 삼중의 시민권을 가져야 한다.

(a) 독특한 문화유산을 보유하고 있는
(b) 지역 주권 문제가 미해결된
(c) 그 시민들이 몰도바와 합쳐지기를 원하는
(d) 3국의 침입을 받을 위험에 처한

해설 몰도바로부터 1990년에 독립을 선언했지만 국제적으로 승인받지 못하고 있는 국가인 트란스니스트리아의 어정쩡한 상황을 설명하는 글이다. 빈칸에는 트란스니스트리아의 현 상황을 가장 잘 묘사한 (b)가 적절하다.

secede 탈퇴하다 **declare** 선언하다 **autonomy** 자치권 **deem** 간주하다 **territory** 영토 **jurisdiction** 사법권, 관할 **legislature** 입법 기관, 의회 **currency** 통화 **heritage** 유산 **unresolved** 미해결의, 미정의 **sovereignty** 주권 **merge** 합쳐지다 **invasion** 침입

2

과학뉴스

쥐의 기억을 연구하는 한 과학자 팀이 쥐에서 실제 사건에 기초하지 않은 기억을 유도해냈다. 그들은 쥐의 두뇌에 저장된 특정 기억과 연결된 세포들을 확인한 후, 그것에 빛을 쏘는 방식(기억 흔적을 담고 있는 뇌의 신경세포를 활성화시키는 기법)으로 그 기억이 떠올려지도록 자극했다. 그리고 나서 과학자들은 특정한 환경을 조성해 쥐의 발에 충격을 주는 한편, 신경세포를 인위적으로 자극했다. 쥐의 잇단 행동을 연구한 끝에 그들은 가짜 공포 기억을 주입하는 것이 가능하다고 결론지었다. 그 증거로 그들은 쥐가 <u>다른 환경에서 발의 충격을 예측하도록</u> 했다.

(a) 기억 흔적 신경세포를 비활성화시켜 기억하도록
(b) 발에 충격을 받은 사건의 기억을 잊어버리도록
(c) 강한 자극에도 두려움 없는 반응을 보이도록
(d) 다른 환경에서 발의 충격을 예측하도록

해설 쥐의 뇌에 가짜 기억을 이식하는 실험이 성공했다는 내용이다. 쥐의 발에 충격을 준 환경을 A라고 하고, 정상적인 환경을 B라고 했을 때, 쥐가 A에서 받은 고통을 B에서 있었던 일로 기억하게 하는 데 성공한다면 가짜 공포 기억을 이식하는 것이 가능하다는 결론이 되므로 빈칸에는 (d)가 적절하다.

induce 유도하다 **associated with** ~와 연관된 **stimulate** 자극하다 **retrieval** 회복, 복구 **target** 겨냥하다 **activate** 활성화시키다 **engram** 기억 흔적(세포 내에 형성된다고 여겨지는) **bear** 지니다 **neuron** 신경세포, 뉴런 **artificially** 인위적으로 **contextual** 배경의, 상황의 **subsequent** 뒤이은 **implant** 주입하다 **deactivate** 비활성화하다 **harsh** 가혹한 **stimuli** stimulus(자극)의 복수 **anticipate** 예상[예측]하다

3

편집진에게,

천문학자로서, 그리고 대중 매체에 실린 과학 기사의 사실성을 엄격히 따지는 사람으로서, '혜성들이 빅 스크린을 때리다'(스카이와쳐스, 11월 호)라는 귀사의 기사를 읽고 <u>개인적으로 만족감과 감사함을 느꼈습니다</u>. 그 이유는 지구 근접 소행성 및 혜성들에 대한 할리우드의 선정적인 묘사를 문제 삼는 것이 귀사의 출판물과 같은 출판물들이 해야 할 일이라고 생각하기 때문입니다. 귀사의 기고자가 지적하였듯이, 지구로 다가오는 어느 혜성이건 폭발해버리는 할리우드의 태만한 전략은 몹시 잘못 인식한 것입니다. 파편들은 혜성이 지닌 모든 운동 에너지로 지구의 대기를 강타할 것이며, 이는 지구상의 모든 핵무기를 합친 것보다 더 큰 폭발을 일으킬 수 있습니다!

니콜라 발레타

(a) 무지를 전혀 믿지 못하였습니다
(b) 할리우드에 대해서 좀 더 많은 것을 기대했습니다
(c) 소행성에 대해서 여전히 감을 잡지 못했습니다
(d) 개인적으로 만족함과 감사함을 느꼈습니다

해설 혜성에 관한 할리우드 영화의 과학적 무지를 비판하는 기사를 읽은 독자가 잡지사에 보내는 편지이다. 기사가 사실에 근거하여 해야 할 일을 했다고 칭찬하고 있으므로 빈칸에는 (d)가 적절하다.

astronomer 천문학자 **stickler for** ~에 까다로운[엄격한] 사람 **factualness** 사실성 **comet** 혜성 **big screen** 영화 **publication** 출판물 **sensationalist** 선정적인 **depiction** 묘사 **near-Earth asteroid** 지구 근접 소행성 **contributor** 기고자 **blow up** 폭파시키다 **grievously** 슬프게도, 몹시 **fragment** 파편 **slam** 강타하다 **kinetic** 운동의, 동적인 **in utter disbelief** 전혀 믿지 못하고 **scratch one's head** 감을 잡지 못하다, 알아내려 애쓰다 **gratitude** 감사

4

스포큰 프리즘은 도서관, 사라질 위기에 처한 언어 사용 공동체들, 그리고 언어 복원 지지자들 간의 협력 관계에 중점을 둔 심포지엄입니다. 희귀 언어 사용자와 사서들, 언어학자들이 금세 사라져버리는 문화적 기록이 잃어버린 유물이 되는 것을 막기 위한 자신들의 노력에 대해 의견을 나눌 것입니다. 개관 이후, 주립 도서관에서는 일반인들이 언어 자료에 쉽게 접근할 수 있게 해주는 호주 토착 언어 컬렉션을 조성해왔습니다. 이 컬렉션에서 선정한 자료들이 원주민 정보 및 자원 네트워크가 후원하는 심포지엄 동안 전시될 것입니다. 이외에도 다른 행사들을 통해 주립 도서관은 <u>토착어 복원에 계속 공헌하고 있습니다</u>.

(a) 전 세계의 주요 언어와 문화를 배우는 것을 촉진합니다
(b) 이 전국적인 언어 학습 프로그램에 사용될 자금을 조성합니다
(c) 소장 도서의 보전으로 여러 곳의 사서들을 돕습니다
(d) 토착어 복원 노력에 계속 공헌하고 있습니다

해설 사라질 위기에 처한 호주 토착어를 보존 및 복원하기 위한 심포지엄 개최를 알리는 공고문이다. 주립 도서관에서는 그 동안 호주 토착언어 컬렉션을 조성해 왔다는 점에서, (d)가 이 기관이 하고 있는 일임을 어렵지 않게 고를 수 있을 것이다.

focused on ~에 중점을 둔 collaborative 협력적인, 공동의 endangered 사라질 위기에 처한 revitalization 재생 advocate 옹호자 linguist 언어학자 fleeting 순식간에 지나가는 artifact 인공물, 유물 indigenous 고유의, 토착의 accessible to ~이 이용하기[접근하기] 쉬운 Aboriginal 오스트레일리아 원주민의 preservation 유지, 보호

5

존 크라카우어는 그의 소설 〈황무지 속으로〉에서, 물질주의를 버리고 알래스카 황무지로 홀로 여행하며 환경이 주는 대로 먹고 사는 청년 크리스토퍼 매캔들리스의 삶과 죽음을 추적한다. 작가는 주인공이 사망한 원인이 독성이 있는 뭣황기 씨앗을 먹었기 때문이라고 암시했다. 하지만 훗날 생화학적 분석을 한 결과 이 가정이 틀렸음이 입증되었고 작가는 강력한 비판을 받았다. 하지만 현재 일부에서는 작가의 원래 판단이 옳았을지도 모른다고 생각하고 있다. 문제의 그 씨앗은 <u>사람을 무력하게 만드는 신경독을 함유한 것으로 최근 증명되었다</u>.

(a) 너무 작아서 치명적인 독을 함유하지 못한다
(b) 알래스카 주 전체에 걸쳐 자라는 것으로 밝혀졌다
(c) 사람을 무력하게 만드는 신경독을 함유한 것으로 최근 증명되었다
(d) 동물들이 섭취한 씨앗의 종과 생화학적으로 유사하다

해설 〈황무지 속으로〉라는 소설에서 주인공이 어떤 씨앗을 먹고 죽었다고 암시하는 내용이 문제가 되었지만 지금은 그 내용이 옳았을지도 모른다고 말하고 있다. 빈칸에는 주인공이 그 씨앗을 먹고 죽었을 거라는 작가의 원래 판단이 옳았음을 뒷받침해주는 근거가 될 말이 필요하므로 (c)가 적절하다.

renounce 버리다 materialism 물질주의 wilderness 황야 live off the land 자급자족해서 먹고 살다 protagonist 주인공 Hedysarum alpinum (식물) 뭣황기 toxic 유독한 biochemical 생화학적인 invalidate 틀렸음을 입증하다 assumption 가정 roundly 강력하게, 대대적으로 suspect ~일 것 같다고 생각하다 estimation 의견, 판단 lethal 치명적인 neurotoxin 신경독 species 종

6

일부 철학자들이 고전 문명에 대해 단순화된 종교적인 믿음을 가졌던 것이 <u>지구에 대한 정확한 이해</u>를 어렵게 하였다. 그들은 세계에 대한 온갖 종류의 허황되고 부정확한 이론들을 제안했다. 그럼에도 불구하고 이러한 고대 사상가들은 내륙 산간에서 발견된 바다 조개껍질의 존재와 같은, 자신들이 직접 관찰한 것에 의해 때때로 올바른 결론에 도달하기도 했다. 즉 이것으로부터 그들은 바다가 과거에 그 땅을 주기적으로 덮쳤다가 드러낸 것으로 정확하게 해석했다. 그들은 또한 물의 순환 과정—증발, 응결, 강우, 그리고 강에서 해역으로의 물의 배수—을 매우 확고하게 인식하고 있었다.

(a) 지구에 대한 정확한 이해
(b) 물의 순환 과정을 캐기 위한 연구
(c) 산의 본질을 올바르게 확인하기
(d) 서로 다른 종교를 가진 학자들 간의 협력

해설 세 번째 문장의 nonetheless를 기준으로 앞뒤의 내용이 상반되고 있다. 즉 앞부분은 고대 사상가들이 지질학에 있어서 정확한 이론을 내지 못하고 중구난방 식이었다는 것, 뒷부분은 그래도 그들이 일부 지질 현상은 정확하게 이해하고 있었다는 내용이다. 이 문제는 고대 사상가들의 고전 문명에 대한 종교적인 믿음으로 인해 어떤 일이 발생했는지를 묻고 있으므로 (a)가 가장 적절하다.

theological 신학적인 classical 고대 그리스 · 로마의 fetter 속박하다 fanciful 상상의, 공상의 inland 내륙의 fairly 매우 solid 확고한 hydrological cycle 물의 순환 과정(water cycle) evaporation 증발 condensation 응결, 응축 precipitation 강우, 강설 draining 배수 basin 유역 ascertain 확인하다 collaboration 협력

7

얼굴 인식은 인간 두뇌 속의 전문적인 인지 영역에서 주관하는 것 같다. 즉 거기서 인지 처리 과정이 반사적으로, 그리고 두뇌의 나머지 부분과는 별개로 진행된다. 건강한 뇌의 기능적 뇌영상 조사를 한 결과, 얼굴 인식 및 처리 과정과 밀접한 연관성이 있는 특정 부위의 위치를 알아냈는데, 면적이 몇 평방 밀리미터에 불과했다. 과학자들은 이것을 방추상 얼굴 영역이라고 부른다. 만약 이 얼굴 인식 장치에 손상이 있다 하더라도, 아마 <u>국지화되어 있어서 그 밖의 인지 장애와는 관련이 없을</u> 것이다.

(a) 안면 근육의 통제 상실과 연관된
(b) 반사 신경의 기능 이상을 초래할
(c) 국지화되어 있어서 그 밖의 인지 장애와는 관련이 없을
(d) 다른 종류의 뇌 손상을 입은 환자들과 유사할

해설 얼굴 인식 및 처리 과정과 밀접한 연관성이 있는 특정 부위인 방추상 얼굴 영역(얼굴을 인식할 때 활성화되는 뇌 영역)이 손상을 입을 경우 발생할 수 있는 현상을 묻는 문제이다. 이곳은 전문화된 인지 영역이고, 뇌의 나머지 부분과는 별개로(in isolation from the rest of the brain) 인지 처리 과정이 진행된다는 점에서 (c)가 적절하다.

cognitive 인지의 domain 영역 reflexively 반사적으로 in isolation from ~와 별개로 functional neuroimaging 기능적 뇌영상 localize ~의 위치를 알아내다 fusiform face area 방추상 얼굴 영역 malfunctioning 기능 부전 impairment 장애 sustain (부상을) 입다, 당하다

8

그렇다. 〈리틀 앤썸〉의 초반에는 나의 마음 한 구석을 만족시켜주는 진실된 감정이입과 부드러움이 아주 잠깐 있다. 나는 이 영화가 심지어 여성 문제에 동조적일 거라고 생각했다. 하지만 여성에 대한 모욕적이고 틀에 박힌 묘사로 반전을 하게 되고, 그 덕분에 나는 별 주저 없이 그리고 정당하게 〈리틀 앤썸〉과 감독을 완전히 묵살할 수 있게 되었다. 이 프로젝트는 영화 제작자인 로날드 리우가 여성 인물들의 묘사에 결함이 있다는 관객의 비판을 스스로 반박할 수 있는 기회였다. 하지만 감독은 제 버릇 개 못 주는 법이라는 속담을 내게 상기시킨다. 〈리틀 앤썸〉은 <u>작품에서 여성의 역할을 경시한다</u>.

(a) 리우의 초기 작품의 비범함을 전혀 보여주지 못한다
(b) 작품에서 여성의 역할을 경시한다
(c) 여성 등장인물을 전개시키는 속도가 너무 느리다
(d) 떠들썩하게 선전한 것과는 차이가 있다

해설 여성에 대해 모욕적이고 틀에 박힌 묘사를 한 〈리틀 앤썸〉이라는 영화와 그 감독을 비판하는 글이다. 빈칸 앞 두 문장에서, 감독은 이번 영화로 예전에 여성 비하적인 영화를 만든 오명을 씻을 기회를 잡았지만, 제 버릇 개 못 주는 법(a leopard cannot change its spots)이라면서 그렇게 하지 못했다고 하므로 (b)가 적절하다.

flicker (어떤 감정이 아주 잠깐) 스침 genuine 진실된 empathy 공감
tenderness 부드러움, 유연함 anthem 성가, 송가 sympathetic
동조적인 take a turn 전환점을 맞다, ~하게 변하다 depiction 묘사
justifiable 정당하다고 인정되는, 정당한 dismiss 무시하다, 묵살하다
rebut 반박하다 shortcoming 결점 a leopard cannot change
its spots 제 버릇 개 못 주는 법, 세 살 버릇 여든까지 간다 genius
천재성, 비범함 remission 경감, 완화 offense 화나게 하는 행위,
모욕 drag on 질질 끌다 fall short of ~에 못 미치다 hype 과대
선전

9

인체 각각의 해부학적인 특성은 두뇌의 일차 운동피질과 일차 체감각피질
의 영역과 일치한다. 하지만 각 신체 부위에 할당된 뇌 자원의 비율은 신
체의 실제 비율과 상당히 다르다. 예를 들면, 손은 우리의 신체적 형태에서
비교적 작은 부분이지만 불균형하게 많은 양의 뇌 공간을 차지한다. 이는
손이 우리의 환경에서 물체와 소통하고 물체를 다루는 데 없어서는 안 될
수단이므로 일리가 있는 말이다. 그 결과 손은 많은 대뇌 피질의 처리 능
력을 도출해낸다.

(a) 대신에
(b) 그렇지 않으면
(c) 게다가
(d) 그 결과

해설 뇌에는 각 신체 부위에 해당하는 영역이 있지만 신체 부위와 뇌 영역
의 크기가 비례하는 것은 아니라고 한다. 빈칸을 중심으로 앞뒤의 내용을
파악해 보면, 뒷부분이 앞부분의 '결과'를 나타내므로 (d)가 적절하다. as a
result나 accordingly로 바꿔 쓸 수 있다.

anatomical 해부학적인 feature 특성, 특질 correspond to ~에
일치하다 primary motor cortex 일차 운동피질 primary
somatosensory cortex 일차 체감각피질 allot 할당하다
considerably 상당히 disproportionately 불균형하게
make sense 일리가 있다, 합당하다 indispensable 필수적인
manipulate 다루다, 조작하다 object 물체 cortical 외피의, 대뇌
피질성의

10

그리스 철학자들은 네 가지 기본 구성 요소, 즉 흙, 공기, 불, 물이 인체에
'체액'으로 존재한다고 추측했다. 이것은 각각 그들이 흑담즙, 혈액, 황담
즙, 점액이라고 밝혀낸 액체였다. 2세기 로마의 의사 클라우디우스 갈렌
은 이들 체액의 불균형이 사람의 정신에 영향을 미칠 거라고 가정하면서,
특정 체액의 과잉 혹은 결여에 따라 정신 문제를 진단하는 요강을 마련했
다. 그는 완전히 틀렸다. 그럼에도 불구하고 어떤 사람들은 병적인 자기중
심주의의 증상을 개선하기 위해 방혈을 하는 등, 정신 문제를 치료하는 데
심각한 결함이 있는 방식을 추종했다.

(a) 사실은
(b) 그럼에도 불구하고
(c) 이와 반대로
(d) 바꿔 말하면

해설 그리스 철학자들이 주장한 4체액설(사람의 몸은 4가지 체액으로 이
루어져 있으며 이들이 균형 잡힌 상태일 때 건강하다는 학설)에 관한 글이
다. 완전히 잘못된 가설이지만 일부 사람들은 그 방식을 선호했다고 하므
로 '양보'의 의미인 (b)가 적절하다.

conjecture 추측하다 component 구성 요소 inhabit ~에 존재하다
humor 체액 fluid 액체 identify 밝히다 bile 담즙 phlegm 점액
respectively 각각 postulate 가정하다 devise 고안하다
protocol (치료 등의) 실시 요강, 계획서 diagnose 진단하다 surfeit
과다, 과잉 atrociously 터무니없이, 심하게 flawed 결함이 있는
ameliorate 개선하다 symptom 증상 egomania 자기 우월 성향,
병적인 자기중심주의

Part II

11

화학자 리누스 파울링은 경력을 쌓기 시작한 1920년대에 두각을 나타냈
다. (a) 그의 가장 획기적인 연구는 화학 결합의 특성에 집중되었으며, 이
연구로 1954년 노벨 화학상을 받았다. (b) 이 상은 1901년 이후로 매년,
가장 많은 결실을 거둔 화학자들에게만 수여되었다. (c) 2차 세계대전 동
안, 그에 못지않게 우수한 다른 과학자들이 최초의 원자 폭탄을 개발하는
동안, 파울링은 평화 운동가가 되었다. (d) 그는 핵무기 실험 금지를 주장
했으며, 1962년에 노벨 평화상을 수상했다.

해설 화학자인 리누스 파울링의 업적에 관한 글이다. (a) 노벨 화학상 수
상, (c) 평화 운동가 활동, (d) 노벨 평화상 수상에 대해 언급하고 있다. (b)
는 노벨 화학상의 역사와 수상자 선정 조건을 말하고 있으므로 글의 주제
와 상관없다.

chemist 화학자 rise to prominence 두각을 나타내다, 유명해지다
groundbreaking 획기적인 center on ~에 집중되다 chemical
bond 화학 결합 prolific 결실이 많은, 다작의 caliber 역량, 우수성
advocate 주장하다 recipient 받는 사람

12

1980년대에 케냐 정부는 상업적인 사탕수수 생산의 경제 효과를 측정하
는 조사에 착수했다. (a) 조사 결과, 사탕수수 생산자가 다른 농부들보다
훨씬 더 많은 소득을 올리는 것으로 나타났다. (b) 이런 차이를 보이는 것
은 사탕수수에 대한 정부의 가격 정책에 기인한다. (c) 정부 정책이 효과적
으로 자국 농부들로 하여금 변동하는 세계 설탕 가격의 영향을 받지 않게
해줌에 따라, 그들의 소득을 보장해 주고 있다. (d) 세계 시장에서 설탕 가
격이 상승하면 농부의 수입도 증가하고, 설탕 가격이 하락하면 그 반대가
된다.

해설 케냐 정부의 사탕수수 정책과 그 효과를 설명하는 글이다. (a), (b),
(c)는 모두 정부의 정책과 관련된 내용이지만, (d)는 자유 시장 경제의 원리
에 대해 말하고 있으므로 글의 흐름에서 벗어난다.

determine 측정하다 sugarcane 사탕수수 considerably 상당히
discrepancy 불일치, 차이 stem from ~에서 기인하다 pricing
policy 가격 정책 insulate 보호하다 fluctuating 변동이 있는, 오르
내리는 follow suit 선례를 따르다, 남을 흉내 내다 vice versa 반대
의 경우도 마찬가지

Part III

13

바이크릭 가족 농장은 70년이 넘게 운영되어 왔습니다. 3대에 걸친 바이크릭 농부의 축적된 지식에 의해 전통은 존속 되었습니다. 수십 년에 걸쳐 저희는 지역 공동체와 강력한 관계를 구축해 왔습니다. 그들은 저희에게 사업체가 이행할 수 있는 가장 중요한 역할 중의 하나를 맡겼습니다. 다름 아닌, 자기 가족들에게 영양분을 공급하는 역할입니다. 이런 이유로, 저희는 농장에서 살충제나 호르몬을 절대 사용하지 않습니다. 저희는 우수한 품질의 천연 무농약 농산물을 고객들에게 자랑스럽게 배달합니다. 고객 여러분은 저희 농산물이 안전하고 (환경 파괴 없이) 지속 가능한 방법에 따라 재배된다는 것을 항상 믿을 수 있습니다.

Q 바이크릭 가족 농장에 대한 핵심 내용은?
(a) 오랜 역사를 지닌 가족 기업이다.
(b) 거기서 나오는 생산물은 정부 기준을 따르고 있다.
(c) 유기농식 농사를 통해 환경 보호주의를 고취한다.
(d) 안전하고 자연적으로 자란 농산물에 전념한다.

해설 친환경 농산물 재배 농장의 광고문으로, 지역 공동체와 깊은 유대 관계를 맺으며 그들에게 안전한 천연의 먹거리를 제공한다는 것이 주된 내용이다.

in operation 운용[가동] 중인 **accumulate** 축적하다 **cultivate** (누구와의 관계를) 쌓다, 구축하다 **entrust A with B** A에게 B의 일을 맡기다 **profoundly** 완전히, 크게 **fulfill** 이행하다 **nourish** 영양분을 공급하다 **pesticide** 살충제 **produce** 농산물 **sustainable** (환경 파괴 없이) 지속 가능한 **organic** 유기농의

14

부엌의 전자레인지는 전자파의 진동을 이용하는데, 식품을 조리하기 위해 좀 더 빠른 속도로 움직인다는 것을 제외하고는 무선 전파와 별반 다를 것이 없다. 마이크로파(전자파)는 특정 형태의 분자, 즉 물처럼 양전하와 음전하를 가진 분자들에게만 영향을 준다. 전자레인지가 작동이 되면, 그것에 의해 방출되는 마이크로파의 진동과 함께 식품에 존재하는 물 분자가 앞뒤로 회전하게 된다. 이것에 의해 자극을 받은 각각의 물 분자들이 자신의 에너지를 다른 인근 분자에게 옮기게 됨으로써 결국 식품이 빠르게 데워진다.

Q 지문의 주된 내용은?
(a) 식품에 존재하는 분자가 균일하게 데워지는 이유
(b) 전자레인지를 기능하게 하는 물리적 과정
(c) 물이 무선 전파와는 다르게 전자파에 반응하는 방식
(d) 서로 다른 에너지파를 이용하는 독특한 전자레인지

해설 전자레인지의 작동 원리(마이크로파를 식품에 가하면 식품에 존재하는 물 분자들이 앞뒤로 회전하게 되고, 이 운동이 주위의 물 분자에 빠르게 전달되어 식품 전체가 신속하게 가열되는 방식)를 설명하고 있으므로 (b)가 정답이다.

microwave 전자레인지; 마이크로파 **oscillating** 진동의 **electromagnetic waves** 전자파 **radio wave** (무선) 전파 **molecule** 분자 **positive** 양전기의 **negative** 음전기의 **operation** 작동 **spin** 회전하다 **physics** 물리적 과정[현상] **underpin** 입증하다

15

비행기가 벼락을 맞는 경우는 매우 흔한데, 미국의 상용 항공기의 경우 한 대당 연 1회꼴 발생한다. 연구진이 수년에 걸쳐 수집한 증거에 의하면, 실제로 비행기가 대전된 적란운 속에 들어가면 벼락을 맞을 수 있는 것으로 나타났다. 이 때문에, 여객기는 모든 민감한 부품들을 전류로부터 보호하는 등, 전기적 충격의 압력을 견뎌내기 위해 특수 제작되어 있다. 벼락을 맞으면, 전류가 최초의 접촉 지점으로부터 전도성을 가진 동체 표면을 따라 퍼지게 되며, 꼬리와 같은 말단부를 통해 밖으로 빠져나간다.

Q 지문의 주제는?
(a) 폭풍이 칠 때 항공기가 비행을 피하는 이유
(b) 항공기가 벼락을 맞았을 때의 대응 방식
(c) 벼락이 비행 중인 항공기를 때렸을 때의 위험
(d) 벼락 맞는 것을 방지하는 비행기 설계의 필요성

해설 비행기가 여러 번 번개를 맞아도 안전한 이유(번개의 전류가 동체 표면을 따라 흐르다 꼬리와 같은 말단부를 통해 밖으로 방전되기 때문)를 설명하는 글이므로 (b)가 정답이다.

incidence 발생 **fleet** 비행대 **charged** 하전된, 대전한 **thunderhead** 적란운, 소나기구름 **induce** 유발하다 **commercial jet** 여객기 **withstand** 견뎌내다 **component** 부품 **shield** 보호하다, 가리다 **current** 전류 **propagate** 전해지다, 퍼지다 **conductive** 전도성의 **outer shell** 외피 **egress** 밖으로 나가다 **terminal** 말단의

16

중세 영어에서 discomfit란 단어는 '전쟁에서의 패배'를 의미했고, 라틴어 접두사 dis-('부정'의 의미)와 어근 conficere('합치다'의 의미)를 합쳐 사용한 고대 프랑스어에서 물려받았다. 하지만 근대에 들어와 그 의미가 '(누군가를) 불안하게 하다'를 뜻하는 discomfort의 의미로 통합되었다. 이 두 단어는 철자와 발음이 유사함에도 불구하고 어원이 다르다. discomfort는 '편안하게 하다'란 뜻의 고대 프랑스어 동사 conforter에서 유래한다. 하지만 표준 미국 영어에서는 그 두 단어를 명사/동사로, 즉 discomfort는 명사, discomfit는 동사로 결합시키는 경향이 있다.

Q 지문의 제목으로 가장 알맞은 것은?
(a) 시간이 지나면서 단어의 의미의 소실
(b) 중세 영어가 고대 프랑스어로부터 받은 영향
(c) 별개의 두 단어가 점진적으로 결합함
(d) discomfort와 discomfit가 서로 짝이 되는 이유

해설 discomfit와 discomfort는 어원상 완전히 별개의 단어이지만 근대에 들어와 의미가 하나로 통합되었고, 표준 미국 영어에서는 두 단어를 품사만 다른 것으로 결합시키는 경향이 있다는 내용으로, 가장 잘 나타내는 제목은 (c)이다.

discomfit 패배, 당황하게 하다 **inherit** 물려받다 **appropriation** 사용, 전용 **prefix** 접두사 **denote** ~을 뜻하다 **negation** 부정 **root** 어근 **put together** 합치다, 모으다 **converge** 하나로 통합되다 **etymologically** 어원적으로 **derive from** ~에서 유래하다 **discrete** 별개의

17

1억 3천만 마리의 물소가 인도와 동남아시아의 농가에서 사육되고 있다. 넓은 발굽과 족부 관절 덕분에 물기 많은 습지에서 마음대로 움직일 수 있고, 토사 속으로 너무 깊이 빠지는 일 없이 진흙 웅덩이에서 뒹굴 수 있다. 이러한 적응 능력에 더하여, 물소는 크기와 체중도 엄청난데, 몸높이가 최고 1.9미터에 달하고 체중이 1,200킬로나 나간다. 이러한 특성 때문에 물소는 오랫동안 짐 나르는 짐승으로 이용되어왔으며, 5천년 넘게 남아시아에서 농부의 논농사를 도왔다.

Q 물소에 대해 바르게 말한 것은?
(a) 아시아에서 그 수가 1억 3천만 마리가 넘는다.
(b) 진흙에서는 육중한 무게 때문에 밑으로 빨려 들어간다.
(c) 아시아에서 사육된 지 5천년이 넘는다.
(d) 몸높이가 최고 1.5미터까지 자라기도 한다.

해설 마지막 문장에서 물소가 남아시아에서 논농사를 도운 지 5천년이 넘었다고 하므로 (c)가 일치한다. five millennia가 5,000 years로 바꿔 표현되었다.

domestic 사육되는 **water buffalo** 물소 **hoof** 발굽 **foot joint** 족부 관절 **maneuver** 기동하다 **sodden** 흠뻑 젖은 **wetland** 습지 **wallow** 뒹굴다 **silt** 토사, 침니 **adaptation** 적응 **stand** (키·높이가) ~이다 **characteristic** 특징 **beast of burden** 짐 나르는 짐승 **till** 경작하다 **rice field** 논 **in excess of** ~을 초과하여 **immense** 엄청난

18

소스 작전이라고 불린 영국 해군의 특별 임무는 X급 초소형 잠수함 6척이 투입된 비밀공작이었다. 1943년에 설계된 이 작전의 목표는 북부 노르웨이에 주둔한 독일 전함 티르피츠, 샤른호르스트, 뤼초우를 무력화시키는 것이었다. 전투 장소에 영국 해군의 초소형 잠수함을 파견하는 것은 전략가들에게 병참학적 문제를 던져 주었다. 왜냐하면 오랫동안 선박에서 승무원 생활을 하기란 실현 불가능한 일이었기 때문이다. 그렇게 비좁고 불편한 선박에서 2주 동안 갇혀 지낸다는 것은 참을 수 없는 일이었다. 또한 작전의 기밀이 노출될 것이므로 수상함이 소형 잠수함들을 북부 노르웨이로 수송할 수도 없었다. 그 대신, 6척의 재래식 잠수함이 X급 잠수정을 노르웨이 해안으로 예인했다.

Q 지문 내용과 일치하는 것은?
(a) 독일은 1943년이 되기 얼마 전에 작전에 대해 알게 되었다.
(b) 독일 함선 3척이 잠수함 12척의 공격을 받고 침몰했다.
(c) 노르웨이가 알고 있는 가운데 소스 작전을 실행했다.
(d) 소형 잠수함을 수송하는 데 대형 잠수함이 사용되었다.

해설 2차 세계대전 때 영국 해군이 노르웨이에 주둔한 독일 전함을 무력화시킬 목적으로 실행한 '소스 작전'을 설명하는 글이다. 6척의 재래식 잠수함이 X급 초소형 잠수함을 노르웨이 해안으로 예인했다는 마지막 문장에서 (d)가 정답임을 알 수 있다.

Royal Navy 영국 해군 **clandestine** 비밀의 **maneuver** 작전 행동, 책략 **midget** 극소형의 **submarine** 잠수함 **devise** 고안하다 **disable** 무력하게 하다 **station** 주둔하다 **strategist** 전략가 **logistical** 병참의, 물류에 관한 **crew** 승무원이 되다 **vessel** (대형) 선박 **feasible** 실현 가능한 **incommodious** 비좁고 불편한 **craft** 배, 선박 **confinement** 감금, 갇힘 **unendurable** 참을 수 없는 **compromise** 위태롭게 하다, 노출시키다 **submersible** 잠수함 **tow** 예인하다 **conventional** 재래식의

19

오랫동안 행방불명이었던 네덜란드 화가 빈센트 반 고흐의 걸작이 20세기 초 이후 처음으로 다시 모습을 드러냈다. 1888년 7월 4일 반 고흐는 작은 참나무들로 둘러싸인 돌밭에 앉아서 〈몽마주의 일몰〉이라는 제목의 풍경화를 그렸다. 이 작품은 반 고흐가 죽은 후 1901년에 그의 동생이 매각했고, 이것을 1908년에 한 노르웨이의 미술품 수집가가 구입하면서 또다시 주인이 바뀌었다. 그는 이 그림을 가짜라고 생각하고 다락방에 놓아두었는데, 미술계에서 사라진 지 1세기가 넘도록 그곳에 방치되어 있었다.

Q 지문의 그림에 대해 바르게 말한 것은?
(a) 뜻밖에도 반 고흐의 동생 집에서 발견되었다.
(b) 위조라는 의심 하에 방치되었다.
(c) 노르웨이의 경치를 배경으로 일몰을 그렸다.
(d) 반 고흐가 사망한 후 한 미술가가 그렸다.

해설 오랜 기간 행방을 알 수 없었던 반 고흐의 풍경화가 노르웨이의 한 다락방에서 발견되었다는 내용이다. 두 번째 주인이 그림을 가짜라고 생각하고 다락방에 방치해 두었으므로 (b)가 정답이다. forgery가 fake로 바꿔 표현되었다.

masterpiece 걸작 **resurface** 다시 부상하다 **oak** 오크, 참나무 **landscape** 풍경화 **change hands** 소유자가 바뀌다, 남의 손에 넘어가다 **forgery** 위조 **deposit** 두다, 놓다 **turn up** (잃어버렸던 물건 등이 뜻밖에도) 나타나다 **estate** 부동산, 재산 **suspicion** 의심 **depict** 묘사하다

20

화가들이 글레이징으로 알려진 기법을 써온 것은 유화의 역사만큼이나 오래됐다. 이는 기본적으로 마른 표면 위에 매우 얇은 투명한 색을 발라 밑색의 색조를 바꾸는 작업이다. 빛이 투명한 상층을 통해 밑면에 반사되면, 글레이즈(이미 칠해져서 건조된 그림 위에 투명하게 덧칠하는 얇은 층)의 색을 띠면서 반짝이게 된다. 게다가, 서로 다른 색깔의 글레이즈를 입히면 환영의 효과까지 볼 수 있다. 즉 안료들이 광학적으로 상호작용해 눈을 속임으로써 실제로 존재하지 않는 혼합된 색을 인식하게 만든다.

Q 글레이징에 대해 바르게 말한 것은?
(a) 유화보다 훨씬 뒤에 발명되었다.
(b) 처음에는 그림의 표면을 보호하기 위해 사용되었다.
(c) 일반적으로 그 색깔이 그림의 색깔과 일치한다.
(d) 빛을 조작해 새로운 종류의 색을 만든다.

해설 유화의 글레이징 기법(유화물감에 오일을 많이 섞어 그림의 마른 물감 위에 묽고 투명하게 덧칠하는 기법)을 설명하는 글이다. 서로 다른 색깔의 글레이즈를 입히면 빛의 효과에 의해 실제로 존재하지 않는 혼합된 색(a blended color that is not actually present)을 인식할 수 있다는 마지막 문장에서 (d)가 정답임을 알 수 있다.

essentially 본질적으로 **application** 바르기, 도포 **translucent** (반)투명한 **layer** 층 **alter** 바꾸다 **hue** 색조 **overlie** ~위에 가로 놓이다 **transparent** 투명한 **aura** 분위기, 기운 **take advantage of** ~에 편승하다 **illusion** 환영, 환상 **pigment** 안료 **interact** 상호작용하다 **optically** 광학적으로 **fool** 속이다 **employ** 이용하다 **typically** 일반적으로 **manipulate** 조작하다 **novel** 새로운 종류의

21

Q 케이스베이스에 대해 바르게 말한 것은?
(a) 차기 버전은 시간 추적 자동화가 특징적일 것이다.
(b) 주로 포괄적인 연구 자원들을 제공한다.
(c) 동료 간의 협력을 용이하게 한다.
(d) 추가 요금을 내면 첨단 보안용 암호화가 가능하다.

해설 법률 회사의 업무 처리를 능률적으로 돕는 소프트웨어를 광고하는 글이다. 동료들끼리 연락처, 기록물, 통신문 등의 사건 정보를 복사를 최소화하는 방식으로 공유할 수 있게 해준다는 점에서 동료 간의 협력을 용이하게 해 준다는 것을 알 수 있다.

law firm 법률 회사 functionality 기능 billing 청구서 작성 intuitive 이해[사용]하기 쉬운 invoice 송장 expedite 신속히 처리하다 collaboration 협력 sync 동기화 correspondence 통신문 duplication 복사 SSL 웹 브라우저와 웹 서버간 데이터를 안전하게 주고받는 표준 프로토콜(secure sockets layer) encryption 암호화 comprehensive 포괄적인 facilitate 가능[용이]하게 하다

22

장님뱀과를 구성하는 장님뱀은 뱀류 아목의 다른 분류군들과 비교했을 때 상대적으로 덜 진화되었다. 관 모양의 몸통과 둥근 끝부분은 지렁이를 연상케 하지만 두 생물은 전혀 연관성이 없다. 이 뱀의 머리와 뭉툭한 꼬리가 거의 구별되지 않으므로, 장님뱀과를 머리가 두 개인 동물로 추정을 해도 무리가 아니다. 구멍 파기에 적합한 형태를 갖고 있는 몸은 내부 장기를 싸고 있는 탄력적인 비늘로 덮여 있는데, 이것 덕분에 이들이 선호하는 서식지인 사양토를 헤치고 나갈 때 마찰을 덜 느낀다.

Q 지문 내용과 일치하는 것은?
(a) 장님뱀의 머리는 꼬리보다 약간 더 크다.
(b) 일부 장님뱀과의 꼬리는 끝으로 갈수록 점점 가늘어진다.
(c) 장님뱀과는 땅속에 산다.
(d) 장님뱀은 가장 최근의 종족에서 진화했다.

해설 장님뱀이 구멍을 파기에 적합한 몸 형태를 갖고 있고 비늘은 이들이 선호하는 서식지인 사양토를 헤치고 나갈 때 마찰을 덜 느끼도록 한다는 마지막 문장으로 보아 서식지가 땅속이라고 해석할 수 있으므로 (c)가 정답이다.

taxa 분류군(taxon의 복수형) suborder 아목 Serpentes 뱀류 blind snake 장님뱀 comprise 구성하다 family Typhlopidae 장님뱀과 tubular 관 모양의 terminal 말단의 be reminiscent of ~을 연상시키다 blunt 뭉툭한 could be forgiven for ~하는 것도 무리가 아니다 body plan 체제(동물 몸의 기본 형식) adapted for ~에 적합한 burrow 구멍을 파다 plate 철판 갑옷을 입히다 resilient 탄력 있는 scale 비늘 sheathe (무엇을 보호하기 위해) 싸다 interior 내장 friction 마찰 plow through 헤치고 나가다 loamy 양토의 habitat 서식 환경, 서식지 tapered 끝이 갈수록 점점 가늘어진 subterranean 지하의

23

Q 보도문에서 추론할 수 있는 것은?
(a) 아이콘 건축 그룹이 법과 대학원의 도서관을 지었다.
(b) 증축 건물이 생기면 더 많은 법대생을 받을 수 있을 것이다.
(c) 법과 대학원의 학과 평가도가 줄곧 하락해왔다.
(d) 법과 대학원은 이 대학 최대의 대학원 프로그램 중 하나이다.

해설 노스다코타 대학의 법과 대학원에 증축 건물을 짓는 이유가 현재 시설로는 제한된 인원의 학생들을 겨우 수용하기 때문이라고 했으므로 (b)를 추론할 수 있다.

draw 다가가다 law school 법과 대학원 panel 패널(특정 문제에 대해 조언·견해를 제공하는 전문가 집단) convene 소집하다 commission 의뢰[주문]하다 architecture firm 건축사 사무소 addition 증축 건물 unmodified 변경되지 않은 intervening 사이에 오는 accommodate 수용하다 Admissions Office 입학처 graduate 대학원생의

24

Q 공지를 통해 차마 씨에 대해 추론할 수 있는 것은?
(a) 집이 번잡한 거리에 위치해 있다.
(b) 강아지가 스스로 빠져나갔을 거라고 생각하지 않는다.
(c) 강아지가 이전에도 동네에서 달아난 적이 있다.
(d) 애완동물을 오랫동안 방치한 채 내버려두는 일이 좀체 없다.

해설 실종된 강아지를 찾는 내용이다. 강아지가 닫혀있는 마당(enclosed backyard)에 혼자 있다가 행방불명 되었고, 정황상 불한당이 유괴했을 가능성(the possibility of her abduction)을 배제할 수 없다는 말에서 (b)를 추론할 수 있다.

in regards to ~에 관해서 go missing 행방불명이 되다 unsupervised 방치된 enclosed 울타리가 있는 grieve 몹시 슬프게 하다 envision 상상하다 confront 직면하다 abduction 유괴 malicious 악의 있는, 심술궂은 passerby 통행인 in the vicinity of ~의 부근에 get in touch with ~와 연락을 취하다 property 부동산

25

〈세계 전망〉은 전 세계 경제 연구원들을 주 독자층으로 한, 누구나 자유롭게 이용할 수 있는 정기간행물입니다. 그 활동은 모범이 될 만한 지식을 출판하는 것뿐만 아니라, 세계 경제 네트워크의 성격에 대한 이해를 재평가하는 독창적인 학술 연구를 증진시키고자 하는 본 간행물의 이념과 맥을 같이 합니다. 이 분야의 기타 대다수 간행물들이 선구적인 연구물의 출판을 터무니없이 수개월씩 지연시키는 구시대적 출판 패러다임을 고수하는 반면, 〈세계 전망〉은 능률적이고 새로운 출판 방식을 채택해 왔습니다. 이 때문에 저희는 편집자 리뷰를 마친 후 새로운 원고에 즉각적이고 자유롭게 다가갈 수 있습니다.

Q 〈세계 전망〉에 대해 추론할 수 있는 것은?
(a) 경제 전문가들에게 무료로 제공된다.
(b) 스스로를 다른 출판업자들보다 더 진보적이라고 생각한다.
(c) 젊은 산업 연구원들에게 거액의 보조금을 제공한다.
(d) 편집 관리를 철저하게 하지 않는다.

해설 지문 중반부에서 경제 분야의 대다수 간행물들이 선구적인 연구물의 출판을 수개월씩 지연시키는 구시대적 관행을 고수하는 반면 〈세계 전망〉은 능률적이고 새로운 출판 방식을 채택한다고 했으므로 정답은 (b)이다.

open-access 누구나 자유롭게 이용할 수 있는 journal 잡지, 정기간행물 consonant with ~와 일치하는 charter 헌장, 선언 redefine 다시 정의하다, 재평가하다 exemplary 모범적인 scholarship 학문, 학식 adhere to ~을 고수하다 antiquated 구식의 impractically 터무니없이 embrace 받아들이다 streamlined 능률적인, 합리화된 accessible 접근[이용]할 수 있는 free of charge 무료로 publisher 출판업자 grant 보조금 oversight 감독, 감시

Part IV

26-27

http://www.simplyjobs.com/job-titles/collections-officers
소개 ∨ 직책 ∨ 위치 ∨ 해외 취업 ∨ 연락

카프리박물관 비(非)상근 수집 담당관

카프리박물관은 '인류의 역사에 대해 배울 수 있는 놀라운 곳'으로 널리 알려져 있습니다. 그런 곳으로서 저희는 다양한 역사 시대로부터의 공예품을 수집하는 데 전념해 왔습니다. 저희는 현재 저희의 사명을 달성하고 모든 지역사회 구성원에게 관련된 역사를 유지하도록 도움을 줄 수 있는, 경력직 자료 수집 담당관을 찾고 있습니다.

■ 책임
• 전시 담당 팀이 다양한 역사 시대의 공예품을 수집하는 것을 지원하기
• 카프리박물관이 아동을 위한 특별 전시회를 조직하는 것을 지원하기
• 박물관 인턴을 교육하고 감독하기
• 지역사회 구성원들이 돈을 기부를 하거나 박물관에서 자원봉사를 하도록 장려하기

■ 지원 요건
• 인류학 학사 학위가 필수이며, 문화인류학 석사 학위 소지자를 우대합니다.
• 지원자는 전시 관련 프로젝트를 수행한 경력이 최소한 2년은 되어야 합니다.
• 지원자는 영어와 프랑스어에 능통해야 합니다.
• 지원자는 대인관계 능력이 뛰어나야 합니다.
• 지원자는 기꺼이 주말에 근무할 수 있어야 합니다.

추가적인 정보를 원하시면, 저희 웹사이트 www.caprimuseum.org 를 방문하시거나 315-555-2500으로 전화를 주십시오.

26 Q 웹페이지에서 추론할 수 있는 것은?
(a) 박물관은 선사 시대의 유물을 수집하는 데 중점을 둔다.
(b) 박물관은 역사가 아동들에게 유의미할 수 있다고 생각하는 것 같다.
(c) 박물관의 인턴십 프로그램에는 지원자들이 많이 몰린다.
(d) 재정적인 어려움 때문에 박물관은 정규 직원을 고용하지 못한다.

해설 (a)는 웹페이지에서 '다양한 역사 시대'라고 밝혔기 때문에 오답이다. (c)는 전형적인 비약인데, 이 구인 광고에서 수집 담당관이 관리를 해야 한다고 해서, 반드시 지원자가 많이 몰린다고 할 수 없기 때문에 정답이 아니다. (d)도 마찬가지로 이렇게 비약해서 이해해서는 절대로 안 된다. 따라서 정답은 웹페이지의 내용으로부터 추론할 수 있는 (b)이다.

27 Q 다음 중 광고된 직책의 지원 요건이 될 수 있는 것은?
(a) 고생태학 석사 학위
(b) 영어와 프랑스어라는 2개 언어를 구사하는 능력
(c) 압박감 속에서도 뛰어나게 업무를 수행하는 능력
(d) 자발적으로 활동하는 능력

해설 NEW TEPS의 주요 출제 문항 유형이므로, 필요한 정보를 빠르고 정확하게 찾는 능력을 길러서 효과적으로 대비하도록 하자. 정답은 (b)이다. (a)에서 말하는 고생태학은 인류학과는 다르다. (c)는 주말 근무를 '압박감 속에서 하는 근무'라고 이해할 수 없기 때문에 오답이다. (d)는 지원 요건에서 직접적으로 말하지 않았기 때문에, 정답이 될 수 없다.

part-time 시간제의 artifact 공예품 era 시대 mission 임무, 사명 relevant 관련된, 유의미한 curatorial 큐레이터의 exhibit 전시회 supervise 감독하다, 지휘하다 anthropology 인류학 proficient 능숙한, 능통한 interpersonal 대인관계의 prehistoric 선사 시대의

28-29

비즈니스 > 지역   아이오와 타임스

온라인 상점과 오프라인 상점이 공존할 수 있을까?

전국 각지에서, 온라인 상점이 오프라인 상점과 맹렬하게 경쟁하고 있고, 그런 경쟁은 때때로 적대감으로 변할 수 있다. 그런 갈등을 해소하는 방법이 있을까?

아이오와에서 가장 오래된 전자제품 상점 가운데 하나인 사라전자는 온라인 상점과 오프라인 상점이 협력함으로써 보다 많은 수익을 창출하는 다양한 방법들이 있다는 사실을 시사한다. 지난 8월 이래로, 사라전자는 북아메리카에서 가장 큰 전자상거래 회사들 가운데 하나인 하모니아와 협력하고 있는데, 그들의 파트너십은 수익의 최대화에 도움을 주고 있다.

고객이 하모니아에서 전자제품을 주문하면, 그 주문은 사라전자에 의해 처리되는데, 사라전자는 고객에게 제품을 배송하는 역할을 맡는다. 동시에 하모니아는 유사한 제품을 그 고객에게 추천한다. 고객이 또 다시 주문하면, 15% 할인을 받을 수 있는 자격을 갖게 된다. 고객이 사라전자에게 제품을 구매하면, 그 구매 정보가 하모니아와 공유된다. 또 다시 전자상거래 회사인 하모니아가 비슷한 제품을 고객에게 추천한다.

하모니아와 사라전자는 모두 파트너십에 완전히 만족하는데, 이는 온라인 상점과 오프라인 상점이 보다 큰 이익을 위해 협력할 수 있음을 시사한다.

28 Q 기사의 주제는?
(a) 경쟁 관계에 있는 두 유형의 소매점이 협력할 수 있는 가능성
(b) 온라인 상점과 오프라인 상점 사이의 격렬한 경쟁
(c) 하모니아와 사라전자 사이의 오래된 반목
(d) 온라인 상점과 오프라인 상점 사이의 위태로운 파트너십

해설 NEW TEPS에서도 이처럼 시사적인 내용들이 비중 있게 출제되고 있음에 유의해야 한다. 정답은 (a)인데, 이 선택지에서 '두 유형의 소매점'이라고 표현한 것에 주목해야 한다. 이와 같이 정답인 선택지를 패러프레이징해서 제시하는 경우가 늘어나고 있기 때문이다. 이렇게 함으로써 문항의 난이도를 높일 수 있다. (b)와 같은 매력적인 오답을 피할 수 있어야 한다. (b)가 정답이라면, '격렬한 경쟁'에 대한 구체적인 설명이 상세하게 제시되어야 한다. 그런데 기사에는 그런 상세한 설명이 없기 때문에 오답이다.

29 Q 기사로부터 추론할 수 있는 것은?
(a) 많은 온라인 상점들은 자체 오프라인 매장이 있다.
(b) 사라전자는 예전에 많은 온라인 상점들과 협력했었다.
(c) 다른 오프라인 상점들이 하모니아와 사라전자 사이의 파트너십으로부터 배우는 바가 있을지도 모른다.
(d) 온라인 상점과 오프라인 상점 사이의 경쟁의 정도는 점점 약해질 것이다.

해설 (a)와 (b)는 기사의 내용만으로는 추론할 수 없으므로 오답이다. (d)는 매력적인 오답이다. 기사의 배경은 온라인 상점과 오프라인 상점 사이의 경쟁인데, 이런 경쟁 관계가 오히려 협력 관계가 될 수 있는 가능성을 주로 다루었다. 그렇다고 해서, 반드시 경쟁의 정도가 약해질 것으로 추론할 수는 없다. 따라서 정답은 무리하지 않고 추론할 수 있는 (c)이다.

coexist 공존하다 **furiously** 맹렬히 **brick-and-mortar** 오프라인 거래의, 소매의 **enmity** 증오, 적대감 **conflict** 갈등, 대립 **collaborate** 협력하다 **maximize** 최대화하다 **entitled** 자격이 있는 **retailer** 소매업자 **long-standing** 오래된 **feud** 반목, 불화 **precarious** 위태로운

30-31

유전자치료가 만병통치약이 될 것인가?

의료기술이 급속히 진전되면서, 점점 더 많은 이들이 유전자치료에 관심을 갖게 되었다. 어떤 이들은 심지어 유전자치료가 모든 질병에 대한 만병통치약이 될 것이라고 생각한다. 그 생각을 검토하기에 앞서, 유전자치료가 무엇인지 살펴봐야 한다.

유전자치료는 '정상적인' 유전자를 인간의 세포에 전달함으로써 비정상적인 유전자가 기능을 회복하도록 만드는 것을 목표로 삼는다. 많은 경우에, 비정상적인 유전자에는 결함이 있는 단백질이 들어 있는데, 그런 단백질을 유전자치료로 고칠 수 있다. 의학자들이 유전자를 직접 인간의 세포에 투입하면, 그런 유전자는 대개 작동을 하지 못한다. 따라서 의학자들은 정상적인 유전자를 인간의 세포에 전달하기 위해서 종종 변형된 바이러스를 이용한다.

유전자치료에는 두 종류의 바이러스가 자주 이용된다. 레트로바이러스가 정상적인 유전자를 인간 세포의 염색체에 더하는 데 반해서, 아데노바이러스는 정상적인 유전자를 인간 세포의 핵에 투입한다. 어떤 종류의 바이러스가 쓰이든, 인간의 조직에 직접적으로 투입할 수 있다.

유전자치료가 먼 미래에 만병통치약이 될지도 모른다. 그렇지만 현재 의학자들이 극복해야 할 장애가 너무도 많다. 예컨대 '정상적인' 유전자를 특정한 인간 세포에 겨냥하는 데 어려움을 겪는다. 그런 장애가 극복될 때까지는 유전자치료가 질병을 효과적으로 치료할 가능성은 높지 않다.

30 Q 지문에 따르면, 다음 중 옳은 것은?
(a) 유전자치료는 이로운 단백질을 만들어내지 못한다.
(b) 유전자치료는 특히 신체증상장애를 치료하는 데 효과적이다.
(c) 정상적인 유전자가 인간 세포의 염색체에 투입될 수 있다.
(d) 아데노바이러스는 인간 세포의 핵에 침투할 수 없다.

해설 NEW TEPS에서도 의학 관련 지문의 출제 비중은 결코 작지 않음에 유의하자. (a)는 오히려 반대라고 이해해야 하므로 오답이다. (b)는 그렇게 이해할 수 있는 설명이 제시되어 있지 않다. (d)는 침투할 수 있다고 분명히 설명했기 때문에 정답이 아니다. 따라서 정답은 (c)인데, 이것은 레트로바이러스와 관련된 설명으로, 지문의 내용과 일치한다.

31 Q 지문으로부터 추론할 수 있는 것은?
(a) 저자는 독자가 유전자치료로 모든 질병이 치료될 것이라고 확신하기를 원한다.
(b) 단백질이 세포의 기능 발휘에 영향을 미칠 수도 있다.
(c) 모든 레트로바이러스는 세포의 비정상적인 성장을 초래한다.
(d) 아데노바이러스는 면역체계를 약화시키는 것으로 널리 알려져 있다.

해설 (a)는 오히려 반대라고 추론하는 것이 타당하기 때문에 오답이다. (c)는 지문에서 레트로바이러스에 대해 그런 취지의 설명을 제공하지 않았기 때문에 정답이 아니다. 설령, 실제로 레트로바이러스가 그렇다고 하더라도, 지문에서 말하지 않은 경우에는 정답으로 골라서는 절대로 안 된다. '지문으로부터'라는 제한 요건이 있기 때문이다. 이는 (d)에 대해서도 마찬가지이다. 따라서 정답은 (b)이다.

panacea 만병통치약 **advance** 진전되다 **cure-all** 만병통치약 **abnormal** 비정상적인 **restore** 회복시키다 **faulty** 결함이 있는 **modify** 수정하다, 변경하다 **retrovirus** 레트로바이러스 **chromosome** 염색체 **adenovirus** 아데노바이러스 **nuclei** 세포핵(nucleus의 복수형) **tissue** (생물의) 조직 **obstacle** 장애 **somatic symptom disorder** 신체증상장애 **debilitate** 쇠약하게 하다

Actual Test 5

32-33

유머로 탁월한?

나를 포함한, 대부분의 미국인들에게 퓰리처상 픽션 부문은 진지한 것, 심오한 것, 접근하기 어려운 것을 뜻한다. 글쎄, 올해의 수상작은 그런 인식을 깨뜨리는 데 기여할지도 모른다.

앤드루 숀 그리어의 〈레스〉가 올해의 퓰리처상 픽션 부문인데, 이 소설은 매우 우습다. 기묘하게도, 그리어는 본래 우스운 소설을 쓰기를 원했던 것은 아니었다. 사실, 이 소설의 주제는 아주 심각하다. 소설의 주제는 청춘의 무상함과 삶의 가혹한 현실을 다룬다.

소설의 주인공인 아서 레스는 전(前) 남자친구의 결혼식에 참석하지 않기 위해 세계 여행을 떠난다. 이 여행은 레스에게 젊음을 붙잡을 수 없다는 것과 평범한 사람들이 직면하는 가혹한 현실에 대한 삶의 교훈을 가르쳐준다. 레스의 여행에서 주목할 만한 점은 자신을 웃음거리로 삼을 수 있는 기회를 많이 제공한다는 것이다.

자신이 올해의 퓰리처상 픽션 부문의 수상 작가라는 사실을 알았을 때, 그리어는 깜짝 놀랐다. 그것은 주로 미국의 문학 평론가들이 익살맞은 소설을 무시하는 경향이 있다는 사실을 그가 알고 있었기 때문이었다. 올해에는 그 평론가들이 생각을 바꿨거나 아니면 그리어의 유머 감각에 깊은 인상을 받았는지도 모른다. 이유야 무엇이든지, 퓰리처상 픽션 부문이 마침내 유머 감각이 뛰어나다는 것의 탁월함을 인정한 셈이다.

32 Q 기사의 요지는?

(a) 퓰리처상 픽션 부문의 명망은 크게 과대평가되어 있다.
(b) 퓰리처상 픽션 부문은 문학에 대한, 마음이 가벼운 접근을 권장할 것이다.
(c) 그리어의 〈레스〉는 미국의 문학 평론가들이 인정한, 가장 우스운 소설이다.
(d) 그리어의 〈레스〉는 어떤 문학상에 대한 사람들의 인식을 바꿔 놓을 수 있다.

해설 (a)는 비약에 해당하기 때문에 오답이다. 기사의 저자가 이렇게 생각한다고 이해할 수 있는 근거가 빈약하다. (b)는 그리어의 〈레스〉라는 작품 하나만으로 이렇게 과장해서 판단할 수 없다. (c)는 '가장 우스운 소설'이라고 이해할 수도 없고, 그것이 기사의 요지도 아니다. 따라서 정답은 기사의 요지를 정확히 포착한 (d)이다.

33 Q 필자가 가장 동의할 것 같은 진술은?

(a) 퓰리처상 픽션 부문은 대부분의 미국인들이 공감할 수 없는 것으로 남아 있다.
(b) 자신을 웃음거리로 삼을 수 있는 것은 위대한 소설가의 특징들 가운데 하나이다.
(c) 그리어의 〈레스〉는 심각한 주제를 익살맞은 방식으로 제시하는 데 성공했다.
(d) 그리어의 〈레스〉는 미국의 문학 평론가들이 자신들의 기준을 심각하게 손상시키도록 할 것이다.

해설 (a)는 공감할 수 없다고 추론하기에는 힘들기 때문에 오답이다. (b)는 필자가 위대한 소설가의 특징을 다루고 있지 않기 때문에 정답이 아니다. (d)는 전형적인 비약에 해당한다. 〈레스〉라는 한 작품을 인정했다는 내용만으로 (d)처럼 일반화할 수가 없다. 따라서 정답은 (c)이다. 기사에서 직접적으로 말한 내용이기 때문이다.

distinguished 빼어난, 뛰어난 **profound** 심오한 **inaccessible** 접근하기 어려운 **shatter** 산산이 부수다 **remarkably** 현저하게, 매우 **transience** 무상함 **protagonist** 주인공 **elusiveness** 포착하기 어려움 **disregard** 무시하다 **distinction** 탁월함 **prestige** 명망, 권위 **compromise** 손상하다; 타협하다

34-35

발신: 알렉산드라 그린 ⟨alexandra_g@jcconstruction.com⟩
수신: 잭 스미스 ⟨j_smith@gaconstruction.com⟩
일자: 7월 13일 금요일 오전 11:33
주제: 프로젝트 조달

안녕, 잭

이미 알고 있을지 모르겠지만, 남호주정부는 국가 조달법 2004를 도입했었는데, 액수가 15만 달러가 넘는 규정 건설 프로젝트는 그 조달법의 규제를 받지 않는 것으로 결정을 내렸어요. 우리 프로젝트의 총액수가 18만 달러이기 때문에, 그 조달법을 따를 필요가 없어요. 그렇지만 기술적인 문제를 논의하기 위해서 여러 정부 기관에 연락을 취해야 해요.

언제 애들레이드에서 저를 방문할 수 있을 것 같아요? 줄리아도 당신과 함께 올 수 있을 것 같아요? 어제 연락을 취한 정부 기관에 따르면, 여러 기술적인 쟁점을 해결하기 위해 두 분이 직접 그 기관을 방문해야 한답니다.

언제 애들레이드에 올 수 있는지 알려주세요. 제 생각에 당신은 그 기관을 방문한 다음에 관광할 수 있는 시간이 있을 것 같아요. 기꺼이 관광 가이드가 되어드릴게요.

곧 다시 만나길 고대해요. 몸조심하시고 건강하시길 빌게요.

행복을 빌면서,
알렉산드라 그린

34 Q 이메일의 주된 목적은?

(a) 수취인에게 줄리아와 기술적인 문제를 논의할 필요가 있다고 통지하는 것
(b) 수취인에게 애들레이드를 방문하여 프로젝트 조달을 도와달라고 요청하는 것
(c) 수취인에게 오락 삼아서 애들레이드를 방문해 달라고 초청하는 것
(d) 잭과 줄리아에게 서로의 껄끄러운 관계를 회복하라고 조언하는 것

해설 (a)가 매력적인 오답인데, 우선 수취인이 '줄리아를 상대로 해서' 기술적인 문제를 논의하는 것이 아니라는 점을 이해해야 한다. 선택지에서 'with Julia'라고 표현한 것을 '줄리아와 함께 정부 기구를 상대로 해서'라고 이해하는 것은 다소 무리가 있다. 설령 그렇게 이해한다고 해도, 이메일의 주된 목적은 이메일의 주제인 '프로젝트 조달'과 연관해서 언급되어야 한다. 따라서 정답은 (b)이다.

35 Q 이메일에 따르면, 다음 중 옳은 것은?

(a) 대부분의 건설 회사들은 국가 조달법 2004를 준수해야만 한다.
(b) 스미스 씨는 기술적인 문제에 익숙할 가능성이 매우 높다.
(c) 그린 씨와 스미스 씨는 동일한 건설 회사에 근무한다.
(d) 그린 씨는 평생 동안 애들레이드에 거주한 사람이다.

해설 (a)는 15만 달러가 넘는 프로젝트를 수행하는 건설 회사들이 더 많을 수도 있기 때문에 오답이다. (c)는 각자의 이메일 주소에 명시된 회사명이 다르기 때문에 서로 다른 건설 회사에서 일하는 것으로 봐야 하므로 정답이 아니다. (d)는 평생 동안 거주했는지를 알 수 없기 때문에 오답이다. 따라서 정답은 자연스럽게 추론이 가능한 (b)이다.

procurement 조달, 입수 **prescribed** 규정된 **regulate** 규제하다 **comply with** ~을 준수하다 **technical** 기술적인 **settle** 해결하다 **lifelong** 평생 동안의

Actual Test 6

청해 Listening Comprehension

p.187

1	(c)	2	(a)	3	(d)	4	(b)	5	(c)	6	(d)	7	(c)	8	(d)	9	(c)	10	(a)
11	(b)	12	(c)	13	(b)	14	(d)	15	(b)	16	(d)	17	(a)	18	(a)	19	(d)	20	(d)
21	(d)	22	(c)	23	(a)	24	(d)	25	(c)	26	(d)	27	(a)	28	(c)	29	(d)	30	(b)
31	(c)	32	(d)	33	(c)	34	(b)	35	(b)	36	(d)	37	(d)	38	(b)	39	(b)	40	(b)

어휘 Vocabulary

p.193

1	(a)	2	(c)	3	(d)	4	(c)	5	(c)	6	(a)	7	(a)	8	(c)	9	(c)	10	(b)
11	(b)	12	(d)	13	(a)	14	(c)	15	(c)	16	(a)	17	(d)	18	(c)	19	(d)	20	(c)
21	(d)	22	(b)	23	(c)	24	(a)	25	(b)	26	(b)	27	(a)	28	(b)	29	(c)	30	(a)

문법 Grammar

p.197

1	(b)	2	(c)	3	(a)	4	(c)	5	(a)	6	(b)	7	(c)	8	(d)	9	(b)	10	(d)
11	(d)	12	(a)	13	(c)	14	(b)	15	(d)	16	(c)	17	(a)	18	(c)	19	(b)	20	(a)
21	(d)	22	(b)	23	(b)	24	(a)	25	(c)	26	(c)	27	(b)	28	(b)	29	(d)	30	(b)

독해 Reading Comprehension

p.201

1	(d)	2	(c)	3	(b)	4	(d)	5	(d)	6	(a)	7	(a)	8	(c)	9	(c)	10	(d)
11	(b)	12	(c)	13	(c)	14	(c)	15	(a)	16	(c)	17	(b)	18	(d)	19	(b)	20	(a)
21	(c)	22	(b)	23	(b)	24	(d)	25	(a)	26	(b)	27	(a)	28	(b)	29	(b)	30	(d)
31	(d)	32	(d)	33	(a)	34	(c)	35	(d)												

Part I

1

M Who's chairing the Wilson committee?

W _____

(a) I'm Melinda, nice to meet you.

(b) No, he's not available right now.

(c) It hasn't been announced yet.

(d) Everyone's expecting that.

M 누가 윌슨 위원회 의장을 맡고 있나요?

W _____

(a) 저는 멜린다이고 만나서 반가워요.

(b) 아니요, 그는 지금 시간이 안 됩니다.

(c) 아직 발표가 안 났어요.

(d) 모든 사람이 그걸 예상하고 있어요.

chair 의장을 맡다 **committee** 위원회 **announce** 발표하다
expect 기대하다, 예상하다

2

W Real-estate prices seem really volatile right now.

M _____

(a) Investing would be risky.

(b) I'll tour the property with you.

(c) That's quite a bargain.

(d) I'd recommend coming over later.

W 지금은 부동산 가격이 정말 변덕스러운 것 같아요.

M _____

(a) 투자는 위험할 겁니다.

(b) 나는 당신과 그 부동산을 둘러볼 거예요.

(c) 정말 싸네요.

(d) 나중에 오시면 좋겠습니다.

volatile 변덕스러운 **invest** 투자하다 **risky** 위험한 **tour** 순회하다,
둘러보다 **property** 재산, 부동산 **bargain** 싸게 사는 물건 **come
over** 들르다, 먼 거리를 오가다

3

M Are this month's sales figures any stronger compared
to last month's?

W _____

(a) All the hard work finally paid off.

(b) It's been puzzling me as well.

(c) Give me just one more month.

(d) There's been no real change.

M 이번 달 판매 수치가 지난달과 비교했을 때 더 좋아졌나요?

W _____

(a) 열심히 한 모든 것이 드디어 결실을 보았네요.

(b) 역시 그건 저를 혼란스럽게 하네요.

(c) 한 달만 더 주세요.

(d) 실제 변화는 없었어요.

sales figures 판매 수치, 판매액 **pay off** 보상을 받다
puzzle 혼란스럽게 하다 **as well** 또한, 역시

4

W Don't put too much faith in that diet drug.

M _____

(a) Sure, put me down for a free trial.

(b) Okay, I understand your skepticism.

(c) Yes, you need to start eating better.

(d) Thanks, I've lost a little weight.

W 저 다이어트 약을 너무 신뢰하지 마세요.

M _____

(a) 그럼요, 저는 무료 체험판으로 해 주세요.

(b) 네, 당신의 회의적인 태도는 이해해요.

(c) 네, 당신은 더 잘 먹기 시작해야 합니다.

(d) 고마워요, 저 살이 좀 빠졌어요.

faith 신뢰, 믿음 **put ~ down for** …을 위한 명단에 ~의 이름을
등록시키다 **trial** 시험, 실험 **skepticism** 회의적인 태도 **lose
weight** 살을 빼다

5

M The plumber called to say he won't be here till 4.

W _____

(a) There's a problem with the sink.

(b) Two o'clock will be fine, then.

(c) I knew he'd be running late.

(d) I don't have his number.

M 배관공한테서 전화가 왔는데, 4시까지는 못 온대요.

W _____

(a) 싱크대에 문제가 있어요.

(b) 그럼 2시가 좋겠는데요.

(c) 늦을 줄 알았어요.

(d) 그의 전화번호를 몰라요.

plumber 배관공 **sink** 싱크대 **run** (어떤 좋지 않은 상태가) 되다

6

M I almost forgot to tell you, but you have a package in
the mailroom, Carmela.

W _____

(a) That's okay since I forgot about it.

(b) No, I won't overlook it again.

(c) Yes, as soon as I finish this.

(d) Great, I've been expecting it.

M 카멜라, 제가 당신에게 말하는 걸 거의 잊을 뻔했군요. 우편물실에 소포가 있어요.

W _____

(a) 내가 그것에 대해 잊었으니 괜찮아요.
(b) 아니요, 다시 간과하지 않을 겁니다.
(c) 네, 제가 이걸 끝내는 대로 빨리요.
(d) 잘됐네요, 기다리고 있었어요.

package 소포   **mailroom** 우편물실   **overlook** 간과하다, 못 보고 넘어가다

7

W What's the latest on the copyright dispute with the publisher?

M _____

(a) She arrived on time as far as I know.
(b) I have a copy of the book right here.
(c) The legal department is handling it.
(d) There's a public machine on the fifth floor.

W 그 출판사와의 저작권 논쟁에 관한 최신 소식은 뭐예요?

M _____

(a) 제가 알기로 그녀는 제시간에 도착했어요.
(b) 지금 여기 책 한 권을 갖고 있어요.
(c) 법무부서가 그 문제를 처리하고 있어요.
(d) 5층에 공공 기기가 한 대 있어요.

copyright 저작권   **dispute** 논쟁   **copy** 한 부, 복사본   **legal** 법적인

8

W How are we going to get downtown with the subway operators on strike?

M _____

(a) The F Line train should take you there.
(b) Downtown living is making a comeback.
(c) I think there's another entrance this way.
(d) We'll have to wait in line for a cab.

W 기관사들이 파업 중인데 우리가 어떻게 시내로 갈 수 있을까요?

M _____

(a) F라인 열차를 타시면 거기에 갈 거예요.
(b) 시내에 사는 것은 다시 유행입니다.
(c) 이쪽으로 가면 다른 출입구가 있는 것 같습니다.
(d) 줄을 서서 택시를 타야겠군요.

get downtown 시내로 가다   **operator** 운영자   **on strike** 파업 중인
comeback 재기   **entrance** 입구   **wait in line** 줄 서서 기다리다

9

M It's getting harder and harder to find a decent babysitter.

W _____

(a) My son is already in the fifth grade.
(b) They say that's the reward of raising a child.

(c) I may have the perfect person for you.
(d) Standard pay is around ten dollars an hour.

M 괜찮은 베이비시터 찾기가 점점 더 어렵네요.

W _____

(a) 제 아들이 벌써 5학년입니다.
(b) 사람들이 말하기를 그게 아이를 키우는 것의 보람이라고 하네요.
(c) 당신에게 딱 맞는 사람을 알고 있어요.
(d) 표준 임금이 시간당 10달러 정도입니다.

decent 괜찮은   **grade** 학년   **raise a child** 자녀를 양육하다

10

M Have you come to a decision regarding the offer we made?

W _____

(a) I'm afraid I have to pass.
(b) He's a bit too wishy-washy.
(c) That's very generous of you.
(d) Weigh the pros and cons.

M 저희 제안에 관해 결정을 내리셨어요?

W _____

(a) 죄송하지만, 사양하겠습니다.
(b) 그는 좀 미온적이에요.
(c) 아주 관대하시군요.
(d) 이해득실을 따져 보세요.

regarding ～에 관한   **pass** 사양[거절] 하다   **wishy-washy** 미온적인, 확고하지 못한   **generous** 관대한   **weigh the pros and cons** 이해득실을 따지다

Part II

11

W Housing prices in this neighborhood are skyrocketing.
M Yes, an average of 25% a year.
W Do you expect that trend to continue?
M _____

(a) Thanks, but I'm not interested.
(b) The market should level off.
(c) Yes, I'll be here until then.
(d) We may be able to discount it.

W 이 동네 집값이 치솟고 있어요.
M 맞아요, 1년에 평균 25퍼센트씩이요.
W 이런 추세가 계속 갈까요?
M _____

(a) 고맙지만 저는 관심이 없어요.
(b) 시장이 안정돼야죠.
(c) 네, 그때까지 제가 여기 있을게요.
(d) 저희가 할인할 수 있을 것 같네요.

skyrocket 급등하다   **trend** 추세, 흐름   **level off** 안정되다, 변동이 없게 되다   **discount** 할인하다

12

M I have to be a full-time student to receive financial aid, right?
W That's university policy.
M What if I drop one of my four courses right now?
W _____

(a) It meets in Miller Hall.
(b) No, it isn't that much.
(c) You'll lose your aid money.
(d) I can do that for you, sure.

M 재정적인 도움을 받으려면 제가 정규 학생이어야 하죠?
W 학교 규정이 그렇습니다.
M 제가 지금 4과목 중 하나를 수강 취소하면 어떻게 되나요?
W _____

(a) 밀러 홀에서 있어요.
(b) 아니요, 그렇게 많진 않아요.
(c) 재정적인 도움을 못 받게 됩니다.
(d) 분명히 제가 해 드릴 수 있어요.

financial aid 금전적인 도움 **policy** 정책 **drop** 빼다, 취소하다

13

W What's this about a tourist visa fee?
M It's 200 dollars, payable on entry.
W How was I supposed to know that?
M _____

(a) Have your ticket ready for the tour bus.
(b) It's clearly stated on the immigration website.
(c) Please take your bag through customs.
(d) That's the policy regarding hotel tax.

W 여행자 비자 수수료가 뭐죠?
M 200달러인데 입장하실 때 내시면 됩니다.
W 제가 무슨 재주로 이걸 아나요?
M _____

(a) 투어 버스 타려면 티켓을 미리 준비하세요.
(b) 출입국 관리소 웹 사이트에 분명히 나와 있습니다.
(c) 세관을 통과할 때 가방을 가져가세요.
(d) 저게 호텔 세금에 관한 규정입니다.

payable 지불할 수 있는 **entry** 입장 **state** 설명하다
immigration 출입국 관리소, 이민 **customs** 세관 **policy** 규정, 정책

14

W Liam, how goes it?
M Just trying to get through this hectic quarter.
W Hectic is an understatement.
M _____

(a) It's a breeze, if you ask me.
(b) Try again in another 15 minutes.
(c) That's not what I said.
(d) It's been pretty crazy, I know.

W 리암, 잘 지내?
M 이 정신없는 분기를 버텨내는 중이야.
W 정신없다는 말로는 부족할 것 같은데.
M _____

(a) 요청만 한다면 식은 죽 먹기야.
(b) 15분 후에 다시 해 봐.
(c) 그건 내가 말한 게 아닌데.
(d) 맞아, 정말 장난이 아니지.

get through 끝내다, 힘든 상황을 버티다 **hectic** 정신없는
quarter 분기 **understatement** 절제된 표현 **breeze** 식은 죽 먹기

15

M Didn't you fill the gas tank yesterday?
W Oh, I meant to but it just slipped my mind.
M I almost ran out of gas on the way to work this morning.
W _____

(a) Fuel prices are way too high these days.
(b) Oh I'm sorry. I apologize for forgetting it.
(c) Well, I'll come right away and pick you up.
(d) Right, that's what I asked you to do.

M 어제 연료 안 채웠어?
W 아, 그러려 했었는데 그만 잊어버렸네.
M 아침 출근길에 연료가 거진 바닥날 뻔했어.
W _____

(a) 요즘 연료비가 너무 비싸.
(b) 오, 미안해. 기름 넣는 걸 잊은 것에 대해 사과할게.
(c) 응. 내가 당장 데리러 갈게.
(d) 맞아, 그게 내가 너에게 요청한 거야.

run out of ~가 다 떨어지다 **fuel** 연료 **besides** ~외에 **apology** 사과

16

M Honestly, I didn't care for the film.
W That heart-warming love story didn't move you?
M I found it a bit contrived.
W _____

(a) I was totally captivated too.
(b) Just because you haven't seen it.
(c) You'll love this romantic comedy.
(d) What a cynical thing to say!

M 솔직히 나는 그런 영화 안 좋아해.
W 마음이 따스해지는 그런 사랑 얘기가 감동적이지 않아?
M 억지로 꾸민 것 같던데.
W _____

(a) 나도 완전히 반했어.
(b) 네가 그걸 못 봤기 때문이야.
(c) 너는 이런 로맨틱 코미디를 좋아할 거야.
(d) 그렇게 냉소적으로 말하다니!

care for ~을 좋아하다 **heart-warming** 마음이 따스해지는 **move**
감동을 주다 **contrived** 억지로 꾸민 듯한, 부자연스러운 **captivate**
사로잡다 **cynical** 냉소적인

17

W Hello, Eric, it's 5:30. Please tell me you're on your way.
M Of course I'm on my way.
W I can tell you're lying. You haven't even left the house yet!
M _____

(a) I promise I'll be there in no time.
(b) It feels like I've been away for a while.
(c) So we'll have some time to kill before it starts.
(d) But I couldn't tell what the traffic was like.

W 여보세요 에릭, 5시 반이야, 제발 오는 중이라고 해줘.
M 물론 가는 중이야.
W 거짓말인 걸 알아. 아직 집에서 나오지도 않았잖아!
M _____

(a) 거기 금방 도착해.
(b) 한동안 떠나있었던 것 같아.
(c) 그래서 시작하기 전에 시간을 좀 보내야 해.
(d) 하지만 교통이 어땠는지 알 수 없었어요.

on one's way 도중인 **in no time** 즉시 **be away** 출타 중인 **tell** 알다

18

W I'll take a cappuccino with extra foam.
M I'm afraid our steamer is broken.
W How much longer till it's fixed?
M _____

(a) It's going to be a while.
(b) Here's your drink, ma'am.
(c) That's kind of you to offer.
(d) It takes two minutes to make.

W 거품을 더 얹은 카푸치노로 할게요.
M 저희 스팀기가 고장 난 것 같습니다.
W 수리하는 데 얼마나 걸릴까요?
M _____

(a) 한참 걸리겠죠.
(b) 여기 음료수 나왔습니다.
(c) 제공해 주셔서 감사합니다.
(d) 만드는 데 2분 걸립니다.

foam 거품 **steamer** 스팀기, 찜통 **broken** 고장 난 **offer** 제공하다

19

M This antihistamine won't make me sleepy, I hope.
W Looks like it may cause drowsiness.
M Where on the box does it say so?
W _____

(a) Let's ask the pharmacist to fill the prescription.
(b) Over there next to the nightstand.
(c) I just can't keep my eyes open.
(d) Beneath the "extra strength" label.

M 이 항히스타민제는 졸리지 않으면 좋겠네요.
W 졸음을 유발하는 것 같은데요.
M 그 상자 어디에 그런 말이 있나요?
W _____

(a) 약사에게 약을 조제해 달라고 얘기합시다.
(b) 저기 침실용 탁자 옆이요.
(c) 도저히 눈을 뜰 수가 없어요.
(d) '강력한 약효' 라벨 밑이에요.

antihistamine 항히스타민제 **drowsiness** 졸림 **fill the prescription** 처방전에 따라 약을 조제하다 **nightstand** 침실용 탁자 **beneath** ~아래에 **extra strength** 약효가 강력한

20

M Are you saying you're able to upgrade my rental?
W Yes, to a minivan at no extra charge.
M That certainly would give my family more room.
W _____

(a) We're ready to service your vehicle now.
(b) Changing the reservation will incur a fee.
(c) I'm afraid we don't have any available.
(d) It's one of our most spacious models.

M 제 렌트를 업그레이드할 수 있다는 말씀인가요?
W 네, 추가 비용 없이 미니밴으로요.
M 확실히 저희 가족들에게 공간이 많아지겠네요.
W _____

(a) 지금 고객님의 차를 수리할 준비가 되어 있습니다.
(b) 예약을 바꾸시면 수수료가 발생합니다.
(c) 지금 이용하실 수 있는 게 없네요.
(d) 가장 공간이 넓은 모델 중 하나죠.

rental 임대, 임대물 **at no extra charge** 추가 수수료 없이 **incur** 초래하다 **spacious** 널찍한

Part III

21

Listen to a conversation between a mother and her son.

W Still reading that textbook, Mitch?
M I've only gotten through half the material.
W Really? But it's almost midnight.
M Looks like I'll be pulling another all-nighter.
W Cramming like this doesn't lead to long-term learning.
M Maybe, but it's too late now.

Q What is mainly being discussed?
(a) Material on tomorrow's test
(b) The man's sleep schedule
(c) Different educational theories
(d) The man's poor study habits

엄마와 아들의 대화를 들으시오.

W 아직도 교과서 읽는 거야, 미치?
M 겨우 반 정도 끝냈어요.
W 정말? 하지만 거의 자정이 됐는데.
M 또 밤새워야 할 것 같아요.
W 이렇게 벼락치기 하면 장기적인 공부가 안돼.
M 그렇겠죠, 하지만 지금은 너무 늦었어요.

Q 주로 얘기하고 있는 것은?
(a) 내일 시험에 관한 교재
(b) 남자의 수면 일정
(c) 여러 교육적인 이론들
(d) 남자의 좋지 않은 학습 습관

textbook 교과서　**pull an all-nighter** 밤샘 공부를 하다　**cram** 벼락치기 공부를 하다　**educational** 교육적인　**poor** 좋지 못한, 형편없는

22

Listen to a conversation between a couple.

M Our electricity bill this month is over 100 dollars.
W You're kidding! Isn't it usually around 50?
M Yes, I wonder what we did differently.
W Well, the air conditioner was on a lot more often.
M Do you think that could be it?
W If so, we need to replace that unit!

Q What are the man and woman mainly talking about?
(a) A home renovation project
(b) An energy-efficient appliance
(c) A high utility charge
(d) A billing error

부부의 대화를 들으시오.

M 이번 달 전기세가 100달러를 넘었어.
W 설마! 보통 50달러 정도 아니었어?
M 그래, 우리가 별다르게 뭘 했는지 궁금해.
W 글쎄, 에어컨이 훨씬 자주 가동되었었네.
M 그것이 원인이라고 생각해?
W 그렇다면 에어컨을 바꿔야겠어!

Q 남자와 여자가 주로 얘기하는 것은?
(a) 집 리모델링 계획
(b) 에너지 효율적인 기구
(c) 높은 공공요금
(d) 청구서 오류

electricity 전기　**replace** 바꾸다　**energy-efficient** 에너지 효율적인
appliance 기구, 도구　**utility charge** 공공요금

23

Listen to a conversation between two club members.

M Did you truly not enjoy *How We Won the War*?
W It was a little slow-moving for my taste.
M I found the battle scenes just riveting.
W I can't get into fiction that's so loosely based on real events.
M So you're saying you'd prefer a nonfiction work?
W When it comes to historical matters, yes.

Q What are the man and woman mainly doing?
(a) Debating a work of historical fiction
(b) Deciding which book to read next
(c) Arguing about a piece of trivia
(d) Pointing out the flaws in a movie

두 클럽 회원의 대화를 들으시오.

M '우리가 어떻게 전쟁을 이겼나'는 정말 재미없었어요?
W 저한테는 좀 질질 끄는 것 같았어요.
M 전 전쟁 장면에서 완전히 빠졌는데요.
W 실제로 일어났던 일에서 많이 벗어난 소설은 흥미가 안 생겨요.
M 그래서 논픽션 작품을 좋아하신다는 거죠?
W 역사적인 사건인 경우에는 그래요.

Q 남자와 여자가 주로 하는 것은?
(a) 한 역사 소설 작품에 관해 얘기하기
(b) 다음에 어떤 책을 읽을지 정하기
(c) 사소한 정보에 대해 다투기
(d) 영화에서 흠 찾아내기

slow-moving 느리게 움직이는, 행동이 굼뜬　**riveting** 관심을 사로잡는, 눈을 못 떼게 하는　**get into** ～에 흥미를 갖게 되다　**trivia** 하찮은 것들, 사소한 정보　**point out** 가리키다, 지적하다　**flaw** 흠, 결함

24

Listen to a conversation between two acquaintances.

W Do you know anything about web design?
M Not too much, actually.
W But I think you have a blog.
M I do, but I use a service that has pre-made templates.
W Could you show me how to do that?
M Absolutely. It's so easy it won't take long at all.

Q Which of the following is correct according to the conversation?
(a) The man is an IT expert.
(b) The woman is an active blogger.
(c) The man designed his own template.
(d) The woman wants to start a website.

두 지인의 대화를 들으시오.

W 웹 디자인에 대해 아는 거 있어요?
M 별로 없어요.
W 하지만 블로그를 하시잖아요.
M 네, 그렇지만 이미 만들어진 템플릿을 이용할 뿐이죠.
W 방법 좀 알려 주시겠어요?
M 그럼요. 쉬워서 오래 안 걸려요.

Q 대화에 따르면 다음 중 옳은 것은?
(a) 남자는 IT 전문가이다.
(b) 여자는 활발한 블로거이다.
(c) 남자는 자신만의 템플릿을 디자인했다.
(d) 여자는 웹 사이트를 시작하고 싶어 한다.

pre-made 미리 만든　**expert** 전문가　**active** 활발한, 적극적인

25

Listen to two friends discuss a photograph.

M This is a really nice picture of you.

W Thanks, I had it professionally done.

M Why not frame it and display it?

W Oh, I didn't think it was good enough for that.

M Seriously? It's quite the portrait.

W If you really think so, I might consider it.

Q Which of the following is correct about the woman according to the conversation?

(a) She had a portrait taken to hang on her wall.

(b) She has requested that the man take her picture.

(c) She had doubts about the quality of the photo.

(d) She once worked as a professional photographer.

두 친구가 사진에 관해 말하는 것을 들으시오.

M 이 사진 정말 잘 나왔다.

W 고마워요, 전문가에게 좀 맡겼지.

M 액자에 넣어 걸어 놓는 게 어때?

W 아, 그 정도로 좋진 않아.

M 정말? 훌륭한 인물 사진인걸.

W 정말 그렇게 생각한다면 한 번 고려해 볼게.

Q 대화에 따르면 다음 중 여자에 관해 옳은 것은?

(a) 여자는 벽에 걸기 위해서 인물 사진을 찍었다.

(b) 여자는 남자에게 사진을 찍어 달라고 요청했다.

(c) 여자는 사진의 품질에 대해 확신이 없었다.

(d) 여자는 한때 전문 사진작가로 일했다.

professionally 전문적으로 **frame** 액자에 넣다 **portrait** 초상화, 인물 사진

26

Listen to a conversation in an office.

W Excuse me, that's my phone you just picked up.

M Is it? Sorry, I have one just like it.

W Really? I thought I had the only XB-2 in this office.

M Actually, mine is the XB-3.

W Wait, that hasn't been released yet.

M I was able to get a hold of an advance unit.

Q Which of the following is correct according to the conversation?

(a) The woman damaged the man's phone.

(b) The woman has lent the man her phone.

(c) The man and woman have the exact same phone.

(d) The man's phone is the newest model.

사무실에서 이뤄지는 대화를 들으시오.

W 실례합니다만 방금 잡으신 거 제 전화기인데요.

M 이게요? 죄송해요, 저도 이렇게 생긴 게 있어서요.

W 정말요? 저는 이 사무실에서 저만 XB-2를 갖고 있는 줄 알았는데요.

M 사실 제 건 XB-3입니다.

W 아니, 그건 아직 출시도 안 되었잖아요.

M 미리 나온 걸 받을 수 있었거든요.

Q 대화에 따르면 다음 중 옳은 것은?

(a) 여자는 남자의 전화기를 파손시켰다.

(b) 여자는 남자에게 자신의 전화기를 빌려 줬다.

(c) 남자와 여자는 정확히 똑같은 전화기를 갖고 있다.

(d) 남자의 전화기는 최신형이다.

get a hold of ~을 입수하다, 잡다 **advance** 사전의

27

Listen to a conversation between a customer and a real estate agent.

M How can this lovely house be offered at such a low price?

W Probably because it backs up to the train tracks.

M You think that's an issue?

W It could cause some pretty terrible noise.

M I'm willing to take that chance.

W Okay, it's your money.

Q Which of the following is correct about the man according to the conversation?

(a) He still wants to buy the house.

(b) He is trying to sell his property.

(c) He is concerned about the noise.

(d) He will take the woman's advice.

고객과 부동산 중개인의 대화를 들으시오.

M 어떻게 이런 멋진 집이 이렇게 낮은 가격에 나왔죠?

W 아마 뒤에 기찻길이 있어서 그런 것 같아요.

M 그게 문제가 될까요?

W 소음이 심할 수 있죠.

M 위험을 감수하겠습니다.

W 그러세요, 집을 살 사람은 당신이니까요.

Q 대화에 따르면 남자에 대해 다음 중 옳은 것은?

(a) 남자는 여전히 집을 사길 원한다.

(b) 남자는 부동산을 팔려고 한다.

(c) 남자는 소음을 염려한다.

(d) 남자는 여자의 충고를 받아들일 것이다.

offer 제공하다 **back** ~의 뒤에 있다 **take the chance** 운에 맡기다, 위험을 감수하다 **property** 재산, 부동산, 소유물

28

Listen to a conversation about a man's boats.

W All of these boats are yours?

M Yes, I have a collection of boats.

W I'm counting at least six canoes, and there must be…

M Actually, it's seven canoes and five kayaks.

W What do you do with all of them?

M I lend them to friends when we go paddling on the river.

Q How many canoes does the man have?

(a) Five

(b) Six

(c) Seven

(d) Eight

남자의 보트에 관한 대화를 들으시오.

W 이 보트들 전부 당신 건가요?

M 네, 제가 보트를 수집했죠.

W 적어도 6척의 카누, 그리고 분명히…

M 카누 7척과 카약 5척이요.

W 이걸로 뭐 하세요?

M 강에서 패들링을 할 때 친구들에게 빌려 주죠.

Q 남자는 소유한 카누는 몇 척인가?

(a) 다섯 척

(b) 여섯 척

(c) 일곱 척

(d) 여덟 척

collection 수집품, 소장품 **paddle** 노를 젓다

29

Listen to two people discuss their petition.

> W Any word from your friend at the tax office?
>
> M No, nothing yet.
>
> W He thought our petition would be approved, though?
>
> M All he said was it seemed to have legal merit.
>
> W I wonder if I shouldn't have gotten my hopes up.
>
> M Well, worrying about it won't do any good.

Q What can be inferred from the conversation?

(a) The man works at a tax office.

(b) The woman wants to stay optimistic.

(c) The man's friend is reluctant about the petition.

(d) They are awaiting some legal advice.

두 사람이 탄원에 관해 말하는 것을 들으시오.

W 세무서에 있는 당신 친구로부터 아무 얘기 없어요?

M 아니오, 아직 없어요.

W 그래도 그는 우리 청원서가 승인될 거라고 보았죠?

M 그게 법적 가치가 있는 것 같다고 말했을 뿐인데요.

W 제가 희망을 가져야 할지 말아야 할지 모르겠네요.

M 그걸 걱정한다고 해서 도움이 되진 않아요.

Q 대화로부터 추론할 수 있는 것은?

(a) 남자는 세무서에서 일한다.

(b) 여자는 낙관하고 싶어 한다.

(c) 남자의 친구는 청원서에 대해 꺼려한다.

(d) 남자와 여자는 법적인 조언을 기다리고 있다.

tax office 세무서 **petition** 탄원서, 청원서 **merit** 가치, 장점
optimistic 낙관하는 **reluctant** 꺼려하는

30

Listen to a conversation about a woman's order for delivery.

> M Paco's Tacos. This is Abel speaking.
>
> W Do you deliver to the Maplewood Park area?
>
> M Yes, all of zip code 02881 is within our delivery radius.
>
> W Great. I'd like to place an order for delivery: one Spicy Beef taco and two Veggie Heaven tacos.
>
> M That'll be 9.75. Expect us in about a half hour.
>
> W Sounds good. Thanks.

Q What can be inferred from the conversation?

(a) Paco's Tacos does not deliver to Maplewood Park.

(b) Maplewood Park is in zip code 02881.

(c) The woman is a regular customer of Paco's Tacos.

(d) The woman will pay extra for delivery.

여자의 배달 주문에 관한 대화를 들으시오.

M 파코스 타코스입니다. 저는 아벨입니다.

W 메이플 우드 파크 지역으로도 배달하시나요?

M 네, 우편번호가 02881이면 저희 배달 구역에 포함돼요.

W 잘됐네요. 배달 주문할게요. 스파이시 비프 타코 하나와 베지 헤븐 타코 두 개요.

M 모두 9달러 75센트입니다. 30분 후에 도착할 겁니다.

W 좋아요. 감사합니다.

Q 대화로부터 추론할 수 있는 것은?

(a) 파코스 타코스는 메이플우드 파크까지 배달하지 않는다.

(b) 메이플우드 파크의 우편번호는 02881이다.

(c) 여자는 파코스 타코스의 단골이다.

(d) 여자는 배송비를 낼 것이다.

zip code 우편번호 **radius** 반경, 범위 **veggie** 채식주의자
regular customer 단골손님

Part IV

31

Environmental Health and Safety inspectors will be making their way through the Jefferson Laboratory Building between April 16th and April 19th. The purpose of these inspections is to protect the lives and health of lab personnel by ensuring that acute hazards in our work environment are addressed expediently. Areas of critical concern include corrosive chemical storage, adequate ventilation, and maintenance of emergency equipment such as eyewash stations and fire extinguishers.

Q What is the main topic of the announcement?

(a) Hazards of a particular lab procedure

(b) The schedule for hiring new personnel

(c) Details concerning an upcoming review

(d) Updates to laboratory safety protocols

환경 문제 및 안전 조사관들은 4월 16일과 19일 사이에 제퍼슨 랩 빌딩으로 갈 것이다. 이 조사의 목적은 우리 작업 환경에서 극심한 위험을 반드시 처리하여 실험실 직원들의 생명과 건강을 보호하기 위함이다. 중대하게 우려되는 분야는 부식성 화합물의 보관, 충분한 환기, 세안기와 소화기 같은 비상 장비의 관리이다.

Q 담화의 중심 소재는?
(a) 특정 실험실 절차의 위험성
(b) 새로운 직원 고용을 위한 일정
(c) 곧 있을 조사에 관한 세부 사항
(d) 실험실 안전 규정 업데이트

make one's way through 나아가다 **personnel** 직원 **acute**
극심한, 급성의 **hazard** 위험 **address** 다루다 **expediently** 편의상,
방편으로 **corrosive** 부식을 일 으키는, 부식성의 **storage** 저장, 보관
ventilation 환기 **eyewash station** 눈 세척대, 세안기

32

In the mid-twentieth century, when the Soviets became
embroiled in the eastern front of World War II, hundreds of
thousands of women were marshaled into readiness for
active military service. At the outset, women primarily held
medical roles. They accounted for about 40 percent of the
Soviets' frontline medical troops, comprising 8 to 10 percent of
the army's forces overall. By the end of the war their roles had
expanded to gunners, engineers, tank crew, snipers, and scouts.

Q What is mainly being introduced in the talk?
(a) Roles off-limits to women in the Soviet army
(b) The Soviet's heavy casualties on the eastern front
(c) Advances made by female medical troops
(d) The contributions of Soviet women during WWII

20세기 중반에 소련이 2차 세계 대전의 동부 전선에 휘말리게 되었을 때
수십만 명의 여성들이 적극적인 군 복무를 하고자 모여들었다. 전쟁 초기
에 여성들이 주로 의료 쪽을 맡았다. 그들은 소련의 최전선 의료 부대의 40
퍼센트에 해당했는데 전체 군대의 8~10퍼센트를 차지했다. 전쟁이 끝날
무렵 그들은 포병, 공병, 탱크 부대, 저격수, 정찰병까지 임무가 확대되었다.

Q 담화에 주로 소개된 것은?
(a) 소련 군대에서 여성들에게 허용되지 않았던 역할
(b) 동부 전선에서의 많은 소련군 사상자
(c) 여성 의료병사들이 이룬 발전
(d) 제2차 세계 대전 동안 소련 여성들의 기여

become embroiled 휘말리게 되다 **marshal** 특정 목적을 위해 사람이나
사물을 모으다 **outset** 시초, 발단 **account for** ~에 해당하다, 차지하다
comprise 구성되다 **off-limit to** (~에게) 출입금지의, 논의 금지의

33

This year, the Department of Statistics and Computation will
be hosting its second annual Summer Statistics Symposium.
The symposium is a professional development workshop
intended for students, faculty, and researchers interested
in building their data analysis skills. Taught by experienced
instructors in the university's Statistics Department, it
offers participants direct access to experts in the field. This
year, our 40 courses will cover topics such as statistical
analysis software and statistical methods such as linear
modeling, advanced regression, and predictive models.

Q Which of the following topics will the symposium NOT
cover?
(a) Statistical analysis software
(b) Linear modeling
(c) Prescriptive models
(d) Advanced regression

올해 통계청은 두 번째 연례 여름 통계 심포지엄을 개최할 것이다. 심포지
엄은 데이터 분석 기술 습득에 관심이 있는 학생, 교직원, 연구원들을 대상
으로 한 전문적인 개발 워크숍이다. 경험이 풍부한 대학의 통계학과 교수
들이 가르치기 때문에 참가자들은 그 분야의 전문가들에게 직접 배울 수
있다. 올해는 우리 40개의 과정이 통계적인 분석 소프트웨어와 선형 모델
링, 고급 회귀 분석, 예측 모델과 같은 통계 방법 등의 주제를 다룬다.

Q 다음 주제 중 심포지엄에서 다뤄지지 않는 것은?
(a) 통계적인 분석 소프트웨어
(b) 선형 모델링
(c) 규범적 모델
(d) 고급 회귀 분석

computation 계산 **host** 개최하다 **analysis** 분석 **instructor** 강사
expert 전문가 **field** 분야

34

On being exposed to a new concept, a person
may perceive it, suddenly, to be ubiquitous in their
life. There's a term for this: the Baader-Meinhof
Phenomenon. At its root is man's natural inclination
to selectively notice concepts to which they have
been previously primed. This is often coupled with the
effect of confirmation bias, the psychological tendency
to construe new information as affirmation of one's
existing beliefs. Together, these contribute to the
strange sense of significance people experience when
confronted with the Baader-Meinhof Phenomenon.

Q Which of the following is correct about the Baader-
Meinhof Phenomenon according to the talk?
(a) It affects how we process information that we learn.
(b) It sometimes acts in concert with confirmation bias.
(c) It causes some people to see themselves as significant.
(d) It is considered an abnormal condition in psychology.

사람이 새로운 개념에 노출되면 곧 그것을 갑자기 그들의 세상에서 흔한
것으로 인지할 수도 있다. 이런 것을 바더마인호프 현상이라고 한다. 이는
인간이 이전에 대비했던 개념에 선별적으로 주목하려는 본성적인 성향에
근거를 두고 있다. 이것은 종종 기존의 믿음에 대한 확신을 갖고 새로운
정보를 해석하려는 심리적인 성향인 확증 편향 효과와 연결된다. 이것들은
모두 바더마인호프 현상과 마주쳤을 때 사람들이 이상하게 중요하다고 느
끼는 원인이 된다.

Q 담화에 따르면 바더마인호프 현상에 관해 일치하는 것은?
(a) 우리가 배우는 정보를 처리하는 방식에 영향을 미친다.
(b) 때때로 확증 편향 효과와 함께 작용한다.
(c) 어떤 사람들이 그들 자신을 중요하게 느끼도록 한다.
(d) 심리학에서 비정상적인 상태로 간주된다.

ubiquitous 어디에나 있는, 아주 흔한 **term** 용어 **prime** 대비시키다
confirmation bias 확증 편향 **construe** 해석하다 **affirmation** 확인,
단언 **contribute to** ~의 원인이 되다 **significance** 중요성 **confront**
직면하다 **in concert with** ~와 협력하여 **abnormal** 비정상적인

35

Traffic remains backed up for miles on 146 East as a result of an overturned tractor trailer. Emergency personnel have been on the scene for over an hour, but it will likely be several more until the site is cleared. Motorists are advised to detour along Highway 4, or to reroute through downtown in order to avoid the area. But remember that we're now approaching rush hour, which will likely see congestion on those surface streets very soon as well.

Q Which of the following is correct according to the report?

(a) Traffic on 146 West remains unaffected.

(b) The downtown will also see congestion soon.

(c) Authorities have yet to reach the scene of the accident.

(d) Highway 4 is usually packed during rush hour.

전복된 견인 트레일러 여파로 이스트 146번 도로의 정체가 수 마일 이어진 상태입니다. 긴급 구조반이 1시간 넘게 현장에 있지만, 완전히 정리되려면 몇 시간 더 걸릴 것 같습니다. 운전자들은 이곳을 피하시려면 4번 고속도로를 따라 우회하시거나 시내를 통하여 경로를 변경하시길 권합니다. 하지만 지금이 점점 차가 막힐 시간이며, 도시 내 일반 도로 또한 이제 금방 차량 정체의 가능성이 높아진다는 점을 기억하십시오.

Q 보도에 따르면 일치하는 것은?

(a) 웨스트 146번 도로의 교통은 영향을 받지 않았다.

(b) 시내 또한 곧 정체될 것이다.

(c) 담당 관리들이 아직 사고 현장에 도착하지 않았다.

(d) 4번 고속도로는 주로 혼잡 시간 때 막힌다.

overturn 뒤집히다; 뒤집다 **tractor trailer** 견인 트레일러 **personnel** 직원, 인원 **site** 현장, 장소 **detour** 우회하다 **surface street** 일반 도로

36

The Alcon blue butterfly experiences a unique growth process. As a larva, it emits a pheromone that mimics that of an ant larva. Adult ants thus transport the butterfly larva into their nest to feed and care for it. The Alcon larva undergoes pupation within the ants' underground nest. Finally, it hatches from its chrysalis and, with the angry ants now in hot pursuit, makes its way out of the nest to safety.

Q What can be inferred from the talk?

(a) The butterfly closely resemble ants in body shape.

(b) Pupation lasts longer underneath the ground than it does above.

(c) Alcon blue butterflies feed on ant larva once they are fully grown.

(d) The hatched butterfly lacks the deceptive pheromone.

앨콘 블루 나비는 독특한 성장 과정을 겪는다. 유충 시절에는 개미 유충을 모방하는 페로몬을 방출한다. 그래서 어른 개미들이 나비 유충을 그들의 집으로 옮겨 먹이고 돌본다. 앨콘 블루 나비의 유충은 개미들이 살고 있는 지하 개미집에서 번데기로 변하게 된다. 마침내 번데기에서 부화하여 이제는 성난 개미들에게 쫓기는 신세가 되고 안전을 위하여 개미집 밖으로 나오게 된다.

Q 담화에서 추론할 수 있는 것은?

(a) 나비는 몸의 형태가 개미와 많이 닮았다.

(b) 번데기로 변하는 과정은 땅 위보다는 아래에서 오래 지속된다.

(c) 앨콘 블루 나비는 완전히 다 자라면 개미 유충을 먹고 산다.

(d) 부화한 나비에게는 다른 동물을 속이는 페로몬이 부족하다.

larva 유충, 애벌레 **emit** 방출하다 **pheromone** 페로몬, 동종 유인 호르몬 **mimic** 흉내를 내다, 모방하다 **transport** 수송하다, 실어 나르다 **pupation** 번데기화 **hatch** 부화되다 **chrysalis** 번데기 **makes one's way out** 밖으로 나오다

Part V
37-38

Almost everyone is familiar with Vincent van Gogh. But did you know he was a genius artist as well as a man of intense emotions? His genius shone through strongly in several of his paintings of flowers. According to Dr. Jennifer Lawson, a world-renowned expert in Impressionism, van Gogh drew those paintings to show off his skills as an artist. She points out that appreciating them helps you understand the artist at a deeper level. That's why the Richville Art Museum has decided to hold an exhibition of those paintings from July 8th through October 15th. For adults, admission to the museum costs $3.00, and tickets to the exhibit cost $6.00. For children up to the age of 17, admission is free, and tickets to the exhibition cost $2.00. Don't miss out on this rare opportunity to understand van Gogh better!

거의 모든 사람들이 빈센트 반 고흐를 잘 알고 있습니다. 그렇지만 그가 강렬한 감정을 갖고 있는 인물이면서 천재 화가였다는 사실을 아셨나요? 그의 천재성은 꽃을 그린 그림들 가운데 여러 작품에서 강렬하게 빛을 발했습니다. 인상파에 대해 세계적으로 유명한 전문가인 제니퍼 로슨 박사에 따르면, 반 고흐는 화가로서 자신의 기량을 과시하기 위해 그 그림들을 그렸다고 합니다. 로슨 박사는 그 그림들을 감상함으로써 화가 반 고흐를 보다 깊은 수준에서 이해하는 데 도움을 받을 수 있다고 지적합니다. 그래서 리치빌미술관은 7월 8일부터 10월 15일까지 그 그림들의 전시회를 개최하기로 결정했습니다. 성인의 경우, 미술관 입장료는 3달러이고, 전시회 입장권은 6달러입니다. 17세까지는 입장료가 무료이고, 전시회 입장료는 2달러입니다. 반 고흐를 보다 잘 이해할 수 있는 이 드문 기회를 놓치지 마세요!

37 Q If you are 21 years old, how much will you have to pay to see the exhibit?

(a) $2.00

(b) $3.00

(c) $6.00

(d) $9.00

Q 21세라면 전시회를 보기 위해서 얼마를 지불해야 할 것인가?

(a) 2달러
(b) 3달러
(c) 6달러
(d) 9달러

해설 NEW TEPS로 전환되면서, 자주 출제되는 문제 유형이다. 문장이 아니라, 단순한 숫자나 한두 단어가 정답으로 제시된다는 특징이 있다. 미술관에 입장하여 전시회를 관람해야 하므로, 미술관 입장료 3달러에 전시회 입장권 가격이 6달러를 더해야 한다. 따라서 정답은 (d)이다.

38 Q Which is correct according to the announcement?

(a) Van Gogh's paintings of flowers were intended to show his affinity for nature.
(b) Dr. Lawson has gained global recognition for her expertise in Impressionism.
(c) The Richville Art Museum is the best museum of Impressionist paintings in the United States.
(d) The exhibit is slated to run from July 8th to October 5th.

Q 안내에 따르면, 다음 중 옳은 것은?

(a) 반 고흐가 꽃을 그린 그림들은 자연에 대한 그의 친밀감을 보여주려는 데 의도가 있었다.
(b) 로슨 박사는 인상파에 대한 전문적인 지식으로 세계적인 인정을 받았다.
(c) 리치빌미술관은 미국에서 인상파 그림들을 전시하는 최고의 미술관이다.
(d) 전시회는 7월 8일부터 10월 5일까지 진행될 예정이다.

해설 이와 같은 유형은 안내를 들으면서, 출제가 예상되는 중요 내용을 간단하게 메모하는 것이 효과적인 대비 전략이다. 특히 숫자 정보와 인과 관계 등이 중요한 메모 사항이다. (a)는 기량을 과시하는 데 의도가 있었으므로 오답이다. (c)는 안내에서 분명하게 제시하지 않은 사항이므로 반드시 오답으로 처리해야 한다. (d)는 10월 15일까지 진행될 예정이기 때문에 정답이 아니다. 따라서 정답은 (b)이다.

familiar 아주 잘 아는, 익숙한 **genius** 천재; 천재성 **intense** 강렬한 **shine through** 빛을 발하다 **world-renowned** 세계적으로 유명한 **Impressionism** 인상파, 인상주의 **show off** 자랑하다, 과시하다 **art museum** 미술관 **miss out on** ~을 놓치다 **well versed in** ~에 정통한

39-40

In the Battle of Hastings, the English army led by King Harold Godwinson was defeated by the invading army led by William, the Duke of Normandy. Different historians have different ideas about why Harold's forces were defeated. Some point out that William had far more military experiences than Harold. As a consequence, the invading army utilized more effective tactics than the English army. Other historians argue that William's forces were superior to Harold's in many ways. The former was superior in numbers to the latter. In addition, unlike the English army, the invading army was able to make skillful use of cavalry. Whatever the reason, the Battle of Hastings marked the beginning of William's control of England.

헤이스팅스전투에서 해럴드 고드윈손왕(王)이 이끄는 영국군은 윌리엄 노르망디공(公)이 이끄는 침략군에 패배하였습니다. 해럴드의 군대가 패배한 이유에 대해서는 역사학자들마다 생각이 다릅니다. 어떤 이들은 윌리엄이 해럴드보다 군사 경험이 훨씬 더 많았다고 지적합니다. 그 결과, 침략군이 영국군에 비해 더 효과적인 전술을 활용했습니다. 다른 역사학자들은 윌리엄의 군대가 해럴드의 군대보다 많은 점에서 월등했다고 주장합니다. 윌리엄의 군대는 해럴드의 군대보다 숫자에서 우월했습니다. 또한 영국군과 달리, 침략군은 기병대를 능숙하게 이용할 수 있었습니다. 이유가 무엇이든지, 헤이스팅스전투는 영국에 대한 윌리엄의 지배가 시작된다는 전조였습니다.

39 Q What is the main point of the lecture?

(a) William, the Duke of Normandy, had far more experiences in battles than King Harold Godwinson.
(b) There might have been many factors leading to the defeat of the English army in the Battle of Hastings.
(c) The Battle of Hastings symbolized the moral deprivation of British society.
(d) The military strategies of the English army were more effective than those of the invading army.

Q 강의의 요점은?

(a) 윌리엄 노르망디공(公)은 해럴드 고드윈손왕(王)보다 전투 경험이 훨씬 더 많았다.
(b) 헤이스팅스전투에서 영국군이 패배하는 결과를 야기한 요인들이 많았을지도 모른다.
(c) 헤이스팅스전투는 영국 사회의 도덕적 빈곤을 상징했다.
(d) 영국군의 군사 전략은 침략군의 군사 전략보다 더 효과적이었다.

해설 NEW TEPS에서도 역사 관련 내용의 비중이 높기 때문에, 역사에 대한 배경 지식을 갖추는 것이 중요한 대비 전략이다. (a)는 세부 사항일 뿐이기 때문에 오답이다. (c)는 강의에서 전혀 말하지 않은 내용이기도 하고, 비약이기도 해서 정답이 될 수 없다. (d)는 잘못된 설명이므로 오답이다. 따라서 정답은 (b)이다.

40 Q What can be inferred from the lecture?

(a) The English forces had long been afraid of William's army.
(b) During the Battle of Hastings, the English army might not have had cavalry.
(c) The Battle of Hastings was the first battle that Harold had to fight for England.
(d) William fought fiercely in the battle, which led to his premature death.

Q 강의로부터 추론할 수 있는 것은?

(a) 영국군은 윌리엄의 군대를 오랫동안 두려워했다.
(b) 헤이스팅스전투를 치를 동안에, 영국군은 기병대가 없었을지도 모른다.
(c) 헤이스팅스전투는 해럴드왕이 영국을 위해 싸워야 했던 최초의 전투였다.
(d) 윌리엄은 전투에서 맹렬하게 싸웠는데, 그 때문에 너무 이른 죽음을 맞이하게 되었다.

해설 세부 사항 유형이든 추론 유형이든, 정답의 근거가 지문에 반드시 나와 있어야 한다. (a)와 (c)는 그런 내용을 전혀 알 수 없으므로 오답이다. (d)는 마지막 문장의 내용으로 보아, 오히려 더 오래 생존했을 가능성이 높으므로 정답이 아니다. 따라서 정답은 (b)이다. 강의에서 침략군이 영국군과 달리 기병대를 이용했다고 말한 것이 근거이다.

invade 침략하다 **duke** 공작 **military** 군사의 **tactic** 전술, 작전 **superior** 우월한 **skillful** 숙련된 **cavalry** 기병(대) **mark** ~의 전조이다 **factor** 요인 **symbolize** 상징하다 **deprivation** 결핍; 손실 **fiercely** 맹렬하게 **premature** 너무 이른

Part I

1 정답 (a)
A 너랑 데이트를 하도록 댄을 잘 구슬릴 수 있었니?
B 아니, 실패한 것 같아.

convince 납득시키다 **go on a date with** ~와 데이트하러 가다
strike out 실패하다 **fall in** 내려앉다 **wind up** ~으로 끝나다
put down 착륙하다, 기록하다

2 정답 (c)
A 당신이 읽고 있는 책의 저자에 대해 들어본 적이 없어요.
B 오, 그는 그냥 18세기 무명의 프랑스 작가에 불과해요.

rustic 소박한, 시골뜨기의 **stellar** 별의 **obscure** 무명의
potential 잠재적인

3 정답 (d)
A 영국산 치즈에 대해 어떻게 생각하세요?
B 와인의 맛을 잘 보완해줘요.

flavor 맛, 향 **moisten** 촉촉하게 하다 **dilute** 묽게 하다 **irrigate**
관개하다, 물을 대다 **complement** 보완하다

4 정답 (c)
A 스티븐과 뭐가 문제야?
B 확실히 모르겠어, 하지만 그가 정말로 나를 열 받게 해.

keep one's chin up 기운을 내게 하다 **count A among B** A를
B 중의 하나로 치다 **rub ~ the wrong way** ~을 열 받게 하다 **stop
~ in one's tracks** ~의 발길을 멈추게 하다

5 정답 (c)
A 학생 중 한 명이 나의 말에 개의치 않고 계속 버릇없이 굴어.
B 보다 엄정한 징계 조치를 취해야 할 때인 것 같아요.

act up 말을 안 듣다, 버릇없이 굴다 **regardless of** ~에 개의치 않고
flagrant 악명 높은, 극악한 **pejorative** 경멸적인 **disciplinary**
규율상의, 징계적인 **subversive** 체제 전복적인

6 정답 (a)
A 최면 요법이 어떻게 작용하는지 이해할 수가 없어.
B 사람의 억눌러진 기억에 접근하는 거라더군.

hypnotherapy 최면 요법 **be supposed to** ~라고들 한다,
~하기로 되어 있다 **access** 접근하다 **repress** (감정을) 억압하다
undermine 약화시키다 **blanket** 덮어 가리다 **entomb** 매장하다

7 정답 (a)
A 상사가 휴가를 늘려주는 데 동의했나요?
B 아니요, 조금도 양보하려고 하지 않았어요.

time off 휴가, 휴식 시간 **refuse to** ~하기를 거부하다
compromise (원칙 등을) 굽히다, 양보하다 **assemble** 모으다, 조립하다
segregate 분리하다 **rectify** (잘못된 것을) 바로잡다

8 정답 (c)
A 넌 분명히 시험 성적이 나빠서 충격을 받았을 거야.
B 충격을 받아? 너무 놀라 말이 안 나올 지경이었어.

sidetrack 곁길로 새게 하다, 탈선시키다 **belittle** 하찮게 만들다,
과소평가하다 **dumbfounded** 너무 놀라서 말이 안 나오는 **heartfelt**
진심 어린, 절실히 느낀

9 정답 (c)
A 비만은 다른 나라들에서도 만연한가요?
B 사실 외국에서 훨씬 더 일반적인 문제예요.

widespread 만연한 **extraneous** 외부로부터의 **fluent** 유창한
prevalent 일반적인, 널리 퍼져 있는 **ample** 충분한

10 정답 (b)
A 그 제품이 마음에 안 드는 이유들을 말해보세요.
B 지금 그걸 모두 열거할 시간이 없어요.

product 제품 **proliferate** 증식시키다 **enumerate** 열거하다
condone 용서하다, 눈감아주다 **legitimize** 정당화하다

Part II

11 정답 (b)
올해 일찍 그 회사에 투자한 사람들은 주가 상승에 따른 이익을 얻고 있다.

reap 거둬들이다, 획득하다 **position** 배치하다 **invest** 투자하다
direct 겨냥하다 **thrive** 번창하다

12 정답 (d)
미들턴에 있는 괜찮은 스시 레스토랑을 찾고 있는 일본 요리 전문가라면
우마미 카페를 방문해야 한다.

cuisine 요리(법) **connoisseur** 감정가, 전문가 **decent** 괜찮은,
제대로 된 **seek** (~을 발견하기 위해) 찾다 **find** (우연히) 찾다 **look**
(발견하기 위해) 찾다 **on the hunt for** ~을 수색 중인

13 정답 (a)
미국은 13년 동안 금주법을 시행하다가, 결국 실패작이었던 이 정책을 폐
지했다.

undergo 겪다 **Prohibition** (미국의) 금주법 시행 시대(1920-33) **ban**
금지 **repeal** (법률 등을) 폐기[폐지]하다 **outdo** 능가하다 **pursue**
추구하다 **upend** (위아래를) 거꾸로 하다

14 정답 (c)
개는 어떤 상황에서 초조하거나 불안감을 느낄 때 매우 독특한 행동을 보
인다.

specific 독특한 **ill at ease** 불안한, 거북한 **conduct** 실시하다
organize 조직하다 **exhibit** (감정 등을) 보이다 **regulate** 규제하다

15 정답 (c)
손님은 웨이터에게 식사를 마쳤다는 것을 알리기 위해 냅킨을 접시 위에
놓았다.

diner 식사 손님 **signal** 신호를 보내다 **past** 지나간 **after** 나중에
through (어떤 것의 사용을) 끝낸 **beyond** ~ 저편에

16 정답 (a)
체즈 데니의 특제 요리는 기름에 볶아 푹 삶은 양고기인데, 이 때문에 그
의 요리가 세계적 명성을 얻었다.

braise (고기를) 기름에 볶아 소량의 물로 뭉근한 불에 끓이다 **earn
renown** 명성을 얻다 **identifiable** 인식 가능한 **caricatured** 희화된
indicative 암시하는, 나타내는 **signature dish** 요리사의 가장 유명한
요리

17 정답 (d)

매일 10분씩 묵상을 하면 스트레스 <u>완화</u>에 큰 도움이 된다.

meditation 명상 **go a long way towards** ~에 크게 도움이 되다
fortify 강화하다 **contradict** 부정[반박]하다 **embellish** 장식하다
alleviate 경감[완화]하다

18 정답 (c)

사장은 정리해고를 하기 전에 모든 선택 방안을 <u>따져보았다</u>.

option 선택 방안 **layoff** 정리해고 **relay** 중계하다, 전달하다 **shift**
이동하다 **weigh** 따져보다 **heft** 들어 올리다

19 정답 (d)

쓰레기를 버리면 <u>최대</u> 500달러의 벌금을 물게 되어 있지만, 대부분 위반
자들에게 부과되는 벌금은 100달러를 넘지 않는다.

litter (쓰레기 등을) 버리다 **fine** 벌금 **violator** 위반자 **assess**
(세금·요금 등을) 부과하다, 매기다 **redundant** 여분의, 과잉의
sufficient 충분한 **excessive** 과도한 **maximum** 최대의

20 정답 (c)

미얀마는 이 나라의 일부 <u>천연자원</u>을 차지하려는 이웃 강국들에 의해 수
십 년 동안 착취를 당해왔다.

exploit 착취하다 **natural resource** 천연자원 **article** 물품, 물건
capability 능력, 역량 **resource** 자원 **artifact** 인공 유물

21 정답 (d)

시장은 생기가 넘치는 연설자였지만, 그의 말은 두서가 없고 종종 <u>비논리
적</u>이었다.

lively 활기찬, 생기 있는 **rambling** 두서없는, 횡설수설하는
stumped 당황스러운 **commendable** 칭찬받을 만한 **languid**
힘없는, 느릿느릿한 **incoherent** 비논리적인, 앞뒤가 맞지 않는

22 정답 (b)

그 협곡은 한때 열차 강도단의 <u>은신처</u>로 유명했다.

canyon 협곡 **blackout** 등화관제, 정전 **hideout** 은신처 **lookout**
경계, 감시 **cutout** 오려내기, (전기) 차단기

23 정답 (c)

멘켄 교수는 다음 학기에는 <u>안식년</u>이어서 수업을 하지 않을 것이다.

semester 학기 **withdrawal** 철회, 취소 **virtuoso** 거장, 명연주자
sabbatical 안식기간 **purgatory** 연옥

24 정답 (a)

심테크 사의 태깅 시스템은 분명히, 여러분이 현재 이용하고 있는 어떤 광
고 서버와도 원활하게 <u>접목될</u> 것이다.

be guaranteed to 필경 ~하게 될 것이다 **seamlessly** 이음매가
없이, 매끄럽게 **currently** 현재 **integrate** 통합[융합, 접목]되다
attune 맞추다, 조율하다 **embody** 상징하다, 구현하다 **mingle** 섞이다

25 정답 (b)

그 법안은 통과 직전에, 실업자 구제 기금을 더 많이 배정하려는 상원에
의해 <u>수정</u>되었다.

passage 통과 **bill** 법안 **Senate** 상원 **relief** 구제, 구호 **the
unemployed** 실업자 **ascend** 오르다 **amend** 수정하다 **attend**
참석하다 **append** 덧붙이다, 첨부하다

26 정답 (b)

디킨스의 많은 장편들은 매주 얼마씩 <u>연재</u> 형식으로 게재되었다.

mete out 할당[배당]하다 **installment** (연재물의) 1회분 **lenient**
관대한 **serial** 연재물 **buoyant** 경기가 좋은, 활황인 **foregone**
기정의, 과거의

27 정답 (a)

그래니 스미스 종 사과는 당도 높은 품종들의 특색이 아닌 시큼함으로 <u>미
각</u>을 자극한다.

tartness 시큼함 **uncharacteristic of** ~의 특징이 아닌 **variety**
품종 **palate** 미각 **essence** 본질 **partition** 칸막이, 분할 **gulley**
도랑, 배수로

28 정답 (b)

최종 결과물이 너무 **빡빡**하지 않도록 하기 위해서는 밀가루 반죽을 손으
로 부드럽게 <u>치대야</u> 한다.

dough 밀가루 반죽 **dense** 조밀한, 밀도가 높은 **buff** (부드러운 천으로)
광을 내다 **knead** (반죽·찰흙 등을) 치대다 **ply** (연장·도구 등을)
부지런히 놀리다 **scour** 문질러 닦다, 윤을 내다

29 정답 (c)

천문학자들은 처음에 우리 <u>은하계</u>에 3천억 개가 넘는 별이 있다는 것을
알았을 때, 믿을 수 없다는 반응을 보였다.

astronomer 천문학자 **incredulity** 쉽사리 믿지 않음, 불신 **orbit** 궤도
nebula 성운 **galaxy** 은하계 **meteorite** 운석

30 정답 (a)

지나고 나서 보니까, 2007년 8월의 유동성 위기는 2008년 시장 붕괴의
<u>전조가 되었다</u>.

in hindsight 지나고 나서 보니까 **liquidity** 유동성 **presage** ~
의 전조가 되다 **convey** 전달하다 **siphon** 빼돌리다, 유용하다
mediate 중재하다

Grammar   p.197

Part I

1 정답 (b)

A 왜 이 연초록 물감 색을 선택했나요?

B 상담가가 그 색이 주황색과 잘 대비될 거라고 해서요.

해설 시제의 일치를 묻는 문제이다. 주절의 동사가 과거(told)일 때 종속
절의 동사는 과거나 과거완료, 혹은 과거진행형이 와야 하므로 정답은 조
동사 will의 과거형을 사용한 (b)이다.

go with ~을 지지하다 **consultant** 상담가 **contrast with** ~와
대조[대비]되다

2 정답 (c)

A 파스타가 약 반 파운드 있어요.

B 그 요리를 하는 데 그 정도로는 충분치 않을 것 같아요.

해설 a half pound of pasta(파스타 반 파운드)는 하나의 단위로 보아
야 하므로 그것을 받는 대명사는 단수이어야 하며, 동사 또한 단수 형태가
되어야 한다. 따라서 정답은 (c)이다. (d)는 시제가 틀렸다.

recipe 요리법

3 정답 (a)

A 노스캐롤라이나에 산 지가 얼마나 되나요?

B 오는 8월이면 8년을 산 셈이에요.

해설 미래의 특정 시점까지 완료나 계속의 의미를 나타낼 때에는 미래완료(will have p.p.) 시제를 사용하므로 (a)가 정답이다.

4 정답 (c)

A 그럼, 우린 직원 몇 명을 정리 해고할 수밖에 없겠지요.

B 네, 수지 균형을 맞추기 위해서는 그래야 한다고 결론 내렸어요.

해설 정리 해고가 필요하다고 회사 측(we)이 결론 내린 것이므로, 문맥상 주어 we 다음에 동사 conclude, 동사의 목적어로 (that) it was necessary가 오는 것이 올바른 어순이다. 따라서 정답은 (c)이다.

lay off 정리 해고하다　**balance the budget** 수지 균형을 맞추다　**conclude** 결론짓다

5 정답 (a)

A 유소년 운동선수로서 경쟁하는 것이 어땠나요?

B 경기 중의 격렬한 분위기에 겁먹을 수 있었어요.

해설 intimidate는 '겁을 주다'라는 타동사이고, 이의 현재분사형 태인 intimidating은 '겁을 주는'이라는 형용사임에 유의하자. (b)는 intimidate의 목적어가 없고, (c)는 them이 지칭하는 바가 애매하며, 수동태인 (d) 역시 의미가 통하지 않는다. 따라서 문맥상 적절한 답은 형용사 intimidating을 활용한 (a)이다.

compete 경쟁하다　**athlete** 운동선수　**intense** 격렬한　**intimidating** 겁먹게 하는

6 정답 (b)

A 넌 TV를 시청하는 시간을 줄여야 해.

B 어젯밤 로렌도 내게 그렇게 말했어.

알맞은 관계절을 고르는 문제이다. 먼저, 빈칸 앞에 선행사가 없는 것으로 보아 선행사를 포함하는 관계대명사 what(= the thing which)이 필요함이 예상되므로 (a)와 (c)는 일단 제외한다. what 이하는 문맥상 '로렌이 내게 말했던 것'이 되어야 하므로 정답은 (b)이다.

7 정답 (c)

A 그 일에 요구되는 자격 조건이 뭐죠?

B 소셜 미디어에 정통한 사람을 찾고 있어요.

해설 find의 목적어, 즉 '소셜 미디어를 잘 아는 사람'에 해당하는 어구를 고르는 문제이므로 familiar with social media가 someone을 수식하는 형태의 (c)가 올바른 어순이다. 물론 여기서 familiar 앞에는 관계대명사와 be동사, 즉 who is가 생략되어 있다.

requirement 필요조건, 요건　**familiar with** ~을 잘 아는

8 정답 (d)

A 들었니? 메리트 교수가 종신 재직권을 수여받았어!

B 학생들의 지지가 없었더라면 분명히 그러지 못했을 거야.

해설 과거 사실과 반대되는 상황을 가정하는 가정법 과거완료의 주절은 〈주어+could[would, might] have p.p. ~〉의 형태를 취하므로 (d)가 올 바르다.

award (상 등을) 수여하다　**tenure** 장기[종신] 재직권

9 정답 (b)

A 카밀라 때문에 아직도 속상하니?

B 그녀에게 많은 공을 들였지만, 눈치도 못 채던걸.

해설 문장의 올바른 어순을 묻는 문제이다. 문맥상, 주어는 I, 동사는 put forth, 목적어는 such an effort, 그리고 맨 뒤에 전치사구 for her가 붙은 (b)가 정답이다.

notice 알아차리다　**put forth** (힘·능력 등을) 발휘하다

10 정답 (d)

A 브랜든이 마을 방범대와 관련된 모든 것을 관리하고 있어.

B 그에게 나를 소개해 준다면 무척 좋겠는데.

해설 put A in touch with B(A를 B에게 소개하다)를 알면 쉽게 풀 수 있는 문제이다. 참고로 keep in touch with ~는 '~와 연락을 취하다'란 뜻이므로 구별할 수 있어야 한다.

related to ~와 관련된　**neighborhood watch** 마을 방범대, 자경단

Part II

11 정답 (d)

알라모 하이츠 드래곤즈는 어느 팀을 상대하더라도 이길 가능성이 크다.

해설 관계형용사 whichever의 용법을 묻는 문제이다. 즉 〈whichever +명사+주어+동사〉는 양보절을 이끌어 '어느 것을 ~하든'의 뜻으로 쓰이므로 정답은 (d)이다.

stand a good chance of ~할 가능성이 충분하다

12 정답 (a)

야생 동물들이 연구자들의 포획에 고분고분하게 반응하지 않은 것은 별반 놀랄 일도 아니었다.

해설 react to(~에 반응하다)의 to는 전치사이므로 그것의 목적어가 동사인 경우에는 동명사 형태를 취해야 한다. 따라서 (c)와 (d)는 일단 제외한다. 문맥상 동물들이 포획되는(be captured) 것이므로 수동태인 (a)가 적절하다.

react to ~에 반응하다　**calmly** 침착하게, 태연하게　**capture** 포획하다

13 정답 (c)

플레처 여사는 할머니로부터 물려받은 고풍의 주방 가구를 전부 팔기로 했다.

해설 sell의 대상인 '고풍의 주방 가구 전부'에 해당하는 말을 어순에 맞게 나열한 선택지를 고르는 문제이다. 형용사의 순서는 일반적으로 〈수량(여기서는 all 혹은 all the)+대소+신구(여기서는 antique)+재료〉이며, 그다음에 그것의 수식을 받는 명사(여기서는 dining room furniture)가 따라오므로 (c)가 정답이다.

inherit 물려받다　**antique** 고풍의, 골동품

14 정답 (b)

여행하는 동안 혹시라도 뭔가 지연되는 일이 생긴다면, 즉시 물류 담당관에게 통보하세요.

해설 should가 앞으로 나오는 가정법 미래의 도치 구문을 묻는 문제이다. 즉 〈if+주어+should+동사원형(혹시라도 ~한다면)〉에서 if가 생략되면 주어와 should의 자리가 바뀌어 〈should+주어〉의 어순이 되므로 (b)가 정답이다.

notify 통보하다　**logistics officer** 물류 담당관

15 정답 (d)

그 탑승객은 공항에 도착하자마자 자신이 항공권 정보를 잘못 읽었다는 것을 깨달았다.

해설 '~하자마자 …하다'란 뜻의 〈No sooner + had + 주어 + p.p.+than+주어+동사의 과거형〉 구문을 묻는 문제이므로 (d)가 정답이다. 이 표현은 부정어구인 no sooner가 문장 앞으로 나옴에 따라 주어와 조동사가 도치된다는 점과 시제에 유의해야 한다.

misread 잘못 읽다　**passenger** 탑승객

16 정답 (c)

보통의 상황에서는 유독한 화학물질이 일단 불활성화 되면 동식물에 해를 주지 않는다.

해설 의미를 명확하게 하기 위해 접속사를 맨 앞에 붙이는 분사구문 문제이다. '~하게 하다'란 뜻의 render는 주로 〈render+목적어+목적격 보어〉의 형태를 취하는데, 이 문제의 경우, 능동태 they render it inert가 수동태 it is rendered inert (by them)으로 바뀐 경우이다. 따라서 빈칸 부분을 분사구문으로 만들어 접속사 once 다음에 주절과 주어가 같은 it과 동사 is를 생략하고 rendered inert만 써주면 되므로 정답은 (c)가 된다.

normally 보통의 상황에서는　**toxic** 유독한　**chemical** 화학물질　**pose harm** 해를 끼치다　**render** ~하게 하다　**inert** 불활성의

17 정답 (a)

모든 국회의원들은 취임 선서를 할 때 헌법을 수호하겠다는 맹세를 해야 한다.

해설 make a pledge(맹세하다)는 그다음에 동사가 올 때는 to부정사를 취한다. 즉 make a pledge to(~할 것을 맹세하다)의 형태로 쓰이므로 (a) to uphold가 정답이다.

lawmaker 입법자, 국회의원　**make a pledge to** ~할 것을 맹세하다　**Constitution** 헌법　**be sworn into office** 선서를 하고 취임하다　**uphold** 지지하다

18 정답 (c)

은퇴한 NBA 올스타 출신의 빌 러셀은 보스턴 셀틱스에서 뛰었으며 팀의 성공에 막대한 기여를 했다.

해설 알맞은 어순을 고르는 문제이다. 문맥상 빈칸에는 '팀의 성공에 크게 기여했다'는 말이 와야 하므로 동사 contribute to(~에 기여하다) 다음에 to의 목적어인 the team's success가 따라온 (c)가 적절하다. 단, 부사(greatly)는 동사 바로 다음이나 문장 끝에 둘 수 있다.

retired 은퇴한　**contribute to** ~에 기여하다

19 정답 (b)

전쟁으로 정신적 충격을 받은 탓에, 많은 군인들은 민간 생활로 돌아가는 것이 대체로 힘들다는 것을 느꼈다.

해설 알맞은 분사구문을 고르는 문제이다. 많은 군인들이 전쟁으로 정신적 충격을 받은 것은 민간 생활로의 복귀가 힘들다고 느낀 것보다 한 시제 앞서는데, 이렇게 종속절의 시제가 주절의 시제보다 빠를 때는 완료형 분사구문(having p.p.)을 사용하므로 (b)가 올바른 형태이다.

largely 주로, 대체로　**unmanageable** 다루기 어려운　**traumatize** 정신적 충격을 주다

20 정답 (a)

칼은 이미 저녁을 짓기로 합의를 본 후에야, 그것이 힘든 일이라는 생각이 머리에 떠올랐다.

해설 occur는 〈occur to+사람〉의 형태로 '(생각 등이) ~의 머리에 떠오르다'란 뜻으로 사용되므로 (a)가 정답이다. 여기서 it은 that 이하를 받는 가주어이다. (c)는 수동태이므로 의미가 통하지 않는다.

occur to ~에게 생각이 떠오르다

21 정답 (d)

화요일에 대통령은 자신이 앞서 했던 말과 거리를 두는 것 같았다. 왜냐하면 정적들이 대통령이 했던 그 말을 비난했기 때문이다.

해설 관계대명사 which의 선행사, 즉 earlier statement가 정적들에 의해 '비난을 당한' 것이므로 수동태이어야 하고, 대통령이 자신의 말에서 거리를 둔 것보다 그의 말이 비난당한 것이 먼저이므로 과거완료 시제를 쓴 (d)가 적절하다.

distance oneself from ~로부터 거리를 두다　**statement** 진술, 발표　**opponent** 반대자, 대항자　**criticize** 비난하다

22 정답 (b)

CEO에게 보내는 사적인 편지에서, 휘태커 씨는 경리부에서 그의 전처와 계속 일하고 싶지 않다고 표명했다.

해설 〈would rather+동사원형(~하기를 좋아하다)〉은 여러 다른 경우보다 한 가지를 더 좋아할 때 사용하는 표현이다. 여기서는 그것의 부정형인 〈would rather not+동사원형(~하지 않는 게 낫다, ~하고 싶지 않다)〉을 묻고 있으므로 정답은 (b)이다.

alongside ~와 함께　**ex-wife** 전처　**financial department** 경리부　**would rather not** ~하고 싶지 않다

23 정답 (b)

만약 그때 사진술이 존재했다면 미국 독립전쟁에 대한 여론이 어떻게 달라졌을지는 아무도 모른다.

해설 how 이하는 문맥상 과거 사실에 반대되는 상황을 가정하는 가정법 과거완료 구문이므로 (b)가 정답이다.

public opinion 여론　**Revolutionary War** 미국 독립전쟁　**photographic** 사진의

24 정답 (a)

기자 회견에서 회사 대변인은 성별이나 연령 때문에 차별받는 직원이 전혀 없다고 주장했다.

해설 빈칸에는 대변인이 주장한 내용이 와야 하므로 선행사와 관계절로 이루어진 (b)와 (d)는 일단 제외한다. 의미상 차별받는 직원이 전혀 없다고 해야 적절하므로 (a)가 정답이다. 이는 they didn't discriminate against any employees를 수동태로 전환한 형태이다.

press conference 기자 회견　**spokesperson** 대변인　**maintain** 주장하다　**on account of** ~때문에　**gender** 성　**discriminate against** ~을 차별하다

25 정답 (c)

전해지는 바에 의하면, 본 씨는 입국 심사대를 통과하면서 관리에게 100달러 지폐를 슬쩍 넣어 주었다.

해설 알맞은 어순을 고르는 문제이다. 빈칸에는 먼저 주절의 동사가 필요하므로 (d)는 일단 제외한다. 문맥상 '슬쩍 넣어 주다(slip)+100달러 지폐를(a bill)+관리에게(to the officer)'의 순서로 된 (c)가 적절하다.

allegedly 전해지는 바에 의하면　**immigration checkpoint** 입국 심사대　**slip** 슬쩍 넣다　**bill** 지폐, 100달러 지폐

Part III

26 정답 (c) must have mentioned → should have mentioned

(a) A 이봐요, 제가 가게에서 산 것 좀 보세요. 새 토스터예요!
(b) B 이런, 그럴 필요가 없었는데. 내가 예전 거를 고쳤거든요.
(c) A 새로 구입하기 전에 그 말을 했어야죠.
(d) B 미안해요, 당신이 그럴 거라고는 생각도 못했어요.

해설 (c)의 must have mentioned that 부분은 문맥상 '그렇게 말했었어야 했는데 그러지 못했다'는 의미가 되어야 하므로, 과거에 하지 못했던 일에 대한 후회나 유감을 나타내는 should have p.p.를 사용해야 한다. 따라서 must를 should로 바꿔야 올바른 문장이 된다.

pick up 사다 **mention A to B** A에 대해 B에게 말하다
replacement 교체 **aware** 알고 있는

27 정답 (b) which seat am I in → which seat I am in

(a) A 방갈로르행 5시 30분 비행기를 탑승하게 됐음을 확인해 드립니다.
(b) B 좋아요, 제가 어느 자리인지 알려 주시겠어요?
(c) A 창가 좌석 15A를 배정받은 것 같군요.
(d) B 가능하다면 통로 쪽 좌석으로 바꿀 수 있을까요?

해설 (b)의 which seat am I in 부분은 tell의 목적어절인 간접의문이 되어야 하므로 〈의문사+주어+동사〉, 즉 which seat I am in의 어순이 되어야 한다.

confirm 확인해주다 **assign** 할당[지정]하다 **aisle** 통로

28 정답 (b) have backed → had backed

(a) 2차 내란에서 승리를 거둔 후 올리버 크롬웰은 이번에는 아일랜드로 관심을 돌렸다. (b) 1649년부터 1650년 사이에 감행된 아일랜드 작전 동안, 크롬웰은 군사를 이끌고 패배한 영국 왕을 지지했던 아일랜드의 가톨릭교도들을 공격했다. (c) 오늘날 다분히 인종 청소 행위로 여겨지는 이 사건에서, 크롬웰의 군대는 여러 번에 걸쳐 수많은 시민들을 학살했다. (d) 전쟁이 끝났을 때 아일랜드인 5만 명이 연한 계약 노동자로서 영국으로 강제 이송되었다.

해설 (b)에서, 아일랜드 가톨릭교도들이 영국 왕을 지지한 것은 크롬웰이 아일랜드를 치기 위해 군사를 이끌었던 것보다 앞선 일이므로 have backed를 대과거인 had backed로 고쳐야 한다.

campaign 작전, 군사 행동 **back** 지지하다 **defeated** 패배한
ethnic cleansing 인종 청소 **massacre** 학살하다 **occasion** 경우, 기회 **deport** 강제 이송하다 **indentured servant** 연한 계약 노동자

29 정답 (d) to feel → to be felt

(a) 1984년 12월 2일, 인도의 보팔 시에서 세계 최악의 산업 재해가 발생했다. (b) 유니온 카바이드사의 한 농약 제조 공장에서 가스가 누출돼 50만 명이 유독성 화학물질에 노출되었고, 최소 2천 2백 명이 즉사했다. (c) 이 사고의 장기적인 영향을 수량화하기란 더욱 어려운 일이지만, 정부는 지금도 50만 명 이상이 후유증을 앓고 있다고 추산하고 있다. (d) 회사와 직원들에게 미칠 심각한 영향이 아직 시작도 안했다.

해설 문장 (d)의 주어 serious repercussions(심각한 영향)는 동사 feel(느끼다)와 수동의 관계이므로 to feel을 to be felt로 바꿔야 한다.

industrial disaster 산업 재해 **take place** 발생하다 **leak** 누출
pesticide plant 농약 제조 공장 **toxic** 유독한 **lead to** 초래하다
quantify 수량화하다 **estimate** 추정, 추산 **be adversely affected** 악영향을 받다 **repercussion** (보통 좋지 못한) 영향 **have yet to** 아직 ~하지 못했다

30 정답 (b) some is the fact that → the fact is that some

(a) 우리는 종종 북극 지방을 생명을 유지하지 못하는 비교적 황량한 지역으로 생각한다. (b) 하지만 사실 약 2만 1천 종의 동물, 식물, 균류, 그리고 미생물들이 북극 지방을 집으로 생각하고 있다. (c) 그런데 이 모든 것이 지구온난화의 결과로 나타나는 환경 변화에 의해 직접적인 위협을 받고 있다. (d) 만약 인간이 긴급히 조치를 취하지 않는다면, 전체 생태 지구의 생물 다양성이 거의 절멸될지도 모른다.

해설 the fact is that ~은 방금 언급된 내용과 반대됨을 강조하여 '사실은 ~이다'라고 할 때 쓰는 표현이다. 따라서 (b)에서 But 다음의 some is the fact that을 the fact is that some으로 고쳐야 문맥상 올바르게 된다. 여기서 some은 about(대략)의 뜻이다.

the Arctic 북극 지방 **desolate** 황량한, 황폐한 **species** 종
fungus 균류 **microbe** 미생물 **unfold** 전개하다 **global warming** 지구온난화 **on the part of** ~측의 **biodiversity** 생물의 다양성
eco-zone 생태 지구 **all but** 거의 **annihilate** 절멸시키다

Reading Comprehension p.201

Part I

1

설암이 다른 방식으로는 완화될 수 없을 때, 의사는 혀 절제술, 즉 <u>혀의 일부 혹은 전부를 제거하는 수술</u>을 실시할 수 있다. 이 치료는 극단적일 수 있지만, 이런 형태의 암은 인근 림프절에 신속히 확산될 수 있기 때문에 매우 적극적인 조치가 필요하다. 적출되어야 할 암 부위의 크기에 따라, 부분적 혀 절제술을 실행할 수 있는데, 이 경우에는 수술 후에 주변 조직을 봉합하게 된다. 더 중증인 경우에는 신체 다른 부위에서 절제한 조직을 이식해 혀를 치료할 수 있다.

(a) 강력한 항암제의 사용
(b) 암 종양 제거
(c) 대부분 환자들이 실제로 선호할 수 있는 것
(d) 혀의 일부 혹은 전부를 제거하는 수술

해설 glossectomy(혀 절제술)의 의미를 몰라도, 뒤이어 나오는 말들(암을 적출하거나, 수술 후에 주변 조직을 봉합하거나, 다른 신체 부위에서 절제한 조직으로 이식한다는 등)에서 혀를 제거하는 수술에 관한 내용임을 짐작할 수 있다.

tongue cancer 설암 **mitigate** 완화[경감]시키다 **surgeon** 외과의
glossectomy 혀 절제(술) **treatment** 치료 **drastic** 극단적인, 과감한
aggressive 대단히 적극적인 **proliferate** 확산되다 **lymph node** 림프절 **extract** 적출하다 **feasible** 실행[실현] 가능한 **tissue** (세포) 조직 **sew** 바느질하다, 깁다 **repair** 치료하다 **graft** 이식 **excise** 잘라내다 **cancerous tumor** 암 종양 **procedure** 수술

2

레이크뷰의 제1회 연례 사운더스 페스티벌이 12월 17일 토요일, 오전 11시부터 자정까지 개최될 것이다. 보조금 후원을 받는 이 행사의 목적은 많은 이 지역 음악을 소개하는 것 외에도, 충분히 이용되지 않은 사우스 레이크뷰의 공연 공간을 전시하기 위함이다. 이곳은 역사적으로 가난과 범죄, 그리고 시의 방치로 낙인 찍혀 내려오는 지역이다. 사운더스 페스티벌 주최 측은 페스티벌 참가자들을 사우스 레이크뷰의 공공 공간들로 초청해, 그들을 공동체 조성에 참여시킴으로써, <u>지역 이미지를 개선하기를 희망하고 있다.</u>

(a) 현지 음악가들만 출연시킬 계획이다
(b) 이번 행사에 기록적인 흥행을 기대한다
(c) 지역 이미지를 개선하기를 희망하고 있다
(d) 새 공연 공간을 건립할 기금을 마련할 것이다

해설 사우스 레이크뷰에서 열리는 지역 페스티벌을 소개하고 있다. 레이크뷰가 가난과 범죄, 시의 방치로 낙인 찍혔지만 페스티벌 참가자들을 초청해 지역 이미지를 개선하려 한다는 (c)가 적절하다.

take place 열리다   serve up 차려내다   healthy 대량의, 큰
grant-sponsored 보조금을 후원받는   showcase 진열[전시]하다
underutilized 충분히 이용되지 않은   district 지구, 지역
stigmatize 오명을 씌우다. 낙인찍다   municipal 시의, 지방 자치의
festival-goer 축제에 가는 사람   engage 관여시키다   feature
주연으로 삼다   ameliorate 개선하다   raise fund 기금을 마련하다

3

부모의 학력과 자녀에 대한 시간 투자는 정비례의 관계를 가진다. 2015년의 경우, 대학을 나온 엄마는 고졸 이하의 학력을 가진 엄마보다 일주일에 평균 4.5시간을 더 자녀를 돌보는 데 할당했다. 흥미롭게도, 이 경향은 취업률의 차이를 반영하지 않고 있다. 왜냐하면, 고등 교육을 받은 엄마는 고등학교를 마치지 않은 엄마보다 취업할 가능성이 높기 때문이다. 자녀에 대한 부모의 시간 할당에서 관찰되는 이런 차이점은, 유급 근로 시간을 제외한 나머지 시간의 유용성보다는 오히려 문화적으로 공고화된 선호성의 차이에서 비롯됨을 암시하고 있다.

(a) 수입 수준과 가족의 행복
(b) 부모의 학력과 자녀에 대한 시간 투자
(c) 고등학교 과정의 성공적인 이수와 장래의 취업
(d) 집에서 보낸 시간과 양육 솜씨

해설 대학을 나온 엄마는 고졸 이하의 학력을 가진 엄마보다 자녀를 돌보는 시간을 더 많이 할애한다는 내용이 이어지므로 정비례 관계에 있는 것은 부모의 학력과 자녀에 대한 시간 투자로 볼 수 있다. 이것은 시간의 유용성보다는 문화적으로 공고해진 선호도의 차이로 보이기 때문에 취업과는 관계가 없다는 결론을 내리고 있으므로 나머지 선택지는 알맞지 않다.

positive correlation 양의[비례] 상관관계   allocate 할당하다
disparity 차이, 불일치   employment rate 취업률   implication
함의, 암시   arise from ~에 기인하다   construct 조성하다
preference 선호   availability 유용성   outside of ~을 제외하고
parenting 양육   prowess 솜씨, 능력

4

스포츠 뉴스

불과 일곱 달 만에 왓퍼드 시티는 아일랜드 출신의 풀백 안톨린 오버빅을 방출하기로 결정했다. 팀이 그와 계약한 것은 그로 인해 왓퍼드의 후위가 좀 더 빨라지기를 바랐기 때문이었다. 이 소식을 접한 오버빅은 비록 훗날에 취소하긴 했지만, 트위터에 자극적인 코멘트를 게재하면서, 자신을 팀에서 내보낸 크리스 압둘라 감독의 결정을 비난했다. 이번 주 초에, 다루기 힘들기로 악명 높은 이 선수는 만약 정상적인 1군 자리를 보장받는다면 자신의 미래를 오직 이 클럽에 헌신하겠다고 약속했다. 이 말과 더불어 시즌 첫 두 경기에서 보여준 그의 실망스런 모습이 그가 팀에서 방출된 이유로 거론되었다.

(a) 오버빅의 계약을 연장하려는 왓퍼드 시티의 결정을 정당화했다
(b) 7개월을 이 선수를 판단할 수 있는 충분한 시간이 아님을 시사했다
(c) 압둘라가 오버빅을 공개적으로 비난할 수밖에 없게 했다
(d) 그가 팀에서 방출된 이유로 거론되었다

해설 한 축구 선수의 방출 소식을 전하는 내용이므로, 시즌 첫 두 경기에서 보여준 실망스런 모습이 그가 방출된 원인이었다는 것을 어렵지 않게 알 수 있다.

opt 선택하다   offload 처분하다   fullback 풀백, 수비수   backline
후위   squad 팀   inflammatory 자극적인   abjure 취소하다
notoriously 악명 높게   fractious 다루기 힘든, 성 잘 내는
stipulate 조건으로서 요구하다. 명기하다   commit 헌신하다   assure
보장하다   first-team spot 1군 자리   vindicate 정당화하다
extend 연장하다   censure 비난하다   exclusion 추방

5

1864년 2월 무렵, 미국 남북전쟁의 형세는 이미 북군 쪽에 유리해진 상태였다. 하지만 백분율로 계산했을 때 북군이 가장 많이 피를 흘린 전투 중의 하나를 치른 것은 바로 이달 동안이었다. 북부 플로리다에서 벌어진 올러스티 전투에서 북군 병사 5천5백 명이 남군 5천 명과 교전을 벌였는데, 이 때 북군은 탤러해시 쪽으로 밀고 나가던 중이었다. 전투가 끝나자 북군은 사망자 203명, 부상자 1152명, 실종자 506명의 피해를 입었다. 천 명당 265명의 사상자가 난 올러스티는 북군 최악의 패배 중의 하나로 기록되었다.

(a) 부상자의 수가 보통보다 많았다
(b) 증원군이 신속히 파견돼 계속 전투를 벌였다
(c) 양측이 상당한 손실을 입은 채 전투에서 퇴각했다
(d) 올러스티는 북군 최악의 패배 중의 하나로 기록되었다

해설 미국 남북전쟁에서 북군에게 가장 큰 타격을 주었던 올러스티 전투를 소개하는 글이다. 이 전투로 북군이 입은 피해가 주제이므로 이와 같은 맥락의 (d)가 오는 것이 적절하다.

tide 정세, 형세   in one's favor ~에게 유리한   Union (남북 전쟁 당시의) 북군   encounter 시합   engage (적과) 교전하다   the
former 전자   lie dead 죽어 있다   considering ~을 감안하면
casualty 사상자   go down 기록되다, 전해지다

6

이스턴 마운틴 기어는 거의 모든 품목에 대해서 반품해 드립니다. 단, 책임 문제로 인해 저희 반품 규정에서 특별히 제외되는 상품이 있습니다. 등산 장비, 스키 및 스노보드 장비, 그리고 자전거가 그런 반품 불가능한 목록에 들어갑니다. 저희 반품 규정에 따르면, 물건을 사용하지 않았고 꼬리표가 부착된 채 원래의 포장 상태로 반품되어야 합니다. 반품되는 물품은 구입일로부터 한 달 이내에 이스턴 마운틴 기어에 접수되어야 하는데, 이 때 고객님은 본인이 구입했던 가격과 동등한 스토어 크레디트를 발급받게 될 것입니다. 하지만 반품 배송 비용은 이 크레디트에서 공제됩니다.

(a) 그런 반품 불가능한 목록에 들어갑니다
(b) 저희 소매 직판점의 특선품입니다
(c) 항상 빠른 배송을 이용해 보냅니다
(d) 현금으로 전액 환불 받고 반품될 수 있습니다

해설 한 상점의 반품 규정을 안내하는 글이다. 빈칸 앞에서는 거의 모든 품목이 반품되지만 예외가 있다면서 등산 장비, 스키 및 스노보드 장비, 자전거를 언급하고 있으므로 이 품목들이 그런 예외에 속한다는 내용이 자연스럽다.

specifically 특별히   debar A from B A를 B에서 제외하다
exchange policy 반품 규정   due to ~때문에   liability 책임
stipulate 규정하다   purchase 구입   store credit 반환하는
물건값이 적힌 표, 반환한 물건의 값을 달아두었다가 나중에 그 상점에서
쓸 수 있게 하는 일종의 쿠폰   deduct 공제하다   constitute 구성하다
inventory 물품 목록   specialty (상점의) 특선품, 명물   retail outlet
소매 직판점   expedite 더 신속히 처리하다   for a full cash refund
현금으로 전액 환불받고

7

사람들은 일반적으로 사회 규범에 순응해, 다른 사람의 생각에 이해가 되고 정당하다고 인정되는 방식으로 행동한다. 하지만 때때로 사람들은 뚜렷한 이유 없이 자멸적인 방식으로 행동, 즉 정신 의학계와 심리학에서 '충동성'으로 구분되는 행동을 한다. 충동적인 사람은 그렇지 않은 사람보다 마약이나 술은 물론 심지어 음식에도 더 쉽게 중독된다. 뇌 과학자들은 충동적인 사람의 행동을 강하게 지배하는 경로, 즉 통상적인 동기 부여 및 보상 시스템의 근저에 있는 신경 화학 구조를 일부 밝혔다. 이와 같은 연구는 <u>의사들이 파괴적인 충동에 대한 새로운 처방책을 개발하는 것을 도울 수 있다.</u>

(a) 의사들이 파괴적인 충동에 대한 새로운 처방책을 개발하는 것을 도울 수 있다
(b) 중독이 충동적인 행동의 일반적인 원인임을 보여 준다
(c) 사람이 사회 규범을 기꺼이 고수하는 것을 택하는 개념에 의문을 제기한다
(d) 정신 의학의 전통적인 관습을 포기하게 만들 수 있다

해설 뇌 과학자들의 연구에 의해 충동적인 사람들의 신경 화학 구조를 일부 밝혀냈다고 하므로, 이러한 연구의 의미는 앞으로 의사들의 처방책 개발에 도움이 될 수 있다는 맥락이 가장 자연스럽다.

conform to ~에 순응하다 **norm** 규범 **comprehensible** 이해할 수 있는 **justifiable** 정당하다고 인정되는 **estimation** 생각, 평가 **unaccountably** 뚜렷한 이유 없이, 불가사의하게도 **self-destructive** 자멸적인 **classify** 분류하다 **psychiatry** 정신 의학 **impulsivity** 충동성 **susceptible to** ~의 영향을 받기 쉬운 **addiction** 중독 **substance** 물질 **elucidate** 해명하다 **neurochemical** 신경 화학의 **pathway** 경로 **wield control over** ~에 지배력을 행사하다, ~을 통제하다 **intervention** 개입 **implicate** (나쁜 것의) 원인임을 보여주다 **adhere to** ~을 고수하다 **abandonment** 단념

8

편집자에게,

이 도시 곳곳의 유서 깊은 식당을 중점적으로 소개한 귀사의 기사는 분명히 어느 정도는 칭찬을 받을 만합니다. 하지만 원통하게도 제가 가장 좋아하는 음식점인, 53번가와 하우젠 사이에 자리 잡은 블루벨이 빠진 것은 큰 실수입니다. 이 도시에서 가장 오랫동안 영업을 해온 식당이자, 초기에 하브 로드리게즈와 도티 브라운과 같은 지역 고관들이 단골로 드나든 블루벨은 <u>이와 같은 기사에서 충분히 최고 자리를 차지할 만합니다.</u> 이 편지로, 저는 귀사가 실수를 사죄하기를 바라며, 데일리 프레스 독자들이 우리 모두가 소중히 여겨야 하는 전설적인 시설을 다시 한 번 상기했으면 합니다.

루크 알바레즈

(a) 마침내 다음 달 문을 닫을 예정입니다
(b) 수많은 출판물에서 특집 기사로 다루어졌습니다
(c) 이와 같은 기사에서 최고 자리를 차지할 만합니다
(d) 편집자의 마음 한구석에 특별하게 자리 잡고 있습니다

해설 유서 깊은 식당을 소개한 기사에 블루벨이라는 음식점이 빠진 것에 대해 독자가 항의하는 편지이다. 빈칸이 들어간 문장에서 블루벨에 대해 칭찬을 늘어놓고 있으므로 (c)가 가장 자연스럽다.

article 기사 **highlight** 강조하다 **diner** 작은 식당 **a measure of** 어느 정도의 **approbation** 칭찬 **omission** 누락, 생략 **joint** 음식점 **mortifying** 분한, 원통한 **blunder** 큰 실수 **continuously** 계속하여 **operate** 영업하다 **patronize** 단골로 삼다, 애용하다 **dignitary** 고위 인사 **expiate** 속죄하다 **oversight** 간과, 실수 **institution** 기관 **cherish** 소중히 여기다 **feature** ~을 특집 기사로 다루다 **merit** ~을 받을 만하다, ~의 가치가 있다

9

애벌레의 탈바꿈은 유기체가 마지막 변태 단계 동안 탈피할 때 드러나는, 번데기라고 불리는 보호 껍질 내에서 일어난다. 라이프 사이클에서 번데기 단계의 특징인 애벌레에서 나비로의 극적인 형태 변화는 이 껍질 속에서 은밀하게 이루어진다. 효소(미생물)가 애벌레의 이전 몸을 소화해, 근본적으로 그것을 새롭게 기능할 수 있는 잠재성을 지닌 가장 기본적인 세포로 변형시킨다. <u>예를 들면,</u> 어떤 세포는 날개가 되고, 또 다른 세포는 다리와 촉각 등 다양한 기관을 이끌어낸다. 나비는 번데기에서 10~14일 만에 극적으로 탈바꿈된 생명체로 나타나게 된다.

(a) 어쨌든
(b) 하지만
(c) 예를 들면
(d) 그럼에도 불구하고

해설 알에서 나비까지의 변태 과정(알-유충-번데기-성충)을 설명한 글이다. 빈칸 앞 문장에서 애벌레의 몸이 가장 기본적인 세포로 변형된다고 했고, 다음 문장에서 어떤 것은 날개가, 다른 어떤 것은 다리나 촉각이 된다고 예를 들고 있다.

metamorphosis 탈바꿈, 변태 **caterpillar** 애벌레, 유충 **transpire** 일어나다 **chrysalis** 번데기 **slough off** 벗어버리다 **molting** 허물 벗기, 털갈이 **pupal** 번데기의 **seclusion** 격리, 고독 **enzyme** 효소 **reduce** 변형시키다, 감수 분열시키다 **slurry** 현탁액 **rudimentary** 가장 기본적인 **functionality** 기능성 **antenna** (곤충의) 촉각 **transmute** 변화시키다

10

빗물 집수를 포함해 물 회수 사업은 건조 혹은 반건조 지역의 수자원 관리에서 중요한 일면을 차지한다. 하지만 수자원 개발은 주의 깊게 관리되어야 한다. 왜냐하면, 자연 서식지의 수문학적 평형이 걸린 문제에서, 물 회수는 물에 의존하는 생태계에 매우 큰 영향을 미칠 수 있기 때문이다. 특히 질병을 옮기는 곤충들이 수집된 물을 이용해 급증할 수 있다. <u>그다음에는</u> 이것이 사람들에게 건강상의 위협을 가한다. 왜냐하면, 점점 더 많은 이런 질병 매개체들이 환경 속에 존재해, 말라리아와 뎅기열과 같은 파괴적인 질병을 퍼뜨리기 때문이다.

(a) 사실
(b) 그렇다 하더라도
(c) 그런데도
(d) 그다음에는

해설 건조한 지역에서 물을 회수하는 사업을 할 때 조심해야 할 점에 관한 글이다. 빈칸을 중심으로 앞과 뒤의 내용을 보면, 질병을 옮기는 곤충들이 급증하여 결과적으로 사람들에게 건강상의 위협이 된다는 내용이다. 따라서 빈칸에는 연속되어 일어나는 사건에서 어떤 일의 결과가 되는(as a result of something in a series of events) 문장을 이끄는 (d)가 적절하다.

water harvesting 물 회수, 집수 **arid** 건조한, 불모의 **hydrological** 수문학의 **habitat** 서식지 **outsized** 큰 **ecology** 생태(계) **rely on** ~에 의존하다 **transmit** 전염시키다 **proliferate** 급증하다 **pose a hazard** 위협을 가하다 **vector** (질병의) 매개체 **devastating** 파괴적인 **dengue fever** 뎅기열

Part II

11

미생물은 인간에게 많은 것을 제공한다. (a) 이제 그런 기여 중의 하나로, 미생물을 통해 독성 화학물질이 환경 및 건강에 큰 위협이 되는 장소의 공업 용제를 말끔히 제거하는 것이 가능해지고 있다. (b) 이전 군사 시설들도 종종 생명을 위협할 수도 있는 물질들을 적절히 처리하지 못하고 있다는 징후를 보이고 있다. (c) 과학자들이 그런 장소에 디할로코코이데 속에 속하는 박테리아 종을 주입한 후, 매우 놀라운 결과를 얻었다. (d) 몇 개월 내에 미생물들이 처리가 어려운 지하수 오염물질을 완전히 중화시킬 것이다.

해설 미생물의 이점에 대해 설명하면서 독극물을 분해하는 미생물 덕분에 환경 및 건강에 위협이 되는 오염물질을 제거할 수 있다는 내용이다. (b)는 미생물의 이점에 대한 지문의 주제와 전혀 상관이 없다.

microbe 미생물 contribution 기여 industrial solvent 공업 용제 toxic 유독한 constitute (위협 등을) 주다, 야기하다 considerable 상당한 installation 시설 disposal 처분, 처리 inoculate 접종하다, 주입하다 genus (생물 분류상의) 속 within a matter of months 몇 개월 이내에 neutralize 중화시키다 refractory 처리하기 어려운 contaminant 오염물질

12

레인 앤 루츠의 목표는 지구에 큰 충격을 주지 않는 양심적인 방식으로 식품을 제조하는 것입니다. (a) 저희는 우리 활동의 지속 가능성을 평가하고 성장의 방향을 조종할 명백한 지침을 만들었습니다. (b) 이런 식으로, 지금까지 저희 회사는 스스로 세웠던 높은 목표에 크게 다가섰습니다. (c) 비판가들이 그런 목표들이 성취 불가능하다고 여길지는 몰라도 저희 생각은 완전히 다릅니다. (d) 예를 들면, 작년에 저희는 유기 폐기물을 관리하기 위해 혐기성 소화법을 이용해, 쓰레기 매립지로부터 회사 폐기물 95퍼센트 이상을 전환했습니다.

해설 한 식품 제조업체가 친환경적인 방법으로 제품을 생산하고 있음을 알리고 있다. 명백한 지침을 만들고 목표를 이루었다면서 그 예를 들고 있다. (c)는 (b)와 (d) 간의 연계성을 흐리고 있다.

objective 목표 conscientious 양심적인 assess 평가하다 sustainability 지속 가능성 steer 조종하다 considerable 상당한 lofty 높은 beg to differ 생각이 완전히 다르다 divert 전환하다 landfill 쓰레기 매립지 anaerobic digestion 혐기성 소화(혐기 상태에서 미생물을 이용하여 폐수를 분해하는 방법) organic waste 유기 폐기물 (버려지는 폐기물 중 유기성 물질, 즉 음식 쓰레기, 식품 부산물 등)

Part III

13

신체가 우주의 진공에 노출되면 어떤 일이 발생할까? 공상과학영화는 비현실적인 사건, 즉 급작스런 압력 감소로 인체가 거꾸로 뒤집히게 된다고 묘사한다. 하지만 사람의 피부는 표준 대기 상태에서 제로 기압에 이르기까지, 실제로 기압이 떨어져도 충분히 견딜 수 있을 만큼 내구력이 있다. 물론 압력 감소는 우주가 가하는 유일한 위협 요소가 아니다. 왜냐하면, 공기가 없는 상태여서 사람이 저산소증, 즉 뇌까지 산소가 충분히 공급되지 않아 급속히 무력해질 것이기 때문이다.

Q 지문의 요지는?
(a) 사람의 뇌는 제로 기압에서 산소를 덜 필요로 한다.
(b) 즉각적인 압력 감소는 저산소증보다 더 위험하다.
(c) 대중문화는 외계의 현실을 잘못 전하고 있다.
(d) 사람의 피부는 초기 연구자들이 생각했던 것보다 더 튼튼하다.

해설 공상과학영화와 같은 대중문화에서 보여 주는 진공 상태에 있는 사람의 모습은 우주의 위험을 잘못 나타낸 것이라는 내용이므로 (c)가 가장 적절하다. science fiction movies가 pop culture로 표현되고 있음에 유의한다.

vacuum 진공 portray 묘사하다 turn inside out 뒤집다 durable 내구력이 있는, 튼튼한 withstand 견디다 pose a hazard 위협을 가하다 hypoxia 저산소증 inadequate 불충분한 incapacitate 무력하게 하다 misrepresent (정보를) 잘못 전하다 instant decompression 즉각적인 압력 감소

14

블랙 코브 프레스는 캔자스 주 위치타에 소재한 인쇄소로, 현지 미술가들과 기관, 출판사들에게 석판 인쇄, 목판, 스크린 인쇄 등의 제작을 위한 최첨단 시설을 제공합니다. 능숙한 인쇄 제작자들이 자신이 원하는 시간만큼 스튜디오를 빌려 독자적으로 인쇄물을 찍을 수 있습니다. 스튜디오 타임은 시간당 10달러로, 시간당, 일당 혹은 주당으로 예약할 수 있습니다. 인쇄 경험이 그다지 많지 않으신 분들은 스튜디오 시간을 빌리는 건 마음대로지만, 항상 블랙 코브 프레스 회원의 도움을 받도록 미리 계획하셔야 합니다.

Q 광고 대상은?
(a) 화보집 출판사
(b) 현지 미술가의 작품
(c) 임대용 아트 스튜디오 공간
(d) 최신식 미술 도구

해설 블랙 코브 프레스라는 인쇄소에서 스튜디오를 빌려 독자적으로 인쇄물을 찍을 수 있는(renting time in the studio to run their own editions) 서비스를 제공한다는 광고이므로 인쇄 작업실을 임대하는 광고임을 알 수 있다.

printing workshop (대규모) 인쇄소 furnish 제공하다 publisher 출판사 state-of-the-art 최신의 facility 시설 lithograph 석판 인쇄 woodcut 목판 screen print 스크린 인쇄(비단이나 발이 고운 인조 섬유로 잉크를 정착시키는 인쇄법) edition (간행물의) 판 book 예약하다 limited 아주 많지는 않은 welcome to 마음대로 ~해도 좋은 in advance 미리 for hire 임대의 top-of-the-line 최고급의, 최신식의

15

리카온을 둘러싼 신화는 피로 흠뻑 젖어 있다. 그의 이름이 늑대를 가리키는 그리스 단어 '리코스'에서 유래한 것 같다는 사실은 이 신화의 무시무시한 주제를 암시한다. 왜냐하면, 늑대는 그리스 신화에서 사람을 잡아먹는 나쁜 평판을 받고 있기 때문이다. 전설에 의하면, 리카온은 향연 때 제우스 신에게 인육을 넣은 음식을 은밀히 바치려고 했다. 리카온의 방약무인에 분노한 제우스는 즉각 그를 늑대로 변신시켜 인간의 수많은 자손을 죽이게 하는 매서운 벌을 내렸다.

Q 지문의 주된 내용은?
(a) 고대 그리스 전설의 이야기
(b) 고대 그리스에서 늑대가 살인자로 여겨진 이유
(c) 반인 반늑대에 관련된 그리스 신화
(d) 특정 그리스 단어가 시간이 흐르면서 진화된 방식

해설 리카온에 얽힌 고대 그리스의 신화를 소개하고 있으므로 (a)가 적절하다. mythology를 legend로 바꿔 표현했다.

drenched in ~로 흠뻑 젖은   derive from ~에서 유래하다   hint at ~을 암시하다   gruesome 소름 끼치는, 무시무시한   disreputable 평판이 나쁜   distinction 특징   covertly 은밀히   cannibalistic 식인의   incorporate 섞다   enrage 격분하게 하다   effrontery 방약무인   vitriolic 통렬한   slay 죽이다   offspring 자손

16

출판사들이 〈되 몽드: 프랑스의 언어와 문화〉 1쇄에 나타난 오류들을 엮는 작업에 독자분들의 도움을 바라고 있습니다. 이것들은 곧 나올 텍스트 재판에서 수정될 예정입니다. 아래에서, 지금까지 모인 광범위한 수정 목록을 찾으세요. 만약 이 요약에서 빠진 오류를 발견한다면 ivy@unf.edu와 martine@unf.edu로 편집자에게 알려 주세요. 출판사는 재판을 위해 정오표를 제출한 모든 독자들에게 감사를 표합니다.

Q 공고 내용은?
(a) 책의 오류에 대한 출판사의 사과
(b) 한 대중적인 작품의 잠정적인 재판 출간일
(c) 대중이 텍스트 개정에 참여할 기회
(d) 잘못된 주장에 대해 독자가 불만을 담을 수 있게 한 의견 게시판

해설 출판사가 어떤 책의 재판에 앞서 독자들에게 초판 책의 오류를 잡아달라고 부탁하는 공고문이다. These errors will be rectified가 revising으로 표현되었다.

solicit 간청하다, 부탁하다   compile 엮다, 모으다   rectify (잘못된 것을) 바로잡다   forthcoming 곧 있을   comprehensive 광범위한, 종합적인   correction 수정   to date 지금까지   omission 생략   compendium 개요서, 요약   apprise 통고하다   gratitude 감사   errata 정오표(erratum의 복수형)   tentative 잠정적인   release date 출간일   revising 개정   erroneous 잘못된

17

기후 변화가 식량 안보에 영향을 미치고 있다. 2012년에, 기나긴 폭염이 북미 옥수수 재배 지역의 작물 생산에 큰 타격을 주었다. 양적인 추정치에 의하면, 열 스트레스 때문에 수확량이 예상치보다 25퍼센트 이상 감소했다. 이와 같은 심각한 기상 사태들이 현재의 기후 변화 모델 하에서 심해질 것으로 예상되며, 따라서 전 세계 식량 생산 시스템에 불안정한 영향을 미칠 것 같다. 심지어 평균 온도에서 비교적 많지 않은 섭씨 1.7도 정도만 상승해도 장기적인 초고온 사태의 발생률이 3배 늘어날 것으로 예상된다.

Q 지문 내용과 일치하는 것은?
(a) 전 세계 식량 생산은 낮은 여름 기온에 달려 있다.
(b) 악천후가 농업에 영향을 줄 것으로 예상된다.
(c) 2012년에 북미에서 기록적인 식량 부족 사태가 여러 차례 발생했다.
(d) 기온이 지금보다 높아지면 장기 폭염 사태가 25퍼센트 늘어날 것이다.

해설 기후 변화의 악영향에 관한 글이다. 앞으로 이상 고온 현상 같은 기상 사태가 계속 심해질 것으로 예상되고, 마지막 문장에서 평균 온도가 1.7도만 상승해도 장기적인 초고온 사태의 발생률이 3배 늘어날 것이라는 말에서 (b)가 일치한다는 것을 알 수 있다.

heat wave 장기간에 걸친 혹서   devastate 완전히 파괴하다   quantitative 양적인   estimates 추정치   thermal 열의   yield 수확량   acute 심각한   meteorological 기상의   be projected to ~할 것으로 예상되다   intensify 심해지다   destabilizing 불안정한   modest 많지 않은   mean 평균의   incidence 발생률   prolonged 장기의   adverse weather conditions 악천후

18

스카이라이트는 휴대용 저장 장치를 갖고 다닐 필요 없이 다양한 장치들 안에 든 중요 파일들에 접속할 수 있게 하는 클라우드 서비스이다. 초보적인 스카이라이트 계정은 5기가바이트의 저장 용량과 끊김 없는 동기화, 그리고 PC와 스마트폰, 기타 안드로이드, 리눅스, iOS 장치들 간의 호환성을 제공한다. 이는 사진과 음악, 문서들을 공유하기 위한 가장 대중적인 옵션이다. 추가 용량은 100기가바이트당 월 5달러에, 혹은 기업의 경우 1테라바이트당 월 16달러에 구입할 수 있다.

Q 스카이라이트를 바르게 설명한 것은?
(a) 장치마다 별도의 계정이 필요하다.
(b) 기업은 개인보다 기가바이트당 한 달에 더 많은 돈을 지불한다.
(c) 서버에 저장된 파일들을 이용하려면 수수료를 내야 한다.
(d) 고객들 대부분은 5기가바이트의 저장 용량을 사용한다.

해설 인터넷으로 연결된 초대형 고성능 컴퓨터에 소프트웨어와 콘텐츠를 저장해 두고 필요할 때마다 꺼내 쓸 수 있는 클라우드 서비스(CSS)인 스카이라이트를 설명하는 글이다. 5기가바이트 상품이 가장 대중적이라고 했으므로 (d)가 적절하다.

cloud 클라우드(온라인 서버)   storage 저장   obviate 불필요하게 하다   portable 휴대용의   access 이용하다   entry-level 초보적인   account 이용 계정, 어카운트(네트워크에서 정보 서비스를 이용할 수 있는 자격)   seamless 끊김이 없는   synching 동기화   integration 통합   application 응용   terabyte 테라바이트(1,000기가바이트)

19

미국 심장 협회에서 발표한 식생활 지침은 적절한 영양 섭취에 과일, 채소, 곡물이 대단히 중요하다는 것을 상세히 기술하고 있다. 소비자들에게 비타민 정제와 같은 건강 보조 식품에 의존하는 대신에, 식단에 자연식품을 골고루 넣어 필수 비타민과 미네랄을 얻도록 권고하고 있다. 또한, 이 지침은 단 음식, 디저트, 탄산음료와 같은 고당분 식품을 먹지 말 것을 촉구한다. 이것들은 보다 건강에 좋은 칼로리 공급원을 대신하게 되어 필수 영양분을 부족하게 만든다.

Q 식생활 지침에 대해서 지문 내용과 일치하는 것은?
(a) 비타민 정제 문제를 다루기 위해 최근에 업데이트되었다.
(b) 인공적인 영양분 공급원을 먹지 못하게 한다.
(c) 사회에 고칼로리 식품이 만연한 것에 대해 경고한다.
(d) 소량의 고당분 식품 섭취를 허용한다.

해설 미국 심장 협회에서 발표한 식생활 지침은 비타민 정제와 같은 건강 보조 식품에 의존하지 말고 식단에 자연 식품을 넣으라고 권고하므로 인공적인 영양분 공급원을 섭취하지 못하게 한다는 (b)가 일치한다.

delineate 정확하게[상세하게] 서술하다   significance 중요성   grain 곡식   nutritional 영양의   adequacy 적절함   procure 획득하다   integrate 합치다   whole food (건강에 좋은) 자연 식품   as opposed to ~에 정반대로   reliance upon ~에 대한 의존   dietary supplement 건강 보조 식품   soft drink 탄산음료   displace 대신하다   correlated with ~와 밀접한 관련이 있는   address (문제 등을) 다루다   prevalence 우세, 만연   inclusion 포함

20

영화 리뷰

깜짝 놀라게 하는 특수 효과조차도 1991년에 나온 저예산 액션 영화 〈닥터, 닥터〉를 김빠지게 개작한 〈닥터〉를 보완할 수 없을 것이다. 이 후속작은 완전히 과녁을 벗어난다. 〈닥터, 닥터〉의 추종 팬을 낳게 한 정치 부패에 대한 체제 전복주의적인 비난과 억압적인 성 역할에 대한 즐거운 공격이 없다. 무엇보다도 최악인 점은, 원작에서 캐시 로비쇼가 진실 되게 연기한 전체주의적 인공두뇌를 가진 마약 경찰관 매릴린 반장이, 로비쇼의 완고하고 주인공답지 않은 주인공의 매력적인 잔인성이 결여된, 퍼석퍼석한 규율 주의자로 배역이 바뀐 것이다.

Q 비평 내용과 일치하는 것은?

(a) 주역 중 한 명을 수정한 것은 특히 실패작이다.

(b) 두 영화는 연이어 보도록 만들어졌다.

(c) 〈닥터, 닥터〉와 〈닥터〉의 주제가 동일하다.

(d) 첫 번째 영화의 성공은 두 번째 영화의 성공을 용이하게 했다.

해설 과거 성공적이었던 영화를 개작한 영화에 대해 비판하는 글이다. Worst of all 이하의 내용을 보면 원작에서 주인공 역할을 맡았던 매릴린 반장이 다른 성격으로 바뀐 것이 최악이라고 했으므로 (a)가 일치한다. 이 영화는 원작을 개작한 것이지 시리즈가 아니므로 (b)는 맞지 않다.

eye-popping 깜짝 놀라게 하는 **vapid** 지루한, 김빠진 **retelling** 개작된 이야기 **subversive** 전복시키는, 파괴적인 **indictment** 고발, 비난 **gleeful** 매우 기쁜, 즐거운 **torpedo** 어뢰로 공격하다 **cybernetic** 인공두뇌의 **narcotic** 마약 **veraciously** 정확하게, 진실하게 **recast** 배역을 바꾸다 **mealy** 창백한, 파삭파삭한 **disciplinarian** 규율 주의자 **magnetize** 매료하다 **impenitent** 완고한, 뉘우치지 않는 **anti-heroine** 주인공답지 않은 여주인공 **back to back** 연이어 **pave the way for** ~을 용이하게 하다

21

비스와바 심보르스카는 1996년 노벨 문학상을 받았다. 세계적으로 유명한 폴란드 시인인 그녀는 문학 평론가들로부터 폴란드의 위대한 시인들 중 선각자로 여겨지고 있다. 유럽에서 2차 세계대전이 끝나고 창작 활동을 시작한 초창기에, 그녀는 독자들이 이해할 수 없는 난해한 운문을 지어 질타를 받았다. 그녀의 첫 시집이 1948년에 완성되었지만, 그녀가 전체를 다시 쓴 4년 후에야 출판되었다.

Q 비스와바 심보르스카에 대해서 바르게 말한 것은?

(a) 전쟁 시기 폴란드의 삶을 주제로 글을 쓴다.

(b) 오늘날 독자들 사이에 널리 알려지지 않았다.

(c) 현대의 비평가들로부터 찬탄을 받고 있다.

(d) 2차 세계대전 전에 본인의 작품에 대한 반대에 부딪혔다.

해설 폴란드의 여류 시인이자 노벨 문학상을 수상한 비스와바 심보르스카를 소개하는 글이다. 두 번째 문장에서 그녀가 문학 평론가들 사이에서 폴란드의 위대한 시인들 중 선각자로 여겨지고 있다(regarded by literary critics as a luminary)고 했으므로 (c)가 일치한다.

recipient 수령인 **of renown** 유명한 **critic** 평론가 **luminary** 선각자, 권위자 **rebuke** 질책하다 **impenetrable** 불가해한 **verse** 운문 **deem** 여기다 **unreadable** 재미가 없어서 안 읽히는, 이해하기 어려운 **entirety** 전체, 전부 **esteem** 존경, 찬탄

22

공지

주민들에게,

폐자원 재활용 연합은 다가오는 3월 15~22일 주에, 여러분의 동네에 거주지 대형 폐기물 수거가 예정되어 있음을 다시 한 번 알려 드립니다. 일 년에 두 번 있는 이 행사에서, 주민들은 일반적으로 매주 차도 가 수거에서 제외되는 크고 무거운 물건들을 버릴 수 있습니다.

· 용인되는 쓰레기는 가전제품, 자동차 부품, 가구 등이 포함됩니다.

· 금지된 품목은 정원 쓰레기, 건축 잔해, 위험 물질 등으로, 이것들은 커닝햄 로에 위치한, 시에서 운영되는 유해 가정 폐기물 시설에서 안전하게 처리될 수 있습니다.

· 폐기물 수거 기간 동안 금지된 품목을 길가에 내놓는 행위는 거주지 폐기물 수거에 방해가 될 것입니다.

감사합니다.

폐자원 재활용 연합

Q 편지의 내용과 일치하는 것은?

(a) 자동차 부품은 일반적으로 매주 수거되는 품목이다.

(b) 주민들은 허용되는 쓰레기만 길가에 내놓아야 한다.

(c) 수거 기간은 동네마다 2주 동안이다.

(d) 모든 품목은 특별 처리 시설로 이송되어야 한다.

해설 평소에는 수거되지 않는 크고 무거운 물건들을 수거해 가는 '대형 폐기물 수거 행사'를 알리는 글이다. 그날은 폐기가 가능한 품목만 내놓아야 한다고 했으므로 정답은 (b)이다.

coalition 연합 **residential** 주거의 **bulk** 부피가 큰 **collection** 수거 **discard** 버리다 **cumbersome** 크고 무거운, 다루기 힘든 **bar** 금지하다 **curbside** 길가 **pickup** 수집 **admissible** 용인되는 **refuse** 쓰레기 **appliance** 가전제품 **detritus** 폐기물 **debris** 잔해 **dispose of** 처리하다 **municipal** 시립의 **restricted** 금지된 **preclude** 방해하다 **duration** 지속 (기간)

23

2월 중순에, 고대 로마인들은 악령을 저지하고 경축자들에게 생명력과 다산을 되찾아주기 위한 의식인 루퍼칼리아 축제를 열었다. 신화 속 인물, 즉 양치기와 관련된 신인 루퍼쿠스를 기리어 이름 지어진 루퍼칼리아는 이들의 보호를 받는 염소를 제물로 사용했다. 그리고 희생된 염소의 가죽은 길쭉하게 찢어두었다. 참가자들은 그 가죽으로 매질을 했는데, 왜냐하면 친구나 이웃을 매질하면 커플이 아이를 밸 가능성이 높아질 거라고 믿었기 때문이다.

Q 지문에서 루퍼칼리아에 대해 추론할 수 있는 것은?

(a) 마을 내에서 고기를 분배하는 방식에서 유래되었다.

(b) 가정을 꾸리고자 하는 사람들에게 유익한 것으로 여겨졌다.

(c) 가축의 신에게 잘 보이기 위해 거행되었다.

(d) 여러 종류의 동물이 희생되었다.

해설 고대 로마의 의식인 루퍼칼리아에 관한 글이다. 마지막 문장에서 염소의 가죽으로 친구나 이웃을 매질하면 커플이 아이를 임신할 가능성이 높아질 거라고 믿었다는 점에서 (b)가 알맞다.

observe (축제 등을) 축하하다, 기념하다 **ritual** 의식 **thwart** 방해하다, 좌절시키다 **vitality** 생명력, 활기 **fertility** 다산 **celebrant** 축하하는 사람 **deity** 신 **ward** 피보호자 **hide** (동물의) 가죽 **slash** 잘라버리다 **administer** (타격을) 가하다 **lashing** 매질(= flogging) **conceive** 임신하다 **originate** 유래하다 **start a family** 가정을 꾸리다 **curry favor with** ~의 비위를 맞추다 **livestock** 가축

24

오하이오 천연자원국에 따르면, 보브캣이 멸종 위기종 목록에서 삭제될지도 모른다. 이번 달 오하이오 야생생물 위원회 앞으로 제출된 보고서에서, 자원국은 그 개체 수가 다시 증가하고 있다는 증거로 주 전체에 걸쳐 보브캣 목격 횟수가 늘고 있음을 지적했다. 야생생물 전문가들은 수십 년간에 걸친 서식지 개선 노력을 멸종 위기에 처한 이 동물을 회복시킨 원동력으로 보고 있다. 2차 세계대전 이전에, 오하이오 주는 삼림 훼손이 심각했다. 하지만 20세기 중반부터 현저히 개선되어, 현재는 삼림 지대가 꽉 찬 것은 아니지만 약 31퍼센트의 삼림이 오하이오 주를 덮고 있다.

Q 보브캣에 대해 추론할 수 있는 것은?
(a) 사냥의 위협을 계속 받고 있다.
(b) 개체 수가 2차 세계대전 동안 절정에 달했다.
(c) 오하이오로 도입된 종이다.
(d) 보브캣의 자연 서식지는 삼림이다.

해설 보브캣의 개체 수가 증가하고 있는 이유를 오하이오 주의 과거와 현재의 삼림 상태에서 찾고 있으므로 삼림이 보브캣의 자연 서식지임을 추론할 수 있다.

bobcat 보브캣(북미산 야생 고양잇과 동물) **endangered** 멸종 위기에 처한 **sighting** 목격, 발견 **resurgence** (활동의) 재기, 부활 **credit** 여기다 **habitat** 서식지 **dynamic** 힘, 원동력 **deforest** 삼림을 없애다 **replete with** ~로 가득한 **woodland** 삼림 지대 **marked** 현저한 **introduced species** 도입종, 외래종

25

하원의원 보우어가 음주 운전으로 체포된 후에 나는 이 불행한 사건을 둘러싼 독설에 한몫 거드는 것을 삼갔다. 내가 이렇게 한 이유는 정의가 이길 것이며 보우어가 해임될 것이라고 잘못 판단했기 때문이었다. 오늘 법원의 결정을 듣고 난 후 나는 더 잠자코 있을 수가 없다. 알코올 및 약물 중독 전문가 알라나 킹이 목요일 증언에서 주장했듯이, 그 하원의원의 행동이 정말로 공공의 이익에 위협이 되지 않는다면, 그렇다면 왜 그가 음주 운전을 하여 유권자들의 생명을 위험에 빠뜨렸을까? 그런 무모한 행위가 대중에게 위협이 되지 않는다면, 과연 무엇이 그렇게 되는지 난 모르겠다.

Q 지문으로부터 추론할 수 있는 것은?
(a) 법원은 그 하원의원을 해임하지 않기로 했다.
(b) 대중은 그 소송에 별로 관심이 없다.
(c) 국원의원 보우어는 음주 운전을 하지 않은 것으로 밝혀졌다.
(d) 필자는 과거에 몇 차례 중독에서 벗어나려고 노력한 적이 있다.

해설 음주 운전을 한 하원의원이 당연히 해임되고 정의가 승리할 것이라는 생각에, 애초에 그에 대한 비방을 하지 않았던 필자가 법원의 판결을 듣고 분개하는 이유를 생각해 보면 (a)가 정답임을 알 수 있다.

representative 하원의원 **refrain from** 삼가다 **acrimony** 신랄함, 악감정 **misguided** 잘못 이해[판단]한 **verdict** 판결 **hold one's tongue** 잠자코 있다 **pose threat to** ~에 위협을 가하다 **addiction specialist** 알코올 및 약물 중독 전문가 **assert** 주장하다 **testimony** 증언 **constituent** 선거 구민 **driving while intoxicated** 음주 운전 **reckless** 무모한 **qualify as** ~의 기준에 부합하다 **proceedings** 소송 **bout** 한 바탕 앓음

Part IV

26-27

◁ 제니

〈나〉

안녕하세요, 제니 씨
지난 목요일에 만나서 아주 기뻤어요. 솔직히 말하자면, 부동산 중개인이 보통 사람을 이용하려고 하는 탐욕스러운 사람이라고 늘 생각했었어요. 이제 제가 얼마나 잘못 생각했는지를 깨달았어요. 모든 도움에 감사드려요. 그리고 확고한 전문성과 대단한 유머 감각에도 감사드려요. 제니와 같은 부동산 중개인은 만난 적이 없어요.
그건 그렇고, 침실이 두 개 있는 아파트를 매달 만 5천 달러에서 2만 달러까지 써서 임차할 계획이에요. 지난주에 보여주었던 아파트가 저한테는 딱 맞을 것 같아요. 어떻게 생각하시나요?

〈제니〉

안녕하세요, 피터 씨
오히려 제가 기뻤어요. 글쎄요, 세상에는 탐욕스러운 부동산 중개인도 정말 있다고 이해해요. 그리고 저 자신이 특별한 부동산 중개인이라고 생각해 본 적은 없어요. 그냥 제 일과 소중한 고객에게 정성을 쏟을 뿐이랍니다. 어떻든 칭찬해 줘서 고마워요.
안타깝지만, 지난주 목요일에 보여드렸던 아파트는 더 이상 임차할 수가 없어요. 그렇지만 피터 씨의 기준에 맞는 다른 아파트를 보여드릴 수 있어요. 언제 시간을 내실 수 있나요?

26 Q 피터는 왜 메시지를 보냈는가?
(a) 제니와 만나서 아파트에 대해 의논하기 위한 약속을 잡기 위해
(b) 임차할 아파트에 대해 제니의 의견을 구하기 위해
(c) 부동산 중개업자들에게 원한이 있었다고 고백하기 위해
(d) 자신의 전문성에 대해 제니가 칭찬해 줘서 고맙다는 뜻을 전하기 위해

해설 NEW TEPS의 출제 경향을 보여주는 문항이다. 특히 (a)를 정답으로 골라서는 안 됨에 유의해야 한다. 메시지에서 피터는 단순히 제니의 의견을 물어보고 있기 때문이다. 만나는 것은 제니가 제시한 내용이다. 이처럼 행위의 주체를 혼동시키는 오답 유형에 특히 유의해야 한다. (c)는 지나친 비약이다. (d)는 '자신'이 아니라 제니의 전문성을 칭찬하고 있기 때문에 오답이다. 따라서 정답은 (b)이다.

27 Q 대화로부터 추론할 수 있는 것은?
(a) 피터가 제니를 만난 것은 부동산 중개인에 대한 피터의 인식에 영향을 미쳤다.
(b) 제니는 피터가 부동산 중개인에게 거들먹거리는 태도에 감정이 상했다.
(c) 제니는 피터가 만난 사람 가운데 가장 익살맞은 사람이다.
(d) 제니는 고객에게 정성을 쏟을 만큼 충분히 자신의 일을 진지하게 받아들이지 않는다.

해설 정답은 (a)인데, 이 문장에 쓰인 inform이 '통지하다'라는 뜻이 아니라, '영향을 미치다'라는 뜻으로 쓰였음에 주목해야 한다. (b)는 제니의 메시지로부터 그렇게 추론할 수 있는 근거가 전혀 없다. (c)는 '사람'이 아니라 '부동산 중개인'이라고 해야 정답으로 생각될 수도 있지만, 지나친 비약이므로 오답으로 처리해야 한다. (d)는 오히려 정반대라고 추론할 수 있다.

to be honest 솔직히 말하자면 **real estate broker** 부동산 중개인 **greedy** 탐욕스러운 **mistaken** 잘못 생각하고 있는 **professionalism** 전문성, 전문가 기질 **exceptional** 특별한; 우수한 **compliment** 칭찬, 찬사 **criterion** 기준 **grudge** 원한 **inform** 영향을 미치다; 알리다 **condescending** 잘난 체하는

28-29

왕과 영국 의회의 애증 관계

영국 대내란 이전에, 왕과 영국 의회 사이의 관계는 복잡했다. 겉보기에는 군주가 원할 때는 언제든지 의회를 해산할 수 있었다는 점에서 의회를 절대적으로 지배하는 것 같았다. 그렇지만 영국 의회에는 저항할 수 있는 재정적인 수단이 있었다.

이 시기 동안에, 의회는 본질적으로 왕의 명령에 의해 설치되는 자문위원회였다. 그럼에도 불구하고, 귀족의 이익을 대변하여, 의회라는 기관은 세금을 징수하려는 군주의 시도를 좌절시킬 수 있었다. 의회가 세금을 인상해 달라는, 왕의 요청을 거부할 때, 왕이 의회로 하여금 그렇게 하도록 강요할 수 있는 방법이 없었다.

따라서 군주는 의회의 협력을 필요로 했는데, 그것이 군주가 의회로 하여금 정책 제안을 하도록 허락한 이유 가운데 하나였다. 그렇지만 왕에게는 그런 제안을 받아들일 수 있는 절대적인 결정권이 있었다. 그런 상호의존적이지만 잠재적으로 대립적인 관계가 영국 대내란의 발발로 귀결된 주된 원동력 가운데 하나였다.

28 Q 기사의 주제는?
(a) 귀족들과 소작농들 사이의 복잡한 관계
(b) 군주와 영국 의회 사이에 긴장이 존재했던 이유
(c) 영국 대내란의 발발에 기여했던 이념적 요인들
(d) 영국에서 입헌군주정이 확립된 방식

해설 NEW TEPS에서 역사 관련 지문의 출제 비중이 높다는 점에 유의하자. 특히 최근에는 영국의 역사에 대한 지문이 자주 출제되고 있다. (a)는 '소작농들'이 전혀 언급되지 않았기 때문에 오답이다. (c)는 기사에서 '이념적 요인들'이 나와 있지 않기 때문에 정답이 아니다. (d)는 입헌군주정의 확립으로 이어졌다는 것이 역사적으로 올바르다고 하더라도, 기사에서 명시하지 않았기 때문에 반드시 오답으로 처리해야 한다. 따라서 정답은 기사의 주제를 정확히 포착한 (b)이다.

29 Q 기사에 따르면, 다음 중 옳은 것은?
(a) 많은 군주들이 영국 의회를 수없이 해산했다.
(b) 영국 의회는 귀족의 이익을 보호하려고 노력했다.
(c) 영국 왕들은 사치스러운 생활방식을 유지하려는 목적으로 높은 세금을 거두려고 했다.
(d) 영국 의회는 영국 사회를 급진적으로 개혁하려고 분투했다.

해설 (a)는 기사에서 분명하게 밝히지 않았기 때문에 오답이다. (c)는 역사적으로 올바른 내용이라고 하더라도, 기사에서 명시하지 않았기 때문에 반드시 오답으로 처리해야 한다. '기사에 따르면'이라는 단서 조항에 특히 유의해야 한다. (d)는 지나친 비약이므로 오답이다. 따라서 정답은 (b)이다.

parliament 의회 **English Civil War** 영국 대내란, 영국의 시민혁명 **on the surface** 겉보기에는 **monarch** 군주 **dissolve** 해산하다 **resist** 저항하다 **in essence** 본질적으로 **advisory committee** 자문위원회 **aristocracy** 귀족 **institution** 기관, 단체 **thwart** 좌절시키다 **consequently** 그 결과, 따라서 **discretion** 재량, 결정권 **confrontational** 대립의

30-31

아동의 정신 건강이 위협을 받고 있다

놀랍게도 정신 건강이 우리나라의 많은 아동들에게 화급한 문제이다. 지난 5년 동안 정신 질환이 있는 아동의 입원이 급격하게 증가하고 있다. 전문가들은 정신질환이 있는 아동의 사례의 대다수가 보고되지 않는다고 생각한다.

많은 점에서, 교사들이 정신질환이 있는 많은 학생들을 다루는 최전선을 담당하고 있다. 이런 학생들의 대부분은 스트레스, 우울증, 그리고 식이장애의 사례가 보고된다. 훌륭한 교사는 당연하게도 이들이 그런 정신질환을 치유하는 것을 돕고 싶어 한다.

초등학교와 중학교가 모두 교사를 위한 정신 건강 프로그램을 제공할 수 있지만, 그런 프로그램은 일반적으로 제공하기에 너무 비용이 많이 든다. 그렇지만 다행스럽게도 정신질환이 있는 학생을 돕기 위해 성실한 교사가 할 수 있는 일들이 많이 있다.

그런 학생을 돕는 가장 효과적인 방법들 가운데 하나는 도움을 주려는 방식으로 정신 건강 문제가 논의될 수 있는 환경을 만드는 것이다. 이 간단한 조치는 또한 정신 건강 교육 프로그램을 제공하는 것과 비교할 때 정신 건강 문제를 다루는, 보다 비용이 적게 드는 방법들 가운데 하나이다.

정신 질환이 있는 아동을 돕는 다른 방법에 대한 정보는 첨부한 기사를 참조하면 된다. 또한 suggestions@mentalhealth.org로 이메일을 보내서 제안을 할 수도 있다.

30 Q 기사의 주된 목적은?
(a) 독자에게 아동의 정신 건강이 놀랄 만한 속도로 악화되고 있음을 알리는 것
(b) 교사들로 하여금 정신 질환이 있는 아동의 사례를 당국에 보고하도록 장려하는 것
(c) 교사들에게 정신 질환이 있는 아동을 돕는 실용적인 방법을 제안하도록 요청하는 것
(d) 특정한 아동 집단을 돕는 효과적인 방법들을 제안하는 것

해설 NEW TEPS에서는 이처럼 시사적인 내용의 출제 비중이 점차 높아지고 있음에 유의해야 한다. (a)는 기사의 주된 목적이 아니라, 기사에서 말하고자 하는 바의 배경에 해당한다. (b)는 기사의 의도가 아니고, (c)는 제안을 할 수도 있다고 했지만, 그것이 기사의 주된 목적이 아니다. 따라서 정답은 (d)이다. 전반적인 글의 초점에 유의해야 한다.

31 Q 저자는 왜 도움을 주려는 환경을 만드는 것이 정신 건강 교육 프로그램을 제공하는 것보다 낫다고 생각하는가?
(a) 그런 프로그램을 제공하는 것보다 더 적은 수의 교사를 관여시키기 때문에
(b) 아동들이 대부분 정신 건강 문제를 논의하는 것을 꺼리기 때문에
(c) 초등학교와 중학교 학생들이 충분히 성숙하지 못하기 때문에
(d) 그런 프로그램을 제공하는 것보다 비용 효과가 더 높기 때문에

해설 NEW TEPS의 주요 출제 유형이다. 해당하는 정보가 있는 부분을 찾아가서 빠르고 정확하게 필요한 정보를 포착하는 연습이 뒷받침되어야 한다. 네 번째 단락에서 정신 건강 문제를 논의할 수 있는 환경을 조성하는 것이 정신 건강 교육 프로그램을 제공하는 것보다 비용적인 장점이 있다고 했으므로 정답은 (d)이다. NEW TEPS의 독해 파트4는 많은 시간이 소요되기 때문에, 효과적인 시간 관리가 필수적이다. 각 단락의 첫 번째 문장을 빠르게 읽어서, 중심 내용에 대한 감각을 얻고, 그에 따라 다소 속도감 있게 문제를 푸는 연습을 해야 실전에서 실력을 제대로 발휘할 수 있다.

hospital admission 입원 mental illness 정신질환
go unreported 보고되지 않다 on the frontline 최전선에
depression 우울증 eating disorder 식이 장애 conscientious
양심적인, 성실한 supportive 따뜻하게 대하는, 지원하는
deteriorate 악화되다 alarming 놀랄 만한; 걱정스러운
authorities 당국

32-33

비즈니스 〉지역   인디애나타임스

커피브레이크는 사회적 책임감이 없는 회사인가?

인디애나주(州) 인디애나폴리스에 본사가 있는 커피브레이크는 지역민
사이에서는 소외 계층을 고용하는, 사회적 책임을 다하는 회사로 잘
알려져 있다. 회사 웹사이트에 따르면, 이 커피점은 매년 훌륭한 대의
를 위해 36만 달러를 기부한다고 한다. 그 때문에 커피브레이크는 미
국에서 가장 존경을 받는 기업들 가운데 하나이다.

지난주에, INN뉴스는 이 커피점이 2014년 이래로 법인세를 납부한
적이 없다고 보도했다. INN뉴스 기자들은 커피브레이크가 모든 종류
의 조세 회피 '협의'에 연루되었다는 사실을 알아냈다. 기자들이 의견
을 구한 여러 명의 세금 전문가들에 따르면, 그런 협의 가운데 일부는
불법일 수도 있다고 한다.

커피브레이크에 대한 이런 충격적인 뉴스에 놀라서, 인디애나폴리스의
여러 소비자 단체들은 세금 회피 시도에 대한 항의로서 그 커피점을
보이콧하겠다고 위협했다. 업계 전문가들은 그 단체들이 실제로 위협
을 실행에 옮기느냐에 상관없이 커피브레이크의 기업 이미지가 심하
게 손상되었다는 데 의견이 일치한다.

커피브레이크는 입장을 제시해 달라는 인디애나타임스의 요청을 거부했다.

32 Q 커피브레이크가 미국에서 널리 존경을 받는 이유는?
(a) 기업의 사회적 책임이라는 개념을 생각해냈기 때문에
(b) 매년 36만 달러가 넘는 수익을 창출하기 때문에
(c) 직장에서의 양성 평등을 계속해서 추구하기 때문에
(d) 재정적 후원을 제공함으로써 사회적 가치를 증진하는 데 도움을 주기
때문에

해설 이 유형은 해당하는 정보를 찾아가서 필요한 정보를 빠르고 정확하
게 확인할 것을 요구하는 유형이다. (a)와 (c)는 전혀 제시되지 않은 내용
이다. (b)는 회사가 주장하는 기부 액수이지, 수익 금액이 아니다. 따라서
정답은 기사에서 분명하게 밝힌 (d)이다.

33 Q 기사로부터 커피브레이크에 대해 추론할 수 있는 것은?
(a) 실제 기부 금액이 인디애나타임스에 의해 독자적으로 확인되지 못했다.
(b) 2014년 이래로, INN뉴스와 껄끄러운 관계를 유지했다.
(c) 조세법을 확실히 준수하기 위해서 세금 전문가들과 정기적으로 상의
한다.
(d) 아주 가까운 장래에 기자회견을 개최할 가능성이 매우 높다.

해설 정답은 (a)이다. 기부 금액은 '회사의 웹사이트'에서 주장하는 금액이
기 때문이다. (b)는 전형적인 비약이다. (c)는 오히려 반대일 가능성이 높기
때문에 오답이다. (d)는 주어진 내용만으로는 확실하게 추론할 수 없다. 이
런 경우는 반드시 오답으로 처리해야 한다.

the disadvantaged 불우한 사람들 **worthy** 훌륭한 **cause** 대의;
원인 **corporation tax** 법인세 **consult** 견해를 묻다 **devastating**
충격적인; 황폐화시키는 **consumer** 소비자 **protest** 항의, 반대
corporate 회사의, 기업의 **corporate social responsibility** 기업의
사회적 책임 **press conference** 기자 회견

34-35

지구의 지리적 극점과 지자기 극점

사람들은 대부분 북극과 남극이라는, 지구의 지리적 극점에 익숙하다.
북극이 지구의 최북단 지점인 데 반해, 남극은 지구의 최남단 지점이
다. 그렇지만 지구에 지자기 극점도 있다는 사실을 아는 사람들은 많
지 않다.

지구의 지자기 극점이 무엇인지 이해하기 위해서는, 지구에 쌍극자장
이 있다는 것을 이해해야 한다. 쌍극자장은 두 개의 서로 다른 극점이
공간에서 분리될 때 형성된다. 지구의 지자기 극점은 지구의 쌍극자장
의 극점이다. 이 쌍극자장의 중심축은 지구의 지자기 극점들에서 지구
의 표면을 가로지른다.

과학자들은 지구의 지자기극이 동일하게 유지된다고 오랫동안 믿고
있었다. 1920년대에 이르러서야 과학자들은 지구의 지자기 극점들이
변화한다는 사실을 관찰했다. 이것은 '지자기 역전'으로 불린다. 1929
년에, 마쓰야마 모토노리라는 일본의 지구물리학자는 지자기 역전이
홍적세 초기에 발생했다고 주장했다.

유감스럽게도 과학계가 그의 생각을 진지하게 받아들여 지자기 역전
을 연구하게 되는 데는 30년이 넘게 걸렸다. 그런 연구들이 『오늘의
지구과학』의 다음 호에서 다뤄질 예정이다.

34 Q 지문에 따르면, 다음 중 옳은 것은?
(a) 사람들은 대부분 지구의 지자기 극점들이 그대로 유지된다고 잘못 생
각한다.
(b) 지구의 지리적 극점들과 지자기 극점들 사이에는 전혀 아무런 관계가
없다.
(c) 공간에서 두 개의 서로 다른 극점이 분리되면 쌍극자장이 형성되는 결
과에 이른다.
(d) 지자기 역전은 역사를 통틀어 여러 번에 걸쳐 발생했다.

해설 과학 관련 중요 사항이므로, 내용까지 꼼꼼하게 익혀 두어야 한다.
(a)는 그에 대한 설명이 없으므로 오답이다. (b)는 지문의 내용만으로는 정
확히 알 수가 없다. 이런 경우는 반드시 오답으로 처리해야 한다. (d)도 마
찬가지다. (d)에서 설명하는 사항이 실제로 올바른 설명이라고 하더라도,
'지문에 따르면'이라는 단서 조항 때문에, 절대로 정답이 될 수 없다. 지문
에서 그 내용을 밝히지 않았기 때문이다.

35 Q 지문으로부터 마쓰야마에 대해 추론할 수 있는 것은?
(a) 지구의 지자기 극점을 처음으로 발견한 지구물리학자였다.
(b) 그의 생각은 1940년대에 과학계에 의해 진지하게 고려되었다.
(c) 세계의 많은 지역에서 현무암 표본을 수집했다.
(d) 1929년에, 그의 생각은 진지하게 고려될 가치가 없는 것으로 인식되
었다.

해설 (a)라고 판단할 수 있는 근거가 없다. (b)는 대략 1950년대 말이나
1960년 대 초로 생각할 수 있으므로 정답이 될 수 없다. (c)는 지문에서
제시한 내용이 아니기 때문에 오답이다. 실제로 마쓰야마가 세계 여러 지
역에서 현무암 표본을 수집했다고 하더라도, 지문에는 그에 대한 설명이
없다. '지문으로부터'라는 말에 특히 유의해야 한다. 따라서 정답은 자연스
럽게 추론할 수 있는 (d)이다.

geographic 지리적인; 지리학의 **southernmost** 최남단의
separate 분리하다 **axis** 중심축, 축 **intersect** 가로지르다
reversal 역전, 전환 **geophysicist** 지구물리학자 **Pleistocene**
홍적세(洪積世) **geoscience** 지구과학 **mistakenly** 잘못하여
basalt 현무암 **specimen** 표본

Actual Test 1

정답 자동 채점

청해 (Listening Comprehension)

문항 1–25: ⓐ ⓑ ⓒ ⓓ
문항 26–40: ⓐ ⓑ ⓒ ⓓ

어휘 (Vocabulary)

문항 1–15: ⓐ ⓑ ⓒ ⓓ
문항 16–30: ⓐ ⓑ ⓒ ⓓ

문법 (Grammar)

문항 1–15: ⓐ ⓑ ⓒ ⓓ
문항 16–30: ⓐ ⓑ ⓒ ⓓ

독해 (Reading Comprehension)

문항 1–25: ⓐ ⓑ ⓒ ⓓ
문항 26–35: ⓐ ⓑ ⓒ ⓓ

수험번호 Registration No.
성명 Name / 한글

문제지번호 Test Booklet No.
감독관확인란

주민등록번호 National ID No.
수험번호 Registration No.
비밀번호 Password
좌석번호 Seat No.
고사실란 Room No.

정답 자동 채점

Actual Test 2

수 험 번 호
Registration No.

성명
Name
한글
한자

문 제 지 번 호
Test Booklet No.

감독관확인란

고사실란
Room No.

좌석번호
Seat No.

청해 Listening Comprehension	어휘 Vocabulary	문법 Grammar	독해 Reading Comprehension

주민등록번호
National ID No.

수험번호
Registration No.

비밀번호
Password

서약

본인은 필기구 및 기재오류와 답안지 훼손으로 인한 책임을 지고, 부정행위 처리규정을 준수할 것을 서약합니다.

답안작성시 유 의 사 항

1. 답안 작성은 반드시 컴퓨터용 싸인펜을 사용해야 합니다.
2. 답안을 정정할 경우 수정테이프(수정액 불가)를 사용해야 합니다.
3. 본 답안지는 컴퓨터로 처리되므로 훼손해서는 안되며, 답안지 하단의 타이밍마크(┃┃┃)를 찢거나, 낙서 등으로 인한 훼손시 발생할 수 있습니다.
4. 답안은 문항당 정답을 1개만 골라 ● 와 같이 정확히 기재해야 하며, 필기구 오류나 본인의 부주의로 잘못 표기한 경우에는 답 관리위원회의 OMR판독기에 따르며, 그 결과는 본인이 책임집니다.

Good ● Bad ◑ ◐ ◉ ⊗ ⊘

5. 감독관의 확인이 없는 답안지는 무효처리됩니다.

Actual Test 3

정답 자동 채점

수험번호 Registration No.
성명 Name
한글
한자

문제지번호 Test Booklet No.

감독관확인란

청해 Listening Comprehension

1	ⓐ ⓑ ⓒ ⓓ
2	ⓐ ⓑ ⓒ ⓓ
3	ⓐ ⓑ ⓒ ⓓ
4	ⓐ ⓑ ⓒ ⓓ
5	ⓐ ⓑ ⓒ ⓓ
6	ⓐ ⓑ ⓒ ⓓ
7	ⓐ ⓑ ⓒ ⓓ
8	ⓐ ⓑ ⓒ ⓓ
9	ⓐ ⓑ ⓒ ⓓ
10	ⓐ ⓑ ⓒ ⓓ
11	ⓐ ⓑ ⓒ ⓓ
12	ⓐ ⓑ ⓒ ⓓ
13	ⓐ ⓑ ⓒ ⓓ
14	ⓐ ⓑ ⓒ ⓓ
15	ⓐ ⓑ ⓒ ⓓ
16	ⓐ ⓑ ⓒ ⓓ
17	ⓐ ⓑ ⓒ ⓓ
18	ⓐ ⓑ ⓒ ⓓ
19	ⓐ ⓑ ⓒ ⓓ
20	ⓐ ⓑ ⓒ ⓓ
21	ⓐ ⓑ ⓒ ⓓ
22	ⓐ ⓑ ⓒ ⓓ
23	ⓐ ⓑ ⓒ ⓓ
24	ⓐ ⓑ ⓒ ⓓ
25	ⓐ ⓑ ⓒ ⓓ
26	ⓐ ⓑ ⓒ ⓓ
27	ⓐ ⓑ ⓒ ⓓ
28	ⓐ ⓑ ⓒ ⓓ
29	ⓐ ⓑ ⓒ ⓓ
30	ⓐ ⓑ ⓒ ⓓ
31	ⓐ ⓑ ⓒ ⓓ
32	ⓐ ⓑ ⓒ ⓓ
33	ⓐ ⓑ ⓒ ⓓ
34	ⓐ ⓑ ⓒ ⓓ
35	ⓐ ⓑ ⓒ ⓓ
36	ⓐ ⓑ ⓒ ⓓ
37	ⓐ ⓑ ⓒ ⓓ
38	ⓐ ⓑ ⓒ ⓓ
39	ⓐ ⓑ ⓒ ⓓ
40	ⓐ ⓑ ⓒ ⓓ

어휘 Vocabulary

1	ⓐ ⓑ ⓒ ⓓ	16	ⓐ ⓑ ⓒ ⓓ
2	ⓐ ⓑ ⓒ ⓓ	17	ⓐ ⓑ ⓒ ⓓ
3	ⓐ ⓑ ⓒ ⓓ	18	ⓐ ⓑ ⓒ ⓓ
4	ⓐ ⓑ ⓒ ⓓ	19	ⓐ ⓑ ⓒ ⓓ
5	ⓐ ⓑ ⓒ ⓓ	20	ⓐ ⓑ ⓒ ⓓ
6	ⓐ ⓑ ⓒ ⓓ	21	ⓐ ⓑ ⓒ ⓓ
7	ⓐ ⓑ ⓒ ⓓ	22	ⓐ ⓑ ⓒ ⓓ
8	ⓐ ⓑ ⓒ ⓓ	23	ⓐ ⓑ ⓒ ⓓ
9	ⓐ ⓑ ⓒ ⓓ	24	ⓐ ⓑ ⓒ ⓓ
10	ⓐ ⓑ ⓒ ⓓ	25	ⓐ ⓑ ⓒ ⓓ
11	ⓐ ⓑ ⓒ ⓓ	26	ⓐ ⓑ ⓒ ⓓ
12	ⓐ ⓑ ⓒ ⓓ	27	ⓐ ⓑ ⓒ ⓓ
13	ⓐ ⓑ ⓒ ⓓ	28	ⓐ ⓑ ⓒ ⓓ
14	ⓐ ⓑ ⓒ ⓓ	29	ⓐ ⓑ ⓒ ⓓ
15	ⓐ ⓑ ⓒ ⓓ	30	ⓐ ⓑ ⓒ ⓓ

문법 Grammar

1	ⓐ ⓑ ⓒ ⓓ	16	ⓐ ⓑ ⓒ ⓓ
2	ⓐ ⓑ ⓒ ⓓ	17	ⓐ ⓑ ⓒ ⓓ
3	ⓐ ⓑ ⓒ ⓓ	18	ⓐ ⓑ ⓒ ⓓ
4	ⓐ ⓑ ⓒ ⓓ	19	ⓐ ⓑ ⓒ ⓓ
5	ⓐ ⓑ ⓒ ⓓ	20	ⓐ ⓑ ⓒ ⓓ
6	ⓐ ⓑ ⓒ ⓓ	21	ⓐ ⓑ ⓒ ⓓ
7	ⓐ ⓑ ⓒ ⓓ	22	ⓐ ⓑ ⓒ ⓓ
8	ⓐ ⓑ ⓒ ⓓ	23	ⓐ ⓑ ⓒ ⓓ
9	ⓐ ⓑ ⓒ ⓓ	24	ⓐ ⓑ ⓒ ⓓ
10	ⓐ ⓑ ⓒ ⓓ	25	ⓐ ⓑ ⓒ ⓓ
11	ⓐ ⓑ ⓒ ⓓ	26	ⓐ ⓑ ⓒ ⓓ
12	ⓐ ⓑ ⓒ ⓓ	27	ⓐ ⓑ ⓒ ⓓ
13	ⓐ ⓑ ⓒ ⓓ	28	ⓐ ⓑ ⓒ ⓓ
14	ⓐ ⓑ ⓒ ⓓ	29	ⓐ ⓑ ⓒ ⓓ
15	ⓐ ⓑ ⓒ ⓓ	30	ⓐ ⓑ ⓒ ⓓ

독해 Reading Comprehension

1	ⓐ ⓑ ⓒ ⓓ
2	ⓐ ⓑ ⓒ ⓓ
3	ⓐ ⓑ ⓒ ⓓ
4	ⓐ ⓑ ⓒ ⓓ
5	ⓐ ⓑ ⓒ ⓓ
6	ⓐ ⓑ ⓒ ⓓ
7	ⓐ ⓑ ⓒ ⓓ
8	ⓐ ⓑ ⓒ ⓓ
9	ⓐ ⓑ ⓒ ⓓ
10	ⓐ ⓑ ⓒ ⓓ
11	ⓐ ⓑ ⓒ ⓓ
12	ⓐ ⓑ ⓒ ⓓ
13	ⓐ ⓑ ⓒ ⓓ
14	ⓐ ⓑ ⓒ ⓓ
15	ⓐ ⓑ ⓒ ⓓ
16	ⓐ ⓑ ⓒ ⓓ
17	ⓐ ⓑ ⓒ ⓓ
18	ⓐ ⓑ ⓒ ⓓ
19	ⓐ ⓑ ⓒ ⓓ
20	ⓐ ⓑ ⓒ ⓓ
21	ⓐ ⓑ ⓒ ⓓ
22	ⓐ ⓑ ⓒ ⓓ
23	ⓐ ⓑ ⓒ ⓓ
24	ⓐ ⓑ ⓒ ⓓ
25	ⓐ ⓑ ⓒ ⓓ
26	ⓐ ⓑ ⓒ ⓓ
27	ⓐ ⓑ ⓒ ⓓ
28	ⓐ ⓑ ⓒ ⓓ
29	ⓐ ⓑ ⓒ ⓓ
30	ⓐ ⓑ ⓒ ⓓ
31	ⓐ ⓑ ⓒ ⓓ
32	ⓐ ⓑ ⓒ ⓓ
33	ⓐ ⓑ ⓒ ⓓ
34	ⓐ ⓑ ⓒ ⓓ
35	ⓐ ⓑ ⓒ ⓓ

주민등록번호 National ID No.

| 0 1 2 3 4 5 6 7 8 9 |

수험번호 Registration No.

| 0 1 2 3 4 5 6 7 8 9 |

비밀번호 Password

| 0 1 2 3 4 5 6 7 8 9 |

고사실란 Room No.

| 0 1 2 3 4 5 6 7 8 9 |

좌석번호 Seat No.

| A B C D E |
| 1 2 3 4 5 6 7 |

정답 자동 채점

Actual Test 4

수험번호 Registration No.

성명 Name
한글
한자

문제지번호 Test Booklet No.

감독관확인란

청 해 Listening Comprehension

1 2 3 4 5 6 7 8 9 10 11 12 13 14 15 16 17 18 19 20 21 22 23 24 25
26 27 28 29 30 31 32 33 34 35 36 37 38 39 40

어 휘 Vocabulary

1 2 3 4 5 6 7 8 9 10 11 12 13 14 15
16 17 18 19 20 21 22 23 24 25 26 27 28 29 30

문 법 Grammar

1 2 3 4 5 6 7 8 9 10 11 12 13 14 15
16 17 18 19 20 21 22 23 24 25 26 27 28 29 30

독 해 Reading Comprehension

1 2 3 4 5 6 7 8 9 10 11 12 13 14 15 16 17 18 19 20 21 22 23 24 25
26 27 28 29 30 31 32 33 34 35

주 민 등 록 번 호 National ID No.

수 험 번 호 Registration No.

비밀번호 Password

좌석번호 Seat No.
A B C D E

고사실번호 Room No.

서 약

본인은 필기구 및 기재오류와 답안지 훼손으로 인한 책임을 지고, 부정행위 처리규정을 준수할 것을 서약합니다.

답안작성시 유 의 사 항

1. 답안 작성은 반드시 **컴퓨터용 싸인펜**을 사용해야 합니다.
2. 답안을 정정할 경우 수정테이프(수정액 불가)를 사용해야 합니다.
3. 본 답안지는 컴퓨터로 처리되므로 훼손해서는 안되며, 답안지 하단의 타이밍마크(∎∎∎)를 찢거나, 낙서 등으로 인한 훼손시 불이익이 발생할 수 있습니다.

4. 답안은 문항당 정답을 1개만 골라 그 같이 정확히 기재해야 하며, 필기구 오류나 본인의 부주의로 잘못 표기한 경우에는 답 관리위원회의 OMR판독기의 판독결과에 따르며, 그 결과는 본인이 책임집니다.

Good ▬ Bad ◐ ◑ ⊗ ◉

5. 감독관의 확인이 없는 답안지는 무효처리됩니다.

Actual Test 5

정답 자동 채점

수험번호 Registration No.

성명 Name
한글
영문

문제지번호 Test Booklet No.

감독관확인란

청해 Listening Comprehension

어휘 Vocabulary

문법 Grammar

독해 Reading Comprehension

주민등록번호 National ID No.

수험번호 Registration No.

비밀번호 Password

고사실란 Room No.

좌석번호 Seat No.

서약

본인은 필기구 및 기재오류와 답안지 채손으로 인한 책임을 지고, 부정행위 처리규정을 준수할 것을 서약합니다.

답안작성시 유의사항

1. 답안 작성은 반드시 **컴퓨터용 싸인펜**을 사용해야 합니다.
2. 답안을 정정할 경우 수정테이프(수정액은 불가)를 사용해야 합니다.
3. 본 답안지는 컴퓨터로 처리되므로 훼손해서는 안되며, 답안지 하단의 타이밍마크(▐▐▐)를 찢거나, 낙서 등으로 인한 훼손시 불이익을 받을 수 있습니다.
4. 답안은 문항당 정답을 1개만 골라 ● 와 같이 정확히 기재해야 하며, 필기구 오류나 본인의 부주의로 잘못 표기한 경우에는 답 관리위원회의 OMR판독기의 판독결과에 따르며, 그 결과는 본인이 책임집니다.

   Good ●   Bad ◖ ◍ ◑ ✕ ⊘

5. 감독관의 확인이 없는 답안지는 무효처리됩니다.